SOVIET MEN OF SCIENCE

Academicians and Corresponding Members
of the Academy of Sciences of the USSR

by

JOHN TURKEVICH

Eugene Higgins Professor of Chemistry
Princeton University

WITH EDITORIAL ASSISTANCE OF

| J. Blanshei | A. Kramer |
| D. Lake | S. Strayer |

GREENWOOD PRESS, PUBLISHERS
WESTPORT, CONNECTICUT

Library of Congress Cataloging in Publication Data

Turkevich, John, 1907-
 Soviet men of science.

 Reprint of the ed. published by Van Nostrand,
Princeton, N. J.
 1. Scientists--Russia. I. Title.
[Q141.T83 1975]   509'.2'2   75-19267
ISBN 0-8371-8246-8

Originally published in 1963 by D. Van Nostrand Company, Inc.,
Princeton, N.J.

Reprinted with the permission of Van Nostrand Reinhold
Company

Reprinted in 1975 by Greenwood Press,
a division of Williamhouse-Regency Inc.

Library of Congress Catalog Card Number 75-19267

ISBN 0-8371-8246-8

Printed in the United States of America

PREFACE

The purpose of this volume is to present to the Western world
the biographies of leading Soviet scientists. This is done in an
attempt to bring a better understanding on the part of the West
of the outstanding achievements of the scientists of the East. It
is further hoped that this volume will facilitate a scientist to
scientist contact and thereby lead to fruitful individual collaboration.

The material presented has been obtained from sources scattered throughout Soviet literature. A copy of the manuscript was
sent to the President of the Soviet Academy of Sciences three
months before presenting it to the publisher. Individual biographies were sent to the Soviet scientists for approval or for cor-
rection. Unfortunately, the Academy was not able to check on
the manuscript. On the other hand, many Soviet scientists have
graciously corrected their biographies. For this we are thank-
ful.

This work was facilitated in its early stages by Professor
George Krugovoy, William Causey, Valentina Kaye, Olga Plos-
chek, Boris Sovetov.

The financial support of the National Science Foundation and
the help of the members of the division of Foreign Science Information of the National Science Foundation, Dr. Arthur Shanahan
and Miss Rita Lupina, are gratefully acknowledged.

AFANAS'YEV, GEORGII DMITRIYEVICH (Geologist)

G. D. Afanas'yev was born March 4, 1906. Upon graduating from the Leningrad Institute in 1930, he worked at the Institute of Petrography, and later at the U.S.S.R. Academy of Sciences Institute of Geological Sciences. From 1948 to 1953, he was scientific secretary at the Department of Geological and Geographic Sciences of the U.S.S.R. Academy of Sciences. He has been a member of the Communist Party of the Soviet Union since 1948, and was elected to the U.S.S.R. Academy of Sciences as a Corresponding Member in 1953. He was assistant to the chief editor of Proceedings of the U.S.S.R. Academy of Sciences, Geological Series, from 1954, and chief editor of a review journal, Geology, from 1956.

Afanas'yev's main works deal with the study of magmetic rocks of the Caucasus and to questions on petrogenesis.

As of 1961, Afanas'yev was Deputy Chief Scientific Secretary of Academy of Sciences U.S.S.R.

Bibliography:
Lake Syevan bottom sedimentation.
Lake Syevan Basin (Gokcha), 3, #2, Leningrad, 1933.
Granitoids of Ancient Intrusive Complexes of North Western Caucasus.' Moscow: 1950.
The importance of granitization as a process leading to the formation of granitoid masses. Congres Geologique International. Comptes rendus de la XIX session. Alger, 1952, Fasc. XV, Alger, 1954, 397-413.
Main results of a study of magmetic geology in the North Caucasus folding territory. Izvest. Akad. Nauk S.S.R., Geol. Ser., 1956, #3.

Office: Institute of Geology of USSR Academy of Sciences
Pyzhevskii 7, Moscow, USSR
Residence: Kotel'nicheskoye nab. 1/15
Moscow, USSR
Telephone: B7 48 82

AGEEV, NIKOLAI VLADIMIROVICH (Metallurgist)

N. V. Ageev was born June 17, 1903. Upon completing the Leningrad Polytechnical Institute in 1926, he started working there. From 1938 to 1940, and again from 1942 to 1951, he worked at the U.S.S.R. Academy of Sciences Institute of General and Inorganic Chemistry. In 1951 he was at the U.S.S.R. Academy of Sciences Institute of Metallurgy. In 1952 he was made

1

Corresponding Secretary for the journal "Problems of Contemporary Metallurgy," and in 1956 was made Chief Editor of the journal "Metallurgy Abstracts." Since 1944 he has been a member of the Communist Party of the Soviet Union. He was elected to the U.S.S.R. Academy of Sciences as a Corresponding Member in 1946.

Ageev's principal works deal with research in metallic alloys. He has specialized in treating problems of physical-chemical analysis of metallic alloys with the aid of x-rays and has studied chemical bonding in metallic alloys by the electron density method.

Bibliography:
Roentgenography of Metals and Alloys. Leningrad: 1932.
Thermal Analysis of Metals and Alloys. Leningrad: 1936.
The Chemistry of Metallic Alloys. Moscow-Leningrad: 1941.
The Nature of Chemical Bonding in Metallic Alloys. Moscow-Leningrad: 1947.
and L. P. Grankova, P. K. Novik. Aluminum's effect on the stability of beta-phase in alloys of Ti-Mo-Fe. Diklady Akad. Nauk S.S.S.R. 146, #2, 351-54 (1962).

Office: A. A. Baykov Institute of Metallurgy
           USSR Academy of Sciences
           Leninskii Prospekt, 49
           Moscow, USSR
Residence: Leninskii Prospekt, 13, Moscow, USSR
Telephone: B2 09 26

AGOSHKOV, Mikhail Ivanovich (Mining Expert)
M. I. Agoshkov was born October 30, 1905. He graduated from the Far East Polytechnic Institute in Vladivostok in 1931. From 1933 to 1941 he worked at the North Caucasus Mining Metallurgical Institute, and at the U.S.S.R. Academy of Sciences Institute of Mining in 1941, where he became deputy Director in 1952.

Agoshkov's works are devoted to exploitation of ore deposits. He has been awarded two orders and also medals. He was head of the foreign section of the U.S.S.R. Academy of Sciences until 1960.

As of 1961, Agoshkov was a Deputy Chief Scientific Secretary of Academy of Sciences U.S.S.R.

In December 1962 it was announced that Agoshkov was appointed acting Chief Scientific Secretary of the Presidium of the U.S.S.R. Academy of Sciences.

3 ALEKSANDROV

Bibliography:
Exploitation of Ore Deposits, 3rd ed. Moscow: 1954 (translated into Rumanian, Bulgarian, Hungarian, and Chinese).
On the Determination of the Productivity of a Mine. Moscow: 1948 (translated into Czech and Polish).
Office: Institute of Mining of USSR Academy of Sciences
Stantsiya Panki
Moscow Oblast', USSR
Residence: nab. Gor'kogo, 32
Moscow, USSR
Telephone: V1 76 99

ALEKIN, OLEG ALEKSANDROVICH (Hydrochemist)
O. A. Alekin was born August 23, 1908. In 1938, he graduated from Leningrad University. From 1929-1951, he worked at the Hydrological Institute in Leningrad. In 1951 he became Director of the U.S.S.R. Academy of Sciences Hydrochemical Institute where he remained until 1961 when he was reassigned to the Laboratory of Limnology. He was rector of Rostov University in 1954. Since 1942, he has been a member of the Communist Party of the Soviet Union. In 1953, Alekin was elected to the U.S.S.R. Academy of Sciences as a Corresponding Member. He received a Stalin Prize in 1951. He has also been awarded three orders and medals.
Alekin's major work is in the chemistry of natural waters, the study of hydrological conditions of rivers and lakes, the development of procedures of chemical analysis of waters (determination of the content of dissolved oxygen, gold, and of pH).
Bibliography:
General Hydrochemistry. Leningrad: 1948.
Hydrochemistry of the Rivers of U.S.S.R., Part 2-3. Leningrad: 1948-49 (Works of the Hydrological Institute, #10, 15).
Basis of Hydrochemistry. Leningrad: 1953.
Chemical Analysis of Inland Waters. Leningrad: 1954.
Office: Laboratory of Limnology
Naberezhnaya Makharova, 2
Leningrad, USSR

ALEKSANDROV, ANATOLII PETROVICH (Nuclear Physicist)
A. P. Aleksandrov was born February 13, 1903. After graduating from Kiev University in 1930, he joined the staff of the Physico-Technical Institute of the U.S.S.R. Academy of Sciences. From 1946 to 1955, he was Director of the Institute

of Physical Problems of the U.S.S.R. Academy of Sciences.
Aleksandrov was a participant at the two Geneva Conferences
of the United Nations on Peaceful Uses of Atomic Energy in
1955 and 1958. In 1959 he visited the United States with the
Soviet delegation of atomic energy experts. After I. V. Kurchatov's death (nuclear physicist, 1902-1960), Aleksandrov was
named his successor as Director of the Kurchatov Institute.
Aleksandrov became a Corresponding Member of the U.S.S.R.
Academy of Sciences in 1943 and in 1953 an Academician. He
is the recipient of a Stalin Prize.

Aleksandrov's scientific work deals with the physical nature
of insulators and investigations of mechanical and electrical
properties of high-polymers. He studied the properties of
polymerized styrene, developed methods of its polymerization
and constructed condensates from polystyrene. Aleksandrov
also investigated the mechanical properties of other polymers
and amorphous substances; he proposed a static theory of stability of solids. He developed a relaxation theory of elasticity,
studied the solidification of polymers and the nature of phase
transitions. He was also active in the development of nuclear
reactors in the post World War II period.

As of 1961, Aleksandrov was a Member of the Presidium of
the U.S.S.R. Academy of Sciences. He was elected as a delegate from R.S.F.S.R. to the Supreme Soviet on March 18, 1962.

Bibliography:
   and Ya. I. Khanin, E. G. Yashin. Observations of spontaneous coherent radiation of ferrite in a resonator. Zhur.
   Exptl. i Teor. Fiz. <u>38</u>, #4, 1334-37 (1960).
   and N. S. Khlopkin, B. Ya. Gnesin, A. I. Gladkov. The
   Atomic-Ice-Breaker "Lenin". Atomnaya Energiya <u>5</u>, #3,
   257-276 (1958).

Biography:
   Aleksandrov, A. P., Vestnik Akad. Nauk S.S.S.R., 1953, #12,
   62.

Office: I. V. Kurchatov Institute of Atomic Energy
                USSR Academy of Sciences
                Moscow, USSR

Residence: Khoroshevskii Serebryannii Bor
                2-aya Lin. 39
                Moscow, USSR

Telephone: D2 10 00 Ext. 50

ALEKSANDROV, BORIS KAPITONOVICH (Hydraulic Engineer)

B. K. Aleksandrov was born August 6, 1889. He graduated
from the Petrograd Polytechnical Institute in 1917. He helped
design the "Moscow" canal and plan the building of the Rybinsk
and Uglich Hydroelectric Plants. In 1939 he was head and chief
engineer of the "Greater Volga" Directorate of the State Trust
for the Planning of Hydroelectric Power Plants and Centers.
In 1918 he taught at a number of secondary and advanced
schools. In 1946 he began teaching at the Moscow Institute of
Energetics, where he became a professor in 1948. In 1953 he
became a Corresponding Member of the U.S.S.R. Academy of
Sciences.

The works of Aleksandrov deal with utilizing the energy of
large plain rivers of the European part of the U.S.S.R. (Volga,
Oka), the transfer of the flow of Northern rivers of Pechora
and Onega into the Volga and Kama, and also with construction
of buildings for hydroelectric buildings and navigable locks. He
is the author of the project of the Kama Hydroelectric Power
Station and dam and of the Kama multi-chambered navigable
lock with utilization of an electric locomotive.

Office: Moscow Institute of Energetics
               Moscow, USSR
Residence: Chistoprudn. bul. 11
               Moscow, USSR
Telephone: B3 10 51

ALEKSEEV, ALEKSANDR EMELYANOVICH (Electronic
      Engineer)

A. E. Alekseev was born November 27, 1891. In 1925, he
graduated from the Leningrad Electrotechnical Institute. From
1908 to 1919, he was employed at an electric plant in Petersburg (Leningrad). Since 1936, he has been professor at the
Leningrad Institute of Railroad Engineers. In 1953, he began
working at the U.S.S.R. Academy of Sciences Institute of
Electromechanics. He has been awarded a medal, the Order of
Lenin and the Order of the Red Banner of Labor. In 1953 he
became a Corresponding Member of the U.S.S.R. Academy of
Sciences.

Alekseev has worked in the field of electric machines. He
worked out the theory and methods of ventilation and heat calculation of electric machines. Under his direction the first Soviet
electric traction machines, turbo and hydro-generators were
built. He is concerned with electric traction on direct and

alternating currents. He participated in designing a rail-welding machine (Stalin Prize 1949).

Bibliography:
Electric Traction Motors, 2nd ed. Moscow: 1951. Construction of Electric Machines. Leningrad-Moscow: 1949 (Lenin Prize 1951).
and M. P. Kostenko. Turbogenerators. Leningrad-Moscow: 1939.

Office: Institute of Electromechanics of USSR Academy
             of Sciences
             Dvortsovaya Naberezhnaya, 18
             Leningrad, USSR

ALEKSEEVSKII, NIKOLAI EVGEN'EVICH (Physicist)
N. E. Alekseevskii was born in 1912. He completed the Leningrad Polytechnical Institute in 1936. From 1936-41, he was at the Ukraine Physico-Technical Institute in Khar'kov. From 1941-42 he worked as an x-ray technician at an evacuation hospital and then as an assistant in the physics department of the Medical Institute in Stalingrad. From 1942 he was at the U.S.S.R. Academy of Sciences Institute of Physical Problems in Moscow. In 1947-60 he was on the staff of the Department of Physics of Low Temperature of the Physics Faculty of Moscow State University, where he became a professor in 1950. In 1960 he became chairman of the department of experimental physics at the Moscow Physico-Technological Institute. In 1960 he was elected a Corresponding Member of the U.S.S.R. Academy of Sciences.
Alekseevskii's works deal with the physics of low temperature.

Bibliography:
and Yu. P. Gaidukov. Anisotropy of the electrical existence of a gold monocrystal in a magnetic field at 4.2^0 K. Zh. eksper. teor. fiz. 35, #2 (8), 554-5 (1958). In Russian Physics-JETP (New York) 35(8), #2383-4 (1959) English translation. Phys. Sci. Abstr. 62, 13334 (1959).
and Yu. P. Gaidukov. Measurement of the electrical conductivity of metals in a magnetic field as a method for investigation of the Fermi surface. Zh. eksper. teor. fiz. 36, #2, 447-50 (1959). Phys. Sci. Abstr. 62, 13335 (1959).
and N. B. Brandt, T. I. Kostina. On the anomalous galvano-magnetic properties of metals at low temperatures. Zh. eksper. teor. fiz. 34, #5, 1339-41 (1958). Phys. Sci. Abstr. 62, 9668 (1959).

and Yu. Gaidukov. The influence of plastic deformation on
the anomalous behaviour of the resistance of gold at low
temperatures. Zh. eksper. teor. fiz. 35, #3 (9), 804-6 (1958).
Soviet Physics-JETP (New York) 35 (8), #3, 558-9 (1959).
English translation. Phys. Sci. Abstr. 63, 2847 (1960).
and Yu. Gaidukov. The anisotropy of magnetoresistance and
the topology of the Fermi surfaces of metals. Zh. eksper.
teor. fiz. 37, #3 (9), 672-7 (1959). Soviet Physics-JETP
(New York) 37 (10), #3, 481-4 (1960). English translation.
Phys. Sci. Abstr. 63, 9939 (1960).
and V. V. Bondar', Yu. M. Polykarov. Superconductivity of
electrodeposited copper-bismuth alloys. Zh. eksper. teor.
fiz. 38, #1, 294-5 (1960). Phys. Sci. Abstr. 63, 10849 (1960).
and M. N. Mikheeva. The critical currents in superconduct-
ing films of tin. Zh. eksper. teor. fiz. 38, #1, 292-3 (1960).
Phys. Sci. Abstr. 63, 12562 (1960).
and A. V. Dubrovin, G. E. Karstens. The application of
mass spectrometers with inhomogenous magnetic fields for
gas analysis. Zhur. Fiz. Khim. 34, 1275-9 (1960). Nuclear
Sci. Abstr. 14, 23096 (1960).
and Fam Zui-Khien, V. G. Shapiro, V. S. Shpinel'. Anisotropy of the Mossbauer Effect in a β-Sn monocrystal. Zhur.
Expt'l. i Teoret. Fiz. 43, #3, 790-93 (1962).
and Yu. P. Gaidukov. Fermi surface of silver. Zhur.
Expt'l. i Teoret. Fiz. 42, #1, 69-74 (1962).
Office: Experimental Physics Department
            Moscow Physico-Technological Institute
            Moscow, USSR
Residence: Vorob'evskoye shosse, 2
            Moscow, USSR
Telephone: B2 13 14

ALEXANDROFF (ALEKSANDROV), PAVEL SERGEIEVICH
    (Mathematician)
P. S. Alexandroff was born May 7, 1896. In 1917 he graduated from Moscow University. He became a lecturer in 1921
and in 1929 was made professor. In 1921 he was elected a
member of the Moscow Mathematical Society, in 1932 President, and in 1946 an Honorary Member. He has been a Corresponding Member of the U.S.S.R. Academy of Sciences since
1929 and since 1953 an Academician. Alexandroff is a member
of the Berlin Academy of Sciences (Associate Member since
1950), the American Philosophical Society in Philadelphia, the
National Academy of Sciences in Washington (since 1947), the

Göttingen Academy of Sciences (1929-38, and from 1945), the
Polish Academy of Sciences and other societies. In 1943 he
was awarded a Stalin Prize.

Alexandroff investigated the theory of point sets and the
theory of the function of the real variable, obtaining such important results as the proof of the theorem on the power of
Borel sets. In collaboration with P. S. Urysohn he developed in
the Soviet Union the field of topology, becoming the head of the
U.S.S.R. School of Topology. Among his former students are:
L. Pontryagin, A. Tychonoff, A. Kurosh, Yu. Smirnov, G.
Chogoshvili, K. Sitnikov and others. Alexandroff originated one
of the main theories of topological spaces--the theory of bi-
compact spaces. He also contributed in an essential way to the
modern theory of dimensionality (in particular he founded the
theory of the homogical dimension); he was the founder of
methods based on combinatory algebraic investigation of sets
and spaces of a general nature; he proved a series of basic
"laws of duality" (combining topological properties of the geometrical figure with topological properties of space comple-
mentary to it).

Bibliography:
> Sur la puissance des ensembles mesurables B. Comptes
> Rendus Acad. Sci. Paris, 1916, 162, p. 323.
> and P. Urysohn. Une condition necessaire et suffisante pour
> qu'une classe (L) soit une classe (D). Compt. Rend. Acad.
> Paris, 1923, 177, p. 1274.
> Ueber die Aequivalenz des Perronschen und des Denjoyschen
> Integralbegriffes, Math. Zeitschrift 1924, 20, p. 213.
> Les ensembles de premiere classe et les espaces abstraits.
> Compt. Rend. Acad. Paris, 1924, 178, p. 185.
> and P. Urysohn. Memoire sur les espaces topologiques
> compacts. Verhandelingen Kon. Acad. Amsterdam, 1929,
> 14:1, p. 1.
> Untersuchungen über Gestalt und Lage abgeschlossener
> Mengen beliebiger Dimension. Annals of Math., 1929, 30,
> p. 101.
> Dimensions theorie. Ein Beitrag zur Geometrie der abge-
> schlossener Mengen. Mathematische Annalen, 1932, 106,
> p. 161.
> On local properties of closed sets. Annals of Math., 1935,
> 36, p. 1.
> On bicompact extensions of topological spaces. Matemati-
> ceski Sbornik, 1939, 5, p. 403.

9 ALEXANDROV

Homological situation properties of complexes and closed
sets. Izvest. Akad. Nauk S.S.S.R., Ser. Mat., 1942, 6 (Stalin
Prize 1943). (English trans. in Transact. Amer. Math. Soc.
1943, 54, p. 286.
Duality theorems for non-closed sets in the n-dimensional
space. Mathematiceski Sbornik, 1947, 21, p. 161.
On the notion of space in topology. Uspekhi Mat. Nauk, 1947,
2, p. 5.
On the dimension of normal spaces. Proceed. Roy. Soc.,
London, 1947, 189, p. 1.
On combinatorial topology of non-closed sets. Matematiceski
Sbornik, 1953, 33, p. 241.
On the homeomorphism of point sets. Trudy Moskovskogo
Matemat. Obshch., 1955, 4, p. 405.
and W. Ponomarev. On certain classes of n-dimensional
spaces. Sibirskij Matematiceskiy Jurnal, 1960, 1, p. 3.
Metrization of topological spaces. Bull. Polish Acad., Sect.
of Math., Phys. and Astronomy, 1960, 8:3, p. 135.
and W. Ponomarev. On dyadic bicompacta. Fundamenta
Mathematicae, 1962, 50, p. 419.
Office: Mechanics-Mathematics Faculty
Moscow University
Moscow V-234, USSR
Residence: Leninskiye gory, sektor "L"
Moscow, USSR
Telephone: V9 30 91

ALEXANDROV, ALEKSANDR DANILOVICH (Mathematician)
A. D. Alexandrov was born August 4, 1912. He is Rector of
Leningrad University. In 1946 he was elected a Corresponding
Member of the U.S.S.R. Academy of Sciences. He has been a
member of the Communist Party of the Soviet Union since 1951.
In 1942 he was awarded a State Prize.
Alexandrov is the founder of the Soviet school of geometry
in the large. He set up an intrinsic geometry of general sur-
faces.
In April 1959, Alexandrov visited the University of California
at Berkeley.
Bibliography:
Inner Geometry of Convex Surfaces. Moscow-Leningrad:
1948.
Convex Polyhedra. Moscow-Leningrad: 1950.

Office: Leningrad State University
Universitetskaya nab. 7/9
Leningrad V-164, USSR

ALIKHANOV, ABRAM ISAAKOVICH (Nuclear Physicist)

A. I. Alikhanov was born March 4, 1904. In 1931 he graduated from Leningrad Polytechnical Institute. He had been on the staff of the Physico-Technical Institute of the U.S.S.R. Academy of Sciences since 1927 and became the Director of its Power Engineering Laboratories. In 1939 Alikhanov was elected a Corresponding Member of the U.S.S.R. Academy of Sciences and in 1943 an Academician. He has also been a member of the Armenian S.S.R. Academy of Sciences since 1943. In 1941 and 1948 he was a recipient of Stalin Prizes.

The first scientific investigations of Alikhanov were in the field of x-rays. In 1934 in collaboration with his brother, Artemii Isaakovich Alikhan'yan, he began research in radioactivity, and in the same year, jointly with M. S. Kozodaev and Alikhan'yan, discovered the pair emission by excited nuclei. In 1935, together with Alikhan'yan, he formulated the relationship between β-spectra and the atomic number of the element. In 1936, with Alikhan'yan and L. A. Artsimovich, Alikhanov proved experimentally the conservation of momentum during pair annihilation. Investigations of cosmic rays (1939) led Alikhanov, together with A. I. Alikhan'yan and S. Ya. Nikitin, to the discovery of unstable mesons. In 1949, he built the first reactor in the U.S.S.R., using heavy water as a moderator. At present Alikhanov is working on the development of nuclear reactors.

As of 1961, Alikhanov was Director of the Institute of Theoretical and Experimental Physics and is Chairman of the Commission on Cosmic Rays.

Bibliography:
and A. I. Alikhan'yan. Investigations in artificial radioactivity. Zhur. Eksptl. i Teoret. Fiz., 1936, 6, #7.
Cosmic rays, recent problems in science and technology. Lectures, Moscow, 1949.
and A. I. Alikhan'yan, M. S. Kozodaev. Measurements of e/m for β particles. Doklady Akad. Nauk S.S.S.R., 1938, 20, #6.
and A. I. Alikhan'yan. New data on the nature of cosmic rays. Uspekhi Fiz. Nauk, 1945, 27, #1.
and A. I. Babaev, M. Ya. Balats, V. S. Kaftanov, L. G. Landsberg, V. A. Lyubimov, Yu. V. Obukov. Further studies

of $\mu \rightarrow e + \gamma$ disintegration. Zhur. Expt'l. i Teoret. Fiz. 42,
#2, 630-31 (1962).
Biography:
    Academician A. I. Alikhanov (on his 50th birthday). Zhur.
    Eksptl. i Teoret. Fiz., 1954, 27, #1.
Office: Institute of Theoretical & Experimental Physics of
              USSR Academy of Sciences
              3 Pyzhevskii Pereulok
              Moscow, USSR
Residence: Dorogmilovskaya, 31
              Moscow, USSR
Telephone: G3 50 22, Ext. 31

ALIKHAN'YAN, ARTEMII ISAAKOVICH (Physicist)
    A. I. Alikhan'yan was born July 24, 1908. He graduated from
Leningrad University in 1931 and began, with A. I. Alikhanov,
work in nuclear physics and cosmic rays. Since 1943 he has
been an Academician of the Armenian SSR Academy of Sciences
and since 1946 a Corresponding Member of the U.S.S.R. Academy of Sciences. In 1941 and 1948 he was awarded Stalin Prizes.
    From 1934, Alikhan'yan, with A. I. Alikhanov and M. S.
Kozodaev, discovered pair emission by excited nuclei. In 1935,
Alikhan'yan, with Alikhanov, established the law of the dependence of beta-spectra on the atomic number of the element.
The main work of Alikhan'yan is devoted to the study of cosmic
rays. In association with Asatiani, he discovered showers with
few particles in cosmic rays (the so-called narrow showers).
Alikhan'yan also showed that in the composition of primary
components of cosmic radiation there are particles present
with energies up to LO^{17} electron-volts. In 1945 Alikhan'yan
helped establish a cosmic ray station on Mountain Aragats,
where he, with associates, conducted a magnetic analysis on
the mass of cosmic ray particles.
    In 1951-52 Alikhan'yan and his associates were successful
in separating particles with a mass $\sim 200m_e$ in cosmic rays
and also in obtaining some indication of the existence of particles with masses of approximately $600m_e$ and $950m_e$.
    As of 1961, Alikhan'yan was Director of the Armenian
Academy of Sciences Institute of Physics.
Bibliography:
    and A. Dadayan. Investigation of narrow showers at an alti-
    tude of 3250 meters above sea level. Zhur. Eksptl. i.
    Teoret. Fiz., 1949, #1.

and S. Ya. Nikitin. Investigation of the end of spectrum RaE with the aid of a double magnetic spectrometer. Izvest. Akad. Nauk S.S.S.R., Ser. Fiz., 1940, 4, #2.

and A. I. Alikhanov and S. Nikitin. Low and high energy components of cosmic rays, and spin of meson. Izvest. Akad. Nauk S.S.S.R., Ser. Fiz., 1940, 6, #1-2.

and T. L. Asatiani, E. M. Matevosyan, R. O. Sharichatunyan. Investigation of the polarization of cosmic rays μ^+-mesons. Zhur. Expt'l. i Teoret. Fiz. 42, #1, 127-29 (1962).

Office: Institute of Physics of Academy of Sciences
Armenian SSR
Yerevan, Armenian SSR

ALIMARIN, IVAN PAVLOVICH (Chemist)

I. P. Alimarin was born September 11, 1903. From 1923 to 1953, he worked at the All-Union Scientific Research Institute of Mineral Raw Materials, and in 1949, at the U.S.S.R. Academy of Sciences Institute of Geochemistry and Analytical Chemistry. From 1929 to 1953, he also taught at the Moscow Institute of Fine Chemical Technology and became a professor there in 1950. In 1953 he was made a professor at Moscow University. He was elected to the U.S.S.R. Academy of Sciences as a Corresponding Member in 1953. He was awarded the Lenin Order, the Order of the Red Banner of Labor, and a medal.

Alimarin has concerned himself with analysis of minerals and ores, analytical chemistry of rare elements, microchemistry and radiochemical analysis.

Bibliography:

and R. L. Podval'naya. Colorimetric determination of small quantities of niobium in the form of a rhodon complex. Zhur. Anal. Khim., 1946, 1, #1, 30-46.

and B. N. Ivanov-Emin and O. A. Alexeeva. Quantitative Chemical Determination of Germanium in the Ash of Fossil Coal. Moscow-Leningrad: 1946.

Utilization of radioactive isotopes in chemical analysis. Utilization of Isotopes in Engineering, Biology and Agriculture. Moscow: 1955 (Reports of the Soviet Delegation at the International Conference for Peaceful Utilization of Atomic Energy, Geneva, 1955).

and V. N. Arkhangel'skaya. Qualitative Semi Microanalysis, 2nd ed. Moscow-Leningrad: 1952.

Office: Chemistry Department
Moscow University
Moscow, USSR

Residence: Leninskiye gory, korp. "I"
                Moscow, USSR
Telephone: B9 18 80

AMBARTSUMIAN, VIKTOR AMAZASPOVICH (Astrophysicist)

V. A. Ambartsumian was born September 18, 1908 in Tbilisi
in the family of the distinguished Armenian philologist, writer
and teacher, A. A. Ambartsumian. Ambartsumian received his
secondary education at Tbilisi. He graduated in 1928 from
Leningrad University, having published, as a student, more
than ten papers on theoretical astrophysics and mathematics.
He pursued graduate studies at Pulkovo Observatory under the
Russian astrophysicist, A. A. Belopolskii (1854-1934). As a
graduate student, he published papers dealing with solar physics, the physics of the stellar atmospheres and gaseous nebulae, and theoretical physics. He completed his graduate work
in 1931, served as docent at Leningrad University, and in 1934
became a professor. Ambartsumian established the chair of
Astrophysics at Leningrad University in 1934, and occupied it
until 1946. He became Director of the Leningrad University
Astronomical Observatory in 1938. He has been a pro-rector
of science at the Leningrad University. From 1943 to 1947 he
was Vice-President of the newly organized Academy of Sciences
of the Armenian S.S.R. He was head of the research branch of
the Leningrad University which was moved to Yelabuga during
World War II. Since 1944 he has served as the Director of
Yerevan Observatory. On his own initiative, he began and
supervised the planning and construction of Byurakan Observatory in 1946, and became the Director. He has held the Chair
of Astrophysics at Yerevan State University since 1947. He
became a member of the Communist Party of the Soviet Union
in 1940. In 1947, he was elected President of the Academy of
Sciences of the Armenian S.S.R. From 1948 to 1955, he was
Vice President of the International Astronomical Union. He
was elected Academician of the Academy of Sciences of the
U.S.S.R. in 1953, having been a Corresponding Member since
1939. He is a Deputy of the Supreme Soviet, since 1950, a
member of the Central Committee of the Communist Party of
Armenia, and President of the Armenian Society for the Propagation of Scientific and Political Knowledge. He has frequently
participated in the work of international congresses, conferences, and meetings, and is an honorary member of corresponding member of academies of science and scientific societies of Austria, Britain, Belgium, Canada, France, Germany,

and the United States. Ambartsumian has twice received a State Prize, in 1946 and in 1950. He has also received two Orders of Lenin and two Orders of the Red Banner of Labor. In 1961 in Berkeley (USA) V. A. Ambartsumian was elected the President of the International Astronomical Union.

The early works of Ambartsumian dealt with the study of stellar physics and gaseous nebulae. He has given a mathematical interpretation of the complex physical processes involved in the luminescence of gaseous nebulae; he has demonstrated the important role of 'L_α' radiation pressure in the nebulae, has developed a solution to the problem of atom accumulation in metastable states, and has elaborated a method for determining the electron temperature of the nebulae. The method he worked out for subdividing the 'L_c' and 'L_α' fields of radiation has enabled him to devise a theory of radiation equilibrium of planetary nebulae. This theory has been the foundation for all subsequent studies in this direction, the most valuable of which is the research conducted by his student, V. V. Sobolev. Ambartsumian has also devised methods of determining the masses of the nebulae and the gaseous envelopes surrounding the stars. These studies have stimulated further research on stellar physics and nebulae both in the Soviet Union and abroad. He was the first in the Soviet Union to have organized a course in Leningrad State University on theoretical astrophysics and is the leader of the Soviet school of theoretical astrophysics.

More recently Ambartsumian's interests extended to include stellar astronomy and cosmogony. A large number of his studies deal with the problem of the evolution of stellar systems. The idea underlying these studies is that of the existence of irregular forces in addition to regular forces in stellar systems. In the case of the double stars and star clusters, these irregular forces often play a decisive role in the process of their development. In order to solve this problem, he elaborated new methods of statistical mechanics of stellar systems and successfully applied them to dual stars and star clusters. The results of these investigations were incorporated by him into lectures during the 1930's at Leningrad University. These investigations and other results have affected previously existing theories of the age of the Galaxy and of the evolution of its component systems. Ambartsumian refuted the "Long Time Scale," according to which the age of the Galaxy was taken to be roughly 10^{13} years, while, according to him, the age of the Galaxy is in the order of 10^{10} years. During 1941-43, he personally conducted extensive research on the theory of light

diffusion in a turbid medium, which is of great importance in
many questions of geophysics, physics, and astrophysics, and
for which he received the State Prize in 1946. This traditionally
well-known problem in science has generally been reduced to
an integral equation for which the solution was found in a very
cumbersome fashion by means of consecutive approximations.
Ambartsumian applied an entirely new method to the solution of
this problem: reducing it to simple functional equations, he obtained an exact solution to it. These equations have become
known as "Ambartsumian's Functional Equations." Also in the
forties, he completed a cycle of studies dealing with the problem
of the structure of the Galaxy which had been partially carried
out during his stay in Leningrad. The structure of the Galaxy
(the basic problem of modern Astronomy) became a more complex question in the 1930's with the discovery of dark, light-
absorbing matter in the interstellar space. In studying (along
with Sh. G. Gordeladze) the distribution of hot stars and of diffuse nebulae, Ambartsumian revealed the patchy structure of
the dark matter, and drew the conclusion that interstellar absorption is conditioned by the total mass of dark clouds, in the
form of separate, obscure nebulae, not a continuous medium,
as had been previously believed. On the basis of the patchy
structure of the dark matter, he elaborated a mathematical
theory of the fluctuations in the distribution of the stars, of the
brightness of the Milky Way, and of the extragalactic nebulae
which was subsequently developed in the work of Ambartsumian's pupils and by a number of foreign scientists (such as
Chandrasekar, Munch). His work also dealt with the relationship between the luminosity of interstellar matter in space and
the neighboring stars, a method to calculate the mass ejected
by Nova (the order of magnitude of only one part in a thousand
of the mass of the sun), a theory on radiation equilibrium in
planetary nebulae, and a theory for determining the space velocity distribution of stars from their radial velocities.

A new development of Ambartsumian is concerned with the
origins and development of celestial bodies. An analysis and
synthesis of observation material accumulated enabled him in
1947 to discover the existence in the Galaxy of a new type of
stellar systems which he designated as stellar associations.
These he found to be subject to break-up through the dropping
out of individual stars, and to be of comparatively recent origin
(State Prize, 1950). He established the continuous process of
star formation at the present stage in the development of the
Galaxy. This was a refutation of the concept held of the

simultaneous origin on the stars in the Galaxy. This work provided a foundation for research in astronomy into the evolution of stars and stellar systems by observation of their development. The theoretical prediction (in 1947-49) by Ambartsumian concerning the dynamic instability of stellar associations and their expansion was confirmed as a result of the analysis of movements of stars carried out in Leyden and Byurakan.

Ambartsumian's finding of the group character of the emergence of stars has permitted clearer study of the physical nature and cosmogonic role of double and multiple stars, star chains and clusters, and gaseous nebulae. It has also resulted in work by Ambartsumian on continuous emission, another aspect of the physical nature of the members of stellar associations. Continuous emission is the excess radiation in a total spectrum observed in stars of the T Tauri and UV Ceti type and also in comet-like nebulae. By synthesis and analysis of uncoordinated data, Ambartsumian established the non-thermal character of continuous emission. This aroused great interest in the origin of this entirely new phenomenon. At the present time, extensive study of continuous emission is under way both at the Byurakan Observatory and at a number of foreign observatories (Lick, Tonantzintla).

In recent years, Ambartsumian began research on the galaxies and on the systems constituted by them. One result of his work is the conclusion (based on the group character of the formation of galaxies) that galaxies form as multiple systems and clusters having in many cases positive energy, that is, constituting systems under disintegration. He interprets radiogalaxies as the result of a process of division--the formation of galaxies counterbalancing the hypothesis of collision of galaxies. The blue galaxies detected by him, a particular kind of dwarf galaxies, enrich our conceptions of the nature of galaxies and may furnish much valuable material for studying the evolution of galaxies. The very important role of nuclei of galaxies in their evolution was shown. In particular it was concluded that the nuclei of galaxies display a number of forms of cosmogonic activity.

In 1960 the composition of degenerate gas with nuclear density and greater was studied. It was shown that with increasing density, different hyperons successively appear and their number in the gas increases. They should be stable due to the Pauli principle.

Then it is proved that in the case of the degenerate superdense gas the configuration of gravitational equilibrium of

out

.

cosmic mass should consist of a hyperon nucleus, neutron layer and outer envelope of usual composition (electrons, protons, and composite nuclei).

The internal structure of equilibrium configurations of stellar masses, with densities of the order of the atomic nucleus and higher, was studied. It was shown that the space metrics inside the configuration essentially deviates from the Euclidian type.

As of 1961, Ambartsumian was a member of the Presidium U.S.S.R. Academy of Sciences, and Chairman of the Commission on Astrophysics of the U.S.S.R. Academy of Sciences.

Bibliography:

Uber eine frage der eigenwerttheorie. Z. f. Phys., 1929, #53.

The radiative equilibrium of a planetary nebula. MN, 1932, 93, #1.

On the radiative equilibrium of a planetary nebula. Leningrad, 1933 (Bulletin of the Main Astronomical Observatory in Pulkovo, 13, #114.

The Excitation of the Metastable States in the Gaseous Nebulae. Circular of Pulkovo Observatory, 1933, #6.

Die Flächenhelligkeiten der Monochromatischen Bilder einiger Gasnebel. Z. f. Ap., 1933, #6.

and N. A. Kosyrev. Uber die Massen der von neuen Sternen ausgestossenen Gashüllen. Z. f. Ap., 1933, #7.

On the derivation of the frequency function of space velocities of the stars from the observed radial velocities. MN, 1935, 96, #3.

and G. A. Shain. On the faint white stars in low galactic latitudes. Astron. Zhur., 1936, 13, #1.

Double stars and the cosmogonic time-scale. Nature, 1936, 137, #3465.

To statistics of double stars. Astron. Zhur., 1937, 14, #3.

On the question of dynamics of open clusters. Scientific Transactions of Leningrad State University, Math. Series (Astronomy), 1938, #22.

Problem of diffuse nebulae and cosmic absorption. Bulletin of the Abastunmani Astrophysical Observatory, 1938, #2.

Diffusion and absorption of light in planetary atmospheres. Scientific Transactions of Leningrad State University, Math. Series (Astronomy), #82, 1941, #11.

On diffusion of light by atmospheres of planets. Astron. Zhur., 1942, #3.

New method of computing the diffusion of light in a turbid
medium. Izvest. Akad. Nauk S.S.S.R., Ser. Geogr. i Fiz.,
1942, #3.
On the problem of the diffuse reflection of light. J. Phys. of
S.S.S.R., 1944, 8, #2.
On the theory of fluctuations of the brightness in milky way.
Doklady Akad. Nauk S.S.S.R., 1944, #6.
Stellar Evolution and Astrophysics. Armenian Academy of
Sciences, Yerevan, 1947.
Stellar associations. Astron. Zhur., 1949, 26, #1.
The Phenomenon of Continuous Emission and Sources of
Stellar Energy. Communications of Byurakan Observatory,
1954, #13.
Multiple Systems of Trapezium Type. Communications of
Byurakan Observatory, 1954, #15.
Stars of T. Tauri and UV Ceti types and Phenomenon of
Continuous Emission. International Astronomical Union
Symposium, Non-Stable Stars, 1957, #3.
Stellar Systems of Positive Total Energy. Observatory,
1955, 75, #885.
On the multiple galaxies. Izvest. Akad. Nauk of Armenian
S.S.R., Fiz-Mat. Nauki, 1956, 9, #1.
On the evolution of galaxies. Report presented to the Solvay
Conference of 1958, Bruxelles, 1959.
and G. S. Saakian. On the degenerate superdense gas of
elementary particles. Astron. Zhur., 1960, 37, #2.
and G. S. Saakian. The internal structure of hyperon con-
figurations of stellar masses. Astron. Zhur., 1961, 38, #6.
Scientific Works in Two Volumes. Armenian Academy of
Sciences, Yerevan: 1960.
Biography:
   V. A. Ambartsumian. Yerevan, 1954 (Academy of Sciences
   of the Armenian S.S.R., Bibliographical Data of U.S.S.R.
   Scientists). Second edition, Yerevan: 1958.
Office: Academy of Sciences Armenian SSR
              Barekmutyan, 24
              Yerevan, Armenian SSR

AMIRASLANOV, ALI AGAMALY OGLY (Deceased, October 16,
      1962.)
   A. A. Amiraslanov was born December 1900. Upon graduat-
ing from the Moscow Mining Academy in 1930, he worked at the
All-Union Institute of Mineral Raw Materials and Scientific
Geological Gold Survey Institute. In 1939-1947 he was a chief
engineer, in 1948-1953 he was Director, and in 1954 he became

chief geologist of the U.S.S.R. Main Geological Survey Directorate of the Ministry of Non-Ferrous Metals. He taught at the
Moscow Geological Survey Institute from 1931 to 1955, and in
1950 became a professor at that institute. He was awarded two
orders as well as medals.
Amiraslanov's major works deal with non-ferrous and rare
metals deposits (chiefly copper, lead and zinc).
Bibliography:
   Levikhin group of pyritic deposits in the Urals. Works of
   the U.S.S.R. Academy of Sciences, 4. Leningrad: 1934.
   Karpushikhinsk Deposit in the Urals and its Prospects.
   Moscow-Leningrad: 1936 (Works of the All-Union Scientific
   Research Institute of Mineral Raw Materials, #99).
   Mineralogical Characteristics of Pyritic Deposits in the
   Urals and Secondary Processes in Them. Moscow-Leningrad:
   1937.
Office: USSR Main Geological Survey
             Directorate of Ministry of Non-Ferrous Metals
             Moscow, USSR
Residence: ul. Chkalova, 18/22
             Moscow, USSR
Telephone: K7 88 77

ANDREEV, NIKOLAI NIKOLAEVICH (Acoustical Physicist)
   N. N. Andreev was born June 28, 1881. In 1909 he graduated
from the University of Basel. From 1917 to 1940 he taught and
directed research in a number of universities and research
institutions. He worked at the Physics Institute of the U.S.S.R.
Academy of Sciences from 1940 to 1954. Beginning in 1945,
Andreev has worked at the Acoustics Institute of the U.S.S.R.
Academy of Sciences. He was elected Corresponding Member
of the U.S.S.R. Academy of Sciences in 1933, and in 1953 Academician.
   Andreev's numerous scientific contributions are mainly in
the field of physical and technical acoustics and in the theory of
vibrations. They are concerned with dispersion problems of
acoustic waves. Andreev established the theory of the diffusion
of sound in moving media; he investigated noise caused by
airplane motors and propellers, problems of architectural
acoustics, and wave acoustics of finite amplitude. Other important contributions of Andreev are in piezo-electricity, in the
theory of the telephone, and in musical acoustics. He is the
author and editor of many popularized scientific articles and

books. He is the founder of the School of Soviet Acoustical
Engineers.
  As of 1961, Andreev was Chairman of the Commission on
Acoustics of the USSR Academy of Sciences.
Bibliography:
  Lattice, prism and resonator. Zhur. Russkogo, Fiz.-Khim.
  Obshchestva, Otdel Fiz., 1918, 47, section 2, #5.
  Electric Oscillations and their Spectra. A Theoretical In-
  vestigation. Moscow: 1917.
  Equilibrium and oscillations of the piezo-electrical crystal
  (a review). Zhur. Priklad. Fiz., 1928, 5, #3-4.
  and I. G. Rusakov. Acoustics of the Moving Medium.
  Leningrad-Moscow: 1934.
Biography:
  Andreev, N. N. Vestnik Akad. Nauk S.S.S.R., 1954, #1.
  Academician N. N. Andreev (on his 75th birthday). Zhur.
  Eksptl. i Teoret. Fiz., 1955, 29, #2.
  N. N. Andreev (on his 75th birthday). Akust. Zhur., 1955, 1,
  #3.
Office: Institute of Acoustics of USSR Academy of Sciences
              Ulitsa Televideniya, 4
              Moscow, USSR
Residence: Leninskii Prospekt, 13
              Moscow, USSR
Telephone: V2 41 96

ANDRIANOV, KUZ'MA ANDRIANOVICH (Chemist)

  K. A. Andrianov was born December 28, 1904. After graduating in 1930 from Moscow University, he worked at the All-
Union Electrotechnical Institute. In 1930-41, he taught at the
Moscow Chemico-Technological Institute. Then, in 1941, he
went to teach at the Moscow Institute of Energetics and in 1946
was made professor there. In 1954 he began work at the Institute of Elemental Organic Compounds. Andrianov has been a
member of the Communist Party of the Soviet Union since 1949.
In 1953, he was elected a Corresponding Member of the U.S.S.R.
Academy of Sciences. In 1943, 1946, 1950, he received Stalin
Prizes.
  The main works of Andrianov are devoted to synthesis and
technology of high molecular compounds, particularly of silicon-
organic polymers. In 1937 he synthesized "polyorganosilox-
anes," and in 1947 he worked out the method of obtaining new
polymers--"polyorganometallosiloxanes." Under his leadership

work was carried out on the synthesis of heat-resistant,
electro-insulating silicon-organic polymers.
In September 1959, Andrianov visited the United States to
attend the American Chemical Society meetings, Atlantic City,
New Jersey.

Bibliography:
Silicon-Organic Compounds. Moscow: 1955.
and D. A. Kardashev. Practical investigation on artificial
polymers and plastics, 2nd ed. Moscow-Leningrad: 1946.
and M. V. Sobolevskii. High Molecular Silicon-Organic
Compounds. Moscow: 1949.
and S. A. Yamanov. Organic Dielectrics and Their Utilization in the Communication Industry. Moscow-Leningrad:
1949.
Heat Resistant Silicon-Organic Dielectrics. Moscow-
Leningrad: 1957.
and N. A. Kurasheva, I. K. Kuznetsova, E. I. Gerkhardt.
Synthesis of regular structural polymers of the polymethyl-
siloxane series. Doklady Akad. Nauk S.S.S.R., 1961, 140,
#3, 365-67.
Ways of synthesizing regular organic polymers with a
spacial structure. Doklady Akad. Nauk S.S.S.R., 1961, 140,
#6, 1310-1313.
and V. I. Savushikina, S. A. Golubtsov, B. A. Charskaya.
Doklady Akad. Nauk S.S.S.R., 1961, 139, #1, 95-99.
and A. A. Zhdanov. Polycondensation as a method for obtaining polydialkylsiloxane and polyalumo dialkylsiloxane elasto-
mers. Doklady Akad. Nauk S.S.S.R., 1961, 138, #3, 361-364.
and V. V. Severnii. Reaction of organocyclosiloxane telo-
merization and dimethyl dichlorsilane. Doklady Akad. Nauk
S.S.S.R. 146, #3, 601-603 (1962).
Office: Institute of Organo-Elemental Compounds of USSR
            Academy of Sciences
            Leninskii Prospekt, 31
            Moscow, USSR

ANITSCHKOW (ANICHKOV), NIKOLAI NIKOLAEVICH (Patho-
    morphologist)
N. N. Anitschkow was born November 3, 1885. In 1909 he
graduated from the Military Medical Academy, where from 1920
to 1946 he was a professor. Also in 1920 he began working at
the Institute of Experimental Medicine at the U.S.S.R. Academy
of Medical Sciences. From 1946 to 1953 he was President of
the U.S.S.R. Academy of Medical Sciences. He has been an

Academician of the U.S.S.R. Academy of Sciences since 1939, and since 1944 an active member of the U.S.S.R. Academy of Medical Sciences. Anitschkow was a Deputy to the Supreme Soviet of the U.S.S.R. second convocation. In 1942 he received a State Prize and in 1952 the I. I. Mechnikov medal from the U.S.S.R. Academy of Sciences.

Anitschkow is the author of a large number of publications on various problems of experimental pathology and pathomorphology, particularly on the pathology of blood vessels. He was first to offer a well organized study of atherosclerosis. Closely related to this field are his investigations on lipid exchange. He has also been concerned with the morphology and functions of the reticulo-endothelial system and its part in deposition of different particles from blood and lymph. In the works concerning the pathology of contagious diseases Anitschkow threw light on the autoinfection in the development of contagious diseases.

Bibliography:

Inflammatory Changes of Myocardium (Study of Experimental Myocarditis). Dissertation. St. Petersburg: 1912.
Study of the Reticulo-endothelial System. Moscow-Leningrad: 1930.
Experimental arteriosclerosis in animals. Reprinted from Arteriosclerosis. A Survey of the Problem. New York: Macmillan, 1933.
Manual of Pathological Physiology, 4th ed. Leningrad: 1938.
Pathology of the Blood Vessels. Moscow-Leningrad: 1940.
and others. Morphology of Wound Healing. Moscow: 1951.
Modern status of the problems of experimental arteriosclerosis. Vestnik Akad. Nauk S.S.S.R., 1956, #2.

Office: Institute of Experimental Medicine of USSR Academy of Medical Sciences
Kirovskii Prospekt 69/71, #24
Leningrad, P-22, USSR

ARBUZOV, ALEKSANDR ERMININGEL'DOVICH (Organic Chemist)

A. E. Arbuzov was born August 30, 1877. He graduated from the Kazan University in 1900 and from 1911 to 1930 was a professor there. He had been a student of A. M. Zaitsev (1841-1910, an outstanding organic chemist and Corresponding Member of the Petersburg Academy of Sciences). In 1930 he became a professor at the Kazan Chemical-Technological Institute. Arbuzov was elected a Corresponding Member of

the U.S.S.R. Academy of Sciences in 1932 and an Academician
in 1942 and was made President, in 1945, of the Kazan' Branch
of the U.S.S.R. Academy of Sciences. He was a delegate from
R.S.F.S.R. to the Supreme Soviet of the U.S.S.R. for the second
through fifth meetings and again as of March 18, 1962. In 1957
he was a Hero of Socialist Labor. Twice, 1943 and 1947, he
has won Stalin Prizes.

Arbuzov's studies are concerned with phosphorous-organic
compounds. In his master's degree thesis "Structure of
Phosphorous Acid and its Derivatives" (1905), Arbuzov determined the structure of phosphorous acid and its esters. He
found a catalytic rearrangement reaction for intermediate
esters of this acid, which is called the Arbuzov Rearrangement.
This isomerization is the widely used method for synthesizing
alkylphosphenic acids and similar compounds. In his doctor's
degree thesis "Catalysis in Conversion of Some Phosphorous
Compounds" (1914), he extended his theory to cover phenyl-
phosphenic and other esters. He identified the forces which
accelerate the catalytic isomerization processes, with the
forces which affect the rates of conventional chemical reactions.
Together with his pupil A. A. Dunin, Arbuzov synthesized
phosphonacetic ester and its homologs. The sodium and potassium derivatives of these esters can be used in syntheses
similar to the acetoacetic and malonic ester. This synthesis
and investigation is related to Arbuzov's work on tautomerism
of dialkyl esters of phosphorous acid and on the reactions of
their metal derivatives. During the investigation of these compounds Arbuzov, in collaboration with B. A. Arbuzov, found a
new method of obtaining free radicals of the triarylmethyl
series. Arbuzov has also studied the tapping and flow of soft
gums from conifers. He found a high pressure (2 to 3 atmospheres) in the gum ducts of these plants and developed a technique for collecting gums without any loss of volatile substances. This technique aided the rapid growth of the resin industry
of the U.S.S.R. Arbuzov wrote a book on the history of chemistry which showed the contributions of N. N. Zenin, A. M.
Butlerov, the Kazan' school as a whole, M. V. Lomonosov,
D. I. Mendeleev, S. V. Lebedev and others. He also studied
extensively the history of free radicals, phosphorous-organic
compounds, and catalysis.

As of 1961 he was Chairman of the Commission on the
History of Chemistry, and Member of the Presidium of the
U.S.S.R. Academy of Sciences.

In 1960 Arbuzov was appointed Director of the Arbuzov Institute of Chemistry of the Kazan' Branch of the U.S.S.R. Academy of Sciences.

Bibliography:

Free radicals. Uspekhi Khim., 1932, 1, #2 & 3.
Selected Works. (This contains a bibliography of Arbuzov's works.) Moscow: 1952.

Biography:

A. F. Bogoyavlenskii and N. N. Aksenov. Aleksandr Erminingel'dovich Arbuzov. Kazan': 1946. (This contains a bibliography of Arbuzov's works.)
G. Kh. Kamai. A. E. Arbuzov's School and its place in Soviet chemical science. Vestnik Vysshei Shkoly, 1948, #2.

Office: Presidium Kazan' Branch USSR Academy of
                Sciences
                Kazan', Tatar ASSR

ARBUZOV, BORIS ALEKSANDROVICH (Organic Chemist)

B. A. Arbuzov was born October 22, 1903. He is the son and pupil of A. E. Arbuzov (an outstanding organic chemist and Academician). In 1926 he graduated from Kazan' Institute of Agriculture and Forestry. He worked at the Kazan' Chemico-Technological Institute from 1930 to 1938 and was made a professor there in 1935. In 1938 he became a professor at the Kazan' University. Beginning in 1945, he has also worked at the Kazan˝ Branch of the U.S.S.R. Academy of Sciences. He was elected in 1943 a Corresponding Member of the U.S.S.R. Academy of Sciences and in 1953 an Academician. The U.S.S.R. Academy of Sciences awarded Arbuzov the D. I. Mendeleev Prize in 1949, and in 1951, he won a Stalin Prize.

Arbuzov's research has been in the field of terpenes, diene compounds and application of physical methods for the study of the composition of organic compounds. Arbuzov discovered the isomerization of α-pinene to allocymene and of α-oxypinene to compholene aldehyde. By the method of diene synthesis he obtained a number of diene products.

As of 1961, B. A. Arbuzov was Director of the Institute of Organic Chemistry of the U.S.S.R. Academy of Sciences Kazan' Branch.

Bibliography:

Research in the Field of Isomeric Conversions of Bicyclic Terpenes and Their Oxides. Kazan': 1936.
and A. N. Pudovik. Silicon-phosphorous organic derivatives. Doklady Akad. Nauk S.S.S.R., 1948, 59, #8.

and A. N. Pudovik. Allylic rearrangements. IX. Effect of
sodium salts of diakyl phosphorous acids and esters of
phosphorous acid on isomeric methoxychloropentanes.
Izvest. Akad. Nauk S.S.S.R., Otdel. Khim. Nauk, 1949, #5,
522-38.
and Z. G. Isaeva. Effect of alcohols on α-oxides of bicycylic
terpenes. Zhur. Obshchei Khim., 1949, #5, 884-905.
Arbusov B. A., Sur la rotation de groupes irreguliers dans
les molecules. Journal de chemie physique, 1953, t. 50,
647-51.

Office: Institute of Organic Chemistry, Kazan' Branch
              USSR Academy of Sciences
              Kazan', Tatar ASSR

ARTOBOLEVSKII, IVAN IVANOVICH (Mechanical Engineer)

I. I. Artobolevskii was born September 26, 1905. In 1926 he
graduated from the Faculty of Agricultural Engineering of K. A.
Timiryazev's Agricultural Academy. He received the degree
of Doctor of Technical Sciences in 1936. In 1927 to 1929 he
taught in the Moscow Electromechanical Institute; and in 1929
to 1932 he taught in the Moscow Chemico-Technological Institute where, in 1932, he was made a professor. In 1932 he became a professor in the Moscow Institute of Chemical Engineering of the N. E. Zhukovskii Air Force Academy and in Moscow
University. He was appointed professor at the Moscow Aviation
Institute in 1941. Beginning in 1937, he directed the Laboratory
of Dynamic Machines of the Institute of Machine Control of the
U.S.S.R. Academy of Sciences. From 1942 to 1954, Artobolevskii was Acting Secretary of the Department of Technical
Sciences of the U.S.S.R. Academy of Sciences. He was Chairman, 1945-1954, of the Department of Mechanical Engineers.
In 1939 he was elected a Corresponding Member of the U.S.S.R.
Academy of Sciences, and in 1946 an Academician. Artobolevskii was an Honored Scientist of the R.S.F.S.R. in 1945. In
1946, the Academy of Sciences awarded him, jointly with V. V.
Dobrovolskii and Z. Sh. Blokh, the P. L. Chebyshev Prize for
the treatises, A Synthesis of Mechanisms (1944) and The Scientific Legacy of Chebyshev (1945 with N. I. Levitskii). He is
also active in public affairs and in 1947 was made Acting Chairman of the All-Union Department for Dissemination of Political
and Scientific Knowledge.
Artobolevskii's field of activity is the theory of machines
and mechanisms. He worked out a classification of three

dimensional mechanisms and developed new methods for their kinematic analysis. He wrote the first Russian monograph on spatial mechanisms (The Theory of Spatial Mechanisms, 1937). He developed new methods for kinematic analysis of complicated multi-element mechanisms (1939). With a group of Soviet scientists, he originated methods for the study of modern automatic machines, especially in the food, printing, and machine-tool industries. He has been working on the theoretical and experimental methods for studying the dynamics of working machines.

Bibliography:

Theory of Three Dimensional Mechanisms. Moscow-Leningrad: 1937.

Methods of Balancing Inertial Forces in Working Machines with Complicated Kinematic Designs. Moscow-Leningrad: 1938.

The Kinematic and Kinetostatic Structure of Multi-Element Plane Mechanisms. Moscow-Leningrad: 1939.

Synthesis of Two Dimensional Mechanisms, I-II. Moscow-Leningrad: 1939-42.

and others. Methods for Analysis of Complicated Machines. Moscow-Leningrad: 1944.

Mechanisms, 1-4. Moscow-Leningrad: 1947-51.

Theory of Mechanisms and Machines, 3rd ed. Moscow: 1953.

Theory of mechanisms for the generation of curves which are hyperbolisms of conic sections. Izvest. Akad. Nauk S.S.S.R., Otdel. Tekh. Nauk, 1955, #11.

Theory of mechanisms for the generation of cissoidal curves. Izvest. Akad. Nauk S.S.S.R., Otdel Tekh. Nauk, 1955, #12.

Biography:

Academy Anniversary of I. I. Artobolevskii. Vestnik Akad. Nauk, S.S.S.R., 1955, #12.

Office: Dept. of Technical Sciences of USSR Academy of Sciences
Malyy Khariton'yevskii Pereulok 4
Moscow, USSR

ARTSIMOVICH, LEV ANDREEVICH (Nuclear Physicist)

L. A. Artsimovich, son of a Moscow professor of statistics, was born February 25, 1909. He graduated at an early age from the Belorussian State University; and at the age of 21, he began to work in the Leningrad Physico-Technical Institute where he was a student of A. F. Ioffe (1880-1960, internationally known physicist), the Director. He also taught at the Leningrad Polytechnical Institute and at Leningrad University. In the postwar years, he gave courses on atomic and nuclear physics, first at the Moscow Engineering and Physics Institute, then more recently at the Moscow University. In 1946 Artsimovich was elected a Corresponding Member and in 1954 an Academician of the U.S.S.R. Academy of Sciences. He was awarded a Stalin Prize in 1953, and in 1958 a Lenin Prize. He has also received a number of orders of the Soviet Union from the government.

Artsimovich's first researches were in x-ray optics, particularly on the problem of complete x-ray reflection. This investigation was carried out together with A. I. Alikhanov. In 1934-1935 Artsimovich, together with I. V. Kurchatov and others, studied the properties of the neutron and in particular the proton capture by a neutron. This study showed that the capture cross section of slow neutrons by protons is very great. In 1936, Artsimovich, with A. I. Alikhanov and A. I. Alikhanyan, examined the conclusions of the American physicist Shenkland on the possibility of the violation of the laws of conservation in the Compton Effect. An original experiment was set up which confirmed the validity of the laws of conservation in the electron and positron annihilation and refuted the ideas of Shenkland.

The main subject of his research at the Leningrad Physico-Technical Institute has been the study of the processes of the interaction of fast electrons with matter. In the mid thirties experimental data on bremsstrahlung and the angular distribution of electrons diverged from accepted theory by two orders of magnitude. Artsimovich did extensive experiments on the dependence of the bremsstrahlung intensity and the total energy losses on the energy of incident electrons. A careful analysis of the results showed that the quantum-mechanical theory of the passage of fast electrons through matter agrees with experimental data within the accuracy of the experiment.

During the war years (1943-46) Artsimovich was concerned with electron optics and the theory of chromatic aberrations of the electron optical system; he carried out theoretical and experimental research in the field of electron optical converters. In 1945, Artsimovich and I. Ya. Pomeranchuk did theoretical research on the role of radiation losses in the betatron. This work permitted the establishment of the maximum energy achieved by this type of electron acceleration. Artsimovich was one of a group who developed an electromagnetic method of isotope separation. From currents then available in the mass spectrometer laboratory (of the order of 10^{-10} amperes), it was necessary to use currents of the order of an ampere. In reaching a solution to this problem, Artsimovich carried out a careful analysis of the problems of the aberrationless focussing of ion beams in axially-symmetric magnetic fields. He designed the optics of the ion source. As a result of this work, the Soviet physicists developed a successful production of separated isotopes. In the beginning of the fifties, Artsimovich began his work on a controlled thermonuclear reaction. The group of physicists under Artsimovich began the study of high current pulse discharge in evacuated deuterium. In the course of these experiments, the group succeeded in obtaining for a short time a highly ionized plasma of a million degrees. In 1952, this group of scientific workers discovered that a powerful pulse discharge in deuterium at low pressure is a source of neutrons and x-ray radiation of short wave length. Further studies showed that the gas-discharge plasma, compressed in the presence of the longitudinal magnetic pole possessed paramagnetic properties. It was also shown that neutrons originate, not as a result of the thermonuclear reaction, but as a result of a specific acceleration process. The work of studying the means of obtaining a controlled thermonuclear reaction is now being conducted extensively under Artsimovich's direction. The report of L. A. Artsimovich at the Second World Conference on the Peaceful Use of Atomic Energy in Geneva in September, 1958, is a survey of the studies of Soviet physicists in this field.

Artsimovich has participated in the Pugwash Conferences. As of 1961, he was Secretary of the Physical Mathematical Sciences Department of the U.S.S.R. Academy of Sciences.

Bibliography:

and A. I. Alikhanov. The complete internal reflections of x-rays from thin films. Zhur. Eksptl. i Teoret. Fiz., #3, 1933.

and A. I. Alikhanov, A. I. Alikhanyan. The law of conservation of momentum in the annihilation of positrons. Doklady Akad. Nauk S.S.S.R., #7, 1936.

and V. A. Khramov. Energy losses for fast electrons. Izvest. Akad. Nauk S.S.S.R., Ser. Fiz., #757, 1938.

Delayed emission for high energy electrons. Zhur. Eksptl. i Teoret. Fiz., 1938, 8, #8-9.

and V. A. Khramov. Bremsstrahlung for high energy electrons. Zhur. Eksptl. i Teoret. Fiz., #8, 1938.

and I. I. Perrimond. Angular distribution of fast electrons
scattered by aluminum atoms. Doklady Akad. Nauk S.S.S.R.,
#52, 303, 1946.

Electron optical properties of emitters. Izvest. Akad. Nauk
S.S.S.R., #8, 313, 1944.

and I. Ya. Pomeranchuk. The radiation of fast electrons in
a magnetic field. Zhur. Eksptl. i Teoret. Fiz., #16, 379,
1946.

and G. Ya. Shchepkin, V. V. Zhukov, B. N. Makov, S. P.
Maksimov, A. F. Malov, A. A. Nikulichev. B. V. Panin,
B. G. Brezhnev. An electromagnetic installation with high
resolution for the separation of isotopes of light elements.
Atomic Energy III (12), #493, 1957.

and A. M. Andrianov, O. A. Basilevskaya, Yu. G. Prokhorov,
N. V. Fillipov. Study of pulse discharges with great electric
current. Atomic Energy I (3), #76, 1956.

and A. M. Andrianov, Ye. I. Dobrokhotov, S. Yu. Lukyanov,
I. M. Podgornii, V. I. Sinitsin, N. V. Filipov. Hard radiation
of impulse discharges. Atomic Energy I (3), #84, 1956.

On the origin of great currents through a plasma with a
longitudinal magnetic pole. Plasma Physics and the Problems of Controlled Thermonuclear Reactions, Handbook, II,
1958, 81.

Magnetic flow in a compressed cylinder. Plasma Physics
and the Problems of Controlled Thermonuclear Reactions,
Handbook, II, 1958, 87.

Analysis of the compression equation of a hole with an external magnetic field. Plasma Physics and the Problems of
Controlled Thermonuclear Reactions, Handbook, II, 1958,
101.

Studies on controlled thermonuclear reactions in the U.S.S.R.
Second International Conference of the UN on the Application
of Atomic Energy for Peaceful Purposes, #2298, 15 pp., 1958.

and K. T. Kartashev. The effect of a transverse magnetic
field on a toroidal discharge. Doklady Akad. Nauk S.S.S.R.
146, #6, 1305-08 (1962).

Biography:
    A. I. Alikhanov. Uspekhi Fiz. Nauk, #2, 367-697, Feb. 1959.
Office: Secretary of Physico-Mathematical Sciences
                 Pyzhevskii Pereulok, 3
                 Moscow, USSR

30

ASRATYAN, EZRAS ACRATOVICH (Physiologist)
     E. A. Asratyan was born May 31, 1903. A pupil of I. P.
Pavlov, he graduated from the Agricultural Institute in 1926
and from the University of Yerevan Medical School in 1930
From 1930 to 1938, he worked in the Physiological Institute,
Academy of Sciences. From 1935 to 1941, he worked at the
Bekhterov Cerebral Institute and from 1936 to 1941, at the
Leningrad Institute of Pedagogy where he became a professor
in 1938. From 1950-52, he was Director of the Institute of
Higher Neuroactivity. In 1944 he was appointed Chief of the
Academy of Sciences Physiological Laboratory, and later be-
came Director of the Institute. He has been professor at the
Second Medical Institute since 1950. He has been an Academician of the Armenian Academy of Sciences since 1947, a
member of the Communist Party of the Soviet Union since 1929,
and was elected to the U.S.S.R. Academy of Sciences as a
Corresponding Member in 1939. As of 1961, he was Director
of the Institute of Neurophysiology of the U.S.S.R. Academy of
Sciences. In 1962 he was awarded the Pavlov Gold Medal for
studies in Pavlovian physiology.
     Using Pavlov's teachings of the evolutionary theory of the
adaptability of the nervous system, Asratyan explained the regenerating aspects in a damaged organism. He and his collaborators proved that in the regeneration of lost and broken
functions of the damaged organism, a deciding role is played
by the cortex of the large hemispheres of the cephalic brain.
He also demonstrated the pathological condition of the organism,
produced by organic trauma (traumatic shock, paralysis, in-
cisions) and offered a new soporific method for treatment of
these conditions. An anti-shock liquid developed by Asratyan
was used in the front lines of the second World War. He, with
collaborators, has been working on the problems of cortical
presentation of unconditioned reflexes, the transfer into conditioned reflex activity, and the relationship of conditional ties
to various functional properties.
Bibliography:
     The influence of extirpation of the cortex of the large hemi-
spheres of the brain in the vegetative and somatic functions
of the organism. Reports on the 20th International Congress of Physiologists, Brussels, 1956. Moscow: 1956.
Outline on Etiology, Pathology and the Therapy of Traumatic
Shock. Moscow: 1945.
On the Adaptive Aspects in a Damaged Organism. Moscow:
1948.

Physiology of the Central Nervous System. Moscow: 1953.
Office: Institute of Neurophysiology of USSR Academy of
        Sciences
        Leninskii Prospekt, 33
        Moscow, USSR
Residence: Leninskii Prospekt, 13
        Moscow, USSR
Telephone: V2 08 65

ASTAUROV, BORIS LVOVICH (Biologist)

B. L. Astaurov was born October 27, 1904. He graduated
from the University of Moscow in 1927. He worked in the
Moscow Branch of the Academy of Sciences Commission for the
Study of Natural Productive Powers from 1926 to 1930. From
1930 to 1935, he was at the Middle East Institute of Sericulture
in Tashkent. Since 1935, he has been an associate at the Institute of Experimental Biology (now the A. N. Severtsov Institute
of Animal Morphology). In 1955, he was laboratory Chief of
Experimental Embryology. He became a Corresponding Member of the U.S.S.R. Academy of Sciences in 1958.

Astaurov's basic works deal with the theory and practice in
the heredity of the mulberry silkworm. He has worked out
methods of thermal artificial parthenoses and found a way of
obtaining complete experimental androgens.

Bibliography:

Problems of Selection and Genetics of the Mulberry Silkworm. Tashkent: 1934.

Works of the Near East Scientific Research of the Institute
of Sericulture, 5th ed.

Tests of the experimental androgens and gynogens in the
mulberry silkworm. Biological Journal, 1937, 6, #1.

Artificial parthogeneses in the mulberry silkworm (experimental succession 1940).

Thermoactivation as an effect and the means of removing the
embryonic dispause. Journal of Natural Biology, 1943, 4,
#6.

Direct proof of the vigorous nature of the biological effect of
X-rays, regardless of the final results of roentgenization
from the primary changes in the cytoplasm. Journal of
General Biology, 1947, 8, #6.

The significance of experiments on merogony and androgenesis to the theory of development and heredity. Accomplishments of Modern Biology, 1948, 25, #1.

and others. Deriving complete heterospermic androgenesis
in interspecific hybrids of the silkworm (experimental
analysis of the relationship between the nucleus and the
cytoplasm in development and heredity). News of the Academy of Sciences Biological Series, 1957, #2.
Office: A. N. Severtsov Institute of Animal Morphology
             Leninskii Prospekt, 33
             Moscow, USSR
Residence: 1-aya Cheremushkinskaya, 3
             Moscow, USSR
Telephone: V7 43 30

AVAKYAN, ARTAVAZD ARSHAKOVICH (Biologist)

A. A. Avakyan was born July 21, 1907. In 1946 he became
a Corresponding Member of the U.S.S.R. Academy of Sciences,
and in 1948 a member of the Lenin All-Union Academy of
Agriculture. He was awarded a Stalin Prize in 1941.
    The studies of Avakyan deal with problems of developing
vegetation. He was very active in the study of hereditary
changes in plants, vegetative hybridization, fertilization, vegetative and sexual reproduction of plants. He has conducted
investigations in the biology and culture of branchy-eared
wheat.
Bibliography:
    and A. Kh. Tagi-Zade. On the so-called "Vernalization" of
    plants by light. Vernalization, 1935, #1.
    The biology of tomato development. Vernalization, 1936,
    #2-3.
    Vernalization of rice. Vernalization, 1936, #1.
    and T. D. Lysenko. Chopping Cotton, 2nd ed. Moscow:
    1949.
    Controlling the development of vegetation organisms.
    Vernalization, 1938, #6.
    Vegetative hybridization of potatoes. Vernalization, 1938,
    #3.
    and M. G. Yastreb. Hybridization by grafting. Vernalization,
    1941, #1.
    and N. I. Feiginson. Step processes and the so-called bloom-
    ing hormones. Agro-Biology, 1948, #1.
    Some questions on the individual development of plants.
    Agro-Biology, 1948, #2.
    Properties hereditarily acquired by organisms. Agro-
    Biology, 1948, #6.

33   BAKULEV

Breeding strains of corn for new cultivated areas. Agro-
Biology, 1956, #1.
The biological nature of the so-called bi-arms. Izvest.
Akad. Nauk S.S.S.R., Biol. ser., 1956, #2.
Office: All-Union Academy of Agriculture
              Moscow, USSR
Residence: Leningradskii Prospekt 75-a
              Moscow, USSR
Telephone: D7 29 71

AVSYUK, GRIGORII ALEKSANDROVICH (Glaciologist)
      G. A. Avsyuk was born in 1906. In 1930 he graduated from
the Moscow Geodesic Institute. From 1928-37 he worked at
the cartographic publishing house of the Ministry of Internal
Affairs (NKVD), and later at the Main Northern Sea Route Administration. In 1937, he began work at the U.S.S.R. Academy
of Sciences Institute of Geography. In 1957, he became deputy
academician-secretary of the U.S.S.R. Academy of Sciences
division of geolo-geographic sciences. Since 1947 he has been
a member of the Communist Party of the Soviet Union. He was
elected, in 1960, a Corresponding Member of the U.S.S.R.
Academy of Sciences.
      Avsyuk visited the United States in February 1958 to attend
the International Arctic Sea Ice Conference in Easton, Maryland.
Bibliography:
      Les investigations glaciologiques en l'URSS. Assoc. Int.
      Hydrol. Sci. Assemblée Gen., Toronto 1957, T. 4 (Pub. #46)
      535-552 (incl. English summary), 1958. Bibliog. & Index of
      Geol. Exclusive of North America. Vol. 23, 1958, p. 23.
Office: Institute of Geography of USSR Academy of Sciences
              Staromonetnii Pereulok, 29
              Moscow, USSR
Residence: Leninskii Prospekt, 25
              Moscow, USSR
Telephone: V4 00 27, Ext. 50

BAKULEV, ALEKSANDR NIKOLAEVICH (Surgeon)
      A. N. Bakulev was born December 7, 1890. He graduated
from the Medical Faculty of Saratov University in 1915 after
which he served for three years as a regimental physician.
From 1919 to 1926 Bakulev was at the hospital surgical clinic
of Saratov University, first as a hospital surgeon and later as a
clinical assistant. He worked, in 1926 to 1943, at the Surgical
Clinical Faculty of the Second Moscow Medical Institute where

he became a professor in 1935. In 1943 he was head of the
Surgical Clinical Faculty of the Pediatric Faculty at the Second
Moscow Medical Institute, and as of 1962 has been Chairman of
the Surgical Clinical Faculty of the Therapeutic Faculty.

During World War II he was a front-line surgeon and subse-
quently chief surgeon of the Moscow Evacuation Hospital and
chief of the surgical division of the Kremlin Therapeutico-
Sanitation Administration Hospital. Bakulev was elected
Corresponding Member of the U.S.S.R. Academy of Medical
Sciences in 1947, and in 1948 Active Member. In 1958 he was
made Academician of the U.S.S.R. Academy of Sciences. In
1954 and in 1957, he was elected President of the U.S.S.R.
Academy of Medical Sciences. He was a Deputy to the Supreme
Soviet of the U.S.S.R., third to fifth convocations. Bakulev was
an Honored Scientist of the R.S.F.S.R. in 1947. He was award-
ed a State Prize in 1949, and in 1957, and two other times Lenin
Prizes. In 1960 he was made a Hero of Socialist Labor.

Bakulev conducted detailed studies on kidney function during
ureter transplantation and worked in the field of bone surgery,
tumors of the posterior mediastinum, and lungs. At the
Moscow Clinic, he studied encephalography and ventriculography
and was one of the first to introduce these methods in clinical
research in the U.S.S.R. He has also proposed the treatment
of brain abscesses by puncture (his doctoral dissertation).

During the second World War he studied the treatment of
firearms wounds, including spinal cord wounds and cranium
damage with exposed tissue where he proposed a closed suture
method.

After the war Bakulev turned to thoracic surgery problems
in lung and heart operations, and in 1948 performed the first
operation in the U.S.S.R. on a congenital defective heart.

In 1956 Bakulev initiated the organization of the Institute of
Thoracic Surgery in Moscow, which in 1960 was reorganized
into the U.S.S.R. Academy of Medical Sciences Institute of
Cardiovascular Surgery. He organized scientific research in
acquired and congenital diseases of the heart and main vessels,
developed surgical methods for their treatment, and incorporated these methods into medical practice (Stalin Prize 1957).

Other activities of Bakulev include Chairmanship of the
Scientific Coordination Council, Academy of Medical Sciences
U.S.S.R. and Membership in the Institute of Chest Surgery,
Moscow, Academy of Medical Sciences U.S.S.R.

Bibliography:
Surgical treatment of spinal cord tumors. Vestnik Khirurgii
im. Grekova, 1939, 58, #3.
Closed suture in retarded treatment of brain wounds.
Khirurgiya, 1942, #11-12.
Diagnosis and treatment of cohesive pericarditis. Khirurgiya, 1948, #10.
and A. V. Gerasimova. Pneumonectomy and Lobectomy
(surgical methods). Moscow: 1949.
and E. N. Meshalkin. Experimental application of angio-
cardiography in chest surgery. Vestnik Khirurgii im. Grekova, 1951, 71, #5.
Surgical Treatment of Cardiac and Main Vessel Disorders
(recognition, experience and perspectives). Moscow: 1952.
Surgery of acquired diseases of heart and aorta. Khirurgiya,
1954, #1.
and E. N. Meshalkin. Congenital Cardiac Deficiencies.
Moscow: 1955.
Conservation Treatment of Marrow Abscesses (by Puncture).
Moscow-Leningrad: 1940.
Office: Institute of Cardio-vascular Surgery
                USSR Academy of Medical Sciences
                Leninskii Prospekt, 8
                Moscow, V-49, USSR
Telephone: B1 13 61
Residence: Pl. Vosstaniya, 1
                Moscow, USSR
Telephone: D5 47 63

BALANDIN, ALEKSEI ALEKSANDROVICH (Organic Chemist)
   A. A. Balandin was born December 8, 1898. In 1923 he
graduated from Moscow University and worked there from 1927,
becoming a professor in 1934. He organized the first laboratory course in the Department of Organic Catalysis at Moscow
State University and in 1959 became Director of the Department.
Balandin is the Chief of the Laboratory of the Kinetics of Catalytic Organic Reactions and the N. D. Zelinskii Laboratory of
the Institute of Organic Chemistry of the Academy of Sciences
of the U.S.S.R. He is a student of N. D. Zelinskii (1861-1953,
an outstanding organic chemist specializing in catalysis and
stereoisomerism.) Balandin has been active in scientific
organizations; he is the Chairman of the Council for the Problem "Scientific Bases of Selecting Catalysts" in the Chemical
Sciences Section of the U.S.S.R. Academy of Sciences. This

Council coordinates all work on catalysts in the U.S.S.R. In 1949 Balandin became a member of the Communist Party of the Soviet Union. He was elected Corresponding Member of the U.S.S.R. Academy of Sciences in 1943 and Academician in 1946. He has received the Order of Lenin, two Orders of the Red Banner of Labor, and a Stalin Prize. For his research in synthetic rubber he was awarded the Mendeleev and Lebedev Prizes.

Balandin formulated the so-called multiplet theory of catalysis, attempting to establish a relationship between the geometry of the atomic groups, which change directly in catalysis during a reaction, and the geometry of active centers on the surface of the catalyst. On the basis of his theory and classification, Balandin studied the dehydrogenation of paraffins, olefins, alkylbenzenes, and those products of dehydrogenation which are important for the industrial synthesis of monomers, for obtaining synthetic rubber and other high-polymers.

Balandin is a Soviet pioneer in the study of the kinetics of organic catalytic reactions. He deduced the general kinetic equation for monomolecular reactions in a flow system. Balandin and his associates carried out extensive research on the kinetics of the dehydrogenation of hydrocarbons, the dehydrogenation and dehydration of alcohols, and the dehydrogenation of amines. Using the method of tagged atoms, the kinetics and mechanism of the dehydration of ethyl alcohol on aluminum oxide and the kinetics of the dehydrogenation of butane and butylene were studied. The reactions of catalytic production of styrene and its homologs were investigated in detail. This study is of great importance for synthetic rubber and plastics. Balandin formulated the theory of the hydrogenation of unsaturated compounds. The multiplet theory proved useful in the studies of Balandin and his co-workers on the hydrogenation of polysaccharides to obtain polyatomic alcohols. It received considerable development with the discovery of the laws for the selection of catalysts. The following are members of his scientific school: Ye. A. Agronomov, O. K. Bogdanova, A. Kh. Bork, I. I. Brusov, V. E. Vasserberg, N. A. Vasiunina, P. G. Ivanov, G. V. Isagulyants, Ye. I. Klabunovskii, S. L. Kiperman, A. I. Kukina, G. M. Marukyan, V. V. Patrikeev, S. Ye. Payk, A. P. Rudenko, T. A. Slovokhotova, N. P. Sokolova, A. A. Tolstopyatova, L. Kh. Freidlin, A. P. Shcheglova, and others.
Bibliography:
Modern problems of catalysis and the theory of multiplets. Uspekhi Khim., 1935, 4, #7.

Catalytic dehydrogenation of hydrocarbons and its applications in synthesis of rubber from gases. Izvest. Akad.
Nauk S.S.S.R., Otdel. Khim. Nauk, 1942, #1.
Theory of organic catalysis from Jubilee Symposium Dedicated to 30 Years Since the October Revolution, Part 1, 637-
58. Moscow-Leningrad: 1947.
Theory of selective catalysis. Uchenie zapiski MGU, 1956,
#175, 97-122.
Concerning the kinetics of alcohol dehydrogenation. Zhur.
Fiz. Khim., 1957, 31, #1.
and O. K. Bogdanov, I. P. Belomestrykh. The effect of
alkylaromatic hydrocarbon structure on the kinetics of their
dehydrogenation. Doklady Akad. Nauk S.S.S.R. 146, #6,
1327-30 (1962).
and V. I. Spitsyn, E. I. Mikhailenko, N. P. Dobrosel'skaya.
Dehydration of isopropyl alcohol on radioactive tricalcium
phosphate catalyst. Doklady Akad. Nauk S.S.S.R. 146, #6,
1128-31 (1962).

Office: N. D. Zelinskii Institute of Organic Chemistry
            Leninskii Prospekt, 31
            Moscow, USSR
Residence: ul. Vesnina, 11
            Moscow, USSR
Telephone: G1 56 76

BARANSKII, NIKOLAI NIKOLAEVICH (Geographer)
    N. N. Baranskii was born July 26, 1881. In 1901, he was
expelled from Tomsk University for participating in a student
political strike. Since that time, he became a professional
revolutionary. In the fall of 1905, he was chosen as a delegate
of the Siberian Bolsheviks to the Irkutsk Conference of the
Siberian Social Democratic Union. He graduated from the
Moscow Commercial Institute in 1914. In 1915, he was a board
member of the People's Commissars of Worker-Peasant Inspection. In 1918, he began to study economic geography which
arose in opposition to the then predominant statistical branch
method. He has been awarded the title Honored Scientist of the
R.S.F.S.R. in 1943. In 1939 he was elected to the U.S.S.R.
Academy of Sciences as a Corresponding Member. He is a
member of the Communist Party of the Soviet Union.
    Baranskii considers the main object of investigations in
economic geography to be not the branches of economics but
economic regions. In economic-geographic studies of various
countries he stresses the internal space difference; he placed

stress on the economic division into districts and the characteristics of these districts. In this connection, he placed great
importance on economic maps and field economic-geographic
investigation of territories. Baranskii compiled a series of
textbooks on economic geography of the U.S.S.R. (among them,
a standard textbook for the eighth grade which until 1955 had
16 editions). He established a series of university courses. He
is the author of questions of methodology of economic geography
and cartography.

In March 1962, Baranskii was awarded the Hero of Socialist
Labor.

Bibliography:
Physical Geography of the U.S.S.R. Textbooks for Junior
High School and High School, 7th ed. Moscow: 1943.
Economic Geography of the U.S.S.R. Textbooks for eighth
grade of High School, 16th ed. Moscow: 1955.
Economic Geography of the United States, Part 1. Moscow:
1946 (Institute of International Relations).
Economic cartography, #1, 3. Moscow, 1939-40 (mimeo-
graphed).
On the methods of teaching a regional course of economic
geography of the U.S.S.R. Bulletin of the All-Union Scientific
Society, 1941, #1.
Economic-geographic study of cities. Questions of Geogra-
phy, 1946, #2.
Generalization in cartography and in the writing of geo-
graphic textbooks. Scientific Papers of the Moscow State
University of M. V. Lomonosov, 1946, #119, Book 2.
Economic Geography--Economic Cartography. Moscow:
1956.
Economic Geography in a Secondary School--Economic
Geography in an Advanced School. Moscow: 1957 (contains
list of works of Baranskii).

Biography:
Geography in the University of Moscow for 200 Years, 1755-
1955, Moscow, 1955.
75th Anniversary of Nikolai Nikolaevich Baranskii. Geography in School, 1956, #4.

Office: USSR Academy of Sciences
Leninskii Prospekt, 14
Moscow, USSR
Residence: Leninskiye gory, korp. "L"
Moscow, USSR
Telephone: V9 32 78

BARMIN, VLADIMIR PAVLOVICH (Mechanical Engineer)
V. P. Barmin was born March 17, 1909. After graduating
from Moscow Technological College in 1930, he worked at the
plant "Compressor" where in 1940-1946 he was chief designer.
Beginning in 1931, he also taught at Moscow Technological
College. He has been a member of the Communist Party of the
Soviet Union since 1944. In 1958 Barmin was elected a Corresponding Member of the U.S.S.R. Academy of Sciences. In 1943
he received a Stalin Prize.
Barmin has been interested in mechanics, in particular construction of compressors.
Bibliography:
   and others. Cooling Machines and Apparatus. Moscow:
   1946.
Office: Moscow Technological College
              Moscow, USSR

BASHKIROV, ANDREI NIKOLAEVICH (Chemist)
A. N. Bashkirov was born December 22, 1903. In 1929 he
graduated from the Moscow Chemico-Technological Institute.
From 1934 to 1938, he worked at the All-Union Scientific Research Institute of Gas and Artificial Liquid Fuel and at its
Siberian branch (Novosibirsk). He was at the U.S.S.R. Academy
of Sciences Institute of Mineral Fuels from 1939 until 1947
when he began work at the Institute of Petroleum of the U.S.S.R.
Academy of Sciences. In 1943, Bashkirov became Chairman of
a Department at the Moscow Institute of Fine Chemical Technology. He has been since 1958 a Corresponding Member of the
U.S.S.R. Academy of Sciences.
Bashkirov worked on desulfurization of gases and petroleum
products and on thermal processing of coal. His main works
are devoted to catalytic synthesis of hydrocarbons, alcohols,
and amines from oxides of carbon and hydrogen; he investigated
the direct oxidation of hydrocarbons, and he worked out an
industrial process for higher aliphatic alcohols by direct oxidation of hydrocarbons.
Bibliography:
   Synthesis of higher alcohols of the aliphatic series by the
   method of direct oxidation of paraffin hydrocarbons. Chemical Science and Industry, 1956, 1, #3.
   and Yu. B. Kagan, L. I. Zvezdkina. Synthesis of higher aliphatic alcohols from CO and H_2. Doklady Akad. Nauk
   S.S.S.R., 1956, 109, #3.

and Yu. B. Kagan, G. A. Kliger. New synthesis of aliphatic
amines. Doklady Akad. Nauk S.S.S.R., 1956, 109, #4.
On some ways of developing synthesis based on oxides of
carbon and hydrogen and on methods of processing synthetic
hydrocarbons. Chemical Processing of Fuel. Works of the
2nd All-Union Congress on Artificial Liquid Fuel and Technological Gases. Moscow: 1957.
and V. V. Kamzolkin. Synthesis of ethanol from carbon dioxide and hydrogen. Doklady Akad. Nauk S.S.S.R.,
1958, 118, #2.

Office: Institute of Petroleum of USSR Academy of Sciences
                Leninskii Prospekt, 31
                Moscow, USSR

BASOV, NIKOLAI GENNADIEVICH (Radio Physicist)
N. G. Basov was born in 1922. He graduated from Moscow
Engineering and Physics Institute in 1950, and in 1957 he
earned the degree of Doctor of Physico-Mathematical Sciences.
In 1948 he began work at the Lebedev Institute of Physics, and
he has been Deputy Scientific Director of this Institute. As of
1962, he was still a member of the Lebedev Institute of Physics.
Basov has been a member of the Communist Party of the Soviet
Union since 1958. In 1962 he was elected a Corresponding
Member of the U.S.S.R. Academy of Sciences. He visited the
United States in September 1959 to attend the International
Conference on Quantum Electronics-Resonance Phenomena,
Bloomingburg, New York. In March 1962 he attended the annual
meeting of the Optical Society of America in Washington, D. C.
   Basov is conducting research in quantum radio physics.
With Corresponding Member A. M. Prokhorov he has developed
quantum optical generators.
Bibliography:
and O. N. Krokhin, L. M. Lisitsyn, E. P. Markin, B. D.
Osipov. Negative conductivity during inducted transfer.
Zhur. Ekspt'l. i Teoret. Fiz. 41, #3, 988-89 (1961).
and A. N. Oraevskii. Investigation of molecules in a mixed
energetic state. Zhur. Ekspt'l. i Teoret. Fiz. 42, #6, 1529-
35 (1962).
and E. P. Markin, D. I. Mash. Certain characteristics of a
generator on a neon and helium mixture. Zhur. Ekspt'l. i
Teoret. Fiz. 43, #3, 1116-1117 (1962).

Office: Lebedev Institute of Physics of USSR Academy of
               Sciences
               Leninskii Prospekt, 53
               Moscow, USSR

BELOUSOV, VLADIMIR VLADIMIROVICH (Geologist)

V. V. Belousov was born October 30, 1907. In 1943 he be-
came Chief of the Laboratory on Theoretical Geotectonics and
on Geodynamics of the USSR Academy of Sciences Institute of
Terrestrial Geophysics. Since 1953, he has been a professor at
Moscow University. In 1953, he was elected to the U.S.S.R.
Academy of Sciences as a Corresponding Member. In 1960 he
was elected President of the International Union of Geodesy and
Geophysics for the term 1960-1963. As of 1961, Belousov was
Chairman of the Soviet Geophysical Committee.

Belousov has worked in tectonics and tectono-physics. He
developed new methods of studying history of oscillatory motion
of the earth's crust and elucidated the history of geological development in the Greater Caucasus and the Russian platform.
In 1942 he advanced, and in 1951 and 1960 he developed the
hypothesis that a prolonged process of differentiation of the
earth's mass with a gradual division according to its density
took place as a main internal process influencing the tectonic
development of the earth's crust.

Belousov visited the United States to attend the American
Geological Society meetings in St. Louis, Missouri, in November
1958, and the Electric Power Delegation at Westinghouse Fermi
Plant in October 1959.

Bibliography:
Outline of the Geochemistry of Natural Gases. Leningrad:
1937.
Greater Caucasus, Part 1-3. Leningrad-Moscow: 1938-40.
Migration of radioelements and development of the structure
of the earth. Izvest. Akad. Nauk S.S.S.R., Geogr. and Geofiz.
Ser., 1942, #6; 1943, #3.
Facies and magnitudes of sedimentary thicknesses of Euro-
pean U.S.S.R. Works of the Institute of Geological Sciences
of the U.S.S.R. Academy of Sciences, 1944, #76.
General Geotectonics. Moscow-Leningrad: 1948.
Basic Problems in Geotectonics. Moscow: 1954. 2nd ed.
1962.
Development of the earth and tectogenesis. Journ. Geophys.
Res. 65, #12, 1960.

The origin of folding in the earth's crust. Journ. Geophys.
Res. 66, #7, 1961.

Office: Soviet Geophysical Committee
             USSR Academy of Sciences
             Molodezhnaya, 3
             Moscow, B-296, USSR
Residence: ul. Frunze, 7
             Moscow, USSR
Telephone: B8 26 33

BELOV, NIKOLAI VASIL'EVICH (Crystallographer)
N. V. Belov was born December 14, 1891. He graduated
from the Petrograd Polytechnical Institute in 1921. In 1938 he
joined the staff of the Crystallography Institute of the U.S.S.R.
Academy of Sciences. He was made professor in 1946 at
Gorkii University and in 1953 at Moscow University. Belov
became in 1954 a member of the Executive Committee and in
1957 vice-president of the International Crystallographic Association. He helped to organize the Leningrad and the Moscow
Crystallographic Museums. In 1946 Belov was elected a Corresponding Member of the U.S.S.R. Academy of Sciences and in
1953 an Academician. He received a Stalin Prize in 1952.

Belov's scientific work is in geometrical crystallography,
x-ray structure work, the practical application of symmetry
groups and Fourier's analysis to crystals. He developed a
theory of close packing of atoms in a crystal. As a result of
this theory a number of structures were established such as
epidote, wollastonite. Belov has trained many Soviet workers
in x-ray crystallography.

Belov visited the United States in January 1960 to attend a
Crystallography Conference at Brooklyn Polytechnical Institute.
Bibliography:
   Crystal structure of tourmaline. Doklady Akad. Nauk
   S.S.S.R., 1949, 69, #2.
   Crystal structure of milarite. Doklady Akad. Nauk S.S.S.R.,
   69, #3.
   Crystal structure of ramsite. Doklady Akad. Nauk S.S.S.R.,
   69, #6.
   Achievements in structural mineralogy. Izvest. Akad. Nauk
   S.S.S.R., Ser. Geol., 1949, #6.
   Structural Crystallography. Moscow: 1951.
   and others. 1651 Shubnikov group, from Trudy Instituta
   Kristallografii, #11. Moscow: 1955.

Outlines of structural mineralogy, from Mineralogicheskii Sbornik. L'voy-Khar'kov: 1950-56, #4 to 10. The Structure of Ionic Crystals and Metallic Phases. Moscow: 1947. and E. A. Pobedimskaya. The structure of epididymite NaBeSi₃O₇(OH). A new kind of infinite silicilic acid chain (strip) [Si₆O₁₅]. Zhur. Strukt. Khim., 1:#1, 51-63 (1960). NSA 15, 11354 (1961). and V. V. Bakakin. Crystal structure of hurlbutite. Doklady Akad. Nauk S.S.R. 135, #3, 587-90 (1960). and L. P. Solov'ev. Crystalline structure of Bertrandite-- Be₄Si₂O₇(OH)₂. Doklady Akad. Nauk S.S.S.R. 140, #3, 685-88 (1961). and V. V. Ilyukhin. Crystalline structure of Rubedium di-(meta)fluoroberyllate RbBe₂F₅. Doklady Akad. Nauk S.S.S.R. 140, #5, 1066-69 (1961). Crystalline structure of evdidimite NaBeSi₃O₇OH. Doklady Akad. Nauk S.S.S.R. 136, #6, 1448-50 (1961). and Kh. S. Mamedov, Yu. A. Akhundov. Crystalline structure of brandisite. Doklady Akad. Nauk S.S.S.R. 137, #1, 167-70 (1961). and K. K. Abrashev. Crystalline structure of Barylite BaBe₂Si₂O₇. Doklady Akad. Nauk 144, #3, 636-38 (1962). Elastic scattering of high energy pions and nucleons. Zhur. Ekspt l. i Teoret. Fiz. 42, 880-81 (1962).

Biography:
Belov, N. V. Vestnik Akad. Nauk S.S.S.R., 1954, #1.
Office: Department of Physics
Moscow University
Moscow, USSR
Residence: Leninskaya slob, 7
Moscow, USSR
Telephone: ZH 5 20 19

BELOZERSKII, ANDREI NIKOLAEVICH (Plant Biochemistry)
A. N. Belozerskii was born August 29, 1905. He graduated in 1927 from the Central Asiatic University. In 1930 he worked at Moscow University and in 1946 was made professor. He was also working in 1946 at the Institute of Biochemistry of the U.S.S.R. Academy of Sciences. In 1958 he became a Corresponding Member of the U.S.S.R. Academy of Sciences, and in June 1962, an Academician.

Belozerskii's investigations are devoted to the chemistry and biochemistry of albumen and chiefly of nucleic acids. He

established the presence of desoxyribonucleic acid in higher
and lower plants and noted the relationship of the change of
nucleic acids in ontogenesis of plants. He showed a specific
characteristic of desoxyribonucleic acid in bacteria.
Bibliography:

Semi-nucleic acids and their connection with the evolution of
nucleus apparatus of the vegetable cell. Uspekhi Sovremennoi Biol., 1944, #18.

and N. I. Proskuryakov. Practical Handbook on the Biochemistry of Plants. Moscow: 1951.

On the metaphosphate-nucleic complexes of yeast and the
chemical nature of volutine. Report at the III International
Biochemical Congress. Brussels. August 1-6, 1955.
Moscow: 1955.

The specific characteristic of nucleic acids in bacteria.
Origin of Life on the Earth. Collection of Reports from an
International Conference, August 1957, Moscow. Moscow:
1957.

Office: A. N. Bakh Institute of Biochemistry
Leninskii Prospekt, 33
Moscow, USSR

Residence: Leninskiye gory, sektor "K", 10th floor
Moscow, USSR

Telephone: V9 17 76

BELYAYEV, ANATOLII IVANOVICH (Metallurgist)

A. I. Belyayev was born in 1906. In 1931 he graduated from
the Kalinin Moscow Institute of Non-Ferrous Metals and Gold.
In 1931-34, he was a plant engineer at Zadorozh'e, and chief
engineer of the Main Aluminum Plant in Moscow. He was,
1934-37, scientific Director of the Moscow branch of the All-
Union Aluminum Institute. In 1941 he began work at the Institute of Non-Ferrous Metals and Gold. He was elected, in 1960,
to the U.S.S.R. Academy of Sciences as a Corresponding
Member.

Belyayev's main works deal with the electrochemistry of
alloy salts and the electrometallurgy of light metals.
Bibliography:

and A. D. Gerasimov. Surface activity of the boundary of
metal and melt, and crystal lattice energy. Izvest. Vysshikh
Ucheb. Zavedenii, Tsvetnaya Met. 2, #5, 45-9 (1959). C. A.
54, 21975c (1960).

and N. I. Grafas. Effect of molten flux on smelting and refining aluminum. Izvest. Vysshikh Ucheb. Zavedenii,
Tsvetnaya Met. 2, #4, 72-82 (1959). C. A. 54, 9561f (1960).
and K. G. Marin. Aluminum oxide behavior in the electro-
lyte of an aluminum bath. Sbornik Nauch. Trudov. Moskov.
Inst. Tsvetnoi Met. i Zolota 1957, #27, 178-92. C. A. 54,
9556b (1960).
and L. A. Firsanova. Melting Al-Si alloys from the sludge
of the secondary aluminum treatment. Sbornik Nauch.
Trudov, Moskov. Inst. Tsvetn. Metal. i Zolota i Vsesoyuz
Nauch. Inzhener.-Tekh. Obshchestvo Tsvetnoi Met. 1957,
#26, 162-71. C. A. 54, 10768a (1960).
and M. A. Kolenkova. Leaching bauxite at high pressures.
Sbornik Nauch. Trudov, Moskov. Inst. Tsvetn. Metal. i
Zolota im. M. I. Kalinina, 1957, #26, 120-31. C. A. 54,
20717g (1960).
and E. A. Zhemchuzhina. Leaching Northern Ural bauxites
at 100 atmospheres pressure. Sbornik Nauch. Trudov,
Moskov. Inst. Tsevtn. Metal. i Zolota 1958, #31, 80-90.
C. A. 54, 18240d (1960).
and E. A. Zhemchuzhina. Effect of graphite and salt ad-
ditions on the quality of carbon anode paste. Izvest. Vys-
shikh Ucheb. Zavedenii, Tsvetnaya Met. 3, #1, 97-100 (1960).
C. A. 54, 24015c (1960).
Office: Institute of Non-Ferrous Metals and Gold
             Moscow, USSR
Residence: B. Serpukhovskaya, 17/44
             Moscow, USSR
Telephone: V1 19 54

BERG, AKSEL IVANOVICH (Radioengineer)
A. I. Berg was born November 10, 1893. He was a submarine
mate during World War I and a submarine Commander in
the Civil War. After graduating from the Naval Academy and
the Naval Engineering School of Leningrad in 1925, he taught
and worked at military and naval institutions. In 1926 he joined
the staff of the Electro-Technical Institute. He also planned and
organized research when he was Chairman of the All-Union
Advisory Committee on Radiophysics and Radioengineering of
the U.S.S.R. Academy of Sciences. Berg was Chairman of the
Board of Directors of the Popov All-Union Technological Society
of Radio Technology and Related Sciences. He has been a member of the Communist Party of the Soviet Union since 1944. In
1943 he was elected Corresponding Member of the U.S.S.R.

Academy of Sciences and in 1946 Academician. He was a recipient in 1951 of the A. S. Popov gold medal.

Berg's scientific work deals with: designing and developing
of tube oscillators; stabilizing frequency; studying amplification
and frequency control of tube oscillators. He formulated and
worked out a number of important problems (grid detection; the
computation of an oscillator with a distorted pulse form of the
anode current) which contributed to the development of radio
engineering. Berg is the author of many textbooks in the field
of radioengineering.

As of 1961, Berg was chairman of the Cybernetics Council
of the U.S.S.R. Academy of Sciences.

Bibliography:

General Theory of Radio Technique, 1925.

The Theory of Vacuum Oscillators of the AC Current, 1925.

Principles of Calculation in Radioengineering. Part I, 1928;
2nd ed. 1930.

Theory and Computation of Tube Oscillators, 1932; 2nd ed.
1935.

Biography:

General Assembly of the U.S.S.R. Academy of Sciences,
Nov. 29 - Dec. 4, 1946. Moscow-Leningrad: 1947.

Academicians elected by the General Assembly of the
U.S.S.R. Academy of Sciences on November 30, 1946. Vestnik Akad. Nauk S.S.S.R., 1947, #1.

Academician A. I. Berg. Radiotekhnika, 1953, 8, #6, 71-74.

I. S. Dzhigit. Academician A. I. Berg (on his 60th birthday).
Izvest. Akad. Nauk S.S.S.R., Otdel. Tekh. Nauk, 1953, #12,
1870-74.

Office: All-Union Scientific Council on Radiophysics &
        Radio Engineers
        Mokhovaya Ulitsa, 2
        Moscow, USSR

Residence: 1-aya Cheremushkinskaya, 3
        Moscow, USSR

Telephone: V7 09 02

BERITASHVILI (BERITOFF), IVAN S. (Physiologist)

I. S. Beritashvili was born December 29, 1884. In 1910 he
graduated from Petersburg University. He became a professor
in 1919 at Tbilisi University. In 1935 he was appointed head of
the Institute of Physiology at the University. This Institute became a part of the Georgian S.S.R. Academy of Sciences in 1941,
and Beritashvili was the Director until 1952. Until recently he

has been Chief of scientific work there. He was elected Academician of the U.S.S.R. Academy of Sciences in 1939 and in 1941
of the Georgian S.S.R. Academy of Sciences. Since 1944 he has
been a member of the Academy of Medical Sciences. In 1938
Beritashvili was awarded the Prize of I. P. Pavlov and in 1941
a Stalin Prize. In 1959 Beritashvili was elected an honorary
member of the New York Academy of Sciences.

The main work of Beritashvili is devoted to muscle physiology and the physiology of the nervous systems, particularly the
central nervous system. He conducted investigations on the
following: the contracting power of various muscles, the relationship of processes of excitation and contraction, functional
differences of nervous and non-nervous sections of the muscle,
plastic and elastic properties of various muscles, functional
properties of peripheral nerves, velocity of distribution of
excitation in the central nervous system, its coordinating action,
the variability of innate reflex actions, the phenomenon of general inhibition of the central nervous system, the higher forms of
behavior in vertebrates, the neuro-psychic processes and their
behavioural role, the conditions of formation of temporary connections, the role of receptors in spatial orientation in vertebrates and in man, the structural basis of the neuro-psychic
activity, the interaction between the imaginal neuro-psychic activity and reflex action in animals, the interaction between the
conscious and reflex action of man and others. He was one of
the first to widely utilize the newest methods of investigating
electric processes in the central nervous system. He is the
author of a treatise "General Physiology of the Muscle and
Nervous System" (1937, Stalin Prize 1941).
Bibliography:
    Study on the Basic Elements of Central Coordination of Skele-
    tal Muscles. Petrograd: 1916.
    Individually Acquired Activity of the Central Nervous System.
    Tbilisi: 1932.
    On the Basic Forms of Nervous and Psychonervous Activity.
    Moscow-Leningrad: 1947.
    Nervous Mechanisms of Spatial Orientation of Mammals.
    Tbilisi: 1959.
    Nervous Mechanisms of Behavior in Higher Vertebrates.
    Moscow: 1961.
Office: I. S. Beritashvili Institute of Physiology of the
                Academy of Sciences Georgian SSR
                Voyenno-Gruzinskaya Doroga 22
                Tbilisi, Georgian SSR

BERNSHTEYN, SERGEI NATANOVICH (Mathematician)
   S. N. Bernshteyn was born March 6, 1880 in Odessa. He did
graduate work in the Sorbonne in 1899 and also at the Paris
Higher Electrical Engineering School in 1901. In 1904 he received the Doctor of Mathematical Science in Paris and in 1914
the Doctor of Pure Mathematics at Kharkov. From 1907 to
1908 Bernshteyn was professor at the Petersburg Women's
Polytechnical School and from 1908 to 1918, professor at the
Higher School for Women at Kharkov. He taught at Kharkov
University from 1907 to 1933 and in 1920 became a professor
there. He was a professor at the Leningrad Polytechnical Insti-
tute during 1933-1941 and about the same time, 1934-1941, at
Leningrad University. In 1935 he joined the staff of the Mathe-
matics Institute of the U.S.S.R. Academy of Sciences. Bern-
shteyn was elected a Corresponding Member of the U.S.S.R.
Academy of Sciences in 1924, and in 1929 an Academician.
Since 1925 he has been a member of the Ukrainian Academy of
Sciences. He was made an Honorary Member of the Moscow
Mathematical Society in 1940. In 1955 he became a Foreign
Member of the Paris Academy of Sciences. He was awarded in
1941 a Stalin Prize.
   Bernshteyn's scientific work deals chiefly with the theory of
differential equations, and the theory of approximations by polynomials of functions. Early investigations (1903) of second
order equations of the elliptical type led him to the conclusion
that under certain general conditions their solutions become
analytical functions which can be represented as a power series.
Bernshteyn developed a new method of solving elliptical differential equations. He also studied the functional approximation of
polynomials, further developing the theory proposed by P. L.
Chebishev and continued by the scientists of the Petersburg
School. This work establishes the accuracy with which a
function can be approximated by polynomials of different powers
and by differential functional properties (as for instance
through derivatives of a definite order). Bernshteyn, with his
students, created a new branch in the theory of functions, which
he called "the constructive theory of functions." His contributions in the field of probability are: the establishment of an
axiomatic structure of the theory of relativity (1917); investigations of finite theorems (continuation and completion of the
work of A. A. Markov, Sr. and A. M. Lyapunov); study of sto-
chastic differential equations and the practical application of
the theory of probability to solutions of problems in physics
and statistics.

49   BERNSHTEYN

Bibliography:
  Collection of Papers, 1, 2. Moscow: 1952-54 (Vol. 1 con-
  tains a bibliography of his work).
  Analytical Approach to Differential Elliptical Equations.
  Kharkov: 1956.
  Sur la nature analytique des équations aux dérivées parci-
  elles de second ordre. Mathématische Annâlen, Berlin-
  Leipzie, 1904, 59, 20-76.
  Investigation and integration of differential equations with
  partial elliptical derivatives of the second order. Reports of
  the Kharkov Mathematical Society, Second Series, 1908-09,
  11.
  The optimum approximation to continuous functions by poly-
  nomials of a given power. Reports of the Kharkov Mathe-
  matical Society, Second Series, 1912, 13, #2-3.
  An experiment in the theory of probability on axiomatic
  grounds. Reports of the Kharkov Mathematical Society,
  Second Series, 1917, 15.
  Specific Properties of Polynomials and the Most Suitable
  Approximation to Continuous Functions of One Compound
  Variable, Pt. 1. Leningrad-Moscow: 1937.
  Theory of Probability, 4th ed. Moscow-Leningrad: 1946.
  and I. G. Petrovskii. The first marginal problem (of Dirich-
  let) to solve elliptical equations and the properties of functions
  explained by these equations. Uspekhi Mat. Nauk, 1940, #8.
Biography:
  On the 70th birthday of S. N. Bernshteyn. Izvest. Akad. Nauk
  S.S.S.R., Ser. Mat., 1950, 14, #3 (list of publications from
  1941).
  R. O. Kuzmin. Mathematical contributions of S. N. Bern-
  shteyn. Uspekhi Mat. Nauk, 1940, #8.
  N. I. Akhiezer. Academician S. N. Bernshteyn and His Works
  on the Constructive Theory of Functions. Kharkov: 1955
  (also contains a list of Bernshteyn's publications).
Office: V. A. Steklov Mathematics Institute of USSR Acade-
              my of Sciences
              1-y Akademicheskii Proyezd, 28
              Moscow, USSR
Residence: Leninskii Prospekt, 13
              Moscow, USSR
Telephone: B2 11 12

BEY-BIENKO (BEI-BIENKO), GRIGORII YAKOVLEVICH (Entomologist)

G. Ya. Bey-Bienko was born February 7, 1903. In 1925 he graduated from the Siberian Agricultural Academy in Omsk. From 1929 to 1938, he worked at the All-Union Research Institute of Plant Protection in Leningrad. In 1938, he became a professor at the Leningrad Agricultural Institute and laboratory chief at the U.S.S.R. Academy of Sciences Institute of Zoology in 1947. From 1946 to 1948, he worked at the Institute of Applied Zoology and Phytopathology. He was awarded the N. A. Kholodkovskii Prize in 1951, and a State Prize in 1952. In 1953 he was elected to the U.S.S.R. Academy of Sciences as a Corresponding Member. He was, in 1954 and 1960, a Vice-President of the All-Union Entomological Society.

Numerous scientific investigations of Bey-Bienko deal with theoretical and applied entomology and ecology. He is the author of monographs on the series: "Fauna of the U.S.S.R.," "Dermapterous Insects" (1936), "Orthoptera. Subfamily of Foliar long-horned Grasshoppers (Phaneropterinae)" (1954), "Cockroaches" (1950).

Bibliography:
and L. L. Mishchenko. Fauna of the U.S.S.R. and of Neighboring Countries. Part 1-2. Moscow-Leningrad: 1951.
and others. Agricultural Entomology, 3rd ed. (V. N. Shchegolev, ed.) Moscow-Leningrad: 1955.
On the general classification of insects. Rev. Entom. Acridoid USSR, XLI, 1, 1962.
Office: Zoological Institute, Academy of Sciences USSR
Universitetskaya Naberezhnaya 1
Leningrad, B-164, USSR

BITSADZE, ANDREI VASILEVICH (Mathematician)

A. V. Bitsadze was born May 22, 1916 in Chiaturskii Rayon, in the Georgian S.S.R. He graduated from the Tbilisi University in 1940 and in 1951 received his Doctor of Physical-Mathematical Science degree. In 1941 he began working at the Institute of Mathematics of the Georgian S.S.R. Academy of Sciences. From 1942 to 1947 he also taught at Tbilisi University. In 1948 he went to work at the Mathematics Institute of the U.S.S.R. Academy of Sciences. Bitsadze has been a member of the Communist Party of the Soviet Union since 1947. In 1958 he was elected a Corresponding Member of the U.S.S.R. Academy of Sciences.

Bitsadze's main work is on the theory of differential
equations with partial derivatives (systems of elliptical
equations, compound equations) and singular integral equations.
Bibliography:
On the Problem of Compound Type Equations. Moscow:
1953.
Terminal problems for systems of linear differential
equations of the elliptical type. Reports of the Georgian
S.S.R. Academy of Sciences, 1944, 5, #8.
On the general compound type problem. Doklady Akad. Nauk
S.S.S.R., 1951, 78, #4.
On elliptical systems of differential equations with partial
derivatives of secondary order. Doklady Akad. Nauk
S.S.S.R., 1957, 112, #6.
Three dimensional mixed-type equations. Doklady Akad.
Nauk S.S.S.R. 143, #5, 1017-19 (1962).
Office: V. A. Steklov Mathematics Institute of USSR Acade-
my of Sciences
1-y Akademicheskii Proyezd, 28
Moscow, USSR

BLAGONRAVOV, ANATOLII ARKADIEVICH (Mechanical
     Engineer)
     A. A. Blagonravov was born June 1, 1894. He is a graduate
of the following institutions: the Mikhailovskoe School of Artillery (1916), Artillery College (1924), and the Military Technical Academy (1929). From 1929 to 1946 he was on the staff of
the Moscow Academy of Artillery and in 1938 was made a professor there. He was President, in 1946-1950, of the Academy
of Artillery Science. Blagonravov was made Director of the
Machine Science Section of the U.S.S.R. Academy of Sciences in
1953. In 1957 he became Academic Secretary of the Technical
Science Division of the U.S.S.R. Academy of Sciences. He has
been a member of the Communist Party since 1937. In 1940 he
was given the permanent rank of lieutenant general in the artillery. Since 1943 he has been an Academician of the U.S.S.R.
Academy of Sciences.
     Blagonravov's scientific contributions are in the field of
machinery and mechanics of armaments. His main work, Basic
Principals of Automatic Weapons (1931), is a valuable source
of fundamental calculations in the construction of weapons.
     In April 1962, Blagonravov was appointed Editor in Chief of
Izvestiya Akad. Nauk S.S.S.R., Otdel. Tekh. Nauk. He has
attended the Pugwash Conferences.

Bibliography:
  Material Part of a Shooting Weapon, I & II. Moscow: 1945-46.
Office: Academic Secretary, Department of Technical
      Sciences
      Malyy Khariton'yevskii Pereulok, 4
      Moscow, USSR

BLINOVA, EKATERINA NIKITICHNA (Dynamic Meteorologist)
  E. N. Blinova was born December 7, 1906. She graduated
from North Caucasus University (Rostov-on-the-Don). In 1935
to 1945, she was senior scientific research associate at the
Main Geophysical Observatory. In 1943 she began working at
the Central Institute of Weather Forecasting in Moscow. Since
1953 she has been a Corresponding Member of the U.S.S.R.
Academy of Sciences.
  Continuing the work of N. E. Kochin (1901-1944, mathematician), Blinova investigated in detail the conditions of atmospheric front stability (1936). Later, from 1938, she studied the
general circulation of the atmosphere and developed a theory of
radiative equilibrium in the atmosphere. She was successful in
making a quantitative explanation of the existence of the so-
called centers of atmospheric action. For this, she studied
wave disturbances occurring in the general east-west atmospheric flow. She utilized the same wave method for a quantitative analysis of such atmospheric macroprocesses as the
origin and development of cyclines and anti-cyclones. Blinova
indicated in her works methods of long-term weather forecasting by means of integration of the so-called vortex equations
proposed by A. A. Fridman (1888-1925, physicist), which are
widely utilized at the present time for weather forecasting with
the aid of electronic computers and for solving other problems
in atmospheric dynamics.
Bibliography:
  Sloping surface of discontinuity of an occlusion. Works of
  the Main Geophysical Observatory, 1935, #4.
  Zonal oscillations of the surface of Margules discontinuity.
  Works of the Main Geophysical Observatory, 1936, #10.
  Theory of cyclone formation. Works of the Main Geophysical Observatory, 1938, #23.
  Determination of the speed of troughs from the non-linear
  equation for a vortex. Priklad. Mat. i Mekh., 1946, 10,
  #5-6.

Hydrodynamic theory of pressure waves, temperature waves and centers of atmospheric action. Doklady Akad. Nauk S.S.S.R., 1943, 39, #7.
Problem of the average annual distribution of temperature in the earth's atmosphere with consideration of continents and oceans. Izvest. Akad. Nauk S.S.S.R., Ser. Geogr. i. Geofiz., 1947, 2, #1.
Problem of determining pressure at sea level. Doklady Akad. Nauk S.S.S.R., New Series, 1953, 92, #3.
Method of solving a non-linear problem of atmospheric movements of a planetary scale. Doklady Akad. Nauk S.S.S.R., New Series, 1956, 110, #6.

Biography:
Ekaterina Nikitichna Blinova. Izvest. Akad. Nauk S.S.S.R., Ser. Geofiz., 1954, #1.

Office: Central Institute of Weather Forecasting
              Moscow, USSR

BLOKHINTSEV, DMITRII IVANOVICH (Physicist)

D. I. Blokhintsev was born January 11, 1908. After graduating from Moscow University in 1930, he taught there and in 1936 was made professor. In 1935-1956 he worked at the Physics Institute and at the Atomic Power Plant of the U.S.S.R. Academy of Sciences. He became Director of the Joint Institute of Nuclear Research in 1956. Since 1943, Blokhintsev has been a member of the Communist Party of the Soviet Union. In 1939 he was elected a Corresponding Member of the Ukrainian S.S.R. Academy of Sciences and in 1958 a Corresponding Member of the U.S.S.R. Academy of Sciences. He was awarded a Stalin Prize in 1952 and in 1957 a Lenin Prize.

Blokhintsev's interests are in the theory of solid bodies, optics, acoustics, field theory, quantum mechanics, philosophy of natural science, atomic physics and technology. He presented (1934) a quantum theory of the phosphorescence of solid bodies, and a theory of spectra of absorption and of fluorescence of complex molecules. A series of investigations by Blokhintsev are devoted to phenomena in semi-conductors; particularly, in the theory of solid rectifiers. Blokhintsev also investigated the distribution of sound in an inhomogeneous moving medium. He directed the construction of the Soviet atomic power plant (1954). Blokhintsev is the author of a text on quantum mechanics for universities.

Bibliography:
On the theory of phosphorescence. Doklady Akad. Nauk S.S.S.R., 1934, 2, #2.

On the theory of solid dry rectifiers. Doklady Akad. Nauk S.S.S.R., 1938, 21, #1-2.

Fluorescence and absorption spectra of complex molecules. Zhur. Eksptl. i Teoret. Fiz., 1939, 9, #4.

Basis of Quantum Mechanics. 2nd ed., Moscow-Leningrad: 1949.

Acoustics of an Inhomogeneous Moving Medium. Moscow-Leningrad: 1946.

Elementary particles in a field. Uspekhi Fiz. Nauk, 1950, 42, #1.

On non-local and non-linear field theories. Uspekhi Fiz. Nauk, 1957, 61, #2.

and N. A. Dollezhal, A. K. Krasin. Atomic energy reactor. Atomic Energy, 1956, #1.

Office: Joint Institute of Nuclear Research
             Moscow, USSR

BOCHVAR, ANDREI ANATOLEVICH (Metallographer)

A. A. Bochvar was born July 26, 1902, son of A. M. Bochvar (1870-1947, founder of the school of metallurgists). In 1923 he graduated from the Moscow Higher Technical School and then taught there. He began teaching at the Moscow Institute of Non-Ferrous Metals and Gold in 1930, and in 1934 he became a professor. In 1939 Bochvar was elected Corresponding Member of the U.S.S.R. Academy of Sciences and in 1946 Academician. He is a Hero of Socialist Labor and a recipient of a Stalin Prize.

Bochvar's basic studies are concerned with the kinetics of eutectic crystallization (doctoral dissertation, 1935), the recrystallization of metals and alloys, the deformation of alloys at high temperatures, the crystallization of alloys under pressure and the relation of the casting properties of alloys to their phase diagrams. Having carried out experimental research in the mechanism of eutectic crystallization, Bochvar constructed a theory for structural peculiarities and anomalies of alloys. He established the temperature patterns of the crystallization of metals and alloys (the so-called "Bochvar Rule"), and formulated the principles of a structural theory of heat-resistance. Studies on the crystallization of alloys under pressure permitted him, jointly with A. G. Spasski, to develop new industrial methods of shaping castings by crystallization under pressure,

thus eliminating porosity of aluminum alloys, and to work out
new principles of casting, ensuring significant metal reduction.
Bochvar wrote a series of textbooks on metallography and the
thermal treatment of metallic alloys.

Bibliography:
A Study of the Mechanism and Kinetics of Crystallization of
Eutectic Alloys. Moscow-Leningrad: 1935.
Basic Treatment of Alloys, 5th ed. Moscow-Leningrad:
1940.
Metallography, 5th ed. Moscow: 1956.
On various mechanisms of plasticity in metallic alloys.
Izvest. Akad. Nauk S.S.S.R., Otdel. Tekh. Nauk, 1948, #5.

Office: Moscow Institute of Non-Ferrous Metals and Gold
Moscow, USSR

BOGOLYUBOV, NIKOLAI NIKOLAEVICH (Mathematician)

N. N. Bogolyubov was born in 1900 in Nizhnii Novgorod (now
Gorkii) and in 1922, he moved with his mother to Kiev, where he
attracted the attention of mathematicians D. A. Grave and N. M.
Krilov. In 1923 he began work in a seminar sponsored by the
department of mathematical physics of the Academy of Sciences
of the Ukrainian S.S.R. under the direction of N. M. Krilov. In
1924, he wrote his first scientific paper. In 1925, by special
permission, he was admitted with no diploma from a higher
educational institution as an associate of the department of
mathematical physics of the Academy of Sciences of the Ukrainian S.S.R. In 1928, he defended his candidate's dissertation on
the subject "The Use of Direct Methods in the Calculus of Variations for Investigation of Irregular Cases of the Problem of
the Extreme." In 1930, the Presidium of the Academy of
Sciences of the Ukrainian S.S.R. awarded him the degree Doctor
of Mathematics honoris causa.
     Starting in 1928, Bogolyubov was employed by the Academy
of Sciences of the Ukrainian S.S.R. In 1936, he became chairman of a department, first at Kiev University, and in 1959 at
Moscow University. From 1946 to 1949, he was Dean of the
Mechanics and Mathematics Division of Kiev University; he
was chairman of a number of departments of the Academy of
Sciences U.S.S.R. (Department of Nonlinear Mechanics of the
Institute of Structural Mechanics, Department of Mathematical
Physics of the Institute of Mathematics). Since 1956, he has
been in charge of the Department of Theoretical Physics of the
Mathematics Institute imeni V. A. Steklov of the Academy of
Sciences U.S.S.R., as well as of the Laboratory of Theoretical

Physics of the Joint Institute of Nuclear Research in Dubno.
He established the School of Nonlinear Mechanics in Kiev and
the School of Theoretical Physics in Moscow. These schools
have made a great contribution both to the development of theoretical science and to the solution of numerous practical problems of modern physics and engineering. Bogolyubov has been
invited many times to deliver lectures on his research at
foreign universities and scientific research institutes, as well
as at international congresses and conferences. A number of
his monographs have been translated into foreign languages.

In 1939, Bogolyubov was elected Corresponding Member of
the Academy of Sciences of the Ukrainian S.S.R., in 1947 Corresponding Member of the Academy of Sciences U.S.S.R., and in
1948 an Academician of the Academy of Sciences of the Ukrainian S.S.R. In 1953, he was elected Academician by the Academy
of Sciences U.S.S.R. He received an honorary doctorate from
the University of Hyderabad. For his research in the field of
nonlinear mechanics and statistical physics, set forth in the
monographs, "On Some Statistical Methods in Mathematical
Physics," and "Problems of Dynamic Theory in Statistical
Physics," Bogolyubov received in 1947 a Stalin Prize, First
Class. For his investigation in superconductivity, he was
awarded the Lomonosov Prize in 1957. In 1958, he was awarded the Lenin Prize for working out the new methods in quantum
field theory and in statistical physics which had led, in particular, to substantiation of the theory of superfluidity and the
theory of superconductivity. Other awards he has received include another Stalin Prize and seven orders, among them three
Orders of Lenin and the Order of the Red Banner of Labor.

The scientific activity of Bogolyubov, which has extended
over more than 30 years, covers varied fields of analysis,
function theory, differential equations, theory of vibrations,
theory of stability, and quantum field theory. During the period
of his productive scientific inquiry, he published over 170 scientific papers, including a series of fundamental monographs.
The following is a brief outline of the principal lines of his
work.

His earliest research was in the field of the calculus of variations. This research was devoted to the development of direct
methods for the solution of extreme problems which do not re-
quire regularity or quasi-regularity of the corresponding operations. At an international congress devoted to problems of the
calculus of variations, his paper entitled "New Methods in the
Calculus of Variations," was awarded the A. Mertani Prize of

the Bologna Academy of Sciences. A number of the investigations by Bogolyubov have dealt with the theory of quasiperiodic functions. He showed that the basic theorems of quasiperiodic functions (for instance, the theorem of the uniform approximation of a continuous quasi-periodic function by trigonometric sums) result from one general theorem in the field of an arbitrary limited function. According to this theorem, certain linear combinations from an arbitrary limited function are capable of being approximated by trigonometric sums. The proof of the approximation theorem for the quasi-periodic functions of Bohr, presented by Bogolyubov, does not rely upon the Parseval equality; in general, it relies upon virtually none of the properties of functions quasi-periodic in the sense of Bohr. In the proof of this theorem, the underlying principle is an original purely mathematical conception of the properties of quasi-periods. In this Bogolyubov has presented a virtually new synthesis of Bohr's theory of quasi-periodic functions.

Bogolyubov has carried out a series of investigations dealing with the theory of differential equations with limiting conditions, directly linked to the application of the differentiation method to the calculus of variations. The basis of these investigations is the estimation of error in the approximate determination of proper values and characteristic functions of the boundary. The approximation method developed here by Bogolyubov is applicable not only to the solution of boundary problems, but also to the solution of partial differential equations. Starting in 1932, he began work with N. M. Krilov on the development of a completely new branch of mathematical physics--the theory of nonlinear oscillations which they called nonlinear mechanics. It should be noted that, in the twenties, the rapid development of radio and electrical engineering required a study of nonlinear oscillations. The use, for this purpose, of methods developed by A. Poincaré and A. M. Lyapunov was completely inadequate. It was necessary to develop new, more flexible methods of investigation of all the complex phenomena originating in nonlinear oscillatory systems. The research of Bogolyubov developed in two principal directions: that of the development of methods for the asymptotic integration of nonlinear equations describing oscillatory processes, and that of the mathematical substantiation of these methods, and this was equivalent to the development of a general theory of dynamic systems.

In the first of these directions, having to do with the study of differential equations with a "small" or "large" parameter,

Bogolyubov was successful in extending the methods of the turbulence theory to general nonconservative systems and in developing new asymptotic methods in the theory of nonlinear oscillations. These asymptotic methods, grounded in mathematics, not only permitted a solution in the first approximation (as, for instance, does the Van der Pohl method) but also in higher degrees of approximation and could be applied to the study of both periodic and quasi-periodic oscillatory processes. These methods were simple for practical use embodying a highly effective principle of equivalent linearization, the symbolic method, etc.

A number of investigations by Bogolyubov in nonlinear mechanics deal with the rigorous foundation of asymptotic methods, the estimation of error over a finite interval, the determination of correspondence of some properties of precise and approximate solutions over an infinite interval, and the proof of some existence and stability theorems of quasi-periodic solutions. Interesting and elegant theorems were proven in the investigation of stationary oscillatory processes. Making use of the Poincaré-Lyapunov theory, as well as of the Poincaré-Danzhua theory of trajectories on a tore, he was successful in investigating the nature of a precise stationary solution in the vicinity of an approximate solution. In the theoretical field of nonlinear mechanics he also investigated the abstract theory of dynamic systems. He made a full investigation of the structure of the invariant dimensions of a compact dynamic system. A study was made of the existence and the basic properties of ergodic numbers emerging in the phase space of a dynamic system, corresponding physically to a stationary oscillation science.

In his first works in theoretical physics, which were related to asymptotic methods, Bogolyubov examined problems dealing with the influence of a random force on a harmonic oscillator, and the establishment of statistical balance in a system connected to a thermostat.

A number of his investigations deal with questions in statistical mechanics of classical systems. Here, he has developed a method of distribution functions, the essence of which lies in the development of analytical calculation methods which give probability distribution function of the particle complexes in the examined system. On the basis of Gibbs' distribution, he arrived at a method for constructing a system of equations for these functions, and indicated methods of their solution for various cases. Extending the technique of distribution functions to the case of unbalanced processes, Bogolyubov approaches from a single point of view the theory of and the calculation of kinetic equations for systems of interacting particles, and provided a general procedure for synthesizing them based on the fundamental theorems of statistical mechanics.

He obtained results of no lesser importance in quantum statistics. Generalizing for the case of quantum systems the method of kinetic distribution functions, he provided a general method of constructing kinetic equations for quantum systems. Interesting results were also obtained by him in questions connected with the behavior of electrons in metal. Here he developed a method of approximate second quantization based on the fact that, under certain assumptions, it is possible to represent the energy spectrum of a Fermi system in the form of an aggregate of elementary excitations that are subject to Boze statistics.

Highly important accomplishments of Bogolyubov are set forth in investigations dealing with superfluidity and superconductivity. It is well known that quantum systems consisting of a large number of identical particles manifest, at low temperatures, the highly unique phenomenon of degeneration. This phenomenon had been studied only for ideal gases. The first results in the theory of the degeneration of non-ideal gases were obtained by him as early as 1947, it being shown that a weakly non-ideal Boze gas can occur in a degenerate state and will then possess the property of superfluidity. In this manner, the first step was made toward the development of the microscope theory of the superfluidity of Helium II.

Development of the ideas and methods which he expressed in his works of 1947 and 1948 made it possible for him to evolve in 1958 a systematic microscopic theory of superconductivity. An important part in understanding the essence of superconductivity was played by Froelich's idea of the decisive role of the interaction of electrons with lattice oscillations, and the prediction on that basis of the isotopic effect. It was, however, impossible to solve the problem on the Hamiltonian basis proposed by Froelich on account of the many difficulties of a purely mathematical nature. Bogolyubov was successful in solving this problem and, as a result, not only developed a systematic theory of superfluidity, but also established the fundamental fact that superconductivity may be regarded as the superfluidity of an electron gas, or more generally, as the superfluidity of Fermi systems. Recently these results have found application in nuclear theory.

In the field of quantum field theory Bogolyubov made an attempt at a completely new synthesis rejecting the Hamiltonian formalism and replacing it by physical conditions, notably that of causality. A systematic exposition of quantum field theory is given by him in the monograph, "Introduction to the Theory of Quantum Fields." Bogolyubov also gave a rigorous proof of the so-called dispersional relations, introducing a new method in quantum field theory. He uncovered the underlying premises of quantum field theory necessary for the derivation of dispersion relationships, and provided rigorous proof for the validity of these relations. He proved a series of theorems lying on the borderline of the theory of multiple complex variables and the theory of generalized functions.

Bogolyubov has attended the Pugwash Conferences.

As of 1961, Bogolyubov was a Member of the Presidium of the Siberian Branch U.S.S.R. Academy of Sciences.

Bibliography:

Problems of Dynamic Theory in Statistical Physics. Moscow-Leningrad: 1946.

New Methods in Variable Calculation. Kharkov-Kiev: 1932.

Statistical Methods in Mathematical Physics. Kiev: 1945.

and N. M. Krylov. Introduction to Non-Linear Mechanics (Approach and asymptotic methods of non-linear mechanics). Kiev: 1937.

and Yu. A. Mitropolskii. Asymptotic Methods in the Theory of Non-Linear Oscillations. Moscow: 1955. (See translation below)

Introduction to the Quantum Field Theory. Moscow: 1957.

and Yu. A. Mitropolskii. Asymptotic Methods in the Theory of Non-Linear Oscillations. (Translated from Russian). Delhi Hindustan Pub. Corp., 1961; (New York, Gordon & Breach) 537 p. (International monographs on advanced mathematics).

Equation with variational derivatives in problems of statistical physics and of quantum theory. Introductory article in The Methods of Functionals in Quantum Theory of Fields, I. V. Novozhilov and A. V. Tulub. New York: Gordon and Breach, 1961. 79 p. (Russian tracts on advanced math. and phys. 5.)

Office: Department of Theoretical Physics
A. V. Steklov Mathematics Institute of USSR
1-y Akademicheskii Proyezd, 28
Moscow, USSR

Residence: Leninskiye gory, Korp. "L"
           Moscow, USSR
Telephone: B9 26 07

BOGOROV, VYENIAMIN GRIGOR'YEVICH (Oceanographer)
    V. G. Bogorov was born December 24, 1904. He graduated
from Moscow University in 1926. From 1930 to 1941 he was
employed at the All-Union Institute of Fisheries and Oceanography. Since 1941 he has been working at the U.S.S.R. Academy
of Sciences Institute of Oceanography (known as the Laboratory
on Oceanography until 1946). In 1958 he was elected to the
U.S.S.R. Academy of Sciences as a Corresponding Member. He
was awarded, in 1951, a Stalin Prize.

    Bogorov's main investigations are the typology of seas, the
geographic zoning of oceans, the productivity of seas, the
twenty-four hour migration of plankton, and biological seasons.
He advanced new methods and instruments for quantitative investigation of plankton, and for undertaking marine expedition-
ary work.

Bibliography:
    Twenty-four hour vertical distribution of plankton in polar
    environments (South East part of the Barents Sea). Works
    of the Polar Scientific Research Institute of Marine Fish
    Industry and Oceanography of N. M. Klinovich, 1938, #2.
    Peculiarities of seasonal occurrence in plankton of polar
    seas and their meaning for ice prognosis. Zoolog. Zhur.,
    1939, 18, #5.
    Role of Biological Indicators for Knowledge of the Hydro-
    logical Regime of the Sea. Moscow-Leningrad: 1945.
    Vertical distribution of zooplankton and vertical separation
    of ocean waters. Works of the Institute of Oceanology
    (U.S.S.R. Academy of Sciences), 1948, 2.
    Production of plankton and characteristics of biogeographic
    territories of the ocean. Doklady Akad. Nauk S.S.S.R., 1958,
    118, #5.
    Sea Life. Moscow: 1954.
Office: Institute of Oceanography of USSR Academy of
              Sciences
              Ulitsa Bakhrushina, 8
              Moscow, USSR
Residence: Leninskii Prospekt, 25
              Moscow, USSR
Telephone: V4 00 27, Ext. 49

BOKII, GEORGII BORISOVICH (Crystallographer Chemist)
G. B. Bokii was born September 26, 1909. He graduated in
1930 from the Leningrad Mining Institute and began working at
the Institute of General and Inorganic Chemistry of the U.S.S.R.
Academy of Sciences. In 1939 he joined the teaching staff of
Moscow University and in 1944 was made professor. Bokii has
been a member of the Communist Party of the Soviet Union
since 1944. In 1958 he was elected a Corresponding Member of
the U.S.S.R. Academy of Sciences. He was awarded two Orders
of the Badge of Honor and also medals.
Bokii has used crystallographic methods for study of complex compounds. Together with S. S. Batsanov he developed a
crystallo-optic method of determining the structure of complex
compounds. For this work he was awarded (in 1954) the Prize
of the Presidium of the U.S.S.R. Academy of Sciences. Bokii
proposed a method of quantitatively determining the values of
trans-influence in measuring interatomic distances in crystals
of complex compounds. This was reported at the International
Congress on Crystallography in 1957 in Canada. He worked out
an atomic structure theory of daltonides and berthollides (1956).
Bibliography:
and E. E. Burova. Crystallographic study of the solid phases
in the system $K_2O-P_2O_5-H_2O$. Izvest. Akad. Nauk S.S.S.R.,
Ser. Khim., 1938, #1.
On the theory of daltonides and berthollides. Zhur. Neorg.
Khim., 1956, 1, #7.
and I. I. Shafranovskii. Russian crystallographers. Works
of the Institute of History of Natural Science and Engineering, 1947.
Crystal chemistry of complex compounds. Proceedings of
the Department of Platinum of the Institute of General and
Inorganic Chemistry of the U.S.S.R. Academy of Sciences,
1948, #21.
and S. S. Batsanov. A new method of determining the structure of complex compounds, 1. Vestnik of the Moscow State
University, 1952, #2.
Office: Chemistry Department
            Moscow University
            Moscow, USSR

BOL'SHAKOV, KIRILL ANDREEVICH (Chemist)
K. A. Bol'shakov was born December 24, 1906. He graduated
from the University of Kazan' in 1930 and from then until 1948

worked at the Institute of Rare Minor Metals in Moscow. He
began teaching at the Moscow Institute of Fine Chemical Technology in 1933 and in 1948 was made professor. In 1958
Bol'shakov was elected a Corresponding Member of the U.S.S.R.
Academy of Sciences. He received a Stalin Prize in 1941.
Bol'shakov's main investigations deal with the physical-
chemical basis of technological processes in obtaining rare
elements.
Bibliography:
and M. N. Sobolev. Extracting vanadium from titanomagne-
tite ores. Rare Metals, 1933, #6.
and V. A. Yazykov. Obtaining ferrovanadium from vanadate
of calcium by a silico-thermal method. Quality Steel, 1934,
#6.
and P. I. Fedorov and G. D. Agashkina. Diagrams of fusibility of double systems: sodium chloride-cobaltous chloride
and sodium chloride-nickel chloride. Zhur. Neorg. Khim.,
1957, 2, #5.
Office: Moscow Institute of Fine Chemical Technology
            Moscow, USSR
Residence: 2ii Shuminskii pr. 2
            Moscow, USSR
Telephone: D4 09 98

BORESKOV, GEORGII KONSTANTINOVICH (Physical Chemist)
    G. K. Boreskov was born April 20, 1907. He graduated from
Odessa Institute in 1928, and from 1928 to 1937 he worked at
the Ukrainian Chemical-Radiology Institute (Odessa; now the
Ukrainian branch of the Institute of Rare Metals). He also
taught at the University of Odessa in 1934-37 and in 1930-37 at
the Odessa Chemical-Technological Institute. From 1937 to
1949 he was Chief of the Laboratory of Catalysis for the Scientific Research Institute of Fertilizers and Insectofungicides. In
1946 he began working at the Karpov Physico-Chemical Institute
and in 1949 became professor at the Moscow Chemico-
Technological Institute of D. I. Mendeleev. Boreskov has been
a Corresponding Member of the U.S.S.R. Academy of Sciences
since 1958. He was awarded a Stalin Prize in 1942, and two
orders and medals.
    The investigations of Boreskov deal with the study of cata-
lytic processes, the development of a scientific basis for selecting and preparing catalysis and designing catalytic reactors.
He proposed a vanadium catalyst for producing sulphuric acid,

which is utilized in contact sulphuric acid plants. He investigated the influence of processes of heat and matter transfer on the speed of contact reactions and selectivity of catalyst action. As of 1961, Boreskov was Director of the Institute of Catalysis, Siberian Branch of U.S.S.R. Academy of Sciences.

Bibliography:
Catalysis in Sulphuric Acid Production. Moscow-Leningrad: 1954.
and K. M. Malin and others. Technology of Sulphuric Acid. Moscow-Leningrad: 1950.
Action mechanism of solid catalysis. Heterogeneous Catalysis in the Chemical Industry. Moscow: 1955.

Biography:
M. G. Slin'ko. Georgii Konstantinovich Boreskov (On the 50th Anniversary since the date of birth). Zhur. Fiz. Khim., 1957, 31, #4.

Office: D. I. Mendeleev Chemico-Technological Institute Moscow, USSR

BRAUNSTEIN, ALEKSANDR EVSEEVICH (Biochemist)

A. E. Braunstein was born May 26, 1902. He graduated in 1925 from the Kharkov Medical Institute. In 1930-1936 he worked as senior scientific worker at the Bakh Biochemical Institute of the People's Commissariat of Public Health of the U.S.S.R. He began working at the All-Union Institute of Experimental Medicine in 1936 as Chief of the Section on Metabolism and subsequently, at the Institute of Biological Medical Chemistry of the U.S.S.R. Academy of Medical Sciences. In 1959, Braunstein became a laboratory Chief at the U.S.S.R. Academy of Sciences Institute of Radiation and Physico-Chemical Biology. He became a Corresponding Member of the U.S.S.R. Academy of Medical Sciences in 1945, and in 1960 a Corresponding Member of the U.S.S.R. Academy of Sciences. In 1941 he received a Stalin Prize.

Braunstein's investigations deal with nitrogen exchange of amino acids and proteins and with enzymology. He discovered the process of enzymatic reamination of amino acids (1937), investigated its biological role, and presented a new view of the assimilation and dissimilation of nitrogen in living and other organisms (1939-1957). He studied other enzymatic transformations of amino acids (1948-1952). He discovered a series of functions of B6 in the transformations of tryptophane oxy-amino acids, and sulphur-containing amino acids (1949-1956).

Bibliography:
and M. G. Kritsman. Formation of amino acids by way of
intermolecular transfer of the amino group. Biokhimiya,
1937, 2, #2.
Biochemistry of Amino Acid Exchange. Moscow: 1949.
and M. M. Shemyakin. Theory on processes of amino acid
exchange, catalyzed by pyridoxine enzymes. Biokhimiya,
1953, 18, #4.
Vitamins of the B Group in processes of amino acid exchange
(report). Ukrainian Biochemical Journal, 1955, 27, #4.
Office: Institute of Biological Medical Chemistry of the
             USSR Academy of Sciences
             Solyanka, 14
             Moscow, USSR
Residence: Novoslobodskaya, 57/65
             Moscow, USSR
Telephone: D1 55 56

BREKHOVSKIKH, LEONID MAKSIMOVICH (Physicist)

L. M. Brekhovskikh was born May 6, 1917. He graduated in
1939 from the University of Perm. In 1953 he was appointed
professor at Moscow University, and in 1954 he was made Director of the Acoustical Institute, U.S.S.R. Academy of Sciences.
Since 1953 he has been a Corresponding Member of the U.S.S.R.
Academy of Sciences and in 1951 he was the recipient of a
Stalin Prize.

Brekhovskikh's early investigations are on scattering of
x-rays in crystals and liquids. From 1942 his main scientific
interest has been in acoustics and wave propagation. He investigated the propagation of sound and electromagnetic waves in
heterogeneous media and developed the theory of wave fields and
point sources in layer-heterogeneous media. In particular, he
presented a theory on the so-called side and head waves, which
play an important role in seismographic surveys. A number of
Brekhovskikh's investigations are in the scattering of sound
electromagnetic waves on uneven surfaces. Together with
others, he discovered (1946) the super-distance propagation of
sound in the sea.

Bibliography:
Reflection of spheric waves from a plane boundary of a
section of two media. Zhur. Tekh. Fiz., 1948, 18, #4.
Wave diffraction on an uneven surface. 1-2, Zhur. Eksptl.
i Teoret. Fiz., 1952, 23, #3 (9), 275-304.

On the field of a point radiator in layer-heterogeneous
media. I-III. Izvest. Akad. Nauk S.S.S.R., Ser. Fiz., 1949,
13, #5, 505-545.
Waves in Layer Media. Moscow: 1957.
Office: Institute of Acoustics of USSR Academy of Sciences
             Ulitsa Televideniya, 4
             Moscow, USSR

BRODSKY (BRODSKII), ALEKSANDR IL'ICH (Physical
    Chemist)
A. I. Brodsky was born June 19, 1895. He graduated from
Moscow University. Since 1938 he has been Director of the
Institute of Physical Chemistry of the Ukrainian S.S.R. Academy
of Sciences. Brodsky has been an Academician of the Ukrainian
S.S.R. Academy of Sciences since 1939 and since 1943 a Corresponding Member of the U.S.S.R. Academy of Sciences. In 1946
he was awarded a State Prize. He was elected, in 1962, Honorable Member of the Polish Chemical Society.
    Brodsky investigated the influence of solvents on chemical
equilibrium, on electrode potentials, and on optical properties
of solutions. He pioneered and organized (from 1934) investigations on chemical reactions using isotopes. He studied isotope exchange reactions, and the isotope composition of natural
waters and rocks. Since 1939 he has investigated the mechanisms of organic and exchange reactions.
Bibliography:
    Investigations in Thermodynamic and Electrochemistry of
    Solutions. Kharkov-Dnepropetrovsk: 1931.
    Contemporary Theory of Electrolytes. Leningrad: 1934.
    Physical Chemistry, 1-2, 6th ed. Moscow-Leningrad: 1948.
    Translations: Ukrainian (Kharkov 2nd ed., 1937); Georgian
    (Tbilisi, 1938); Latvian (Riga, 1950); Bulgarian (Sophia,
    1952); Polish (Warsaw, 2nd ed., 1954).
    Calculation of Thermodynamic Functions. Moscow: 1948.
    Chemistry of Isotopes, 2nd ed. Moscow: 1957. Trans-
    lations: Polish (Warsaw, 1957); Chinese (Peking, 1956);
    German (Berlin, 1961).
    and L. L. Gordienko. Nitrogen isotope exchange in amides
    of acids. Doklady Akad. Nauk S.S.S.R. 134, 595-98 (1960).
    Isotopic investigations of mechanisms of reactions, produc-
    ing hydrogen peroxide and peroxy acids. Kernenergie 3,
    822-27 (1960).
    Isotopic investigations on mechanisms of some oxidation-
    reduction reactions. Kernenergie 3, 827-33 (1960).

and V. A. Lunenok-Burmakina, A. P. Potemskaja. Investigation of the mechanism of anodic ozone formation in sulfate
solutions. Doklady Akad. Nauk S.S.S.R. 137, 1402-04 (1961).
and I. F. Franchuk. Isotopic investigation of oxides and
peroxides of uranium. Doklady Akad. Nauk S.S.S.R. 138,
1345-48 (1961).
and M. M. Aleksankin, I. P. Gragherov. Mechanism of the
oxidation of pyruvic acid with hydrogen peroxide. Zhur.
Obshchei Khim. 32, 829-32 (1962).
Biography:
Aleksandr Il'ich Brodsky, Specialist in the Area of Physical
Chemistry. (On the 60th Anniversary Since the Date of
Birth). Ukr. Zhur. Khim., 1955, 21, #4.
Office: (L. V. Pisarzhevskiy) Institute of Physical Chemis-
                try
                Ukrainian SSR Academy of Sciences
                Bolshaja Kitajevskaya Str. 97
                Kiev 28, Ukrainian SSR

BRUEVICH, NIKOLAI GRIGOREVICH (Mechanical Engineer)
N. G. Bruevich was born November 12, 1896 in Moscow. He
graduated from Moscow University in 1922 and from Moscow
Aviation Institute in 1930. In 1937 he received the degree of
Doctor of Technical Sciences and became professor. He joined
the teaching staff in 1929 of the Zhukovskii Academy of Military
and Air Engineering. In 1951 he began teaching at the Machine
Institute of the U.S.S.R. Academy of Sciences. During World
War II (1941-1945), he was in charge of evaluating and resolving
problems pertaining to aviation. He is a lieutenant general of
engineers. Since 1921 Bruevich has been a member of the
Communist Party of the Soviet Union. In 1939 he was elected a
Corresponding Member of the U.S.S.R. Academy of Sciences,
and in 1942 an Academician.
    In the 1930's Bruevich developed general methods of kine-
matic and kinetostatic analyses for plane and space mechanisms. While working on computing machines and precision
movements of mechanisms, he established a theory of precision
in machinery. The application of this theory provides a rational
approach for planning and manufacturing mechanical devices
and precision instruments. He also instituted a course dealing
with working principles of computing machines.

Bibliography:
Kinematics of the simplest space mechanisms with fifth
grade couples. Works of the Zhukovskii Air Force Academy
RKKA, 1937, #18.
Kinetostatics of space mechanisms. Works of the Zhukovskii
Air Force Academy RKKA, 1937, #22.
Precision of Mechanisms. Moscow-Leningrad: 1946 (also
Bruevich's bibliography).
and B. G. Dostupov. Installation of Computing Instruments.
Moscow-Leningrad: 1954.
Office: Institute of Machine Studies of USSR Academy of
Sciences
Malyy Kharitonyevskii Pereulok, 4
Moscow, USSR

BRUK, ISAAK SEMYONOVICH (Electrical Engineer)

I. S. Bruk was born November 9, 1902. He graduated from
the Moscow Technical College in 1925, and has been working at
the U.S.S.R. Academy of Sciences Institute of Energetics since
1935. In 1956, he became Chief of the U.S.S.R. Academy of
Sciences Laboratory on Directing Machines and Systems, and
later was made Director of the Institute. He was elected, in
1939, to the U.S.S.R. Academy of Sciences as a Corresponding
Member.
Bruk has worked on power electric and mathematical machines. In 1936-38, the first U.S.S.R. machines for integrating
ordinary differential equations were built according to the design of Bruk. A computing device, "computing table of alternating current" for investigating electrical systems was built in
1945-1947 under his leadership. From 1948 he has conducted
work on high speed electronic computers. The M-1, M-2, M-3
machines were built in 1950-55.
Bibliography:
Machine for Integrating Differential Equations. Moscow-
Leningrad: 1941.
The stability of electric systems. Electricity, 1945, #9.
Electric minimizer. Doklady Akad. Nauk S.S.S.R., 1948, 62,
#4.
High speed electronic computer M-2. Electricity, 1956, #9.
Office: Institute of Electronic Controlling Machines
Leninskii Prospekt, 16
Moscow, USSR

Residence: ul. Chkalova, 21
        Moscow, USSR
Telephone: K7 48 37

BUDKER, GERSH ITSKOVICH (Physicist)
    G. I. Budker was born May 1, 1918. He graduated in 1941
from Moscow University. In 1946 he began work at the Institute
of Atomic Energy of the U.S.S.R. Academy of Sciences. He also
became a professor, in 1956, at the Moscow Engineering Physics Institute. In 1957 Budker was made Director of an Institute of the Siberian branch of the U.S.S.R. Academy of Sciences.
Since 1958 he has been a Corresponding Member of the U.S.S.R.
Academy of Sciences.

    Budker has investigated the theory of heterogeneous uranium-
graphite reactors, the theory on kinetics and control of atomic
reactors, and the theory and calculation of a circular-orbit
accelerator of charged particles. From 1951 he has worked on
plasma physics, the design of new types of accelerators and the
realization of controlled thermonuclear reactions. He has investigated the theory of a stabilized electron beam, and a kinetic equation for relativistic plasma.

    As of 1961, Budker was a Member of the Siberian Branch
Presidium and the Director of the Institute of Nuclear Physics
of the Siberian Branch U.S.S.R. Academy of Sciences.
Bibliography:
    Relativistic stabilized electron beam. Atomic Energy, 1956,
    #5.
    and S. T. Belyaev. Relativistic kinetic equation. Doklady
    Akad. Nauk S.S.S.R., 1956, 107, #6.
Office: Institute of Nuclear Physics of the Siberian De-
               partment of USSR Academy of Sciences
               Novosibirsk, Siberia

BUDNIKOV, PYOTR PETROVICH (Inorganic and Industrial
    Chemist)
    P. P. Budnikov was born October 21, 1885. He graduated in
1911 from the Riga Polytechnical Institute. From 1919 to 1926
he was professor at the Ivanova-Voznesensk Institute and from
1926 to 1941 at the Khar'kov Chemico-Technological Institute.
In 1943 he became professor at the Moscow Chemico-
Technological Institute. Since 1939 he has been a Corresponding Member of the U.S.S.R. Academy of Sciences and Academician of the Ukrainian S.S.R. Academy of Sciences. Budnikov

was an Honored Scientist of the Ukrainian S.S.R. in 1943. In 1942, 1950, and 1952, he was awarded Stalin Prizes. The chief emphasis of the works of Budnikov is given to a complex study of the mineral wealth of the U.S.S.R. and establishing a method for its utilization. The long study of Budnikov on the investigation of gypsum broadened the latter's use in the building and chemical industries. He invented an anhydridic cement. As a result of his study of the chemical processes during hydration and solidification of blast furnace slag, Budnikov discovered new types of hydraulic cement--sulfated non-clinker and low-clinker slag cements, high quality, quick hardening and expanding cement--which were widely utilized. Work was carried out by Budnikov in the field of hydrothermal processing of building materials, and refractory material for the coke, chemical and metallurgical industries. A series of his works is devoted to the thermo-chemistry of binding agents, the chemical and thermal stability of refractory material, and corrosion of cements and concrete. He studied reactions in solid phases in silicate systems and developed new methods of investigating silicates.

Bibliography:
Gypsum, Its Study and Utilization, 3rd ed. Moscow-Leningrad: 1943.

and A. S. Bereznoi. Reactions in Solid Phases. Moscow: 1949.

and others. Technology of Ceramics and Refractory Material, 2nd ed. Moscow: 1954.

Technology of Ceramic Products, ed. Moscow-Leningrad: 1946.

Biography:
D. S. Belyankin, ed. Collection of Works Devoted to the 60th Anniversary Since the Date of Birth of P. P. Budnikov. Moscow: 1946.

G. V. Kukolev. Pyotr Petrovich Budnikov. Zhur. Priklad. Khim., 1956, 29, #1.

Collection of Scientific Work in Chemistry and Technology of Silicates Devoted to the 70th Anniversary Since the Date of Birth of P. P. Budnikov. Moscow: 1956.

Office: Moscow Chemico-Technical Institute
Moscow, USSR
Residence: Troilinskii p. 3
Moscow, USSR
Telephone: G1 40 58

BUSHUYEV, KONSTANTIN DAVYDOVICH (Physicist)
    K. D. Bushuyev was born in 1914. In 1941 he graduated from
the Moscow Aviation Institute. Since 1941 he has been a member of the Communist Party of the Soviet Union. In 1960 he was
elected to the U.S.S.R. Academy of Sciences as a Corresponding
Member.
    Bushuyev's works deal with theoretical and applied me-
chanics.
Office: USSR Academy of Sciences
            Leninskii Prospekt, 14
            Moscow, USSR

BYKHOVSKII, BORIS EVSEEVICH (Parasitologist)
    B. E. Bykhovskii was born in 1908. In 1930 he graduated
from the biological department of the Leningrad State University
Institute of Physico-Mathematics. From 1929 to 1939, he was
a laboratory worker, scientific worker, senior scientific worker
of the Fishing Industry Institute in Leningrad. He was, in 1939-
40, senior scientific worker of the U.S.S.R. Academy of Sciences
Zoological Institute. From 1940-44 he was deputy chairman of
the Presidium of the Tadzhik branch of the U.S.S.R. Academy
of Sciences. He was deputy Director of the U.S.S.R. Academy
of Sciences Zoological Institute and chief of the Laboratory on
Helminth Parasitology at this Institute from 1942 to 1959, when
he was reappointed deputy Director of the U.S.S.R. Academy of
Sciences Zoological Institute. In September 1962 he was made
Acting Director of this Institute.
    Since 1941 he has been a member of the Communist Party of
the Soviet Union. In 1960 he was elected to the U.S.S.R. Academy of Sciences as a Corresponding Member.
    Bykhovskii's main works deal with the study of parasitic
lower helminths.
Bibliography:
    and A. V. Gusev. Contributions to knowledge about mono-
    genetic trematodes with a primitive fastening armature.
    Trudy Zool. Inst. Akad. Nauk S.S.S.R. 1955 (21): 110-118,
    1955; Referat. Zhur. Biol., 1956, #82221. Biol. Abstr. 33,
    21376 (1958).
    Information on monogenetic trematodes in the fishes in
    Tadzhikstan. Izv. Vses. N. I. Inst. Oz. i Rechn. Rybn. Kh-
    va 42: 109-123, 1957. Biol. Abstr. 35, 30659 (1960).
    and L. F. Nagibina. The monogenetic trematoda of the sheat-
    fish, silarus glanis. Parazitol. Sb. 1957 (17). Biol. Abstr.
    35, 5131 (1960).

and Yu. I. Polianskii. Results and perspectives of work of Soviet parasitologists in the field of the study of parasites of fish in the seas of the U.S.S.R. Trudy Soveshchanii Ikhtiol. Komiss. Akad. Nauk S.S.S.R. 9. 177-183. 1959. Referat Zhur., Biol., 1960, #105717. Biol. Abstr. 36, 46537 (1961).

and G. K. Petrashevskii, Yu. I. Polianskii. V. A. Dogel' and his role in the investigation of parasites and diseases of fish in the U.S.S.R. Trudy Soveshchanii Ikhtiol. Komiss. Akad. Nauk S.S.S.R. 9. 7-12. 1959. Referat Zhur., Biol., 1960, #115052 (Trans.)

CHELOMEI, VLADIMIR NIKOLAEVICH (Mechanical Engineer)

V. N. Chelomei was born June 30, 1914. Upon graduating from the Kiev Aviation Institute in 1938, he taught there. From 1941 to 1944, he worked at the Central Institution of Aircraft Engines, and subsequently in a number of scientific research organizations. He has been a professor at Moscow Technical College since 1952. Since 1941 he has been a member of the Communist Party of the Soviet Union. In 1958 he was elected a Corresponding Member of the U.S.S.R. Academy of Sciences, and in June 1962, an Academician.

Chelomei's main work deals with mechanics, dynamics of machinery, theory of pneumatic and hydraulic servomechanisms.

Bibliography:

Elastic oscillations of bending. Works of the Kiev Aviation Institute, 1936, #6.

One problem of quasi-harmonic oscillations. Works of the Kiev Aviation Institute, 1936, #6.

Oscillations subjected to the action of periodically changing longitudinal forces. Works of the Kiev Aviation Institute, 1937, #8.

Theory of springs. Works of the Kiev Aviation Institute, 1938, #8.

Stability of rods, subjected to the action of longitudinal, periodically changing forces distributed longitudinally. Works of the Kiev Aviation Institute, 1938, #10.

Stability of plates in special cases. Doklady Akad. Nauk Ukr. S.S.R., 1938, #1.

Dynamic Stability of Elements in Aviation Construction. Moscow: 1939.

Pneumatic servomechanisms. Izvest. Akad. Nauk S.S.S.R., Otdel. Tekh. Nauk, 1954, #5.

Possibilities of raising the stability of elastic systems with the aid of vibration. Doklady Akad. Nauk S.S.S.R., 1956, 110, #3.

Investigation of pneumatic and hydraulic servomechanisms. Automatic Control and Computing Techniques, Moscow, 1958, #1.

Office: Moscow Technical College
              Moscow, USSR

CHEPIKOV, KONSTANTIN ROMANOVICH (Geologist)

K. R. Chepikov was born January 6, 1901. He graduated from the Moscow Mining Academy in 1929. He conducted geological surveys for locating oil on the Kerch Peninsula, Northern Caucasus, Siberia, and particularly in the Ural-Povolzh'e region. In 1947 he became Chief of the Laboratory on Oil Geology at the Institute of Geological Sciences, and in 1954 was made deputy Director of the U.S.S.R. Academy of Sciences Oil Institute. He was awarded a Stalin Prize in 1946, has been a member of the Communist Party of the Soviet Union since 1919, and was elected to the U.S.S.R. Academy of Sciences as a Corresponding Member in 1953.

Bibliography:
and A. D. Arkhangel'skii and others. Brief outline of geological structure and oil deposits of the Kerch Peninsula. Works of the Main Directorate of Geological Surveys of the U.S.S.R. National Economic Council. #13. Moscow-Leningrad: 1930.

Question of separation of the Upper Permian red beds by the fauna tetrapoda. Izvest. Akad. Nauk S.S.S.R., Geol. Ser., 1946, #4.

Age of Ufimskii deposits. Izvest. Akad. Nauk S.S.S.R., Geol. Ser., 1948, #4.

Office: Oil Institute of USSR Academy of Sciences
              Moscow, USSR
Residence: Leninskii Prospekt, 25
              Moscow, USSR
Telephone: V4 00 27, Ext. 44

CHERNIGOVSKII, VLADIMIR NIKOLAEVICH (Physiologist)

V. N. Chernigovskii was born March 1, 1907. He graduated from Perm University Medical College in 1930; in 1930 to 1932 he was assistant at the Orenburg Veterinary Institute and in 1932 to 1937 at the Sverdlovsk Medical Institute. From 1937 to 1941 he was senior research associate and in 1944 professor in the Department of General Physiology at the All-Union Institute of Experimental Medicine (Leningrad). Chernigovskii also worked in the Naval Academy, Leningrad, from 1941 to 1953 and at the same time at the Institute of Physiology (reorganized into the Institute of Normal and Pathological Physiology of the Academy of Medical Sciences). In 1953, he was made Director of this Institute. He was elected a Corresponding Member of the U.S.S.R. Academy of Sciences in 1953 and in 1960 an Academician. Chernigovskii has been a Corresponding Member of the Academy of Medical Sciences since 1948, and an Academician since 1950. From 1953 to 1957 he was Vice-President of the Academy of Medical Sciences. In 1944 the Academy of Sciences awarded him the I. P. Pavlov Prize for his "Afferent System of Internal Organs." As of 1961 he was Director of the I. P. Pavlov Institute of Physiology. In March 1962 he was elected to the Supreme Soviet as a delegate from R.S.F.S.R.

The basic works of Chernigovskii are devoted to the research on interoceptive reflexes and functional interrelations between the cortex of the cephalic brain and internal organs. He studied interoceptive reflexes and their mechanisms in detail. New reflexes were described and characteristics given of the interoceptive analyzer. Extensive investigations were made of reflex control in the blood system and the role of the nervous system in the pathogeneses of a number of diseases.

Bibliography:
Afferent System of Internal Organs. Kirov: 1943.
and Yaroshevsky. The Problem of Nerve Control in the Blood System, 1953.
and S. M. Zarayskaya. Presentation of the vagus nerve in the central cortex and radial lobe of feline brain. Doklady Akad. Nauk S.S.S.R. 147, #3 (1962).
Office: I. P. Pavlov Institute of Physiology
              Tuchkova Naberezhnaya, 2-a
              Leningrad, USSR

CHERNYAEV, IL'YA IL'ICH (Inorganic Chemist)
I. I. Chernyaev was born January 20, 1893. In 1915 he graduated from Leningrad University and taught there becoming a professor in 1932. He was a student of L. A. Chugaev (1873-1922, professor of Inorganic Chemistry at Leningrad University and founder and director of the Institute for the Study of Platinum of the U.S.S.R. Academy of Sciences). Beginning in 1918, he also worked at the Institute on the Study of Platinum of the U.S.S.R. Academy of Sciences. From 1934 Chernyaev worked

at the Institute of General and Inorganic Chemistry of the
U.S.S.R. Academy of Sciences and in 1941 became its Director.
In addition, he was professor of Moscow Petroleum Institute
from 1935 to 1941. And in 1945 he was made professor at
Moscow University. Chernyaev was elected Corresponding
Member of the U.S.S.R. Academy of Sciences in 1933 and in
1943 Academician. In 1946 and 1952 he won Stalin Prizes.
    Chernyaev has investigated the chemistry of complex com-
pounds. In 1915 Chernyaev completed an investigation of
hydroxylamine compounds of divalent platinum. In 1926 Chernyaev published his work on the study of nitro compounds of
divalent platinum. Using these compounds he discovered trans-
influence. It is constituted by the fact that the dependence of
the reaction ability of any substitute in the internal sphere of a
complex compound depends upon the nature of the substitute
which is in contraposition to it. This phenomenon, associated
with his name, was found to be applicable to a series of compounds of tetravalent platinum, palladium, rhodium, iridium and
cobalt. Using transinfluence, Chernyaev and his students synthesized many complex compounds. Chernyaev discovered the
change in the sign of the rotation of a plane of polarization by
optically active amino compounds of tetravalent platinum during
their transformation into amido- (or imido-) compounds. He
studied the oxidation reaction of complex compounds of platinum,
reduction of iridium, proved that the binding of the nitro group
with platinum takes place through nitrogen, and studied the heat
of reactions of complex compounds. A considerable number of
Chernyaev's investigations are devoted to refining of platinum
metals. As a result he obtained platinum, palladium, gold and
rhodium in a spectrally pure state.
    As of 1961, Chernyaev was Chairman of the Commission for
Considering Works Submitted in Competition for the N. S.
Kurnakov Award.
    As of September 1962, Chernyaev, at his own request, was
relieved of the directorship of the U.S.S.R. Academy of Sciences
Institute of General and Inorganic Chemistry and resumed his
former position as Chief of the Section on Simple and Complex
Inorganic Compounds of this Institute.
Bibliography:
    Questions on chemistry of complex compounds. Uspekhi
    Khim., 1936, 5, #9, 1169-1215.
    On the geometric isomerization of compounds of tetra-
    valent platinum. Uspekhi Khim., 1947, 16, #4, 385-402.

Aqua-carbonate complex compounds of uranyl. Zhur. Neorg.
Khim., 1956, #12.
with G. S. Muraveiskaya. On the reactions of dinitro-
dimethyl amine compounds of tetravalent platinum. Zhur.
Neorg. Khim., 1957, 2, #3.
Biography:
V. V. Lebedinskii and A. M. Rubinshtein. Academician Il'ya
Il'ich Chernyaev (on 60th Anniversary since date of birth).
Uspekhi Khim., 1953, 22, #3, 241-252.
A. V. Babaeva. Leading Soviet Scientist I. I. Chernyaev (on
the 60th Anniversary since the date of birth). Zhur.
Obshchei Khim., 1953, 23, #5.
Office: N. S. Kurnakov Institute of General and Inorganic
Chemistry
Leninskii Prospekt, 31
Moscow, USSR

CHERNYI, GORIMIR GORIMOVICH (Mechanics Specialist)
In 1960 G. G. Chernyi was at the Moscow State University
im. M. V. Lomonosov. He visited the United States in January
1960 to attend the International Symposium on Magneto-Fluid
Dynamics in Washington, D. C. In June 1962 he was elected a
Corresponding Member of the U.S.S.R. Academy of Sciences.

CHIBISOV, KONSTANTIN VLADIMIROVICH (Scientific
Photographer)
K. V. Chibisov was born March 1, 1897. He graduated from
Moscow University in 1922. From 1918 to 1930 he worked at
the Air Force Scientific Testing Institute of Scientific Aero-
photography and during the same period taught at a number of
colleges. In 1950 he became a professor at Moscow University.
Chibisov began working, in 1930, at the All-Union Scientific Research Cinema-Photo Institute and was one of its founders. In
1948 he became Chairman of the U.S.S.R. Academy of Sciences
Commission on Scientific Photography and Cinematography. In
1945 he was awarded the title Honored Scientist of the
R.S.F.S.R., and in 1950 a Stalin Prize. He has been a Corresponding Member of the U.S.S.R. Academy of Sciences since
1946.
The main work of Chibisov is devoted to photographic sensi-
tometry, synthesis of photographic emulsions and the nature of
photographic sensitivity. Of particular importance are the
works of Chibisov on determining the chemical composition and

the role of centers of light sensitivity, which form in micro-
crystals of silver halides in photographic emulsions as a result
of interaction with active components of gelatin. Chibisov also
investigated the light sensitivity of photographic emulsions.
Bibliography:
Theory on Photographic Processes, 1. Moscow: 1935.
Theory of synthesis of photographic emulsions. P. V.
Kozlov's Technology of Photo-Cinema Film, 2. Moscow-
Leningrad: 1937.
The nature of centers of light sensitivity of photographic
emulsions. Uspekhi Khim., 1953, 22, #10. Works of the
Scientific Research Cinema-Photo Institute, #8.
and others. The Nature of Photographic Sensitivity.
Moscow: 1948.
Investigating the nature of photographic sensitivity. Suc-
cesses of Scientific Photography, 5, Moscow, 1957.
Biography:
V. I. Sheberstov. K. V. Chibisov. Journal of Scientific and
Applied Photography and Cinematography, 1957, 2, #1.
Office: Moscow University
               Moscow, USSR

CHINAKAL, NIKOLAI ANDREEVICH (Mining Engineer)

N. A. Chinakal was born November 19, 1888. Upon his
graduation from the Simferpol Gymnasium, he studied from
1907 to 1912 at the Dnepropetrovsk Mining Engineers Institute,
and after his graduation worked at the Donbas Mines.

Chinakal's work on improving the working conditions of
miners promoted him to the rank of progressive specialist, and
in 1920, he was appointed assistant to the authorized representative of the Central Administration of the Coal Industry in
the Makeevskii Region; later in 1921, he was elected member
of the Central Committee of the All-Russian Union of Miners
(VSG) and served as Chief of the Economic Section of the VSG
Central Committee. At the end of 1921, Chinakal was appointed
a member of the governmental commission of the Council of
Labor and Defense, and developed a plan for restoring the
Donbas. Upon completion of this assignment, he was transferred to the Donugol Combine, where from 1923 to 1928, he
headed the Mechanization Section and concurrently served on
the editorial board of Gornii Tekhnik. In 1924-1925, Chinakal
was a member of a Soviet delegation of mining engineers who
went to the U. S., Britain and Germany to study coal mining
processes. From 1940 to 1944 he taught at the Kirov

Polytechnical Institute at Tomsk as a professor and Director of
the Chair of Advanced Mining Construction. Since 1957, he
has been Director of the U.S.S.R. Academy of Sciences Siberian
Branch Institute of Mining. Chinakal was awarded the degree
of Doctor of Technical Sciences without presenting a dissertation, and in February 1958, was elected to the U.S.S.R. Academy of Sciences as a Corresponding Member. He received a
Stalin Prize for his shield system in 1942. Other awards include the Order of Lenin, the Order of the Red Banner of Labor,
and a medal for "Valorous Work in the Great Patriotic War"
(WWII). He has been a member of the Communist Party of the
Soviet Union since 1944.

In the Kuzbas, Chinakal commenced work in 1930 on project
administration, first as a deputy, and later as chief engineer
of the planning administration of Kuzbassugol. In 1935, he
formulated a scheme of shield reinforcement for the exploitation of the thick strata of precipitous slopes. The shield
system of exploitation, suggested and introduced by Chinakal
in close collaboration with the collective of coal mines and the
Kuzbassugol Combine, was a contribution in the exploitation of
thick precipitous coal strata. In 1943, as a member of the
Government Commission, he took an active part in the organization of the West Siberian branch of the U.S.S.R. Academy of
Sciences, and from 1944 was a permanent Director of the Mining and Geological Institute of the West Siberian affiliate of the
Academy of Sciences. Chinakal has contributed 106 scientific
works. His major works are devoted to questions on development and improvement of systems of utilization and mechanization of coal deposits.

Bibliography:
> System of Exploitation with Shield Reinforcement. Moscow-
> Leningrad: 1943.
> Light, non-sectional shield. Coal, 1954, #2.
> Shield method of exploitation. Progressive Method Using
> Systems of Exploitation in the Kuzbas. Moscow: 1957.
> and N. V. Marevich. Shield method of exploitation with
> gravity filling of worked-out space. Progressive Method
> Using Systems of Exploitation in the Kuzbas. Moscow: 1957.

Office: Institute of Mining of the Siberian Department of
> USSR Academy of Sciences
> Irkutsk, Siberia

79 | **CHMUTOV**

CHIZHIKOV, DAVID MIKHAILOVICH (Metallurgist)

D. M. Chizhikov was born November 17, 1895. In 1924 he graduated from the Moscow Mining Academy and subsequently worked at the copper electrolytic plant in Moscow and at a lead-zinc works in Vladikavkaz. From 1928 to 1930, he was chief engineer of the planning and construction of the Konstantinovskii Zinc Works in the Donbas. In 1930, he participated in the organization of the Scientific Research Institute of Non-Ferrous Metallurgy and was its first Director. From 1933 to 1941, he was a professor at the Moscow Institute of Non-Ferrous Metals and Gold. In 1939, he began working at the U.S.S.R. Academy of Sciences Institute of Metallurgy. He has been a member of the Communist Party of the Soviet Union since 1921. In 1939 he was elected a member of the U.S.S.R. Academy of Sciences. He was awarded Stalin Prizes in 1942 and 1950.

Bibliography:
Metallurgy of Heavy Non-Ferrous Metals. Moscow-Leningrad: 1948.
Metallurgy of Zinc. Moscow-Leningrad: 1938.
Metallurgy of Lead. Moscow: 1944.
Chlorine Method and Processing of Polymetallic Ores and Concentrates. Moscow-Leningrad: 1936.
and G. S. Frents. Chlorine Method of Processing Tin Ores and Concentrates. Moscow-Leningrad: 1941.
Office: A. A. Baykov Institute of Metallurgy
Leninskii Prospekt, 29
Moscow, USSR
Residence: Kotel'nicheskaya nab. 1/15
Moscow, USSR
Telephone: B7 42 54

CHMUTOV, KONSTANTIN VASIL'EVICH (Physical Chemist)

K. V. Chmutov was born March 21, 1902. He graduated in 1928 from the Moscow Technological College. In 1930-51 he taught there and in other colleges. He began working in 1950, at the Institute of Physical Chemistry of the U.S.S.R. Academy of Sciences. In 1953 Chmutov was elected a Corresponding Member of the U.S.S.R. Academy of Sciences. He has been a member of the Communist Party of the Soviet Union since 1947.

The major work of Chmutov is the study of surface phenomena and of sorption processes.

As of 1961, Chmutov was Chairman of the Commission on Chromatography.

Bibliography:
and M. Dubinin. Physico-Chemical Basis of Gas Protection.
Moscow: 1939.
Technics of Physico-Chemical Investigations. 3rd edition.
Moscow: 1954.

Office: Institute of Physical Chemistry of USSR Academy of
            Sciences
            Leninskii Prospekt, 31
            Moscow, USSR
Residence: 1-aya Cheremuskhinskaya, 3
            Moscow, USSR
Telephone: B7 44 25

CHUFAROV, GRIGORII IVANOVICH (Physical Chemist)
G. I. Chufarov was born November 14, 1900. He graduated
in 1928 from the Ural Polytechnic Institute. In 1931-36 he
worked at the Ural Physico-Chemical Institute and in 1936-39
at the Ural Physico-Technical Institute. He was Director, in
1939-46, of the Institute of Chemistry of the Ural Branch of the
U.S.S.R. Academy of Sciences. In 1946-56, he was Rector of
the Ural University. As of 1962, he has been working at the
Ural Branch of the U.S.S.R. Academy of Sciences. He has been
a member of the Communist Party of the Soviet Union since
1939. In 1953 he was elected a Corresponding Member of the
U.S.S.R. Academy of Sciences. He was a Deputy to the U.S.S.R.
Supreme Soviet, fourth convocation.
    The works of Chufarov are devoted to physico-chemical
problems of metallurgical and related processes. He studied
corrosion of metals in acids and the action of inhibitors and hot
tinning, zincing, and decarbonization of ferrosilicon steel.
Chufarov investigated the mechanism and kinetics of dissociation and reduction of metal oxides.
Bibliography:
    Production of cast iron, iron, and steel by way of reducing
    carburized ores. Izvest. Akad. Nauk S.S.S.R., Otdel. Tekh.
    Nauk, 1946, #6.
    and E. P. Tatievskaya. Absorption-catalytic theory of re-
    ducing oxides of metals. Problems of Metallurgy. Moscow:
    1953.
    and E. P. Tatievskaya. Mechanism and kinetics of reducing
    oxides of metals. Physico-Chemical Basis of the Blast
    Furnace Process and Contemporary Practice in Production
    of Cast Iron. Sverdlovsk: 1956.

Office: Ural Branch of USSR Academy of Sciences
              Severnaya Kovalevskaya Ulitsa, 13
              Sverdlovsk 49, USSR

CHUKHANOV, ZINOVII FEDOROVICH (Heat Engineer)
      Z. F. Chukhanov was born October 21, 1912. He graduated
in 1932 from Moscow Chemical-Technological Institute. In
1931-1934 he worked in the All-Union Power Engineering Institute and in 1932-1937 in the State Institute of Nitrogen. He began working in 1938 at the Power Institute of the U.S.S.R.
Academy of Sciences. In 1939 he was elected a Corresponding
Member of the U.S.S.R. Academy of Sciences. He has been a
member of the Communist Party of the Soviet Union since 1944.
      Chukhanov studied the theory of burning and vaporization of
solid fuels and worked out new complex methods in the utilization of fuels. He has also studied heat exchange and diffusion.
Bibliography:
      and M. K. Grodzovskii. Process of vaporization of fuel.
      Doklady Akad. Nauk S.S.S.R., New Series, 1934, 3, #5.
      Thermal conditions for burning and vaporization of a layer
      of solid fuel. Doklady Akad. Nauk S.S.S.R., New Series,
      1944, 44, #7.
      The theory of burning of coke carbon and methods of de-
      veloping techniques in burning and vaporization of solid
      fuels. Izvest. Akad. Nauk S.S.S.R., Otdel. Tekh. Nauk, 1953,
      #4.
      Succession of individual stages in the burning process of
      solid fuel. Process of Coal Burning (A. S. Predvoditelev,
      editor). Moscow-Leningrad: 1938.
      and S. E. Khaikina. Oxidation. Process of Coal Burning.
      Moscow-Leningrad: 1938.
      Question of underground vaporization of sub-Moscow coal
      and schist. Izvest. Akad. Nauk S.S.S.R., Otdel. Tekh. Nauk,
      1939, #8.
      Energo-Technological Utilization of Fuel. Moscow: 1956.
Office: G. M. Krzhizhanovskii Power Engineering Institute
              Leninskii Prospekt, 19
              Moscow, USSR
Residence: Leninskii Prospekt, 13
              Moscow, USSR
Telephone: B2 41 56

CHUKHROV, FYODOR VASIL'YEVICH (Geochemist)

F. V. Chukhrov was born July 15, 1908. He graduated from the Moscow Geological Survey Institute in 1932. Since 1936, he has been working at the U.S.S.R. Academy of Sciences Institute of Geological Sciences where he became deputy Director in 1950. In 1955, he became Director of the U.S.S.R. Academy of Sciences Institute of Geology of Ore Deposits, Petrography, Mineralogy and Geochemistry. He has been a member of the Communist Party of the Soviet Union since 1953. In that year he was also elected to the U.S.S.R. Academy of Sciences as a Corresponding Member.

Chukhrov has made mineralogical and geochemical investigation of ore deposits of Kazakhstan, studied colloids of the earth's crust, and the mineralogy of oxidized ozone.

In 1950 he was the recipient of a Stalin Prize.

Bibliography:

Colloids in the Earth's Crust, 2nd ed. Moscow: 1955.

Ore Deposits of Dzhyezkazgan-Ulutavsk Region of Kazakhstan. Moscow-Leningrad: 1940.

The significance of leaching of molybdenum for appraisal of molybdenum deposits in Central Kazakhstan. Soviet Geology, 1947, #14-15.

East Konuradsk deposit as a representative of quartz-molybdenum formation in Central Kazakhstan. Soviet Geology, 1948, #31.

Oxidized Zone of Sulphide Deposits of the Kazakhstan Steppe Region. Moscow: 1950.

Office: Institute of Geology of Mineral Deposits, Petrography, Mineralogy and Geochemistry
Staromonetnyy Pereulok, 35
Moscow, USSR
Residence: ul. Chkalova 21/2
Moscow, USSR
Telephone: K7 68 26

DANILOV, STEPAN NIKOLAEVICH (Organic Chemist)

S. N. Danilov was born January 6, 1889. He was a student of A. E. Favorskii (1860-1945, organic chemist). In 1914 he graduated from Petersburg University, where from 1915 he taught and subsequently became a professor. He was made professor at the Leningrad Technological Institute in 1930. In 1949 he became Chief of the Laboratory at the Institute of High Molecular Compounds of the U.S.S.R. Academy of Sciences. Since 1943, Danilov has been a Corresponding Member of the

U.S.S.R. Academy of Sciences. He became editor, in 1946, of
the Journal of General Chemistry (Zhur. Obshchei Khim.).
Danilov discovered that aldehydes of the chain and cyclical
construction with secondary and tertiary radicals can be isomerized into ketones. He established that oxy-aldehydes under
the influence of catalysts are isomerized into oxy-ketones and
into monocarboxylic acids. These investigations elucidated
some biochemical processes such as the transformation of
sugars. Danilov worked out new methods of obtaining ethyl
cellulose. He conducted investigations in the area of analysis,
stabilization, and transformation of viscose.

Bibliography:
Dehydration of secondary - tertiary alpha glycols, deriva-
tives of hydro-benzoin. Journal of Russian Physico-
Technical Society, Chem. sec., 1917, 49, #3-4.
Dehydration of cyclohexylhydrobenzoin in connection with
isomerization of aldehydes into ketones. Journal of Russian
Physico-Technical Society, Chem. Sect., 1926, 58, #1-2.
and A. M. Gakhokidze. Isomerization of oxyaldehydes. VI--
Saccharinic rearrangement of mannose. Zhur. Obschei
Khim., 1936, 6, #5.

Biography:
V. V. Razumovskii. Corresponding member of the U.S.S.R.
Academy of Sciences S. N. Danilov (On the 60th Anniversary
Since the Date of Birth). Priroda, 1949, #4.

Office: Institute of High Molecular Compounds
               Birzhevoy Prospekt, 6
               Leningrad, USSR

DELONE, BORIS NIKOLAEVICH (Mathematician)
      B. N. Delone was born in Leningrad March 15, 1890. He
graduated from Kiev University in 1913 where he was a pupil
of V. P. Ermakov (1845-1922, mathematician), and D. A. Grave
(1863-1939, mathematician). In 1934, he was awarded the degree of Doctor of Physical-Mathematical Sciences. He became
a professor in 1926. He was employed at Kiev University from
1913 to 1916, and at Kiev Polytechnic Institute from 1916 to
1922. He has been a professor at Moscow University since
1935, and since 1932, has been employed at the U.S.S.R. Academy of Sciences Institute of Mathematics. In 1929 he became a
Corresponding Member of the U.S.S.R. Academy of Sciences.
      On number theory Delone obtained a solution in whole
numbers of indefinite equations of the third power, with two
unknowns. His geometric works are concerned with a theory of

DERYAGIN 84

G. F. Voroni, the correct breaking up of a space, the geometry
of numbers, and mathematical crystallography. Delone presented an important method in structural analysis of crystals. He
has been concerned with geometrizing the theories of Galois.

Bibliography:
  and D. K. Faddeev. Theory on Irrationality of the Third
  Power. Moscow-Leningrad: 1940.
  and A. D. Aleksandrov. Mathematical Basis in Structural
  Analysis of Crystals and Determination of the Basic Repeat-
  ing Parallelepiped with the Use of X-rays. Moscow-
  Leningrad: 1934.
  Petersburg School of Number Theory. Moscow-Leningrad:
  1947.

Biography:
  On the 60th Anniversary of Boris Nikolaevich Delone. Izvest.
  Akad. Nauk S.S.S.R., Mat. Ser., 1950, 14, #4. (contains
  bibliography of the works of Delone).

Office: V. A. Steklov Mathematics Institute of USSR
           Academy of Sciences
           1-y Akademicheskii Proyezd, 28
           Moscow, USSR
Residence: Pyatnitskaya, 12
           Moscow, USSR
Telephone: B1 16 57

DERYAGIN, BORIS VLADIMIROVICH (Physical Chemist)

B. V. Deryagin was born August 4, 1902. In 1922 he graduated from Moscow University. He was appointed, in 1935, Chief
of the Laboratory of Surface Forces at the Institute of Physical
Chemistry of the U.S.S.R. Academy of Sciences.

Deryagin studied properties of thin layers of liquids. He
discovered (together with M. M. Kusakov) the "unwedging
action" of these layers. He proposed a theory of coagulation of
dispersed systems by electrolytes (1935-41) and the theory of
agglomeration of solid particles. He investigated the mechanism of lubrication by thin layers and boundaries. He worked
out the molecular theory of external friction of solid bodies
(1933-34) and (together with N. A. Krotova) the electric theory
of adhesion.

Deryagin became a Corresponding Member of the U.S.S.R.
Academy of Sciences in 1946.

Bibliography:
and N. A. Krotova. Adhesion. Investigations of adhesion and gluing action. New ideas in the study of aerosols. Moscow-Leningrad: 1949.

and others. On the radius of action of molecular surface forces and polymolecular solvate layers. Doklady Akad. Nauk S.S.S.R., 1939, 23, #7.

and others. Boundary phases as a particular state of aggregation of liquids. Collection Devoted to the Memory of Academician P. P. Lazarev. Moscow: 1956.

On the question of determining the concept and the degree of unwedging pressure and its role in statics and kinetics of thin layers of liquid. Kolloid Zhur., 1955, 17, #3.

and I. I. Abrikosova. Direct measurement of molecular attraction of solid bodies, Part 1-2. Zhur. Eksptl. i Teoret. Fiz., 1956, 30, #6, 31, #1 (7).

What is Friction? Outlines on the Nature of Friction. Moscow: 1952.

and Ya. P. Toporov. Application of two-membered law of cracking to friction properties of polymers. Doklady Akad. Nauk S.S.S.R. 146, #6, 1356-59 (1962).

Office: Laboratory of Surface Forces
             Institute of Physical Chemistry
             Leninskii Prospekt, 31
             Moscow, USSR

DEVYATKOV, NIKOLAI DMITRIEVICH (Electronic Engineer)

N. D. Devyatkov was born April 11, 1907. He graduated from the Leningrad Polytechnical Institute in 1931. In 1925 he worked at the U.S.S.R. Academy of Sciences Physico-Technical Institute and subsequently in a number of other scientific research institutes. In 1954, he became head of a scientific research institute and also the Department of Ultra-High Frequency Electronics at the U.S.S.R. Academy of Sciences Institute of Radio Engineering and Electronics. Since 1944 he has been teaching at the Moscow Institute of Energy. He became a Corresponding Member of the U.S.S.R. Academy of Sciences in 1953.

Devyatkov has studied the gaseous discharge, the construction of gaseous discharge devices for protecting lines of communication from over voltage and acoustic shock, and also gaseous discharge devices for modulated radiation in the infrared part of a spectrum. He has worked out ultra high frequency devices for detecting, generating and converting frequencies of

electromagnetic oscillations in range from decimetric to mili-
metric wave lengths.
Bibliography:
Dischargers for protecting weak current lines. Electricity,
1931, #22.
On radiation of a helium gas-discharge tube with a hot
cathode. Zhur. Tekh. Fiz., 1934, 4, #10.
Gaseous acoustic shock absorbers for protection against
acoustic shock. Works of the All-Union Electro-Technical
Association, 1935, 5.
Three-electrode metallic tube of a decimetric range.
Zhur. Tekh. Fiz., 11, #8.
Office: Dept. of Ultra-High Frequency Electronics
Institute of Radio Engineering and Electronics
Mokhovaya Ulitsa 11, K-9
Moscow, USSR

DIKUSHIN, VLADIMIR IVANOVICH (Machine-tool Engineer)
V. I. Dikushin was born July 26, 1902. In 1928 he graduated
from the Moscow Higher Technical School and in 1932 began
working at the Experimental Scientific Institute of Metal Cutting Machines. He became a Corresponding Member of the
U.S.S.R. Academy of Sciences in 1943, and in 1953 Academician.
In 1941 and again in 1951 he received a Stalin Prize.
Dikushin's scientific works are devoted to basic problems
of machine tool design, in particular to working out scientific
bases of metal cutting machine design. Under Dikushin's direction, systems were worked out for the assembly line work
of machine tools and of standard machines for handling rotating bodies in automatic lines. Dikushin is the head of the
first engineering project in the U.S.S.R. for automatic pro-
duction.
Bibliography:
Machine-Building. Encyclopedic Reference-Book, 9.
Moscow: 1949 (Chapter 12).
Biography:
Dikushin Vladimir Ivanovich. Vestnik Akad. Nauk S.S.S.R.,
1954, #4.
I. I. Petrov. Vladimir Ivanovich Dikushin (On his 50th birth-
day and his 25th year of scientific activity). Telemekhanika
i Avtomat, 1953, 14, #3.
Office: Experimental Scientific Institute of Metal Cutting
Machines
Moscow, USSR

Residence: Kotel'nicheskaya nab. 1/15
   Moscow, USSR
Telephone: B7 44 89

DOLGOPLOSK, BORIS ALEKSANDROVICH (Organic Chemist)
   B. A. Dolgoplosk was born November 12, 1905. He graduated
in 1931 from Moscow University. In 1932-46 he worked at synthetic rubber plants. He taught at the Yaroslavl' Technological
Institute in 1944-46 and in 1945 became professor there. In
1946 he began work in the All-Union Scientific Research Institute of Synthetic Rubber and also, in 1948, at the Institute of
High Molecular Compounds of the U.S.S.R. Academy of Sciences.
Dolgoplosk has been a member of the Communist Party of the
Soviet Union since 1945. He was elected in 1958 a Corresponding Member of the U.S.S.R. Academy of Sciences. In 1941 and
1949 he received Stalin Prizes and in 1947 the S. V. Lebedev
Prize.
   Dolgoplosk has studied the polymerization processes and
their practical application. He investigated the initiation of
radical processes under the influence of oxidizing-reducing
reactions. He also studied reactions of free radicals in solutions, the determination of the connection between the structure of the radicals and their relative reaction ability, and the
determination of the mechanism of initiating and inhibiting
radical processes. In catalytic polymerization, Dolgoplosk
ascertained the role of complex formation during polymerization
under the influence of lithium - organic compounds. Dolgoplosk
conducted a series of investigations on the connection between
the structure and the properties of rubber and developed
methods of obtaining new types of rubber. He completed work
on the synthesis of carboxylic rubber, obtaining from it properties close to those of natural rubber.
Bibliography:
   and B. L. Erusalimskii, R. A. Krol', L. M. Romanov. Reactivity of free radicals and the role of their polar factor.
   Questions of chemical kinetics, catalysis and reaction ability. Moscow: 1955.
   and E. I. Tinyakova. Main types of oxidizing-reducing systems for initiating radical processes in water and hydrocarbon media and the mechanism of their action. Chemical
   Science and Industry, 1957, 2, #3.
   and B. L. Erusalimskii, E. I. Tinyakova. Generation of free
   radicals in solutions and their reactions in model systems.

DOLLEZHAL 88

Doklady Akad. Nauk S.S.S.R., Otdel. Khim. Nauk, 1958, #4, 469-481.
and E. I. Tinyakova. Mechanism of complex catalysts in polymerization. Doklady Akad. Nauk S.S.S.R. 146, #2, 856-59 (1962).
and E. I. Tinyakova. Mechanism of diene polymerization and structure of polymer chains. Doklady Akad. Nauk S.S.S.R. 146, #2, 362-65 (1962).
Office: Institute of High Molecular Compounds
Birzhevoy Prospekt, 6
Leningrad, USSR.

DOLLEZHAL, NIKOLAI ANTONOVICH (Power Engineer)

N. A. Dollezhal was born October 15, 1899. Upon graduating from Moscow Higher Technical School (MVTU), he became engaged in designing thermopower installations. From 1932 to 1934, he was Technical Director of the Institute of Nitrogen Machine Building. In 1935-1938, he was Chief Engineer of the "Bolshevik" Plant in Kiev. He was Director of the Scientific Institute of Chemical Machine Building in Moscow from 1942 to 1953. In 1923, he taught at the Institute of the National Economy in Moscow as well as at the Moscow Higher Technical School. He was awarded a Stalin Prize in 1952, and a Lenin Prize in 1957. In 1953, he was elected to the U.S.S.R. Academy of Sciences as a Corresponding Member, and in June 1962, an Academician.

Dollezhal has planned steam power plants and designed compressing machines for the chemical industry. He worked out the theory of self-acting valves of reciprocating compressors. He is working in nuclear energy in the above-mentioned cities, and was the chief designer of the reactor installed in the first atomic electric power station in the U.S.S.R.

Dollezhal visited the United States on a Nuclear Scientists Exchange program in New York City November 1959.

Bibliography:
Foundations of Planning Steam Power Installations. Moscow-Leningrad: 1933.
Toward a theory of self-acting laminated valves of piston compressors. Chemical Machine-Building, 1939, #7.
Higher pressure compressors. Chemical Machine-Building, 1940, #4-5.
Calculation of the basic parameters of self-acting laminated valves of a piston compressor. General Machine-Building, 1941, #9.

Applied theory of an intake valve of a piston compressor.
General Machine-Building, 1941, #1.
and others. The atomic reactor of the electric power station
of the U.S.S.R. Academy of Sciences. Atomic Energy, 1956,
#1.
Office: Scientific Institute of Chemical Machine Building
              Moscow, USSR

DORODNITSYN, ANATOLII ALEKSEEVICH (Hydrodynamicist)
A. A. Dorodnitsyn was born December 2, 1910. In 1931 he
graduated from the Groznenskii Petroleum Institute. Since
1936 he has been teaching and carrying out work in higher educational and scientific institutions of Moscow and Leningrad.
He started working in 1941 at the Central Aerodynamic Institute. From 1944 to 1955 he worked at the Mathematical Institute of the U.S.S.R. Academy of Sciences, and in 1955, he was
appointed Director of the Computer Center of the U.S.S.R.
Academy of Sciences now the Institute of Cybernetics. Dorodnitsyn was made professor in 1947 at the Moscow Physico-
Technical Institute. He has been an Academician of the U.S.S.R.
Academy of Sciences since 1953. In 1946, in 1947, and in 1951,
he was awarded Stalin Prizes.
    The investigations of Dorodnitsyn deal with problems of dy-
namic meteorology, aerodynamics, and applied mathematics.
His study of the influence of uneven land surfaces on air
streams is very important. He explained theoretically the formation of descending currents over mountain ridges. He is
concerned with a study of boundary strata in compressible gas
and supersonic flows of compressible gas; he also studied
asymptotic behavior of derivatives of several classes of non-
linear differential equations.
    As of 1961, Dorodnitsyn was Chairman of the Commission
on Computing Techniques of the U.S.S.R. Academy of Sciences.
    In June 1958, Dorodnitsyn visited the United States to attend
a Conference on Digital Computers at Michigan University.
Bibliography:
    Border strata in compressible gas. Priklad. Mat. i Mekh.,
    1942, 6, #6.
    Asymptotic laws of the distribution of discrete values for
    several special kinds of differential equations of the second
    order. Uspekhi Mat. Nauk, 1952, 7, #6.
    Asymptotic derivations of the Van Der Pohl equations.
    Priklad. Mat. i Mekh., 1947, 11, #3.

Office: Director, Computer Center
              1-y Akademicheskii Proyezd, 28
              Moscow, USSR

DUBININ, MIKHAIL MIKHAILOVICH (Physical Chemist)
    M. M. Dubinin was born December 20, 1900. In 1921 he
graduated from a technical institute in Moscow and began teaching there. He was a pupil of N. A. Shilov (1872-1930, outstanding physical chemist in catalysis and surface adsorption).
Dubinin taught at the Military Academy of Chemical Defense in
1932 and became a professor there in 1933. From 1946 to 1950
he was President of the All-Union D. I. Mendeleev Chemical
Society. He was made Chief of the Sorption Processes Laboratory at the Institute of Physical Chemistry of the U.S.S.R.
Academy of Sciences in 1946. Since 1943 he has been an Academician of the U.S.S.R. Academy of Sciences. And from 1948 to
1957 he was Secretary-Academician of the Division of Chemical
Sciences at the U.S.S.R. Academy of Sciences. In 1942 and in
1950 he was awarded Stalin Prizes. In 1961, he was awarded
the Red Banner of Labor.
    Since 1925 Dubinin has studied phenomena of absorption of
gases, vapors and dissolved substances by porous solids. He
proposed new methods of preparation of pure activated charcoal. These samples helped him study adsorption and formation of surface oxides of the acid type. They also helped him
to develop the basis for charcoal porosity characteristics.
Dubinin determined the mechanism of vapor absorption as a
function of the porosity factor of the absorbent structure. From
1932 to 1935 he investigated gas and vapor absorption from an
air stream which passes through a bed of granular absorbent.
He also developed basic concepts of vapor mixture absorption
and devised methods and designed equipment for vapor mixture
separation. In 1936 and 1937 he studied the effect of absorbent
ultraporosity on vapor absorption of substances with different
molecule sizes. Since 1940 Dubinin has worked on scientific
and practical problems of chemical defense. Since 1946 Dubinin
and his co-workers have been successfully investigating the dependence of sorption qualities of activated charcoals on their
structure and of vapor absorptivity on its physical properties.
Dubinin and his associates classified structural types of absorbents.
    As of 1961, Dubinin was a Member of the Presidium of the
U.S.S.R. Academy of Sciences.
    Dubinin has attended the Pugwash Conferences.

Bibliography:
Physical-Chemical Principles of Sorption Techniques, 2nd ed. Moscow-Leningrad: 1935.
and K. V. Chmutov. Physical-Chemical Principles of Gas Defence. Moscow: 1939.
and E. D. Zverina. Sorption and structure of activated carbons. Zhur. Fiz. Khim., 1947, 21, #11-12; 1949, 23, #1, 4, 9, 10; 1950, 24, #4, 10.

Office: Sorption Processes Laboratory
Institute of Physical Chemistry of USSR Academy of Sciences
Leninskii Prospekt, 31
Moscow, USSR

DUBININ, NIKOLAI PETROVICH (Biologist)

N. P. Dubinin was born January 1907. He has worked at the Moscow Zootechnical Institute where he became a professor in 1935. From 1932 to 1948, he worked at the U.S.S.R. Academy of Sciences Institute of Cytology, Histology and Embryology, and at the Forestry Institute from 1949-1955. He has been working at the Institute of Biophysics since 1955. He was elected, in 1946, a Corresponding Member of the U.S.S.R. Academy of Sciences.

Dubinin's basic work is in genetics, cytogenetics, genetic principles of selectivity, and the theory of evolution.

Bibliography:
Problems of physical and chemical organs of heredity. Biofizika, 1956, 1, #8.
Questions and problems of radioactive genetics. Vestnik Akad. Nauk S.S.S.R., 1956, #8.
Forest birds in the lower valley of the Ural. I. Works of the Institute of Forestry,Academy of Sciences, 1953, 18.
and T. A. Terapanov. Birds of the Ural Valley. II-III. Works of the Institute of Forestry, Academy of Sciences, 1956, 32.
and N. N. Sokolov. Chromosomic mutations and the system of species. Zhur. Obshchei Biol., 1940, 1, #4.
and B. N. Sedorov. The dependence of a gene's activity on its position in a system. Biol. Zhur., 1934, 3, #2.

Office: Institute of Biophysics
Leninskii Prospekt, 33
Moscow, USSR

Residence: 2-aya Meshchanskaya, 87
             Moscow, USSR
Telephone: Il 39 31

DUKHOV, NIKOLAI LEONIDOVICH (Mechanical Engineer)

N. L. Dukhov was born October 13, 1904. Upon graduating from the Leningrad Polytechnical Institute in 1932, he worked as a designer at the Leningrad Plant, and in 1941 at the Chelyabinsk Plant. He was awarded the title Hero of Socialist Labor, and became a member of the Communist Party of the Soviet Union in 1941. In 1953, he was elected to the U.S.S.R. Academy of Sciences as a Corresponding Member.

The basic works of Dukhov deal with the development of new designs.

Office: USSR Academy of Sciences
              Leninskii Prospekt, 14
              Moscow, USSR

DUMANSKII, ANTON VLADIMIROVICH (Colloidal Chemist)

A. V. Dumanskii was born April 20, 1880. He is one of the founders of colloidal chemistry in Russia. He graduated in 1903 from Kiev Polytechnical Institute where, until 1913, he conducted his investigations. In 1913 he organized in Voronezh a Laboratory of Colloidal Chemistry which was reorganized in 1932 into the All-Union Scientific Research Institute of Colloidal Chemistry. Until 1942 he was Director of this Institute. In 1946 he became Director of the Institute of General and Inorganic Chemistry, Ukrainian S.S.R. Academy of Sciences. Dumanskii has been a Corresponding Member of the U.S.S.R. Academy of Sciences since 1933, and since 1945 an Academician of the Ukrainian S.S.R. Academy of Sciences. He is the founder and editor, since 1935, of the Colloidal Journal.

While studying dispersed, chiefly colloidal systems, Dumanskii introduced physical methods for research in colloidal chemistry. He observed an increase in the concentration of salts with the introduction of gelatin to their solution, which was helpful subsequently in explaining the role of water, bound to colloidal particles. Instead of using animal membranes for investigating the properties of a medium surrounding colloidal particles (a dispersed medium), Dumanskii introduced, in 1908, the use of collodion membranes, later widely utilized in chemistry and biology. He introduced the use of a powerful centrifuge for measuring the size of colloidal particles. Dumanskii's widespread investigations in the utilization of physico-chemical diagrams (allowing to clearly outline the conditions of sedimentation and formation of colloidal solutions) in colloidal systems had considerable practical significance. The works of Dumanskii, and his students on the solvation of colloidal systems lead to considerable changes in the theory under question and in the technology of a number of fields in practical colloidal chemistry (agronomy, sugar, fermentation, starch-molasses, bread baking and other industries).

Bibliography:

Methods of determining dispersion of sols, emulsions and suspensions. Papers of the Voronezh Agricultural Institute, 1928, 11.

Liophilicity of Dispersed Systems. Voronezh: 1940.

Study of Colloids. 3rd edition. Moscow-Leningrad: 1948.

Utilizing colloidal-chemical approaches in the study of technological processes. Uspekhi Khim, 1935, 4, #2.

and I. A. Dumanskii. Bibliographical Outline of the Development of Domestic Colloidal Chemistry. #1, 2nd edition. Kiev: 1951.

Biography:

Z. Vashchenko. Anton Vladimirovich Dumanskii. Introductory Article by P. A. Rebinder. Kiev: 1955.

B. A. Dogadkin. Anton Vladimirovich Dumanskii. Kolloid. Khim., 1950, #5.

B. A. Dogadkin, S. M. Lipatov, P. A. Rebinder. On the 70th Anniversary Since the Date of Birth of Anton Vladimirovich Dumanskii. Kolloid. Khim., 1955, 17, #3.

S. M. Lipatov, A. V. Dumanskii. On the 70th Anniversary Since the Date of Birth. Uspekhi Khim., 1950 #6.

E. M. Natanson. Anton Vladimirovich Dumanskii, On the 75th Anniversary Since the Date of Birth. Ukr. S.S.R. Zhur. Khim., 1955, 21, #3.

Office: Institute of General and Inorganic Chemistry of
              Ukrainian SSR Academy of Sciences
              Ulitsa Leontovicha 9
              Kiev, Ukrainian SSR

DZHELEPOV, BORIS SERGEEVICH (Physicist)

B. S. Dzhelepov was born December 12, 1910. He graduated from Leningrad University in 1931, and from then until 1943, he worked at the Physico-Technical Institute of the U.S.S.R. Academy of Sciences. In 1935-1941 and again in 1944, he taught at Leningrad University. He worked in 1939-1941 and also in 1946 at the All Union Scientific Research Institute of Metrology.

Beginning in 1945, Dzhelepov has worked at the Radium Institute of the U.S.S.R. Academy of Sciences. He was elected, in 1953, a Corresponding Member of the U.S.S.R. Academy of Sciences. Dzhelepov's field is nuclear physics. In 1932-41 he studied the energy spectra of electrons emitted by artificially created radioactive elements. In 1938 he designed a gamma spectrometer, based on pair formation. In 1948, together with Orbeli, he developed a gamma spectrometer, based on the measurement of recoil electron energy knocked out by gamma rays in the direction of its initial movement. In 1954 this method was improved and a new device was built. Dzhelepov and associates studied beta and gamma spectra and spectra of conversion electrons of more than thirty radioactive isotopes. Together with N. A. Vlasov, he studied the angular distribution of quanta formed during positron annihilation, which permitted the evaluation of the velocities of positrons at which they are annihilated in solid bodies. Dzhelepov analysed data on beta disintegration, on mirror nuclei, and on isotopic spin.

Bibliography:

and L. N. Syryanova. Influence of the Electric Field of an Atom on Beta Disintegration. Moscow-Leningrad: 1956.

and O. E. Kraft. Positrons in inner conversion of radioactive isotopes Sb 124. Izvest. Akad. Nauk S.S.S.R., Ser. Fiz., 1956, 20, #3.

and S. A. Shestopalova. Magnetic gamma spectrometer with improved focussing-electron. Izvest. Akad. Nauk, Ser. Fiz., 1956, 20, #3.

and I. A. Yaritsyna. The study of hard gamma rays with low intensity with the aid of the photoneutron effect. Izvest. Akad. Nauk, Ser. Fiz., 1956, 20, #3.

and others. Spectrum of gamma rays Sb^{124}. Izvest. Akad. Nauk, Ser. Fiz., 1956, 20, #8.

and S. A. Shestopalova. About $0 \longrightarrow 0$ transformation into RaC. Izvest. Akad. Nauk, Ser. Fiz., 1956, 20, #8.

and others. A new method of improving the focusing properties of a lens spectrometer. Izvest. Akad. Nauk, Ser. Fiz., 1956, 20, #8.

and L. K. Peker. On equally solved beta-transformations. Doklady Akad. Nauk, 1956, 106, #4.

and I. M. Vokhanskii, A. I. Medvedev, I. F. Uchevatkin. The nature of Er^{167} at a level of 531.8 kev. Doklady Akad. Nauk S.S.S.R. 146, #2, 789-92 (1962).

95 ELYUTIN

Office: V. G. Khlopin Radium Institute of USSR Academy of
Sciences
Ulitsa Roentgena, 1
Leningrad, USSR

ELISEEV (YELISSEEV), NIKOLAI ALEKSANDROVICH (Geologist & Petrographer)
N. A. Eliseev was born December 19, 1897. He graduated
in 1924 from Leningrad University. In 1938-47 he was professor at Leningrad Mining Institute and in 1947 became professor at Leningrad University. He has also been working,
beginning in 1949, in the Laboratory of Precambrian Geology of
the U.S.S.R. Academy of Sciences. Since 1953 he has been a
Corresponding Member of the U.S.S.R. Academy of Sciences.
Eliseev's field of work is the petrography of ore on the
Altai, Kol'skii Peninsulas, Krivoi Rog, and also the methodology
of petrographic investigations.
Bibliography:
Petrography of Ore Altai and Kalba. Petrography of the
U.S.S.R. Series 1, Regional Petrography, #6. Moscow-
Leningrad: 1938.
and A. A. Polkanov. Petrology of Pluton of Gremyakha-
Vyrmes, Kol'skii Peninsula. Leningrad: 1941.
Structural Petrology. Leningrad: 1953.
Methods of Petrographic Investigation. Leningrad: 1956.
Metamorphism. Leningrad, Publ. Leningrad University,
1959, 415 pp., 224 figs.
and G. I. Gorbunov, E. N. Eliseev, W. A. Maslenikov, K. N.
Utkin. Ultrabasic and basic intrusions of Pechenga. Acade-
my of Sciences, Moscow and Leningrad, 1961. 357 pp. 175
figs.
and A. P. Nikolskii, V. G. Kushev. The metasomatites of
the Krivoi Rog ore belt. Academy of Sciences, Moscow and
Leningrad, 1961. 204 pp. 85 figs.
Office: Laboratory of Precambrian Geology of USSR
Academy of Sciences
Leningrad, USSR

ELYUTIN, VYACHESLAV PETROVICH (Metallurgist)
V. P. Elyutin was born 1907. In 1930 he graduated from the
Moscow Institute of Steel. He has been working at the Moscow
Institute of Steel, and from 1945 to 1951 he was Director of this
Institute. He holds the degree of Doctor of Technical Sciences,
and in 1947 he became a professor. He has been a member of

the Communist Party of the Soviet Union since 1929. From
1951 to 1954 he was Deputy Minister and from 1954 to 1959
U.S.S.R. Minister of Higher Education. In 1959 he became
Minister of Higher and Middle Special Education. Elyutin was
a delegate to the Supreme Soviet of R.S.F.S.R. Fourth Convocation in 1958. He had been a Member Candidate of the Central
Committee of the Communist Party of the Soviet Union since
1956, and in 1961 he became a Member. Elyutin is Deputy
Chairman of the Committee for Lenin Prizes for Science and
Technology and of the Soviet Chinese Friendship Society. He
was awarded a Stalin Prize in 1952, Order of Lenin in 1957,
Red Banner of Labor, and two Badges of Honor. In 1959 Elyutin
accompanied Nikita Khrushchev to the United States. He was
elected a Corresponding Member of the U.S.S.R. Academy of
Sciences in 1962.

Bibliography:
　　Ferrous Alloys Production (Textbook). Moscow: 1951, 2nd
edition 1957.
　　and V. F. Funke. The equilibrium diagram of the chromium-
niobium system. Izvest. Akad. Nauk S.S.S.R., Otdel. Tekh.
Nauk 1956, #3, 68-76. C. A. 51, 830c (1957).
　　and V. F. Funke. Method for the determination of the melting point of refractory metals and alloys. Zavodskaya Lab.
22, 1444-8 (1956). C. A. 51, 1769e (1957).
　　and Yu. A. Pavlov, P. F. Merkulova. Determination of the
temperature of beginning of reduction of oxides with carbon.
Primenenie Radioaktiv. Izotopov i Met. (Moscow: Metallur-
gizdat) Sbornik 34, 48-52 (1955; Referat. Zhur., Met. 1956,
#5131. C. A. 51, 14501f (1957).
　　and G. A. Grigor'ev, M. A. Maurakh. The viscosity of fused
titanium. Izvest. Akad. Nauk S.S.S.R., Otdel. Tekh. Nauk
1957, #8, 95-101. C. A. 52, 3444i (1958).
　　and M. A. Maurakh, Yu. A. Pavlov. Interaction of molten titanium with graphite. Primenenie Radioaktiv. Izotopov i
Met., Moskov. Inst. Stali im. I. V. Stalina, Sbornik 1955, #34,
115-21. C. A. 53, 1040b (1959).
　　and others. Proizvodstvo ferrosplavov. Elektromettallur-
giya (Production of Ferroalloys. Electrometallurgy).
Moscow: Gosudarst. Nauch. Tekh. Izdatel. Lit. po Chernoi i
Tsvetnoi Met. 1957. 436 pp. C. A. 53, 925i (1959).
　　and P. F. Merkulova, Yu. A. Pavlov. The temperature of the
beginning of metal oxides reduction by solid carbon. Proizvodstvo i Obrabotka Stali i Splavov, Moskov. Inst. Stali im.
I. V. Stalina, Sbornik 38, 79-87 (1958). C. A. 53, 7894g (1959).

and E. I. Mozzhukhin, V. I. Shulepov. Proizvodstvo i Obrabotka Stali i Splavov, Moskov. Inst. Stali im. I. V. Stalina,
Sbornik 38, 427-32 (1958). C. A. 53, 7936c (1959).
and Yu. A. Pavlov, B. V. Glukhovtsev. Castability and density of nickel-vanadium alloys. Nauch. Doklady Vysshei
Shkoly, Met. 1958, #4, 12-16. C. A. 53, 9972d (1959).
and I. I. Kitaigorodskii, E. I. Mozzhukhin, V. B. Rabkin. The
composition of microlite and metallic compound NiAl. Zhur.
Priklad. Khim. 33, 559-63 (1960). C. A. 54, 17183b (1960).
and R. F. Merkulova, Yu. A. Pavlov. Reduction of metal
oxides with carbon. Nauch. Doklady Vysshei Shkoly, Met.
1958, #3, 10-14. C. A. 54, 15159f (1960).
and Yu. A. Pavlov, B. S. Lysov. Free energy of formation
of vanadium-oxygen solutions. Izvest. Vysshikh Ucheb.
Zavedenii, Chernaya Met. 1960, #1, 5-11. C. A. 54, 14885f
(1960).
and E. I. Mozzhukhin, Ya. S. Umanskii. Strength of carbide-
base alloy bond with NiAl or CoAl compounds. Izvest.
Vysshikh Ucheb. Zavedenii, Chernaya Met. 1960, #3, 131-5.
C. A. 54, 24269a (1960).
Office: Ministerstvo Vysshego Srednogo Spetsia'lnogo
              Obrazovaniya
              ul. Zhdanova, 11
              Moscow, USSR

EMANUEL', NIKOLAI MARKOVICH (Physical Chemist)
    N. M. Emanuel' was born October 1, 1915. After graduating
from the Leningrad Polytechnical Institute in 1938, he worked
at the Institute of Chemical Physics of the U.S.S.R. Academy of
Sciences. In 1944 he began teaching at Moscow University and
in 1950 became a professor there. Emanuel' has been a member of the Communist Party of the Soviet Union since 1948. In
1958 he was elected a Corresponding Member of the U.S.S.R.
Academy of Sciences. He was awarded the A. N. Bakh Prize in
1948, and in 1958 the Lenin Prize for investigating the properties and peculiarities of chain reactions.
    The main works of Emanuel' are in the field of chemical
kinetics. He discovered the formation of intermediate products
of a free radical type in slow chain reactions of oxidation, and
developed a kinetic method of investigating these products, thus
confirming a number of important rules of the chain theory.
He also worked on intramolecular hydrogen bonding. He discovered a new mechanism of homogeneous catalysis in hydrocarbon oxidation reactions, the peculiarities of negative

catalysts when introduced during various stages of chain reactions. Emanuel' proposed methods for controlling complex
chain reactions by changing the conditions during the process.
He developed a number of methods for stimulating slow, branching chain reactions, utilizing the capability of these processes
for self-support and self-acceleration. The investigations of
Emanuel' are of significance for improving and creating new
processes in Soviet chemical technology. Recently Emanuel'
has used concepts of chemical kinetics for the study of pathological processes such as the development and inhibition of malignant tumor.

Bibliography:
Intermediate Products of Complex Gaseous Reactions.
Moscow-Leningrad: 1946.
Macroscopic stages, particular role of the initial period and
the mechanisms of the action of inhibitors and positive cata-
lysts in chain reactions. Questions of Chemical Kinetics,
Catalysis and Reaction Ability. Moscow: 1955, 117-136.
New problems in the area of chain reactions. Doklady Akad.
Nauk S.S.S.R., Otdel. Khim. Nauk, 1957, #11.

Office: Chemistry Department
            Moscow University
            Moscow, USSR
Residence: Vorob'evskoye shosse, 2
            Moscow, USSR
Telephone: B2 46 63

EMEL'YANOV, VASILII SEMENOVICH (Metallurgist)
    V. S. Emel'yanov was born February 12, 1901. Upon gradu-
ating from the Moscow Mining Academy in 1928, he worked
there until 1931. In 1935 he started working on various important projects in industry and personnel. From 1940 to 1946,
he worked as a Deputy Chairman and Chairman of the U.S.S.R.
Council of People's Commissars Council on Standards. In
1957-60, he was Chief of the Main Administration on the Use of
Atomic Energy under the USSR Council of Ministers. He became, June 1960, Chairman of the State Committee of the USSR
Council of Ministers on the Use of Atomic Energy, and in 1962
he was made Deputy Chairman of that Committee. He has been
the representative of the Soviet Union at UN discussions on
Atomic Energy, and the chief delegate of the U.S.S.R. at the International Atomic Energy Agency in Vienna. He was a recipient of
a Stalin Prize in 1942 and in 1950, and in 1954 Hero of Socialist
Labor. Since 1919 he has been a member of the Communist

Party of the Soviet Union. He was elected, in 1953, a Corresponding Member of the U.S.S.R. Academy of Sciences. He has
participated in the Pugwash Conferences.

Emel'yanov's main scientific work deals with developing new
grades of steel, technology of producing armor, study of the
role of nitrogen and other gases in special steel and ferroalloys.
Under the direction of Emel'yanov, new electric furnaces for
smelting of steel and ferroalloys were developed, the technology was worked out and high grade ferroalloys were introduced in industry.

Bibliography:
> and K. P. Grigorovich. Experiment in the smelting of ferro-
> manganese in electric furnaces. Journal of the Metal
> Industry, 1929, #12.
> Influence of nitrogen on properties of steel. Quality Steel,
> 1935, #5.
> Production of manganese steel. Quality Steel, 1934, #3.
> and Yevstyukhin, eds. Metallurgy and Metallorgraphy of
> Pure Metals. Trans. from the Russian. English ed. Rev.
> and edited by Bruce Chalmers. New York, Gordon and
> Breach, 1962. 340 p.

Office: Council of Ministers of USSR
              Moscow, USSR

ENGEL'GARDT, VLADIMIR ALEKSANDROVICH (Biochemist)

A. V. Engel'gardt was born December 3, 1894. In 1919 he
graduated from Moscow University. From 1929 to 1933 he was
professor at the University of Kazan' and the Kazan' Medical
Institute and from 1934 to 1940 professor at Leningrad University. He was made professor at Moscow University in 1936.
Beginning in 1933, he worked in departments of the U.S.S.R.
Academy of Sciences: in 1935, Chief of the Laboratory of Biochemistry of the Animal Cell at the Institute of Biochemistry,
1944-50 at the Institute of Physiology. He was Chairman of the
Department of Biochemistry of the Institute of Experimental
Medicine at the U.S.S.R. Academy of Medical Sciences from
1945 to 1952. From 1955 to 1960 he was Academician-
Secretary of the Department of Biological Sciences of the
U.S.S.R. Academy of Sciences. Engel'gardt was elected Corresponding Member of the U.S.S.R. Academy of Sciences in 1946
and Academician in 1953. Since 1944 he has also been a member of the U.S.S.R. Academy of Medical Sciences. He was made
chief editor of the journal Biochemistry in 1944. He is a member of many domestic and foreign scientific societies. For

investigations of muscle activity, he (with M. N. Lyabimova) was awarded in 1943 a Stalin Prize.

Engel'gardt's main investigations are devoted to the study of the regularities in the transformation of organic phosphorous compounds in processes of cellular metabolism, their role in the exchange of energy and in the physiological functioning of the cell, the study of the interrelation of energy processes and the mechanical reaction of muscle protein. His investigations aided the establishment of definite ties between chemical phenomena in the muscle fiber and its function. Engel'gardt discovered the process of aerobic resynthesis of adenosine triphosphoric acid. He established that the contracting protein of the muscle, myosin, has the properties of an adenylpyrophosphatase enzyme and by splitting the adenosine triphosphoric acid, obtains energy for its functioning. Engel'gardt also investigated vitamins, and studied the technology for vitamin production and their quantitative determination.

As of 1961, Engel'gardt was Chairman of the U.S.S.R. Academy of Sciences Presidium Commission on Radiobiology, and Director of the Institute of Radiation and Physico-Chemical Biology of the U.S.S.R. Academy of Sciences.

In September 1958, he visited the United States to attend the 8th General Assembly of Scientific Union in Washington, D. C., and January 1959, he visited the University of California at Berkeley.

Bibliography:

Anerobic disintegration and aerobic resynthesis of pyrophosphate in red blood cells of birds. Kazan' Med. Zhur., 1931, 27, #4-5.

Reversible and conjugated reactions in the energy exchange of cells. Izvest. Akad. Nauk S.S.S.R., Ser. Biol., 1936, #4.

and A. P. Barkhash. Oxidizing disintegration of phosphaglucovanillic acid. Biokhimiya, 1938, 3, #4.

and M. N. Lyubimova. Adenylpyrophosphatase and myosin of the muscle. Biokhimiya, 1939, 4, #6.

Phosphoric acid and functions of the cell. Izvest. Akad. Nauk S.S.S.R., Ser. Biol., 1945, #2.

with I. M. Seits. Phosphorylization during respiration and the Pasteur effect. Biokhimiya, 1949, 14, #6.

and M. N. Lyubimova. On the mechano-chemistry of the muscle. Biokhimiya, 1942, 7, #5-6.

Biography:
Academician V. A. Engel'gardt. On the 60th Anniversary
since the date of birth. Uspekhi Sovremennoi Biol., 1954,
38, #3 (6).
On the 60th Anniversary since the date of birth and the 35th
Anniversary of scientific activity of Academician Vladimir
Aleksandrovich Engel'gardt. Voprosy Med. Khim., 1955, 1,
#1.
A. E. Oparin, N. M. Sisakyan et al. Vladimir Aleksandrovich
Engel'gardt (On the 60th Anniversary since the date of birth).
Doklady Akad. Nauk S.S.S.R., 1954, #6.
Office: Institute of Radiation and Physico-Chemical Biology
Moscow, USSR

EYKHFEL'D, IOGAN GANSOVICH (Botanist)
I. G. Eykhfel'd was born January 25, 1893. Upon graduation
from the Petrograd Agricultural Institute, he became Director
of the Polar Division (Murmansk Territory) of the All-Union
Institute of Plant Growing from 1923 to 1940 (until 1930, known
as the All-Union Institute of Applied Botany and New Cultures).
From 1940-1951, he was Director of the Institute at Leningrad.
In 1950 he became President of the Estonian S.S.R. Academy of
Sciences. In 1953 he was awarded the title Honored Scientist of
the Estonian S.S.R., and has been a member of the Lenin All-
Union Academy of Agricultural Sciences since 1935. He became
an Academician of the Estonian S.S.R. Academy of Sciences in
1946 and was elected to the U.S.S.R. Academy of Sciences as a
Corresponding Member in 1953. In 1942, he was awarded a
Stalin Prize. He was a deputy to the third and fifth convocations
of U.S.S.R. Supreme Soviet, and was elected again March 1962.
Eykhfel'd is a specialist in the field of Polar plant cultivation
and agriculture. He aided a study on moving agricultural cultures into the Northern regions of the country and proved the
possibility of creating a vegetable and feed base in severe
climatic environments of the Kola Peninsula and the Northern
part of the Karelian A.S.S.R. He conducted work on the study
and selection of a special set of early ripening cultures for
the far North, and of utilizing Khibin rocks as mineral fertilizer,
and presented an outline of field cultures of Scandinavia.
Bibliography:
Selection at the Polar Circle. Works of Applied Botany and
Breeding, 1925, 14, #5.

Cultured Pastures and Method of Selection of Pasture Grasses in Scandinavia. Leningrad: 1929 (Proceedings of Experimental Agriculture in the Leningrad Territory, #10).
Problems of agriculture in the far North. Soviet North, 1931, #5.
Struggle for the Far North. . . Leningrad: 1933.
Problems of agricultural science in the Estonian S.S.R. in farming. Resume. in Pollumajanduslik Sessioon. 16-18 jaanuarini, 1947; Agricultural Session, January 16-18, 1947, Tartu, 1947, 212-214.
Establishment of a summer feeding base for dairy cattle. Proceedings of the Latvian S.S.R. Academy of Sciences, 1955, #2 (91).
Experiment in establishing pastures for many years in Estonia. Journal of Agricultural Science, 1956, #2.
Office: Academy of Sciences Estonian SSR
Kokhtu Ulitsa, 6
Tallin, Estonian SSR

FEDOROV, SERGEI FILIPPOVICH (Geologist)
S. F. Fedorov was born July 13, 1896. He graduated from the Moscow Mining Academy in 1924. From 1934 to 1954, he was a professor at the Moscow Oil Institute. Since 1934, he has been working at the U.S.S.R. Academy of Sciences. Since 1920 he has been a member of the Communist Party of the Soviet Union. He became a Corresponding Member of the U.S.S.R. Academy of Sciences in 1939. In 1950 and 1952 he received Stalin Prizes. In 1952 the U.S.S.R. Academy of Sciences awarded him the I. M. Gubkin Prize.
Fedorov studied mud volcanism and the genetic connection of mud volcanos to oil deposits.
Bibliography:
and I. M. Gubkin. Mud volcanoes of the Soviet Union and their oil content. International Geological Congress. Works of the XVIIth Session. U.S.S.R. 1937, 4, Moscow, 1940.
Oil Deposits of the Soviet Union, 2nd ed. Moscow-Leningrad: 1939.
Methodology of compiling maps for oil prognosis. Vestnik Akad. Nauk S.S.S.R., 1940, #3.
and others. Geological Structure of the Southern Part of the Siberian Platform. Moscow: 1953.
New data on the genesis of oil deposits. Doklady Akad. Nauk S.S.S.R., New series, 1953, 88, #1.

Office: Dept. of Geological and Geographical Sciences of
              USSR Academy of Sciences
              Leninskii Prospekt, 14
              Moscow, USSR
Residence: Leninskii prospekt, 13
              Moscow, USSR
Telephone: V2 44 49

FEDEROV, YEVGENII KONSTANTINOVICH (Geophysicist)
    Ye. K. Federov was born April 10, 1910. In 1932 he gradu-
ated from Leningrad University. He worked as a magnetologist
in Polar stations on the Land of Franz and Joseph in 1932-33
and on the Cape of Chelyuskin in 1934-35. As a geophysicist-
astronomer in 1937-38, he participated in the operations of the
first Soviet drifting scientific station, "North Pole-1." From
1939 to 1947 he was in charge of the Hydrometeorological
Service of the U.S.S.R. Council of Ministers. Fedorov worked
from 1947 to 1955 at the Institute of Applied Geophysics of the
U.S.S.R. Academy of Sciences and in 1955 became Director of
that Institute. He became a member of the Communist Party of
the Soviet Union in 1938. In 1939 he was elected a Corresponding Member of the U.S.S.R. Academy of Sciences and in 1960 an
Academician. Also in 1960 he became Chief Scientific Secretary
of the U.S.S.R. Academy of Sciences Presidium; however, in
December 1962 it was announced that Federov was relieved of
his position of Chief Scientific Secretary of the Presidium of
the Academy of Sciences and reassigned as Chief of the U.S.S.R.
Council of Ministers Main Administration of Hydrometeorological Services. He has been Chairman of the Soviet delegation of
Experts on Control of Atomic Tests. In 1938 he was made a
Hero of the Soviet Union.
    His main investigations are concerned with magnetology,
meteorology and practical astronomy.
Bibliography:
    Astronomical definitions, Works of a Drifting Station "North
    Pole," 1, 209-334. Leningrad: 1940.
    Meteorological instruments and observations, Works of a
    Drifting Station "North Pole," 2, 5-30. Leningrad-Moscow:
    1941-45.
    Main problems of hydrometeorological services, General
    Session of the U.S.S.R. Academy of Sciences, July 1-4, 1946.
    Moscow-Leningrad: 1947, 93-110.
    The influence of atomic explosions on meteorological
    processes. Atomic Energy, 1956, #5.

Office: Institute of Applied Geophysics
Glebovskaya Ulitsa, 20-b
Moscow, USSR

FEDOROV, YEVGRAF YEVGRAFOVICH (Climatologist)

Ye. Ye. Fedorov was born Nov. 8, 1880. He graduated from
the University of Petersburg in 1910. From 1911 to 1934, he
worked at the Magneto-Meteorological Observatory in Pavlovsk,
and from 1934 to 1951, at the U.S.S.R. Academy of Sciences
Institute of Geography. He became a Corresponding Member
of the U.S.S.R. Academy of Sciences in 1946.

Fedorov's main works are concerned with the study of cloud
and solar radiation. He also developed methods for studying
climate by means of simultaneous observation of temperature,
humidity, etc.

Bibliography:

Climate as an aggregate of weather. Journal of Meteorology,
#7 (1925).

Distribution and type of precipitation in the plains of the
European part of the USSR in the summer. Works of the
U.S.S.R. Academy of Sciences Institute of Geography, #28
(1938).

and A. I. Baranov. Climate and Weather of the European
Part of the USSR. Moscow-Leningrad: 1949.

Biography:

Ya. I. Fel'dman. Yevgraf Yevgrafovich Fedorov (On the
occasion of the 75th year since the date of birth). Izvest.
Akad Nauk S.S.S.R., Ser. Geogr., #1 (1956).

Office: Dept. of Geological and Geographical Sciences of
USSR Academy of Sciences
Leninskii Prospekt, 14
Moscow, USSR

Residence: Prospekt Mira 70-a
Moscow, USSR

Telephone: I1 45 78

FERDMAN, DAVID LAZAREVICH (Biochemist)

D. L. Ferdman was born January 7, 1903. He graduated in
1925 from Khar'kov University. He began working in 1928 at
the Institute of Biochemistry of the Ukrainian S.S.R. Academy
of Sciences. In 1944, he became professor at Kiev University.
He was elected a Corresponding Member of the Ukrainian S.S.R.
Academy of Sciences in 1939, and in 1946 a Corresponding
Member of the U.S.S.R. Academy of Sciences.

Investigations of Ferdman and his associates are devoted to the study of muscle chemistry, especially phosphorous compound metabolism and the formation and elimination of ammonia, and to the biochemistry of diseased muscles. They ascertained the presence of glutamine in the tissues of animals and studied its role.

Bibliography:
Biochemistry of Phosphorous Compounds. Kiev: 1935.
Exchange of Phosphorous Compounds. Moscow-Leningrad: 1940.
Biochemistry of Muscle Disease. Kiev: 1953.
On processes of formation and elimination of ammonia in the animal organism. Uspekhi Biokhim., 1950, 1, 216-242.
Biokhimia (Biochemistry). Textbook. Moscow: Sovetskaya Nauka. 1959. 600 pp. 1st edition. Moscow: Vysshaya Shkola. 1962. 625 pp. 2nd edition.
Contributions to functional biochemistry of muscles. Izvest. Akad. Nauk S.S.S.R., Ser. Biol. 3, 346-354 (1960).
Office: Kiev University
Kiev, Ukrainian SSR
Residence: Ulitsa Leontovicha 9, Apt. 3
Kiev, Ukrainian SSR

FESENKOV, VASILII GRIGOR'EVICH (Astrophysicist)

V. G. Fesenkov was born January 13, 1889. In 1911 he graduated from Khar'kov University. He is a member of many committees of the International Astronomical Union. In 1927 he became a Corresponding Member of the U.S.S.R. Academy of Sciences and in 1935 an Academician. Since 1946 he has been a member of the Kazakh S.S.R. Academy of Sciences, and a Member of the Presidium of Kazakh Academy of Sciences as of 1961.

Fesenkov's research deals with the physical properties of planets, meteors, physics of the sun and stars, evolution of stars, and the structure of gas and dust nebulae. He studied the structure of galaxies, cosmogony, celestial mechanics, and optics of the atmosphere. Fesenkov pioneered in the photometric investigation of the zodiac light and formulated a dynamic theory of zodiac light. He also investigated twilight of our atmosphere, the structure of the atmosphere, the brightness of the sky during the day, and the luminescence of the sky during the night. He introduced a hypothesis of corpuscular photogenesis of stars and developed a criterion of the influx stability of celestial bodies, thus explaining the peculiar structure of the solar system and the formation and evolution of galactic nebulae. Fesenkov also advanced the hypothesis of star formation from the interstellar gas and dust medium. He is the author of numerous popular publications in the field of cosmogony.

As of 1961, Fesenkov was Chairman of the U.S.S.R. Academy of Sciences Committee on Meteorites and Director of the Astrophysical Institute of Kazakh S.S.R. Academy of Sciences.

Bibliography:
La lumière Zodiacale. Thèse de doctorat. Petersburg: 1914.

Cosmogony problems in modern astronomy. Astron. Zhur., 1949, 26, #2.

The atmospheric shadow of the earth. Astron. Zhur., 1949, 26, #4.

Corpuscular radiation, a factor in the evolution of the sun and the stars (Paper presented at the VIII International Congress of the Astronomical Association in Rome, Sept. 1952). Moscow: 1952.

and D. A. Rozhkovskii. Star formation from the filaments of gaseous and dust nebulae. Astron. Zhur., 1952, 29, #4.

Office: Astrophysics Institute of Academy of Sciences
                Kazakh SSR
                Shevchenko Ulitsa, 28
                Alma-Ata, Kazakh SSR

FLEROV, GEORGII NIKOLAEVICH (Physicist)

G. N. Flerov was born March 2, 1913. After graduating from the Leningrad Industrial Institute, he worked at the Leningrad Physico-Technical Institute. From 1944 he worked in several departments of the U.S.S.R. Academy of Sciences, and is working at the Joint Institute of Nuclear Research. In 1953 Flerov was elected a Corresponding Member of the U.S.S.R. Academy of Sciences. He has been a member of the Communist Party of the Soviet Union since 1955. In 1946 he was awarded a Stalin Prize.

Flerov works in nuclear physics and cosmic rays. He investigated the energy dependence of cross section radiative-capture of slow neutrons. In 1940, with L. I. Rusinov, Flerov showed that during nuclear fission there is emission of secondary neutrons. In the same year, together with K. A. Petrzhak, he discovered the phenomena of spontaneous fission of heavy nuclei. He discovered nuclear fission under influence of a neutral component of cosmic rays.

Bibliography:
Absorption of slow neutrons by cadmium and mercury. Zhur. Eksptl. i Teoret. Fiz., 1939, 9, #2.

and K. A. Petrzhak. Spontaneous fission of uranium. Zhur. Eksptl. i Teoret. Fiz., 1940, 10, #9-10.

and L. I. Rusinov. Experiments in uranium fission. Izvest. Akad. Nauk S.S.S.R., Ser. Fiz., 1940, 4, #2.

and I. S. Panasyuk. Spontaneous fission of thorium. Doklady Akad. Nauk S.S.S.R., 1941, 30, #8.

and F. A. Alekseev. The Utilization of Radioactive Radiation in Prospecting and Exploitation of Oil Deposits in the U.S.S.R. Moscow: 1955.

and others. Spontaneous fission of thorium. (Letter to the editorial board) Zhur. Eksptl. i Teoret. Fiz., 1955, 28, #4.

and V. V. Volkov, L. Pomorskii, Ya. Tys. Observation of a three neutron capture reaction and a rupture reaction of three protons in the interaction of N^{14} and Ne^{20} ions with C, Al, Cu, and Ta nuclei. Zhur. Ekspt'l. i Teoret. Fiz. 1962, 42, #2, 635-37.

Office: Department of Physico-Mathematical Sciences of
            USSR Academy of Sciences
            Pyzhevskii Pereulok, 3
            Moscow, USSR

FLORENSOV, NIKOLAI ALEKSANDROVICH (Geologist)

N. A. Florensov was born in 1909. In 1936, he graduated from the Irkutsk State University, where he was an assistant from 1937-38, senior instructor 1938-40, a docent and departmental chairman 1940-56, and from 1956 to 1959, a professor and departmental chairman. From 1945 to 1947, he was also the Chief Geologist of the Irkutsk Geological Administration. In 1949 he also began work at the Eastern-Siberian branch of the U.S.S.R. Academy of Sciences, and in 1959 became the director of the division on regional geology of the U.S.S.R. Academy of Sciences East-Siberian Geological Institute. Florensov was awarded the title of Honored Scientist and Technologist by the Buryat A.S.S.R. in 1959, and in 1960 was made a Corresponding Member of the U.S.S.R. Academy of Sciences.

Florensov's work has been in the field of East-Siberian tectonics and neotectonics.

FOCK   108

Bibliography:
  and M. M. Odintsov, P. M. Khrenov. Nekotorye geologi-
  cheskie zakonomernosti razmeshcheniya poleznykh isko-
  paemykh na yuge vostochnoi Sibiri (Some geological consider-
  ations in deposits of useful minerals in South-Eastern
  Siberia). Akad. Nauk S.S.S.R. Vostoch. Filial, Izv. #2, 29-
  42. Bibliog. & Index of Geology Exclusive of North America.
  Vol. 23, 1958. p. 417.
  Nekotorye strukturnye osobennosti ugknoshykh tolshch Pri-
  baikalya (Certain structural peculiarities of coral basins of
  Lake Baikal region). Akad. Nauk S.S.S.R., Lab. Geol. Uglya,
  Tr. Vyp. 6, p. 558-567, 1956. Bibliog. & Index of Geology
  Exclusive of North America. Vol. 22, p. 163.
  Office: East Siberian Geological Institute
               Ulitsa Krasnoyzvezdy 18
               Irkutsk, East Siberia

FOCK, VLADIMIR ALEXANDROVITCH (Theoretical Physicist)
    V. A. Fock was born December 22, 1898. In 1922 he gradu-
ated from Petrograd University and remained there for further
study, becoming a professor in 1932. He worked at the following institutions: the State Institute of Optics (1919-23, 1928-41),
the Leningrad Institute of Physics and Technology (1924-36),
and the Institute of Physics of the U.S.S.R. Academy of Sciences
(1934-41, 1944-53). In 1954 he was appointed to the staff of the
Institute of Physical Problems of the U.S.S.R. Academy of
Sciences. Fock became a Corresponding Member of the
U.S.S.R. Academy of Sciences in 1932 and in 1939, an Academician. He was awarded, in 1946, a Stalin Prize, and a Lenin
Prize in 1960. As of 1960, he was still teaching at Leningrad
University. In April 1959, he visited the United States to attend
Harvard University as a Leningrad exchange scientist. In 1958
he was elected a Foreign Member of the Norwegian Royal Society in Trondheim.
    The basic research of Fock deals with quantum mechanics,
quantum electro-dynamics, the theory of electromagnetic diffraction and radio-wave propagation, the general theory of relativity, mathematics, and mathematical physics. His early work
is devoted to mechanics of elastic bodies and to theoretical
optics. In 1924 he established basic concepts of the theory of
the illumination vector in the optical field. Fock's most important contribution to mechanics is the solution of two-
dimensional static problems in the theory of elasticity. This
he carried out using the integral equation of Fredholm. In 1926

Fock worked out a theoretical approach to the wave equation of
quantum mechanics for a charged particle in a magnetic field,
proving for the first time its "gauge-invariant" properties. As
a consequence of the above investigation Fock arrived at the
scalar relativistic wave equation for a particle with no spin in
an electromagnetic field, independently of similar work by
the Swedish physicist O. Klein. This equation is often referred
to as the Klein-Fock equation. In 1930 Fock derived from a
variational principle the equations of the self-consistent field
in the quantum theory of the atom, taking due account of the
symmetry properties of the wave function; he developed an approximation method for determining the energy states and
transition probabilities of polyelectronic atoms. The method is
also used in the theory of molecular structure and in the theory
of solids. Fock's most important contributions to the field
theory are investigations in second quantization and quantum
electrodynamics. In 1932 and 1934 Fock developed a method
permitting a quantum description of systems with a variable
number of Bose particles (e.g. photons); he uses a functional,
dependent on an infinite set of wave functions in spaces of increasing number of dimensions (Fock space) and on an auxiliary
function (the field variable). In 1939 Fock solved Einstein's
gravitational equations for an "insular" distribution of masses
(like the Solar system), proving that gravitation equations also
include equations of motion. In his monograph "The theory of
space, time and gravitation" (1955) Fock interprets Einstein's
gravitation theory from his own point of view, drawing a sharp
distinction between the physical principle of relativity and the
mere co-variance of differential equations; he also insists on
the importance of the idea of unity between metric and gravitation, as opposed to the idea of relativity of motion, which is of
limited application only (according to Fock, a general principle
of relativity does not exist). Fock's other scientific achievements are in the integral equations, the various applications of
conformal representation, the theory of the puncture of dielectrics, the methods based on electricity to detect mineral
resources, the theory of core sampling by electrical means,
and the theory of diffraction of radio-waves. He also published
a number of papers on the interpretation of quantum mechanics.
Bibliography:
    The problem of many electrons in quantum mechanics and
    atomic structure. The 30th Anniversary of the October
    Revolution, Part I. Moscow-Leningrad: 1947.

The motion of finite masses in the theory of relativity. Zhur.
Ekspt'l. i Teoret. Fiz., 1939, 9, #4, p. 375.
and A. P. Kotel'nikov. Some Applications of Lobachevsky's
ideas in Mechanics and Physics. Moscow-Leningrad: 1950.
Zur Quantelektrodynamik. Physikalische Zeitschrift der
Sowjetunion (Charkow), 1934, 6, #5, p. 425.
Investigations in the Quantum Field Theory. Leningrad:
1957.
Theory of Space, Time and Gravitation. Moscow, 1955 and
1961. London, 1959 and 1963.
Criticism of an attempt to disprove the uncertainty relationship between time and energy. Zhur. Ekspt'l. i Teoret. Fiz.
42, #4, 1135-39 (1962).

Office: Physical Institute
           University of Leningrad
           Leningrad 164, USSR
Residence: Vassili Ostrov, 12th line 37, apt. 6
           Leningrad 178, USSR

FOTIADI, EPAMINOND EPAMINONDOVICH (Geophysicist)

E. E. Fotiadi was born January 23, 1907. He graduated
from Leningrad University in 1933. From 1927 to 1939, he
worked in the Emba Oil Trust, and in 1946 at the Scientific Research Institute of Geophysics. In 1951 he worked at the All-
Union Scientific Institute of Geophysical Methods for Prospecting. Since 1958, he has been working at the U.S.S.R. Academy
of Sciences Institute of Geology and Geophysics of the Siberian
Branch where he is Deputy Director. He has been a member
of the Communist Party of the Soviet Union since 1945. In 1958
he was elected to the U.S.S.R. Academy of Sciences as a Corresponding Member.

Fotiadi has worked on geophysical methods of prospecting
for oil deposits, and the geological explanation of gravity and
magnetic anomalies. He is the author of manuals and in-
structions for gravimetric and topogeodesic work. He has compiled summaries on geophysical data on the Southern part of
Emba territory, and has studied the structure of crystalline
base and associated sedimentary cover of the Russian platform.
Bibliography:
    and others. Course of Gravitational Prospecting. Moscow-
Leningrad: 1941.

Problem of geological interpretation of the anomalies of
gravity on the Russian platform. Applied Geophysics, #12,
Moscow, 1955.
Results of geophysical research. Volga-Ural Oil Bearing
Territory. Tectonics. Leningrad: 1956 (Works of the All-
Union Scientific Research Institute of the Oil Industry, #100).
Appraisal of gravitational influence of large facial-lithological
complexes of the sedimentary cover of various regions of
the Russian platform and of the South European part of the
U.S.S.R. Applied Geophysics, #17, Leningrad, 1957.
Structure of the crystalline base of the Russian platform.
Outlines on Geology of the U.S.S.R., 2. Leningrad: 1957
(Works of the All-Union Scientific Research Geological
Survey Institute for Oil, #101).
Office: Institute of Geology and Geophysics of Siberian
               Branch of USSR Academy of Sciences
               Novosibirsk, Siberia

FRANK, GLEV MIKHAILOVICH (Biophysicist)

G. M. Frank was born May 24, 1904. He graduated from
Crimean University in 1925. In 1929 he worked at the Physico-
Technical Institute in Leningrad and subsequently at the All-
Union Institute of Experimental Medicine and at the U.S.S.R.
Academy of Medical Sciences. He began working at the U.S.S.R.
Academy of Sciences in 1943. From 1946 to 1948 he was Chief
of the Radiation Laboratory of the U.S.S.R. Academy of Sciences. In 1948 he was on the staff of the U.S.S.R. Academy of
Medical Sciences Biophysics Institute where he became laboratory Chief in 1953 to 1958, acting Director, then Director, in
1958. Frank became a Corresponding Member of the U.S.S.R.
Academy of Medical Sciences in 1945, and in 1960 a Corresponding Member of the U.S.S.R. Academy of Sciences. He has been
a member of the Communist Party of the Soviet Union since
1947. In 1949 and 1951 he was awarded a Stalin Prize.
     Frank investigated the effect of ultra-violet and ionizing
radiation on living organisms and the biophysical basis of
nervous excitation and muscle contraction. He was one of the
first in the U.S.S.R. to use radioactive isotopes in biological
investigations.
Bibliography:
On Early Reactions of the Organism from Irradiation De-
pending Upon the Localization of Influence. Reports. . .
Moscow: 1955.

and others. Investigating the physico-chemical processes
of nervous activity. Biochemistry of the Nervous System.
Kiev: 1954.
Office: Institute of Biophysics
              Leninskii Prospekt, 33
              Moscow, USSR

FRANK, IL'YA MIKHAILOVICH (Physicist)

I. M. Frank was born October 23, 1908. After graduating in
1930 from Moscow University, he worked in the State Optical
Institute. In 1934 he went to work at the Physics Institute of
the U.S.S.R. Academy of Sciences. He became a professor in
1944 at Moscow University. Since 1946 he has been a Corresponding Member of the U.S.S.R. Academy of Sciences. He was
awarded a Stalin Prize in 1946, and in 1958 the Nobel Prize.
  Frank's major work is in physical optics and nuclear physics. Together with the Soviet scientist, I. E. Tamm, he gave
the theory of the Cherenkov effect. In cooperation with L. V.
Groshev, he studied pair formation. Frank, and his associates,
studied the physics of neutrons.

Bibliography:
Function of excitation and curve of absorption in optical
disassociation of thallium iodide. Works of the State Optical
Institute, 1933, 9, #87.
and I. E. Tamm. Coherent radiation of fast electrons in a
medium. Doklady Akad. Nauk S.S.S.R., New Series, 1937, 14,
#3.
and L. V. Groshev. Formation of pairs in krypton under the
action of gamma rays. Izvest. Akad. Nauk S.S.S.R., Otdel.
Mat. i Estest. Nauk, Ser. Fiz., 1938, #1-2, 57-65.
and L. V. Groshev, E. L. Feinberg. Multiplication in
uranium-graphite systems. Session of the Academy of Sciences on the Peaceful Utilization of Atomic Energy, July 1-5,
1955, Moscow, 1955.
The Doppler effect in a refractive medium. Izvest. Akad.
Nauk S.S.S.R., Ser. Fiz., 1942, 6, #1-2, 3-31.
Office: Physics Department
              Moscow University
              Moscow, USSR
Residence: Nab. Gor'kogo 32/34
              Moscow, USSR
Telephone: B1 36 17

FREIDLINA, RAKHIL' KHATSKELEVNA (Organic Chemist)
R. K. Freidlina was born September 20, 1906. She graduated
from Moscow University in 1930 and worked from then until
1934 at the Scientific Research Institute of Insectofungicides.
In 1935-39 and in 1941-54, she was at the Institute of Organic
Chemistry of the U.S.S.R. Academy of Sciences. Freidlina also
taught at the Moscow Institute of Fine Chemical Technology in
1938-41. In 1945 she became Chief of the Laboratory of the
Institute of Organo-Elemental Compounds of the U.S.S.R. Academy of Sciences. Since 1958 she has been a Corresponding
Member of the U.S.S.R. Academy of Sciences. In 1954 she became a member of the Communist Party of the Soviet Union.

Freidlina has synthesized and investigated the structure and
properties of organic compounds of mercury, arsenic, tin,
antimony, lead, titanium, silicon, zirconium, boron, fluorine
and chlorine. Of theoretical interest are her discoveries of
homolytic isomerization of organic compounds in solutions, investigation of adduct of metallic salts to olefin and acetylenes,
which led to the establishment of the concept of quasi-complex
compounds. Freidlina's investigations of reactions of telo-
merization of olefins and chemical transformations of telomers
made possible the development of an industrial method of synthesizing intermediate products for production of Soviet synthetic
fibers—enanth and pelargon.

Bibliography:
    Synthetic Methods in the Field of Organo-Metallic Com-
    pounds of Arsenic. Moscow-Leningrad: 1945.
    and A. N. Nesmeyanov and A. E. Borisov. Chemistry of
    quasi complex organo-metallic compounds and phenomenon
    of tautomerism. Anniversary Collection of the U.S.S.R.
    Academy of Sciences, Devoted to the 30th Anniversary of
    the Great October Socialist Revolution, I. Moscow-
    Leningrad: 1947.
    and A. N. Nesmeyanov and L. I. Zakharkin. Study of chemi-
    cal transformations of polychlorocarbons and related com-
    pounds. Uspekhi Khim., 1956, 25, #6.
    Reaction of telomerization and chemical transformations of
    telomers. Izvest. Akad. Nauk, S.S.S.R., Otdel. Khim. Nauk,
    1957 #11.
Office: Institute of Organo-Elemental Compounds
              Leninskii Prospekt, 31
              Moscow, USSR

Residence: 1-aya Cheremushkinskaya, 3
           Moscow, USSR
Telephone: B7 48 54

FRISH, SERGEI EDUARDOVICH (Physicist)
    S. E. Frish was born June 19, 1899. He graduated in 1921
from Petrograd University. From 1919 to 1939, he worked at
the State Optical Institute. In 1933 he became a professor at
Leningrad University where he had taught since 1924. Since
1946 he has been a Corresponding Member of the U.S.S.R.
Academy of Sciences.
    Frish studied atomic spectra of the Zeeman effect, the hyper-
fine structure of spectra lines, nuclear moments, spectroscopy
of gaseous discharge, and gas spectral analysis. From 1953 he
has been studying elementary processes in atomic excitation by
electronic impact.
Bibliography:
    Analysis of complex spectra (Ne II and Na II). Works of the
    State Optical Institute, Leningrad, 1932, 8, #81.
    Atomic Spectra, 1933.
    Techniques of Spectroscopy, 1936.
    and Yu. M. Kagan. Spectroscopy of gaseous discharge.
    Vestnik of the Leningrad University, 1948, #1.
    Spectroscopic study of the movement of ions in plasma, I-II.
    Zhur. Eksptl. i Teoret. Fiz., 1947, #6, 577-84; 1948, #6,
    519-24.
    Spectroscopic Determination of Nuclear Moments, 1948.
    and A. V. Timoreva. Course of General Physics. 1-2, 6th
    ed., 1955-56, 3, 4th ed., 1957.
    Role of effective cross-section during excitation of spectra.
    Uspekhi Fiz. Nauk, 1957, 61, #4.
Office: Department of Physics
           Leningrad University
           Leningrad, USSR

FRUMKIN, ALEKSANDR NAUMOVICH (Physical Chemist)
    A. N. Frumkin was born October 24, 1895. In 1915 he gradu-
ated from Odessa University. He was professor at the Institute
of Odessa University from 1920 to 1922, and from 1922 to 1946,
he was on the staff of the L. Karpov Physico-Chemical Institute
in Moscow. Frumkin spent 1928-29 at the University of Wis-
consin, U.S.A., as a lecturer in colloidal chemistry. In 1930,
he was elected to the chair of electrochemistry at the Moscow
University. He was appointed, in 1939, to the staff of the

Institute of Physical Chemistry of the U.S.S.R. Academy of Sciences, and from 1939 to 1949 was the Director. Since 1932 he has been an Academician of the U.S.S.R. Academy of Sciences. He received a Lenin Prize in 1931, and in 1941 a Stalin Prize.

Frumkin's research is primarily in surface phenomena and in the theory of electrochemical processes. He applied the Gibbs equation to adsorption and derived the equation for absorbed molecules on a surface. He developed the concept of the structure of the electrical double layer at the solid-liquid interface. In his experiments, he established the quantitative theory of the influence of the electric field on molecular adsorption. By means of measurements of potential jumps on the liquid-gas interface, he studied the nature of chemical bonds in molecules. In 1929, Frumkin developed the theory of kinetics in electrochemical reactions based on the composition of the solution and the structure of the double layer. He also recognized the importance of the zero potentials at the metallic electrodes. With V. G. Levich, Frumkin developed a theory of diffusion processes which take place in solutions while under the influence of an electrical field. He explained the mechanism of a number of electrochemical reactions, such as the reduction of oxygen and other anions. He has many pupils among the Soviet electrochemists. His scientific work found application in the generation of electrical energy by chemical sources, the wetting of metals by electrolytes, flotation, polarography, heterogeneous catalysis, and colloidal chemistry.

In 1958 Frumkin was appointed Director of the Institute of Electro-Chemistry of the U.S.S.R. Academy of Sciences.

Frumkin visited the United States in May 1960 to attend the Electrochemical Society meetings in Chicago.

Bibliography:

Electrocapillary Effects and Electrode Potentials. Odessa: 1919.

Adsorption and oxidation reactions. Uspekhi Khim., 1949, 18, #1.

with others. Kinetics of Electrochemical Processes. Moscow: 1952.

Kinetics of electrochemical processes and phenomena on the interface of a metal-solution, from the book: Electrochemical Conference of Dec. 19-25, 1950. Moscow: 1953, pp. 21-46.

Adsorption and electrochemical kinetics. Uspekhi Khim., 1955, 24, #8, pp. 933-50.

Office: Institute of Electrochemistry
              Leninskii Prospekt, 31
              Moscow, USSR

GALIN, LEV ALEKSANDROVICH (Mechanical Engineer)

L. A. Galin was born September 28, 1912. Upon graduation
from the Moscow Technological Institute of Light Industry, he
worked at the U.S.S.R. Academy of Sciences Institute of Mechanics. In 1956 he became a professor at Moscow University.
He has been a member of the Communist Party since 1951, and
was elected to the U.S.S.R. Academy of Sciences as a Corresponding Member in 1953.

The main work of Galin is in the theory of elasticity. He has
investigated the elastic-plastic problems in unsettled filtration
of liquids.

Bibliography:
   Contact Problems of the Theory of Elasticity. Moscow:
   1953.

   Plane elastic-plastic problem. Priklad. Mat. i Mekh., 1946,
   10, #3.

Office: Moscow University
              Moscow, USSR
Residence: Sr. Pervomaiskaya, 21
              Moscow, USSR
Telephone: E5 50 38

GEL'FAND, IZRAIL MOISEEVICH (Mathematician)

I. M. Gel'fand was born August 20, 1913 in Krasnie Okni,
Odessa Oblast. He was a postgraduate student at Moscow University in 1935, where in 1940, he was granted the degree of
Doctor of Physical-Mathematical Sciences. He was made a
professor in 1943. In 1932 he began his employment with Moscow University, and since 1939 has been working at the U.S.S.R.
Academy of Sciences Institute of Mathematics. He is also
working at the Institute of Biophysics. In 1951 he was awarded
a Stalin Prize for his work in the theory of representation of
groups. He was elected to the U.S.S.R. Academy of Sciences as
a Corresponding Member in 1953.

In his thesis for the candidate's degree, Gel'fand developed
the theory of integration of functions. His thesis for the
Doctor's degree was devoted to the theory of normalized rings.
This theory served as a basis for functional analysis in the
most varied areas of mathematics: theory of trigonometric
series, group theory, theory of differential equations. Since

1943, he has been working on the theory of unitary infinitely
measureable representations of continuous groups. At the same
time, he has been occupied with the theory of generalized functions and their application in differential equations, and also in
quantum mechanics.

Bibliography:
Normierte ringe. Mathematical Collection, 1941, 9, 3-24.
and A. M. Yaglom. General relativistic invariant equations
and infinitely measurable representations of the group of
Lorentz. Zhur. Ekspt. i Teoret. Fiz., 1948, 18, #8.
Lectures on Linear Algebra. Moscow-Leningrad: 1948.
and M. A. Neimark. Unitary Representation of Classic
Groups. Moscow-Leningrad: 1950.
and D. A. Raikov. Non-reducible unitary representation of
locally bi-compact groups. Mat. Sbornik, 1943, 13, #2-3.
and G. E. Shilov. Fourier's transformation of quickly rising
functions and questions on the sole method for solving the
problem of Cauchy. Uspekhi Mat. Nauk, 1953, 8, #6.
Lectures on Linear Algebra. Translated from the rev. 2nd
Russian ed. by A. Shenitzev. New York Interscience Publishers, 1961. 185 p. (Interscience tracts in pure and applied mathematics, #9).
and M. I. Graev. Constructions of irreducible concepts of
simple algebraic groups over a finite field. Doklady Akad.
Nauk S.S.S.R. 147, #3, 529-32 (1962).
and M. I. Graev. Categories of group concepts and the
problem of classifying irreducible concepts. Doklady Akad.
Nauk S.S.S.R. 146, #4, 757-60 (1962).

Biography:
Thirty Years of Mathematics in the U.S.S.R., 1917-1947.
Moscow-Leningrad: 1948 (Collection of articles edited by
A. G. Kurosh and others).
A. N. Kolmogorov. Works of I. M. Gel'fand on algebraic
questions of functional analysis. Uspekhi Mat. Nauk, 1951,
6, #4.

Office: V. A. Steklov Mathematics Institute of USSR Acade-
                my of Sciences
                1-y Akademicheskii Proyezd, 28
                Moscow, USSR

GELFOND, ALEKSANDR OSIPOVICH (Mathematician)

A. O. Gelfond was born October 24, 1906, in Leningrad. He
graduated from Moscow University in 1927, and received the
degree of Doctor of Physical-Mathematical Sciences in 1935.

He became a professor in 1931. In 1930 he began to work at the U.S.S.R. Academy of Sciences Mathematics Institute. Since 1940 he has been a member of the Communist Party of the Soviet Union. He was elected to the U.S.S.R. Academy of Sciences as a Corresponding Member in 1939.

Gelfond has worked in number theory and the theory of functions of a complex variable. He established new methods of analyzing transcendence of numbers. In his works (1929 and 1934) Gelfond solved the problem of Euler-Hilbert, proving the transcendence of logarithms of algebraic numbers with algebraic bases.

Bibliography:

Transcendent and Algebraic Numbers. Moscow: 1952.
Calculation of Terminal Differences. Moscow-Leningrad: 1952.

Biography:

Yu. V. Linnik and A. I. Markushevich. Aleksandr Osipovich Gelfond (50th Anniversary since the date of birth). Uspekhi Mat. Nauk, 1956, 11, #5, 239-45 (contains a bibliography of the published works of Gelfond).

Office: V. A. Steklov Mathematics Institute of USSR
              Academy of Sciences
              1-y Akademicheskii Proyezd, 28
              Moscow, USSR
Residence: Chkalova 1
              Moscow, USSR
Telephone: K7 38 33

GERASIMOV, INNOKENTII PETROVICH (Physical and Soil
    Geographer)

I. P. Gerasimov was born December 9, 1905. After graduation from the Leningrad University in 1929, he worked in various departments of the U.S.S.R. Academy of Sciences; first at the Soil Institute and later at the Institute of Geography. Gerasimov has been a member of the Communist Party since 1944. In 1946 he was elected a Corresponding Member of the U.S.S.R. Academy of Sciences and in 1953 an Academician. He was made an Honored Scientist of Kazakh S.S.R. in 1944.

Gerasimov's field of investigation is paleogeography, geomorphology, geology of Quaternary deposits and geography of soils of Central Asia, Kazakhstan, Russian Plain, Western Siberia, Southern and Central Ural, and also some foreign territories. Gerasimov is working on the development of natural physico-geographical zones, the history of the development of topography of the U.S.S.R., the principles of geomorphological zoning, general question of geography, cartography and the classification of soils.

As of 1961, Gerasimov was Chairman of the Permanent Commission for the Complex Utilization of Experimental Stations and Bases Operated under Academic Management. He also has been Chairman of the State Committee of Soviet Geographers, U.S.S.R. Academy of Sciences, and a member of Moscow State University.

Bibliography:
Basic Outlines of the Development of Contemporary Surface of Turan. Moscow-Leningrad: 1937 (Works of the Institute of Geography, #25).
and K. K. Markov. Glacial Period on the Territory of the U.S.S.R. Moscow-Leningrad: 1939 (Works of the Institute of Geography, #33).
State soil map of the U.S.S.R. and contemporary problems of the Soviet cartography of soils. Pochvovedenie, 1950, #4.
Origin of the nature of contemporary geographical zones of the territory of the U.S.S.R. Izvest. Akad. Nauk S.S.S.R., Ser. Georg., 1951, #2.
Contemporary Problems of Geomorphology of Kazakhstan, Lessons. . . Alma-Ata, 1943.
World soil map and general law of soils. Pochvovedenie, 1945, #3-4.
Scientific basis of systematization of soils. Pochvovedenie, 1952, #11.
Brown Soils of the Mediterranean Territories. Report on the Fifth International Congress of Pedologists. Moscow: 1954.

Biography:
E. M. Murzaev. On the 50th Anniversary of Academician Gerasimov. Proceedings of the All-Union Geographical Society, 1956, 88, #2.
Gerasimov, Innokentii Petrovich. Akad. Nauk S.S.S.R., 1953, #12, 69.

Office: Institute of Geography
               Staromonetnyy Pereulok, 29
               Moscow, USSR
Residence: Leninskii Prospekt, 13
               Moscow, USSR
Telephone: V2 41 36

GERASIMOV, YAKOV IVANOVICH (Physical Chemist)

Ya. I. Gerasimov was born September 23, 1903. In 1925, upon graduation from Moscow University, he joined the faculty and became a professor in 1942. He became a member of the Communist Party of the Soviet Union in 1952. In 1953, he was elected to the U.S.S.R. Academy of Sciences as a Corresponding Member. He has been awarded the Order of Lenin and other medals.

Gerasimov's main works deal with the study of thermodynamic properties of non-ferrous metals.

Bibliography:

and A. N. Krestovnikov. Chemical Thermodynamics of Non-Ferrous Metallurgy, #1-3. Moscow-Leningrad, Sverdlovsk, 1933-34.

Thermodynamic properties of tungstates of bivalent metals. Reports at XIII International Congress of Theoretical and Applied Chemistry, Stockholm, 1953, Moscow, 1953.

and A. V. Nikol'skaya. Investigation of thermodynamic properties of double-metallic systems using EMF. System of Cadmium—Bismuth. Zhur. Fiz. Khim., 1954, 28, #4, 713-728.

Office: Chemistry Department
Moscow University
Moscow, USSR
Residence: Lomonosovskii pr. 14
Moscow, USSR
Telephone: B9 21 83

GINZBURG, VITALII LAZAREVICH (Physicist)

V. L. Ginzburg was born October 4, 1916. He graduated in 1938 from Moscow University. In 1940 he began working at the Physics Institute of the U.S.S.R. Academy of Sciences. He was made professor in 1945 at Gorkii University. Since 1944 Ginzburg has been a member of the Communist Party of the Soviet Union. In 1953 he was elected a Corresponding Member of the U.S.S.R. Academy of Sciences. At the present time he is continuing his work at the Physics Institute and teaching at Gorkii State University.

Ginzburg's investigations are in the theory of radio propagation in the ionosphere, radio astronomy, the origin of cosmic rays, ferroelectric phenomena, the theory of super conductivity, the theory of elementary particles, and some questions of optics.

In 1962, Ginzburg was awarded the M. V. Lomonsov Prize for
work in the illumination theory and surface light movement.
Bibliography:
Origin of cosmic rays. Izvest. Akad. Nauk S.S.S.R., Ser.
Fiz. 20, #1, 5-16 (1956).
The Origin of cosmic rays. Uspekhi Fiz. Nauk 62, 37-98
(1957).
and B. N. Geshman. The effect of a magnetic field on convective instability in stellar atmospheres and in a terrestrial
ionosphere. Trudy Radiofiz. Fak. Gor'kogo Gos. Univ. 30,
3-29 (1956).
and V. M. Fain. The problem of quantum effects during high
frequency field interaction in resonators. Radiotekh. i
Electronika 2, #6, 780-789 (1957).
Relativistic wave equations with a mass spectrum. Trudy
Gor'kogo Gos. Univ. 35, 51-63 (1957).
and G. G. Getmantsev, I. S. Shklovskii. Radio astronomical
research with the aid of artificial earth satellites. Uspekhi
Fiz. Nauk 66, #2, 157-161 (1958).
Mechanisms of sporadic solar radio emission. Izvest.
Vuzov, Radiofizika, 1, #5-6, 9-16 (1958).
and V. V. Zheleznyakov. Possible mechanisms of sporadic
solar radio emission (emission in isotropic plasma). Astron.
Zhur. 35, #5, 694-712 (1958).
and V. V. Zheleznyakov. The absorption and emission of
electromagnetic waves by magnetically active plasma.
Izvest. Vuzov, Radiofizika, 1, #2, 59-65 (1958).
and B. N. Gershman, N. G. Denisov. The distribution of
electromagnetic waves in plasma (ionosphere). Uspekh. Fiz.
Nauk 61, #4, 561-612 (1957).
and V. V. Zheleznyakov. The distribution of electromagnetic
waves in the solar corona while estimating the effect of a
magnetic field. Astron. Zhur. 36, #2, 233-246 (1959).
Radio astronomy and the origin of cosmic rays. Izvest.
Vuzov, Radiofizika, 1, #5-6, 3-8 (1959).
and V. Ya. Eidman. The force of an emission reaction during the movement of a charge in a medium. Zhur. Ekspt'l. i
Teoret. Fiz. 36, #6, 1823-1833 (1959).
and V. Ya. Eidman. Certain features of electromagnetic
wave emission by particles moving at the speed of light.
Izvest. Vuzov, Radiofizika, 2, #3, 331-343 (1959).
and B. N. Gershman. On the formation of ionospheric heterogeneities. Izvest. Vuzov, Radiofizika, 2, #1, 8-13 (1959).

The possible determination of a magnetic field's current in
the external solar corona during its illumination by polarized
radio emission of discreet sources. Izvest. Vuzov, Radiofizika, 3, #2, 341-342 (1960).
and V. M. Fain. The theory of ferro- and antiferromagnetism. Zhur. Ekspt'l. i Teoret. Fiz. 39, #5, 1323-1338 (1960).
The Distribution of Electromagnetic Waves in Plasma.
Moscow: 1960.
The law of conservation and an expression for energy density
in the electrodynamics of absorptive dispersing media.
Radiofizika 4, #1, 74-89 (1961).
and V. V. Zheleznyakov. Noncoherent mechanisms of sporadic solar radio emission in the case of a magnetically
active coronal plasma. Astron. Zhur. 38, #1, 3-20 (1961).
and E. A. Benediktov, G. G. Getmantsev. Radio astronomical research with the aid of artificial earth satellites.
Artificial Earth Satellites, #7, 3-22 (1961).
Light scattering near phase transfer points in a solid state.
Uspekh. Fiz. Nauk 77, #4 (1962).
The law of conservation of energy in the electrodynamics of
media with spatial dispersion. Izvest. Vuzov, Radiofizika,
5, #6 (1962).
and V. M. Agranovich. Crystallo-optics with consideration
of spatial dispersion and the theory of excitons. Parts I and
II. Uspekh. Fiz. Nauk 76, #4 (1962), and 77, #4 (1962).
Office: Scientific Research Radiophysical Institute of
            Gor'kii State University
            ul. Lyadova 25/14
            Gor'kii, USSR

GLUSHKO, VALENTIN PETROVICH (Power Engineer)
V. P. Glushko was born August 20, 1908. In 1956 he became
a member of the Communist Party of the Soviet Union. He was
elected a Corresponding Member of the U.S.S.R. Academy of
Sciences in 1953, and in 1958 an Academician.
Glushko's basic works are concerned with various divisions
of power engineering.
Office: Dept. of Technical Sciences of USSR Academy of
            Sciences
            Malyy Khariton'yevsky Pereulok, 4
            Moscow, USSR
Residence: Leninskiye gory, sektor "M"
            Moscow, USSR
Telephone: V9 21 63

GOLDANSKII, VITALLI IOSIFOVICH (Physical Chemist)
V. I. Goldanskii is a member of the U.S.S.R. Academy of
Sciences Institute of Chemical Physics as of 1962. In June
1958 he visited the United States to attend the Gordon Research
Conference on Nuclear Chemistry at Meriden, New Hampshire.
He was elected in June 1962 a Corresponding Member of the
U.S.S.R. Academy of Sciences.

Bibliography:
Direct neutron exchange reactions of complex nuclei. Zhur.
Eksptl. i Teoret. Fiz. 36, 526-8 (1959). C. A. 53, 15792g
(1959).
Direct neutron exchange interaction of complex nuclei involving a possible large change of the nuclear spins. Nuclear Phys. 9, 551-7 (1959). C. A. 53, 13805b (1959).
and P. S. Baranov, V. S. Roganov. Yield and angular distribution of fast photoneutrons from deuterium and carbon.
Phys. Rev. 109, 1801-6 (1958). C. A. 53, 14762d (1959).
and A. S. Belousov, B. B. Govorkov. Generalized form of
the relation for the cross section of π-meson photogeneration on complex nuclei to the number of nucleons. Zhur.
Eksptl. i Teoret. Fiz. 36, 244-8 (1959). C. A. 53, 12865g
(1959).
(γ, ρ) reactions leading to nuclei in the ground state. Acta
Phys. Acad. Sci. Hung. 9, 177-84 (1958) (in Russian). C. A.
53, 11035a (1959).
and E. Leikin. Prevrashcheniya atomnykh yader (Transformations of Atomic Nuclei). Moscow: Izdatel. Akad. Nauk
S.S.S.R. 1958. 426 pp. C. A. 53, 5908i (1959).
and M. I. Podgoretskii. Method for the identification of new
transuranium elements. Zhur. Eksptl. i Teoret. Fiz. 37,
315-17 (1959). C. A. 54, 8341a (1960).
and Ya. A. Smorodinskii. Peculiarities in the S-matrix and
the ρ° meson. Zhur. Eksptl. i Teoret. Fiz. 36, 1950-1
(1959). C. A. 54, 8345g (1960).
and R. G. Vasil'kov, B. B. Govorkov. Photogeneration of
neutral π mesons on hydrogen for γ-quanta energies from
the threshold energies to 240 m.e.v. Zhur. Eksptl. i Teoret.
Fiz. 37, 11-22 (1959). C. A. 54, 8344d (1960).
and A. V. Kutsenke, M. I. Podgoretskii. Statistika otschetov
pri registratsii yadernykh chastits (Counting Statistics in
the Registration of Nuclear Particles.) Moscow: Gosudarst.
Fiz.-Mat. Izdatel. 1959. 411 pp. C. A. 54, 17103f (1960).

Superheavy isotopes of hydrogen and helium. Zhur. Eksptl. i Teoret. Fiz. 38, 1637-9 (1960). C. A. 54, 18096g (1960).

and M. V. Kazarnovskii. Intrashell-interaction levels and their excitation by multi-charged ions. Nuclear Phys. 13, 117-24 (1959). C. A. 54, 20527d (1960).

and B. B. Govorkov, R. G. Vasil'kov. Photoproduction of neutral pions on hydrogen near the threshold. Nuclear Phys. 12, 327-32 (1959). C. A. 54, 7367f (1960).

The tenth trans-uranium element. U. S. At. Energy Comm. UCRL-Trans-492, 17 pp. (1959). C. A. 54, 22080c (1960).

Temperature dependence of the rate of reversible processes of spontaneous predissociation. Doklady Akad. Nauk S.S.S.R. 127, 1242-4 (1959). C. A. 54, 21954a (1960).

and A. M. Balkin, I. L. Rozental. Kinematika yadernykh reaktsii (Kinematics of Nuclear Reactions). Moscow: Gosudarst. Fiz.-Mat. Izdatel. 1959. 296 pp. C. A. 54, 20567d (1960).

Stability limits of proton and two-proton radioactivity of neutron-deficient isotopes of light nuclei. Zhur. Eksptl. i Teoret. Fiz. 39, 497-501 (1960). C. A. 55, 139g (1961).

and I. M. Barkalov, B. G. Dzantiev. Joining Polymeric Materials. U.S.S.R. Patent No. 129,015, June 1, 1960. C. A. 55, 1091a (1961).

and A. A. Berlin, B. G. Dzantiev. Radiation polymerization of phenylacetylene. Vysokomolekulyarnye Soednineniya 2, 1103-7 (1960). C. A. 55, 8919h (1961).

Role of the tunnel effect in the kinetics of low-temperature chemical reactions. Doklady Akad. Nauk S.S.S.R. 124, 1261-4 (1959). C. A. 55, 7996g (1961).

and O. A. Karpukhin, G. G. Petrov. Positronium reactions in aqueous solutions. Zhur. Ekspt'l. i Teoret. Fiz. 39, 1477-8 (1960). C. A. 55, 9013h (1961).

and I. M. Barkalov, B. G. Dzantiev, E. V. Egorov. Welding of Teflon and other polymeric materials by the localized action of neutron irradiation. Vysokomolekulyarnye Soedineniya 2, 1801-4 (1960). C. A. 55, 26511d (1961).

and Yu. M. Kagan. Thermochemical action of ionizing radiation. Intern. J. Appl. Radiation Isotopes 11, 1-9 (1961). C. A. 55, 25532i (1961).

and O. A. Karpukhin, V. V. Pavlovskaya. Determination of energy characteristics of the efficiency of registration of high-energy γ-quanta. Pribory i Tekh. Eksperimenta 1960, #3, 23-6. C. A. 55, 4178i (1961).

and R. G. Vasil'kov, B. B. Govorkov. Photoformation of $\pi°$
mesons on carbon near the threshold. Zhur. Ekspt'l. i
Teoret. Fiz. 37, 1149-51 (1959). C. A. 55, 5182d (1961).
and A. I. Baz, Ya. B. Zel'dovich. Isotopes of light nuclei.
Uspekhi Fiz. Nauk 72, 211-34 (1960). C. A. 55, 6173a (1961).
Neutron-deficient isotopes of light nuclei and the phenomena
of proton and 2-proton radioactivity. Nuclear Phys. 19, 482-
95 (1960). C. A. 55, 11114e (1961).
Tunnel transitions between systems described by the Morse
potential curves. Doklady Akad. Nauk S.S.S.R. 127, 1037-40
(1959). C. A. 55, 20578c (1961).
and L. K. Peker. The isomerism of atomic nuclei. Uspekhi
Fiz. Nauk 73, 631-53 (1961). C. A. 55, 20663d (1961).
and O. A. Karpukhin, A. V. Kutsenko, V. V. Pavlovskaya.
Elastic $\gamma - \rho$ scattering at 40 to 70 m.e.v., and polarizability
of the proton. Nuclear Phys. 18, 473-91 (1960). C. A. 55,
13102h (1961).
and V. A. Bryukhonov, N. N. Delyagin, E. F. Makorov, V. S.
Shpinel'. Observation of Mossbauer effect in a stannous-
containing polymer. Zhur. Eksptl. i Teoret. Fiz. 42, #2,
637-39 (1961).
Office: Institute of Chemical Physics of USSR Academy of
               Sciences
               Vorob'evskoye Shosse, 2
               Moscow, USSR

GOLUBTSOV, VYACHESLAV ALEKSEEVICH (Power Engineer)
     V. A. Golubtsov was born April 10, 1894. After he graduated
in 1925 from the Leningrad Electro-Technical Institute, he
worked in the building and operation of a series of electric
power stations. In 1934-1936 he was Chief Engineer at Kash-
mira and subsequently at Chelyabinsk state electric power
plant. He was also chief engineer in the building of the
Dneprodzerzhinsk state electric power plant in 1936-1937. In
1944 he began teaching at the Moscow Power Institute and in
1945 was made a professor. He became Chief of the laboratory
on complex methods of utilizing fuel in power stations of the
Energy Institute of the U.S.S.R. Academy of Sciences in 1955.
Since 1931 Golubtsov has been a member of the Communist
Party of the Soviet Union. In 1953 he was elected a Corresponding Member of the U.S.S.R. Academy of Sciences. He has been
awarded two orders as well as medals, and in 1950 he received
a Stalin Prize.

The scientific works of Golubtsov are devoted to questions on water preparation, air preheating, deaeration, dust preparation, utilization of ash, particularly the use of ash of the coal fields of Moscow in order to obtain alumina. He participated in developing new methods for softening water for industrial boilers.

Bibliography:

and I. Ya. Zalkind. Refractory Material and Cinders in Power Engineering. Moscow-Leningrad: 1953.

and P. P. Elizarov. Operation of Boiler Plants of Power Stations. Moscow-Leningrad: 1950.

and T. Kh. Margulova. Salt water for current control of purity in high pressure saturated steam. Power Stations, 1953, #10.

and M. M. Sendik. Question of selecting rational schemes for preparing water for thermal networks. Thermal Energetics, 1954, #4.

Some questions of rational use of fuel. Works of the Moscow Energy Institute of V. M. Molotov, #25, Moscow-Leningrad: 1955.

Complex power-technological utilization of fuel. Vestnik Akad. Nauk S.S.S.R., 1956, #1.

Some questions on rational utilization of fuel. Works of the Moscow Energy Institute, 1955, #25.

Office: Energy Institute of USSR Academy of Sciences
              Moscow, USSR

Residence: ul. Osipenko, 31
              Moscow, USSR

Telephone: B1 72 15

GORBACHEV, TIMOFEI FEDOROVICH (Mining Engineer)

T. F. Gorbachev was born June 23, 1900. In 1928, he graduated from the Tomsk Polytechnical Institute, and subsequently worked in the coal industry. From 1946 to 1950, he was chief engineer of a group of enterprises known as Kuzbas Coal. From 1950 to 1954, he was Director of the Kemerovo Mining Institute. In 1954, he was Chairman of the Presidium of the U.S.S.R. Academy of Sciences West Siberian branch (dissolved January 1959). In 1949 he was awarded a Stalin Prize. He has also received the Order of Lenin, two other orders, and medals. He was made a Hero of Socialist Labor in 1948. Since 1942 he has been a member of the Communist Party of the Soviet Union. He was elected, in 1958, a Corresponding Member of the U.S.S.R. Academy of Sciences.

Gorbachev has worked in the exploitation of systems of thick, steeply dipping beds and movable shoring. He developed a self-propelled machine "Kuzbas" which utilizes water.
As of 1961, Gorbachev was a Vice-President of the Siberian Branch U.S.S.R. Academy of Sciences.

Bibliography:
Ways of Improving Systems of Exploitation of Thick, Steeply Dipping Beds of South Kuzbas. Moscow: 1949.
Preliminary Results of Observing the Undermining of Coal Beds, Mine Working, Constructions and Sources of Water in the Kuzbas. Moscow: 1951.
Experience in Exploitation of Thick Beds in the U.S.S.R. and Abroad. Moscow: 1957.
Combined system of exploitation with whields. . . Improvement of the Shield Method of Exploitation. Moscow: 1954.
Office: Siberian Branch of USSR Academy of Sciences
                 Novosibirsk, Siberia

GORINOV, ALEKSANDR VASIL'EVICH (Railway Engineer)

A. V. Gorinov was born August 4, 1902. After graduating from the Moscow Institute of Communication Engineers, he worked in a series of expeditions for surveying new railroads (Chardzhou-Kungrad, Ulan-Ude-Naushki, Ural'sk-Iletsk). He was chief-construction engineer for the Moscow-Donbass Railroad. He taught at Leningrad Institute of Railroad Engineers in 1931-1946, and in 1937 became professor. He taught also at the Military-Transport Academy of the Soviet Army from 1932 to 1938. In 1941 he became professor at Moscow Institute of Railroad Engineers. He also worked in a number of scientific research organizations. Gorinov has been a member of the Communist Party of the Soviet Union since 1920. In 1939 he was elected a Corresponding Member of the U.S.S.R. Academy of Sciences.

The main work of Gorinov is in the complex design of railroads, the theory of inertia calculations and the reserve utilization of a train's kinetic energy, the improvement of transportation with gradually increasing railroad power, and the scientific basis for classifying railroads.

Bibliography:
Large reserves for increasing the weight of trains over complete routes. Railroad Transport, 1954, #8.
Classification of the railroads of the U.S.S.R. Izvest. Akad. Nauk S.S.S.R., Otdel Tekh. Nauk, 1946, #5.

Scientific basis for the classification of railroads. Construction of Railroads and Track Equipment. Moscow: 1948. Designing of Railways, 3rd ed., 1-3. Moscow: 1948.

Office: Moscow Institute of Railroad Engineers
Moscow, USSR
Residence: Arbat, 20
Moscow, USSR
Telephone: G1 41 11

GORSKI, IVAN IVANOVICH (Paleontologist)

I. I. Gorski was born September 12, 1893. In 1935, he became a professor at the Leningrad Mining Institute. From 1943 to 1947, he was Director of the All-Union Scientific Research Institute of Geology. He was Chairman of the Karelo- Finnish Branch of the U.S.S.R. Academy of Sciences from 1947 to 1952. In 1950, he became Director of the Laboratory on Coal Geology of the U.S.S.R. Academy of Sciences, and in 1954 he was elected Chairman of the All-Union Paleontological Society. Since 1943, he has been a Corresponding Member of the U.S.S.R. Academy of Sciences.

Gorski is a specialist in the geology of the Urals, particularly of the Ural coal deposits. He investigated coral fauna of upper Paleozoic U.S.S.R. He has studied the geology of coal bearing regions of the Urals, Kazakhstan and Central Asia; stratigraphy and tectonics of the Urals, Kazakhstan and other parts of U.S.S.R.; coral and other fauna of the Carboniferous Urals, Kazakhstan, Central Asia and the Arctic. He took part, as a Chief Editor, in compiling geological maps of the Urals (scale of 1/500,000-1939), of the European section of the U.S.S.R., of the Urals and Caucasus (scale of 1/1,500,000-1948), a map for the survey of coal regions in the U.S.S.R. (scale of 1/5,000,000-1956), etc. Total amount of works is over 200 titles.

Bibliography:
Detailed Geological Survey of the Kamensk Works Region. Moscow-Leningrad: 1931.
Coral from Lower Carboniferous Deposits of the Kirkhiz Steppes. Moscow-Leningrad: 1932.
Geological outline of the Kizelovskii region. Coal Bearing Deposits of the Western Slope of the Urals. Leningrad-Moscow: 1932.
Carboniferous corals of Novaya Zemlya, Leningrad, 1938. (Works of the All-Union Arctic Institute, 93).

Geotectonic conditions in the formation of coal deposits of
the Urals, and peculiarities of the geological structure of de-
posits associated with them. Izvest. Akad. Nauk S.S.S.R.,
Geol Ser., 1943, #4-5.
Belts and groups of coal accumulation in light of contempo-
rary data. Works of the Laboratory of Coal Geology of the
U.S.S.R. Academy of Sciences, 1956, #5.
History of Coal Accumulation on the Territory of the
U.S.S.R. Leningrad: 1956.

Office: Department of Geology and Geography
              Presidium, USSR Academy of Sciences
              Lenin Prospekt, 14
              Moscow, USSR

GRASHCHENKOV, NIKOLAI IVANOVICH (Neurologist)

N. I. Grashchenkov was born March 26, 1901. He graduated
in 1926 from the University of Moscow and until 1933 was a
member of the Medical Faculty of the University (which later
was reorganized into the first Medical Institute of Moscow). He
also worked at the Institute of Experimental Medicine, and in
1939-1944 was Director of this Institute. In 1937-1939 Grashchenkov was First Deputy Public Commissar for Health and
Welfare. During World War II, 1941-45, he was consultant on
problems of neuro-pathology and neuro-surgery in the army.
He conducted epidemiological work in the prophylaxis and
treatment of tick-borne diseases and Japanese encephalitis.
From 1944 to 1948, he was Director of the Neurological Institute of the Academy of Medical Sciences of the USSR. In 1951
he became professor at the Central Institute of the Advancement
of Physicians in Moscow. Grashchenkov has been a member of
the Communist Party of the Soviet Union since 1918. In 1939
he was elected a Corresponding Member of the U.S.S.R. Academy of Sciences, in 1944 an Active Member of the U.S.S.R.
Academy of Medical Sciences, and in 1947 a member of the
Belorussian Academy of Sciences. From 1948 to 1951 he was
President of the Academy of Sciences of the Belorussian S.S.R.
From 1959 to 1961 he was Assistant Director General of W.H.O.
in Geneva.

Grashchenkov's basic work deals with the physiology and
pathology of the sense organs, electro-physiology of the central
nervous system, traumatic shock and infectious diseases of the
nervous system.

In September 1962, Grashchenkov visited the United States
to attend the 5th World Congress of Sociology in Washington.

Grashchenkov's other activities in his field include being
Director of the Laboratory of Clinical Neurophysiology, Mos-
cow, Academy of Sciences U.S.S.R.; member, the Moscow City
Clinical Hospital, Moscow City Health Department, Ministry of
Health R.S.F.S.R.; member of the First Moscow Medical Insti-
tute im. I. M. Sechenov, Moscow Ministry of Health R.S.F.S.R.,
member of Ministry of Health.
Bibliography:
   Anaerobic Infection of the Brain. Moscow: 1944.
   Firearm Wounds of the Spine and Spinal Cord and Methods
   for their Treatment. Moscow: 1946.
   Craniocerebral Wounds and Method for Treatment. Moscow:
   1947.
   Mosquito (Japanese) Encephalitis and Methods for Treat-
   ment. Moscow: 1947.
   Interneural Synapses and their Role in Physiology and Path-
   ology. Minsk: 1948.
   Outline of Virus Effects on the Central Nervous System.
   Minsk: 1951.
Biography:
   Nikolai Ivanovich Grashchenkov. On his 60th birthday. I. M.
   Sechenov Physiological Journal of the USSR, 4, 1961.
   (English version).
Office: Academy of Medical Sciences USSR
              Solyanka 14, Moscow, USSR
Residence: Kotel'nicheskaya nab. 1/15
              Moscow, USSR
Telephone: B7 45 25

GRIGOLYUK, EDUARD IVANOVICH (Mechanical Engineer)
   E. I. Grigolyuk was born December 13, 1923. After graduating from Moscow Aviation Institute in 1934, he taught there. In
1946-1950 he taught at the Moscow Technological College. He
began work at the Experimental Construction Bureau in 1948,
and in 1953 at the Institute of Mechanics of the U.S.S.R. Academy of Sciences. In 1952 he was made editor of an abstract
journal "Mechanics." He was elected, in 1958, a Corresponding
Member of the U.S.S.R. Academy of Sciences.
   Grigolyuk's main works are concerned with the theory of
shells. He is also concerned with the theory of elasticity and
the theory of plasticity.
Bibliography:
   Thin bimetallic shells and plates. Engineering Collection,
   1953, 17.

Equation of axiosymmetric bimetallic elastic shells. Engineering Collection, 1954, 18.
Non-linear oscillations and stability of sloping rods and shells. Izvest. Akad. Nauk S.S.S.R., Otdel. Tekh. Nauk, 1955, #3.
On the bulging of thin shells beyond the limits of elasticity. Izvest. Akad. Nauk S.S.S.R., Otdel. Tekh. Nauk, 1957, #10.
Terminal deflection of three layer shells with a stiff filler. Izvest Akad. Nauk S.S.S.R., Otdel. Tekh. Nauk, 1958, #1.
Stability of elastic plastic heterogeneous shells. Doklady Akad. Nauk S.S.S.R., 1958, 119, #4.

Office: Institute of Mechanics of USSR Academy of Sciences
              Leningradskii Prospekt, 7
              Moscow, USSR
Residence: Pushkinskaya 7/5
              Moscow, USSR
Telephone: B9 25 98

GRIGOREV, ANDREI ALEKSANDROVICH (Geographer)
     A. A. Grigorev was born November 1, 1883. In 1907 he graduated from Petrograd University. He organized in 1918 the Geographic Institute in Petrograd where he was a professor and dean until 1925. From 1925 to 1936 he was a professor at Leningrad University. In 1918 Grigorev organized in the Academy of Sciences an industrial geography department of the commission which studied the natural productive forces of Russia. This department became in 1931 the Geographic Institute of the U.S.S.R. Academy of Sciences, and until 1951, Grigorev was the Director. He has been an Academician of the U.S.S.R. Academy of Sciences since 1939. In 1946 he became a member of the Communist Party of Soviet Russia. He was awarded a Stalin Prize in 1947. He is a member of a number of scientific societies including the Geographic Society of the U.S.S.R. Grigorev is on the main editorial board of the Bol'shaya Sovetskaya Entsykl. (Great Soviet Encyclopedia). He has been active in the Society for the Dissemination of Political and Scientific Knowledge. Also he is interested in the history of Russian geography.
     In 1904, and again in 1921, Grigorev completed an expedition to the Bolshezemelskaya tundra. At various times, he investigated little-known regions of the South Urals (1923), Yakutsk, ASSR (1925-26), the Kolskii Peninsula (1928-29 and 1931), and Kazakhstan, carefully studying the elements of the geographical environment. His results have been useful to soil scientists,

paleographers, geomorphologists, and geobotanists. Grigorev
has published more than 300 articles. His monograph, The
Subartic, sums up the material on the tundra belt, and was the
first geography treatise to be awarded a Stalin Prize. In his
articles from 1928-1930, he introduced a new direction in geography, subsequently named "dynamic geography," in which
great stress is paid to natural processes. He has attempted to
convert geography from a descriptive science to one which establishes general laws of physico-geographical processes,
based on studies of the paleography of the Quaternary Period,
on discoveries of fresh-water diatomites, and on the evolution
of physico-geographic processes on the earth's surface since
the Devonian Period.

Bibliography:

Soviet geography up to the XVIIIth Congress of the Commu-
nist Party of the Soviet Union (Bolsheviks). Vestnik Akad.
Nauk S.S.S.R., 1939, #2-3.
Soviet geography during the Second Five Year Plan. Izvest.
Akad. Nauk S.S.S.R., Ser. Georg-GeoFiz., 1939, #2.
An Attempt at an Analytical Characterization of the Com-
ponents and Structure of the Physico-Geographic Sphere of
the Earth. Leningrad-Moscow: 1937.
Subartic. Experiment to Characterize the Main Types of
Physico-Geographic Environment. Moscow-Leningrad:
1946.
On some questions of physical geography. Voprosi Filosofii,
1951, #1.

Biography:

G. D. Rikhter. On the 60th Anniversary of Academician
A. A. Grigorev. Priroda, 1944, #2.

Office: Institute of Geography
Staromonetnyy Pereulok, 29
Moscow, USSR

GRINBERG, ALEKSANDR ABRAMOVICH (Chemist)

A. A. Grinberg was born April 20, 1898. In 1924 he graduated from Leningrad University. He became, in 1936, professor
at Lensovet Leningrad Technological Institute. From 1943 until
1958 he was a Corresponding Member of the U.S.S.R. Academy
of Sciences, and in 1958 he was elected Academician. In 1946
he was awarded a Stalin Prize.

Grinberg investigated the structure of platinum salts and
isomerism of platinum and palladium divalent derivatives.
Also he has studied acid-base and redox properties of complex

compounds, equilibria of their aqueous solutions, and use of tracers in chemistry of complex compounds.

Bibliography:
Introduction to Chemistry of Complex Compounds, 2nd ed. Leningrad-Moscow: 1951. (Trans. by J. R. Leach. Ed. by D. H. Busch & R. F. Trimble, Jr. Oxford, London. Pergamon Press, 1962, 363 p.)
New data on the kinetics of substitution reactions and on the mutual influence of coordinated groups. Zhur. Neorg. Khim. 4, 1517-32 (1959). C. A. 54, 9454a (1960).
and M. I. Gel'fman. Stability of complex compounds of bivalent platinum. Doklady Akad. Nauk S.S.S.R. 133, 1081-3 (1960). C. A. 54, 23632c (1960).
and V. E. Mironov. Ligand exchange in HgX_4^{--}. Radiokhimiya 2, 249-54 (1960). C. A. 54, 17140d (1960).
and A. M. Trofimov, L. N. Stepanova. Determination of the charge magnitude of polynuclear complex ruthenium ions by the ion-exchange method. Radiokhimiya 2, 78-82 (1960). C. A. 54, 18033c (1960).
and D. N. Bykhovskii. Coprecipitation of trivalent cerium with uranium oxalate. Radiokhimiya 2, 164-74 (1960). C. A. 54, 16975h (1960).
and L. V. Vrublevskaya, Kh. I. Gil'dengershel, A. I. Stetsenko. New data on the acid-base properties of complex compounds. Zhur. Neorg. Khim. 4, 1018-27 (1959). C. A. 54, 9588c (1960).

Office: Lensovet Technological Institute
             Zagorodnyi Prospekt 49
             Leningrad, USSR

GRINBERG, GEORGII ABRAMOVICH (Physicist)

G. A. Grinberg was born June 16, 1900. He is the brother of Academician A. A. Grinberg (chemist). He graduated in 1923 from Petrograd Polytechnic Institute and in 1935 received a Doctor of Physical-Mathematical Sciences degree. From 1919 to 1930 Grinberg worked in the State Roentgenological and Radiological Institute and in the Physico-Technical Institute in Leningrad. In 1924-1955 he taught at Leningrad Polytechnic Institute where in 1930 he became professor. He also worked during 1929-1941 at the plant "Svetlana" in Leningrad. In 1941 he began working at the Physico-Technical Institute of the U.S.S.R. Academy of Sciences. Grinberg has been a Corresponding Member of the U.S.S.R. Academy of Sciences since 1946. In 1949 he was awarded a Stalin Prize.

Grinberg's major work is in theoretical electronics, the theory of electromagnetic wave propagation, and in the theory of elasticity. He formulated a general theory for the focusing effect of electric and magnetic fields. He proposed the theory of coastal refraction. He studied the problem of radio propagation in heterogeneous spheres. Grinberg originated a unique method of integrating equations of mathematical physics. He is the author of the work, "Selected Questions on the Mathematical Theory of Electrical and Magnetic Phenomena" (1948) (Stalin Prize, 1949).

Bibliography:

Theory on the coastal refraction of electromagnetic waves. Zhur. Fiz., 1942, 6, #5.

Basis of the general theory on the focusing effect of electrostatic and magnetic fields. I-III. Doklady Akad. Nauk S.S.S.R., 1942, 37, #5-6, 9; 38, #2-3.

A new method of solving some peripheral problems in the equation of mathematical physics which allow division of variables. Izvest. Akad. Nauk S.S.S.R., Ser. Fiz., 1946, 10, #2.

Theory of established processes in electronic devices or in circuits which contain such devices. Zhur. Tekh. Fiz., 1955, 25, #12.

and B. E. Vonshtedt. The basis of an exact theory on the wave field of transmission lines. Zhur. Tekh. Fiz., 1954, 24, #1.

Methods proposed by P. F. Papkovich for solving plane problems of the theory of elasticity for a rectangular area and for problems of bending a thin rectangular slab with two fixed edges, and some generalizations from these. Priklad. Mat. i Mekh., 1953, 17, #2, 211-28.

Office: Physico-Technical Institute of the USSR Academy
of Sciences
Sosnova 2
Lesnoy, Leningrad, USSR

GROSS, EVGENII FYODOROVICH (Physicist)

E. F. Gross was born October 20, 1897. He graduated from Leningrad University in 1924, and in 1938 became a professor at this University. Beginning in 1944, he has been working also at the Physico-Technical Institute of the U.S.S.R. Academy of Sciences. In 1946 he was elected a Corresponding Member of the U.S.S.R. Academy of Sciences and that same year a recipient of a Stalin Prize.

In 1940 Gross proposed a spectroscopic method for determining orientational relaxation times of molecules from anisotropic scattering. In 1951, he discovered an optic spectrum of excitons which transmit energy of excited states in crystals. In 1954-55, he discovered in excitons the Zeeman and Stark effect and the disassociation of excitons under the influence of an external electrical field. In 1956, he discovered the radiation spectrum of excitons, their large diamagnetism, and their role in inner photo-effect.

Bibliography:

Light scattering. XV Anniversary of the State Optical Institute (Collection of articles under the general editorship of Academician S. I. Vavilov). Leningrad-Moscow: 1934, 34-107.

Transverse thermal Debye waves and the scattering of light in crystals. Doklady Akad. Nauk S.S.S.R., 1940, 26, #8.

Fluctuation of entropy in a liquid and the Rayleigh line. Zhur. Eksptl. i Teoret. Fiz., 1946, 16, #2.

Light scattering and relaxational phenomena in liquids. Doklady Akad. Nauk S.S.S.R., 1940, 28, #9.

and S. M. Fuks. Sur le nouveau type de spectre de diffusion des cristaux et la structure des liquides. Le Journal de Physique et le Radium, 1936, 7, #3.

Optical spectrum of excitons in the crystal lattice. Nuovo Cimento, Supplemento, Ser. 10, 1956, #3.

and others. Exciton structure of spectrum curves of inner photoelectric effect in crystals. Doklady Akad. Nauk S.S.S.R., 1956, 110, #5.

and B. P. Zakharechnaya. Linear and quadratic Zeeman effects and exciton diamagnetism of cuprous oxide. Doklady Akad. Nauk S.S.S.R., 1956, 111, #3.

and Czhan Guan-in, L. E. Soloviev. Absorption spectra in the azure and blue regions of the spectrum and deformation effects in refined samples of copper oxide. Doklady Akad. Nauk S.S.S.R. 146, #2, 577-80 (1962).

and D. S. Nadzvetskii. Resonance and non-resonance irradiation of centers in crystalline GaP and their interaction with lattice phonons. Doklady Akad. Nauk S.S.S.R. 146, #3, 1047-50 (1962).

Office: Physico-Technical Institute of USSR Academy of
                Sciences
                Sosnova 2
                Lesnoy, Leningrad, USSR

GRUSHIN, PETR DMITRIEVICH (Mechanics Specialist)
    In June 1962, P. D. Grushin was elected Corresponding
Member of the U.S.S.R. Academy of Sciences.

GUTYRYA, VIKTOR STEPANOVICH (Chemist)
    V. S. Gutyrya was born September 11, 1910. After graduating
from the Azerbaijan Industrial Institute in 1932, he worked at
the Azerbaijan Oil Research Institute (now the Azerbaijan
Scientific Research Institute of Oil-Refining Industry). In 1937-
54 and again in 1955 he was made Director of the Institute. He
has been an Academician of the Azerbaijan S.S.R. Academy of
Sciences since 1949, and since 1953 a Corresponding Member
of the U.S.S.R. Academy of Sciences. In 1942 he received a
Stalin Prize.
    Gutyrya has studied chemistry of oil and technology of
petrochemical synthesis.
Bibliography:
    and others. Oil of Azerbaijan. Baku: 1945.
    Catalytic Refining of Distillates of Thermal Reforming.
    Baku: 1946.
    Ya. Masumyan, S. M. Lisovskaya. Distillation Curves of
    Baku Oil. Baku: 1947.
Office: Academy of Sciences Azerbaijan SSR
               Kommunisticheskaya Ulitsa 10
               Baku 1, Azerbaijhan SSR

IERUSALIMSKII, NIKOLAI DMITRIEVICH (Microbiologist)
    N. D. Ierusalimskii was born in 1901. He graduated from
Moscow State University in 1931. From 1930-35, he was a
microbiologist at the Chemico-Pharmaceutical Institute in
Moscow. In 1935 he began to work at the U.S.S.R. Academy of
Sciences Institute of Microbiology, where he became in 1950
deputy director. From 1935-38 he was also deputy section
chief of the Scientific-Research Laboratory on Industrial
Fermentation, and in 1954, became a professor at Moscow State
University. Since 1946 he has been a member of the Communist
Party of the Soviet Union. He was elected, in 1960, to the
U.S.S.R. Academy of Sciences as a Corresponding Member.
    Ierusalimskii's work is primarily concerned with the study
of microorganism development in connection with nutritive
conditions.
Office: Moscow State University
               Moscow, USSR

Residence: 1-aya Cheremushkinskaya 4/34
        Moscow, USSR
Telephone: B7 51 77

IL'YUSHIN, ALEKSEI ANTONOVICH (Mechanical Engineer)
    A. A. Il'yushin was born January 20, 1911. In 1934 he gradu-
ated from Moscow University and became a professor there in
1938. In 1943, he became Chief of the Department of Strength
of Materials of the U.S.S.R. Academy of Sciences Institute of
Mechanics of which he became Director in 1953. He has been
a member of the Communist Party of the Soviet Union since
1940. He was elected, in 1943, a Corresponding Member of the
U.S.S.R. Academy of Sciences. In 1948 he was awarded a Stalin
Prize.
    Il'yushin has worked in the theory of elasticity and plasticity.
In 1936-38 he obtained important results in the area of viscous-
plastic flow and its stability for metals. In 1937 he designed a
pile-driver for testing materials and construction models at
high speeds of deformation. In 1942-48 he formulated a theory
on small, elastic-plastic deformations which appear as the
basis for calculating structures which work beyond the limits
of elasticity. He also proposed a method for solving these
problems. He developed a theory on the stability of plates, and
shells beyond the limits of elasticity. In 1951-52 he formulated
a theory of modeling in the processes of preparing metals by
pressure. In 1953-54 he established a postulate on isothropy in
general theory on plasticity. Il'yushin also solved a number of
problems in gaseous dynamics.
Bibliography:
    Deformation of a viscous-plastic body. Scientific Research
    Papers of Moscow University. Mechanics, 1940, #39.
    Several questions on the theory of plastic deformations.
    Applied Mathematics and Mechanics, 1943, 7, #4.
    Elastic-plastic stability of plates. Applied Mathematics and
    Mechanics, 1946, 10, #5-6.
    Plasticity, Part I—Elastic-Plastic Deformation. Moscow-
    Leningrad: 1948.
    Modeling of hot and high speed processes of preparing
    metals by pressure. Applied Mathematics and Mechanics,
    1952, 16, #4.
    Connection between tension and small deformations in me-
    chanics of solid media. Applied Mathematics and Mechanics,
    1954, 18, #6.

Questions on the theory of flows of plastic substances on
surfaces. Applied Mathematics and Mechanics, 1954, 18, #3.
Law of plane sections in aerodynamics of high supersonic
speeds. Applied Mathematics and Mechanics, 1956, 20, #6.
Biography:
   V. S. Lenskii. Elasticity and Plasticity. On the works of
Stalin Prize Laureate, A. A. Il'yushin, Moscow-Leningrad,
1950.
Office: Institute of Mechanics of USSR Academy of Sciences
              Leningradskii Prospekt, 7
              Moscow, USSR
Residence: Chistoprudnyii Bul'v. 9
              Moscow, USSR
Telephone: B3 71 52

IMSHENETSKII, ALEXANDRE ALEKSANDROVICH (Microbiologist)

   A. A. Imshenetskii was born January 8, 1905. He graduated
from the University of Voronezh in 1926. In 1930 he worked at
the U.S.S.R. Academy of Sciences Institute of Microbiology,
where he became Director in 1949. He was elected to the
U.S.S.R. Academy of Sciences in 1946 as a Corresponding Member, and in June 1962, an Academician.
   Imshenetskii's researches are in the structure, biology, individual growth, variation and physiology of micro-organisms.
In studying the construction of bacteria, he proved that the majority of them retain a significant amount of vital substance but
lack an individual morphological nucleus and that the latter is
found only in complex bacteria. He explored changes in the
structure of bacteria in the process of ontogeneses under the
influence of various external factors which enabled him to discover the metaphysical essence, the so-called theory of cyclogenics. His other work is the study of the biology of bacteria
which attack cellulose. His work includes a study on the influence of increased temperatures on the course of microbiological processes (a comparable study of the nature of mesophilic
and thermophilic bacteria was made). He has explored groups
of cellulose, amylolytic, proteolytic and thermophilic bacteria,
which are of practical value. He showed ways of replacing the
mesophilic bacteria with the thermophylic which hastens the
course of microbiological processes (for example—fermentation). A series of his research deals with the biology and
physiology of nitrifying bacteria; the variability and selectivity
of yeast, mold fungus and bacteria.

In April 1960, Imshenetskii visited the United States on an
exchange program at the Rockefeller Institute for Medical Research in New York City.

Imshenetskii was in the United States again in April 1961 to
attend the Third International Space Science Symposium
(COSPAR), Washington; the Brain Research Institute of University of California, Los Angeles Medical Center; a conference
of the New York State Medical Society, New York City; and the
Space Medicine Program of the New York Medical College.
Bibliography:
    Structure of Bacteria. Moscow-Leningrad: 1940.
    Microbiological Processes at High Temperatures. Moscow-
    Leningrad: 1944.
    Variability in the selectivity of micro-organisms. Works on
    the Conference on the Directed Changeability and Selection
    of Micro-organisms. Moscow: 1951; Moscow: 1952, 11-37.
    Cellulose Microbiology. Moscow: 1953.
Office: Institute of Microbiology
                Leninskii Prospekt, 33
                Moscow, USSR

ISAKOV, IVAN STEPANOVICH (Naval Officer)
I. S. Isakov was born August 22, 1894. In 1929 he graduated
from the Naval Academy. From 1933 to 1938, he was Chief of
Staff and subsequently Commander of the Baltic Fleet, and at
the same time head of the Naval Academy. During World War II,
he was Chief of Staff of the Naval Forces. In 1947, he was
deputy to the Commander-in-Chief of the Naval Forces. He
has been a member of the Communist Party of the Soviet Union
since 1939, and was a delegate to the first convocation of the
Supreme Soviet. In 1958, he was elected to the U.S.S.R. Academy of Sciences as a Corresponding Member.

In 1947-55, Isakov was the main editor of the Naval Atlas,
for the publication of which he received the Stalin Prize (1951).
In 1950-54, he was a member of the editorial board of the Atlas
of the World. Isakov is a consultant for a number of scientific
institutions. He is the author of works on military geography.
Office: USSR Academy of Sciences
                Leninskii Prospekt, 14
                Moscow, USSR

ISHLINSKII, ALEKSANDR YUL'EVICH (Mechanics Scientist)
A. Yu. Ishlinskii was born August 6, 1913. After graduating
from Moscow University in 1935, he taught there and in 1945

became a professor. From 1948 to 1955 he was Director of the Institute of Mathematics of the Ukrainian S.S.R. Academy of Sciences and also a professor at Kiev University. In 1955 he was appointed director of a scientific research institute. He has been a member of the Communist Party of the Soviet Union since 1940. He was elected Academician of the Ukrainian S.S.R. Academy of Sciences in 1948, and in 1960 Academician of the U.S.S.R. Academy of Sciences.

Ishlinskii's main investigations are in general mechanics, elasticity, and oscillations. He presented a theory of gyroscopic devices, investigated the behavior of complex gyroscopic systems on a movable base, and gave the theoretical basis for a space gyroscope.

Bibliography:

Mechanics of Special Gyroscopic Systems. Kiev: 1952.

Dynamical forms of stability loss of elastic systems. Doklady Akad. Nauk S.S.S.R., 1949, 64, #6.

On the dynamics of soil masses. Doklady Akad. Nauk S.S.S.R., 1954, 95, #4.

General theory of plasticity with a linear strengthening. Ukr. Mat. Zhur., 1954, #3.

Sketches in History of Technology. Kiev: 1955.

On the theory of a horizon-compass. Priklad. Mat. i Mekh., 1956, #4.

The theory of a gyroscopic pendulum. Priklad. Mat. i Mekh., 1957, #1.

Theory of a bigyroscopic gyrovertical. Priklad. Mat. i Mekh., 1957, #2.

Office: Academy of Sciences Ukrainian SSR
Vladimirskaya Ulitsa 5
Kiev, Ukrainian SSR

IVANOV, LEONID ALEKSANDROVICH (Deceased, April 12, 1962).

L. A. Ivanov was born February 24, 1871. He graduated from Moscow University in 1895. From 1904 to 1941, he was professor at the Institute of Forestry (now the S. M. Korov Forest-Technical Academy). From 1938 to 1947, he headed the photosynthesis laboratory of the Institute of Plant Physiology of the U.S.S.R. Academy of Sciences. Since 1944, he has been the chief of the Laboratory on the Physiology and Ecology of Wood Strains of the U.S.S.R. Academy of Sciences Institute of Forests. He became a Corresponding Member of the U.S.S.R. Academy of Sciences in 1922.

Ivanov studied the influence of light and moisture on wood
and established the relationships in the distribution and absorption of physiologic radiation in forests under variable conditions. He established an original method of investigating
photosynthesis, designed new devices—phytoactinometer for
studying photosynthesis, phytoatmometer for studying evaporation, and others. Ivanov developed the theoretical basis of
tapping confiers, which he presented in the work Biological
Basis of Utilizing Confiers of U.S.S.R. in the Turpentine Industry (1934). He has also carried out researches on the anatomy
of wood strains, the systematics of simple plants, investigation
of the processes of fermentation and respiration, and the
transformation of phosporus in plants.

Bibliography:
Light and Moisture in the Life of Our Wood Strains. Moscow-
Leningrad: 1946.
Physiology of Plants, 2nd ed. Leningrad: 1936.
General Course on the Systematics of Plants. Moscow-
Leningrad: 1937.
Anatomy of Plants, 3rd ed. Leningrad: 1939.

Biography:
N. A. Maximov. Physiology of Plants. Outline on the History
of Russian Botany. Moscow: 1947.
N. L. Kossovich. Half a Century of Uninterrupted Creative
Activity of Professor L. A. Ivanov in the Forest-Technical
Academy of S. M. Kirov. Works of the Forest-Technical
Academy of S. M. Kirov, 1948, #64.

Office: Laboratory of Forest Studies
Moscow, USSR
Residence: nab. Gor'kogo 40/42
Moscow, USSR
Telephone: V3 29 97

KABACHNIK, MARTIN IZRAILOVICH (Organic Chemist)

M. I. Kabachnik was born August 27, 1908. In 1931 he graduated from the Chemical Technological Institute in Moscow and
began to work for the U.S.S.R. Academy of Sciences. He was a
member of the Institute of Organic Chemistry from 1939 until
1954, when he became a member of the Institute of Elementary
Organic Compounds. In 1953 he was elected a Corresponding
Member of the U.S.S.R. Academy of Sciences and in 1958 an
Academician. He won a Stalin Prize in 1946.

The principal research of Kabachnik deals with the study of tautomerism of organic compounds and with synthesis of organic phosphorous insecticides.

Bibliography:

and T. A. Mastryukova. Theory of tautomeric equilibrium, Communication #3. Problem of pseudomerism. Izvest. Akad. Nauk S.S.S.R., Otdel. Khim. Nauk, 1953, #1.

and A. N. Nesmeyanov. Dual reaction properties and tautomerism. Zhur. Obshchei Khim., 1955, 25, #1. Concerning some problems of tautomerism. Uspekhi Khim., 1956, 25, #2.

New ways for the practical application of basic organic compounds. Vestnik Adak. Nauk S.S.S.R., 1956, #1.

Office: Institute of Organo-Elemental Compounds
Leninskii Prospekt, 31
Moscow, USSR

Residence: ul. Chkalova 21/2
Moscow, USSR

Telephone: K7 36 25

KADOMTSEV, BORIS BORISOVICH (Physicist)

B. B. Kadomtsev was elected a Corresponding Member of the U.S.S.R. Academy of Sciences in June 1962.

Bibliography:

Convective instability of a plasma column (stream). Zhur. Ekspt'l. i Teoret. Fiz. 37, #4, 1096-1101 (1959). NSA 14: 5958, 1960.

Plasma equilibrium in helical symmetry. Zhur. Ekspt'l. i Teoret. Fiz. 37, #5, 1352-54 (1959). NSA 14:7058, 1960.

Stabilization of plasma with the aid of heterogenous magnetic fields. Nuclear Physics, Moscow 1959, 175-183.

Low pressure plasma stability. Zhur. Ekspt'l. i Teoret. Fiz. 37, #6, 1646-51 (1959). NSA 14:12311, 1960.

Instability of an electron cloud in a magnetron. Zhur. Tekh. Fiz. 29, #7, 833-44 (1959). NSA 14:388, 1960.

Magnetic stability of plasma in a magnetic dipolar field. Doklady Akad. Nauk S.S.S.R. 133, #1, 68-70 (1960). NSA 14: 26345, 1960.

and A. V. Timofeev. Drift of unstable heterogenous plasma in a magnetic field. Doklady Akad. Nauk S.S.S.R. 146, #2, 581-84 (1962).

Office: USSR Academy of Sciences
Leninskii Prospekt, 14
Moscow, USSR

KALESNIK, STANISLAV VIKENT'EVICH (Geographer)

S. V. Kalesnik was born January 23, 1901. He graduated from Leningrad University in 1929, where he became a professor in 1938. In 1940-1959 he was scientific secretary, and in 1952 he became vice president of the All-Union Geographical Society. In 1953, he was elected a Corresponding Member of the U.S.S.R. Academy of Sciences.

Kalesnik's main research is concerned with glaciology, geomorphology and geology of Central Tien Shan, Dzhungarskii Alatau, and also with general glaciology and physical geography. He studied signs of regressive phases in the evolution of glaciers, and introduced new ideas and terminology (chionosphere, energy of glaciation) into glaciology.

Kalesnik has been Director of the Laboratory on Limnology since 1955.

Bibliography:
Mountainous and Glacial Regions of the U.S.S.R. Leningrad-Moscow: 1937.
General Glaciology. Leningrad: 1939.
Basis of General Geography, 2nd ed. Leningrad: 1955.
Short Course in General Geography. Moscow: 1957.

Office: 1) Laboratory of Limnology
Naberezhnaya Makarova 2
Leningrad, USSR
2) Department of Geography
Leningrad University
Krasnaia ulitsa, 60
Leningrad, USSR

Residence: ul. prof. Popova 4, Apt. 3
Leningrad, USSR

KANTOROVICH, LEONID VITALEVICH (Mathematician)

L. V. Kantorovich was born January 19, 1912. He graduated from Leningrad University in 1930, and received the degree of Doctor of Physical-Mathematical Science in 1935. From 1930-1939, he taught at the Leningrad Institute of Industrial Construction Engineers. He began teaching at Leningrad University in 1932, and became a professor there in 1934. He has been working at the Leningrad Branch of the U.S.S.R. Academy of Sciences Institute of Mathematics since 1940. In 1958, he was made a Corresponding Member of the U.S.S.R. Academy of Sciences. He was the recipient of a Stalin Prize in 1949, for work on functional analysis.

The main work of Kantorovich is in theory of functions of a
real variable, and to approximate methods of analysis, functional analysis, semi-ordered spaces, the theory of methods of
approximation, utilization of computers, particularly automation
of programming, and application of mathematics in planned
economic analysis.

Bibliography:
Mathematical Methods of Organizing and Planning Industry.
Leningrad: 1939.
and V. I. Krylov. Methods of Approximation of Advanced
Analysis, 4th ed. Moscow: 1952.
and others. Functional Analysis of Semi-Ordered Spaces.
Moscow-Leningrad: 1950.
Functional analysis and applied mathematics. Uspekhi Mat.
Nauk, 1948, 3, #6.
and L. I. Gor'kov. Some functional equations arising in the
analysis of a one-product economic model. Doklady Akad.
Nauk S.S.S.R. 129, #4, 732-35 (1959).

Office: Institute of Mathematics, Leningrad Branch
              USSR Academy of Sciences
              Leningrad, USSR

KAPELYUSHNIKOV, MATVEI ALKUNOVICH (Petroleum
        Engineer)
M. A. Kapelyushnikov was born September 13, 1886. He
graduated from the Tomsk Technological Institute in 1914, after
which he worked at a scientific research institute in Baku until
1937 as the Director of the Office of Turbodrilling and Cracking. He was awarded the title Honored Scientist of the
R.S.F.S.R. in 1947, and was elected to the U.S.S.R. Academy
of Sciences as a Corresponding Member in 1939.
    In 1912 he proposed turbodrilling of oil wells. The first
turbodrills had a single-stage turbine and a reducer for di-
minishing the speed of the working shaft connected to a drill.
Later, a group of engineers under the leadership of P. P.
Shumilov developed a multi-stage reducerless turbodrill, which
was widely utilized. In 1924-31 Kapelyushnikov, together with
V. G. Shukhov, designed and built the first Soviet cracking plant.
In 1933, together with S. D. Zalkin, Kapelyushnikov developed
pneumatic control of a drilling rig. In 1952, he established
the fact that dissolving oil in gas under considerable pressure
makes it possible to explain the conditions in the migration of
oil and formation of deposits.

Bibliography:
The mechanization and automation of drilling. Oil Economy,
1945, #7.
Physical conditions of oil, gas and water in conditions of oil
bedding. Izvest. Akad. Nauk S.S.S.R., Otdel. Tekh. Nauk,
1952, #11.
The question of migration and accumulation of dispersed oil
in sedimentary rock. Doklady Akad. Nauk S.S.S.R., 1954, <u>99</u>,
#6.
Office: Academy of Sciences USSR
              Leninskii Prospekt, 14
              Moscow, USSR
Residence: Leninskii Prospekt, 13
              Moscow, USSR
Telephone: V2 50 76

KAPITSA, PYOTR LEONIDOVICH (Physicist)
P. L. Kapitsa was born July 8, 1894. In 1918 he graduated
from the Polytechnic Institute in Petrograd (Leningrad) and
began scientific work under A. F. Ioffe (1880-1959, solid state
physicist). He was sent in 1921 on a scientific trip to England
where he worked until 1930 under E. Rutherford in the Caven-
dish Laboratory at Cambridge University. From 1930 to 1934
he was Director of the Monde Laboratory at Cambridge University. In 1935 Kapitsa was persuaded to remain in the Soviet
Union. From 1935 to 1946 and again in 1955 he was Director of
the Institute of Physics Problems of the U.S.S.R. Academy of
Sciences. He was elected a Corresponding Member of the
U.S.S.R. Academy of Sciences in 1929 and an Academician in
1939. In 1941 and in 1943 he received Stalin Prizes. He was
made a Hero of Socialist Labor in 1945. Kapitsa is editor of
the Soviet Journal of Experimental and Theoretical Physics.
He was a member of and honored by many foreign organizations
including: London Royal Society (1929), Danish Academy of
Sciences (1946), National Academy of Sciences of the U. S. A.
(1946), English Institute of Metals (1943), Franklin Institute in
the U. S. A. (1944), Paris University, University of Oslo, University of Algiers.
    The first investigations of Kapitsa are devoted to the study
of the inertia of electrons and properties of radiation. In 1920,
in the article, "The Possibility of Determining the Magnetic
Moment of the Atom," Kapitsa, together with N. N. Semenov,
proposed an experiment on the determination of magnetic
moments of atoms in atomic beams. Kapitsa constructed an

installation for creating very powerful magnetic fields. He observed the splitting of spectral lines in fields up to 320 kilogauss, discovered linear increase of electrical resistance of metals with the field, and studied magnetostriction of diamagnetic bodies in these fields. Kapitsa developed a large capacity hydrogen liquifier of helium by using the adiabatic principle. He proposed a new method of liquifying air in a low pressure cycle and for using a turbine engine driven by compressed gas. Using a turbine engine driven by compressed gas to liquify air, Kapitsa built an installation (1939) for obtaining large quantities of liquid oxygen by way of fractionation. He is the author of the treatise on "Turbine Engine Driven by Compressed Gas for Obtaining Low Temperatures and Its Application in Liquification of Air" (1939; Stalin Prize 1941). He conducted investigations on the properties of liquid helium II and discovered (1938) the phenomenon of super fluidity. The results of these investigations are in "Heat Transfer and Super Fluidity of Helium II" (1941) and "Investigating the Mechanism of Heat Transfer in Helium II" (1941; Stalin Prize 1943). In connection with the study on the operation of a fractionating column, Kapitsa conducted investigations on the wave heat processes in moving thin layers of liquid. Later development of this work led to the establishment of a quantitative theory on interaction of marine waves with the wind. Kapitsa developed a hydro-dynamic theory of lubricating bearings. In 1951 he published studies on the movement of a pendulum with a vibrating suspension device and proposed a hypothesis on the nature of ball lightning (1955).

In 1960 Kapitsa was awarded the Lomonosov Gold Medal for his work in low temperature physics.

As of 1961, Kapitsa was a Member of the Presidium of the USSR Academy of Sciences.

In June 1958, he visited the United States to attend the Gordon Research Conference on Polymer Research at New London, New Hampshire. He has also attended the Pugwash Conferences.

Biography:

Academician Pyotr Leonidovich Kapitsa. Vestnik Akad. Nauk S.S.S.R., 1939, #2-3, 193.

Academician Pyotr Leonidovich Kapitsa (On the 60th Anniversary since the date of birth). Zhur. Eksptl. i Teoret. Fiz., 1954, 27, #3.

E. V. Shpol'skii. Pyotr Leonidovich Kapitsa (On the 60th Anniversary since the date of birth). Uspekhi Fiz. Nauk, 1954, 54, #4.

Office: S. I. Vavilov Institute of Physics Problems
                Vorob'evskoye Shosse, 2
                Moscow, USSR
Telephone: B2 32 30

KARANDEEV, KONSTANTIN BORISOVICH (Electrical Engineer)

K. B. Karandeev was born July 18, 1907. He graduated in
1930 from Leningrad Polytechnic Institute. In 1929-1935 he
worked in the Electro-Physical Institute in Leningrad. He was
professor at the Leningrad Institute of Signal Engineering in
1937-42 and also deputy director of the All-Union Scientific
Research Institute of Metrology. In 1944 he became professor
at L'vov Polytechnic Institute. Beginning in 1952, he worked in
the Institute of Machine Studies and Automation of the Ukrainian
S.S.R. Academy of Sciences. Karandeev was made Director of
the Institute of Automation and Electrometry of the Siberian
branch of the U.S.S.R. Academy of Sciences in 1957. He was
elected a Corresponding Member of the Ukrainian S.S.R. Academy of Sciences in 1957 and in 1958 a Corresponding Member of
the U.S.S.R. Academy of Sciences. In 1954 he was made an
Honored Scientist of the Ukrainian S.S.R.

Karandeev's main works deal with developing exact methods
of electrical measurement, methods of measuring low and high
currents, low electromotive forces, and the theory of bridge
methods. He has been concerned with semiconductor rectifiers,
telemetry, use of computors in measuring schemes and devices,
and with geophysical apparatus.

Bibliography:
   Methods of Electrical Measurement (Differential, Bridge,
   and Compensation). Moscow-Leningrad: 1952.
   Bridge Methods of Measurement. Kiev: 1953.
   Semiconductor Rectifiers in Measuring Techniques. Kiev:
   1954.
   Direct Current Galvanometers (Theory and Practice).
   L'vov: 1957.
Office: Institute of Automation and Electrometry, Siberian
                Branch of USSR Academy of Sciences
                Novosibirsk, Siberia

KARAVAEV, NIKOLAI MIKHAILOVICH (Fuel Chemist)

N. M. Karavaev was born June 7, 1890. After graduating
from the Moscow Technological College in 1920, he taught there
until 1930. From 1925 to 1932 he was at the Moscow Chemico-
Technological Institute, and from 1924 to 1932 he also worked

at the All-Union Heat Engineering Institute. In 1939-41 Karavaev was at the Institute of Fuel Minerals of the U.S.S.R. Academy of Sciences. He became a professor in 1949 at the Moscow
Institute of Chemical Machine Building where he had worked
since 1946. In 1946 he was elected a Corresponding Member
of the U.S.S.R. Academy of Sciences.

Karavaev has studied the origin, chemistry, and technology
of solid fuels and products obtained from them. Since 1926 he
has been investigating the coal of the Kuznets, Irkutsk, and other
basins. In 1929 he proposed industrial marking of coal of the
Kuznets basin. In 1933-36, Karavaev directed the work on
hydrogenation of solid fuels and tars and also on hydrocarbon
synthesis from water gas. He has been engaged in the study of
semicoking of Siberian coal in industrial conditions. Together
with associates, Karavaev proposed a new scheme of processing raw benzene from chemical-coke plants. He worked out a
new scheme of periodic rectification. He also worked in the
pyrolysis of fuels.

Bibliography:
   Coal of the Kuznets basin. Proceedings of the Heat Engi-
   neering Institute, 1929, #8 (51).
   Question of marking coal of the Kuznets basin. Proceedings
   of the Heat Engineering Institute, 1929, #7 (50).
   Properties and quality of coal in the U.S.S.R. Works of the
   XVIIth Session of the International Geological Congress of the
   U.S.S.R., 1937, 1, Moscow, 1939.
   and others. Machines and Devices of the Chemical-Coke
   Industry. 1, Moscow: 1955.
   Investigating the Phase Equilibrium of the System Naphtha-
   lene-Beta-Methylnaphthalene. Ukr. Khim. Zhur., 1955, 21,
   #2.Method of Determining the Ratio of Heat Emission in a
   Layer of Granular Material. Izvest. Akad. Nauk, S.S.S.R.,
   Otdel. Tekh. Nauk, 1956, #6.
   Lignites. Chemistry and Technology of Fuels and Oils,
   1957, #1.

Office: Moscow Institute of Chemical Machine Building
              Moscow, USSR

KARGIN, VALENTIN ALEKSEEVICH (Chemist)
   V. A. Kargin was born January 23, 1907. After graduating
from Moscow University in 1930, he worked at the L. Karpov
Physico-Chemical Institute in Moscow. He became a Corresponding Member of the U.S.S.R. Academy of Sciences in 1946
and in 1953, Academician.

Kargin's fields of scientific work are colloidal chemistry
and chemistry of high-molecular compounds. He has developed
methods of purification of substances, investigated the formation and properties of alumino-silicates, and worked on the
coagulation and stabilization of hydrophobic colloids. He studied
the formation of colloidal particles in solutions. He applied
these results to the study of the ion exchange in soils, working
out a method of strengthening water soaked sand. In his
thermodynamic studies Kargin and his associates showed that
polymer solutions are true solutions, and determined the sorb-
tive properties of polymers. He has investigated the nature of
the phase condition of polymers and their mechanical and rheological properties. The results of these investigations are
widely applied in the synthetic fiber, plastics, rubber and
paper industries.

In June 1958, Kargin visited the United States to attend the
Gordon Research Conference on Polymer Research at New
London, New Hampshire. He has also attended the Pugwash
Conferences.

Bibliography:

and A. I. Rabinovich. On activity of compensating ions in
colloidal systems. Zhur. Fiz. Khim., 1935, 6, #9.

and A. I. Rabinovich. On the changes in colloidal systems
during their interaction with electrolytes. Zhur. Fiz. Khim.,
1935, 6, #9.

and N. V. Mikhailov, V. M. Bukhman. Roentgenographic
study of the orientation of synthetic fiber. I-II. Zhur. Fiz.
Khim., 1940, 14, #2.

and T. I. Sogolova. On the question of three physical conditions of amorphously-liquid linear polymers. Zhur. Fiz.
Khim., 1949, 23, #5.

Adsorption of electrolytes on silica gel, sesquioxides, and
their mixed gels. Uspekhi Khim., 1939, 8, #7.

and G. D. Slonimskii. On the crystalline condition of polymers. Uspekhi Khim., 1955, 24, #7.

and Z. Ya. Berestneva. On the mechanisms of formation of
colloidal particles. Uspekhi Khim., 1955, 24, #3.

and T. A. Matveeva. High voltage, many-chambered electro-
dialysis. Doklady Akad. Nauk S.S.S.R., 1955, 105, #2.

and V. G. Zhuravlova, Z. Ya. Berestneva. Electromicroscopic investigation of the structure of isotactic polybuty-
lene. Doklady Akad. Nauk S.S.S.R. 146, #2, 366-67 (1962).

and G. P. Andrianova. Supramolecular structures in films of isotactic polypropylene. Doklady Akad. Nauk S.S.S.R. 146, #6, 1337-40 (1962).

Biography:

Kargin, Valentin Alekseevich. Vestnik Akad. Nauk S.S.S.R., 1954, #3.

V. L. Karpov. On the 20th anniversary of the scientific activity of the Corresponding Member of the U.S.S.R. Academy of Sciences, V. A. Kargin. Kolloid. Zhur., 1949, 11, #4.

Z. Ya. Berestneva, G. D. Slonimskii. On the 50th anniversary since the date of birth of Valentin Alekseevich Kargin. Kolloid. Zhur., 1957, 19, #2.

Office: L. Karpov Physico-Chemical Institute
              Moscow, USSR

Residence: p. Arkadiya Gaidara, 5/7
              Moscow, USSR

Telephone: K7 62 78

KAZANSKII, BORIS ALEKSANDROVICH (Organic Chemist)

B. A. Kazanskii was born April 13, 1891. In 1918 he graduated from Moscow University where he was a pupil of N. D. Zelinskii, the leader of Russian organic chemistry in the first part of this century. He was made professor in 1935 at Moscow University. And in 1936 he was in charge of and organized the catalytic synthesis laboratory at the Institute of Organic Chemistry at the U.S.S.R. Academy of Sciences. In 1954 he became Director of the Zelinskii Institute of Organic Chemistry. Since 1946 he has been an Academician. He was awarded, in 1949, a Stalin Prize.

Kazanskii has specialized in the conversion of hydrocarbons. In particular, he has investigated hydrogen cleavage of five-membered hydrocarbons in the presence of platinum catalyst. This reaction points the way for conversion of these hydrocarbons into branched paraffins. In 1936 Kazanskii studied the aromatization of paraffins in the presence of platinized carbon at 300° to 310° Later he determined that an intermediate of this reaction is cyclohexane. In 1954 he showed that in the presence of platinum, paraffins can also convert to hydrocarbons of the cyclopentane series. This cyclization goes to the greatest extent for branched paraffins (isooctane). He also studied aromatization in the presence of different oxides as catalysts. He investigated selective hydrogenation of compounds with several double bonds in the presence of platinum, palladium, and nickel. Recently he has investigated the conjugation of

151   KAZARNOVSKII

trimembered cyclic hydrocarbons with a double bond in the side
chain (vinylcyclopropane) or in the aromatic nucleus (phenyl-
cyclopropane). With G. S. Landsberg, he developed a method
for detailed study of petroleum, using Raman spectra.

In 1961 Kazanskii was awarded the Order of Lenin and two
orders of the Red Banner of Labor. He was also a member of
the steering Committee of International Union on Pure and
Applied Chemistry.

Bibliography:
with A. F. Plate. Aromatization of some cyclopentane and
paraffin homologues in the presence of platinized carbon.
Zhur. Obshchei Khim., 1937, 7, #2.
with G. T. Tatevosyan. Catalytic hydrogen addition to compounds with several double bonds. Zhur. Obshchei Khim.,
1938, 8, #14-51.
Catalytic hydrogenation of cyclopentanes with ring cleavage.
Uspekhi Khim., 1948, 17, #6.
with others. Catalytic conversion of hydrocarbons. Khim.
Nauka i Promyshlennost', 1957, 2, #2.

Biography:
A. M. Rubinshtein. Academician Boris Aleksandrovich
Kazanskii (for 60th birthday). Vestnik Akad. Nauk S.S.S.R.,
1951, #5.
A. F. Plate. Academician Boris Aleksandrovich Kazanskii.
Izvest. Akad. Nauk S.S.S.R., Otdel. Khim. Nauk, 1951, #3.

Office: N. D. Zelinskii Institute of Organic Chemistry
             Leninskii Prospekt 31
             Moscow, USSR
Residence: Leninskii Prospekt 13
             Moscow, USSR
Telephone: B2 21 89

KAZARNOVSKII, ISAAK ABRAMOVICH (Chemist)
I. A. Kazarnovskii was born September 29, 1890. He graduated in 1914 from Zurich University. In 1922 he began working
at the Karpov Physico-Chemical Institute in Moscow. He has
been a Corresponding Member of the U.S.S.R. Academy of
Sciences since 1939. In 1941 he was awarded a Stalin Prize.

Kazarnovskii's main work deals with problems in the formation of metal chlorides and peroxides. He discovered new,
higher oxides such as the peroxide of sodium NaO_2, 1936, and
the ozonides of alkali metals such as ozonide of potassium KO_3
and elucidated their structure; he worked out methods of producing sodium peroxide, anhydrous aluminum chloride from

clays, and a new method of regenerating air (which was used on an industrial scale).

Bibliography:

Structure of inorganic peroxides. Zhur. Fiz. Khim., 1940, 14, #3.

and S. I. Raikhchtein. Higher oxides of potassium (Inorganic Peroxides. 11). Zhur. Fiz. Khim., 1947, 21, #3.

and G. P. Nikol'skii, T. A. Abletsova. New oxide of potassium. Doklady Akad. Nauk., New Series, 1949, 64, #1.

and others. Kinetics of spontaneous decay of the ozonide of potassium. Doklady Akad. Nauk, 1956, 108, #4.

and others. Isotope exchange of oxygen between a free hydroxyl radical and water. Zhur. Fiz. Khim. 1956, 30, #6.

Office: L. Karpov Physico-Chemical Institute
Moscow, USSR

KELDYSH, MSTISLAV VSEVOLDOVICH (Mathematician and Specialist in Mechanics)

M. V. Keldysh was born February 10, 1911 in Riga (now in Latvian S.S.R.). He is the son of Vsevolod Mikhaylovich Keldysh (1878, a specialist on ferro-concrete construction and a professor). In 1931 he graduated from Moscow University. Joining the N. Ye. Zhukovskii Central Aero-Hydrodynamics Institute (TsAGI), Keldysh worked during 1934-35 in its Department of Flutter Engineering and in 1943 and in 1945 was a department chief in the Institute. In 1939 he became associated with the V. A. Steklov Mathematics Institute of the U.S.S.R. Academy of Sciences and in 1954 was made Director of that institute's Department of Applied Mathematics.

He has been a member of the Communist Party of the Soviet Union since 1949. In 1943 he was elected a Corresponding Member of the U.S.S.R. Academy of Sciences and in 1946 an Academician. He was named academician-secretary of the Academy's Department of Physico-Mathematical Sciences in 1953, has served on the Academy's Presidium since 1953, and in 1960 was elected one of the vice presidents. In 1961 Keldysh replaced A. N. Nesmeyanov as President of the U.S.S.R. Academy of Sciences.

In 1957 Keldysh was named to membership on the Presidium of the newly formed U.S.S.R. National Committee on Theoretical and Applied Mechanics, U.S.S.R. Academy of Sciences. The following year he was cited as a member of the organization committee of the All-Union Conference on Theoretical and Applied Mechanics, and when that conference convened in Moscow during January 27-February 3, 1960, he served as chairman of the Section on General and Applied Mechanics. Since 1956 he has been a member of the editorial boards of the journals Matematicheskii Sbornik, Novaya Seriya, and Prikladnaya Matematika i Mekhanika.

Among the honors and awards that have been conferred upon Keldysh are the Order of Labor Red Banner (in 1943, 1945 and 1953) and the Order of Lenin (in 1945, 1954 and 1960). He received a Stalin Prize in 1941 for scientific works in predicting the breakdown of airplanes. In 1960 he was made a member of the Presidium of the Committee for Awarding Lenin Prizes in the Field of Science and Engineering of the Council of Ministers U.S.S.R.

Keldysh's interests in mechanics and mathematics are theory of oscillations, aerodynamics, theory of waves on the surface of a heavy liquid, impact against water, investigation of an approximate integration of differential equations, potential theory, conformal representation mapping, theory of eigenfunctions and eigenvalues of parameters for non self-conjugate differential equations. In hydromechanics, he worked on the theory of non-stabilized motion of a wing. He proved, for gas, the theorem of Zhukovskii. He presented a theory on the solvability of the Dirichlet problem in its dependence on boundary conditions. He solved the basic problems of the stability of solutions of the Dirichlet problem. Keldysh developed a theory of approximation of functions of a complex variable by a series of polynomials. Of considerable importance is the work of Keldysh on the theory, calculation and working out of methods for avoiding various types of vibration in an airplane. Since 1953 his papers have discussed such topics as thermal excitation of sounds, speed of approximation of functions by polynomials on arbitrary continua, point character of the spectrum of a certain class of matrices in an analytical space and series of rational fractions. He has been directing work on the theory of rocket propulsion and on the development of a ballistic theory of space flight. During September 1957, at a meeting celebrating the 100th anniversary of the birth of K. E. Tsiolkovskii, Keldysh spoke on the use of artificial earth satellites in scientific research.

In June 1961, Keldysh received the Hammer and Sickle Gold Medal, and in March 1962, he was elected a delegate from R.S.F.S.R. to the Supreme Soviet.

Bibliography:
On the solvability and stability of the problem of Dirichlet.
Uspekhi Mat. Nauk, 1940, #8.
Shimmy of the front wheel of a three-wheeled chassis, 1945.
On the presentation of functions of a complex variable by
series of polynomials in closed domains. Mat. Sbornik,
1945, 16, #3.
On the proper meanings and proper functions of some class-
es of non-self-conjugate equations. Doklady Akad. Nauk
S.S.S.R., 1951, 77, #1.
Vibrations in the air flow of a braced wing. Works of the
Central Aerohydrodynamic Institute, #357. Moscow: 1938.
Office: President, USSR Academy of Sciences
Leninskii Prospekt, 14
Moscow, USSR

KELL', NIKOLAI GEORGIEVICH (Geodesy and Photogrammetry
Scientist)
N. G. Kell' was born January 20, 1883. In 1915 he graduated
from Petrograd (Leningrad) Mining Institute, and in 1923 he
became a professor at this Institute. He worked as a topograph-
er in 1908-1911 on the Kamchatka expedition of the Russian
Geographical Society, and in 1922 he was made a member of
this society. In 1921 he was made Head of the Chair of Geodesy
at the Leningrad Mining Institute. In 1917-1922, Kell' worked
at the Ural Mining Institute in Sverdlovsk and in 1919-1920 was
the Director. In 1947 he became Chief of the Laboratory on
Aeromethods, and in 1958 he was chairman of the Joint Committee on Aerial Survey. Since 1946, he has been a Corresponding Member of the U.S.S.R. Academy of Sciences.
Kell's researches are in geodesy, photogrammetry, development of aerial photogrammetric methods and their application
in geographic and geological mapping.
As of 1961, Kell' was Chairman of the Interdepartmental
Commission for Aerial Surveys.
Bibliography:
Map of Kamchatka Volcanos. Leningrad: 1928.
Advanced Geodesy and Geodesic Works, Part 1-2. Lenin-
grad: 1932-33.
Photography and Photogrammetry. Leningrad-Moscow:
1937.
Graphic Method in Work with Errors, and Laws (Distri-
bution). Moscow-Leningrad: 1948.

Utilization of Results from Topographico-geodesic Work for
Engineering Purposes. Leningrad-Moscow: 1950.
Indications for Using Geometrical and Geodesical Proper-
ties of Aerial Photo-materials for Geological Mapping.
Leningrad-Moscow: 1950.
Measurement Deciphering of Aerial Photos in Field Con-
ditions. Moscow-Leningrad: 1959.
and V. G. Zdanovich, K. A. Zvonarev, A. N. Belolikov, N. A.
Gusev. Higher Geodesy. Moscow: 1961.
Biography:
L. S. Khrenov. Nikolai Georgievich Kell'. Proceedings of
the All-Union Geographic Society, 1953, 85, #3.
Office: Laboratory of Aeromethods
            USSR Ministry of Geology and Mineral Conservation
            Birzhevoi Proyezd, 6
            Leningrad, V-164, USSR
Telephone: A2 45 64

KHARITON, YULII BORISOVICH (Nuclear Physicist)

Yu. B. Khariton was born February 27, 1904. In 1925 he
graduated from Leningrad Polytechnic Institute. While still a
student, in 1921, he began scientific work at the Laboratory of
N. N. Semenov of the Leningrad Physico-Technical Institute.
In 1927-28 Khariton was sent to England where he studied the
scintillation of alpha-particles under E. Rutherford. In 1931 he
began working at the Institute of Chemical Physics of the
U.S.S.R. Academy of Sciences. He was elected a Corresponding Member of the U.S.S.R. Academy of Sciences in 1943 and
an Academician in 1953. He was also a Deputy to the U.S.S.R.
Supreme Soviet, and was elected again in March 1962.

The first investigation of Khariton was the study of condensation of metallic vapor molecular beams in a vacuum on cooled
surfaces. The result was the basis for the theory on condensation, later developed by Khariton and other Soviet scientists.
In 1925 Khariton, while studying the phenomena of chemi-
luminescence of vapors of phosphorus at low oxygen pressures,
discovered the phenomenon of the lower limit of cold ignition
of phosphorous vapors. He showed that below a certain pressure of oxygen, the reaction of oxidation does not take place,
and above a certain pressure, moves with noticeable speed.
Together with Ya. B. Zel'dovich, Khariton made calculations
for a chain reaction of uranium fission. Khariton, and associates, worked on the theory of excitation and spreading of explosion detonations; in particular he established the principle

which links the explosive ability of substances with the speed of
the chemical reaction in the explosive wave front.
Bibliography:
   On the question of detonation due to impact. Collection of
   Articles on the Theory of Explosives. Moscow: 1940.
   and Ya. B. Zel'dovich. On the question of chain decay of the
   main isotope of uranium. Zhur. Eksptl. i Teoret. Fiz., 1939,
   1, 9, #12.
   and Ya. B. Zel'dovich. On the chain decay of uranium under
   influence of slow neutrons. Zhur. Eksptl. i Teoret. Fiz.,
   1940, 10, #1.
Office: Institute of Chemical Physics
             Vorob'evskoye Shosse 2
             Moscow, USSR

KHARKEVICH, ALEKSANDR ALEKSANDROVICH (Radio
     technologist)
     A. A. Kharkevich was born in 1904. In 1930 he graduated
from the Leningrad Electro-Technical Institute. He worked,
1932-41, at various teaching institutions of Leningrad, and from
1941-44 he was at the Physico-Technical Institute of Leningrad,
Kazan', and Moscow. From 1944-48, he was professor and departmental head of the L'vov Polytechnical Institute, and from
1948-52, he was the departmental Director of the (Ukraine)
U.S.S.R. Academy of Sciences Institute of Physics in Kiev. In
1952-54, Kharkevich was professor and departmental chairman
of the Electro-Technical Institute of Communications in Moscow. In 1954 he started to work in the Laboratory on the Treatment of Scientific Communication Problems (now the Laboratory
on Systems of Information Transmission), where he became
Chief in 1957. He was elected in 1960 a Corresponding Member
of the U.S.S.R. Academy of Sciences. In 1962, Kharkevich was
appointed acting Director of the U.S.S.R. Academy of Sciences
Institute of Problems of Information Transmission.
     Kharkevich's works deal with the theory, design and con-
struction of electro-acoustical apparatus.
Bibliography:
   and E. L. Blokh. Geometric theory of the threshold of trans-
   missibility of communications systems. Radiotekhnika 10,
   #7, 3-7 (1955). Elec. Engr. Sci. Abstr. 59, 811 (1956).
   On the calculation of the spectra of random processes.
   Radiotekhnika 12, #5, 5-11 (1957). Elec. Engr. Sci. Abstr.
   60, 6323 (1957).

and E. L. Blokh. On the question of a geometric proof of
Shannon's theorem. Radiotekhnika 11, #11, 5-16 (1956).
Elec. Engr. Sci. Abstr. 60, 3026 (1957).
Kotel'nikov's theorem. Radiotekhnika 13, #8, 3-10 (1958).
Elec. Engr. Sci. Abstr. 62, 1719 (1959).
Pattern recognition. Radiotekhnika 14, #5, 12-22 (1959).
Elec. Engr. Sci. Abstr. 62, 6673 (1959).
Principles of construction for reading machines. Radio-
tekhnika 15, #3, 3-9 (1960).
Office: Laboratory on Systems of Information Trans-
                 mission
                 Shosse Entuziastov 156
                 Moscow, USSR

KHEL'KVIST, GERMAN AVGUSTOVICH (Oil Geologist)
    G. A. Kehl'kvist was born October 5, 1894. He graduated
from Tomsk Technological Institute in 1923 and in 1924 worked
in the oil industry. From 1950 he worked in scientific research
institutions. In 1956-58 he was professor at Moscow Oil Institute. He was made Director of the Sakhalin Complex Scientific
Research Institute of the U.S.S.R. Academy of Sciences in 1957.
Khel'kvist has been a member of the Communist Party of the
Soviet Union since 1946. In 1958 he was elected a Corresponding Member of the U.S.S.R. Academy of Sciences. He received
in 1958 a Stalin Prize.
    Khel'kvist took part in studying and prospecting for oil de-
posits of the Azerbaijan S.S.R., Northern Caucasus, the Ukraine,
and the territory along the Volga and Sakhalin. His scientific
research is devoted to the study of oil and gas deposits, the relationships of oil beds, and methodology of prospecting. Khel'-
kvist introduced the concept of zoned oil beds.
Bibliography:
    Zoned Oil Deposits and the Methodology of Prospecting.
    Moscow-Leningrad: 1944.
    Geological Structure of Zoned Oil Deposits. Moscow-
    Leningrad: 1946.
    and others. General and Oil Geology. Moscow-Leningrad:
    1951.
    and A. V. Ul'yanov. Geology of Oil and Gas Deposits. Mos-
    cow: 1955.
    and others. Basis of Geology of Oil and Gas. Moscow: 1957.

Office: Sakhalin Complex Scientific Research Institute of
USSR Academy of Sciences
Yuzhno-Sakhalinsk
Sakhalin, USSR

KHITRIN, LEV NIKOLAEVICH (Heat Engineer)
L. N. Khitrin was born February 20, 1907. He graduated in
1930 from Moscow University. From 1931 to 1941 he worked
at the All-Union Heat Engineering Institute. He taught at Moscow University in 1936 and in 1953 became professor. In 1945
he began working at the Institute of Energetics of the U.S.S.R.
Academy of Sciences. Since 1953 he has been a Corresponding
Member of the U.S.S.R. Academy of Sciences. He received in
1950 a Stalin Prize.

His main works deal with the physics of burning processes.
He worked on the theory of heterogeneous burning, new intensive methods of burning, and on complex electro-
technological methods of utilizing fuels. He studied carbon
burning processes; his results, together with those of A. S.
Predvoditelev and others, appeared in 1949 in the treatise,
"Burning of Carbon". He has been engaged in developing new,
highly intensive furnaces.

Bibliography:
Experimental study of the influence of pressure on the normal speed of flame distribution. Zhur. Tekh. Fiz., 1937,
7, #1, 30-42.
Lighting gas flow mixtures by incandescent bodies. Doklady
Akad. Nauk S.S.S.R., 1955, 103, #2.
Main characteristics of the process of burning of carbon.
Izvest. Akad. Nauk S.S.S.R., Otdel. Tekh. Nauk, 1953, #4,
543-568.
and others. Complex energo-technological utilization of
fuel. Vestnik Akad. Nauk S.S.S.R., 1956, 26, #1.
and Z. F. Chukhanov. Energo-Technological Utilization of
Fuel. Methods of Effective Utilization of Fuel. Moscow:
1956.
Physics of Burning and Explosion. Moscow: 1957.
Office: Moscow University
Moscow, USSR
Residence: Novopeschanaya, 17
Moscow, USSR
Telephone: D7 24 38

KHOMENTOVSKII, ALEKSANDR STEPHANOVICH (Geologist)

A. S. Khomentovskii was born in 1908. In 1930 he graduated
from the Siberian Technological Institute in Tomsk. From
1930-37 he directed geological research parties. He taught,
1938-41, at the Krasnoyarsk State Pedagogical Institute. He
served in the Soviet Army from 1941-43. He worked, 1943-
1954, at the "Yuzhuraluglerazvedka" (South Urals Coal Prospecting) trust in Orensburg. From 1955-57 he was chairman of the
department on Geology and Useful Minerals at the Saratov State
University; and from 1957 to 1960, of the Perm Mining Institute. In 1960 he became chairman of the Presidium of the Far-
Eastern branch of the U.S.S.R. Academy of Sciences. Since
1941 he has been a member of the Communist Party of the
Soviet Union. In 1950 Khomentovskii was awarded a Stalin
Prize. He was elected in 1960 a Corresponding Member of the
U.S.S.R. Academy of Sciences.

Khomentovskii's main works deal with the classification,
tectonics, formation and distribution of coal deposits in Siberia
and the Urals.

Office: USSR Academy of Sciences
                 Leninskii Prospekt, 14
                 Moscow, USSR

KHRENOV, KONSTANTIN KONSTANTINOVICH (Electric
        Welding Engineer)

K. K. Khrenov was born February 25, 1894. He graduated
in 1918 from Petrograd Electrotechnical Institute and in 1921-
25 taught there. From 1928 to 1947 he taught at the Moscow
Electromechanical Institute of Railroad Transport Engineers,
where in 1933, he was made professor. In 1931 he also began
teaching in the Moscow Higher Technical School. He worked in
the Institute of Electric Welding of the Ukrainian Academy of
Sciences in 1945-1948; and in 1952 he began working in the
Institute of Electrotechnics of the Ukrainian Academy of Sciences. In 1947 he was made professor at Kiev Polytechnic
Institute. Khrenov has been an Academician of the Ukrainian
S.S.R. Academy of Sciences since 1945 and since 1953 a member of its presidium. In 1953 he was elected a Corresponding
Member of the U.S.S.R. Academy of Sciences. Since 1955, he
has been a member of the Communist Party of the Soviet Union.

He is an Honored Scientist of the Ukrainian S.S.R. and in 1946
was the recipient of a Stalin Prize.

The basic works of Khrenov are concerned with electric
welding of metals. He originated methods of electric welding
and cutting of metals under water. These methods are being
broadly applied in the restoration of bridges and the repair of
ships.

As of 1961, Khrenov was Academician Secretary of the
Technical Science Department of SSR Ukrainian Academy of
Sciences.

Bibliography:

and V. I. Yarko. The Technology of Arc Electric Welding.
Moscow-Leningrad: 1940.

Underwater Electric Welding and Cutting of Metals. Moscow: 1946.

The electric Welding Arc. Kiev-Moscow: 1949.

and S. T. Nazarov. Automatic Arc Electric Welding. Moscow: 1949.

New Developments in Informational Technology. Kiev: 1949.

Welding, Cutting and Soldering of Metals. Kiev-Moscow:
1952. (Translated into Bulgarian, Chinese, German, Rumanian).

and D. M. Kushnerev. Ceramic Fluxes for Automatic Arc
Welding. Kiev: 1954.

and D. M. Kushnerev. Ceramic Fusing Agents. Kiev: 1961.

Office: Academy of Sciences Ukrainian SSR
              Vladimirskaya Ulitsa, 54
              Kiev, Ukrainian SSR

KHRISTIANOVICH, SERGEI ALEKSEEVICH (Mechanical Engineer)

S. A. Khristianovich was born October 27, 1908. In 1930 he
graduated from the Leningrad Institute and then worked in the
State Hydrological Institute in Leningrad. From 1937 to 1953,
he was at the Central Aerohydrodynamic Institute. He was a
Member of the Presidium of the U.S.S.R. Academy of Sciences
in 1946 to 1956. In 1956 he started working in the Institute of
Chemical Physics of the U.S.S.R. Academy of Sciences.
Khristianovich has been a member of the Communist Party of
the Soviet Union since 1949. He was elected a Corresponding
Member of the U.S.S.R. Academy of Sciences in 1939, and in
1943 an Academician. In 1942, 1946, and 1952 he was awarded
Stalin Prizes.

161   KHRUSHCHOV

Khristianovich's field of work is mechanics of liquids and
gases. In his monograph, "Irregular Movement in Canals and
Rivers" (1938) he solved the problem of spreading and reflection of waves and applied these results to hydrotechnical
structures. In plasticity, he solved the surface problem of the
determination of the tension arising in a plastic medium in
terms of the forces set in a closed contour. On the theory of
filtration, Khristianovich wrote in 1940 "The Movement of Sub-
soil Waters, Not Following the Darcy Law" and in 1941 "On the
Movement of Aerated Liquids in Porous Rocks." In aerodynamics, he studied the flow of gas at high subsonic speeds
around a profile in the presence of lifting force, and worked out
a method of calculating the effect of compressibility on the
characteristics of wing profiles. He carried out important
studies on the flow of gas at supersonic speed, and also in
aviation technology.

As of 1961, Khristianovich was a Vice President of the Siberian Department of the U.S.S.R. Academy of Sciences, Director of the Institute of Theoretical and Applied Mechanics
(Novosibirsk), and a Member of the Presidium of the U.S.S.R.
Academy of Sciences.

Bibliography:
The surface problem of the mathematical theory of plasticity
under external forces set in a closed contour. Mat. Sbornik,
New Series, 1936, 1 (43), #4.
Flow of Gas Around Bodies at High Subsonic Speeds. Mos-
cow: 1940 (Works of the N. E. Zhukovskii Central Aero-
Hydrodynamic Institute, #481).
On Supersonic Flow of Gas. Moscow: 1941 (Works of the
N. E. Zhukovskii Central Aero-Hydrodynamic Institute,
#543).
and I. M. Yurevii. Flow around a wing profile at subcritical
speeds. Priklad. Mat. i Mekh., 1947, 11, #1.
Approximate integration of equations of the supersonic flow
of gas. Priklad. Mat. i Mekh., 1947, 11, #2.
Office: Siberian Branch of USSR Academy of Sciences
              Novosibirsk, Siberia

KHRUSHCHOV, GRIGORII K. (Deceased, December 22, 1962.)
G. K. Khrushchov was born March 3, 1897. He graduated in
1919 from Moscow University and until 1930 continued to work
there. From 1933 to 1945 he was professor at the Moscow
Animal-Veterinary Institute. In 1939-1949 he was Director of
the Institute of Cytology, Histology and Embryology. Krushchov

became a professor in 1945 at the second Moscow Medical
Institute. In 1949 he was made Director of the Severtsov Institute of Morphology of Animals of the U.S.S.R. Academy of Sciences. He has been a member of the Communist Party of the
Soviet Union since 1940. He was elected, in 1953, a Corresponding Member of the U.S.S.R. Academy of Sciences. In 1947
he was an Honored Scientist of the R.S.F.S.R. The U.S.S.R.
Academy of Sciences awarded him, in 1949, the I. I. Mechnikov
Prize.

Krushchov has worked in comparative and experimental histology and cytology. He has been working on the stimulating
role of leucocytes of blood in restoration processes.
Bibliography:
   Physical Properties of the Living Cell and Methods of Their
   Investigation. Moscow-Leningrad: 1930.
   Role of Leucocytes in Restoration Processes in Tissue,
   1945.
   Leucocytic systems of mammals and their evolution. Works
   of the Fifth All-Union Congress of Anatomists, Histologists,
   and Embryologists in Leningrad, July 5-11, 1949. Leningrad: 1951.
Office: A. N. Severtsov Institute of Morphology of Animals
              USSR Academy of Sciences
              Leninskii Prospekt, 33
              Moscow, USSR

KIBEL', IL'YA AFANAS'EVICH (Meteorologist)

   I. A. Kibel' was born October 19, 1904. He graduated from
the University of Saratov in 1925. From 1925 to 1943, he
worked at the Main Geophysical Observatory. In 1943, he started to work at the Central Institute of Weather Forecasting in
Moscow, where he was made a professor in 1949. In 1941, he
was awarded a Stalin Prize, and in 1943, he was elected to the
U.S.S.R. Academy of Sciences as a Corresponding Member.

   Kibel' compiled a closed simplified system of equations in dynamic meteorology in order to obtain some specific solutions in
this system. In 1940 he obtained the first approximate solution
to the problem of precalculating a field of pressure and temperature for a time interval of approximately twenty-four hours,
basing the proximity of actual wind to geostrophic wind.
Bibliography:
   Theoretical Hydromechanics, Part I, 4th ed., Part II, 3rd
   ed. Moscow-Leningrad: 1948.

Utilization of the method of long waves in a compressible
liquid. Prikl. Mat. i Mekh., 1944, 7, #5.
Distribution of temperature in the earth's atmosphere. Dok-
lady Akad. Nauk S.S.S.R., 1943, 39, #1.
Conditions for a dynamic possibility of movement of a com-
pressible liquid at an assigned inflow of energy. Geophysical
Collection, 1932, 5, #3.
Application to meteorology of mechanics of baroclinic
liquid. Izvest. Akad. Nauk S.S.S.R., Georg. i Geofiz. Ser.,
1940, #5.
On the adjustment of air movement to the geostrophic.
Doklady Akad. Nauk S.S.S.R., 1955, 104, #1.
Introduction to Hydrodynamic Methods of Short-Range
Weather Forecasting. Moscow: 1957.
Office: Central Institute of Weather Forecasting
              Moscow, USSR

KIKOIN, ISAAK KONSTANTINOVICH (Physicist)

I. A. Kikoin was born March 28, 1908. In 1932 he graduated
from Leningrad Polytechnic Institute. He then taught and did
research in Leningrad and Sverdlovsk until 1944 when he became professor at the Moscow Engineering and Physics Institute. In 1943 he was elected Corresponding Member of the
U.S.S.R. Academy of Sciences and in 1953 Academician. He
was awarded in 1942 a Stalin Prize.

Most of Kikoin's work has been on electric and magnetic
properties of metals and semiconductors, particularly liquid
metals. He measured the gyromagnetic coefficient for super-
conductors and proved that the Hall effect in ferromagnetic
substances is affected by magnetizing the material. He discovered a photomagnetic effect; the production of an electromotive force when a conductor, placed in a magnetic field, is
exposed to light. He showed experimentally that the absolute
charge of a positron is equal to that of an electron. Kikoin also
developed methods for measuring electric quantities in high
current direct current systems and then found application in
electrolysis (Stalin Prize, 1942).

Bibliography:
    and Ya. G. Dorfman. Physics of Metals, Moscow-Leningrad:
    1934.

Biography:
    Kikoin, I. K. Vestnik Akad. Nauk S.S.S.R., 1954, #1.
Office: Moscow Engineering and Physics Institute
              Moscow, USSR

KIRILLIN, VLADIMIR ALEKSEEVICH (Thermal Physicist)

V. A. Kirillin was born January 20, 1913. He graduated in
1936 from Moscow Energetics Institute. He taught at this Institute in 1938-1941 and again in 1943, and in 1952 became professor. In 1954-1955 he was Deputy Minister of Higher Education in the U.S.S.R. In 1954-1956 he was Deputy Chairman of
the State Committee on New Technology. He became, in 1955,
Chairman of the Department of Science of Universities, Technical Schools, and Colleges of the Central Committee of the
Communist Party. He has been Chief of the Laboratory on High
Temperatures at the Moscow Institute of Energetics. At the
XXth Congress of the Communist Party he was chosen a mem-
ber of the Inspection Commission of the Central Committee of
the Communist Party. Since 1937 he has been a member of the
Communist Party. In 1953 he was elected a Corresponding
Member of the U.S.S.R. Academy of Sciences and in June 1962
an Academician. In March 1962, Kirillin was elected to the
Council of Nationalities. From 1956 to 1961 he was a member
of the Central Committee on Revisions of the Communist Party.
He was elected, in 1961, a Candidate Member of the Central
Committee of the Communist Party and a Deputy to the 6th
session of the Supreme Soviet. He received, in 1951, a Stalin
Prize, and in 1959, a Lenin Prize.

Kirillin has studied thermal and physical properties of heat
carriers in power plants, in wide intervals of temperature and
pressure. Kirillin has also carried out experimental and theoretical research of the thermal properties of water and steam.
He and his associates developed new standard data on water and
steam, necessary for modern designing in super-pressure
steam electric power stations.

Bibliography:

and A. E. Sheindlin. Collection of Problems on Technical
Thermodynamics. Moscow-Leningrad: 1949.

and A. E. Sheindlin. Basis of Experimental Thermodynamics. Moscow-Leningrad: 1950.

and others. Thermodynamic Properties of Gases. Moscow:
1953.

and A. E. Sheindlin. Cycles of Internal Turbine Combustion.
Moscow: 1949.

and A. E. Sheindlin, V. Ya. Chekhovskii. Experimental determination of molybdenum enthalpy at temperatures of 700-
2337°. Doklady Akad. Nauk S.S.S.R. 139, #3, 645-47 (1961).

and A. E. Sheindlin, V. Ya. Chekhovskii. Enthalpy and the
specific heat of tungsten in the temperature range of 0-
2400°C. Doklady Akad. Nauk S.S.S.R. 142, #6, 1323-26
(1962).
Office: Moscow Energetics Institute
Moscow, USSR
Residence: ul. Kazakova, 29
Moscow, USSR
Telephone: El 65 24

KISHKIN, SERGEI TIMOFEEVICH (Metallurgist)
S. T. Kishkin was born in 1906. In 1931 he graduated from
the Bauman Moscow Higher Technical Institute. He has been a
member of the Communist Party since 1939. He was elected,
in 1960, to the U.S.S.R. Academy of Sciences as a Corresponding Member.
Kishkin's work is in the field of metallurgy and metal sciences.
Bibliography:
and S. Z. Bokshtein, L. M. Moroz. Autoradiography of
chromium self-diffusion and diffusion in some metals.
Zavodskaya Lab. 23, 316-18 (1957). C. A. 52, 207c (1958).
and A. A. Klypin, A. M. Sulima. The influence of plastic
deformation on the heat resistance of alloy EI 437. Metalloved. i Obrabotka Metal. #6, 18-21 (1958). C. A. 53, 6022c
(1959).
and S. Z. Bokstein, L. M. Moroz. Effect of metal composition and structure on grain boundary diffusion. Radio-
isotopes Sci. Research, Proc. Intern. Conf., Paris, 1957, I,
232-48 (Pub. 1958). C. A. 53, 13934d (1959).
and S. Z. Bokshtein, A. A. Zhukhovitskii, E. R. Mal'tsev.
The effect of phase changes on self-diffusion rate. Nauch.
Doklady Vysshei Shkoly, Met. #4, 158-61 (1958). C. A. 53,
16882a (1959).
Effect of Radiation on the Structure and Properties of
Structural Metals. Moscow: Gosudarst. Izdatel. Oboronnoi
Prom. 1958, 39 pp. C. A. 54, 4334b (1960).
and S. Z. Bokshtein, L. M. Moroz. Study of Metal Structure
by the Method of Radioactive Isotopes. Moscow: Gosudarst.
Izdatel. Oboronnoi Prom. 1959, 218 pp. C. A. 54, 11948g
(1960).
and S. Z. Bokshtein, V. B. Osvenskii. The effect of poly-
morphic transformation on diffusion in titanium. Metalloved.

i Termichesk, Obrabotka Metal. #6, 21-6 (1960). C. A. <u>54</u>,
18265f (1960).
Office: USSR Academy of Sciences
            Leninskii Prospekt, 14
            Moscow, USSR
Residence: M. Pionerskii p. 5
            Moscow, USSR
Telephone: D1 65 92

<u>KISUN'KO, GRIGORII VASILEVICH (Radio Technologist)</u>
    G. V. Kisun'ko was born in 1918. In 1938 he graduated from
the Voroshilovgradskii University. From 1938-41, he was an
instructor at the Leningrad Pedagogical Institute. He has been
a member of the Communist Party of the Soviet Union since
1944. He was elected, in 1958, a Corresponding Member of the
U.S.S.R. Academy of Sciences.
Office: USSR Academy of Sciences
            Leninskii Prospekt, 14
            Moscow, USSR

<u>KNUNYANTS, IVAN LYUDVIGOVICH (Organic Chemist)</u>
    I. L. Knunyants was born June 4, 1906. In 1928 he graduated
from Moscow Technological College and continued work there.
He began, in 1931, working at the Institute of Organic Chemistry
of the U.S.S.R. Academy of Sciences. In 1941, he became a
Member of the Communist Party of the Soviet Union. From
1946 he was a Corresponding Member of the U.S.S.R. Academy
of Sciences until 1953 when he was made an Academician.
Three times, 1943, 1948, 1950, he won a Stalin Prize.
    Knunyants synthesized pyridine analogs of triphenylmethane
and carbocyanine dyes and studied the relation of their color
and structure. He produced a series of new transformations of
aliphatic oxides, which led to the synthesis of gamma-
acetopropyl alcohol; this synthesis is used in production of
vitamin B1 and in anti-malaria substance. Also he studied
methods of introducing fluorine into organic compounds, such
as the reaction of aliphatic oxides with hydrogen fluoride. At
present he is concerned with reactions of fluoroolefins. Many
of his inventions, such as photosensitizers and caprone, are
used in Soviet industry.
Bibliography:
    <u>and O. V. Kild'sheva</u>. Methods of introducing fluorine in
    organic compounds. Uspekhi Khim., 1946, <u>15</u>, #6.

On interrelation of aliphatic oxides with hydrogen fluoride.
Doklady Akad. Nauk S.S.S.R., 1947, 55, #3.
and R. N. Sterlin. On reactions of organic oxides with hydrogen fluoride. Doklady Akad. Nauk S.S.S.R., 1947, 56, #1.
Some theoretical problems of contemporary organic chemistry. Vestnik Akad. Nauk S.S.S.R., 1953, #4, 15-29.
and N. P. Gambaryan. Reaction of hydrodimerization.
Uspekhi Khim., 1954, 23, #7, 781-820.
and E. Ya. Perova. Successes in establishing the structure
and synthesis of proteins. Uspekhi Khim., 1955, 24, #6,
641-72.
and others. On the facility and distribution of four-term
cycle formation. Uspekhi Khim., 1955, 25, #7, 785-844.
and others. Transformation of mercaptoamino acids. Report I-V in Proc. Acad. Sci. U.S.S.R., Sect. Chem., 1955,
#1-4.
and N. P. Gambaryan. A new method for obtaining beta-
lactams. Proc. Acad. Sci. U.S.S.R., Sect. Chem., 1955, #6.
and others. Nitrating of perfluorineolefin with nitrogen dioxide. Doklady Akad. Nauk S.S.S.R., 1956, 111, #5.
and A. V. Fokin. On nitroperfluorinealkylnitrite. Doklady
Akad. Nauk S.S.S.R., 1957, 112, #1.
and A. V. Fokin, V. S. Blagoveshchenskii, Yu. M. Kosyrev.
New formations of nitroso compounds. Doklady Akad. Nauk
S.S.S.R. 146, #5, 1088-91 (1962).
Biography:
   Knunyants, Ivan Lyudvigovich. Vestnik Akad. Nauk S.S.S.R.,
   1954, #3.
Office: N. D. Zelinskii Institute of Organic Chemistry of
              USSR Academy of Sciences
              Leninskii Prospekt, 31
              Moscow, USSR
Residence: Kotel'nicheskaya nab., 1/15
              Moscow, USSR
Telephone: B7 46 47

KOBZAREV, YURII BORISOVICH (Radio Engineer)
   Yu. B. Kobzarev was born December 8, 1905. After he
graduated from Khar'kov University in 1926, he worked until
1943 at the Physico-Technical Institute of the U.S.S.R. Academy
of Sciences in Leningrad. From 1944 to 1955 he was professor
at Moscow Institute of Energetics. In 1955 he began working at
the Institute of Radio Engineering and Electronics of the
U.S.S.R. Academy of Sciences. He has been a Corresponding

Member of the U.S.S.R. Academy of Sciences since 1953. In
1941 he was awarded a Stalin Prize.
   In 1926-31 Kobzarev developed frequency stabilization by
means of quartz crystals in tube generators. He worked on the
theory of oscillation of oscillator plates. Kobzarev studied the
phenomena in non-linear systems and indicated the high efficiency of "quasi-linear" method of treating these phenomena
based on the concept of complex amplitudes and resistance. He
played an active role in the development of radar.

Bibliography:
   Parameters of piezoelectric crystal resonators. Zhur.
   Priklad. Fiz. 1929, 6, #2.
   Peculiarities of crystal resonators. Zhur. Priklad. Fiz., 6,
   #6.
   Representation of a tube characteristic by a power series.
   Zhur. Tekh. Fiz., 1933, 3, #6.
   and A. Ageev. Transient processes in resonance amplifiers.
   Zhur. Tekh. Fiz., 1935, 5, #8.
   The theory of a tube generator with two degrees of freedom.
   Radiotechnics, 1950, #2.

Office: Institute of Radio Engineering and Electronics of
             USSR Academy of Sciences
             Mokhovaya Ulitsa 11, K-9
             Moscow, USSR

KOCHESHKOV, KSENOFONT ALEKSANDROVICH (Chemist)

   K. A. Kocheshkov was born December 12, 1894. He graduated from Moscow University in 1922 and in 1935 became a professor there. In 1946 he was elected a Corresponding Member
of the U.S.S.R. Academy of Sciences. He was awarded a Stalin
Prize in 1948.
   The investigations of Kocheshkov deal with the chemistry of
metallo-organic compounds. He discovered new methods of
synthesis of compounds of lead, tin, silicon, alkali metals, zinc,
thallium, antimony, bismuth. He also developed syntheses for
amines and mercaptans using metallo-organic compounds.
Kocheshkov is one of the editors for "Synthetic Method in the
Area of Metallo-Organic Compounds."

Bibliography:
   and N. I. Sheverdina. Interaction of α-benzyl-hydroxylamine
   with magnesium- and lithium organic compounds as a method
   of synthesis of primary amines. Izvest. Akad. Nauk S.S.S.R.,
   Otdel. Khim. Nauk, 1941, #1.

and A. N. Nesmeyanov. Synthetic Methods in the Area of
Metallo Organic Compounds. #4. Moscow-Leningrad: 1945.
and A. P. Skoldinov. Synthetic Methods in the Area of
Metallo Organic Compounds. #5. Moscow-Leningrad: 1947.
and A. P. Skoldinov. Synthetic Methods in the Area of
Metallo Organic Compounds. #8. Moscow-Leningrad: 1947.
and T. V. Talalaeva. Synthetic Methods in the Area of
Metallo Organic Compounds. #1. Moscow-Leningrad: 1949.
Office: Department of Chemistry
                 Moscow University
                 Moscow, USSR

KOCHETKOV, NIKOLAI KONSTANTINOVICH (Organic
     Chemist)
N. K. Kochetkov was born in 1915. In 1939 he graduated
from the M. V. Lomonosov Moscow Institute of Fine Chemical
Technology. He served in the Soviet Army from 1939 to 1945.
In 1945-1959, he was an assistant, docent, and then professor,
in 1956, at the Moscow State University. In 1959 he became
deputy Director and Chief of the Laboratory on Hydrocarbons
and Nucleotides at the U.S.S.R. Academy of Medical Sciences
Institute of Natural Compound Chemistry. He was also, from
1954 to 1960, Director of the chemical section at the U.S.S.R.
Academy of Medical Sciences Institute of Pharmacology and
Chemotherapy. He has been a Corresponding Member of the
U.S.S.R. Academy of Medical Sciences since 1957, and was
elected in 1960 to the U.S.S.R. Academy of Sciences as a Corresponding Member.
     Kochetkov's work is concerned with organic synthesis, in-
vestigation and synthesis of new medicinal preparations, and
studies of carbon and carbon containing compounds and nucleotides.
Bibliography:
     and N. N. Semenov, M. M. Shemyakin. Academician Alek-
sandr Nikolaevich Nesmeyanov. Zhur. Obshchei Khim. 29,
2811-16 (1959).
     and E. E. Nifant'ev, N. V. Molodtsov, L. I. Kudryashov.
Ethylene acetals of α-(bromoaryl) acetaldehydes and their
transformations. Doklady Akad. Nauk S.S.S.R. 130, 94-7
(1960).
     and A. M. Likhosherstov, A. M. Kritsyn. Pyrrolizidine
alkaloids. Doklady Akad. Nauk S.S.S.R. 141, #3, 361-63
(1961).

and I. G. Zhukova, I. S. Glukhoded. Thin-layer chromatography of cerebrosides. Doklady Akad. Nauk S.S.S.R. <u>139</u>, #3, 608-11 (1961).
and Acad. A. N. Nesmeyanov, R. B. Materikova. Acetyl derivatives of pentaethonodifenocene. Doklady Akad. Nauk S.S.S.R. <u>136</u>, #5, 1096-98 (1961).
and E. Ye. Nifant'ev. Chemistry of β-ketoacetals. Uspekhi Khim. #1, 31-47 (1961).

Office: Institute of Natural Compound Chemistry
Academy of Medical Sciences USSR
Solyanka, 14
Moscow, USSR

KOCHINA, PELAGEYA YAKOVLEVNA (Hydrodynamicist)

P. Ya. Kochina was born May 1, 1899. In 1921 she graduated from Petrograd University. From 1919 she worked in the main geophysical observatory. She taught at the Ways of Communication Institute, at the Institute of Civil Fleets, and at Leningrad University where she was made professor in 1934. Beginning in 1935 she worked in the Mathematics Institute and subsequently in the Institute of Mechanics of the U.S.S.R. Academy of Sciences. She was elected a Corresponding Member of the U.S.S.R. Academy of Sciences in 1946 and in 1958 an Academician. In 1945 she was awarded a Stalin Prize.

Kochina's major interest is the theory of filtration. She has solved many important problems, which are associated with the movement of ground waters and oil in porous media. In 1952, she wrote a monograph on the "Theory of Ground Water Movement," summarizing the Soviet work in the field of filtration. She has also worked in dynamic meteorology, stability of plates, and theory of tides in basins. Kochina was the editor of the first collection of the works of Kovalevskaya, the Russian mathematician, and published articles of Kovalevskaya's life and work.

Bibliography:
Some Problems of Flat Moving Ground Waters. Moscow-Leningrad: 1942.
Life and Works of S. V. Kovalevskaya, 1850-1891 (Centennial since the date of birth). Moscow-Leningrad: 1950.

Biography:
To the 50th Anniversary since the date of birth of P. Ya. Polubarinova-Kochina. Priklad. Mat. i Mekh., 1949, #3.

Office: Institute of Mechanics of USSR Academy of Sciences
              Leningradskii Prospekt, 7
              Moscow, USSR
Residence: Leninskii Prospekt, 13
              Moscow, USSR
Telephone: V2 46 79

KOLMOGOROV, ANDREI NIKOLAEVICH (Mathematician)

A. N. Kolmogorov was born April 25, 1903. In 1925 he graduated from Moscow University where he was a student of N. N. Luzin (1883-1950), Professor at the University. Kolmogorov became a professor there in 1931. In 1939 he was elected an Academician of the U.S.S.R. Academy of Sciences. He was awarded in 1941 a Stalin Prize.

Kolmogorov's scientific works began in the field of the theory of a real variable, where he worked on the convergence of trigonometric series, the theory of measure, generalization of the concept of the integral and general theories of operation on sets. Returning in 1956 to the theory of functions, Kolmogorov obtained important results on the representability of functions of a number of variables by superposition of functions with a smaller number of variables. Kolmogorov made contributions to constructive logic; in topology he created the theory of the so-called "upper" or V-homologies. Kolmogorov also worked on the theory of the approximation of functions and functional analysis. His more outstanding works are concerned with the theory of probability, where he, together with A. Ya. Khinchin, began from 1925 to apply the methods of the theory of functions of a real variable. This permitted the solution of some difficult problems and construction of a system of axiomatic foundation to the theory of probability (1933). From the beginning of the 1930's, analytical methods which were found essential for constructing the theory of the Markov processes with continuous time predominate in the works of Kolmogorov. Later he developed the theory of stationary, accidental processes, which led to results used in automatic control, and to the establishment (together with a group of students) of a theory of "branching," accidental processes. Kolmogorov worked together with A. M. Obukhov on the statistical theory of turbulence; he also investigated the theory of fire, statistical methods of controlling mass production, the theory of conveying information along communication channels. He is interested in the teaching of mathematics in secondary schools. Among his students are:

A. I. Mal'tsev, S. M. Nikol'skii, I. M. Gel'fond, B. V. Gnedenko,
A. M. Obukhov, M. A. Millionshchikov, E. B. Dynkin, Yu. V.
Prokhorov.

Bibliography:
Main Concepts on the Theory of Probability. Moscow-
Leningrad: 1936.

and P. S. Aleksandrov. Introduction to the Theory of
Functions of a Real Variable, 3rd ed. Moscow-Leningrad:
1938.

and P. S. Aleksandrov. Algebra, Part 1. Moscow: 1939.

and B. V. Gnedenko. Assymptotic Distribution for Sums of
Independent Accidental Quantities. Moscow-Leningrad:
1949.

and S. V. Fomin. Elements of the Theory of Functions and
Functional Analysis. V. II, Measure. The Lebesque Integral.
Hilbert Space. Trans. from 1st (1960) Russian ed. by Hyman
Kamel & Horace Komm. Rochester, N. Y.: Graylock Press,
1961.

and M. Arato, Ya. G. Sinai. Evaluating parameters of a
complex stationary Gauss-Markow process. Doklady Akad.
Nauk S.S.S.R. $\underline{146}$, #4, 747-50 (1962).

Biography:
P. A. Aleksandrov and A. Ya. Khinchin. Andrei Nikolaevich
Kolmogorov (On the 50th Anniversary since the date of
birth). Uspekhi Mat. Nauk, 1953, $\underline{8}$, #3 (contains bibliography
of the works of Kolmogorov).

On the 50th Anniversary of Andrei Nikolaevich Kolmogorov.
Izvest. Akad. Nauk S.S.S.R., Ser. Mat., 1953, $\underline{17}$,#3 (contains
bibliography of the works of Kolmogorov).

Office: Department of Mathematics
              Moscow University
              Moscow, USSR
Residence: Leninskiye gory, sekt. "L"
              Moscow, USSR
Telephone: B9 30 82

KOLOSOV, NIKOLAI GRIGOR'EVICH (Histologist)
    N. G. Kolosov was born April 29, 1897. In 1924 he graduated
from and continued to work at Kazan' University. He was made
professor at Stalingrad Institute in 1940, and in 1945-1950 at
Saratov Medical Institute. In 1950 he began work at the Institute of Physiology of the U.S.S.R. Academy of Sciences. He became a professor, in 1953, at the Leningrad University. In
1945 he was elected a Corresponding Member of the U.S.S.R.

Academy of Medical Sciences and in 1953 Corresponding Member of the U.S.S.R. Academy of Sciences.

Kolosov is a specialist in the area of neurohistology. He has been studying the structure of the autonomic nervous system and its interactions with the central nervous system; he has been an advocate of the neuron structure theory of the nervous system. He studied in detail the double innervation of the alimentary canal and pelvic organs. Kolosov has also worked on the afferent innervation of the human alimentary canal.

In recent years he has studied afferent innervation of vegetative ganglia and vegetative neurons.

Bibliography:
Materials on the autonomic innervation of the alimentary canal of some vertebrates. Works of the Tatar Institute of Theoretical and Clinical Medicine, 1935, #2.

Some Chapters on the Morphology of the Autonomic Nervous System. Saratov: 1948.

Innervation of Internal Organs and the Cardiac Vascular System. Moscow-Leningrad: 1954.

Afferent Innervation of the Human Alimentary Canal. Moscow-Leningrad: 1962.

Office: Leningrad University
                 Leningrad, USSR

KONDRAT'EV, VIKTOR NIKOLAEVICH (Physical Chemist)

V. N. Kondrat'ev was born February 1, 1902. He graduated from the Leningrad Polytechnical Institute in 1924 and then worked at the Physico-Technical Institute of the U.S.S.R. Academy of Sciences. In 1931, he began working at the Institute of Chemical Physics of the U.S.S.R. Academy of Sciences. Also he has been professor at the Moscow Engineering Physics Institute. In 1948 he became a member of the Communist Party of the Soviet Union. From 1943 to 1953 he was a Corresponding Member of the U.S.S.R. Academy of Sciences, and in 1953 he became an Academician. In 1944 he received a Stalin Prize.

Kondrat'ev has worked in chemical kinetics, molecular spectroscopy and structure, and photochemistry. He studied the elementary processes during chemical transformation. Also he developed methods of determining concentrations and reaction velocity of free atoms and radicals, which are intermediate in photochemical reactions and combustion processes. Kondrat'ev showed that the velocity of an over-all reaction is

determined by the speed of reactions of free radicals whose
concentration is considerably greater than at equilibrium. In
the field of molecular structure, Kondrat'ev with aid of the
spectroscopic method, determined the heats of disassociation
and established a geometric structure of a series of molecules.
He also worked out an optical method for studying unstable conditions of molecules and photo-chemical dissociation of molecules.

In 1961, Kondrat'ev was elected to the bureau, the executive
committee and editorial board of the International Union of
Pure and Applied Chemistry.

Bibliography:

N. N. Semenov, Yu. B. Khariton. Electronic Chemistry.
Moscow-Leningrad: 1927.

Photochemistry. Moscow-Leningrad: 1933.

and M. El'yashevich. Elementary Processes of the Exchange
of Energy in Gases. Moscow-Leningrad: 1933.

Free Hydroxyl. Moscow: 1939.

Spectroscopic Study of Chemical Gas Reactions. Moscow-
Leningrad: 1944.

Structure of Atoms and Molecules. Moscow-Leningrad:
1946.

Energy levels of atomic nuclei. Uspekhi Fiz. Nauk, 1949, 38,
#2.

Utilization of Tagged Atoms in the Study of the Mechanism of
Chemical Reactions, Moscow, 1955. (Reports presented by
the U.S.S.R. at the International Conference on Peaceful
Uses of Atomic Energy, Geneva, August 8-20, 1955). Moscow: 1956.

History of the Development of Kinetics of Chemical Reactions. Questions of History of Natural Science and Techniques, 2nd ed. Moscow: 1956.

Ways of Development of the Theory of a Chemical Process
(Homogeneous Reactions). Vestnik Akad. Nauk S.S.S.R.,
1956, #5.

and N. M. Emanuel. Chain reactions and processes of burning and explosions. Uspekhi Khim., 1956, 25, #4.

Elementary Chemical Processes. Leningrad: 1936.

Biography:

N. Ya. Buben, V. V. Voevodskii, N. D. Sokolov. Scientific
Activity of V. N. Kondrat'ev. Uspekhi Khim., 1952, #8.

Kondrat'ev, Viktor Nikolaevich. Vestnik Akad. Nauk S.S.S.R.,
1953, #12.

175   KONOBEEVSKII

Office: Institute of Chemical Physics of USSR Academy of
           Sciences
           Vorob'evskoye Shosse, 2
           Moscow, USSR
Residence: Leninskii Prospekt, 30
           Moscow, USSR
Telephone: B2 21 14

KONOBEEVSKII, SERGEI TIKHONOVICH (Physicist)

S. T. Konobeevskii was born April 26, 1890. In 1913 he
finished at Moscow University. From 1919-23, he taught at the
University of National Economy in Moscow. He worked, in
1923-1929, at the All-Union Technical Institute, and in 1929-
1941, at the State Institute of Dyed Metals. In 1926 he began
teaching at Moscow University where, in 1935, he became a
professor. In 1948 he started work at various institutions of
the U.S.S.R. Academy of Sciences. Since 1946 he has been a
Corresponding Member of the U.S.S.R. Academy of Sciences.
In 1948 he became a member of the Communist Party of the
Soviet Union.

Konobeevskii's main work deals with X-ray-structural investigation of metals and alloys and their structural change during plastic deformation, tempering, and phase transformations.
He developed a theory of aging of alloys, the decomposition of
solid solutions, and the effect of radiation on materials.

Bibliography:
   Crystallization of metals during their conversion in a solid
   state. Izvest. Akad. Nauk S.S.S.R., Ser. Khim., 1937, #5,
   1909-1944.
   The theory of phase conversions, 1-3. Zhur. Exptl. i Teor.
   Fiz. 1943, 13, #6, 11-12.
   Solid phases of a variable composition and basic consider-
   ations of their structure. Bulletin of Physico-Chemical
   Analysis, 1948, 16, #4.
   Effect of radiation on the structure and properties of sepa-
   rating materials. Research in Geology, Chemistry and
   Metallurgy. Moscow: 1955 (Report of the Soviet delegation
   at the International Conference on the Peaceful Use of
   Atomic Energy, Geneva, 1955).
   The nature of radiative disturbances in separating materials.
   Atomic Energy, 1956, #2.

Office: Department of Physics
           Moscow University
           Moscow, USSR

KONSTANTINOV, BORIS PAVLOVICH (Physicist)

B. P. Konstantinov was born July 6, 1910. He graduated in
1929 from the Mechanical-Mathematical Faculty of the Leningrad Polytechnic Institute. Beginning in 1930 he worked at the
Leningrad Electro-Physical Institute as well as at some other
scientific research institutes. As of 1961, he has been Director
of the Leningrad Physico-Technical Institute of the U.S.S.R. Academy of Sciences where he has worked since 1940. In 1947 he
became a professor at Leningrad Polytechnic Institute. He was
elected Corresponding Member of the U.S.S.R. Academy of
Sciences in 1953 and in 1960 Academician.

Konstantinov's main investigations are theoretical and applied acoustics and physical chemistry. In 1934 he developed a
quantitative theory of the sound of a propeller. He investigated
in 1936 the equation of non-linear acoustics. In 1935-43 he
studied auto-oscillary phenomena and the process of sound formation in musical instruments and in sound signaling devices,
non-planar waves in wind instruments, and resonant absorption.
He also studied the influence of viscosity and thermal conductivity on the propagation and absorption of sound in an organic
medium. Konstantinov obtained results important for measurement in acoustics.

Bibliography:

On several applications of the continuity equation of energy
in acoustics. Zhur. Eksptl. i Teoret. Fiz., 1936, 6, #9.
On the auto-oscillation and sound formation of the tongue of
an accordion. Zhur. Tekh. Fiz., 1939, 9, #20.
On absorption of sound waves during reflection from a solid.
Zhur. Tekh. Fiz., 1939, 9, #3.
On the attenuation of sound in a room with hard walls and on
the diffusion coefficient of sound absorption. Zhur. Tekh.
Fiz., 1939, 9, #5.
and L. V. Rotova. Role of longitudinal mixing in exchange
columns for separation of isotopes. Doklady Akad. Nauk
135, #4, 896-98 (1960).

Office: Leningrad Physico-Technical Institute
Sosnovka, 2
Lesnoy, Leningrad, USSR

KOROLEV, SERGEI PAVLOVICH (Mechanics Specialist)

S. P. Korolev was born December 30, 1906. In 1930 he
graduated from the Moscow Higher Technical School. He has
been a member of the Communist Party of the Soviet Union

since 1953. In 1953 he was elected a Corresponding Member of
the U.S.S.R. Academy of Sciences, and in 1958 an Academician.
The basic works of Korolev are in mechanics.

Office: USSR Academy of Sciences
               Leninskii Prospekt, 14
               Moscow, USSR

KOROTKOV, ALEKSEI ANDREEVICH (Organic Chemist)

A. A. Korotov was born February 25, 1910. He graduated in
1938 from the Leningrad Chemico-Technological Institute.
From 1931-45 he worked in synthetic rubber plants. In 1945 he
began working at the All-Union Scientific Research Institute of
Synthetic Rubber and in 1953 at the Institute of High Molecular
Compounds of the U.S.S.R. Academy of Sciences. Korotov has
been a member of the Communist Party of the Soviet Union
since 1942. In 1958 he became a Corresponding Member of the
U.S.S.R. Academy of Sciences.

Korotkov is concerned with reprocessing by-products from
production of synthetic rubber, synthesis based on ethylene
oxide, the study of production of isoprene, and the catalytic
polymerization of vinyl compounds and bi-ethylene hydrocarbons. He worked out a method for obtaining a polyisoprene
synthetic rubber, with properties similar to those of natural
rubber.

Bibliography:
> and L. B. Trukhmanova. Question of the nature of action of
> complex catalysts. Doklady Akad. Nauk S.S.S.R., 1957, 117,
> #4.
> and M. P. Burova. Determining the structure of rubber by
> the method of infra-red spectroscopy. Izvest Akad. Nauk
> S.S.S.R., Otdel Khim. Nauk, 14, #4, 1950.
> and K. B. Piotrovskii, D. P. Feringer. Influence of the
> microstructure of isoprene on its properties. Doklady Akad.
> Nauk S.S.S.R., 1956, 110, #1.

Office: Institute of High Molecular Compounds of USSR
               Academy of Sciences
               Birzhevoy Prospekt, 6
               Leningrad, USSR

KORSHAK, VASILII VLADIMIROVICH (Organic Chemist)

V. V. Korshak was born January 9, 1909. He was a student
of P. P. Shorygin (1881-1939, organic chemist). He graduated
in 1931 from the Moscow Chemico-Technological Institute and
in 1942 became a professor at this Institute. In 1935 he also

started working at the Institute of Organic Chemistry of the
U.S.S.R. Academy of Sciences. In 1954 he began work at the
Institute of Organo-Elemental Compounds of the U.S.S.R. Acade-
my of Sciences. Korshak has been a member of the Communist
Party of the Soviet Union since 1940. In 1953 he was elected a
Corresponding Member of the U.S.S.R. Academy of Sciences.
He was awarded Stalin Prizes in 1949 and in 1951.

Korshak's main works deal with the chemistry of high molecular compounds. He investigated the process of polycondensation of dicarboxylic acids with diamines and glycols, and also
dihalide derivatives with aromatic hydrocarbons. He worked
out a theory of linear polycondensation. He proposed a classification and nomenclature for high molecular compounds. A part
of Korshak's work deals with the mechanism of the Friedel-
Crafts-reaction and with methods for synthesis of various organic substances.

In August 1956, Korshak visited the United States to attend
the Sixth International Conference on Coordination Compounds,
New York.

Bibliography:
and G. S. Kolesnikov. Tetraethyl Lead. Preface by A. N.
Nesmeyanov. Moscow-Leningrad: 1946.
and S. R. Rafikov. Synthesis and Investigation of High Molecular Compounds. Moscow-Leningrad: 1949.
Chemistry of High Molecular Compounds. Moscow-
Leningrad: 1950.
General Methods of Synthesis of High Molecular Compounds.
Methods of High Molecular Organic Chemistry, 1. Moscow:
1953.
and D. Ya. Tsvankin, S. P. Krukovskii. Investigation of poly-
ethelene terepthalate ("lavsan") coating with grafted polystyrene. Doklady Akad. Nauk S.S.S.R. 146, #6, 1347-48
(1962).

Office: Institute of Organo-Elemental Compounds of USSR
              Academy of Sciences
              Leninskii Prospekt, 31
              Moscow, USSR
Residence: Novopeschanaya, 25
              Moscow, USSR
Telephone: D7 19 30

KORZHINSKII, DMITRII SERGEIVICH (Geographer and
    Petrographer)
D. S. Korzhinskii, son of S. I. Korzhinskii (1861-1900,

Russian botanist) was born September 13, 1899. After graduating from the Leningrad Mining Institute in 1926, he worked on the Geological Committee. Then, until 1937, he was with the Central Scientific Research Geological Survey Institute. In 1937 he began working in the Institute of Geology at the U.S.S.R. Academy of Sciences, and in 1956 in the Institute of Geology for Ore Deposits, Petrography, Mineralogy and Geochemistry of the U.S.S.R. Academy of Scientists. Also during these years, 1929 to 1940, he taught at the Leningrad Mining Institute. Korzhinskii became a Corresponding Member of the U.S.S.R. Academy of Sciences in 1943, and in 1953 an Academician. He was awarded in 1946, a Stalin Prize, in 1949, the A. P. Karpinskii Prize by the U.S.S.R. Academy of Sciences, and in 1958, a Lenin Prize.

Korzhinskii studied pre-Cambrian crystalline rock formations and associated mineral resources of Yakutiya and Eastern Siberia, Skarn ore beds of the Urals, and Central Asia. His main works are devoted to physico-chemical analysis of the process of mineral formation (mainly the metamorphic and metasomatic processes). He has studied the thermodynamics of natural systems and methods of analyzing mineral paragenesis.

As of November 1962, he has been made chief editor of the journal, Geology of Ore Deposits.

Bibliography:
Factors of Mineral Balance and Mineralogical Facies of the Depths. Moscow: 1940 (Works of the Mining Institute of the U.S.S.R. Academy of Sciences, #12.)
Bimetasomatic, Phlogopite and Lazurite Deposits of the Archean Baikal Territory. Moscow: 1940 (Works of the Mining Institute of the U.S.S.R. Academy of Sciences, #29.)
The Petrology of Tur'inski Skarn Copper Beds. Moscow: 1948 (Works of the Mining Institute of the U.S.S.R. Academy of Sciences, #68.)
Sketch of metasomatic processes. Main Problems in the Study of Magmatogene Ore Beds, 1955.
Physico-Chemical Basis in Analyzing Mineral Paragenesis. Moscow: 1957.

Biography:
Korzhinskii, Dmitrii Sergeivich. Vestnik Akad. Nauk S.S.S.R., 1954, #2.

Office: Institute of Geology of Mineral Deposits, Petrography, Mineralogy and Geochemistry
Staromonetnyy Pereulok, 35
Moscow, USSR

Residence: Leninskii Prospekt, 13
          Moscow, USSR
Telephone: V2 42 55

KOSTENKO, MIKHAIL POLIEVKTOVICH (Electrical Engineer)
     M. P. Kostenko was born December 16, 1889. Before gradu-
ating in 1918 from the Electrical Engineering Institute of the
Petersburg Polytechnic Institute, Kostenko had been banished
for a period to a remote corner of the Urals by the Tsarist
Government for having participated in student revolutionary
demonstrations. After graduating with distinction, he remained
at the Institute to prepare for teaching activities. In 1930, he
was appointed to the Chair of Electrical Machines in the M. I.
Kalinin Polytechnic Institute. More than 400 electrical engineers (specialists in constructing electrical machines) have
graduated from there under his direction. Kostenko was Chief
Electrician of the Kharkov Electromechanical Plant, and, in
1942-44, professor in the Central Asiatic Industrial Institute
(Tashkent). He is Director of the Institute of Electromechanics
of the U.S.S.R. Academy of Sciences. He has consulted and
taught in Rumania, Hungary, Bulgaria, and Poland. He was a
delegate to the Paris Conference on Large-Scale Electrical
High-Tension Systems. In 1939 he was elected a Corresponding
Member of the U.S.S.R. Academy of Sciences and in 1953 an
Academician. He is an Honored Scientist of the Uzbek S.S.R.
He was a Deputy of the Supreme Soviet of the U.S.S.R., fifth
convocation. In 1949 and 1951, Kostenko was awarded Stalin
Prizes and in 1958 a Lenin Prize.
     Under the Lenin Plan, GOELRO (State Plan for Electrifi-
cation of Soviet Russia), Kostenko was one of the originators
(and is chief) of the office for new designs at the "Electrosila"
Plant, where he worked from 1929-30, and where he has been
consultant since 1932. In this connection, the office designed
four of the eight generators for the then new Volkhov hydroelectric power plant. Their success assured the beginning of
Soviet manufacture of heavy power machinery construction.
Similarly, Kostenko has participated in the development of all
the basic electrical machines produced in Russia: generators
for plants such as the Dneprovskaya, Ribinskaya, Uglichskaya,
and the Volga Cascade. He was consulted in the manufacture of
motors for the atomic ice-breaker "Lenin," and for generators
of the Kuibishev and Stalingrad power stations. He is a member
of the technical council of Electrosila.

At the Institute of Electromechanics of the Academy of Sciences of the U.S.S.R., located in laboratories in a private residence on the Palace Embankment of the Neva [Leningrad], Kostenko works on the combined operation of AC and DC transmission lines and the automatic regulation of superpower generators. The laboratories contain models of the Stalingrad power stations and of the future Volga, Krasnoyar, Bukhtarin, and Bratskaya plants. Stalingrad will transmit AC and DC simultaneously; AC to Moscow and DC to the Don Basin. The modelling methods are used there to work out the electrification of the main Russian railroad lines under the Seven Year Plan. Kostenko is working on problems of the utilization of alternating current electric traction for this purpose.

Kostenko's basic works are concerned with the theory of electrical machines and methods for their experimental study and planning. He gave a theory of transformers, polyphase asynchronous and commutating machines; worked out an original scheme of commutative generators for alternating current. He has been concerned with electric traction using alternating current, electrodynamic modelling of energy systems in connection with the stability and reliability of the operation of distant electric transmission, and with the rectification of alternating current. He has written a monograph on the universal transformer. In all, he has written over 100 scientific works, which have become indispensable manuals for Soviet engineers, especially his Commutators, printed a quarter of a century ago.

As of 1961, Kostenko was a Member of the Presidium of the U.S.S.R. Academy of Sciences.

Bibliography:

Alternating Current Commutator Machines, Part 1. Leningrad: 1933.

Electric Machines (part 1-2). Moscow-Leningrad: 1944-49.

and others. Electromagnetic Processes in Systems with Powerful Rectifiers. Moscow-Leningrad: 1946.

and E. D. Treivish. Transformer and Electric Machine Designing in Experimental Research in Stabilizing Parallel Work of Electric Plants. Trudy Lenin. politekh. inst., 1946, #1.

Electrodynamic model for research in stability. Electricity, 1950, #9.

Designing electrical equipment in irradiation of parallel stability of energy systems for long-distance transmission. Izvest. Akad. Nauk S.S.S.R., Otdel. Tekh. Nauk, 1953, #12.

and A. E. Alekseev. Turbogenerators. Leningrad-Moscow: 1933.

Biography:
  Kostenko Mikhail Polievktovich. Vestnik Akad. Nauk
  S.S.S.R., 1954, #3, 52.
  Electric machine-building. Trudy Lenin. politekh. inst.,
  1953, #3. (This issue is dedicated to Prof. M. P. Kostenko
  in connection with his 30th year of scientific activity).
Office: Institute of Electromechanics of USSR Academy of
              Sciences
              Dvortsovaya Naberezhnaya, 18
              Leningrad, USSR

KHOSTENKO, MIKHAIL VLADIMIROVICH (Power Specialist)
  In June 1962, M. V. Khostenko was elected Corresponding
Member of the U.S.S.R. Academy of Sciences.

KOSYGIN, YURII ALEKSANDROVICH (Geologist)
  Yu. A. Kosygin was born January 22, 1911. After graduating
from Moscow Oil Institute in 1931, he worked in the oil industry.
From 1935 to 1941, he worked in the Institute of Fuel Minerals
of the U.S.S.R. Academy of Sciences and at the Moscow Oil
Institute. He began working, in 1945, at the Geological Institute
of the U.S.S.R. Academy of Sciences. Since 1958 he has been a
Corresponding Member of the U.S.S.R. Academy of Sciences.
  Kosygin has studied the tectonics of platforms and foredeeps,
mainly in oil-bearing regions. His works on salt tectonics
facilitated recognition of regularities in arrangement of oil deposits on salt domes. He has also studied oil-bearing deposits
and the presence of gas in various regions of the U.S.S.R. He
took part in compiling tectonic maps of the U.S.S.R.
  In May 1960, Kosygin visited the U. S. to participate in geo-
logical studies at the U. S. Geological Survey, Denver, Colo-
rado.
Bibliography:
  Oil Deposits of Turkmen S.S.R. Moscow-Leningrad-Novo-
  Sibirsk: 1933.
  Salt Tectonics of Platform Territories. Moscow-Leningrad:
  1956.
  Basis of Tectonics of Oil-Bearing Territories. Moscow-
  Leningrad: 1952.
  Tectonics of Oil-Bearing Territories, 1. Moscow: 1958.

Office: Institute of Geology of USSR Academy of Sciences
Pyzhevskii Pereulok, 7
Moscow, USSR

KOTEL'NIKOV, VLADIMIR ALEKSANDROVICH (Radio
Engineer)
V. A. Kotel'nikov was born August 24, 1908. After graduating
from Moscow Institute of Energetics, he worked at the Radio-
engineering and Electronics Institute of the U.S.S.R. Academy
of Sciences and became the Director in 1954. Since 1948 he
has been a member of the Communist Party of the Soviet Union.
In 1953 Kotel'nikov was elected an Academician of the U.S.S.R.
Academy of Sciences. He received Stalin Prizes in 1943 and in
1946.
Kotel'nikov has been concerned with errors in radio reception and with the development of radio communication apparatus. He introduced (1946) the concept of potential error stability as characteristic of given method of transmission. The
method of analysis suggested by him has had wide application
and great significance for the development of new methods of
radio communication. Under his direction, a multi-channel
telephon-telegraphic line of radiocommunication on a single
frequency side band was worked out.
Bibliography:
and A. M. Nikolaev. Foundations of Radio-Engineering. I,
Moscow: 1950; II, Moscow: 1954.
On the traffic capacity of the ether and wire in communication. Materials for the First All-Union Congress on
Questions of the Technical Reconstruction of Communi-
cations and of the Improvement of Weak Industry. Mos-
cow: 1933.
Problems of error free radio communication, Radio-
Engineering Collection. Moscow-Leningrad: 1947.
The Theory of Potential Freedom from Error (dissertation).
Moscow-Leningrad: 1956.
and V. M. Dubrovich, M. D. Kislick, E. B. Korenberg, V. P.
Minashin, V. A. Morozov, N. I. Nikitin, G. M. Petrov, O. N.
Rzhiga, A. M. Shakhovskii. Radar observation of Venus.
Doklady Akad. Nauk S.S.S.R. 145, #5, 1035-39 (1962).
Biography:
Kotel'nikov Vladimir Aleksandrovich. Vestnik Akad. Nauk,
1954, #4.

Office: Institute of Radio Engineering and Electronics,
              USSR Academy of Sciences
              Mokhovaya Ulitsa 11, K-9
              Moscow, USSR
Residence: 1-aya Cheremushkinskaya, 3
              Moscow, USSR
Telephone: B7 25 11

KOTON, MIKHAIL MIKHAILOVICH (Chemist)

M. M. Koton was born in 1908. In 1935 he graduated from
the Leningrad State University. In 1934-36, he worked at the
Leningrad Institute of High Pressures. He was, from 1936-39,
at the Leningrad Pediatric Medical Institute, where in 1946, he
became a professor, and then chairman of the Department of
General and Analytical Chemistry. In 1937-52, he worked at
the U.S.S.R. Academy of Sciences Leningrad Physico-Technical
Institute. In 1952, he became Laboratory Chief at the U.S.S.R.
Academy of Sciences Leningrad Institute of High Molecular
Weight Compounds, where he was made deputy Director in
1959, and Director in 1960. From 1952-60, he was a professor
at the Leningrad Polytechnical Institute. In 1960 he was elected
a Corresponding Member of the U.S.S.R. Academy of Sciences.

Koton's main works are concerned with the chemistry of
organic, metallo organic, and high molecular weight compounds.
Bibliography:

and N. A. Glukhov, A. N. Baburina, L. M. Shcherbakova.
Synthesis and polymerization of β-oxides. I. Synthesis and
polymerization of 3, 3-bis (chloromethyl) oxyacyclobutane.
Zhur. Priklad. Khim. 33, 182-5 (1960). C. A. 54, 10988b
(1960).

and T. M. Kiseleva. Synthesis of polyorganostannoxanes.
Doklady Akad. Nauk S.S.S.R. 130, 86-7 (1960). C. A. 54,
10839c (1960).

and T. M. Kiseleva. Synthesis of polymerizable unsaturated
organomercury compounds. Doklady Akad. Nauk S.S.S.R.
131, 1072-3 (1960). C. A. 54, 20936h (1960).

and T. M. Kiseleva, F. S. Florinskii. Mercurated styrenes.
Izvest. Akad. Nauk S.S.S.R., Otdel. Khim. Nauk, 948 (1959).
C. A. 54, 1378f (1960).

and T. M. Kiseleva, N. P. Zapevalova. Reactivity of unsaturated compounds of tin and lead. Zhur. Obshchei Khim. 30,
186-90 (1960). C. A. 54, 22436e (1960).

and K. A. Sivograkova, Z. D. Tolstikova, E. N. Eremina. Preparation of large-surface scintillators from polymeric materials. Platicheskie Massy, #2, 48-52 (1960). C. A. 54, 25965e (1960).

and N. A. Adrova, V. N. Andreev, Yu. N. Panov, N. S. Musalev. Optical and scintillation characteristics of some oxadiazoles. Optika i Spektroskopiya 7, #1, 128-9 (1959). C. A. 54, 23816g (1960).

and N. A. Adrova. Synthesis and polymerization of 3-vinyl-2, 5-diphenylfuran. Vysokomolekulyarnye Soedineniya 2, 408-10 (1960). C. A. 54, 24629b (1960).

and S. E. Bresler, A. T. Os'minskaya, A. G. Popov, N. N. Savitskaya. The increase of thermostability of polymers by cyclization in macromolecular chains by partial decomposition. Vysokomolekulyarnye Soedineniya 1, #7, 1070-3 (1959). C. A. 54, 15998c (1960).

and A. F. Dokukina. Synthesis of chloro-substituted dimethylstyrenes. Zhur. Obshchei Khim. 29, 2201-4 (1959). C. A. 54, 10904i (1960).

and A. F. Dokukina. Relation between structure and polymerizability of substituted styrenes. II. Polymerization of tri- and tetra-substituted halomethylstyrenes. Vysokomolekulyarnye Soedineniya 1, 1129-32 (1959). C. A. 54, 19014h (1960).

and P. A. El'tsova, O. I. Mineeva, O. L. Surnina. Polymerization of vinyl derivatives of biphenyl, diphenyl oxide, and diphenyl sulfide. Vsyokomolekulyarnye Soedineniya 1, 1369-73 (1959). C. A. 54, 17954c (1960).

and Yu. N. Panov, N. A. Adrova. Optical characteristics of compounds of the oxazole, oxadiazole, and furan series. Optika i Spektroskopiya 7, #1, 29-34 (1959). C. A. 54, 23814i (1960).

and N. P. Zapelvalova. Synthesis and polymerization of nuclear methoxy substituted styrenes. III. Synthesis and polymerization of trimethoxystyrenes. Zhur. Obshchei Khim. 29, 2900-5 (1959). C. A. 54, 12036c (1960).

and I. V. Andreeva, D. F. Andreev, E. M. Rogozina. Polyacrolene complexes with salts of heavy metals. Doklady Akad. Naul S.S.S.R. 139, #6, 1372-74 (1961).

and I. V. Andreeva, P. F. Andreev, L. G. Danilov, E. M. Rogozina. Reaction between an aqueous solution of polyacrolein and inorganic salts. Doklady Akad. Nauk S.S.S.R. 146, #3, 608-610 (1962).

and F. S. Florinskii. Synthesis of polymerizing thallium-
organic compounds. Doklady Akad. Nauk S.S.S.R. 146, #4,
820-21 (1962).

Office: Institute of High Molecular Weight Compounds of
USSR Academy of Sciences
Birzhevoy Prospekt, 6
Leningrad, USSR

KOVALENKOV, VALENTIN IVANOVICH (Electrical Engineer)

V. I. Kovalenkov was born March 25, 1884. He graduated
from Petersburg Electro-Technical Institute in 1909, and from
Petersburg University in 1911. From 1940 to 1948 he worked
at the Institute of Automation and Remote Control of the
U.S.S.R. Academy of Sciences. In 1946 to 1956, he was Director of the U.S.S.R. Academy of Sciences Laboratory in Solving Problems in Wire Communications. He was awarded a
Stalin Prize in 1941, and was awarded the title Honored Scientist of the R.S.F.S.R. in 1935. He holds the rank of Major
General in the Technical Engineering Service, and has been a
member of the Communist Party of the Soviet Union since 1945.
He was elected, in 1939, to the U.S.S.R. Academy of Sciences as
a Corresponding Member.

The main works of Kovalenkov are concerned with the theory
of wire transmission of communication, to analysis of processes in them and to analyzing of magnetic chains. In addition, Kovalenkov worked on the origination of telephone translation (from 1909; first Soviet translation of the system of
Kovalenkov was established in 1922 on the telephone line of
Moscow-Petrograd). He has a series of inventions in the area
of electrotechnics and sound movies.

Bibliography:
Theory of Transmission in Electro-communication Lines,
I-II. Moscow: 1937-38.
Basis of Theory on Magnetic Chains, and Its Use in Analysis
of Relay Schemes. Moscow-Leningrad: 1940.
Electro-magnetic Processes Established Along Wire Lines.
Moscow-Leningrad: 1945.

Biography:
V. S. Kulebakin. V. I. Kovalenkov. Journal of Communi-
cation, 1954, #4.
Corresponding Member of the U.S.S.R. Academy of Sciences,
V. I. Kovalenkov. Avtomat. i Telemekh., 1954, 15, #3.

Corresponding Member of the U.S.S.R. Academy of Sciences,
V. I. Kovalenkov (On the 70th Anniversary since the date of
birth). Electricity, 1954, #4.
Office: Laboratory in Solving Problems in Wire Communi-
                 cations, USSR Academy of Sciences
                 Moscow, USSR

KOVALEV, NIKOLAI NIKOLAEVICH (Hydroturbine Specialist)

N. N. Kovalev was born February 22, 1908. After graduating
from Leningrad Technological Institute in 1933, he worked at
the Leningrad Metal Plant until 1959. From 1945 to 1959 he
was the Chief Constructor of hydroturbines at this plant. He
also taught at the Leningrad Polytechnic Institute. In 1959 he
supervised the hydroturbine section in the Central Scientific
Research Steam Turbine Institute. Kovalev has been a member
of the Communist Party of the Soviet Union since 1942. In
1953, he was elected a Corresponding Member of the U.S.S.R.
Academy of Sciences. He received, in 1946 and 1951, State
Prizes; in 1957, Hero of Socialist Labor award; in 1959, a
Lenin Prize; and three medals.

The major works of Kovalev are devoted to designing hydroturbines. Under his leadership, swing-blade hydroturbines
were built for hydroelectric power plants, among them the
Volga and Dnieper. After World War II, he supervised the construction of hydroturbines for Mingechaur, Tsimlyanskaya and
Kuibishev hydroelectric power stations.

Bibliography:
        and others. Exploitation of Hydroturbines. Leningrad-
        Moscow: 1941.
        Contemporary condition and main questions of the future de-
        velopment of hydroturbines. Boiler-Turbine Construction,
        1950, #4.
        Hydroturbines. Moscow: 1961.
Office: Polzunov Technical Institute
                 Konstantinogradskaya, 16
                 Leningrad S-167, USSR

KOVAL'SKII, ALEKSANDR ALEKSEEVICH (Physical Chemist)

A. A. Koval'skii was born September 10, 1906. He graduated
in 1930 from the Leningrad Polytechnic Institute. He had been
working since 1929 at the Institute of Chemical Physics of the
U.S.S.R. Academy of Sciences and in 1947 was made professor
there; in 1957 he became Director of the Institute of Chemical
Kinetics and combustion of the Siberian branch of the U.S.S.R.

KOVDA

Academy of Sciences. Koval'skii has been a member of the Communist Party of the Soviet Union since 1949. In 1958 he was elected a Corresponding Member of the U.S.S.R. Academy of Sciences.

Koval'skii's major works are in the field of kinetics and chemical reaction and nuclear physics. His investigations on the study of upper and lower limits of ignition constituted an important experimental base for establishing the theory of branching chain reactions. He studied the mechanism of a number of heterogeneous catalytic reactions. In the field of nuclear physics he conducted investigations on high energy particles.

Bibliography:

and M. L. Bogoyavlenskaya. Initiation of homogeneous reaction in gas by solid catalysts. Zhur. Fiz. Khim., 1946, 20, #11.

and V. I. Gol'danskii and others. Cross sections of nonelastic interaction of neutrons with energy of 120 and 380 million electron-volts with nuclei. Doklady Akad. Nauk S.S.S.R., 1956, 106, #2.

Office: Institute of Chemical Kinetics and Combustion Novosibirsk, Siberia

KOVDA, VIKTOR ABRAMOVICH (Soil Scientist)

V. A. Kovda was born December 29, 1904. He graduated in 1927 from Kuban Agricultural Institute in Krasnodar. In 1931 he became a scientific worker at the Soil Institute of the U.S.S.R. Academy of Sciences. He was professor at Moscow University in 1939-1941 and again in 1953. He was Director of the Institute of Botany and Pedology of the Uzbek branch of the U.S.S.R. Academy of Sciences in 1941-1942, and in 1943-1948 he taught at Moscow Hydromeliorative Institute. Kovda has been a member of the Communist Party of the Soviet Union since 1927. In 1953 he was elected a Corresponding Member of the U.S.S.R. Academy of Sciences. He was an Honored Scientist of the Uzbek S.S.R. in 1943, and in 1951 he received a Stalin Prize.

Kovda's main research interest is the study of soils of the Southern regions of the U.S.S.R., the solonetz, solonchak, and the soils of irrigated regions. His work elucidated the origin of solonetz and solonchak soils and suggested methods of their melioration. Kovda's investigations are important in reclamation of new lands, in the construction of irrigation systems,

and in melioration of solonetz soil and saline lands of the
U.S.S.R.

Bibliography:
Solonchak and Solonetz Soil. Moscow-Leningrad: 1937.
Origin and Regime of Saline Soils. Vol. 1-2. Moscow-
Leningrad: 1946-47.
Lowland Soils Near the Caspian Sea (North-West part).
Moscow-Leningrad: 1950.
The Geochemistry of U.S.S.R. Deserts. Moscow: 1954 (this
edition contains a bibliography).
Mineral Composition of Flora, and Pedogenesis in Pochvove-
denie. 1956, #1.
Office: Moscow University
Moscow, USSR
Residence: M. Yakimanka, 3
Moscow, USSR
Telephone: B1 05 99

KRASIL'NIKOV, NIKOLAI ALEKSANDROVICH (Microbiologist)

N. A. Krasil'nikov was born December 18, 1896. He graduated in 1926 from Leningrad University and in 1929 began working at the Institute of Microbiology of the U.S.S.R. Academy of
Sciences. For a number of years he participated in expeditions
for the study of soil microorganisms in various parts of the
country. Since 1946 he has been a Corresponding Member of
the U.S.S.R. Academy of Sciences. He is also a member of
Moscow State University. In 1951 he was awarded a Stalin
Prize.

The scientific work of Krasil'nikov is the field of biology of
microorganism, mainly the study of actinomycetes and bacteria.
Krasil'nikov studied their structure, development, variability,
physiological properties; he worked out a new principle of
classification of actinomycetes and bacteria, and compiled tables
for determining their series and species. He investigated the
interrelation of microorganisms and higher plants and proposed
a series of practical measures for increasing crop yields. He
investigated antagonism between microorganisms and worked
out the method for protecting plants against phytopathogenic
bacteria and fungi. He also carried out investigations in antibiotics and described antibiotics of actinomycetic origin.

Bibliography:
Actinomycetes and Related Organisms, Actinomycetales.
Moscow-Leningrad: 1938.

Guide of Actinomycetes. Actinomycetales. Moscow-
Leningrad: 1941.
Microbiological Bases of Bacterial Fertilizers. Moscow-
Leningrad: 1945.
Guide of Actinomycetes and Bacteria. Moscow-Leningrad:
1949.
Actinomycetes-Antagonists and Antibiotic Substances.
Moscow-Leningrad: 1950.
Soil Microorganisms and Higher Plants. Moscow, Academy
of Sciences of the U.S.S.R., 1958. [i.e. Jerusalem, Israel
Program for Scientific Translations; available from the
Office of Technical Services, Washington] 474 p.

Office: Institute of Microbiology of USSR Academy of
             Sciences
             Leninskii Prospekt, 33
             Moscow, USSR

KRASNOVSKII, ALEKSANDR ABRAMOVICH (Biochemist)

A. A. Krasnovskii was born in Odessa in 1913. He studied
at the Mendeleev Chemical and Technological Institute, Moscow.
In 1948 he earned his Doctor of Biological Science degree. He
became, in 1951, a deputy Laboratory Chief in the U.S.S.R.
Academy of Sciences Institute of Biochemistry. Krasnovskii
was elected a Corresponding Member of the U.S.S.R. Academy
of Sciences in 1962. In 1950 he was awarded the A. N. Bakh
Prize.

Krasnovskii's main work is in chlorophyll chemistry and
photosynthesis.

Bibliography:

Reversible formation of absorption bands in red and near-
infrared regions of spectrum in photoreduction of chlorophyll, protochlorophyll, and their analogs. Doklady Akad.
Nauk S.S.S.R. 112, 911-14 (1957). C. A. 51, 12239a (1957).
Proc. Acad. Sci. U.S.S.R., Sect. Biochem. 112, 49-53 (English
translation). C. A. 52, 5561g (1958).
and L. J. Vorob'eva, E. V. Pakshina. Investigation of the
photochemically active form of chlorophyll in plants of
different systematic groups. Fiziol. Rastenii 4, #2, 124-33
(1957). C. A. 51, 16744h (1957).
Development of mode of action of photocatalytic system in
organisms. Repts. Intern. Symposium, Moscow, 1957 (Publishing House of Academy of Sciences of USSR, Moscow),
391 pp. (351-62.-41 ref.) C. A. 52, 1332c (1958).

and G. P. Brin. Chlorophyll- and pheophytin-sensitized photooxidation. Biokhimiya 22, 776-88 (1957). Biochemistry (U.S.S.R.) 22, 728-38 (1957) (English translation). C. A. 52, 13828h (1958).

and F. F. Litvin. Intermediate stages of formation of chlorophyll in etiolated leaves as studied by fluorescence spectra. Doklady Akad. Nauk S.S.S.R. 117, 106-9 (1957). C. A. 52, 5555i (1958). Proc. Acad. Sci. U.S.S.R., Sect. Biochem. 116-17, 251-5 (1957) (English translation). C. A. 52, 17422b (1958).

and F. F. Litvin. Investigation of the process of chlorophyll formation and of its state in plant leaves by means of fluorescence spectra. Izvest. Akad. Nauk S.S.S.R., Ser. Fiz. 23, 82-5 (1959). C. A. 53, 13291d (1959).

and E. S. Mikhailova, G. P. Brin, N. M. Sisakyan. Light reactivation of cytochrome oxidase activity of plants containing and not containing chlorophyll. Biokhimiya 24, 3-8 (1959). C. A. 53, 11534b (1959).

and A. V. Umrikhina. Utilization of compounds of bivalent iron and ascorbic acid as donors of electrons in photochemical reactions of porphyrins and chlorophyll in aqueous media. Doklady Akad. Nauk S.S.S.R. 122, 1061-4 (1958). C. A. 53, 1929f (1959).

and L. M. Vorob'eva. Reversible photoreduction of chlorophyll and sensitized reactions in sugar beet leaf homogenates. Biokhimiya 23, 760-70 (1958). C. A. 53, 2375c (1959).

and A. V. Umrikhina. Formation of free radicals during photoreduction of chlorophyll or its derivatives by the method of initiation of chain polymerization. Biofizika 3, 547-57 (1958). C. A. 53, 2382i (1959).

Participation of chlorophyll in photochemical hydrogen (electron) transfer. Proc. Intern. Symposium Enzyme Chem., Tokyo and Kyoto 2, 355-8 (1957) (Pub. 1958) (in English). C. A. 53, 10389a (1959).

Reversible photochemical reduction and its analogs and the mechanism of photosensitization. J. chim. phys. 55, 968-79 (1958). C. A. 54, 11657h (1960).

and E. M. Belavtseva, L. M. Vorob'eva. Structure of aggregated chlorophyll. Biofizika 4, 521-32 (1959). C. A. 54, 11164b (1960).

and E. V. Pakshina. Photochemical and spectroscopic properties of bacterioviridin of green sulfur bacteria. Doklady Akad. Nauk S.S.S.R. 127, 913-16 (1959). C. A. 54, 2487c (1960).

KRASNOVSKII192

and F. F. Litvin, G. T. Rikhireva. Formation and transformation of protochlorophyll in green plant leaves. Doklady Akad. Nauk S.S.S.R. 127, 699-701 (1959). C. A. 54, 2506g (1960).

and M. I. Bystrova. Chlorophyll formation in the homogenates of etiolated leaves by the method of fluorescent spectrophotometry. Biokhimiya 25, 168-79 (1960). C. A. 54, 21356d (1960).

and G. P. Brin. Chlorophyll-photosensitized oxidation-reduction transformations of pyridine nucleotides in chlorophyll solutions and in leaf homogenates. Biokhimiya 24, 1085-93 (1959). C. A. 54, 13283f (1960).

and E. V. Pakshina. Reversible photoreduction of bacteriochlorophyll and its participation in photochemical electron transfer. Doklady Akad. Nauk S.S.S.R. 135, 1258-61 (1960). C. A. 55, 11542d (1961).

and F. F. Litvin, G. T. Rikhireva. Luminescence of various forms of chlorophyll in plant leaves. Doklady Akad. Nauk S.S.S.R. 135, 1528-31 (1960). C. A. 55, 11558a (1961).

Primary processes of photosynthesis in plants. Ann. Rev. Plant Physiol. 11, 363-410 (1960). C. A. 55, 13571a (1961).

and Yu. E. Erokhin, I. B. Fedorovich. Fluorescence of green photosynthesizing bacteria and the state of bacterioviridin. Doklady Akad. Nauk S.S.S.R. 134, 1232-5 (1960). C. A. 55, 9560g (1961).

and N. G. Doman, A. K. Romanova, L. M. Vorob'eva, E. V. Pakshina, Z. A. Terent'eva. Synthesis of chlorophyll and fixation of CO_2 in etiolated barley seedlings under illumination. Fiziol. Rastenii, Akad. Nauk S.S.S.R. 8, #1, 3-12 (1961). C. A. 55, 21267e (1961).

Photobiochemical paths of participation of pigments in photosynthesis reactions. Storage of light energy in the reaction of reversible photochemical reduction of chlorophyll. Problemy Fotosinteza, Doklady 2-oi [Vtoroi] Konf., Moscow 1957, 30-43 (Pub. 1959). C. A. 55, 26141b (1961).

and M. I. Bystrova, A. D. Sorokina. Fractionation of various pigments in homogenates of etiolated and illuminated leaves. Doklady Akad. Nauk S.S.S.R. 136, 1227-30 (1961). C. A. 55, 16697i (1961).

and N. N. Drozdova, E. V. Pakshina. Effect of carotene on the photochemical properties of chlorophyll. Biokhimiya 25, 282-4 (1960). C. A. 55, 3737g (1961).

and Yu. E. Erokhin, Khun-Yui Tsyun. Fluorescence of aggregated forms of bacterio-chlorophyll, bacterioviridin and chlorophyll in relation to pigmentation in photosynthesizing organisms. Doklady Akad. Nauk S.S.S.R. 143, #2, 456-59 (1962).

Office: A. N. Bakh Institute of Biochemistry
                  Leninskii Prospekt, 33
                  Moscow, USSR

KREPS, EVGENII MIKHAILOVICH (Physiologist)

E. M. Kreps was born April 30, 1899. He graduated in 1923 from the Military Medical Academy and in 1924-1931 taught there. From 1923 to 1934 he was Chief of the Physiology Laboratory of the Murmansk Biological Station. During 1931-1951 he worked in the Emergency Rescuing Commission of the Naval Fleet. In 1934-1937 he was professor at Leningrad University. Beginning in 1935, he has worked at the Sechenov Institute of Evolutionary Physiology of the U.S.S.R. Academy of Sciences, and in 1960 he became the Director. In 1946 he was elected Corresponding Member of the U.S.S.R. Academy of Sciences, and is also a member of the U.S.S.R. Academy of Medical Sciences.

Kreps' works are concerned with the comparative physiology and biochemistry of the nervous system and with functions of blood in breathing. He established the regulation of enzyme activity by the central nervous system. Kreps also studied the physiology of divers and marine chemistry. He designed oxyhemometers and utilized them in medical practice.

Bibliography:
The reaction of astsidii on external irritations. Archives of Biological Sciences, 1925, 25, #4-5.
Change in the activity of enzymes as a method of regulating the functions of a living organism. Izvest. Akad. Nauk S.S.S.R. Ser. Biol., 1945, #2.
and others. Biochemical evolution of the brain in ontogeny and nervous activity. Zhur. Vysshei Nervnoi Deyatel'. im I. P. Pavlova, 1952, #1.
Comparative biochemistry of muscle activity. Physiological Journal of the U.S.S.R., 1933, 16, #4.
Breathing Enzyme-Carbon anhydrosis and its meaning in physiology and pathology. Uspekhi Sovremennoi Biol., 1944, 17, #2.
Phospholipids of the nervous system. Uspekhi Sovremennoi Biol., 1956, 41, #3.

Office: I. M. Sechenov Institute of Evolutionary Physiology,
              USSR Academy of Sciences
              Prospekt Maklina, 32
              Leningrad, USSR

KRETOVICH, VATSLAV LEONOVICH (Biochemist)

V. L. Kretovich is a Doctor of Biological Sciences. He has
worked at the Technological Institute of Food Industry, Moscow,
and as of 1962, also at the U.S.S.R. Academy of Sciences A. N.
Bakh Institute of Biochemistry. In June 1962 he was elected a
Corresponding Member of the U.S.S.R. Academy of Sciences.
He received the A. N. Bakh Prize in 1958 for his "Principles
of the Biochemistry of Plants."

Bibliography:

Osnovy biokhimii rastenii (Principles of the Biochemistry
of Plants. 2nd ed. Moscow: Sovet. Nauka. 1956. 497 pp.
C. A. 53, 1480a (1959).

The biosynthesis of dicarboxylic amino acids and enzymatic
transformations of amides in plants. Advances in Enzymol.
20, 319-40 (1958). C. A. 53, 3331d (1959).

and T. G. Florenskaya. Effect of heating on proteins and
enzymes of wheat grain. Biokhim. Zerna, Sbornik 1958, #4,
56-85. C. A. 53, 595e (1959).

and T. I. Smirnova, M. K. Veinova. Electrochemical properties of soybean and hemp seed proteins. Biokhim. Zerna,
Sbornik 1958, #4, 5-21. C. A. 53, 478a (1959).

and A. P. Prokhorova. Enzymatic processes in stored dry
vegetable materials. Biokhim. Zerna, Sbornik 1958, #4, 132-
7. C. A. 53, 602f (1959).

and R. R. Tokareva. Improvement of breadmaking quality of
four by the use of fungal enzyme preparations. Biokhim.
Zerna, Sbornik 1958, #4, 241-61. C. A. 53, 596a (1959).

and E. Galyas. Synthesis of amino acids from oxalecetic
acid in sprout extracts. Doklady Akad. Nauk S.S.S.R. 124,
217-19 (1959). C. A. 53, 8318g (1959).

and I. S. Petrova, R. R. Tokareva, K. I. Chizhova. Semi-
micromethod of determining volatile organic acid in the
control of bakery production. Trudy Vsesoyuz. Nauch.-
Issledovatel. Inst., Khlebopekar. Prom. 1958, #7, 98-102.
C. A. 53, 8464d (1959).

and Zh. V. Uspenskaya. Synthesis of phenylalanine and
transformation of phenylpyruvic acid in the ripening wheat
spike. Biokhimiya 24, 116-22 (1959). C. A. 53, 9380f (1959).

and V. I. Yakovleva. Biosynthesis of glutamic acid and glutamine in pea and wheat seedlings. Fiziol. Rastenii, Akad. Nauk S.S.S.R. 6, 165-70 (1959). C. A. 53, 19054c (1959).

and O. L. Polyanovskii. Biosynthesis of tryptophan in ear wheat. Izvest. Akad. Nauk S.S.S.R., Ser. Biol. 1959, #3, 428-30. C. A. 53, 19058f (1959).

Biokhimiya zerna i khleba (Biochemistry of Grain and Bread). Moscow: Izdatel. Akad. Nauk S.S.S.R. Nauch.-Populyar. Ser. 1958, 176 pp. C. A. 53, 18332b (1959).

and Z. G. Evstigneeva, K. B. Aseeva, I. G. Savkina. Nitrogen substances in drawing pumpkin sap. Fiziol. Rastenii, Akad. Nauk S.S.S.R. 6, 13-19 (1959). C. A. 53, 13288d (1959). Enzymatic synthesis of glutamic acid and phenylalanine in plants. Proc. Intern. Symposium Enzyme Chem. Tokyo and Kyoto 2, 468-70 (1957) (Pub. 1958) (in English). C. A. 53, 15235a (1959).

and A. A. Bundel, M. R. Frasheri, N. V. Borovikova. Participation of hydroxylamine in the synthesis of amino acids in plants. Doklady Akad. Nauk S.S.S.R. 122, 1065-7 (1958). C. A. 53, 2373h (1959).

and A. A. Bundel, M. R. Frasheri, N. V. Borovikova. Competitive inhibition of transamination in plants by hydroxylamine. Zhur. Obshchei Biol. 19, 414-16 (1958). C. A. 53, 2380c (1959).

and M. P. Popov, D. A. Cheleev. Interaction of lipases and lipoxidases in the oxidation process of fats. Izvest. Vysshikh Ucheb. Zavedenii, Pishchevaya Tekhnol. 1958, #5, 23-7. C. A. 53, 11697f (1959).

Origin of dicarboxylic and aromatic amino acids in vegetables. Qualitas Plant. et Materiae Vegetables 3-4, 79-90 (1958) (in French). C. A. 53, 5414f (1959).

and V. I. Yakovleva. Biosynthesis of glutamic acid and glutamine in ripening wheat ear. Doklady Akad. Nauk S.S.S.R. 125, 210-12 (1959). C. A. 53, 20301i (1959).

Osnovy biokhimii rastenii (Principles of Plant Biochemistry), 2nd ed. Kiev: Gosudust. Izdatel. sel'sk.-Khoz. Lit. U.S.S.R. 1959. 479 pp. C. A. 54, 1673i (1960).

and T. I. Smirnova, B. F. Poglazov. Amperometric titration of sulfhydryl groups of glycinin. Biokhimiya 24, 758-60 (1959). C. A. 54, 3551i (1960).

and Z. S. Kagan. The biosynthesis of valine and of isoleucine in the ripening wheat spike. Biokhimiya 24, 717-21 (1959). C. A. 54, 3610d (1960).

and O. L. Polyanovskii. Tryptophan synthesis from indolyl-
pyruvic acid in plants. Biokhimiya 24, 995-1001 (1959).
C. A. 54, 14374g (1960).

and A. N. Ponomareva. Quantitative determination of free
amino acids in grain and flour. Izvest. Vysshikh Ucheb.
Zavedenii, Pishchevaya Tekhnol. 1960, #1, 132-4. C. A. 54,
15742d (1960).

and V. I. Yakovleva. Biosynthesis of glutamic acid in homogenates of wheat and pea sprouts. Biokhimiya 24, 842-8
(1959). C. A. 54, 15546d (1960).

and E. A. Morgunova, A. I. Starodubtseva. Effect of heating
on physiological and biochemical properties of sunflower
seeds. Masloboino-Zhirovaya Prom. 26, #2, 8-11 (1960).
C. A. 54, 25080h (1960).

and E. Galyas. Synthesis of amino acids from oxalacetic
and pyruvic acids in barley sprouts. Doklady Akad. Nauk
S.S.S.R. 130, 1144-7 (1960). C. A. 54, 17573f (1960).

and Z. S. Kagan. Biosynthesis of valine and ammonium ion
utilization in wheat sprouts. Doklady Akad. Nauk S.S.S.R.
131, 673-5 (1960). C. A. 54, 17573h (1960).

and K. I. Klechkovskii. Ornithine cycle of amino acid transamination in pea and wheat seedlings. Biokhimiya 25, 164-7
(1960). C. A. 54, 21344i (1960).

and A. I. Starodubtseva, E. A. Vetkina. The dependence of
the respiratory intensity of sunflower seeds on their oil
content. Biokhim. Zerna, Sbornik 5, 256-62 (1960). C. A.
54, 21795f (1960).

and Zh. V. Uspenskaya. Biosynthesis of phenylalanine in
Gramineae and Leguminosae. Biokhim. Zerna, Sbornik 5,
5-46 (1960). C. A. 55, 1811h (1961).

and Z. G. Evstigneeva, K. B. Aseeva. Assimilation by the
root system of labeled ammonium [compounds] in the soil.
Biokhimiya 25, 476-81 (1960). C. A. 55, 3737g (1961).

and Z. G. Evstigneeva, K. B. Aseeva. Incorporation of soil
ammonia nitrogen into seed protein reserve. Biokhimiya 25,
878-83 (1960). C. A. 55, 3738b (1961).

and R. R. Tokareva. Method for determining aromatic substances in bread. Khlebopekar. i Konditer. Prom. 5, #6,
11-13 (1961). C. A. 55, 21405c (1961).

and R. R. Tokareva. Utilization of concentrated enzyme
preparations from molds in bread baking. Biokhim. Zerna i
Khlekopecheniya, #6, 241-8 (1960). C. A. 55, 21405i (1961).

Modern concepts in the nature and mechanism of enzyme action. Izvest. Akad. Nauk S.S.S.R., Ser. Biol. 26, #3, 425-40 (1961). C. A. 55, 18819e (1961).

and E. Krauze. Biosynthesis of amino acids from pyruvic acid and ammonia in yeast. Doklady Akad. Nauk S.S.S.R. 136, 1474-7 (1961). C. A. 55, 16668b (1961).

and A. N. Ponomareva. Amino acid participation in melanoidin formation in bread making. Biokhimiya 26, 237-42 (1961). C. A. 55, 16843f (1961).

and T. I. Smirnova. Glycinin—a reversibly dissociating system. Biokhim. Zerna i Khlebopecheniya, #6, 66-74 (1960). C. A. 55, 27467e (1961).

and A. A. Bundel, M. R. Frasheri, N. V. Borovikova. Effect of hydroxylamine on growth of wheat. Fiziol. Rastenii, Akad. Nauk S.S.S.R. 7, 261-8 (1960). C. A. 55, 4862h (1961).

and A. P. Prokhorova. Biochemical characteristics of grains possessing different odors. Izvest. Akad. Nauk S.S.S.R., Ser. Biol. 1960, 446-50. C. A. 55, 6714i (1961).

and K. M. Stepanovich. Serine synthesis from pyruvic acid in plants. Doklady Akad. Nauk 139, #2, 488-90 (1961).

and Z. S. Kagan. Biosynthesis of valine from its keto analog in sunflower sprouts. Doklady Akad. Nauk 143, #3, 727-79 (1962).

Office: A. N. Bakh Institute of Biochemistry
Leninskii Prospekt, 33
Moscow, USSR

KRUZHILIN, GEORGII NIKITICH (Heat Engineer)

G. N. Kruzhilin was born June 6, 1911. He graduated in 1934 from Leningrad Physico-Mechanical Institute. He worked at the Central Boiler-Turbine Institute in Leningrad in 1933-1946, and in 1936-1938 at its branch in the Urals. Since 1946 he has worked in various departments of the U.S.S.R. Academy of Sciences, and in 1955 at the Krizhanovskii Institute of Energetics. In 1960 he was made Director. Kruzhilin has been a member of the Communist Party of the Soviet Union since 1944. In 1953 he became a Corresponding Member of the U.S.S.R. Academy of Sciences.

The main works of Kruzhilin are devoted to experimentally establishing the distribution of the ratio of heat emission along the surface of a body, the calculation of a terminal heat layer, the theory of heat emission on condensation of steam and a boiling liquid, and the investigation of removal of moisture by steam from boilers.

Bibliography:

and V. A. Shvab. New method of calculating the range of the ratio of heat emission on a surface of a body washed by a liquid flow. Zhur. Tekh. Fiz., 1935, 5, #3.

and V. A. Shvab. Investigation of the alpha field on the surface of a round cylinder washed by a cross air blast. Zhur. Tekh. Fiz., 1935, 5, #4.

Investigation of the terminal heat layer. Zhur. Tekh. Fiz., 1936, 6, #3.

Theory of heat emission of a round cylinder in a cross liquid stream. Zhur. Tekh. Fiz., 1936, 6, #5.

Exacting Nussel'ton's theory on heat exchange under condensation. Zhur. Tekh. Fiz., 1937, 7, #20-21.

Heat emission from the heating surface to a boiling single-component liquid under free convection. Izvest. Akad. Nauk S.S.S.R., Otdel. Tekh. Nauk, 1948, #7.

Summary of experimental data on heat emission during the boiling of liquids in conditions of free convection. Izvest. Akad. Nauk S.S.S.R., Otdel. Tekh. Nauk, 1949, #5.

Theory of removing and separating moisture in steam boilers. Soviet Boiler-Turbine Construction, 1945, #1, 4.

Reactor for physical and technical research. Moscow: 1955. (Reports presented by the U.S.S.R. at the International Conference for Peaceful Utilization of Atomic Energy).

Office: Krzhizhanovskii Power Engineering Institute of
USSR Academy of Sciences
Leninskii Prospekt, 19
Moscow, USSR

KRYLOV, ALEKSANDR PETROVICH (Petroleum Engineer)

A. P. Krylov was born August 14, 1904. He graduated in 1926 from Leningrad Mining Institute. He began teaching at the Moscow Petroleum Institute in 1933 and in 1949 he became professor. In 1953 he was made deputy Director of the All Union Scientific Research Petroleum Institute and Chief of a laboratory at the Institute of Petroleum at the U.S.S.R. Academy of Sciences. Since 1953 he has been a Corresponding Member of the U.S.S.R. Academy of Sciences. He was awarded a Stalin Prize in 1949.

Krylov's main works deal with rational methods in exploiting oil deposits.

Bibliography:

and I. M. Murav'yov. Textbook in Exploitation of Oil Deposits, Part II. Moscow-Leningrad: 1940.

and others. Scientific Basis for the Exploitation of Oil Deposits. (Stalin Prize). Moscow-Leningrad: 1948.
and I. M. Murav'yov. Exploitation of Oil Deposits. Moscow-Leningrad: 1949.
Main principles of exploiting oil beds by pumping a working agent into the bed. Works of the Moscow Oil Institute of I. M. Gubkin, 1953, #12.
and G. I. Barenblatt. The Elastic Plastic Regime of an Oil Bed. Moscow: 1955.
Office: Moscow Petroleum Institute of USSR Academy of Sciences
              Moscow, USSR
Residence: Dorogomilovskaya nab. 1/2
              Moscow, USSR
Telephone: G3 50 14, Ext. 199

KULEBAKIN, VIKTOR SERGEEVICH (Electrical Engineer)

V. S. Kulebakin was born October 18, 1891. In 1914 he graduated from the Moscow Higher Technical School where in 1917 he began teaching. He also taught in other higher educational institutions and in 1921 became a professor. In 1923 he was appointed professor at the Air Force Engineering Academy. Kulebakin organized the All-Union Electrotechnical Institute, the Moscow Energy Institute, and the Institute of Automatics and Telemechanics of the U.S.S.R. Academy of Sciences. He had been a Corresponding Member of the U.S.S.R. Academy of Sciences since 1933, and in 1939 he was elected Academician. He is a Major General in the Engineer-Technical Service. In 1950 he was awarded a Stalin Prize.

Kulebakin has worked on electronic computers, automatic regulation and design of regulators. He has studied the electrical ignition of aircraft engines. Investigations of Kulebakin on the reflection of light from the earth's surface and from rotating propellers, and on illumination of open spaces for making night flying practical. Kulebakin has also worked on the automation of electrical drive. His accomplishment in the electrification of airplanes was the basis of electrical engineering in Soviet aviation. He participated in the development of electric locomotion in mines (Stalin Prize, 1950).

Bibliography:
Testing Electric Machines and Transformers, 2nd ed. Moscow-Leningrad: 1935.
Electric Apparatus. I. Moscow-Leningrad: 1932.

and A. M. Senkevich. Electrical Equipment of Airplanes,
Pt. 1. Moscow: 1945.
and L. M. Snideev, V. D. Nagorskii. Electrification of Air-
planes. 1952.
Biography:
Academician V. S. Kulebakin. To his 60th Birthday. Elec-
tricity, 1951, #12.
Office: Air Force Engineering Academy
              Moscow, USSR
Residence: B. Khariton'evskii p. 12/1
              Moscow, USSR
Telephone: B3 64 75

KUPREVICH, VASILII FEOFILOVICH (Botanist)
V. F. Kuprevich was born January 24, 1897. From 1934 to
1938, he worked in the Biological Institute of the Byelorussian
S.S.R. Academy of Sciences. In 1938, he was made chief of a
laboratory of the Botannical Institute of the U.S.S.R. Academy
of Sciences, and from 1949 to 1952, he was Director of this
Institute. In 1952 V. F. Kuprevich was elected an Academician
of the Byelorussian S.S.R. Academy and President of the Academy of Sciences of Byelorussian S.S.R. Since 1953 he has been
a Corresponding Member of the U.S.S.R. Academy of Sciences.
In 1945 V. F. Kuprevich became a member of the Communist
Party of the Soviet Union. He is presently a Deputy of the
U.S.S.R. Supreme Soviet.
Kuprevich has studied the physiology and biochemistry of
diseased plants and the classification of mushrooms. He has
investigated the physiology of diseased plants. He was the first
to discover the presence of extracellular enzymes in obligate
parasites and proposed progressive curtailment and specializ-
ation of extracellular enzymatic apparatus in parasitic mushrooms in the process of their evolution. The basis of the
pathological process is the action of extracellular enzymes of
a parasite on the protoplast of the host and responsive reactions
of the latter which led to necrosis, or the suppression of the
activity of the parasitic enzymes. Kuprevich showed that leaves
can assimilate carbon dioxide transmitted along with water
from other parts of the plant. These investigations led to the
discovery of the feeding process of plants by carbon dioxide
from the soil. Kuprevich discovered extracellular enzymes
which are secreted by the thinnest roots of higher plants. He
proved the possibility of heterotrophenous feeding of higher
plants in natural environments and eliminated the principal

difference in the method of feeding of autotrophic and hetero-
trophic plants.
Bibliography:
   Physiology of a Diseased Plant in Connection with General
   Questions on Parasitism. Moscow-Leningrad: 1947.
   Problem of Species in Heterotrophic and Autotrophic Plants.
   Moscow-Leningrad: 1949.
   Influence of higher plants on the substratum with the aid of
   enzymes secreted by roots. Questions of Botany, 2, Moscow-
   Leningrad: 1954, 91-99.
   and V. H. Tranzschel. Flora plantarum cryptogamarum
   U.R.S.S., V. IV, Fungi (I). Uredinales fasc. I, familia
   Melampsoraceae, p. 420, 1957, Moscow-Leningrad.
Biography:
   President of the Byelorussian S.S.R. Academy of Sciences,
   V. P. Kuprevich. Vestnik Akad. Nauk S.S.S.R., 1952, #1.
   V. P. Ssavitch. V. F. Kuprevitch--the President of the
   Academy of Sciences of the Byelorussian Republic. Botani-
   cal Journal, 1957, 2, p. 325.
Office: President Academy of Sciences Byelorussian S.S.R.
              Leninskii pr. 66
              Minsk, Byelorussian S.S.R.
Telephone: 3-21-03

KURDYUMOV, GEORGII VYACHESLAVOVICH (Metallurgist)

   G. V. Kurdyumov was born February 1, 1902. In 1926 he
graduated from the Leningrad Polytechnic Institute. He had
been working since 1925 at the Physico-Technical Institute of
the U.S.S.R. Academy of Sciences. In 1932 he began working at
the Dnepropetrovsk Physico-Technical Institute, and from 1932
to 1941 he taught at Dnepropetrovsk University. Kurdyumov
was appointed Director of the Institute of Metalworking and the
Physics of Metals of the Central Scientific Institute of Ferrous
Metallurgy (Moscow) in 1944. In 1939 he was elected Academician of the Ukrainian S.S.R. Academy of Sciences. He has
been a Corresponding Member of the U.S.S.R. Academy of
Sciences since 1946 and since 1953 an Academician. He was
awarded, in 1949, a Stalin Prize.
   Kurdyumov has studied the processes arising in the hardening and tempering of steel and the phenomena of phase transformations, hardening, and diffusion in metals and alloys. Together with N. Y. Gudtsov and N. Ya. Selyakov, he defined
(1926) the crystalline structure of martensite. The existence
of the regular orientation of the crystalline lattice of martensite

in relation to austenite was revealed by Kurdyumov together
with A. A. Ivens and G. Zaks (1929-30). He further established
that the normal mutual orientation of crystal lattices of the
initial and resulting phases occurs according to a general pattern of phase transformations in solids. In 1932-39, Kurdyumov
made studies of metastable states and phase transformations in
copper alloys. The theory of these transformations permitted
Kurdyumov to discover in 1948 the isothermic transformation
of martensite at low temperatures and the thermoelastic
equilibrium in martensite transformation.

In February 1962, Kurdyumov visited the United States to
attend the Aluminum Symposium and annual meeting of the
American Institute of Mining, Metallurgical, and Petroleum
Engineers. (University of Illinois at Urbana and AIME, New
York).

Bibliography:

Thermal treatment of steel in light of X-ray study. Journal
of the Metal Industry, 1932, #9.
Common patterns of phase transformations in eutectoid al-
loys. Izvest. Akad. Nauk S.S.S.R., Otdel. Mat. i Estest.
Nauk, Ser. Khim., 1936, #2.
Toward a theory of hardening and tempering steel. Col-
lection of Scientific Papers of the Section of Metal-Working
and Thermal Treatment of the VNITO Metallurgists. Mos-
cow: 1940.
Application of methods of X-ray structural analysis for
study of tempering of hardened steel. Questions of the
Physics of Metals and Metalworking, Collection of Scientific
Papers of the Section of Metalworking. . ., #2. Kiev: 1950.
Non-diffused (martensitic) transformations in alloys. Zhur.
Tekh. Fiz., 1948, 18, #8.
On the nature of hardened steel. Zhur. Tekh. Fiz., 1954, 24,
#7.
Application of radioactive isotopes for study of diffusion and
interatomic interactions in alloys. Application of Isotopes
in Technology of Biology and Agriculture. Moscow: 1955
(Reports of the Soviet Delegation to the International Confer-
ence on Peaceful Use of Atomic Energy, Geneva, 1955).
Über den Mechanismus der Phasenumwandlungen in den
Eutectoidlegierungen. Physikalische Zeitschrift der Sowjet-
union, 1933, 4, #3.

Biography:

Kurdyumov Georgii Vyacheslav. Vestnik Akad. Nauk
S.S.S.R., 1954, #3, 48.

On the Fiftieth Birthday of G. V. Kurdyumov. Problems of
Metalworking and the Physics of Metals (Collection 3).
Moscow: 1952.
Office: Academy of Sciences Ukrainian SSR
              Vladimirskaya Ulitsa, 54
              Kiev, Ukrainian SSR

KURSANOV, ANDREI L'VOVICH (Biochemist)

A. L. Kursanov, son of L. I. Kursanov, was born November 8,
1902. He graduated in 1926 from Moscow University. First he
worked at the Scientific Research Institute. From 1929 to 1938
he taught at the Moscow K. A. Timiryazev Agricultural Academy. Beginning in 1935 he was also at the A. N. Bakh Institute
of Biochemistry. He started teaching at Moscow University in
1944. In 1952 Kursanov was made Director of the Timiryazev
Institute of Plant Physiology of the U.S.S.R. Academy of Sciences. He was elected in 1946, a Corresponding Member of the
U.S.S.R. Academy of Sciences and in 1953, an Academician.

Kursanov's investigations are in plant metabolism. He
ascertained the dependence between assimilation of carbon dioxide and emission of high polymer substances from leaves,
studied the action of enzymes in a living plant, and investigated
the process of assimilation of carbon dioxide by soils through
a root system. From 1940 Kursanov conducted investigation of
tanning substances of the tea leaf, important in control of tea
production.

Kursanov is currently Chairman of the Scientific Council of
Exhibitions.

As of 1961, Kursanov was a Member of the Presidium of the
U.S.S.R. Academy of Sciences.

Bibliography:
Reversible Action of Enzymes in the Living Plant Cell.
Moscow-Leningrad: 1940.
Synthesis and Transformation of Tanning Substances in
Tea Leaves. (Bakh Studies #7) Moscow: 1952.
Movement of organic substances in the plant. Botan. Zhur.,
1952, #5.
Biological synthesis of disaccharides in Successes of Bio-
logical Chemistry, 2. Moscow: 1954.
with others. On the possibility of Carbonates. Doklady
Akad. Nauk S.S.S.R., 1951, 79, #4.
with B. B. Vartapetyan. Participation of oxygen of water
and the oxygen of the atmosphere in the respiration of plants.
Doklady Akad. Nauk S.S.S.R., 1955, 104, #2.

Carbohydrate--phosphorous exchange and synthesis of amino
acids in the roots of a pumpkin (Cucurbita pepo). Fiziol.
Rastenni, 1954, #1.

Office: L. A. Timiryazev Institute of Plant Physiology of
USSR Academy of Sciences
Leninskii Prospekt, 33
Moscow, USSR

Residence: M. Yakimanka, 3
Moscow, USSR

Telephone: B1 30 30

KURSANOV, DMITRII NIKOLAEVICH (Organic Chemist)

D. N. Kursanov was born April 3, 1899. He graduated in
1924 from Moscow University. From 1930 to 1947 he worked
at the Moscow Textile Institute and in 1936 was made professor.
Beginning in 1943, he has worked at the Institute of Organic
Chemistry and in 1953 at the Institute of Scientific Information
of the U.S.S.R. Academy of Sciences. In 1953 he was elected a
Corresponding Member of the U.S.S.R. Academy of Sciences.

The main emphasis of Kursanov's work lies in studying reaction mechanisms of organic substances, and in particular,
alcohol-dehydration, the reactions catalyzed by aluminum
chloride, and the splitting and exchange of quaternary ammonium compounds. He discovered a number of new reactions of
practical importance, in the formation of hydrophobic derivatives of cellulose and reactions in chemical dyeing of cellulose.
Kursanov has also investigated with isotopes the intramolecular
mutual influence of atoms in organic compounds.

Bibliography:

and S. S. Namyotkin. Experiment in utilizing the xanthogene
method for dehydrating benzyl alcohol. Journal of the
Russian Physico-Chemical Society, 1926, 57, #6-9
Benzylidene-Cyclohexane. Zhur. Obshchei Khim., 1931, 1,
#7.

and R. R. Zel'vin. New type of condensation reaction under
the influence of aluminum chloride. Doklady Akad. Nauk
S.S.S.R., 1942, 36, #1.

and others. Reactions of exchange and splitting in the group
of quaternary ammonium salts. Izvest. Akad. Nauk S.S.S.R.,
Otdel. Khim. Nauk, 1948, #2.

and V. V. Voevodskii. New data on reactions of hydrogen
exchange of free organic radicals and ions. Uspekhi Khim.,
1954, 23, #6.

and Z. I. Parnes. Reaction of cyclopentadiene hydrogen exchange. Doklady Akad. Nauk S.S.S.R., 1956, 109, #2.
Hydrogen exchange of ions of carbonium with acids and
hydrogen exchange of carbonyl compounds with deuterium
oxide in an alkaline medium. Ukr. S.S.R. Zhur. Khim., 1956,
22, #1.

Office: Moscow Textile Institute
              Moscow, USSR
Residence: Kotel'nicheskaya nab. 1/15
              Moscow, USSR
Telephone: B7 44 01

KUZIN, ALEKSANDR MIKHAILOVICH (Radiobiologist)

A. M. Kuzin was born in 1906. In 1929 he graduated from
the first Moscow State University. From 1930-1938, he was at
the first Moscow Medical Institute, and from 1938-42, at the
third. He was professor, 1942-43, at the Izhevsk Medical
Institute. From 1943 to 1950, he was Chief of the biochemical
section of the Moscow Control Institute. He worked, 1945-1951,
at the Moscow Medical Institute of the R.S.F.S.R. Ministry of
Health and as a consultant to the U.S.S.R. Academy of Medical
Sciences Laboratory on Cancer Biotherapy. From 1950 to 1952,
he was Chief of the U.S.S.R. Academy of Sciences Laboratory
on Isotopes and Irradiation. In 1952-1957, he was Director and
Chief of the Radiobiology Laboratory of the U.S.S.R. Academy
of Sciences Institute of Biophysics. In 1954 he became chief
editor of the journal "Biophysics," and in 1961 chief editor of
the journal "Radiobiology." He has been a member of the
Communist Party of the Soviet Union since 1946. In 1960 he
was elected a Corresponding Member of the U.S.S.R. Academy
of Sciences.

Kuzin visited the United States in January 1958 to participate in the UN session on Atomic Radiation in New York City.
He has also attended Pugwash Conferences.

Bibliography:
Biochemical fundamentals of the biological action of ionizing
radiations. U. S. At. Energy Comm. AEC-tr-3353, 4-11
(1958). C. A. 53, 4373h (1959).
Initial mechanisms of the biological effect of ionizing radi-
ation. Trudy Vsesoyuz. Nauch. -Tekh. Konf. Primenen.
Radioaktiv. i Stabil. Izotopov i Izluchenii v Narod. Khoz. i
Nauke, Radiobio., Moscow, 1957, 3-13 (Pub. 1958).

and N. I. Krusanova, A. I. Krasovskaya. Changes in structural viscosity of desoxyribonucleoproteins of sarcoma 45 of
rats. Voprosy Onkol. 4, 276-9 (1958). C. A. 53, 6442b
(1959).

Radiobiologiya, biologicheskoe destvie ioniziryushchikh
izluchenii (Radiobiology, Biological Effect of Ionizing Radiation). Moscow: Izdatel. Akad. Nauk S.S.S.R. 1957. 434 pp.
C. A. 53, 9328b (1959).

and V. I. Tokarskaya. Complete labeling of organic plant
substances with radioactive carbon in the study of disturbed
metabolism. Biokhimiya 24, 80-6 (1959). C. A. 53, 9380b
(1959).

and V. A. Struchkov, N. B. Strazhevskaya. Character of the
change of polymer spectrum of desoxyribonucleic acid (DNA)
after γ-irradiation of its solutions. Doklady Akad. Nauk
S.S.S.R. 130, 895-7 (1960). C. A. 54, 20295c (1960).

and V. I. Tokarskaya-Merenova. Destruction of pyrimidine
metabolism in radiation injury. Biofizika 4, 446-53 (1959).
C. A. 54, 2464h (1960).

and V. I. Tokarskaya, N. G. Doman, S. E. Demina. Assimilation of organic phosphorous compounds (sugar phosphates)
by higher plants. Mechenye Atomy v Issledovan. Pitaniya
Rastenii i Primenen. Udobrenii, Trudy Soveshchaniya Akad.
Nauk S.S.S.R. 1955, 58-60. C. A. 54, 5842h (1960).

and I. I. Kolomiitseva, L. P. Kayushin. Free radicals in rat
tissue before and after irradiation by γ-rays of Co^{60}. Doklady Akad. Nauk S.S.S.R. 140, #1, 230-31 (1961).

and L. M. Kryukova. Mutation effect of metabolites, formed
in irradiated vegetation. Doklady Akad. Nauk S.S.S.R., 137,
#4, 970-71 (1961).

Nuclear Explosions, a World-Wide Hazard. Trans. by G.
Yankovsky. Moscow, Foreign Languages Pub. House, 1959,
138 p.

Office: Institute of Biophysics of USSR Academy of Sciences
             Leninskii Prospekt, 33
             Moscow, USSR
Residence: Novopeschanaya, korp. 55
             Moscow, USSR
Telephone: D7 51 60

KUZNETSOV, SERGEI IVANOVICH (Microbiologist)
    S. I. Kuznetsov was born in 1900. He graduated from Mos-
cow State University in 1923. He worked, 1920-25, as a
chemist-bacteriologist at a hydrobiological station. In

1925-1931, he was a postgraduate student and assistant at Moscow State University. He was chief of the Microbiological Laboratory of a limnological station from 1931 to 1941. In 1941-46, he was a senior scientific worker at the Lublin plant for the decontamination of sewer water. In 1942 he worked at the U.S.S.R. Academy of Sciences Institute of Microbiology where in 1946 he became section chief. He was elected, in 1960, a Corresponding Member of the U.S.S.R. Academy of Sciences.
Kuznetsov's works are concerned with the geological activity and physiology of microbes.

Kuznetsov has also been a member of the Institute of Biology of Reservoirs, Verkhnye-Nikolskoye, Academy of Sciences as well as a member of the U.S.S.R. Academy of Sciences Institute of Microbiology.

Bibliography:
The question of the possibility of "radiosynthesis." Mikrobiologiya 25(2): 195-199 (1956). Referat. Zhur., Biol., 1957, #475 (Translation). Biol. Abstr. 32, 31081 (1958).
and V. A. Kuznetsova, K. B. Ashirov, V. A. Gromovich, I. V. Ovchinnikova. An experiment on suppressing the development of sulfate-reducing bacteria in the oil strata of the Kabriva field. Mikrobiologiya (trans.) 26(3): 334-341 (1957). Biol. Abstr. 33, 002663 (1959).
Principal results in the investigation of the microflora of oil deposits. Mikrobiologiya (trans.) 26(6): 630-636 (1957). Biol. Abstr. 33, 20219 (1959).
The geological activity of microorganisms. Izvest. Akad. Nauk S.S.S.R., #2, 30-33 (1959).
and V. I. Zhadin, N. V. Timofeevresovsky. The role of radioactive isotopes in solving the problems of hydrobiology. Proc. Ind. Internatl. Conf. Peaceful Uses Atomic Energy 27: 200-207 (1958). Biol. Abstr. 35, 40271 (1960).
and Ye. N. Kabanova, N. M. Pishchurina. Fluorescent antibodies and their use in cytology and microbiology. Izvest. Akad. Nauk Ser. Biol. 1957(6): 718-732 (1957). Biol. Abstr. 35, 67448 (1960).
and G. A. Sokolova. Contributions to the physiology of thiobacillus thioparus. Mikrobiologiya (trans.) 29(2): 131-134 (1960). Translated from Microbiologia 29(2): 170-176. Biol. Abstr. 36, 17782 (1961).
Dynamics of the quantity of bacteria in Rybinskoye Reservoir in 1958. Bull. Inst. Biol. Vodokhranilishch Akad. Nauk

KUZNETSOV

S.S.S.R. 5, 3-6. Referat. Zhur., Biol., 1961, #6B155. Biol.
Abstr. 36, 69444 (1961).
and E. S. Pantskhava. Effect of methane-forming bacteria
on increasing the electrochemical erosion of metals. Doklady Akad. Nauk S.S.S.R. 139, #2, 478-80 (1961).

Office: Institute of Microbiology of USSR Academy of
Sciences
Leninskii Prospekt, 33
Moscow, USSR
Residence: M. Kolkhoznaya pl. 1/3
Moscow, USSR
Telephone: K5 81 99

KUZNETSOV, VALERII ALEKSEEVICH (Geologist)

V. A. Kuznetsov was born April 12, 1906. After graduating
from the Tomsk Geological Survey Institute in 1932, he worked
in geological establishments of Siberia. Since 1945, he
has worked at the Mining and Geological Institute of the Siberian
branch of the U.S.S.R. Academy of Sciences. Since 1958 he has
been a Corresponding Member of the U.S.S.R. Academy of Sciences. The Presidium of the U.S.S.R. Academy of Sciences, in
1946 and in 1953, awarded Kuznetsov several prizes including
the V. A. Obruchev Prize.

Kuznetsov's main works deal with mercury deposits, metallogenesis of mercury, and also the distribution of mercury in
West Siberia. He is also concerned with teotectonics and magmatism of the Altai Mountains, Tuva, and Altai-Sayansk folded
territory in general.

Bibliography:
Main questions on stratigraphy and tectonics of central and
western Tuva. Materials on Geology and Minerals of the
Tuva Autonomous Region., #2, Moscow: 1953.
G. V. Pinus and I. M. Volokhov. Hyperbassets of Tuva.
Moscow: 1955 (U.S.S.R. Academy of Sciences. The study of
productive forces. West Siberian branch. Works of the
Tuva Complex Expedition, #2.
Main Stages of Geotectonic Development of Southern Altai-
Sayansk Mountain Region. Works of the Mining and Geological
Institute (U.S.S.R. Academy of Sciences. West Siberian
Branch), 1952, #12.
Geotectonic division into districts of the Altai-Sayansk folded
region. Questions on Geology of Asia, 1, Moscow: 1954.

Office: Mining and Geological Institute of Siberian Branch,
              USSR Academy of Sciences
              Novosibirsk, Siberia

KUZNETSOV, VLADIMIR DMITRIEVICH (Physicist)

V. D. Kuznetsov was born April 30, 1887. In 1910 he graduated from Petersburg University and in 1911 began working in
higher educational institutions of Tomsk. He became a professor at Tomsk University where he had been since 1917. Beginning in 1929, he has directed the Siberian Physico-Technical
Institute organized by him. Since 1945 Kuznetsov has been a
member of the Communist Party of the Soviet Union. Having
been a Corresponding Member of the U.S.S.R. Academy of Sciences since 1946, he became an Academician in 1958. He was
made an Honored Scientist of RSFSR in 1945 and Hero of Socialist Labor in 1957, and in 1942 he was awarded a Stalin Prize.

The basic direction of Kuznetsov's work is comprehensive
investigation of the properties of solids and the phenomena occurring in solids during their technological treatment. Kuznetsov studied surface energy, hardness, and other properties of
crystals; internal friction of solids; plasticity and strength of
metallic single crystals and poly-crystals; the mechanism of
crystallization and recrystallization; external friction and wear
of metals and alloys; and the cutting of metals. He wrote a
multi-volume monograph, The Physics of Solids. Kuznetsov
worked out a basic physical theory of cutting which showed both
theoretically and experimentally the possibility of rapid cutting
of metals. This was later confirmed in practice.

As of 1961, Kuznetsov was a Member of the Presidium of the
Siberian Branch USS.S.R. Academy of Sciences.

Bibliography:

and others. The Physics of Solids, 1-5. Tomsk: 1937-1949.
Crystals and Crystallization. Moscow: 1953.
Surface Energy of Solids. Moscow: 1954.
Excrescences in Cutting and Wearing. Moscow: 1956.

Biography:

Studies in the Physics of Solids, Collection of Articles.
Dedicated to the 70th Birthday of Corresponding Member
V. D. Kuznetsov of the Academy of Sciences U.S.S.R.
Moscow, 1957.

Office: Presidium of the Siberian Department of USSR
              Academy of Sciences
              Novosibirsk, Siberia

KUZNETSOV, V. I. (Mechanical Engineer)
  V. I. Kuznetsov was born April 27, 1913. After graduating
in 1938 from Leningrad Polytechnic Institute, he worked in
scientific research and construction organizations. Since 1942
he has been a member of the Communist Party of the Soviet
Union. He was elected, in 1958, a Corresponding Member of
the U.S.S.R. Academy of Sciences. In 1923 and in 1946 he received Stalin Prizes.
  His main works are devoted to various questions of applied
mechanics.

Office: USSR Academy of Sciences
              Leninskii Prospekt, 14
              Moscow, USSR
Residence: Leninskii Prospekt, 2
              Moscow, USSR
Telephone: V1 97 49

KUZNETSOV, YURII ALEKSEEVICH (Geologist)
  Yu. A. Kuznetsov was born April 19, 1903. He graduated in
1924 from Tomsk University. In 1930 he began working at the
Tomsk Polytechnic Institute (in 1930-1933 this Institute was the
Geological Survey Institute, and in 1933-1938, the Industrial
Institute). He was made professor in 1938 at the Tomsk Polytechnic Institute. He has also participated in the work of geological survey organizations of Siberia. Since 1958 he has been
a Corresponding Member of the U.S.S.R. Academy of Sciences.
  Kuznetsov's works deal with stratigraphy, tectonics, petrology and metallogenesis of the Altai, Kuznets-Alatau, Upper
Sayan and the Yenisei ridge. He paid particular attention to
elucidating conditions in the formation of intrusions and their
role in ore mineralization. He studied deposits of iron ore,
rare and non-ferrous metals, gold, and refractory clay. He
studied magmatic rock facies and also magmatic formations.
He systematized and elucidated the characteristics of
tectonic structures.
Bibliography:
  Pre-Cambrian petrology of the south Yenisei Ridge. Materials on the Geology of West Siberia, #15. Moscow: 1941.
  Origin of magmatic rocks. Magmatism and Minerals Associated with it. Moscow: 1955.
  Facies of magmatic rocks. Questions on the Geology of
  Asia, 2. Moscow: 1955

211 LANDAU

Office: Tomsk Polytechnic Institute of USSR Academy of
Sciences
Tomsk, USSR

LANDAU, LEV DAVIDOVICH (Physicist)

L. D. Landau was born January 22, 1908 in Baku. In 1927 he
graduated from Leningrad State University. He began working
in 1937 at the Institute of Physical Problems of the U.S.S.R.
Academy of Sciences. In 1943 he became a professor at Moscow State University. He has been an Academician since 1946.
He was awarded a State Prize in 1946, Lenin Prize in 1962,
and two Orders of Lenin. In November 1962 Landau was
awarded the Nobel Prize in physics. He is a member of numerous foreign scientific organizations including: the National
Academy of Sciences of the United States, the English Physical
Society, the English Royal Society, the Danish Royal Academy
of Sciences, the Dutch Academy of Sciences, and the French
Physical Society.

Landau's investigations are in solid state theory and physics
of low temperatures. He has worked out a thermodynamic theory of the phase transitions of a secondary kind in solids bodies,
and elucidated their profound connection with the qualitative
change of a body's symmetry during transition. In 1940-41
Landau developed the macroscopic theory of liquid helium
superfluidity which takes place in this fluid at temperatures
close to absolute zero. Landau predicted the possibility of dif-
fusing sound waves with two unequal speeds (phenomenon of
secondary sound) in liquid helium. In his works on superconductivity, Landau presented a theory on the intermediate condition of superconductors. In conjunction with A. Abrikosov,
I. Pomeranchuk and I. Khalatnikov, Landau found a solution to
the main equations of the quantum field theory, without the use
of the perturbation theory, and he proved that the concept of
point interaction is groundless because it leads to the absence
of any interaction. Recently, in connection with the discovery of
the nonconservation of parity in weak interactions, Landau proposed the theory of combined inversion and the theory of a "two
component neutrino." A considerable number of his investigations are in nuclear physics and cosmic rays.

Bibliography:
Continuum Mechanics, Hydrodynamics and the Theory of
Elasticity. Moscow-Leningrad: 1944.
and E. M. Lifshits. Field Theory, 2nd ed. Moscow-
Leningrad: 1948.

and E. M. Lifshits. Quantum Mechanics, Part I. Moscow-Leningrad: 1948.

and E. M. Lifshits. Statistical Physics (Classic and Quantum). Moscow-Leningrad: 1951.

On the theory of phase transition. Zhur. Eksptl. i Teoret. Fiz., 1937, #1, 5.

Theory of helium superfluidity. Zhur. Eksptl. i Teoret. Fiz., 1941, #6.

On the theory of intermediate condition of superconductors. Zhur. Eksptl. i Teoret. Fiz., 1943, #11-12.

and A. Abrikosov, I. Khalatnikov. On the quantum theory of fields. Nuovo cimento, supplement, 1956, 3, #1, 80.

On the laws of conservation at weak interactions. One possibility for polarized properties of neutrons. Zhur. Eksptl. i Teoret. Fiz., 1957, #2.

and L. Pyatigorskii. Mechanics. Moscow-Leningrad: 1940.

and E. M. Lifshits. Mechanics of Continuous Media. Moscow-Leningrad: 1944.

Biography:

V. B. Berestetskii. Lev Davidovich Landau (To the 50th Anniversary since the date of birth). Uspekhi Fiz. Nauk, 64, #3 (1958).

Office: S. I. Vavilov Institute of Physics Problems of USSR
            Academy of Sciences
            Vorob'evskoye Shosse, 2
            Moscow, USSR

Telephone: B2 18 86

LARIONOV, ANDREI NIKOLAEVICH (Electrical Engineer)

A. N. Larionov was born July 16, 1889. He graduated in 1919 from Moscow Technical College and until 1930 taught there. From 1921 to 1941 he also worked at the All Union Electro-Technical Institute. In 1930 he assisted in the organization of the Moscow Institute of Energetics and in 1933 was made a professor there. He began working in 1953 at the Institute of Automation and Telemechanics of the U.S.S.R. Academy of Sciences. Since 1953 he has been a Corresponding Member of the U.S.S.R. Academy of Sciences.

The major works of Larionov deal with the theory, calculation, and construction of special electric machines and electric drive. Under the leadership and participation of Larionov there were developed a series of electric machines which are distinguished by their light weight and small size (high voltage, direct current machines, high voltage direct-current

convertors, machines with excitation by permanent magnets,
alternating current generators, special machines). In 1924 he
proposed a three-phase bridge scheme of current rectification.
He took part in the planning of electrical equipment in the airplane "Maxim Gorki", in the solution of technical problems
associated with the starting of turbo and hydro generators in
power plants, and in the solution of the electrification of oil
fields.
Bibliography:
  Utilization of Electricity in Aviation and Motor Transport.
  Moscow-Leningrad: 1954.
  and others. Basis of Electrical Equipment in Aircraft and
  Automobiles. Moscow-Leningrad: 1955.
  and others. Hysteresis of Electric Motors. Works of the
  Moscow Institute of Energetics of V. M. Molotov. #16,
  Moscow-Leningrad: 1956.
  Selection of single optimum frequencies for autonomous
  systems of alternating current with special elements and
  electric machines of automation. Session of the U.S.S.R.
  Academy of Sciences on Scientific Problems of Automation
  in Industry, October 15-20, 1956. Moscow: 1957. (Works
  of a Session of the U.S.S.R. Academy of Sciences, 5.
Biography:
  Professor A. N. Larionov (On the 60th Anniversary since the
  date of birth and 30th Anniversary of his scientific-
  pedagogical activity. Electricity, 1950, #1.
Office: Institute of Automation and Remote Control of USSR
              Academy of Sciences
              Kalanchevskaya Ulitsa 15-a
              Moscow, USSR
Residence: Krasnokazarmennaya, 12
              Moscow, USSR
Telephone: ZH 4 38 00

LAVRENKO, EVGENII MIKHAILOVICH (Geobotanist)
  E. M. Lavrenko was born February 24, 1900. In 1921-1928,
he worked at the Botanical Gardens in Khar'kov. He was assistant professor in 1929, and in 1931-1934 professor at Khar'-
kov Agricultural Institute. In 1934 he started working at the
Botanical Institute of the U.S.S.R. Academy of Sciences. Since
1946 he has been a Corresponding Member of the U.S.S.R.
Academy of Sciences.
  Lavrenko developed a new classification for steppe vegetation of the U.S.S.R. and proposed the zonal and provincial

division of vegetation of European-Asiatic Steppe Regions. He
investigated zoning and compiled vegetation maps. His work on
the history of flora and vegetation threw light on the origin of
vegetative cover of the U.S.S.R. He introduced the concept of
phytogeosphere as a part of the biosphere.
Bibliography:
   History of flora and vegetation of U.S.S.R. according to the
   data of the contemporary distribution of plants. Vegetation
   of the U.S.S.R. (Collection of Articles), 1. Moscow-
   Leningrad: 1938, 235-296.
   Steppes of the U.S.S.R. Vegetation of the U.S.S.R. (Col-
   lection of Articles), 2. Moscow-Leningrad: 1940, 1-265.
   On the phytogeosphere. Questions of Geography, Moscow,
   1949, #15, 53-66.
   Age of botanical regions in non-tropical Eurasia. Izvest.
   Akad. Nauk S.S.S.R., Ser. Geog., Moscow, 1951, #2, 17-28.
   and V. B. Sochava, eds. Steppes and agricultural lands in
   the steppe regions. Vegetative Cover of the U.S.S.R.
   Explanatory text to "Geobotanical Map" of the U.S.S.R.,
   Scale 1:4,000,000. Moscow-Leningrad: 1956, 595-730.
Office: V. L. Komarov Institute of Botany of USSR Academy
            of Sciences
            Ulitsa Popova, 2
            Leningrad, P-22, USSR

LAVRENTEV, MIKHAIL ALEKSEEVICH (Mathematician)

   M. A. Lavrentev was born November 19, 1900 in Kazan. In
1922 he graduated from Moscow University. He received the
Doctor of Physical-Mathematical Sciences degree in 1933 and
the Doctor of Technical Sciences degree in 1932. From 1931 to
1941, he was professor at Moscow University. He was made
Chairman in 1934 of the Department on Theory of Functions at
the Mathematical Institute of the U.S.S.R. Academy of Sciences.
From 1939 to 1948 he was Director of the Institute of Mathematics and Mechanics of the Ukrainian S.S.R. Academy of Sci-
ences, and from 1945 to 1948 he was Vice President of this
Academy. Lavrentev was Director of the Institute of Exact
Mechanics and Computing Techniques of the U.S.S.R. Academy
of Sciences from 1950 to 1953. He was, in 1951-53 and in 1955-
57, Academician Secretary of the Department of Physico-
Mathematical Sciences of the U.S.S.R. Academy of Sciences.
In 1957 he became Vice President of the U.S.S.R. Academy of
Sciences and Chairman of the Siberian branch of the U.S.S.R.
Academy of Sciences. He was elected Academician of the

Ukrainian S.S.R. Academy of Sciences in 1939, and in 1946
Academician of the U.S.S.R. Academy of Sciences. Lavrentev
has been a member of the Communist Party of the Soviet Union
since 1952. In 1957 he became a member of the Czechoslovaki-
an Academy of Sciences. He was a deputy to the U.S.S.R. Supreme Soviet (5th Convocation). Lavrentev was elected again a
deputy from RSFSR to the Supreme Soviet in March 1962. In
1946 and 1949, he was awarded Stalin Prizes, and in 1960 received the Order of Lenin.

Lavrentev has been interested in the theory of the function
of a complex variable, the metric study of the conformity of the
boundaries at conformal mapping, and the properties of
functions that can be represented by converging series of polynomials. He worked out the theory of quasi-conformal mapping, which is the basis of geometric methods of solving a wide
range of problems in mathematics and mathematical physics.
Lavrentev did a great deal of work on problems of the mechanics of a continuous medium and on hydrodynamics such as
the theory of flows and a new theory of non-linear waves.

As of 1961, Lavrentev was Director of the Institute of Hydrodynamics of the Siberian Branch U.S.S.R. Academy of Sciences
and, in the same year, he was elected to the Central Committee
of the Communist Party.

Bibliography:
On the theory of conformal mapping. Works of the Physico-
Mathematical Institute of V. A. Steklov, 1934, 5.
Some properties of single leaf functions with application to
the theory of flows. Mat. Sbornik, 1938, 4, #3.
General problem of the theory of quasi-conformal mapping
of plane regions. Mat. Sbornik, New Series, 1947, 21, #2.
Main theorem of the theory of quasi-conformal mapping of
plane regions. Izvest. Akad. Nauk S.S.S.R., Ser. Mat., 1948,
12, #6.

Biography:
M. V. Keldysh. On the 50th birthday of M. A. Lavrentev.
Izvest. Akad. Nauk S.S.S.R., Ser. Mat., 1951, 15, 1.
Mathematics in the U.S.S.R. during the last 30 Years. Col-
lection of Articles. Moscow-Leningrad: 1948.

Office: President, Siberian Department of USSR Academy
                of Sciences
                Novosibirsk, Siberia

LAVROVSKII, KONSTANTIN PETROVICH (Organic Chemist)

K. P. Lavrovskii was born December 31, 1898. He graduated in 1926 from Moscow University. In 1930-34 he worked at the State Scientific Research Oil Institute and in 1933 became a professor there. He also worked for a number of years in the oil industry. Beginning in 1942 he was at the U.S.S.R. Academy of Sciences, first at the Institute of Mineral Fields, then at the Institute of Oil. Since 1953 he has been a Corresponding Member of the U.S.S.R. Academy of Sciences. He has been a member of the Communist Party of the Soviet Union from 1920. He was awarded M. V. Frunze and N. D. Zelinskii Prizes.

Lavrovskii's investigations are concerned with the field of chemistry and technology of oil refining and organic catalysis. His work on the synthesis of tetraethyl lead was the basis for the Soviet production of this antiknock agent. He developed the commercial production of aviation gasoline from sulfur crude of "Second Baku." His studies of catalytic hydrocarbon transformations was a theoretical basis for the production of unsaturated gases and high octane fuels.

Bibliography:

and A. M. Brodskii. Physico-chemical investigation of high velocity cracking. Reports at the IVth International Oil Congress in Rome. Moscow: 1955.

and A. M. Brodskii. Processing of gaseous paraffins under conditions of high velocity cracking. Works of the Institute of Oil of the U.S.S.R. Academy of Sciences, 1954, 4, 176-198.

and Yu. L. Fish, N. N. Naimushin. Catalytic cracking of cyclical hydrocarbons under pressure. Works of the Institute of Oil of the U.S.S.R. Academy of Sciences, 1952, 2.

and A. L. Rozenthal' and A. Kh. Eglit. Interaction of iron ores with methane in conditions of a 'boiling' layer. Doklady Akad. Nauk S.S.S.R., 1957, 112, #4.

Office: USSR Academy of Sciences Institute of Petrochemical Synthesis
Leninskii Prospekt, 29
Moscow, USSR

Residence: 1st Donskoi pr. 15
Moscow, USSR

Telephone: B2 51 90

LEBEDEV, ALEKSANDR ALEKSEEVICH (Physicist)

A. A. Lebedev was born November 26, 1893. In 1916 he graduated from Petersburg University and remained there to prepare for a professorship. Except for a few years, he has

217   LEBEDEV

been working at Leningrad University until the present time.
He was a Corresponding Member of the U.S.S.R. Academy of
Sciences from 1939 to 1943 when he was elected an Academici-
an. Lebedev was twice a Deputy to the U.S.S.R. Supreme Soviet.
He received a Stalin Prize in 1947 and again in 1949. In 1957
he was made a Hero of Socialist Labor.

In 1919, at the State Optical Institute, Lebedev began a varied
study of the processes of annealing optical glass. He formulated a theory of temperature conditions for annealing various
types of glass. Lebedev investigated the use of interference
for measuring wave lengths and indices of refraction. In 1931
he designed a polarized interferrometer which was based on
light passing through a birefringent lens. He is a prominent
Soviet specialist in the area of electronic optics. In 1931, while
studying the diffraction of fast electrons, Lebedev used the
focusing action of a magnetic lens in an electron diffraction
camera. Together with associates, Lebedev designed a Soviet
electronic microscope (Stalin Prize 1947). He has also studied
photoelectric phenomena, and he directed the construction of a
Soviet photographic camera (Stalin Prize 1949).

In 1958 Lebedev was appointed Chief of the U.S.S.R. Academy of Sciences Commission Staff on Radiobiology. As of 1961,
he was Chairman of the Permanent Commission for Electron
Microscopy.

Bibliography:
On structural transformations in glass, in Structure of
Glass. Collection of Articles. Moscow-Leningrad: 1953.

Biography:
Academician A. A. Lebedev, in General Conference of the
U.S.S.R. Academy of Sciences, September 25-30, 1943.
Moscow-Leningrad: 1944.
Academician Aleksandr Alekseevich Lebedev (On the 60th
Anniversary since the date of birth). Zhur. Eksptl. i Teoret.
Fiz., 1953, 25, #6(12).

Office: Department of Physics
              Leningrad University
              Leningrad, USSR

LEBEDEV, SERGEI ALEKSEEVICH (Radio Engineer)

S. A. Lebedev was born November 2, 1902. After graduating
in 1928 from Moscow Technological College, he worked until
1945 in the All-Union Electrotechnical Institute. In 1946 to
1951 he was Director of the Institute of Electroengineering at
the Ukrainian S.S.R. Academy of Sciences. Lebedev became

Director, in 1953, of the Institute of Exact Mechanics and Computing Technicians of the U.S.S.R. Academy of Sciences. Also in 1953 he was made professor at the Moscow Physico-Technical Institute. He has been a member of the Communist Party of the Soviet Union since 1946. In 1945 he was elected Academician of the Ukrainian S.S.R. Academy of Sciences and in 1953 an Academician of the U.S.S.R. Academy of Sciences. He was awarded a Stalin Prize in 1950 and in 1956 he was a Hero of Socialist Labor.

Lebedev was one of the first in the U.S.S.R. to work on the stability of power systems. He is the author of a theory on the stability of synchronous machines, and a specialist in automation of power systems. He has been working on computer techniques and the design and construction of computer devices. He directed the construction of high speed computers.

In December 1958 and April 1959, Lebedev visited the United States to attend the Joint Computer Conference in Philadelphia.

In November 1962 Lebedev was awarded the Order of Lenin.
Bibliography:
and P. S. Zhdanov. Stability of Parallel Action of Electrical Systems, 2nd ed. Moscow-Leningrad: 1934.
Artificial stability of synchronous machines (speech at 12th session of International Conference on Large Electric Networks, Paris, June 24-July 3, 1948, published in Moscow, 1948).
Biography:
Lebedev, Sergei Alekseevich. Vestnik Akad. Nauk S.S.S.R., 1954, #1, 42.
A. D. Nesterenko and I. T. Shvets. Sergei Alekseevich Lebedev. Questions of Electro-automation and Radio Technics. Kiev: 1954.
Office: Institute of Precision Mechanics and Computation Techniques
USSR Academy of Sciences
Leninskii Prospekt, 51
Moscow, USSR
Residence: Novopeschanaya, 17
Moscow, USSR
Telephone: D7 53 75

LEONTOVICH, MIKHAIL ALEKSANDROVICH (Physicist)
M. A. Leontovich was born March 9, 1903, son of A. V. Leontovich (1869-1943, physiologist). In 1923 he graduated from Moscow University. He worked on the Commission for

Investigation of the Kursk Magnetic Anomoly. Beginning in
1929, he was a scientific worker at the Physics Institute of
Moscow University. He was a professor from 1934 to 1935 and
again in 1955 at Moscow University. From 1934 to 1941 and
1946 to 1952, he worked at the Physics Institute of the U.S.S.R.
Academy of Sciences. Leontovich began working at the Institute
of Atomic Energy, U.S.S.R. Academy of Sciences in 1951. In
1939 he was elected Corresponding Member of the U.S.S.R.
Academy of Sciences and in 1946 Academician. He received
the Gold Medal of A. S. Popov in 1952, and in 1958 a Lenin
Prize.

Leontovich's investigations are in electrodynamics, optics,
statistical physics, radiophysics. Important investigations by
Leontovich are on the theory of molecular dispersion of light
(until 1935), in ultra-acoustics [absorption of sound in gases
(1936), in liquids (1936 and 1939)], on the theory of fluctuations
and statistical physics [on the basis of thermodynamic statistics
(1932), on gas-kinetic equations derived from the theory on sto-
chastic processes (1935)], and in various aspects of radiophysics
[thermal fluctuations of the electromagnetic field in solids (together with S. M. Rytov)]. Leontovich also studied the theory of
radiowave propagation and the theory of antennae. He determined
the approximate ratios between the components of the electromagnetic field on the surface of a conducting medium, thus considerably simplifying mathematical treatment of the problem of
radiowave propagation along the earth's surface and allowing
solution of many special problems. A theory of fine wire antennae was completed by Leontovich jointly with his student,
M. L. Levin, and published as "On the Theory of Excitation of
Oscillations in Antennae Vibrators" (1944). Leontovich participated in solving practical problems in radioengineering. For
his work in radiophysics and radioengineering Leontovich was
awarded the Gold Medal of A. S. Popov (1952). Recently he has
been investigating powerful pulse discharges in gas in an effort
to obtain high-temperature plasma (Lenin Prize 1958).

Bibliography:
   Statistical Physics. Moscow-Leningrad: 1944.
   Introduction to Thermodynamics, 2nd ed. Moscow-
   Leningrad: 1952.
Biography:
   Mikhail Aleksandrovich Leontovich. On the 50th Anniversary
   since the date of birth. Zhur. Eksptl. i Teoret. Fiz., 1953,
   <u>24</u>, #1 (7).

S. Khaikin. Laureate of the Gold Medal of Popov. Radio,
1952, #6.

Office: I. V. Kurchatov Institute of Atomic Energy of USSR
               Academy of Sciences
               Moscow, USSR

LEVICH, VENIAMIN GRIGOR'EVICH (Physical Chemist and
        Theoretical Physicist)

V. G. Levich was born March 30, 1917. He graduated in
1937 from Kharkov University. In 1940-1958 he worked at the
Institute of Physical Chemistry at the U.S.S.R. Academy of
Sciences. He taught in 1940-1949 at Moscow State Pedagogical
Institute. He was made Departmental Chairman of the Moscow
Engineering-Physical Institute in 1950, and in 1951 professor.
In 1958, Levich became Chairman of the Theoretical Depart-
ment of the Institute of Electrochemistry of the U.S.S.R. Acade-
my of Sciences. Since 1958 he has been a Corresponding Mem-
ber of the U.S.S.R. Academy of Sciences.

The works of Levich deal with the investigation of physico-
chemical processes and are mainly concerned with problems of
physico-chemical hydrodynamics. He formulated a theory of
mass transfer to the phase contacting area, a theory of concentrated polarization with the passing of a current through solutions, a theory of the influence of surface-active substances
on the movement of a liquid, a theory of a non-equilibrium
double layer, coagulation of aerosols and colloids in turbulent
flows, and other questions on the theory of mutual influence of
physico-chemical processes and the movement of a medium.
Bibliography:
    Physico-Chemical Hydrodynamics. Moscow: 1952.
    Statistical Physics. Moscow: 1950.
    and B. M. Grafov. Effect of rectification on an ideally
    polarized electrode. Doklady Akad. Nauk S.S.S.R. 146, #6,
    1372-73 (1962).
Office: Theoretical Department
               Institute of Electrochemistry of USSR Academy of
                   Sciences
               Leninskii Prospekt, 31
               Moscow, USSR
Residence: Zhitnaya, 10
               Moscow, USSR
Telephone: B3 02 68

221   LIFSHITS

LIFSHITS, IL'YA MIKHAILOVICH (Physicist)

I. M. Lifshits was born in 1917. In 1936 he graduated from
the Khar'kov State University, and in 1938 from the Khar'kov
Mechanico-Machine-Building Institute. He started, in 1937, as
a scientific worker, and in 1941, became a section chief at the
Ukraine S.S.R. Academy of Sciences Physico-Technical Institute in Khar'kov. Also in 1941 he received his Doctor of Science Degree. In 1944 he became Chairman of the Theoretical
Physics Department of Khar'kov State University. He is a
Corresponding Member of the Ukrainian SSR Academy of Sciences and was elected, in 1960, a Corresponding Member of the
U.S.S.R. Academy of Sciences. In 1952 Lifshits was awarded
the Mandelshtam Memorial Prize of the U.S.S.R. Academy of
Sciences for work on dynamic theory of nonideal crystals. For
his research on electronic structure of metals, he received, in
1961, the Simon Memorial Prize of the Physical Society of
London.

Lifshits' works deal with the theory of solid state physics
and low temperature physics.

Bibliography:

On the theory of X-rays scattering by crystals with variable
structure. Sow. Phys. $\underline{12}$, (1937).
Optical behavior of non-ideal crystal lattices in infra-red.
Zhur. Eksper. i Teor. Fiz. $\underline{12}$, 117 (1942). (English trans.
Jour. of Phys. $\underline{7}$, 215, 1943). Zhur. Eksper. i Teor. Fiz. $\underline{12}$,
137 (1942). (English trans. Jour. of Phys. 7, 86, 1943).
Zhur. Eksper. i Teor. Fiz. $\underline{12}$, 156 (1942). (English trans.
Jour. of Phys. $\underline{8}$, 82, 1944).
On the theory of degenerate regular perturbation. I, II.
Zhur. Eksper. i Teor. Fiz. $\underline{17}$, 1017 (1947). Zhur. Eksper. i
Teor. Fiz. $\underline{17}$, 1076 (1947).
and I. V. Obreimov. On the theory of crystal twinning.
Jour. of Phys. $\underline{11}$, 121 (1947).
Short elastic waves scattering in a crystal lattice. Zhur.
Eksper. i Teor. Fiz. $\underline{18}$, 293 (1948).
and L. N. Rosentzveig. Dynamics of crystals lattice filling
a semi-space. Zhur. Eksper. i Teor. Fiz. $\underline{18}$, 1012 (1948).
On kinetics of superconductivity destruction in magnetic
field. Zhur. Eksper. i Teor. Fiz. $\underline{20}$, 834 (1950).
On a problem of perturbation theory, connected with quantum
statistics. Uspekhi Mat. Nauk $\underline{7}$, 171 (1952).
On thermal properties of chain and layer structure at low
temperature. Zhur. Eksper. i Teor. Fiz. $\underline{22}$, 475 (1952).

On determination of energy spectrum of Bose-system from
its thermal heat capacity. Zhur. Eksper. i Teor. Fiz. 26, 5
(1952).

and A. M. Kosevich. On the theory of the De-Haas-van-
Alphen effect for the particles with arbitrary dispersion low.
Doklady Akad. Nauk S.S.S.R. 96, 5 (1954).

and A. V. Pogorelov. On determination of Fermi-surface
and velocities in metals from magnetic susceptibility oscillations. Doklady Akad. Nauk S.S.S.R. 96, 6 (1954).

On the theory of magnetic susceptibility in metals at low
temperatures. Zhur. Eksper. i Teor. Fiz. 29, 6 (1955).

Some problems of dynamic theory of non-ideal crystal lattices. Supplemento del Nuovo-cimento 3, 4 (1956).

and M. Ja. Azbel', M. I. Kaganov. The theory of galvano-
magnetic phenomena in metals. Zhur. Eksper. i Teor. Fiz.
31, 22 (1956).

and G. I. Stepanova. On the oscillation spectrum of the dis-
ordered crystal lattices. Zhur. Eksper. i Teor. Fiz. 30, 5
(1956).

and M. Ja. Azbel', V. I. Gerasimenko. Paramagnetic resonance and polarization of nuclei in metals. Jour. of Phys.
and Chem. of Solids (1957).

and G. I. Stepanova. The correlation in solid solutions.
Zhur. Eksper. i Teor. Fiz. 33, v2(8), 485 (1957).

Quantum theory of galvanomagnetic effects in metals. Jour.
of Phys. and Chem. of Solids 4, 11 (1958).

and A. M. Kosevich. Theory of Shubnikov-De-Haas effect.
Jour. of Phys. and Chem. of Solids, 4, 1 (1958).

and V. V. Slesov. On the kinetics of diffusional decay of
supersaturated solid solutions. Zhur. Eksper. i Teor. Fiz.
35, v2(8) (1958). Jour. of Phys. and Chem. of Solids 19,
#112, p. 35 (1961).

and M. Ja. Azbel'. The electronic resonances in metals.
Progress in Low Temperature Physics v. III, 1961.

The theory of quantum cyclotronic resonance in metals.
Zhur. Eksper. i Teor. Fiz. 40, #4 (1961).

and V. G. Pestcharsky. The galvanomagnetic characteristics
of metals with open Fermi-surfaces. Zhur. Eksper. i Teor.
Fiz. 35, #5(11), 1958.

and M. I. Kaganov, L. V. Tanatarov. On the theory of the
radiation effects in metals. Atomnaya Energia 6, #4 (1959).

and M. I. Kaganov. Some problems of electron theory of
metals. I. Uspekhi Fiz. Nauk 69, #3 (1959). II. Uspekhi
Fiz. Nauk 78, #3 (1962).

High-pressure anomalies of electron properties of metals.
Zhur. Eksper. I Teor. Fiz. 38, #5 (1960).
The kinetics of ordering at phase transition of second order.
Zhur. Eksper. i Teor. Fiz. 42, #5 (1962).
and V. V. Slezov. Dynamic equilibrium of a fog cloud over
a liquid surface. Doklady Akad. Nauk S.S.S.R. 146, #2, 799-
802 (1962).
Office: Ukrainian SSR Academy of Sciences Physico-
               Technical Institute of USSR Academy of Sciences
               Yumovskii Tupik, 2
               Khar'kov 24, Ukrainian SSR

LINNIK, VLADIMIR PAVLOVICH (Physicist)
V. P. Linnik was born July 6, 1889. In 1914 he graduated
from Kiev University. He began working at the State Optical
Institute in 1926. Until 1941 he was a professor at Leningrad
University. Since 1939 he has been an Academician of the
U.S.S.R. Academy of Sciences. Twice, in 1946 and in 1950, he
was awarded Stalin Prizes.
   Linnik's research is in optics and its application in the
instrument-making industry. He constructed the following optical devices: a double microscope (1929), microinterferometer
(1933) for controlling the exactness of the processing of surfaces, a microscope for studying the surface of red-hot bodies,
interferometers for measuring double stars and the angular
diameter of the sun. He has developed methods of laboratory
investigation and testing of optical devices such as the aber-
ration of optical systems, the centering of optical systems, and
the assembling of microscope lenses. He designed control
devices for optical-mechanical industry. Linnik also worked
on the physics of X-rays and, in particular, on the investigation
of crystals with X-rays.
Bibliography:
   Device for interference investigation of the reflecting objects
   under the microscope ("Microinterferometer"). Doklady
   Akad. Nauk S.S.S.R., 1933, #1.
   Device for interference investigation of the microprofile of a
   surface ("Microprofilometer"). Doklady Akad. Nauk S.S.S.R.,
   1945, 47, #9.
   Interferometer for controlling large machine details. Doklady Akad. Nauk S.S.S.R., 1942, 35, #1.
   Interference passage instrument. Doklady Akad. Nauk, 1946,
   53, #3.

On the fundamental possibility of lessening the influence of
the atmosphere on the image of a star. Optika i Spektro-
scopy, 1957, 3, #4.
Statistically similar zones of a linear type. Doklady Akad.
Nauk S.S.S.R. 144, #5, 974-76 (1962).
Theory of statistical similar zones. Doklady Akad. Nauk
S.S.S.R. 146, #2, 300-03 (1962).
and V. F. Skubenko. Asymptote of whole number third order
matrices. Doklady Akad. Nauk S.S.S.R. 146, #5, 1007-08
(1962).
Biography:
  V. P. Linnik. Uspekhi Fiz. Nauk, 1939, 21, #2.
  Academician Vladimir Pavlovich Linnik. Vestnik Akad.
  Nauk S.S.S.R., 1939, #2-3.
Office: Department of Physics
              Leningrad University
              Leningrad, USSR

LINNIK, YURII VLADIMIROVICH (Mathematician)
  Yu. V. Linnik was born January 8, 1915. He graduated from
Leningrad University in 1938 and did postgraduate work there
in 1940, in which year he was granted the Doctor of Physical-
Mathematical Sciences degree. Since 1940, he has been em-
ployed at the Leningrad branch of the U.S.S.R. Academy of
Sciences Mathematics Institute, and has been a professor at
Leningrad University since 1944. In 1947 he was awarded a
Stalin Prize. He was elected, in 1953, a Corresponding Member
of the U.S.S.R. Academy of Sciences.
  In the theory of numbers, Linnik was occupied with the
presentation of numbers in quadratic form and gave an estimation of the smallest prime number in an arithmetical pro-
gression with a large difference. He also worked in the calcu-
lus of probability, on heterogeneous Markov chains and on
mathematical statistics.
Bibliography:
  Asymptotic distribution of whole points on a sphere. Doklady Akad. Nauk S.S.S.R., 1954, 96, #5.
  Asymptotic distribution of reduced binary forms in connection with the geometry of Lobachevskii. I-III. Vestnik of
  Leningrad University, 1955, #2, 3-23; #5, 3-32; #8, 15-28.
Office: Leningrad Section
              Mathematical Institute of USSR Academy of Sciences
              Nab. Fontanki, 25
              Leningrad D-11, USSR

LIVANOV, MIKHAIL NIKOLAEOVICH (Human and Animal
_____Physiologist)
     As of 1962, M. N. Livanov has been working at the Institute
of Biophysics, Moscow, Academy of Medical Sciences and at the
Institute of Higher Nervous Activity, Moscow, Academy of Sciences U.S.S.R. He was elected a Corresponding Member of the
U.S.S.R. Academy of Sciences, June 1962.

LURIE (LUR'YE), ANATOLII ISAKOVICH (Mechanics Specialist)
     A. I. Lurie was born in 1901. Upon graduating from the
Leningrad Polytechnical Institute (Faculty of Physics and Mechanics) in 1925, he began working there. In 1935, he became
a professor, and chairman of the Department of Theoretical
Mechanics and later (1944) of Machine Strength and Dynamics.
He was elected, in 1960, a Corresponding Member of the
U.S.S.R. Academy of Sciences.
     Lurie's basic work deals with the theory of tensile strength,
stability of automatic control systems and analytical mechanics.
Bibliography:
     and L. G. Loitsianskii. Theoretical Mechanics, v. 1, 2, 3.
     Six editions Gostekhizdat 1932-1955, translated into Bulgarian (1958) and Chinese (1954).
     Operational Calculus with Application to Mechanical Problems. Gos. Izd. Tekh. Teor. Lit: 1st ed. 1938, 2nd ed. 1950.
     Statics of thin-walled elastic shells. (U. S. Atomic Energy
     Commission, Translation series AEC Tr-3798) Washington,
     D. C., Office of Technical Services, Dept. of Commerce,
     1959, 210 pp. Translated into Chinese, 1957. Goz. Izdat.
     Tekh.-Teor. Lit: Moscow, 1947, 252 pp. Applied Mechanics
     Rev. 13, 3324 (1960).
     Some nonlinear problems of the theory of automatic control.
     Translated from the Russian (Gostekhizdat, 1951): Akademie
     Verlag Berlin 1957; Ministry of Supply, Her Majesty's
     Stationary Office, London, 1957. Applied Mechanics Rev. 13,
     3259 (1960).
     Three-dimensional problems of the theory of elasticity.
     Moscow, Gostekhizdat, 1955, 494 pp. Ref. Zh. Mekh. #4,
     1957, Rev. 4562. Applied Mechanics Rev. 12, 45 (1959).
     Analytical Mechanics. Gos. Izd. Phys. Math. Lit.: 1961,
     824 pp.
     Bibliography of journal publications can be found in: Prik.
     Mat. i Mekh. 25, #4, 1961. Journal of Applied Mathematics
     and Mechanics, Pergamon Press Inc., N. Y., 25, #4, 1961.

Office: Department of Machine Strength and Dynamics
           Leningrad Polytechnical Institute
           Leningrad, USSR
Residence: Polytechnical Road 3; app. 90
           Leningrad K-64, USSR

LYSENKO, TROFIM DENISOVICH (Biologist and Agriculturist)

T. D. Lysenko was born September 17, 1898. He graduated from Uman School of Horticulture in 1921 and in 1925 from Kiev Institute of Agriculture. He worked on an experimental selection station in Gandzha (now Kirovobad), Azerbaidzhan S.S.R. then at the All-Union Genetic Institute in Odessa. From 1938 to 1956 he was President of the Lenin All-Union Academy of Agricultural Sciences, and was elected a Member of the Presidium in 1960. In 1940 Lysenko was made Director of the Genetics Institute of the U.S.S.R. Academy of Sciences. He has been an Academician of the Ukrainian S.S.R. Academy of Sciences since 1934 and of the U.S.S.R. Academy of Sciences since 1939. In 1935 he became an Active Member of the Lenin All-Union Academy of Agricultural Sciences. Lysenko was Deputy to the Supreme Soviet of the U.S.S.R., first through fifth convocations. In March 1962, he was again elected deputy from the Ukrainian SSR to the Supreme Soviet. In 1941, 1943, and 1949 he was awarded Stalin Prizes and in 1945 he was a Hero of Socialist Labor.

Lysenko works are in the following fields: heredity and its variability, individual development of organisms, intra- and inter-species relationships, plant nutrition. Lysenko enunciated a theory on stagewise development of plants. He proposed a method of seed treatment (vernalization) before sowing and of cotton stamping. He developed a number of new grains (vernalized wheat "lyutestsens 1173," "odesskaya 13," barley "odesskii 14," cotton "odesskii 1." Based on a hypothesis of the connection between an organism and the surrounding medium he attempted to develop methods of direct changes of organic nature in agricultural plants. He attempted to convert vernalized non-wintering farm crops into cold-resistant winter crops. He proposed a method of soil fertilization by organic-mineral mixtures. While working on questions of vegetative and sexual hybridization Lysenko formed a number of theories on heredity and its variability. In addition to finding rules for individual development of plants, Lysenko also studied the laws of species' formation and intra- and interspecies relationships. After studying relationships among individual organisms within a

species, Lysenko proposed a theory that in nature there is no
overpopulation within the species and the struggle for survival
is absent. He also postulated that the existing biological species
can directly produce other species under the influence of the
surrounding medium changes. These ideas are not shared by
many Soviet scientists.

Bibliography:
Report on the position in biological science, in the book:
Position in Biological Science. Stenographic report of the
session of V. I. Lenin All-Union Academy of Agricultural
Sciences, July 31-August 7, 1948. Moscow: 1948.
Agricultural Biology. Works on Genetics, Selection and
Seed Cultivation, 6th ed. Moscow: 1952.
Successive Development of Plants. Works on the Theory of
Successive Development and Vernalization of Agricultural
Plants. Moscow: 1952.
Selected Works. Moscow: 1953.

Biography:
B. A. Keller. Plant Nature Reformers. K. I. Timiryazev,
I. V. Michurin, T. D. Lysenko. Moscow: 1944.
A. Molodchikov. Reformers of Nature (I. V. Michurin,
T. D. Lysenko, L. Burbank). Moscow: 1948.
M. S. Voinov. Academician T. D. Lysenko. Moscow: 1950.

Office: Institute of Genetics of USSR Academy of Sciences
Leninskii Prospekt, 33
Moscow, USSR

LYUL'KA, ARKHIP MIKHAILOVICH (Aeronautical Engineer)

A. M. Lyul'ka was born March 24, 1908. After graduating
in 1931 from the Kiev Polytechnic Institute, he worked at the
Kharkov Turbo-Generator Plant. In 1933-1939 he worked at
the Kharkov Aviation Institute. Lyul'ka worked at the Central
Boiler-Turbine Institute in Leningrad in 1939-1941, and subsequently in other scientific research and designers' organizations. In 1958 he received his Doctor of Technical Sciences
degree. He is a professor. Since 1947 he has been a member
of the Communist Party of the Soviet Union. In 1948 and 1951,
he was awarded Stalin Prizes and in 1957 Hero of Socialist
Labor. He was elected, in 1960, a Corresponding Member of
the U.S.S.R. Academy of Sciences.

While at the Kharkov Aviation Institute, Lyul'ka began working on the problem of utilizing a gas turbine as an aviation
engine. In this period he worked out a theory and method of
constructing high altitude and high-performance characteristics

for a turbo-compression air fed engine and the expediency of
using this engine as a power plant for a high-performance jet
plane. In 1937-39 Lyul'ka designed the first Soviet experimental turbo-compression jet aviation engine. In postwar
years, powerful, contemporary turbojet engines AL-3, AL-5
were built under the leadership of Lyul'ka. He has been working on a series of basic engineering problems such as the analytic dependence of the degeneration of a turbojet engine on the
speed of flight as in its transfer into a ramjet.

Office: USSR Academy of Sciences
               Leninskii Prospekt, 14
               Moscow, USSR

LYUSTERNIK, LAZAR ARONOVICH (Mathematician)

L. A. Lyusternik was born December 31, 1899 in Zdunska
Wola, Poland. He graduated from Moscow University in 1922
and received the degree of Doctor of Physical-Mathematics in
1935. In 1931, he became a professor at Moscow University.
He was awarded a Stalin Prize in 1946, and was made a Corresponding Member of the U.S.S.R. Academy of Sciences in 1946.

Lyusternik utilized topological methods for calculus of variations "in the whole." In 1924, he applied the method of finite
differences to the solution on the problem of Dirichlet. He
proved, together with L. G. Shnirelman, the theorem of three
geodesics. He also works in the area of functional analysis,
differential equations, and computing mathematics.

Bibliography:
   Problem of Dirichlet. Uspekhi Mat. Nauk, 1940, #8.
   Topology of functional spaces and calculus of variations in the
   whole. Works of the Mathematical Institute of V. A. Steklov,
   1947, 19.

Biography:
   Thirty Years of Mathematics in the U.S.S.R. 1917-1947.
   Moscow-Leningrad: 1948 (Collection of articles under
   editorship of A. G. Kurosh et al.)
   A. N. Kolmogorov. Lazar Aronovich Lyusternik (50th Anniversary since the date of birth). Uspekhi Mat. Nauk, 1950,
   5, #1.

Office: Mathematics Department
               Moscow University
               Moscow, USSR
Residence: ul. Chkalova 14/16
               Moscow, USSR
Telephone: K7 50 75

MAKAREVSKII, ALEKSANDR IVANOVICH (Aeronautical Engineer)

A. I. Makarevskii was born April 6, 1904. He graduated in 1929 from Moscow Technical School. In 1927 he began working at the Central Aero-Hydrodynamic Institute and in 1950 became Director of this Institute. In 1952 he was made professor at the Moscow Physico-Technical Institute. He has been a member of the Communist Party of the Soviet Union since 1943. In 1953 he was elected a Corresponding Member of the U.S.S.R. Academy of Sciences. He was the recipient in 1943 of a Stalin Prize.

Makarevskii has investigated the external loads acting upon aircraft in flight. He presented an analysis of possible overloads in the aircraft in connection with characteristics of the stability and maneuverability of the aircraft. In his paper, "Questions on Durability of an Aircraft at High Speeds" (1947) he examined the influence of the compressibility of air on the magnitude of aerodynamic loads. The most important result of the works of Makarevskii was the establishment of domestic standards on durability, including that of high speed aircraft. He took part in compiling a work "Manual for Constructors" (1940-42).

Bibliography:
Permissible General Deformation in Construction of Aircraft. Techniques of the Air Force, 1936, #8-9 and 12.
Load of the Wind and Empennage of Fighters in Flight. Works of the Central Aero-Hydrodynamic Institute, 1940, #41.

Office: Moscow Physico-Technical Institute
Moscow, USSR

MAKSUTOV, DMITRII DMITRIEVICH (Astronomical Equipment Designer)

D. D. Maksutov was born April 23, 1896. He graduated from the Military Engineering School in 1914. In 1930 he organized and directed the Laboratory of Astronomical Optics at the State Optical Institute in Leningrad. In 1941 he became a doctor and in 1944, a professor. He began working in 1952 at the Main Astronomical Observatory of the U.S.S.R. Academy of Sciences (Pulkova). In 1946 he was elected a Corresponding Member of the U.S.S.R. Academy of Sciences. He received State Prizes in 1941 and 1946.

Maksutov investigated the improvement of shadowing and other optical methods, the technology of producing large, exact

optical devices, and the theory and practice of producing
aspherical surfaces. He invented the catadioptric (meniscus)
systems for optical devices, which bear his name. These systems received wide use in a number of fields in science and
technology. Maksutov also created optical systems for a number of large unique instruments.
Bibliography:
    Anaberration reflecting surfaces and systems and new
    methods of testing them. Works of the State Optical Insti-
    tute, 1932, 8, #86.
    Shadow Methods of Investigating Optical Systems.
    Leningrad-Moscow: 1934.
    New catadioptric meniscus systems. Works of the State
    Optical Institute, 1944, 16, #124.
    Astronomical Optics. Moscow-Leningrad: 1946.
    Production and Investigation of Astronomical Optics.
    Leningrad-Moscow: 1948.
Office: Main Astronomical Observatory of USSR Academy
              of Sciences
              Leningrad M-140, Pulkovo, USSR

MAL'TSEV, ANATOLII IVANOVICH (Mathematician)
    A. I. Mal'tsev was born November 14, 1909. In 1931 he
graduated from Moscow University. He was on the staff of the
Pedagogical Institute Imeni Ivanovo from 1932 and in 1943 became professor. In 1942 he started working at the Mathematics
Institute of the U.S.S.R. Academy of Sciences. Mal'tsev was
elected a Corresponding Member of the U.S.S.R. Academy of
Sciences in 1953, and in 1958 an Academician. He was a Deputy
of the Supreme Soviet U.S.S.R. (fourth and fifth convocations).
In 1946 he received a Stalin Prize, and in 1956 he was an
Honored Scientist of the R.S.F.S.R.
    Mal'tsev is a specialist in algebra, related questions of
mathematics logic, and theories of continuous groups. He has
published results in the theory of abstract groups, rings, and
general algebraic systems.
Bibliography:
    Untersuchungen aus dem Gebiete der mathematischen Logik.
    Mat. Sbornik, New Series, 1936, 1, (43), #3, 323-36.
    On the inclusion of associative systems in groups. Mat.
    Sbornik, 1939, 6 (48), #2, 331-36; 1948, 8 (50), #2, 251-53.
    On one general method of derivation of local theorems of
    group theory. Scientific Research Papers of the Ivanovo

Pedagogical Institute, Physico-Mathematical Faculty, 1941,
1, #1, 3-9.
On semi-simple sub groups of lie groups. Izvest. Akad.
Nauk S.S.S.R., Ser. Mat., 1944, 8, #4, 143-74.
On one class of homogeneous spaces. Izvest. Akad. Nauk
S.S.S.R., Ser. Mat., 13, #1, 9-32.
On the general theory of algebraic systems. Mat. Sbornik,
1954, 35 (77), #1, 3-20.
Basis of Linear Algebra, 2nd ed. Moscow-Leningrad: 1956.
Insolubility of the elementary theory of finite groups. Dok-
lady Akad. Nauk 138, #4, 771-4 (1961).
Elementary theories of locally free universal algebrae.
Doklady Akad. Nauk 138, #5, 1009-12 (1961).
Effective inseparability of a set of identically true formulae
from a set of finitely refutable ones in some elementary
theories. Doklady Akad. Nauk 139, #4, 802-05 (1961).
Strictly related models and recursively perfect algebrae.
Doklady Akad. Nauk S.S.S.R. 145, #2, 276-79 (1962).
Recursive Abel groups. Doklady Akad. Nauk S.S.S.R. 146,
#5, 1009-1010 (1962).
Biography:
Mathematics in the U.S.S.R. During 30 Years, 1917-1947.
Collection of Articles, Moscow-Leningrad: 1948 (contains
bibliography of the works of Mal'tsev).
Office: V. A. Steklov Mathematics Institute
1-y Akademicheskii Proyezd 28
Moscow, USSR

MAN'KOVSKII, GRIGORII IL'ICH (Mining Engineer)

G. I. Man'kovskii was born in 1897. Upon completion of his
studies at the Leningrad Mining Institute in 1924, he worked
until 1932 as chief of mine construction in the Donets and Lower
Moscow basins. During 1932-39, he participated in the building
of the Moscow subway. From 1939 to 1954, he again worked in
mine construction for the coal industry. In 1954 he took a position at the U.S.S.R. Academy of Sciences Skochinskii Mining
Institute. He received a Stalin Prize in 1946, and in 1948 was
awarded the title of Honored Scientist and Technologist of the
R.S.F.S.R. In 1944 he became a Doctor of Technical Sciences
and in 1957, a professor. He was elected, in 1960, a Corresponding Member of the U.S.S.R. Academy of Sciences.
Bibliography:
Means of technical development for special methods of mining. Ugol, 32, #7, 1957, 1-4. Engineering Index, 1959, p. 1113.

Theoretical investigations into rock freezing process. Inst.
of Min. Engrs. - Proc. of Symposium July 1959, 439-55
(discussion) 455-6. Engineering Index, 1960, p. 1331.
Office: Skochinskii Mining Institute of USSR Academy of
               Sciences
               Moscow, USSR
Residence: Dorogomilovskaya nab., 9
               Moscow, USSR
Telephone: G3 53 27

MARCHUK, GURII IVANOVICH (Atomic Energy Specialist)
    G. I. Marchuk has been a member of the U.S.S.R. Council of
Ministers' Main Administration for the Use of Atomic Energy
as of 1961. In June 1962 he was elected a Corresponding Member of the U.S.S.R. Academy of Sciences.
Bibliography:
    Multigroup method of calculations used in the design of the
    reactor for an atomic electric power station.   Soviet J.
    Atomic Energy #2, 149-61 (1956). NSA 11:677, 1957.
    On finite-differential diffusion equations. Fizika i Teplo-
    tekhnika Reaktorov, pp. 22-44. Moscow: Publishing House
    on Atomic Power. 1958. 213 p. NSA 12:15718, 1958.
    On the multigroup calculation method for nuclear reactors.
    Fizika i Teplotekhnika Reaktorov, pp. 7-21. Moscow:
    Publishing House on Atomic Power. 1958. 213 p. NSA 12:
    15895, 1958.
    and F. F. Mikhailus. Resonant neutron capture in an infinite
    uniform medium. Atomnaya Energ. 4, 520-30 (1958). NSA
    12:16783, 1958.
    and V. Ya. Pupko, E. I. Pogudalina, V. V. Smelov, I. P.
    Tyuterev, S. T. Platonova, G. I. Druzhinina. Certain prob-
    lems in the physics of nuclear reactors and methods for
    their solution. Nuclear Reactors and Nuclear Energy.
    Moscow: 1959, 588-612.
    Numerical methods of designing nuclear reactors "Chislen-
    nye Metody Rascheta Yadernykh Reaktorov," pp. 279-317,
    Chap. XII. Trans. from a publication of the Publishing
    House of Atomic Energy. Moscow: 1958. 43 p. NP-tr-482.
    NSA 15, 1013, 1961.
    and G. A. Ilyasova, V. E. Kolesov, V. P. Kochergin, L. I.
    Kuznetsova, E. I. Pogudalina. Critical masses of uranium-
    graphite reactors. English trans. 1960. 18 p. NSA 16,
    2404, 1962.

Review of nuclear reactor calculating methods. Atomnaya
Energ. <u>11</u>, 356-69 (1961). NSA 16, 3897 (1962).

Office: U.S.S.R. Council of Ministers' Main Administration
            for the Use of Atomic Energy
        Moscow, USSR

MARKOV, ANDREI ANDREEVICH (Mathematician)

A. A. Markov was born September 22, 1903. He is the son
of A. A. Markov (1856-1922, the Russian mathematician usually
referred to as A. A. Markov Sr.). He has been a professor at
Leningrad University since 1935. In 1953, he was elected to
the U.S.S.R. Academy of Sciences as a Corresponding Member.

Markov has worked in topology, topological algebra, theory
of algorithms, and theory of dynamic systems. He proved by
methods of mathematical logic the impossibility of algorithmic
solution of some problems in the theory of associative systems
and problems which are concerned with whole number matrices.

Biography:
    Yu. V. Linnik and N. A. Shanin. Andrei Andreevich Markov
    (50th Anniversary since the date of birth). Uspeki Mat.
    Nauk, 1954, <u>9</u>, #1.
    Thirty Years of Mathematics in the U.S.S.R. 1917-1947.
    Moscow-Leningrad: 1948 (Collection of articles under the
    editorship of A. G. Kurosh <u>et al.</u>) (contains bibliography of
    the works of Markov)
    Theory of Algorithms. Moscow, USSR Academy of Sciences,
    1954 [i.e. Jerusalem, Israel Program for Scientific Trans-
    lations, 1961; available Office Tech. Services, U. S. Dept.
    Commerce, Washington] 444 p.
    Calculated invariants. Doklady Akad. Nauk S.S.S.R. <u>146</u>, #5,
    1017-1020 (1962).

Office: Mathematics Department
        Leningrad University
        Leningrad, USSR

MARKOV, MOISEI ALEKSANDROVICH (Theoretical Physicist)

M. A. Markov was born May 13, 1908. He graduated in 1930
from Moscow University. In 1934 he went to work at the Physics Institute of the U.S.S.R. Academy of Sciences. Since 1953
he has been a Corresponding Member of the U.S.S.R. Academy
of Sciences. Markov has also been a member of the Joint
Institute of Nuclear Research, Dubna.

The major work of Markov is concerned with the relativity
theory of elementary particles and quantum electrodynamics.

He proposed the theory of the so-called non-local fields and established the necessary conditions which had to be satisfied by the theory of extended particles. Other investigations of Markov deal with the study of particles and antiparticles, interaction of hard gamma-quanta with matter, and the systematics of elementary particles.

Bibliography:

'Tetra-dimensionally extended' electron in a relativistic quantum area. Zhur. Eksptl. i Teoret. Fiz., 1940, 10, #12.
One criterion of relativistic invariance. Zhur. Eksptl. i Teoret. Fiz., 1946, 16, #9.
Mon-local fields and complex nature of 'elementary' particles (dynamically deformable formfactor). Uspekhi Fiz. Nauk, 1953, 51, #3.
Hyperons and K-Mesons. Moscow: 1958.

Office: P. N. Lebedev Physics Institute of USSR Academy
              of sciences
              Leninskii Prospekt, 53
              Moscow, USSR
Residence: 3ii Akademicheskii pr., 35
              Moscow, USSR
Telephone: B7 53 07

MATULIS, YUOZAZ YOUZASOVICH (Chemist)

Yu. Yu. Matulis was born March 31, 1899. He has been an Academician of the Lithuanian S.S.R. Academy of Sciences since 1941 and in 1946 became President. In 1946 he was elected Corresponding Member of the U.S.S.R. Academy of Sciences. He became a member of the Communist Party of the Soviet Union in 1950. In 1945 Matulis was an Honored Scientist of the Lithuanian S.S.R. He has been a Deputy to the U.S.S.R. Supreme Soviet, third through fifth convocations and Chairman of the Lithuanian S.S.R. Society for the Propagation of Political and Scientific Knowledge.

The main investigations of Matulis are concerned with the photochemistry, electrochemistry, and kinetics of reaction in solutions. He is the author of a textbook on colloidal chemistry, and handbook on physical chemistry, and also the author of a number of articles on questions of the influence of surface-active substances on the electrodeposition of metals.

Bibliography:

Text of Practical Physical Chemistry. Kaunas: 1948.
Colloid Chemistry. Kaunas: 1947.

Office: Academy of Sciences Lithuanian SSR
            K. Pizhelos Ulitsa 28
            Vilnyus, Lithuanian SSR

MEDVEDEV, SERGEI SERGEEVICH (Chemist)

S. S. Medvedev was born May 17, 1891. In 1919 he graduated
from Moscow University. He began working at the L. Karpov
Physico-Chemical Institute in 1922 and at the same time taught
at the Moscow Institute of Fine Chemical Technology. In 1943
he was made an Honored Scientist of the RSFSR. He was elected a Corresponding Member of the U.S.S.R. Academy of Sciences in 1943 and in 1958, an Academician. In 1946 he won a
Stalin Prize.

Medvedev has been concerned with polymerization processes, which are the bases of many important chemical industries--
synthetic rubber and plastics. He has studied the mechanism
of many radical chain reactions and emulsion polymerization.
He synthesized new elastic materials with increased heat resistance. In the area of radiation chemistry, Medvedev investigated the influence of nuclear radiation on the processes of
polymerization. Recently he has done research on the theory
of slow oxidation of hydrocarbons.

In 1961 he received the Order of Lenin and two orders of the
Red Banner of Labor.

Bibliography:

and Yu. A. Aleksandrova, Y. L. Huan, A. N. Pravednikov.
Reactions of oxygen-containing radicals of type RO. Doklady Akad. Nauk S.S.S.R. 123, 1029-32 (1958). C. A. 53,
7736a (1959).

and A. R. Gantmakher, E. B. Lyudvig. Mechanism of initiation of cationic polymerization in the presence of metal
halides. Doklady Akad. Nauk S.S.S.R. 127, 100-3 (1959).
C. A. 53, 21099e (1959).

and V. M. Yur'ev, A. N. Pravednikov. Effect of side chains
on rate of oxidation of carbon chain polymers. Doklady
Akad. Nauk S.S.S.R. 124, 335-7 (1959). C. A. 53, 8781b
(1959).

and G. D. Berezhnoi, P. M. Khomikovskii. Kinetics of the
emulsion polymerization of styrene. Vsyolomolekulyarnye
Soedineniya 2, 141-52 (1960). C. A. 54, 19015a (1960).

and A. N. Pravednikov, Yin-Shen Kan. Crossing polymer
chains with γ-radiation. Proc. U. N. Intern. Conf. Peaceful
Uses At. Energy, 2nd, Geneva, 1958, 29, 192-5 (1959).
C. A. 54, 20431e (1960).

and Yu. L. Spirin, A. R. Gantmakher. Electron absorption
spectra of carbanions in polymerization of styrene in the
presence of metal-organic compounds. Vysokomolekulyarnye Soedineniya 2, 310-12 (1960). C. A. 54, 20474a (1960).
Office: L. A. Karpov Physico-Chemical Institute
              Obukha Street, 10
              Moscow, USSR
Residence: Khoroshevskoye Shosse 1/2
              Moscow, USSR
Telephone: D3 00 80, Ext. 128

MEISEL', MAKSIN NIKOLAEVICH (Microbiologist)
    N. N. Meisel' was born in 1901. He graduated from the first
Leningrad Medical Institute in 1926, where he completed his
postgraduate studies in histology in 1929. In 1932 he completed
additional postgraduate work in microbiology and cytology at
the U.S.S.R. Academy of Sciences. In the same year he worked
as one of the organizers of the Far-Eastern branch of the
U.S.S.R. Academy of Sciences, where from 1932 to 1934, he
was a member of the Presidium and Academic-Secretary. In
1934 he began work at the U.S.S.R. Academy of Sciences Institute of Microbiology, and in 1959 became Laboratory Chief of
the U.S.S.R. Academy of Sciences Institute of Radiation and
Physico-Chemical Biology. He undertook a teaching position at
the Moscow State University in 1946, and in 1947 received the
degree of Doctor of Biological Sciences at that institution. In
1960 he was elected to the U.S.S.R. Academy of Sciences as a
Corresponding Member.
    Meisel' has worked in microbiology and nucleic acids.
    In August 1958, Meisel' visited the United States to attend
the International Radiation Research Congress at Buckington,
Vermont.
    Meisel' is a member of the Institute of Biological Physics
of the U.S.S.R. Academy of Sciences, Moscow.
Bibliography:
    Luminescent microscopy. Vestnik Akad. Nauk S.S.S.R., #10,
    3-10 (1953).
    Ionizing radiations and cellular metabolism. All-Union
    Conference on the Application of Isotopes and Radiation,
    1957. Mikrobiologiya [trans.] 26(4): 502-505. Biol. Abstr.
    33, 020295 (1959).
    and Ye. N. Sokurova. Combined effect on ultraviolet and
    x-rays on bacillus anthracoides spores. Biofizika 2(4):
    483-486. 1957. Biol. Abstr. 35, 35178 (1960).

and T. S. Sokolova. Inherited cytoplasmic variations in
yeast caused by berberine and acriflavin. Doklady Akad.
Nauk S.S.S.R. 131, #2, 436-39 (1961).
and L. S. Agroskin, N. V. Korolev, I. S. Kulaev, N. A.
Pomoshchnikova. Ultraviolet fluorescence of nucleic acids
and polyphosphates. Doklady Akad. Nauk S.S.S.R. 131, #6,
1440-43 (1961).
Office: Institute of Radiation and Physico-Chemical Biology
             of USSR Academy of Sciences
             Moscow, USSR

MELENT'EV, LEV ALEKSANDROVICH (Energetics Specialist)
L. A. Melent'ev was born in 1908. In 1930 he graduated
from the Leningrad Polytechnical Institute. From 1929-33, he
worked at the Leningrad Energetics Institute. He was, 1933-
35, bureau chief of the Leningrad Commission on Energetics.
From 1936 to 1942, he was a senior instructor, docent, and then
professor of the Leningrad Engineering-Economics Institute.
In 1942-60, he was a senior scientific worker at the U.S.S.R.
Academy of Sciences Institute of Energetics, and from 1945-60,
he was also Chairman of the Thermo-Energetics Department,
and professor at the Leningrad Engineering Economics Institute. In 1960 he became Director of the U.S.S.R. Academy of
Sciences Siberian Branch Institute of Energetics. Since 1947
he has been a member of the Communist Party of the Soviet
Union. He was elected to the U.S.S.R. Academy of Sciences as
a Corresponding Member in 1960.
Melent'ev has concerned himself with power plants in the
Soviet Union.
As of 1962, he has been Chairman of the Presidium of the
East Siberian Branch of Siberian Department. In March 1962,
he was elected delegate from R.S.F.S.R. to the Supreme Soviet.
Bibliography:
40 years of Soviet power engineering. District heating development in USSR. Teploenergetika 4, #11, 1957, 35-40.
Engineering Index, 1958, p. 972.
and G. B. Levental. Correlation between the thermodynamic
and power indices of heat-power plant efficiency. Engineering Index, 1958, p. 1180. Also in Applied Mechanics Review,
#2022, 1959.
Office: Institute of Energetics
             Siberian Branch USSR Academy of Sciences
             Irkutsk, Siberia

MEL'NIKOV, NIKOLAI VASIL'EVICH (Mining Engineer)

N. V. Mel'nikov was born February 28, 1909. He graduated in 1933 from Sverdlovsk Mining Institute and has the degree of Doctor of Technical Sciences. From 1950 to 1956 he was professor at the Academy of Coal Industry. In 1955 he became Deputy Director of the Institute of Mining at the U.S.S.R. Academy of Sciences. Mel'nikov has been a member of the Communist Party of the Soviet Union since 1944. In 1953 he was elected a Corresponding Member of the U.S.S.R. Academy of Sciences and in June 1962 an Academician. From 1949 to 1954 he was a member of the Council of Ministers Bureau on Fuel and Metallurgical Industries. In 1961 he was Minister of the U.S.S.R. He was elected Deputy to the Supreme Soviet, sixth session. As of 1961, Mel'nikov was Director of the U.S.S.R. Academy of Sciences Institute of Mining. In March 1962, he was elected to the Council of Nationalities. As of 1962 he is Chairman of the U.S.S.R. Council of Ministers State Committee on Fuel Industries. He was awarded, in 1946, a Stalin Prize.

Mel'nikov's main works deal with the investigation of new systems of open pit mineral deposits and of rational methods in utilizing techniques of open pit mining.

Bibliography:

Mineral Output by the Open Pit Method. Moscow-Leningrad: 1948.

Drilling of Wells and Holes in Open Pit Mining. Moscow: 1953.

Mechanization of Dumping Operations in Open Pit Mining. Moscow: 1954.

Development of Mining Science in the Area of Open Pit Mining of Deposits in the U.S.S.R. Moscow: 1957.

Office: Institute of Mining of the USSR Academy of Sciences
             Stantsiya Panki
             Moscow Oblast', USSR

Residence: ul. Vorovskogo 33/35
             Moscow, USSR

Telephone: D5 02 27

MEL'NIKOV, OLEG ALEKSANDROVICH (Astronomer)

O. A. Mel'nikov was born in 1912. Upon his graduation in 1933 from Khar'kov State University, he began working at the U.S.S.R. Academy of Sciences Main Astronomical Observatory (Pulkovo). In 1946 he also became a professor at Leningrad State University (Department of Astrophysics). In December 1961, he became Assistant Director of the U.S.S.R. Academy of

Sciences Astronomical Observatory (Pulkovo). In the same
year, he was elected to the U.S.S.R. Academy of Sciences as a
Corresponding Member. He was awarded the degree of Doçtor
of Physico-Math Sciences in 1945.

Mel'nikov's principal works are concerned with stellar and
solar physics, interstellar matter, construction of astronomical apparatus, and the history of astrophysics and astronomical
equipment building.

Bibliography:
On the reddening of early c-stars and the law of cosmic absorption. Circ. Pulkovo obs. 21, 1937, pp. 3-14.

and V. P. Vyasanitsyn. Modern solar spectrographs. Vistas
in Astr. U.S.S.R. Acad. Sci., 13, 1947, pp. 3-85.

On some characteristics of interstellar gases. Astron.
Journal U.S.S.R., 24, 1947, pp. 73-81.

A new determination of the solar reversing layer excitation
temperature. Bull. Pulkovo Obs. 142, 1949, pp. 36-39.

Spectrophotometry of δ Cephei, η Aqulae and the K-effect
for Cepheids. Publ. Pulkovo obs. 64, 1949, pp. 3-144.

and B. K. Ioannisiany. A new telescope with slitless spectro-
graph for the ultraviolet. Its testing in high mountain conditions. Bull. Pulkovo obs. 147, 1951, pp. 55-63.

and S. S. Zhuravlev. Spectrophotometry of faculae in active
solar regions in 1955. Vestnik of the Leningrad Univ. 13,
1956, pp. 124-133.

On the history of development of astrospectroscopy in
Russia and U.S.S.R.-Astro-historical investigation. Ed. by
P. G. Kulikovsky and I. E. Rahlin, 3, 1957, Moscow, U.S.S.R.,
pp. 9-258.

Soviet astronomical apparatus construction. Izvest. Acad.
of Sci. U.S.S.R., 1, 1958, pp. 54-59.

The calibration of the gradient (spectrophotometric) stellar
temperature scale by reference to the sun. Astron. Zh. 35,
#2, 218-21 (1958). Soviet Astron.-AJ (New York) 2, #2, 195-
8 (1958). Phys. Sci. Abstr. 62, 9166 (1959).

Investigation of the ultraviolet spectrum of the sun. Priroda, #6, 1959, pp. 75-78.

Astronomical seeing, ed. (253 p., Illustr.), 1959, Leningrad,
U.S.S.R., pp. 63-115.

History of the Telescope. Leningrad; USSR: 1960, pp. 1-51.

On the new law of selective absorption in the galaxy. Bull.
Pulkovo obs. 163, 1960, pp. 119-132.

On the relation between general and selective light absorption
in the galaxy. Bull. Pulkovo obs. 167, 1961, pp. 129-138.

Office: Astronomical Observatory of USSR Academy of
            Sciences
            Pulkovo, USSR

MENSHOV, DMITRII EVGENEVICH (Mathematician)

D. E. Menshov was born in Moscow April 18, 1892. He
graduated from Moscow University in 1916 and in 1935 he received the Doctor of Physical-Mathematical Sciences degree.
He was made professor in 1928 at Moscow University where he
had taught since 1922. In 1953 he was elected a Corresponding
Member of the U.S.S.R. Academy of Sciences. He was awarded
a Stalin Prize in 1951.

Menshov's main work is in orthogonal functions and trigonometric series. He obtained a basic result in the uniqueness of
representing functions by trigonometric series (1916), and gave
a complete solution to the problem of representation of
functions by trigonometric series (1940). Menshov is also the
author of an important work on the theory of analytical functions.

Bibliography:

Biography:

N. K. Bari and L. A. Lusternik. Dmitrii Evgenevich
Menshov (60th Anniversary since the date of birth). Uspekhi
Mat. Nauk, 1952, 7, #3.

Office: Mathematics Department
            Moscow University
            Moscow, USSR

MERGELYAN, SERGEI NIKITOVICH (Mathematician)

S. N. Mergelyan was born May 19, 1928 in Simferopol. He
graduated from Yerevan University in 1947, and received the
degree of Doctor of Physical-Mathematical Sciences in 1949.
From 1949 to 1956, he was employed at Yerevan University,
and since 1945, at the Mathematics Institute of the Armenian
Academy of Sciences. In 1953, he became a professor at Moscow University. He was made an Academician of the Armenian
S.S.R. Academy of Sciences in 1956, and was elected to the
U.S.S.R. Academy of Sciences as a Corresponding Member in
1953. He received a Stalin Prize in 1952.

Mergelyan worked on the theory of the best approximation of
functions of a complex variable by polynomials.

As of 1961, Mergelyan was Director of the Scientific Research Institute of Mathematical Computers and a member of
the Presidium of the Armenian S.S.R. Academy of Sciences.
Sciences.

Bibliography:
Some Questions on the Constructive Theory of Functions.
Moscow: 1951.
Even approximations of functions of a complex variable.
Uspekhi Mat. Nauk, 1952, 7, #2.
The completeness of systems of analytical functions. Uspekhi
Mat. Nauk, 1953, 8, #4.

Office: Scientific Research Institute of Mathematical
              Computers
              Yerevan, Armenian SSR

MESHCHERYAKOV, MIKHAIL GRIGOR'EVICH (Physicist)

M. G. Meshcheryakov was born September 17, 1910. He
graduated from Leningrad University in 1936. In 1937-1947, he
worked at the U.S.S.R. Academy of Sciences Radium Institute.
He became a professor at Moscow University in 1954, and has
been working at the Joint Institute of Nuclear Research since
1956. He has been a member of the Communist Party of the
Soviet Union since 1940. In 1953 he was elected to the U.S.S.R.
Academy of Sciences as a Corresponding Member.

Meshcheryakov has worked on the physics of high energy
particles. He and his associates experimentally showed the
change in the interaction of nucleons with nucleons at 460-660
million electron volts.

Bibliography:
On the absorption of fast neutrons by heavy nuclei. Doklady
Akad. Nauk S.S.S.R., 1945, 48, #8.
and I. I. Gurevich. On the absorption of slow neutrons in
dysprosium and cadmium. Physikalische Zeitschrift der
Sowejetunion, 1938, 13, #2.
Investigation of nuclear processes at high energies in accelerators. Session of the U.S.S.R. Academy of Sciences on
the Peaceful Utilization of Atomic Energy, July 1-5, 1955,
Plenum Session, Moscow, 1955.
and others. Investigation of interaction of protons with protons at high energies. Izvest. Akad. Nauk S.S.S.R., Ser. Fiz.,
1955, 19, #5.
and others. Energy spectra of π^+-mesons in reaction pp $\longrightarrow$
npπ+ at 556 and 657MEV. Journal of Experimental and
Theoretical Physics, 1956, 31, #1(7), 45-54.
and others. Polarization of protons with energy of 660MEV
in nuclear scattering. Journal of Experimental and Theoretical Physics, 1956, 31, #3, 361-70.

and others. Six-meter synchrocyclotron of the Institute of
Nuclear Problems of the U.S.S.R. Academy of Sciences.
Atomic Energy, 1956, #4.
and L. G. Azhgirei, Yu. P. Kumekin, S. B. Narashev, G. D.
Stoletov, Chuan De-Tsyan. C^{12} nuclei excitation by protons
with an energy of 660 MeV. Doklady Akad. Nauk S.S.S.R.
145, #6, 1249-54 (1962).

Office: Joint Institute of Nuclear Research
              Dubno, Moscow, USSR

MIGDAL, ARKADII BEISUNOVICH (Physicist)

A. B. Migdal was born March 11, 1911. He graduated from
Leningrad University in 1936. In 1944 he became a professor
at Moscow Engineering Physical Institute. He has been working
at the U.S.S.R. Academy of Sciences since 1945. In 1953, he
was elected to the U.S.S.R. Academy of Sciences as a Corresponding Member.

Migdal has been concerned with nuclear theory and quantum
mechanics. He developed a theory on dipole radiation of atomic
nuclei and a theory on ionization of atoms during nuclear reactions. He has also worked in cosmic rays and on the use of
the quantum field theory in the many body problems.

Bibliography:

Ionization of atoms during alpha and beta disintegration.
Zhur. Eksper. i Teoret. Fiz., 1941, 11, #2-3.
Quadrupole and dipole gamma radiation of nuclei. Zhur.
Eksper. i Teoret. Fiz., 1945, 15, #3.
and Ya. A. Smorodinskii. Artificial π-mesons. Uspekhi
Fiz. Nauk, 1950, 41, #2.
Theory of nuclear reactions with formation of slow particles.
Zhur. Eksper. i Teoret. Fiz., 1955, 28, #1.
Quantum kinetic equation for multiple scattering. Doklady
Akad. Nauk S.S.S.R., 1955, 105, #1.
Bremsstrahlung and pair production in condensed media at
high energies. The Physical Review, 1956, 103, 2 series,
#6, Sept. 15, 1811-20.

Office: Physics Department
              Moscow Engineering Physical Institute
              Moscow, USSR
Residence: ul. Chkalova, 52
              Moscow, USSR
Telephone: K7 42 41

MIKHAILOV, ALEKSANDR ALEKSANDROVICH (Astronomer)

A. A. Mikhailov was born April 26, 1888. He graduated from Moscow University in 1911, and from 1918 to 1948 he was a professor at the University. In 1939 he became Chairman of the Astronomical Council of the U.S.S.R. Academy of Sciences and in 1947 Director of the Main Astronomical Observatory of the U.S.S.R. Academy of Sciences in Pulkovo. In 1949 Mikhailov was made a member of the main editorial board of the Great Soviet Encyclopedia. He was elected a Corresponding Member of the U.S.S.R. Academy of Sciences in 1943. Since 1956 he has been a member of the Communist Party of the Soviet Union. In 1934-1959 he was Chairman of the Central Council of the All Union Astronomic-Geodesic Society. He was, from 1946 to 1948, vice president of the International Astronomical Union.

Mikhailov is a specialist in the prediction of solar eclipses. He presented a theory of solar and lunar eclipses, the occultations of planets by the moon, the transits of planets across the solar disk, and compiled a table for precalculating eclipses. He headed five expeditions for observations of total solar eclipses. In 1936 he investigated the deflection of light rays in the field of solar gravity for which he constructed a special unit. He was one of the initiators of a general gravimetric survey in the U.S.S.R. (1932). He developed a method of determining the shape of the earth from determinations of gravity. He edited several stellar atlases.

Bibliography:

Course on Gravimetry and the Theory on the Shape of the Earth. 2nd ed. Moscow: 1939.

Theory of Eclipses. 2nd ed. Moscow-Leningrad: 1954.

On the observation of the effect of Einstein. Astron. Zhur., 1956, 38, #6.

Stellar Atlas of Stars up to 8.25 Magnitude. 2nd ed. Moscow: 1959.

Biography:

Molodenskii, M. A. Work of A. A. Mikhailov in the Area of Gravimetry and the Theory on the Shape of the Earth. Collection of Scientific-Technical and Industrial Articles for Geodesy, Cartography, Topography, Aero-Photography and Gravimetry, 1948, #17.

Office: Main Astronomical Observatory of USSR Academy of Sciences

Leningrad M-140, Pulkovo, USSR

MIKHEEV, MIKHAIL ALEKSANDROVICH (Physical Power Engineer)

M. A. Mikheev was born May 25, 1902. In 1927 he graduated from the Leningrad Polytechnic Institute. From 1925 to 1934 he worked in the Physico-Technical Institute of the U.S.S.R. Academy of Sciences. Beginning in 1936, he has also worked at the Moscow Energy Institute. Mikheev was elected a Corresponding Member of the U.S.S.R. Academy of Sciences in 1946 and in 1953 an Academician. In 1941 and in 1951 he was awarded Stalin Prizes.

The scientific work of Mikheev is in the field of heat transfer. He studied the processes of heat transfer of various heat carriers under free and forced convection.

Bibliography:

and M. V. Kirpichev. Modelling Heat Equipment (1936, Stalin Prize 1941).

and M. V. Kirpichev. Bases of Heat Transfer, 2nd ed. (1949, Stalin Prize 1951).

Heat production in turbulent motion of liquids in turbines. Izvest. Akad. Nauk S.S.S.R., Otdel. Tekh. Nauk, 1952, #10.

Biography:

Mikheev, Mikhail Aleksandrovich. Vestnik Akad. Nauk S.S.S.R., 1953, #12.

Office: Moscow Energy Institute
Moscow, USSR

Residence: 1-aya Cheremushkinskaya, 3
Moscow, USSR

Telephone: B7 28 77

MIKOYAN, ARTYOM IVANOVICH (Aeronautical Engineer)

A. I. Mikoyan was born August 5, 1905. He graduated in 1936 from the N. E. Zhukovskii Military Air Academy. He is a Major General in the Engineering-Technical Service. Since 1925 he has been a member of the Communist Party of the Soviet Union. In 1953, Mikoyan was elected Corresponding Member of the U.S.S.R. Academy of Sciences. He was Deputy to the U.S.S.R. Supreme Soviet, third through fifth convocations. He has been awarded a Stalin Prize.

In 1939-40 Mikoyan, together with M. I. Gurevich, designed the fighter plane, MIG-1, for aerial combat at high altitudes. In the same year, 1940, the plane was modified and under the name, MIG-3, found wide front line use during World War II (1941-45). Mikoyan is one of the pioneers of jet aviation in the

U.S.S.R. In 1946, at the Tushinskii Air Field, the first turbojet plane designed by Mikoyan was demonstrated.

In March 1962, Mikoyan was elected to the Council of Nationalities.

Bibliography:
Biography:
    A. Minaev. Planes of A. E. Mikoyan Design. Vestnik of the
    Air Force, 1951, No. 7.
Office: USSR Academy of Sciences
             Leninskii Prospekt, 14
             Moscow, USSR

MIKULIN, ALEKSANDR ALEKSANDROVICH (Aeronautical Engineer)

A. A. Mikulin was born February 2, 1895. He is a Major
General in Engineer-Technical Service. In 1934 he was elected
an Academician of the U.S.S.R. Academy of Sciences. He was
a Hero of Socialist Labor in 1940. Since 1952 he has been a
member of the Communist Party of the Soviet Union.

In 1923 Mikulin began to work as a designer in the Scientific
Automotor Institute. In 1929, he worked out a plan for AM-34
engines, which in 1931 successfully underwent tests. This
engine was installed in aircraft in which, in 1937, V. P. Chkalov
and M. M. Gromov carried out distant non-stop flights across
the North Pole to the U.S.A., and in airplanes which, in 1937,
flew from Moscow to the North Pole. Constructed under Mikulin's direction, an AM-35 engine was installed in a MIG aircraft. At the time of the World War II, 1941-45, he directed
the design of powerful aircraft engines, AM-38f (which were
installed in the Sturmovik IL-2) and other designs for aircraft
engines. Mikulin introduced the use of rotating blades for the
regulation of superchargers and high pressure feed and cooling
of intake air. He worked out the first Soviet turbocompressor
and variable pitch propeller. After 1945, a group directed by
Mikulin developed jet engines.

Biography:
    A. A. Mikulin, Hero of Socialist Labor, Major General of the
    IAS. Technics of the Air Fleet, 1945, #2.
Office: USSR Academy of Sciences
             Leninskii Prospekt, 14
             Moscow, USSR
Residence: Pugoshvinikov p. 15
             Moscow, USSR
Telephone: G6 03 38

MILLIONSHCHIKOV, MIKHAIL DMITRIEVICH (Mechanical Engineer and Physicist)

M. D. Millionshchikov was born January 16, 1913. He graduated from Groznyi Oil Institute in 1932 and taught there. In 1934-1943 he taught at the Moscow Aviation Institute and subsequently at the Moscow Engineering-Physics Institute where he became professor in 1949. From 1944 to 1949 he worked at the Institute of Mechanics of the U.S.S.R. Academy of Sciences. Millionshchikov has been a member of the Communist Party of the Soviet Union since 1947. In 1953 he was elected a Corresponding Member of the U.S.S.R. Academy of Sciences, and in June 1962, an Academician. He is the recipient of a Stalin Prize.

Millionshchikov's main work is in theory of turbulence, the theory of filtration, and applied gas dynamics. He investigated isotropic turbulence in the terminal stages of its degeneration. In the theory of filtration, he developed methods for exploiting oil wells. In applied gas dynamics, he studied gas ejectors and their use.

As of 1961, Millionshchikov was a Vice President of the U.S.S.R. Academy of Sciences.

Bibliography:

and S. A. Khristianovich and others. Applied Gas Dynamics. Moscow: 1948.

Degeneration of homogeneous isotropic turbulence in a viscous non-compressible liquid. Doklady Akad. Nauk S.S.S.R., New Series, 1939, 22, #5.

Theory of homogeneous isotropic turbulence. Doklady Akad. Nauk S.S.S.R., 1941, 32, #9.

Office: Moscow Engineering Physics Institute of USSR
              Academy of Sciences
              Moscow, USSR

MINTS, ALEKSANDR LVOVICH (Engineer)

A. L. Mints was born December 27, 1895. In 1918 he graduated from the Don University and in 1932 from Moscow Institute of Communication Engineers. From 1920 to 1928, he served in radio-technical units and in scientific establishments of the Red Army. He worked in laboratories of the radio industry and in construction of radio stations from 1928 to 1934 and during some of that time, 1929 to 1930, he was also teaching in the Leningrad Institute of Communications. He became Director, in 1946, of the Radio-Engineering Institute of the

Academy of Sciences U.S.S.R. In 1946 Mints was elected a Corresponding Member of the U.S.S.R. Academy of Sciences, and in 1958 an Academician. He was a recipient of Stalin Prizes in 1946 and in 1951. In 1950 he was awarded Popov Gold Medal by the U.S.S.R. Academy of Sciences for his work in the construction of radio stations and in radio-engineering. The basic work of Mints is concerned with radiotelephone modulation, design of high power radio broadcasting stations, directional antennae for long and short wave radio stations, demountable transmitting tubes, new methods of radio-measurement, and with radio-engineering and electronics of elementary particle accelerators. Mints directed the planning and construction of powerful radio stations (i.e., VTsSPS, 1929; Comintern, 1933; RV-96, 1938; Kuibishevskii, 1943), and also participated in the design of accelerators of the Joint Institute of Nuclear Studies, 680 MEV Phasotron (1949, 1953) and the 10 BEV Synchrotron (1957).

Bibliography:
  and I. G. Klyashkin. Foundations for Calculation of Modulation on the Anode. Moscow-Leningrad: 1926.
  and I. G. Klyashkin. Foundations for Calculation of Modulation on the Grid. Moscow: 1928.
  500 Kwt Radio Stations. Moscow: 1934.
  Improvement of the technology of radio broadcasting installations (in the book) 50 Years of Radio. Scientific-Technical Collection. Moscow: 1945.
  Problems of radio-engineering and electronics of powerful cyclical accelerators of heavy charged particles. Radiotekh. i Elektron., 1956, #5.

Biography:
  Laureate of the Popov Gold Medal. Radio, 1950, #6.
  Distinguished Soviet radio specialist. Vest. Svyazi. Tekhnika Svyazi, 1950, #6.
  Laureate of the Popov Gold Medal. Radiotekh., 1950, #4.
  A. L. Mints. To his 60th Birthday. Radiotekh., 1955, 10, #2.

Office: Radio Engineering Institute of USSR Academy of
             Sciences
             Moscow, USSR

MIRCHINK, MIKHAIL FEDOROVICH (Oil Geologist)

M. F. Mirchink was born June 15, 1901. He graduated in 1930 from Moscow Mining Academy. In 1943 he became professor at Moscow Mining Institute. Since 1941 he has been a member of the Communist Party of the Soviet Union. In 1953

Mirchink was elected a Corresponding Member of the U.S.S.R. Academy of Sciences. In 1949 and 1950 he received Stalin Prizes.

The works of Mirchink deal with regional geology of oil-bearing territories of the Caucasus and the Russian Platform, and also with the exploitation of oil deposits. He established in 1932 a course on oil field geology at the Azerbaijan Industrial Institute. He combined scientific work with large-scale practical activity; he has participated in the discovery of oil. He, together with others, published the work, "Scientific Basis for Development of Oil Deposits" (1948).

As of 1961, Mirchink was Director of the Institute of Geology and Processing of Mineral Fuels.

Bibliography:
Stratigraphic Deposits of Oil. Baku: 1943.
Oil Field Geology. Moscow-Leningrad: 1946.
Office: Moscow Mining Institute
Moscow, USSR

MISHIN, VASILII PAVLOVICH (Mechanical Engineer)

V. P. Mishin was born January 18, 1917. After graduating in 1941 from the Moscow Aviation Institute, he worked in various designing and scientific research organizations. Since 1943 he has been a member of the Communist Party of the Soviet Union. In 1958 he was elected a Corresponding Member of the U.S.S.R. Academy of Sciences.

Mishin's main works are devoted to various problems of applied mechanics.

Office: USSR Academy of Sciences
Leninskii Prospekt, 14
Moscow, USSR

MISHUSTIN, EVGENII NIKOLAEVICH (Microbiologist)

E. N. Mishustin was born February 22, 1901. He graduated in 1924 from Moscow Timiryazev Agricultural Academy. In 1939 he began working at the Institute of Microbiology of the U.S.S.R. Academy of Sciences. Since 1953 he has been a Corresponding Member of the U.S.S.R. Academy of Sciences. In 1951 he was awarded a Stalin Prize.

Mishustin's main works deal with agricultural microbiology. He is the author of the work "Thermophilic Microorganisms in Nature and Practice" (1950).

Bibliography:
Scientific Basis of Processing Feed in Silos. 2nd ed.
Moscow-Leningrad: 1933.
Course on Agricultural Microbiology. Moscow-Leningrad:
1934.
Ecologic-Geographic Change of Soil Bacteria. Moscow-
Leningrad: 1947.
Thermophilic Microorganisms in Nature and Practice. 1950.
and M. I. Pertsovskaya. Microorganisms and Self-
purification of Soil. Moscow: 1954.
Microorganisms and the Fertility of Soil. Moscow: 1956.
Office: Institute of Microbiology of the USSR Academy of
Sciences
Leninskii Prospekt, 33
Moscow, USSR
Residence: Leninskii Prospekt, 13
Moscow, USSR
Telephone: V2 58 78

MOLODENSKII, MIKHAIL SERGEEVICH (Geophysicist)

M. S. Molodenskii was born June 16, 1909. Upon graduating
from Moscow University in 1932, he worked at the Central
Scientific Research Institute of Geodesy, Aero Photography and
Cartography. In 1946 he worked at the U.S.S.R. Academy of
Sciences Geophysical Institute, and in 1956, at the U.S.S.R.
Academy of Sciences Institute of Terrestrial Physics. He was
awarded a Stalin Prize in 1946 and 1951. In 1946 he became a
Corresponding Member of the U.S.S.R. Academy of Sciences.
Molodenskii worked out a theory on utilization of measure-
ments of the gravitational field of the earth for geodesic pur-
poses. He proposed a method of astronomic-gravimetric level-
ling, a new method of determining the shape of the earth. He
designed the first spring gravimeter in the U.S.S.R. He investigated the elastic properties of the earth and the earth's
core.
Bibliography:
Main questions on geodesic gravimetrics. Works of the
Central Scientific Research Institute of Geodesy, Aero
Photography and Cartography, 1945, #42.
Methods of simultaneous treatment of gravimetric and geodesic materials in studying the gravitational field of the
earth and its shape. Works of the Central Scientific Research Institute of Geodesy, Aero Photography and Cartography, 1951, #86.

Elastic movement, free mutation, and some questions on the structure of the earth. Trudy Geofiz. Inst. Akad. Nauk S.S.S.R., 1953, #19.

Office: O. Yu. Shmidt Institute of Terrestrial Physics of USSR Academy of Sciences
Bol'shaya Gruzinskaya Ulitsa 10
Moscow, USSR

Residence: Kotel'nicheskaya nab. 1/15
Moscow, USSR

Telephone: B7 45 73

MOSHKIN, PANTELEIMON AFANAS'EVICH (Chemical
    Technologist)

P. A. Moshkin was born February 13, 1891. He graduated in 1918 from the Moscow Technological College where he taught until 1930. From 1928 to 1931 he was professor at the Moscow Chemical-Technological Institute. In 1943 he became Chief of the Laboratory of the Scientific-Research Institute of Plastics. Since 1953, Moshkin has been a Corresponding Member of the U.S.S.R. Academy of Sciences. In 1948 he was awarded a Stalin Prize.

Moshkin's main investigations are devoted to the development of industrial methods for chemical synthesis. His works on the synthesis of aliphatic acids by oxidation of paraffins aided in the organization of producing valuable raw materials for the soap and the chemical industries. He developed methods of separating and characterizing phenols in primary tar of humus coal. He proposed industrial methods for the synthesis of intermediate products and plasticizers for plastics.

Bibliography:
and others. Paraffin of sulfur oil as a raw material for producing synthetic aliphatic acids. Chemistry and Technology of Fuel and Oil, 1957, #6.

and N. I. Velizar'eva. Obtaining synthetic aliphatic acids by means of paraffin oxidation. Chemistry and Technology of Fuel and Oil, 1957, #8.

Phenols of humus coal primary tar. Works of the All-Union Scientific-Research Institute of Artificial Liquid Fuel and Gas (All-Union Scientific-Research Institute of Gas), #1. Moscow-Leningrad: 1948.

and S. A. Chyornaya. Determining the simultaneous presence of two phenyl groups. Chemistry and Technology of Artificial Liquid Fuel and Gas. Moscow-Leningrad: 1952.

and O. B. Kol'tsevaya. Separating 3.5-dimethylphenol by
alkylation. Chemistry and Technology of Fuel and Oil,
1957, #2.
Office: Scientific-Research Institute of Plastics
              Moscow, USSR

MURATOV, MIKHAIL VLADIMIROVICH (Geologist)

M. V. Muratov has been working at the U.S.S.R. Academy of
Sciences Institute of Geology. In June 1962 he was elected a
Corresponding Member of the U.S.S.R. Academy of Sciences.
Bibliography:
    and P. V. Fedorov, A. R. Geptner. Time appearance of
    Mediterranean elements in the fauna of the Black Sea.
    Doklady Akad. Nauk 138, #1, 181-83 (1961).
Office: Institute of Geology of USSR Academy of Sciences
              Pyzhevskii Pereulok, 7
              Moscow, USSR

MUSKHELISHVILI, NIKOLAI IVANOVICH (Mathematician and Mechanics Expert)

N. I. Muskhelishvili was born February 16, 1891. In 1914
he graduated from Petersburg University. He became a professor at Tbilisi State University in 1922 and also at the Polytechnic Institute in Tbilisi. On his initiative, the Tbilisi Mathematics Institute was established in 1935. Muskhelishvili was
elected a Corresponding Member of the U.S.S.R. Academy of
Sciences in 1933 and in 1939 an Academician. In 1941 he became the President of the Georgian S.S.R. Academy of Sciences.
He has been a member of the Communist Party of the Soviet
Union since 1940 and a Deputy to the U.S.S.R. Supreme Soviet
during all the six convocations. In 1945 he was a Hero of
Socialist Labor and in 1941 and 1947, a recipient of Stalin
Prizes.
    Muskhelishvili's main investigations are in the theory of
elasticity, integral equations, and boundary-value problems in
the theory of functions. He utilized the theory of functions of a
complex variable in problems of the theory of elasticity. With
the aid of complex representation of displacements and ten-
sions, the main problems of a two dimensional theory of elasticity in a static case are reduced. The work of Muskhelishvili
and his students solved the major problems of the two-
dimensional theory of elasticity in a static case. Investigations
were also carried out by Muskhelishvili and his students in the
theory of linear boundary-value problems of analytical functions

and in the theory of one-dimensional integral equations with specific nuclei.

As of 1961 Muskhelishvili was Chairman of the National Committee of the U.S.S.R. for Theoretical and Applied Mechanics. In 1962 he was elected to the Council of Nationalities. Muskhelishvili was a Member of the Presidium of the U.S.S.R. Academy of Sciences as of 1961, and was Director of the A. M. Razmadze Institute of Mathematics of the S.S.R. Georgian Academy of Sciences.

Bibliography:
Course in Analytical Geometry, 3rd ed. Moscow-Leningrad: 1947.
Some Basic Problems of the Mathematical Theory of Elasticity, 4th ed. Moscow-Leningrad: 1954.
Singular Integral Equations. Moscow-Leningrad: 1962, 2nd ed.

Biography:
M. V. Keldysh and S. L. Sobolev. Nikolai Ivanovich Muskhelishvili (On the 60th Anniversary since the date of birth). Uspekhi Mat. Nauk, 1951, 6, #2 (42).
Editorship of A. G. Kurosh and others. Thirty Years of Mathematics in the U.S.S.R. 1917-1947. Collection of Articles. Moscow-Leningrad: 1948.
Thirty Years of Mechanics in the U.S.S.R. 1917-1947. Collection of Articles. Moscow-Leningrad: 1950 (contains bibliography of the works of Muskhelishvili).
Problems of Continuum Mechanics. (Contributions in honor of the seventieth birthday of Academician N. I. Muskhelishvili, February 16, 1961.) Philadelphia, Pa., 1961.

Office: Academy of Sciences Georgian SSR
              Ulitsa Dzerzhinskogo, 8
              Tbilisi 2, Georgian SSR
Telephone: 3-54-64

MUSTEL', EVAL'D RUDOL'FOVICH (Astrophysicist)

E. R. Mustel' was born June 3, 1911. He graduated from Moscow University in 1935 and in 1939 returned there to work. From 1944-1951 he was a professor at Moscow University. In 1946 he went to work at the Astrophysical Observatory of the U.S.S.R. Academy of Sciences and in 1957 at the Astronomical Council of the U.S.S.R. Academy of Sciences. He has been a Corresponding Member of the U.S.S.R. Academy of Sciences since 1953. In 1952 he was awarded a Stalin Prize.

Mustel' developed a theory of radiant equilibrium of stellar atmospheres for the absorption coefficient dependent upon frequency. Mustel' offered a physical picture of the processes occurring during new star's formation. He investigated corpuscular radiation from the sun and the physical phenomena in the active areas of the sun.

Bibliography:

Theory of Radiant Equilibrium of Stellar Atmospheres for the Absorption Coefficient dependent Upon Frequency. Works of The State Astronomical Institute of P. K. Sternberg, 1940, 13, #2.

Investigation of the Question of Ejection of Matter by New Stars After Maximal Brilliance. Proceedings of the Crimean Astro-Physical Observatory, 1948, 1, 2, 91-171.

and others. Theoretical Astrophysics. Moscow: 1952.

Physical Nature of Calcium Floccules. Proceedings of the Crimean Astro-Physical Observatory, 1952, 9, 25-40.

Magnetic fields of new stars. Astron. Zhur., 1956, 33, #2, 182-204.

Physical nature of differences between geomagnetic disturbances with a sudden and a gradual beginning. Astron. Zhur., 1957, 34, #1.

Office: USSR Academy of Sciences Council for Astronomy
Pyzhevskii Pereulok, 3
Moscow, USSR

Residence: Sokol'nicheskaya slob. 14/18
Moscow, USSR

Telephone: E1 40 76

NALIVKIN, DMITRII VASIL'EVICH (Geologist and Paleontologist)

D. V. Nalivkin was born August 25, 1889. He graduated from the Petrograd Mining Institute in 1915, and in 1920 became a professor at this Institute. From 1917 to 1949, he worked on the Geological Committee (All-Union Scientific Research Geologic Institute). He was chairman from 1946 to 1951 of the Presidium of the Turkmen branch of the U.S.S.R. Academy of Sciences. From 1946 to 1953 he was the Director of the Laboratory on Limnology of the U.S.S.R. Academy of Sciences. Nalivkin was elected a Corresponding Member of the U.S.S.R. Academy of Sciences in 1933 and in 1946 an Academician. Since 1951 he has been a Honorary member of the Turkmen S.S.R. Academy of Sciences. In 1937 he became the chief editor of a geological survey map of the Soviet Union. He was the

recipient of a Stalin Prize in 1946. In 1949 Nalivkin was awarded the Gold Medal of A. P. Parpinskii by the U.S.S.R. Academy
of Sciences. He was given a Lenin Prize in 1957 for scientific
leadership in compiling a geological map of the U.S.S.R. (in
scale of 1/2,500,000, published 1956).

Nalivkin's major work is devoted to stratigraphy and paleogeography of the Paleozoic Era of the Urals, of the territory
close to the Urals, of Central Asia, and of the Russian plateau.
Nalivkin is an authority on the Devonian deposits of the U.S.S.R.
Detailed study of Devonian fauna, brachiopods, has allowed him
to work out the details of the stratigraphy of mid-Devonian and
upper Devonian deposits in sections of the Timan Mountain
ridge and the Russian plateau. His research in the Urals made
the stratigraphy and paleogeography of this territory more precise, has permitted separation of middle and upper Devonian
and lower Carboniferous deposits by layers and showed considerable spreading of Silurian and earlier deposits. Studies
made by Nalivkin resulted in greater knowledge of the geology
and minerals of Central Asia, and also aided in the determination of stratigraphic positions of Ural bauxite deposits and oil
deposits in the territories close to the Urals.

Nalivkin was Chairman of the National Committee for
U.S.S.R. Geologists as of 1961.

Bibliography:

Outline of Turkistan Geology. Tashkent-Moscow: 1926.

Brachiopods of Upper and Middle Devonian in Turkistan.
Moscow-Leningrad: 1930.

Semilukski and Voronezh layers. Proceedings of the Main
Directorate of Geologic Surveying, 1930, 49, #1.

Past Don and Elets Layers. Moscow-Leningrad-
Novosibirsk: 1934.

Brachiopods of Upper and Middle Devonian and Lower
Carboniferous of North East Kazakhstan. Leningrad-
Moscow: 1937.

Brachiopods of the main Devonian field. Fauna of the Main
Devonian Field, 1. Moscow-Leningrad: 1941.

Devonian deposits of the U.S.S.R. Atlas of the Leading
Forms of Fossile Fauna of the U.S.S.R., 3. Moscow-
Leningrad: 1947.

Study of Facies. Geographic Conditions for Deposition, 1-2.
Moscow-Leningrad: 1955-56.

Short Outline of the Geology of the U.S.S.R. Moscow: 1957.

Biography:

Dmitrii Vasil'evich Nalivkin. Moscow-Leningrad: 1950.

Office: National Committee for Geologists USSR
USSR Academy of Sciences
Leninskii Prospekt, 14
Moscow, USSR

NAMETKIN, NIKOLAI SERGEEVICH (Organic Chemist)
N. S. Nametkin has been working at the Institute of Petrochemical Synthesis of the U.S.S.R. Academy of Sciences. He
visited the United States in 1959 to attend the Chemical Society
meetings at Atlantic City, New Jersey. In June 1962 he was
elected a Corresponding Member of the U.S.S.R. Academy of
Sciences.

Bibliography:
and A. V. Topchiev, L. S. Povarov, G. V. Garnishevskaya.
Synthesis of compounds with silazine links. Doklady Akad.
Nauk S.S.S.R. 109, 787-90 (1956). C. A. 51, 4936e (1957).
Proc. Acad. Sci. U.S.S.R., Sect. Chem. 109, 477-80 (1956)
(Eng. trans.). C. A. 52, 5284d (1958).
and A. V. Topchiev, T. I. Chernysheva, S. G. Durgar'yan.
Some derivatives of disilanopropane. Doklady Akad. Nauk
S.S.S.R. 110, 97-100 (1956). C. A. 51, 4979g (1957). Proc.
Acad. Sci. U.S.S.R., Sect. Chem. 110, 545-8 (1956) (Eng.
trans.) C. A. 52, 5284b (1958).
and A. V. Topchiev, L. S. Povarov. Bis(tetraalkyldisilano-
methane) cyclodioxides. Doklady Akad. Nauk S.S.S.R. 109,
332-5 (1956). C. A. 51, 1826g (1957). Proc. Acad. Sci.
U.S.S.R., Sect. Chem. 109, 405-8 (1956) (Eng. trans.). C. A.
52, 5414d (1958).
and A. V. Topchiev, T. I. Chernysheva. Synthesis of some
compounds of silicon with cycloalkyl radicals. Doklady
Akad. Nauk S.S.S.R. 111, 1260-3 (1956). C. A. 51, 9477e
(1957). Proc. Acad. Sci. U.S.S.R., Sect. Chem. 111, 767-70
(1956) (Eng. trans.). C. A. 52, 6160i (1958).
and A. V. Topchiev, F. F. Machus. Some silicohydrocarbons
of the series of disilanomethane and disilanoethane. Doklady
Akad. Nauk S.S.S.R. 116, 248-50 (1957). C. A. 52, 6162f
(1958).
and A. V. Topchiev, Chan-Li Gu, N. A. Leonova. Synthesis
and properties of mono-, di- and tri-p-tolylalkylsilanes.
Doklady Akad. Nauk S.S.S.R. 115, 107-9 (1957). C. A. 52,
5323a (1958).
and A. V. Topchiev, T. I. Chernysheva. Synthesis of some
alkylhalosilanes and silicohydrocarbons. Doklady Akad.
Nauk. S.S.S.R. 115, 326-9 (1957). C. A. 52, 4473f (1958).

and A. V. Topchiev, T. I. Chernysheva. Addition of dialkyl-
(phenyl) silanes to ethylene hydrocarbons. Doklady Akad.
Nauk S.S.S.R. 118, 517-19 (1958). C. A. 52, 10922d (1958).
and A. V. Topchiev, Chan-Li Gu, N. A. Leonova. Synthesis
and properties of phenyl-, 3,4-xylyl-, and 4-(isopropylphenyl)
alkylsilanes. Doklady Akad. Nauk S.S.S.R. 118, 731-4 (1958).
C. A. 52, 11769i (1958).
and A. A. Gundyrev, A. V. Topchiev. Dipole moments of
hexa alkyl derivatives of disiloxane. Doklady Akad. Nauk
S.S.S.R. 121, 1031-3 (1958). C. A. 52, 19307d (1958).
and A. V. Topchiev, L. S. Povarov. Preparation of compounds with silathiacarbon links. Doklady Akad. Nauk
S.S.S.R. 117, 245-8 (1957). C. A. 52, 8943g (1958). Proc.
Acad. Sci. U.S.S.R., Sect. Chem. 117, 1011-14 (1957). C. A.
53, 5107b (1959).
and A. V. Topchiev, T. I. Chernysheva, S. G. Durgar'yan.
Synthesis and properties of disilylpropanes. Trudy Moskov.
Neft. Inst. im. I. M. Gubkina 1958, #23, 22-30. C. A. 53,
18894b (1959).
and Z. A. Aleksandrova, A. A. Gundyrev, G. M. Panchenkov,
A. V. Topchiev. Relation between the surface tension of
certain types of organosilicon compounds and their structure. Khim. i Prakt. Primenenie Kremneorg. Soedinenii,
Trudy Konf., Leningrad, 1958, #3, 96-103. C. A. 53, 16040a
(1959).
and Chan-Li Gu, N. A. Leonova, A. V. Topchiev, V. V.
Bazilevich. Synthesis of silicon hydrocarbons with alkylbenzyl substituents and the study of the possibility of the
chloromethylation of organosilicon compounds. Khim. i
Prakt. Primenenie Kremneorg. Soedinenii, Trudy Konf.,
Leningrad 1958, #1, 249-55. C. A. 53, 17026f (1959).
and A. V. Topchiev, L. I. Kartasheva. Reaction of ethyl
bromide with silicon. Izvest. Akad. Nauk S.S.S.R., Otdel.
Khim. Nauk 1958, 949-53. C. A. 53, 1117b (1959).
and A. V. Topchiev, S. G. Durgar'yan, S. S. Dyankov. Polymerization of dialkyldiallylsilanes with a complex catalyst:
triethylaluminum-titanium tetrachloride. Khim. i Prakt.
Primenenie Kremneorg. Soedinenii, Trudy Konf., Leningrad,
1958, #2, 118-24. C. A. 53, 8686i (1959).
and V. V. Bazilevich, A. A. Gundyrev, G. M. Panchenkov,
A. V. Topchiev. Raman spectra of certain silicon hydrocarbons and hexaalkyldisiloxanes. Khim. i Prakt. Primenenie Kremneorg. Soedinenii, Trudy Konf., Leningrad, 1958,
#3, 103-8. C. A. 53, 12833d (1959).

and A. V. Topchiev, T. I. Chernysheva. Addition of tri-
benzylsilane to olefins. Doklady Akad. Nauk S.S.S.R. 126,
1001-3 (1959). C. A. 53, 21746c (1959).

and A. V. Topchiev, S. G. Durgar'yan. Addition of trichlorosilane to dialkyl (phenyl, chloro) diallylsilanes in the presence of $H_2PtCl_6 . 6 H_2O$. Doklady Akad. Nauk S.S.S.R. 130,
105-8 (1960). C. A. 54, 10833f (1960).

and A. V. Topchiev, Chan-Li Gu, N. A. Pritula. Preparation
of some organosilicon compounds with alkylbenzyl radicals
from chloromethylated alkylbenzenes. Zhur. Obshchei Khim.
29, 2820-6 (1959). C. A. 54, 12031c (1960).

and A. V. Topchiev, T. I. Chernysheva, L. I. Kartasheva.
Addition reaction of trialkoxysilanes to olefins. Doklady
Akad. Nauk S.S.S.R. 126, 794-7 (1959). C. A. 54, 262b
(1960).

and A. V. Topchiev, S. G. Durgar'yan, I. M. Tolchinskii.
Copolymerization of dimethyl- and methylphenyldiallylsilane
with propylene on the composite Et_3Al + $TiCl_4$ catalyst.
Vysokomolekulyarnye Soedineniya 1, #11, 1739-44 (1959).
C. A. 54, 14767a (1960).

and A. V. Topchiev, T. I. Chernysheva, S. G. Durgar'yan.
Addition of silicon hydrides to unsaturated compounds. J.
prakt. Chem. [4] 9, 82-5 (1959). C. A. 54, 4359h (1960).

and A. V. Topchiev, S. G. Durgar'yan. Synthesis of organo-
silicon polymers on a complex catalyst, Et_3Al + $TiCl_4$.
Mezhdunarod. Simpozium po Makromol. Khim., Doklady,
Moscow 1960, Sektsiya 1, 152-5. C. A. 55, 7329e (1961).

and S. G. Durgar'yan, Yu. P. Egorov, A. V. Topchiev.
Structure determination of organosilicon compounds (prepared by addition of trichlorosilane to mono- and diallyl
derivates of silicon) by infrared spectroscopy. Zhur.
Obshchei Khim. 30, 2600-8 (1960). C. A. 55, 14341d (1961).

and A. V. Topchiev, S. G. Durgar'yan, N. A. Kuz'mina. Addition of trichlorosilane to trialkyl (phenyl or chloro)-
diallysilanes. Some silicohydrocarbons prepared from the
addition products. Zhur. Obshchei Khim. 30, 2594-600
(1960). C. A. 55, 14345g (1961).

and A. V. Topchiev, S. G. Durgar'yan. Addition of trichlorosilane to trialkyl (phenyl or chloro)-allylsilanes. Some
silicohydrocarbons of disilanepropane series. Zhur. Obshchei Khim. 30, 927-32 (1960). C. A. 55, 430b (1961).

and A. A. Gundyrev, G. M. Panchenkov, A. V. Topchiev.
Dielectric permeability and the dipole moments of some

silicon organic compounds. Doklady Akad. Nauk S.S.S.R.
129, 1325-7 (1959). C. A. 55, 26503b (1961).
and I. N. Lyashenko, L. S. Polak, A. V. Topchiev, A. S.
Fel'dman, T. I. Chernysheva. Catalytic and radiation polymerization and copolymerization of allylhydrosilanes.
Vysokomolekulyarnye Soedineniya 3, 833-40 (1961). C. A.
55, 26504d (1961).
and A. V. Topchiev, Chang-Li Ku, N. A. Pritula. Chloromethylation of trialkylbenzylsilanes and some transformations of chloromethylbenzyltrialkylsilanes. Zhur. Obshchei Khim. 31, 1303-9 (1961). C. A. 55, 23402g (1961).
and A. V. Topchiev, T. I. Chernysheva, I. N. Lyashenko.
Hydrisilane addition to allylamine. Doklady Akad. Nauk 140,
#2, 384-86 (1961).
Office: Institute of Petrochemical Synthesis
            Leninskii Prospekt, 29
            Moscow, USSR

NEKRASOV, BORIS VLADIMIROVICH (Chemist)
    B. V. Nekrasov was born September 18, 1899. In 1924 he
graduated from the Institute of the National Economy of Plek-
hanov and continued to work there. Subsequently, he worked
at the Moscow Textile Institute. In 1939 he became Chairman
of the Department of the Kalinin Moscow Institute of Non-
Ferrous Metals and Gold. He was elected in 1946 a Corresponding Member of the U.S.S.R. Academy of Sciences.
    Nekrasov works on coorelation of structure and properties
of chemical compounds. He proposed in 1955 an explanation of
the trans influence in complex compounds, in 1948 a theory of
the structure of boranes, in 1946 an equation for the polarity of
bonds and effective charges of atoms in molecules of the AB_m
type. He is the author of a text book, "Course on General
Chemistry" which has had 12 editions (2 vols., 1935, 12th edition, 1955) which has been translated into many languages.
Bibliography:
    Properties of Ions. Part 1-5. Bulletin de la Societe chimi-
    que de France, Paris, 1936, Febr. 5 Serie, V. 3 (Part 1-2);
    Zhur. Obshchei Khim., 1937, #7 (Part 3), 1940, #13 (Part 4);
    1940, #15 (Part 5).
    Theory of the structure of boranes. Zhur. Obshchei Khim.,
    1940, #11.
    Electro affinity of chemical elements. Zhur. Obshchei
    Khim., 1946, #11.

Unusual Valency of Some Metals. Report. . . Izvest. Akad.
Nauk S.S.S.R. Otdel. Khim. Naul, 1956, #2., 137-144.
Office: Chemistry Department
        Kalinin Moscow Institute of Non-Ferrous Metals
        and Gold
        Moscow, USSR
Residence: Zubovskii bulv. 16/20
        Moscow, USSR
Telephone: G6 07 93

NENADKEVICH, KONSTANTIN AVTONOMOVICH (Chemist-Mineralogist)

K. A. Nenadkevich was born June 2, 1880. In 1902 he graduated from Moscow University. Since 1906 he has been working
in various geological departments of the U.S.S.R. Academy of
Sciences (Geological and Mineralogical Museum, Geological Institute, Institute of Mineralogy and Geochemistry of Rare Metals).
He was elected in 1946 a Corresponding Member of the U.S.S.R.
Academy of Sciences. In 1948 he received a Stalin Prize.

Nenadkevich studied new types of mineral raw materials
and developed methods for obtaining rare metals from ores.
In 1916-20 Nenadkevich worked out the technology of producing
metallic bismuth from domestic raw materials and conducted
its first experimental smelting. In 1926 he chemically ascertained the age of one of the most ancient minerals—uraninite.
Bibliography:
    Question of the U.S.S.R. soda industry (Doroninskoe soda
    lake). Zhur. Priklad. Khim., 1924, 1, #3-4.
    Electrolytic methods of separating nickel and cobalt. Dok-
    lady Akad. Nauk S.S.S.R., 1945, 49, #1.
Office: Institute of Mineralogy, Geochemistry and Crystal-
            lography of Rare Elements
            Ulitsa Kubysheva, 8
            Moscow, USSR
Residence: M. Yakimanka, 3
            Moscow, USSR
Telephone: V1 94 84

NESMEYANOV, ALEKSANDR NIKOLAEVICH (Organic Chemist)

A. N. Nesmeyanov was born September 9, 1899. He graduated from Moscow University in 1922 and began his work there.
In 1930 he was instrumental in establishing a Laboratory of
Organic Chemistry at the Institute of Fertilizers and Insectofungicides and was its Chief until 1934. He helped the

University of Moscow organize a Laboratory of Metallo-
Organic Compounds in 1934. In 1935 he was made professor
at the University. At the same time, beginning in 1934, he
worked at the Institute of Organic Chemistry of the U.S.S.R.
Academy of Sciences where in 1935 he organized a Laboratory
of Metallo-Organic Compounds. He became Director of the
Institute in 1939. From 1948 to 1951 he was President of Moscow University and was active in acquiring a new building. In
1953, Nesmeyanov helped found the Institute of Scientific Information of the U.S.S.R. Academy of Sciences. Through his initiative, in 1954, an Institute of Organo-Elemental Compounds of
the U.S.S.R. Academy of Sciences was set up and he was made
the Director. Nesmeyanov has been active in social and political work. He became a member of the Communist Party of the
Soviet Union in 1944 and was Deputy to the U.S.S.R. Supreme
Soviet. Also he was a member of the All-World Council for
Peace and the Soviet Committee in Defense of Peace. In 1939
Nesmeyanov was made a Corresponding Member, and in 1943
an Academician of the U.S.S.R. Academy of Sciences. He was
elected President of the U.S.S.R. Academy of Sciences in 1951.
Nesmeyanov is the leader of the Soviet school of metallo-
organic specialists. In 1943 he was a winner of a Stalin Prize.

Nesmeyanov's main scientific work is in chemistry of
metallo-organic compounds: lithium, boron, nitrogen, sodium,
magnesium, aluminum, silicon, phosphorus, sulfur, selenium,
titanium, chromium, iron, copper, zinc, germanium, arsenic,
zirconium, molybdenum, cadmium, tin, antimony, tungsten,
mercury, thallium, lead, bismuth. In 1929 Nesmeyanov proposed a diazo method of synthesis of mercury-organic compounds, which he and his associates later used for synthesis of
metallo-organic compounds of thallium, tin, lead, germanium,
arsenic, antimony and bismuth. He also studied mutual transformations of metallo-organic compounds, utilizing these reactions for synthesis of previously unknown types of metallo-
organic compounds of zinc, cadmium, aluminum, thallium, tin
and others from mercury-organic compounds. He proved that
products of addition of salts of non-transition metals to unsaturated compounds are metallo-organic and not complex compounds, discovered new classes of these compounds, and studied
their chemistry. Nesmeyanov also investigated unsaturated
metallo-organic compounds. He made a detailed study of the
steriochemistry of their mutual transformations. Through his
study of metallic derivatives of oxo-enol systems and alpha-
mercurated oxo-compounds, he showed the relation between the

structure and the reactivity of metallic derivatives of tautomeric systems and later of the tautomeric systems themselves.
Nesmeyanov, and his associates, ascertained the mechanism of
electrophilic replacement in saturated carbon atoms. He obtained diphenylchloronium, diphenylbromium, triphenyloxonium
salts and studied the mechanism of decomposition of these
-onium salts and of various diazonium and iodonium compounds.
Nesmayanov and associates made a thorough study of the reactions of the new metallo-organic, "sandwich" compounds, the
ferrocene, and ascertained their aromatic character. He also
carried out a series of syntheses based on olefin telomeriz-
ation. He and K. A. Kocheshkov edited a series of monographs
"Synthetic Methods in the Field of Metallo-Organic Compounds." Based on his experiment, Nesmeyanov advanced a
series of theoretical ideas on the future development of the
theory of chemical structure.

    Nesmeyanov was Chairman of the Council for Coordinating
Scientific Work of the Academies of Sciences of Union Re-
publics. He was Chairman of the Editorial Publishing Council
of the U.S.S.R. Academy of Sciences.

    In 1962, Nesmeyanov was awarded the M. V. Lomonosov
Gold Medal.

Bibliography:

    A new synthesis method for aromatic mercury-organic
    salts. Zhur. Russ. Fiz.-Khim. Obshchestva (Khim. chast'),
    1929, 61, #8.

    and E. I. Kan. Fluorine formyl. Zhur. Obshchei Khim.,
    1934, 4, #9.

    and I. F. Lutsenko. On reactions of metallic derivatives of
    oxo-compounds and the phenomenon of tautomerism. Dok-
    lady Akad. Nauk S.S.S.R., 1948, 59, #4.

    and A. E. Borisov. On saving the steriochemical configu-
    ration during reactions of electrophylic and radical substi-
    tution in the olefin carbon atom. Doklady Akad. Nauk
    S.S.S.R., 1948, 60, #1.

    and V. A. Sazonova. On the quasi-complex compounds,
    hyperconjugation and tautomerism. Proc. Acad. Sci.
    U.S.S.R., Sect. Chem., 1949, #4.

    and L. G. Makarova. Synthesis of aromatic compounds of
    thallium through diazo-compounds. Doklady Akad. Nauk
    S.S.S.R., 1952, 87, #3.

    and L. G. Markova. Synthesis of aromatic compounds of tin
    with the aid of aryldiazoniumboric fluoride. Doklady Akad.
    Nauk S.S.S.R., 1952, 87, #3.

and N. A. Kochetkov, M. I. Rybinskaya. Synthesis of benzoni-
trile and flavilic salts on the base of betavinyl chloride of
ketones. Doklady Akad. Nauk S.S.S.R., 1953, 93, #1.
and O. A. Reulov, O. A. Ptitsina. On new possibilities of
synthesis of antimonous-organic compounds through didia-
zone salts of trichloride antimony. Doklady Akad. Nauk
S.S.S.R., 1953, 91, #6.
and E. G. Perevalova, R. V. Golovnya, O. A. Nesmeyanova.
Reaction of substitution of hydrogen of ferrocene. Doklady
Akad. Nauk S.S.S.R., 1954, 97, #3.
and T. P. Tolstaya. Diphenyl chloronium salts. Doklady
Akad. Nauk S.S.S.R., 1955, 105, #1.
and M. I. Kabachnik. Dual reaction ability of tautomerism.
Zhur. Obshchei Khim., 1955, 25, #1.
and T. P. Tolstaya, L. S. Isaeva. Diphenyl bromonium salts.
Doklady Akad. Nauk S.S.S.R., 1955, 104, #6.
and N. A. Kochetkova. Alkylation of ferrocene. Doklady
Akad. Nauk S.S.S.R., 1956, 109, #3.
and R. Kh. Freidlina, L. I. Zakharkin. Study of chemical
transformation of polyhydrocarbon chlorides and relative
compounds. Uspekhi Khim., 1956, 25, #6.
and V. A. Sazonova, A. V. Gerasimenko. α Pyridil ferrocene and 1,1'-di(α-pyridil)-ferrocene. Doklady Akad. Nauk
S.S.S.R. 147, #3, 634-35 (1962).
Office: Institute of Organo-Elemental Compounds of USSR
                Academy of Sciences
                Leninskii Prospekt, 31
                Moscow, USSR
Residence: Lomonosovskii Prospekt, 14
                Moscow, USSR
Telephone: B9 13 47

NEUMANN (NEYMAN), LEONID ROBERTOVICH (Electrical
       Engineer)
    L. R. Neumann was born April 6, 1902. He graduated from
the Leningrad Polytechnical Institute in 1930, and in 1940 began
teaching there as a professor. From 1931 to 1935 he was Director of a group of high voltage centers of the Leningrad
Electro-Physical Institute. He worked at the U.S.S.R. Academy
of Sciences Institute of Energetics from 1946 to 1960 and since
then has been working at the Leningrad Institute of Electromechanics. In 1953, he was elected to the U.S.S.R. Academy of
Sciences as a Corresponding Member.

Neumann's main works deal with investigating phenomena in non-linear electric circuits, the study of the skin-effect in ferromagnetic bodies, the electromagnetic processes in electric systems with powerful ion converting units, and with direct current transmissions. He has participated in the work of the International Electrotechnical Commission in the fields of scientific terminology and of systems of electric and magnetic units.

Bibliography:
and P. L. Kalantarov. Theoretical Basis of Electrical Engineering, 5th ed. Leningrad-Moscow: 1959.
and M. P. Kostenko, G. N. Blavdzevich. Electromagnetic Processes in Systems with Powerful Rectifying Units. Moscow-Leningrad: 1946.
Skin-Effect in Ferromagnetic Bodies. Leningrad-Moscow: 1949.
and S. R. Glinternick, A. V. Emelyanov, V. G. Novitski. Direct Current Power Transmission as a Part of Power Systems. Moscow-Leningrad: 1962.

Biography:
Professor L. R. Neumann. On the 50th Anniversary Since the Date of Birth. Electricity, 1952, #8.
L. R. Neumann. On the 60th Anniversary Since the Date of Birth and 35th Anniversary of the Scientific and Pedagogical Activity. Electricity, 1962, #6.

Office: Electromechanical Institute
              Dvorzovaja naberezhnaja, 18
              Leningrad, USSR

NIKITIN, NIKOLAI IGNAT'EVICH (Chemist)

N. I. Nikitin was born March 12, 1890. He graduated in 1913 from the Institute of Forestry in Petersburg. In 1929 he became professor at the S. M. Kirov Leningrad Forest-Technical Academy. He has been a Corresponding Member of the U.S.S.R. Academy of Sciences since 1939 and of the Finnish Chemical Society since 1959.

Nikitin has worked in cellulose and wood chemistry. He obtained new solutions of cellulose derivatives in alkali by weak esterification and freezing, obtained the fibers from the solutions of low-substituted xanthogenates and obtained the films of alkali-soluble low-substituted nitrocellulose and carboxymethylcellulose. He investigated the role of packing of cellulose molecules on the lyophilic properties of fibers and their relation to the quantity of nonfreezing water in the fibers. He

also studied the reactivation of cellulose by means of freezing
and inclusion and slight esterification of the fibers. He investigated the chemical composition of many wood species of the
U.S.S.R. and developed methods for obtaining sulfate and sulfite
cellulose from wood of larch (Larix daurica and L. sibirica)
with the utilization of its gum. He also developed a new synthesizing reaction of acetylene and alkali on lignin and described
the action of ethylene-oxide on lignin. Nikitin was one of the
pioneers in the development of wood and cellulose chemistry
in the U.S.S.R. and he wrote several monographs on this subject.

Bibliography:

Colloidal Solutions and Esters of Cellulose, 2nd ed. Leningrad: 1933.

Chemistry of Wood. Moscow-Leningrad: 1951.

and N. I. Klenkova. Quantity of non-freezing water in cellulose fibers after swelling. Zhur. Priklad. Khim., 1954, 27,
#2, 171-180.

and G. A. Petropavloskii. The production and the properties
of slightly substituted methyl- and carboxylmethyl cellulose.
1-2. Zhur. Priklad. Khim., 1956, 29, #10-11.

Methods of a Scientific Chemical Worker (Outlines from the
Past). Moscow-Leningrad: 1955.

Die Chemie des Holzes. Akademie-Verlag: Berlin, 1955
(Germ. trans.)

Chemistry of Wood and Cellulose. Moscow-Leningrad:
1962.

Biography:

F. P. Komarov and S. D. Antonovskii. Nikolai Ignat'evich
Nikitin. Zhur. Obshchei Khim., 1950, #4, 557-562.

N. You. Solechnie. Nikolai Ignat'evich Nikitin. J. Appl.
Chem. U.S.S.R. 33, 521-528 (1960). (English trans.)

Office: Institute of Highmolecular Compounds of USSR
              Academy of Sciences
              Birzhevoi proezd 6
              Leningrad, B-164, USSR

NIKOLAYEV, ANATOLII VASIL'EVICH (Chemist)

A. V. Nikolayev was born November 27, 1902. He graduated
in 1924 from Leningrad University. In 1927-31 he was a leader
of the Pavlodar Salt Expedition of the Commission on the Study
of Natural Productive Forces of the U.S.S.R. Academy of Sciences and in 1931-35, of the Complex Kulundinsk Expedition of
the Soviet on the Study of the Productive Forces of the U.S.S.R.

Academy of Sciences. He started working in 1934 at the Institute of General and Inorganic Chemistry of the U.S.S.R. Academy of Sciences. In 1936-41 he taught at the Moscow Polygraphic Institute and in 1945-57 at the Moscow Institute of Non-Ferrous Metals and Gold, where he was made professor in 1946. In 1957 Nikolaev became Director of the Institute of Inorganic Chemistry of the Siberian branch of the U.S.S.R. Academy of Sciences. He was elected in 1958 a Corresponding Member of the U.S.S.R. Academy of Sciences. In 1947 he was awarded the V. I. Vernadskii Prize for his research summarized in the monograph "Physico-Chemical Study of the Natural Borates."

Nikolayev's main work deals with physico-chemical analysis of salt systems for the purpose of elucidating the formation of natural salt and its industrial processing, thermal analysis, radiochemistry. He developed thermal analysis of complex compounds of platinum, investigated the chemistry and separation of rare-earth elements, and studied the extraction of inorganic substances by organic solvents.

As of 1961, Nikolayev was a Member of the Presidium of the Siberian Branch U.S.S.R. Academy of Sciences.

Bibliography:

Pre-Irtysh Salt Region. Part I. Leningrad: 1931.

Kolundinsk Salt Lakes and Methods of Processing. Novosibirsk: 1935.

and others. Thermography. Curves of Heating and Cooling. Moscow-Leningrad: 1944.

Protective films on salts and their utilization. Akad. Nauk S.S.S.R., 1944, #4-5, 57-65.

Physico-Chemical Study of the Natural Borates. Moscow: 1947.

Characteristics of heterogeneous equilibria in the extraction of inorganic substances. Izvest. Sibir. Otdel. Akad. Nauk S.S.S.R., #4, 51-63 (1960). C. A. 54, 22128d (1960).

and A. G. Kurnakova. Extraction of boric acid. Bor. Trudy Konf. Khim. Bora i Ego Soedinenii, 157-61 (1955). (Pub. 1956). C. A. 54, 25615d (1960).

and A. G. Kurnakova, Z. G. Rumyantseva. The chemistry of protactinium. Zhur. Neorg. Khim. 4, 1682-6 (1959). C. A. 54, 8394b (1960).

and S. M. Shubina. Isotope exchange of tributyl phosphate with tagged phosphoric acid. Zhur. Neorg. Khim. 4, 956-8 (1959). C. A. 54, 8397h (1960).

and N. M. Sinitsyn. Distillation of ruthenium from highly
diluted nitrate solutions. Zhur. Neorg. Khim. 4, 1935-6
(1959). C. A. 54, 11790c (1960).

Office: Institute of Inorganic Chemistry, Siberian Branch
              of USSR Academy of Sciences
              Novosibirsk, Siberia

NIKOLAEV, IVAN IVANOVICH (Railroad Engineer)

I. I. Nikolaev was born April 11, 1893. Upon graduating
from the Moscow Institute of Communication and Line Engineers in 1921, he taught there until 1957, having become a professor in 1935. From 1921 to 1938, he taught at the Moscow
Technical College. From 1947 to 1951 he was professor at the
Academy of Railroad Transport. In 1955 he began work at the
Institute of Complex Transport Problems of the U.S.S.R. Academy of Sciences. He became a member of the Communist Party
of the Soviet Union in 1942. In 1947 he was awarded the title
Honored Scientist of R.S.F.S.R. He was elected, in 1953, a
Corresponding Member of the U.S.S.R. Academy of Sciences.

The works of Nikolaev deal with questions of dynamics and
steam distribution of locomotives.

Bibliography:
Dynamics and Steam Distribution of a Locomotive, 2nd ed.
Moscow: 1953.
and E. G. Kestner. Experimental Investigation of a Loco-
motive. Moscow-Leningrad: 1933.
Designing locomotives. Complex Modernization and Con-
temporary Methods of Designing Locomotives. Moscow:
1945.
Theory and Construction of Locomotives. Moscow: 1939.
and others. Rolling Stock and Traction of Trains, 2nd ed.
Moscow: 1955.
and others. General Course on Railroads. Moscow: 1956.
Biography:
60th Anniversary of Professor I. I. Nikolaev. Railroad
Transport, 1953, #5.
Office: Institute of Complex Transport Problems of USSR
              Academy of Sciences
              Moscow, USSR
Residence: Durasovskii p. 7
              Moscow, USSR
Telephone: K7 35 36

NIKOL'SKII, BORIS PETROVICH (Physical Chemist)

B. P. Nikol'skii was born October 14, 1900. After graduating from Leningrad University in 1924, he worked there and in 1939 became professor. In 1953 he was elected Corresponding Member of the U.S.S.R. Academy of Sciences. Nikol'skii investigated processes of ion exchange between aqueous solutions and various solid systems—soils, ionites, and others. He developed a theory on these processes, which is used in ion-exchange chromatography. He also proposed an ion-exchange theory for a glass electrode. As of 1961, Nikol'skii was Director of the Institute of Mechanics of the U.S.S.R. Academy of Sciences.

Bibliography:
Laws of ion-exchange between the solid phase and solutions. Uspekhi Khim., 1939, 8, #10.
Theory of a glass electrode. Zhur. Fiz. Khim., 1953, 27, #5-6.
Office: Chemistry Department
              Leningrad University
              Leningrad, USSR

NOVIKOV, IVAN IVANOVICH (Physicist)

I. I. Novikov was born January 29, 1916. In 1930 he graduated from Moscow University, and worked for scientific organizations of the Soviet Navy from 1940 to 1948. In 1950 he became a professor at the Moscow Institute of Physical Engineering of which he was made Director in 1956. From 1954 to 1957, he was assistant to the Chief Academic Secretary of the U.S.S.R. Academy of Sciences Presidium. He was Editor-in-Chief of the journal "Atomic Energy" in 1956, and since 1957 has been the Director of the Institute of Thermal Physics of the Siberian branch of the U.S.S.R. Academy of Sciences. In 1958, he was elected a Corresponding Member of the U.S.S.R. Academy of Sciences. He has been awarded a Stalin Prize.

Novikov has studied thermodynamics of gases, gas dynamics, heat transfer, use of the theory of similarity in the study of thermophysical properties of substances, investigation of the thermodynamic properties of heat carriers and atomic energy.

Bibliography:
and M. P. Vukolovich. Equations of the State of Real Gases. Moscow-Leningrad: 1948.
Index of the adiabatic curve of saturated and moist steam. Doklady Akad. Nauk S.S.S.R., 1948, 59, #8.

Existence of Impact Waves of Disturbance. Doklady Akad.
Nauk S.S.S.R., 1948, 59, #9.
and M. P. Vukolovich. Technical Thermodynamics, 2nd ed.
Moscow-Leningrad: 1955.
and others. Heat emission and thermophysical properties of
molten alkali metals. Atomic Energy, 1956, #4.
and others. Liquid-metal Heat Carriers. Moscow: 1958.
Office: Institute of Thermophysics, Siberian Branch of
        USSR Academy of Sciences
        Novosibirsk, Siberia

NOVIKOV, PYOTR SERGEEVICH (Mathematician)

P. S. Novikov was born August 28, 1901. He graduated in
1927 from Moscow University. In 1934 he started working at
the Mathematical Institute of the U.S.S.R. Academy of Sciences.
He was elected a Corresponding Member of the U.S.S.R. Academy of Sciences in 1953 and in 1960 an Academician. In 1957 he
was awarded a Lenin Prize, and again in 1961.

Novikov's main works are concerned with set theory and
mathematical logics.

Bibliography:
Fonctions implicites mesurables. Fundamenta Mathematicae, Warszava, 1931, Bd. 17, 8-25.
Sur la séparabilité des ensembles projectifs du seconde
classe. Fundamenta Mathematicae, Warszava, 1935, Bd. 25,
459-466.
On the non-contradiction of some positions of descriptive
set theory. Works of the V. A. Steklov Institute of Mathe-
matics, 1951, 38, 279-316.
On the algorithmical insolubility of the problem of identity
of words in group theory. Moscow: 1955.
Office: V. A. Steklov Mathematics Institute of USSR
        Academy of Sciences
        1-y Akademicheskii Proyezd, 28
        Moscow, USSR
Residence: ul. Chkalova, 21/2
        Moscow, USSR
Telephone: B7 06 85

NOVOSELOVA, ALEKSANDRA VASIL'EVNA (Chemist)

A. V. Novoselova was born March 24, 1900. She graduated
from Moscow University in 1924 and had worked there since
1920. In 1946 she was made professor at the University. She

was elected in 1953 a Corresponding Member of the U.S.S.R.
Academy of Sciences. In 1948 she was awarded a Stalin Prize.
Novoselova developed analytical methods for beryllium, and
for complexes in system $MoO_3 - H_2O$.

Bibliography:
and M. E. Levina. Thermal analysis of the system NaF-
BeF_2. Zhur. Obshchei Khim., 1944, 14, #6.
and D. F. Kirkina, Yu. P. Simanov. Polymorphism of beryllium fluoride. Doklady Akad. Nauk S.S.S.R., 1956, 107, #6.
and Yu. P. Simanov. Structure and transformation of fluorine
compounds of beryllium. Scientific Papers of Moscow State
University, #174, 1955, 7-16.
and Yu. P. Simanov, N. N. Semenenko, N. N. Krasovskaya.
Compounds of hydroxyacetate of beryllium with pyridine dioxane. Zhur. Neorg. Khim., 1956, 1, #4.
and K. N. Semenenko. Interaction of hydroxy-acetate of
beryllium with hydroxymonochloracetate of beryllium. Zhur.
Neorg. Khim., 1956, 1, #10.
Office: Chemistry Department
                Moscow University
                Moscow, USSR
Residence: Lomonosovskii pr. 14
                Moscow, USSR
Telephone: B9 15 80

NOVOZHILOV, VALENTIN VALENTINOVICH (Mechanics Specialist)

V. V. Novozhilov was born May 18, 1910. After graduating
from Leningrad Physico-Technical Institute, he worked in a
series of scientific research establishments. He started teaching at the Leningrad University in 1946 and in 1949 became a
professor. Since 1958 he has been a Corresponding Member of
the U.S.S.R. Academy of Sciences.

Novozhilov's major works deal with the theory of elasticity,
theory on plasticity, theory of shells, and also their application
to problems in ship building.

Bibliography:
Theory of Thin Shells. 2nd ed. Leningrad: 1951.
Basis of Non-Linear Theory of Elasticity. Leningrad-
Moscow: 1948.
Office: Leningrad University
                Leningrad, USSR

NUZHDIN, NIKOLAI IVANOVICH (Biologist)

N. I. Nuzhdin was born April 17, 1904. He graduated in 1929 from Teachers Institute in Yaroslavl. In 1935 he began working in the Institute of Genetics at U.S.S.R. Academy of Sciences. He has been a member of the Communist Party since 1927. In 1953 he was elected a Corresponding Member of the U.S.S.R. Academy of Sciences.

Nuzhdin's works are in the field of genetics, radiobiology, and evolution.

Bibliography:

Hereditary changes in ontogenesis. Zhur. Obshchei Biol., 1945, #6.

Criticism of the idealogical theories of genes. Versus Reactionary Mendelism-Morganism. Moscow-Leningrad: 1950.

Darwin and Mitchurian biology. Izvest. Akad. Nauk S.S.S.R., Ser. Biol., 1952, #3.

The role of hybridization in variability. Zhur. Obshchei Biol., 1946, 7, #2.

Interdependence between the condition of the chromosome cellular nucleotide, speed of growth and development. Doklady Akad. Nauk S.S.S.R., New Series, 1948, 60, #3.

Office: Institute of Genetics of USSR Academy of Sciences
          Leninskii Prospekt, 33
          Moscow, USSR

Residence: 1-aya Cheremushkinskaya, 3
          Moscow, USSR

Telephone: V7 52 78

OBREIMOV, IVAN VASIL'EVICH (Physicist)

I. V. Obreimov was born March 8, 1894. In 1915 he graduated from Petrograd University. He worked at the State Optical Institute from 1919 until 1924 when he began work at the Leningrad Physico-Technical Institute. Subsequently he worked at the Physico-Technical Institute and from 1929 to 1937 was the Director. In 1933 Obreimov was elected a Corresponding Member of the U.S.S.R. Academy of Sciences and in 1958 an Academician. He was awarded a Stalin Prize in 1946.

Obreimov conducted scientific investigations on the physics of crystals and molecular spectroscopy. He studied plastic deformation and optical properties of single crystals and spectroscopy of crystals at low temperatures. In his monograph, On the application of Fresnel diffraction for physical and Technical measurements (1945), (Stalin Prize 1946),

Obreimov proposed and developed a method for determining dispersion which can be applied to a study of crystals undergoing chemical reactions and to control of fractionation of mixtures.

In 1960 Obreimov was awarded the S. I. Vavilov Gold Medal.

Bibliography:

and T. N. Shkurina. Identification of hydrocarbons by a dispersion curve. Proc. Acad. Sci. U.S.S.R., Sect. Chem., 1955, #5.

Formation of ultramicroscopic heterogeneities during plastic deformation of rock salt. Doklady Akad. Nauk S.S.S.R., 1956, 108, #3.

Office: Leningrad Physico-Technical Institute of USSR Academy of Sciences

Sosnovka 2

Lesnoy, Leningrad, USSR

OBRUCHEV, SERGEI VLADIMIROVICH (Geologist)

S. V. Obruchev was born February 3, 1891. He is the son of the Russian geologist V. A. Obruchev, 1863-1956. S. V. Obruchev graduated from Moscow University in 1915. While conducting geological studies of the Yenisei basin from 1917 to 1924, he delineated and described the Tungusskii coal basin. He was awarded a Stalin Prize in 1946, and became a Corresponding Member of the U.S.S.R. Academy of Sciences in 1953.

In 1926-35 Obruchev studied the practically unknown regions of Northeastern U.S.S.R., the river basins of Indigirka and Kolyma, Chukotskii region. He developed schemes of ore description, geomorphology and geological structure of Northeastern Asia. He proposed uniting the mountain structures of the middle of Indigirka River and Kolyma under the name of Cherskii Ridge. In 1937-54 he studied the ridge of Eastern Sayan, Khamar-Daban and Eastern Tuva. He also did research on the geology and geomorphology of other regions of the U.S.S.R. He is the author of a series of scientific-popular books (Unknown Mountains of Yakutiya, 1928; On the Persei Through Polar Seas, 1929; Kolyma Land, 1933; A Plane in Eastern Arctic, 1934; Into Unexplored Territories, 1954.) He compiled a Handbook of a Traveler and Student of Local Lore (2 volumes, 1949-1950).

Bibliography:

Tungusskii basin (South and Western part), I-II, Works of the All-Union Geological Prospecting Society of the People's

Commissariat of Heavy Industry of the U.S.S.R., #164, 178.
Moscow-Leningrad: 1932-1933.
New orographic scheme of North Eastern Asia. Research
Papers of the Leningrad State University. Series on Geo-
graphic Sciences, 1940, 56, #3.
Outline of the tectonics of North Eastern Asia. To Acade-
mician V. A. Obruchev, on the 50th Anniversary of Scientific
and Pedagogical Activity, 1. Moscow-Leningrad: 1938.
Main characteristics of the tectonics and stratigraphy of
Eastern Sayan. Izvest. Akad. Nauk S.S.S.R., Geol. Ser.,
1942, #5-6.
Orography and Geomorphology of the Eastern Half of Eastern
Sayan. Proceedings of the All-Union Geographic Society of
the U.S.S.R., 1946, #7-8.
New data on orography of North Eastern Tuva. Questions on
the Geology of Asia, 2. Moscow: 1955.
Office: USSR Academy of Sciences
             Leninskii Prospekt, 14
             Moscow, USSR

OBUKHOV, ALEKSANDR MIKHAILOVICH (Geophysicist)
     A. M. Obukhov was born May 5, 1918. After having gradu-
ated from Moscow University in 1940, he worked at the Geophysical Institute of the U.S.S.R. Academy of Sciences. He holds
a doctorate in physical-mathematical sciences. In 1956, he
became director of the U.S.S.R. Academy of Sciences Institute
of Atmospheric Physics. In 1953, he became a Corresponding
Member of the U.S.S.R. Academy of Sciences.
     Obukhov has been concerned with the statistical theory of
turbulence and its application in meteorology. Together with
A. N. Kolmogorov, he developed a theory of the local structure
of turbulence. He also experimentally investigated atmospheric
turbulence and worked in dynamic meteorology and the theory
of probability.
     As of 1961, Obukhov was Chairman of the Commission on
Physics of Atmosphere.
Bibliography:
     Distribution of Energy in the Spectrum of a Turbulent Flow.
     Izvest. Akad. Nauk S.S.S.R., Ser. Geogr. i Geofiz., 1941,
     #4-5.
     Structure of the Temperature Field in a Turbulent Flow.
     Izvest. Akad. Nauk S.S.S.R., Ser. Geogr. i Geofiz., 1949, 13,
     #1.

Question of Geostrophic Wind. Izvest. Akad. Nauk S.S.S.R.,
Ser. Geogr. i Geofiz., 13, 1949, #4.
Dynamics of stratified fluids. Doklady Akad. Nauk S.S.S.R.
145, #6, 1239-42 (1962).
Biography:
    Aleksandr Mikhailovich Obukhov (Meteorologist). Izvest.
    Akad. Nauk S.S.S.R., Ser. Geofiz., 1954, #1.
Office: Institute of Physics of the Atmosphere of USSR
              Academy of Sciences
              Bol'shaya Gruzinskaya Ulitsa, 10
              Moscow, USSR

ODING, IVAN AVGUSTOVICH (Metallurgist)

I. A. Oding was born July 6, 1896. He graduated in 1921
from the Technological Institute of Petrograd. From 1930 to
1942 he was professor at the Leningrad Polytechnic Institute.
In 1942-1947 he was the Director of the Central Scientific Re-
search Institute of Technology and Machine Building; in 1947-
1953 he worked at the Institute of Machine Studies of the
U.S.S.R. Academy of Sciences. Beginning in 1953, he has carried out research at the Institute of Metallurgy of the U.S.S.R.
Academy of Sciences. He has been a member of the Communist
Party of the Soviet Union since 1942. In 1946 he was elected a
Corresponding Member of the U.S.S.R. Academy of Sciences.
He received a Stalin Prize in 1946, and in 1956 was an Honored
Scientist of the R.S.F.S.R.
    Oding's main works are concerned with problems in the
strength of metals. He worked on the establishment of new
methods for testing mechanical properties of metals, such as
cyclical viscosity and relaxation.
Bibliography:
    Strength of metals. Study of Metals, 3rd ed. Moscow-
    Leningrad: 1937.
    Permissible Stresses in Machine Building and Cyclical
    Strength of Metals. 3rd ed. Moscow-Leningrad: 1947.
    Basis of Strength of Metals of Boilers, Turbines and Turbo-
    generators. Moscow-Leningrad: 1949.
    Contemporary Methods of Testing Metals. 4th ed. Moscow-
    Leningrad: 1944.
Biography:
    Ivan Avgustovich Oding (On the 60th Anniversary Since the
    Date of Birth) in Factory Laboratory. 1956, #8.

On the 60th Anniversary of the Corresponding Member of the
U.S.S.R. Academy of Sciences I. A. Oding. Study of Metals
and Metal Processing, 1956, #9.
Office: A. A. Baykov Institute of Metallurgy of USSR Acade-
              my of Sciences
              Leninskii Prospekt, 49
              Moscow, USSR
Residence: B. Ordynka 34/38
              Moscow, USSR
Telephone: B1 72 80

OKHOTSIMSKII, DMITRII YEVGEN'EVICH (Mechanics
    Specialist)
    D. Ye. Okhotsimskii was born in 1921. In 1946 he graduated
from the mechanical-mathematics faculty of Moscow State University. In that year he also initiated postgraduate studies,
later became a junior, and then senior scientific worker, and
in 1953 departmental Chief of the U.S.S.R. Academy of Sciences
Mathematics Institute. He became, in 1959, a professor of the
theoretical mechanics department of Moscow State University.
He was awarded a Lenin Prize in 1957, and has been a member
of the Communist Party of the Soviet Union since 1951. In 1960
he became a Corresponding Member of the U.S.S.R. Academy of
Sciences.
    Okhotsimskii has worked on earth satellites.
Bibliography:
    Theory of the motion of a body with cavities partially filled
    with a liquid. Prikl. Mat. Mekh. 20, 1, 3-20 (1956). Applied
    Mechanics Reviews 11, 760 (1958).
    and T. M. Eneev. Some variation problems connected with
    the launching of artificial satellites of the earth. J. Brit.
    Interplanetary Soc. 16, 5, 263-294 (1958). Uspekhi Phys.
    Nauk 63, suppl. la, 5-32 (1957). Proc. 8th International
    Astronautical Congr., Barcelona, 1957. Applied Mechanics
    Reviews 12, 1055 (1959).
    and I. L. Kondrasheva, Z. P. Vlasova, R. K. Kazakova.
    Calculations for a precision explosion, taking into account
    the counter resistance. Trudy Matem. In-ta Akad. Nauk
    S.S.R. #50, 66 pp. & others 1957, Ref. Zh. Mekh. #3, 1958,
    Rev. 2659. Applied Mechanics Reviews 12, 5798 (1959).
    and T. M. Eneev, G. P. Taratyrova. The determination of
    the period of existence of an earth satellite and an investi-
    gation of the secular perturbations of its orbit. Uspekhi Fiz.

Nauk 63, 1a, 33-50 (1957). Ref. Zh. Mekh. #8, 1958. Rev.
8371. Applied Mechanics Reviews 13, 6634 (1960).
Office: Theoretical Mechanics Department
             Moscow State University
             Moscow, USSR

OPARIN, ALEKSANDR IVANOVICH (Organic Chemist)

A. I. Oparin was born March 3, 1894. In 1917 he graduated
from Moscow University, and in 1929 he became a professor
there. He helped organize the Institute of Biochemistry of the
U.S.S.R. Academy of Sciences, began working there in 1935,
and became the Director in 1946. He was elected Corresponding Member of the U.S.S.R. Academy of Sciences in 1939 and in
1946 an Academician. From 1949 to 1956 he was Academician-
Secretary of the Department of Biological Sciences of the
U.S.S.R. Academy of Sciences. Oparin has been a prominent
national figure in the Soviet Union. In 1950 he was appointed a
member of the Soviet Committee in Defense of Peace and a
member of the International Council for Peace. He became, in
1952, Vice-President of the International Federation of Scientists and was elected again in September 1962. In 1950 he was
awarded the A. N. Bakh and I. I. Mechnikov Prizes.

Oparin's work is devoted to the biochemical basis of processing of vegetative raw materials, to the action of enzymes
in a living vegetative organism, and to the origin of life on the
earth. His work laid the basis for technical biochemistry in
the U.S.S.R. The study by Oparin and his students gave a
rational biochemical basis for the production of sugar, bread,
tea, wine, and tobacco. Oparin advanced a hypothesis on the
origin of life on earth based on investigations in the field of
astronomy, chemistry, geology and biology.

Bibliography:
    Origin of Life on Earth, 3rd ed. Moscow: 1957.
    Changes of the Action of Enzymes in the Living Cell under
    Influence of External Action. Moscow: 1952.
    Life: Its Nature, Origin, and Development. Edinburgh:
    Oliver and Boyd Co., 1961. 224 p. (English trans.)

Biography:
    Aleksandr Ivanovich Oparin. On 60th Anniversary since date
    of birth. Biokhimya, 1954, 19, #2.

Office: A. N. Bakh Institute of Biochemistry of USSR
             Academy of Sciences
             Leninskii Prospekt, 33
             Moscow, USSR

Residence: Cheremushkinskaya, 3
            Moscow, USSR
Telephone: B7 25 22

ORLOV, YURII ALEKSANDROVICH (Paleontologist and
       Histologist)
   Yu. A. Orlov was born June 12, 1893. In 1917 he graduated
from the Petrograd (Leningrad) University. He taught in Perm'
University until 1924, and from 1924 to 1935 at the Military
Medical Academy in Leningrad. Orlov was a professor at the
Leningrad University 1933-1941 and in 1943 at the Moscow Uni-
versity. In 1929 he began working in the Paleontological Insti-
tute of the U.S.S.R. Academy of Sciences and in 1945 he became
Director of this Institute. He was elected Corresponding Mem-
ber of the U.S.S.R. Academy of Sciences in 1953 and in 1960 an
Academician. In 1946 he was awarded the title of Honored
Scientist of the R.S.F.S.R.
   Orlov is the author of comparative-morphological investi-
gations of the nervous system of invertebrates and on paleon-
tology of invertebrates and vertebrates.
Bibliography:
   Perunilnae, new subfamily of marten is from Neogene Eur-
   asia. Moscow-Leningrad: 1947 (Works of the Paleontologi-
   cal Institute of the U.S.S.R. Academy of Sciences, 10, #3).
Office: Institute of Paleontology of USSR Academy of
            Sciences
            Leninskii Prospekt, 33
            Moscow, USSR
Residence: Leninskii Prospekt, 13
            Moscow, USSR
Telephone: V2 05 38

PALLADIN, ALEKSANDER VLADIMIROVICH (Biochemist)
   A. V. Palladin was born September 10, 1885. He graduated
in 1908 from the University of Petersburg. In 1916 he was
made professor at the Institute of Agriculture and Forestry in
Kharkov and in 1921 professor at the Kharkov Medical Institute.
He helped found the Ukrainian Biochemical Institute (since
1931, the Institute of Biochemistry of the Ukrainian S.S.R.
Academy of Sciences) and in 1925 became the Director. Begin-
ning in 1934, he was also a professor at the University of Kiev.
He became a member of the Communist Party of the Soviet
Union in 1932. Since 1929 he has been a Member of the Acade-
my of Sciences of the Ukrainian S.S.R. From 1946 to 1962 he

was the President of this Academy of Sciences. In 1942 he be-
came a Member of the U.S.S.R. Academy of Sciences. Palladin
was named, in 1935, an Honored Scientist of the Ukrainian
S.S.R. He has been a member of the U.S.S.R. Academy of Medical Sciences since 1944. In 1950 he was an Honored Member
of the Belorussian S.S.R. Academy of Sciences. Also he is an
Honorary Member of the Academies of Sciences of Bulgaria,
Hungary, and Rumania and a foreign Member of the Polish
Academy of Sciences. He has been a Deputy to the U.S.S.R.
Supreme Soviet. The Supreme Soviet of the U.S.S.R. awarded
him in 1955 the title of "Hero of Socialist Labor."

Palladin's work is in animal biochemistry. He was the first
in the U.S.S.R. to study experimentally the biochemistry of
vitamins and the intermediate chemical transformations in
metabolism (intracellular carbohydrate and phosphorous exchange). In the study of vitamins, he investigated the processes
of their transformation in the tissues of animals, and the dis-
order of metabolism during avitaminosis and hypovitaminosis.
He produced a synthetic vitamin preparation "vikasol," which
is utilized in medicine. His earlier work was devoted to the
study of creatin. In the area of biochemistry of the muscle he
investigated the role of creatin in the muscle and the questions
of muscular activity and muscle training. In the area of biochemistry of the nervous system, Palladin and associates
showed the biochemical difference of separate, functionally-
dissimilar parts of the central nervous system; conducted comparative biochemical investigations on tissues of the nervous
system in different types of animals; and studied the chemical
composition of tissues of the nervous system in the process of
embryonic development of animals. Palladin studied the biochemistry of the brain under various functional conditions, such
as inhibition and excitation, and investigated proteins and enzymes of the nervous system.

Palladin is the author of Textbook on Biological Chemistry
(1924, 12th ed., 1946). In 1926, he was instrumental in establishing the first Soviet biochemical journal, "Scientific
Notes of the Biochemical Institute," later renamed (1934) the
"Ukrainian Biochemical Journal." He is its editor at the present time.

As of 1961 Palladin was a Member of the Presidium of the
U.S.S.R. Academy of Sciences.

Bibliography:

Investigations on the Formation and Secretion of Creatin in
Animals. Kharkov: 1916.

Basis of Nutrition, 3rd ed. Moscow: 1927.
Investigations on the Biochemistry of Muscles and the Nervous System Under Various Conditions. The Anniversary Collection devoted to the 30th Anniversary of the Great Socialist October Revolution, Part 2. Moscow-Leningrad: 1947.
Chemical Nature of Vitamins, 3rd ed. Kiev: 1941.
Metabolism in the brain under various functional conditions. Vestnik Akad. Nauk, 1952, #10.
Der Stoffwechsel im Gehirn bei verschiedenen functionellen Zuständen. Wien Klini Wochensch. 66, 473, 1954.
Metabolism of Nucleic Acids in the Brain during its Development. "Biochemistry of the developing nervous system," New York, 1955.
La biochimie du cerveau. Conferences et Rapports du III Congres International du Biochimie. Bruxelles. Liege, 1956. p. 375.
Proteins of the Nervous System under Various Conditions. "Metabolism of the nervous system." Ed. by Richter.
London: Pergamon Press, 1957.
Zur Kenntnis der Proteine des Nervensystems. IV Intern. Congress of Biochemistry. Symposium III, Biochem. of the Nervous System. 1959, p. 185.
Protein metabolism of the Nervous System. III Symposium of Biochemistry of Nervous System. Erevan (USSR): 1962.
Metabolism in the brain by excitation and inhibition. Ukrainskii Biochem. Journ. 34, 621 (1962).
Biography:
D. L. Ferdman. Scientific, pedagogical and social activity of the Member of the Academy of Sciences A. V. Palladin. Uspekhi Sovremennoi Biol. 1955, 40, #1.
M. F. Gulii. On the 70th Anniversary since the date of birth and the 50th Anniversary of scientific of hero of Socialist labor, Member of the Academy of Sciences A. V. Palladin. Vestnik Akad. Nauk Ukrain. S.S.R., 1955, #9.
A. M. Uterski. A. V. Palladin. 2nd ed., Kiev, 1961. Academy of Sciences of Ukrainian S.S.R.
Office: Institute of Biochemistry of the Academy of Sciences
              Ukrainian S.S.R.
              Ulitsa Leontovicha 9
              Kiev, Ukrainian SSR
Telephone: 5-80-67

PATON, BORIS EVGEN'EVICH (Metallurgist)

B. E. Paton was born November 27, 1918. He graduated in 1941 from Kiev Polytechnical Institute. In 1942 he began work at the Ukrainian S.S.R. Academy of Sciences Institute of Electro-Welding and in 1953 was made Director. He has been a member of the Communist Party of the Soviet Union since 1952. He became a Corresponding Member of the Ukrainian S.S.R. Academy of Sciences in 1952 and in 1958 an Academician. In February 1962, he was elected President of the Ukrainian S.S.R. Academy of Sciences. As of June 1962 he is an Academician of the U.S.S.R. Academy of Sciences. In 1950 he received a State Prize and in 1957, a Lenin Prize.

Paton's work has been concerned with electro-technical problems of contact, arc, and gas-electric welding of metals. From 1942-1945, he investigated the basic methods of closed arc welding. In 1945-1951 he developed a theory for controlling automatic electric arc welding and methods for pipe welding (State Prize 1950). He also participated in developing new methods of electric-slag welding of massive pieces of metal (Lenin Prize 1957).

He was a deputy to the fifth session of the Ukrainian Supreme Soviet and the sixth session of the Supreme Soviet of the U.S.S.R. In 1961 he was elected to the Central Committee of the Communist Party.

Bibliography:

and A. M. Makar. Experimental Research in Automatic Welding Under a Flux Layer. Kiev: 1944.

Investigating Conditions and Control of Stable Combustion of a Welding Arc. Kiev: 1951.

and E. L. Lebedev. Estimating the Chain and Apparatus of an Alternate Current for Arc Welding. Kiev: 1953.

and others. Programmatic and Cybernetic Control of Welding Processes. Kiev: 1960.

Electro-slag Rewelding of Metals. Moscow: 1961.

Production of Two-Layer Sheets for Electro-slag Welding. Moscow: 1962.

Office: Institute of Electrowelding im. E. O. Paton
              ul. Gor'kogo, 69
              Kiev, Ukrainian SSR
Telephone: 7-90-01

PAVLOV, IGOR' MIKHAILOVICH (Metallurgist)

I. M. Pavlov, son of M. A. Pavlov (1863-1950, a Russian metallurgist) was born June 23, 1900. After graduating from

PAVLOVSKY

Petrograd Polytechnic Institute in 1923, he worked in Metallurgical plants. In 1928 he began teaching at and in 1934 was made professor at the Leningrad Polytechnic Institute. He became a professor in 1943 at the Moscow Institute of Steel. In 1953 he went to work at the Institute of Metallurgy of the U.S.S.R. Academy of Sciences. Since 1946 he has been a Corresponding Member of the U.S.S.R. Academy of Sciences.

Pavlov's main works deal with the theory of the rolling and with pressure processing of metals and also with the general problems of metallurgy and metals.

Bibliography:

Theory of Rolling. 3rd ed., Moscow: 1950.

Composition of a Furnace Charge for Non-Ferrous Casting. 2nd ed., Moscow-Leningrad: 1932.

Rolling of Non-Ferrous Metals and Alloys. Leningrad-Moscow: 1932.

and Ya. S. Gallai. Forward Flow During Rolling. Moscow-Leningrad: 1936.

and others. Processing of Metals by Pressure. Moscow: 1955.

Grundlagen der Metallverformung durch Druck. Bd 1-2, B., 1954.

Office: A. A. Baykov Institute of Metallurgy of USSR
             Academy of Sciences
             Leninskii Prospekt, 49
             Moscow, USSR

Residence: ul. Gor'kogo, 8
             Moscow, USSR

Telephone: B9 44 96

PAVLOVSKY (PAVLOVSKII), EVGENII NIKANOROVICH
(Zoologist and Parasitologist)

E. N. Pavlovsky was born March 5, 1884. In 1909 he graduated from the Medical Military Academy and in 1921 became a professor there. From 1933 to 1944 he worked at the All-Union Institute of Experimental Medicine (Leningrad) and at the same time (until 1951) in the Tadzhik branch of the U.S.S.R. Academy of Sciences. He was made Director in 1942 of the Zoological Institute of the U.S.S.R. Academy of Sciences and Chairman, in 1946, of the Department of Parasitology and Medical Zoology at the Institute of Epidemiology and Microbiology of the U.S.S.R. Academy of Medical Sciences. Pavlovsky has been a member of the Communist Party of the Soviet Union since 1940. He is a lieutenant-general in the medical service.

In 1939 he became an Academician of the U.S.S.R. Academy of
Sciences, in 1944 a member of the U.S.S.R. Academy of Medical Sciences, and in 1951 an honorary member of the Tadzhik
S.S.R. Academy of Sciences. The U.S.S.R. Geographic Society
elected him President in 1952. Pavlovsky has been made an
honorary member of many Russian and other scientific societies including: the Royal Society of Tropical Medicine and
Hygiene, Societe Pathologie exotique, Societe France de Zoo-
logie, Parasitological Society of USA, the Iranian Academy
(Teheran), Leopoldina Academy, the Academy of Zoology. He
has received honorary doctorate degrees from the Sorbonne
University (Paris) and the University in Delhi (India). He is a
Deputy of the U.S.S.R. Supreme Soviet, second through fourth
convocations. In 1935 he was an Honored Scientist of the
R.S.F.S.R. Pavlovsky received a Stalin Prize in 1941 and again
in 1950. The U.S.S.R. Academy of Sciences awarded him the
gold medal of I. I. Mechnikov in 1949, and in 1954 the U.S.S.R.
Geographic Society awarded him a gold medal.

As of 1961, Pavlovsky was Chairman of the Commission on
Icthyology of the U.S.S.R. Academy of Sciences. He is also
President of the All-Union Entomological Society, Academy of
Sciences U.S.S.R. In 1962, Pavlovsky asked to be relieved of
the directorship of the Zoological Institute of the U.S.S.R.
Academy of Sciences and was appointed the Senior Scientific
Consultant of this Institute.

Pavlovsky's main work is in parasitology. He organized and
conducted many complex expeditions to Middle Asia, to Zakav-
kaz'ye, to the Crimea, the Far East and other regions of the
country in order to study endemic parasitic and communicable
diseases (tick fever, tick encephalitis, mosquito fever, leush-
maniosis). Pavlovsky, his students, and associates collected
voluminous materials on the fauna, biology and ecology of parasites and carriers of sickness. They studied natural reservoirs of pathogenic organisms and the routes of their circulation in nature and in the organisms of humans and domestic
animals. He investigated natural breeding grounds for communicable diseases of man and helped to organize prophylactic measures. He investigated intestinal protozoan and worm infesta-
tion, flying, bloodsucking insects (gnus) and protective measures
against these insects (protective nets of Pavlovsky), and eradi-
cation of bloodsuckers in their breeding ground and habitats.
Pavlovsky also studied poisonous animals and the properties
of their poison ("Poisonous Animals and their Meaning for
Man," 1923, and "Poisonous Animals and their Venoms," 1927).

He is the author of a series of textbooks and manuals on parasitology and of studies on the natural sources of diseases.
Bibliography:

Course on the Parasitology of Man (Works on Carriers of
Infection and Invasion), 2nd ed. Leningrad: Moscow: 1934.
Short Textbook on the Biology of Man's Parasites. Moscow-
Leningrad: 1941.
Manual on Man's Parasites Including Work on the Carriers
of Communicable Diseases, 1-2, 5th ed. Moscow-Leningrad:
1946-48.
Papatachi Fever and its Carriers. Leningrad: 1947.
Gnus (Bloodsucking, two-winged), Its Meaning and Methods
of Extermination. Leningrad: 1951.
Textbook on Man's Parasites with Works on the Carriers of
Communicable Diseases, 6th ed. Leningrad: 1951.
Biography:

Evgenii Nikanorovich Pavlovsky, 2nd ed. Moscow: 1956.
To the Seventieth Anniversary Since the Date of Birth of
E. N. Pavlovsky. Medical Parasitology and Parasitic Diseases, 1954, #2. J. N. Pawlowski, Leben und Werk. Berlin,
1959.

Office: Institute of Zoology of USSR Academy of Sciences
Universitetskaya Naberezhnaya, 1
Leningrad, B-164, USSR
Residence: Prosp. K. Marksa 3, Apt. 5
Leningrad, USSR
Telephone: G-216-52

PETROV, ALEKSANDR DMITRIEVICH (Organic Chemist)

A. D. Petrov was born August 28, 1895. He graduated in
1922 from Petrograd University. In 1943 he became a professor at the Moscow Chemico-Technological Institute. Since
1946 he has been a Corresponding Member of the U.S.S.R.
Academy of Sciences. In 1947 he was awarded a Stalin Prize.

Petrov's work is in organic synthesis. He conducted syntheses of pure hydrocarbons in motor fuel and established the
manner in which the composition and structure of these hydrocarbons are related to their properties. He conducted syntheses
and investigated properties of silicon hydrocarbons.
Bibliography:

Means of developing organic synthesis. Industry of Organic
Synthesis of the Aliphatic Series Compounds. Moscow-
Leningrad: 1943.
Chemistry of Motor Fuels. Moscow: 1953.

Office: Chemistry Department
           Moscow Chemico-Technological Institute
           Moscow, USSR

PETROV, ALEKSANDR PETROVICH (Railroad Transportation Engineer)

A. P. Petrov was born September 1, 1910. He graduated in 1934 from the Moscow Institute of Transportation Engineers. From 1935 to 1940 he worked at the Scientific Research Institute of Railroad Transportation. In 1936 he formed the teaching staff of the Moscow Institute of Transportation Engineers. He worked in the Ministry of Transportation in 1941-1946 and in 1949 began working at the All Union Scientific Research Institute of Railroad Transportation. He has been a member of the Communist Party of the Soviet Union from 1945. In 1953 he was elected a Corresponding Member of the U.S.S.R. Academy of Sciences.

The work of Petrov is in national use of railroads, particularly the organization of the car turnover. He worked out a method of calculating plans for formation of trains. He formulated a theory of schedules, and traffic carrying capacity of railroads.

Bibliography:
   Plan on Formation of Trains. Experiment, Theory, Methodology of Calculation. Moscow: 1950.
   Investigation of a Two-Track Schedule in Connection with the Scheduling of Passenger Trains. Moscow: 1941.
   Organization of Traffic in Railroad Transport. Moscow: 1952.
Office: All Union Scientific Research Institute of Railroad
           Transportation
           Moscow, USSR
Residence: Leningradskii Prospekt, 28
           Moscow, USSR
Telephone: D3 60 00, Ext. 420

PETROV, BORIS NIKOLAEVICH (Automation Specialist)

B. N. Petrov was born March 11, 1913. In 1939 he graduated from Moscow Institute of Energetics and began working at the Institute of Automation and Remote Control of the U.S.S.R. Academy of Sciences. He has taught at Moscow Aviation Institute, starting in 1944, and in 1948 became a professor. He was elected a Corresponding Member of the U.S.S.R. Academy of Sciences in 1953, and in 1960 an Academician.

Petrov's investigations are in automation and in approximate integration of differential equations.

Bibliography:

and others. Automatic Control of Linear Dimensions of Objects. Moscow: 1947.

On construction and transformation of structural schemes. Izvest. Akad. Nauk S.S.S.R., Otdel. Tekh. Nauk, 1945, #12.

Office: Moscow Aviation Institute
             Moscow, USSR

PETROV, GEORGII IVANOVICH (Engineer in Hydro-Aeromechanics and Gas Dynamics)

G. I. Petrov was born May 31, 1912. After graduation from Moscow University in 1935 he worked in scientific research institutes. In 1953 he became a professor at Moscow University. He was elected a Corresponding Member of the U.S.S.R. Academy of Sciences in 1953, and in 1958 an Academician. In 1949 he received a Stalin Prize.

The earlier works of Petrov were concerned with the question of stability of vortex layers, the propagation of oscillations in a viscous liquid, elucidation of physical conditions in the destruction of laminar flow. He proved the convergence of Galerkin's method for seeking the characteristic value in a wide class of equations, including non-conservative systems (particularly equations of oscillations in a viscous liquid).

Bibliography:

On the Propagation of Oscillations in a Viscous Liquid and the Appearance of Turbulence. Moscow: 1938.

Utilization of Galerkin's method in the problem of the stability of flow of a viscous liquid. Priklad. Mat. i Mekh., 1940, 4, #3.

Office: Moscow University
               Moscow, USSR
Residence: Prospekt Mira, 73
               Moscow, USSR
Telephone: I1 93 31

PETROV, NIKOLAI NIKOLAEVICH (Surgeon-oncologist)

N. N. Petrov was born December 14, 1876. He graduated in 1899 from the Military Medical Academy in Petersburg (Leningrad). In 1913 he became professor at the Institute of Advanced Training of Doctors in Petersburg. He founded the Oncology Institute in Leningrad in 1926 and was a scientific leader in this Institute. He was elected a Corresponding Member of the

U.S.S.R. Academy of Sciences in 1939 and in 1944 a Member of the U.S.S.R. Academy of Medical Sciences. In 1935 Petrov was an Honored Scientist of the R.S.F.S.R., and in 1942 recipient of Stalin Prize. The Academy of Sciences of the U.S.S.R. awarded him the I. I. Mechnikov Prize in 1953 for his work on the experimental rendering of malignant tumors in monkeys. In 1957 he was a Hero of Socialist Labor.

Petrov's works are on questions of origin, prophylaxis and treatment of malignant tumors, and surgery of stomach and duodenal ulcers.

Petrov is a Member of the Institute of Experimental Pathology and Therapy, Sukhumi, U.S.S.R. Academy of Medical Sciences.

Bibliography:

Editorship of Petrov and others. Stomach Duodenum Ulcers and Surgical Treatment. 1941.

Editorship of Petrov and others. Malignant Tumors. 2 vols. 1932-34.

Editorship of Petrov and others. Malignant Tumors. 3 vols. 1947-52.

Editorship of Petrov and others. Treatment of War Injuries. 1939, 7th edition, 1945.

Biography:

A. I. Serebrov, S. A. Kholdin, A. S. Chechulin. Nikolai Nikolaevich Petrov (On the 50th Anniversary of Scientific, Pedagogical Medical and Social Activity). Questions on Oncology, #3, Moscow, 1951 (contains bibliography of the scientific works of Petrov).

Office: Academy of Medical Sciences of USSR Academy of Sciences
                    Solyanka, 14
                    Moscow, USSR

Residence: 5-aya Cheremushkinskaya, 3
                    Moscow, USSR

Telephone: V5 14 61

PETROVSKII, IVAN GEORGIEVICH (Mathematician)

I. G. Petrovskii was born January 18, 1901. In 1927 he graduated from Moscow University. He became a professor there in 1933, and in 1951 he was appointed Rector of the University. In 1943, Petrovskii was elected a Corresponding Member of the U.S.S.R. Academy of Sciences and, in 1946, an Academician. He was awarded, in 1946 and in 1952, Stalin

Prizes. He is a member of the Soviet Committee on Defense of Peace.

The work of Petrovskii is concerned with the theory of partial differential equations, algebraic geometry, qualitative theory of differential equations, and theory of probability. He studied the various classes of elliptical systems (1937), studied problems with initial conditions for parabolic and hyperbolic systems of equations (1936); investigated the dependence of solutions on initial conditions; indicated for hyperbolic equations with constant coefficients the necessary and adequate conditions of existence of lacunae, that is, those regions in the base of the characteristic cone, the initial conditions of which do not influence the significance of the solution at the cone vortex (1944). For his studies on the theory of partial differential equations Petrovskii was awarded, in 1946, a Stalin Prize. Petrovskii has also solved the first boundary-value problem for the equation of heat conductivity using the most general assumptions concerning the boundary of the domain (1935), gave the solution of the Dirichlet problem for the Laplace equation by the method of finite differences in an n-measured domain (1941), studied the behavior of integral curves for the system of ordinary differential equations in the vicinity of a singular point (1934), and obtained a series of results in the theory of probability. In the area of algebraic geometry, Petrovskii studied the distribution of ovals of the algebraic curve of the sixth order (1935). The method allowed solution of a more general problem which gives the distribution of ovals of an algebraic curve of any order, and establishes the topological properties of algebraic surfaces and algebraic manifolds of any number of dimensions (1949). Petrovskii, together with E. M. Landis, obtained (1955-57) evaluations of the number of limiting cycles in the ordinary differential equations, the right part of which is a ratio of two polynomials of the nth power; in the case where $n = 2$, their evaluation is exact. He is the author of textbooks, Lectures on the Theory of Ordinary Differential Equations (1939), Lectures on the Theory of Integral Equations (1948), Lectures on Equations with Partial Derivatives (1950), which were published many times in the U.S.S.R. and translated to foreign languages (Stalin Prize 1952).

In 1961 Petrovskii was awarded the Order of Lenin. In March 1962, he was elected delegate from R.S.F.S.R. to the Supreme Soviet.

As of 1961, Petrovskii was a Member of the Presidium of the U.S.S.R. Academy of Sciences.

Bibliography:
Uber das Cauchysche Problem für Systeme von partiellen
Differentialgleichungen. Mathematical Collection. New
Series, 1937, 2 (44), #5.
On the topology of real plane algebraic curves in Annales of
Mathematics. Princeton-New York: 1938, 39, #1, 197-209.
Sur l'analyticité des solutions des systèms d'équations
differéntielles. Mathematical Collection. New Series, 1939,
5 (47), #1.
On the diffusion of waves and the lacunas for hyperbolic
equations. Mathematical Collection, New Series, 1945, 17
(59), #3.
and E. M. Landis. On the number of limiting cycles of the
equation $\frac{dy}{dx} = \frac{P(x, y)}{Q(x, y)}$, where P and Q are polynomials of the
second power. Mathematical Collection, 1955, 37, #2, 209-
250.
and E. M. Landis. On the number of limiting cycles of
equation $\frac{dy}{dx} = \frac{P(x, y)}{Q(x, y)}$, where P and Q are polynomials. Doklady Akad. Nauk S.S.S.R., 1957, 113, #4.
Biography:
S. D. Sobolev. On the 50th Anniversary of Ivan Georgievich
Petrovskii. Izvest. Akad. Nauk S.S.S.R., Ser. Mat., 1951,
15, #3.
A. N. Kolmogorov. Ivan Georgievich Petrovskii. On the
50th Anniversary since the date of birth. Uspekhi Mat.
Nauk, 1951, #3 (43) (contains bibliography of the works of
Petrovskii).
Office: Moscow University
              Moscow, USSR
Residence: Leninskii Prospekt, 13
              Moscow, USSR
Telephone: V2 14 47

PETRYANOV-SOKOLOV, IGOR' VASIL'EVICH (Physical Chemist)

I. V. Petryanov-Sokolov was born June 18, 1907. After
graduating from Moscow University in 1930, he worked at the
Karpov Physico-Chemical Institute. In 1947 he became professor at the Moscow Chemico-Technological Institute. He has
been a Corresponding Member of the U.S.S.R. Academy of
Sciences since 1953. In 1941 he received a Stalin Prize.

The main works of Petryanov-Sokolov deal with the study of aerosols with a liquid dispersed phase, i.e., fog. He developed new methods of investigating them and studied the appearance of charges in them and the influence of charges on their stability.

Bibliography:

and N. Fuks. Determining the size and charge of particles in fog. Zhur. Fiz. Khim., 1933, 4, #5.

and N. M. Tunitskii. Formation of Aerosols During Condensation of Supersaturated Vapors. Zhur. Fiz. Khim., 1939, 13, #8.

and N. Rozenbyum. Edge angles of small drops. Doklady Akad. Nauk S.S.S.R., 1948, 61, #4.

Office: Moscow Chemico-Technological Institute
             Moscow, USSR

PEYVE, ALEKSANDR VOL'DEMAROVICH (Geologist)

A. V. Peyve was born February 9, 1909. After graduating from Moscow Geological Survey Institute in 1930, he worked in the Scientific Institute on Fertilizers. In 1934-1935, he took part in the Tadzhik-Pamir Expedition of the U.S.S.R. Academy of Sciences. He began working at the Geological Institute of the U.S.S.R. Academy of Sciences in 1935 and in 1952 became deputy Director. In 1961 Peyve was named director. He has been a member of the Communist Party of the Soviet Union since 1953. In 1958 he was elected a Corresponding Member of the U.S.S.R. Academy of Sciences. He was awarded a Stalin Prize in 1946.

Peyve's main work is in regional tectonics, and also stratigraphy of magmas and metalogenesis. He has conducted investigations of various types of faults in the earth's crust, particularly deep faults. He is the author of works on the asymmetry of abyssal structures and on the conditions for the formation and development of geosynclines. The name of Peyve is associated with the discovery of a series of deposits of bauxite, phosphorite, and potassium salts. He took part in the compilation of a tectonic map of the U.S.S.R. on the sale of 1/5,000,000 (1956).

Bibliography:

Scheme of Tectonics of Western Tien Shan. Izvest. Akad. Nauk S.S.S.R., Otdel Mat. i Estest. Nauk, 1938, #5-6.

Main types of abyssal faults. Izvest. Akad. Nauk S.S.S.R., Otdel Mat. i Estest. Nauk, 1956, #1 and 3.

Tectonics of the North Urals Bauxite Belt. Moscow: 1947.

Office: Institute of Geology of USSR Academy of Sciences
              Pyzherskii Pereulok, 7
              Moscow, USSR
Residence: 1-aya Cheremushkinskaya, 3
              Moscow, USSR
Telephone: V7 43 26

PEYVE, YAN VOL'DEMAROVICH (Agricultural Chemist)
      Y. V. Peyve was born August 3, 1906. He graduated in 1929
from the Moscow Agricultural Academy of K. A. Timiryazev.
In 1930-1944, he worked in the All-Union Scientific Research
Institute of Flax; in 1944-1950 he was President of the Latvian
Agricultural Academy. Peyve has been a doctor of sciences
and a professor of agrochemistry since 1940. He has been an
Academician of the Latvian S.S.R. Academy of Sciences from
1946 and in 1951 was made President. In 1953 he was elected
Corresponding Member of the U.S.S.R. Academy of Sciences.
Peyve has been a Deputy to the U.S.S.R. Supreme Soviet, fourth,
fifth, and sixth convocations. In 1949 he became a member of
the Soviet Committee in Defense of Peace, and in 1951 Chairman of the Latvian Republican Committee on the Defense of
Peace. He was elected in 1958, Chairman of the Council of the
Nationalities of the U.S.S.R. Supreme Soviet.
      Peyve's main work is in agrochemistry, biochemistry, soil
science, and increasing harvest of industrial crops such as flax
and sugar beets. He established methods of determining mobile
forms of potassium, aluminum, humous acids, and microelements in soils of the Podzol zone and invented apparatus for
making these analyses under production laboratory conditions
on collective farms. He worked out principles of differential
use of fertilizer for flax and other agricultural crops in relation
to soil conditions. Peyve also studied use of microelements
such as boron, molybdenum, zinc, and copper and plant nutrition and cobalt, copper, zinc, molybdenum and boron in the
soils of the Latvian S.S.R. and U.S.S.R.
      In 1961 Y. V. Peyve published a monograph "Biochemistry of
the Soils" in which he presents experimental works dealing with
biochemistry of soil humus, biochemistry of microelements and
other elements of plant nutrition as well as biochemistry of
enzymes.
      In 1961 he was a Candidate Member of the Central Committee
of the Communist Party.

Bibliography:
Soil conditions and effect of applying microfertilizers.
Trace elements in plant nutrition. Transactions of the Laboratory of Biochemistry of Soils and Trace Elements. Riga: 1958.
Microelements and enzymes. Izdanie, Academy of Sciences of Latvian S.S.R. Riga: 1960.
Boron and Molybdenum in Latvian Soils. Riga: 1960.
Trace elements in agriculture. Primenenie Mikroelementov v Sel'sk. Khoz. i Med., Trudy Vsesoyuz. Soveshchaniya, Baku (Ya. V. Peyve, ed.). 1958, 5-15 (Pub. 1959). C. A. 54, 25455g (1960).
and N. N. Ivanova, L. V. Karelina. Boron in the soils of Latvian S.S.R. Latvijas PSR Zinatnu Akad. Vestis 1959, I, 35-47 (in Russian). C. A. 54, 4987g (1960).
Biochemical role of molybdenum and its application in agriculture. Trace elements and yields. Transactions of the Laboratory of Biochemistry of Soils and Trace Elements. Riga: 1961.
Biochemistry of the Soils. Moscow: 1961.
and G. Zhiznevskaya. Effect of molybdenum and copper on nitratreductase activity in plants. Riga: 1961.

Office: Academy of Sciences Latvian SSR
                Riga, Latvian SSR

PILYUGIN, NIKOLAI ALEKSEEVICH (Automation Specialist)
    N. A. Pilyugin was born in 1908. In 1935 he graduated from the Moscow Higher Technical School, and subsequently worked in various scientific-research organizations. He has been a member of the Communist Party of the Soviet Union since 1940. In 1960 he was elected to the U.S.S.R. Academy of Sciences as a Corresponding Member.
    Pilyugin's principal works deal with problems of automatic controls.

Office: USSR Academy of Sciences
                Leninskii Prospekt, 14
                Moscow, USSR

PISTOL'KORS, ALEKSANDR ALEKSANDROVICH (Radio Engineer)
    A. A. Pistol'kors was born October 10, 1896. He became acquainted with radio engineering in World War I in the Officers Electrochemical School in Petersburg and on the Caucasus front while working at a radio station. He entered the Moscow

Technical College in 1923 and in 1927 graduated. In 1926-1928
he worked in the Nizhnii-Novgorod Radio Laboratory, and in
1929-1942 at the Central Radio Laboratory in Leningrad. In
1931 to 1945 Pistol'kors also taught at the Leningrad Electro-
Technical Institute and at the Leningrad Institute of Engineers
of Communication. He was professor from 1945 to 1950 at the
Moscow Institute of Communication Engineers. Since 1946
he has been a Corresponding Member of the U.S.S.R. Academy
of Sciences. In 1956 for his work in radio technics, he was
awarded the A. S. Popov Gold Medal.

The scientific work of Pistol'kors is in the theory of antennae and feeder lines, the calculation of resistence of radiation
in complex antennae, the theory of two-wire non-symmetrical
lines, the calculation of antennae according to a given directional diagram, and the theory of slot antennae. He proposed a
number of new type antennae, including a bent vibrator which is
utilized in television reception antennae.

Bibliography:
Antennae. Moscow: 1947.
Problems of non-contact electric attraction. Electricity,
1938, #10.
Calculating the resistance of radiation for directed short-
wave antennae. Wireless Telegraphy and Telephony, 1928,
9, #3.
Theory of non-symmetrical two-wire line. Scientific-
Technical Collection on Electric Communication, #16.
Leningrad-Moscow: 1937. (Electro-Technical Institute of
Communication in Leningrad).
General theory of diffraction antennae. Zhur. Tekh. Fiz.,
1944, 14, #12.
Application of the functions of Mathieu for calculating the
distribution of the field in the antenna according to a given
directional diagram. Doklady Akad. Nauk S.S.S.R., 1953, 89,
#5.

Biography:
Laureate of the Gold Medal of A. S. Popov. Radiotechnics,
1956, 11, #6.
I. Dzhigit. Laureate of the Gold Medal of A. S. Popov.
Radio, 1956, #7.

Office: USSR Academy of Sciences
               Leninskii Prospekt, 14
               Moscow, USSR

Residence: ul. Gor'kogo, 43
             Moscow, USSR
Telephone: D3 74 35

PIYP, BORIS IVANOVICH (Volcanologist)
        B. I. Piyp was born November 6, 1906. After graduating
from the Leningrad Mining Institute in 1931, he conducted field
studies on the Kamchatka peninsula and the Urals. He began
working in the Laboratory of Volcanology of the U.S.S.R. Academy
of Sciences in 1940, and in 1940-46 and 1950-54 was Chief of the
Kamchatka Volcanological Station. Since 1945 Piyp has been a
member of the Communist Party of the Soviet Union. In 1958
he was elected a Corresponding Member of the U.S.S.R. Academy of Sciences. For his monograph on the volcanoes of the
Klyuchevskaya group in 1956, he was awarded the Prize of the
Presidium of the U.S.S.R. Academy of Sciences. He has also
received the Order of the Red Star and medals.
        Piyp studied the volcanoes, hot springs and geologic struc-
ture of Kamchatka. He investigated in detail a number of
eruptions of volcanoes of various types.
        As of 1961, Piyp was a Member of the Presidium of the Si-
berian Branch U.S.S.R. Academy of Sciences, and Director of
the Kamchatka Joint Expedition.
        In 1962 he was appointed Director of the Siberian Branch
Institute of Volcanology.
Bibliography:
        Hot Springs of Kamchatka. Moscow-Leningrad: 1937.
        (U.S.S.R. Academy of Sciences. Council for the Study of
        Productive Forces. Kamchatka Series, #2)
        Materials on the Geology and Petrography of the Regions of
        Avachi, Rassoshina, Gavanka, and Nalacheva Rivers on the
        Kamchatka. Moscow-Leningrad: 1941 (U.S.S.R. Academy
        of Sciences, Council for the Study of Productive Forces.
        Works of the Kamchatka Complex Expedition, 1936-37, #2).
        Klyuchevsk Volcano and Its Eruption in 1944-45 and in the
        Past. Moscow: 1956. (Works of the Laboratory of Volcan-
        ology of the U.S.S.R. Academy of Sciences, #2)
Office: Laboratory of Volcanology
             Staromonetnyy Pereulok, 35
             Moscow, USSR
Residence: Leninskii Prospekt, 25
             Moscow, USSR
Telephone: V4 00 27, Ext. 60

PLAKSIN, IGOR' NIKOLAEVICH (Metallurgist and Mining
        Engineer)
    I. N. Plaksin was born October 8, 1900. He graduated in
1926 from the Far East University. In 1930 he became a professor at the Moscow Institute of Nonferrous Metals and Gold.
He began working, in 1944, also at the Mining Institute of the
U.S.S.R. Academy of Sciences. He has been a member of the
Communist Party of Soviet Union since 1945. In 1946 he was
elected a Corresponding Member of the U.S.S.R. Academy of
Sciences. He was awarded Stalin Prizes in 1951 and in 1952.
    Plaksin has worked in hydrometallurgy and on the concen-
tration of commercial minerals. He studied the influence of
forms in which minerals are found in ores on their concen-
tration and has used microradiography and radiometry.
Bibliography:
    Interaction of Alloys and Natural Gold with Mercury and
    with Cyanide Solutions. Moscow-Leningrad: 1937.
    Metallurgy of Noble Metals. Moscow: 1943.
    and D. M. Yukhtanov. Hydrometallurgy. Moscow: 1949.
    On Testing and Testing Analysis. Moscow: 1947.
    Influence of gases and reagents on minerals in flotation
    processes. Izvest. Akad. Nauk S.S.S.R. Otdel. Tekh. Nauk,
    1950, #12.
    Results and Perspectives of Investigation on Interaction of
    Reagents with Minerals in Flotation. Izvest. Akad. Nauk
    S.S.S.R. Otdel. Tekh. Nauk, 1955, #1.
    and G. A. Myasnikova and A. M. Okolovich. Flotation Con-
    centration of Arsenic-Pyrite Ores. Moscow: 1955.
    Using microantoradiography for the study of interaction re-
    agents with minerals in flotation. Reprinted from the Pro-
    ceedings of the Second Internation Congress of Surface Ac-
    tivity, 2. Leningrad: 1957.
    and S. V. Bessonov. Role of gases in flotation reactions.
    Reprinted from the Proceedings of the Second Internation
    Congress of Surface Activity, 2. Leningrad: 1957.
    Résultats généraux de travaux sur la flotation des charbons
    et perspectives scientifiques et techniques de son expansion.
    Revue de l'industrie minérale, 1955, 36, #626.
    Office: Mining Institute of USSR Academy of Sciences
                Stantsiya Panki
                Moscow Oblast', USSR
    Residence: Staromonetry pr. 3
                Moscow, USSR
    Telephone: B1 53 30

PLAUDE, KARL KARLOVICH (Thermal Engineer)

K. K. Plaude was born March 26, 1897. Upon graduating from the Leningrad Institute of Civil Engineering in 1926, he worked at the "Gidravlika" plant until 1936. From 1928-34, he lectured at the Leningrad Institute of Civil Engineering, and from 1932 to 1938, at the Leningrad Institute of Industrial Construction Engineers. From 1937 to 1941, he worked at "Lengosproektstroi" and during 1942-44 was chief of the Construction Directorate in Moscow. From 1941 to 1953, he was lecturer at the University of Latvia, and in 1950 was Director of the Latvian S.S.R. Academy of Sciences Institute of Energetics and Electrotechnics. He is a holder of the title Honored Scientist of the Latvian S.S.R., awarded in 1955. Since 1946 he has been a member of the Communist Party of the Soviet Union. He became Academician of the Latvian S.S.R. Academy of Sciences in 1951. From 1958 to 1960 he was Vice-President, and since 1960 has been President of the Latvian S.S.R. Academy of Sciences. In 1960 he was elected Corresponding Member of the U.S.S.R. Academy of Sciences. He is a Deputy of the Supreme Soviet of the U.S.S.R. In March, 1962, he was elected to the Council of Nationalities.

Professor Plaude's main work lies in the field of heat supply. He has studied heat exchange for heat plants using a high temperature heat carrier. Plaude developed a two-step system of heat supply, electricity systems, and automatic thermoregulators for local regulation of radiators. He has elaborated principles of automation of heat supply. He is the author of many scientific works in the field of the thermal engineering.

Bibliography:

Scheme of a step system of distant heat supplying. Izvest. Akad. Nauk Lat. S.S.R., 1950, #12.

System of heat supply according to a two-step scheme. Questions of Energetics, #2, Riga, 1953.

Characteristics of the heating of radiators in central water heating at increased temperatures of the heat-carrier. Questions of Energetics, #4, 1956.

Automatic thermo-regulator for radiators of a central water heating system. Questions of Energetics, #4, 1956.

Calculated temperature of water in radiators of a central heating system. Izvest. Akad. Nauk Lat. S.S.R., 1957, #1.

Padomju savienibas energetikas attistiba. Riga: 1957.

Automatic regulation of a central water heating system. Riga: 1960.

Automation of subscriber centres in district heated buildings. Riga: 1960.
Application of water at high temperatures in heating systems. Riga: 1962.
Latvijas energetikas attistiba PSRA energosistema. Riga:
1961.
Office: President, Latvian S.S.R. Academy of Sciences
              ul. Turgeneva, 19
              Riga, Latvian SSR

POGORELOV, ALEKSEI VASIL'EVICH (Mathematician)

A. V. Pogorelov was born in 1919. In 1945 he completed his
studies at the Zhukovskii Air Force Academy. From 1947 to
1959, he was chief of the geometry section and Chairman of the
Geometry Department of the Khar'kov State University. In 1959
he became head of the geometry section of the Ukrainian S.S.R.
Academy of Sciences Institute of Mathematics, and the Ukrainian S.S.R. Academy of Sciences Institute of Physico-Technology.
He is a Corresponding Member of the Ukrainian S.S.R. Academy of Sciences, and in 1960, was elected a Corresponding Member of the U.S.S.R. Academy of Sciences. In 1950 he was
awarded a Stalin Prize.

Pogorelov's works are primarily concerned with problems
of solid geometry.

Bibliography:

Geometric imbedding in the large of a two-dimensional Rie-
mannian manifold into a tri-dimensional one. Vestnik Lenin-
grad Univ. Ser. Mat. Mek. Astr. 12 (1957) #7, 156-163.
Mathematical Reviews 20, 4302 (1959).
Some questions in geometry in the large in a Riemannian
space. Izdat. Harvosh University, Kharkov, 1957, 90 p.
Mathematical Reviews 20, 4304 (1959).
On a transformation of isometric surfaces. Doklady Akad.
Nauk S.S.S.R. 122, 20-21 (1958). Mathematical Reviews 20,
5507 (1959).
On the regularity of convex surfaces with a regular metric
in spaces of constant curvature. Doklady Akad. Nauk
S.S.S.R. 122, 186-187 (1958). Mathematical Reviews 20,
5508 (1959).
The rigidity of general convex surfaces. Doklady Akad. Nauk
S.S.S.R. 128, 475-477 (1959). Mathematical Reviews 21,
7542 (1960).

The rigidity of closed surfaces non-homeomorphic to Rie-
mannean space. Doklady Akad. Nauk S.S.S.R. 138 (1961), #1,
51-52.
Transcritical deformations of cylindrical shells under ex-
ternal pressure. Doklady Akad. Nauk S.S.S.R. 138 (1961),
#6, 1325-27.
Transcritical deformations of cylindrical shells in torsion.
Doklady Akad. Nauk S.S.S.R. 142 (1962), #2, 302-03.
Office: Ukrainian Physico-Technical Institute
            Yumovskii Tupik, 2
            Khar'kov, Ukrainian SSR

POMERANCHUK, ISAAK YAKOVLEVICH (Physicist)
I. Ya. Pomeranchuk was born May 20, 1913. He graduated
from the Leningrad Polytechnic Institute in 1936 and then
worked in departments of the U.S.S.R. Academy of Sciences.
In 1946 he became professor at Moscow Physical Engineering-
Physical Institute. Since 1953 he has been a Corresponding
Member of the U.S.S.R. Academy of Sciences. He is a recipient
of a Stalin Prize.
    The works of Pomeranchuk deal with theoretical physics of
low temperatures, theory of radiation, nuclear physics, and
cosmic rays. He obtained important results in the theory of
heat conductivity of dielectrics and the theory of neutron scattering in crystals. Pomeranchuk in 1939 showed that the radiation of electrons in the earth's magnetic field limited the
possible energy of the electrons of cosmic rays reaching the
atmosphere. He also worked on the theory of collisions and
radiation at high energies.
Bibliography:
    and A. A. Akhizer. Some Questions on Nuclear Theory.
    2nd ed. Moscow-Leningrad: 1950.
    Equality to zero of a renormalized charge in quantum
    electrodynamics. Doklady Akad. Nauk S.S.S.R., 1955, 103,
    #6.
    On renormalization of a meson charge in pseudo-scalar
    theory with pseudo-scalar coupling. Doklady Akad. Nauk
    S.S.S.R., 1955, 104, #1.
    On transforming into zero of a renormalized meson charge
    in pseudo-scalar theory with pseudo-scalar coupling. Dok-
    lady Akad. Nauk S.S.S.R., 105, #3.
    Solution of equations of pseudo-scalar meson theory with
    pseudo-scalar coupling. Zhur. Eksptl. i Teoret. Fiz., 1955,
    #6.

and L. Landau. Limits of utilization of the theory of Bremsstrahlung of electrons and pair production at high energies.
Doklady Akad. Nauk S.S.S.R., 1953, 92, #3.
On the theory of liquid He^3. Zhur. Eksptl. i Teoret. Fiz.,
1950, #10.
Maximal energy which can be possessed on the surface of
the earth by primary electrons of cosmic rays because of
radiation in the earth's magnetic field. Zhur. Eksptl. i Teoret. Fiz., 1939, #8.

Office: Moscow Physical Engineering-Physical Institute
             Moscow, USSR
Residence: Nab. Gor'kogo 4/22
             Moscow, USSR
Telephone: B1 75 76

PONTEKORVO, BRUNO MAKSIMOVICH (Physicist)
      B. M. Pontekorvo was born August 22, 1913. After graduat-
ing in 1933 from the University of Rome, he taught there. In
1936-1940 he worked in scientific organizations in France,
1940-1948 in the United States, and in 1948-50 at the Harwell
Laboratories in England. Since 1950 he has been working in
the U.S.S.R. In 1955 he became a member of the Communist
Party of the Soviet Union. He was elected in 1958 a Corresponding Member of the U.S.S.R. Academy of Sciences.
      Pontekorvo showed, in 1936-39 while studying nuclear iso-
merism, that isomeric transitions have a large internal conversion ratio. He obtained a beta-stable isomer by neutron
irradiation of cadmium. Exciting nuclei by X-ray radiation, he
discovered the phenomena of "nuclear phosphorescence". He
proposed in 1943 neutron logging. In 1948, while measuring the
beta spectrum of tritium, Pontekorvo showed that the mass of
neutrino does not exceed 1/500 electron mass. He was the first
to observe L-capture. While studying decay of υ-mesons, he
ascertained that during this process there was no emission of
gamma rays, but the product of the decay was the electron.
Pontekorvo pointed out the analogy between the processes of
the capture of the υ-meson with a K-shell and the usual K-
capture of the electron. After 1950 Pontekorvo investigated the
production of π°-mesons by neutrons. He predicted in 1951
production of heavy mesons with hyperons. From 1955 he
studied the interaction of π-mesons with nucleons.

Bibliography:
and others. Artificial radioactivity produced by neutron
bombardment. II. Proceedings of the Royal Society of
London, 1935, Ser. A, 149, #868.
and A. Lazard. Isomerie nucleaire produit par les rajons x
du Spectre Continu. Comptes Rendus Hebdomadaires des
Seances de l'Academie des Sciences, Paris, 1939, 208, #2.
On the processes of formation of heavy mesons and particles. Zhur. Eksptl. i Teoret. Fiz., 1955, 29, #2 (8).
and A. I. Mukhin, E. B. Ozerov. Scattering of π+-mesons on
hydrogen. I. Zhur. Eksptl. i Teoret. Fiz., 1956, 31, #3.
and Mukhin. Scattering of π+-mesons on Hydrogen. II.
Zhur. Eksptl. i Teoret. Fiz., 1956, 31, #4.
Office: USSR Academy of Sciences
Leninskii Prospekt, 14
Moscow, USSR

PONTRYAGIN, LEV SEMYONOVICH (Mathematician)

L. S. Pontryagin was born September 3, 1908 in Moscow.
At the age of 14 he lost his sight in an accident. In 1929 he
graduated from Moscow University and in 1935 became a professor. He was elected a Corresponding Member of the U.S.S.R.
Academy of Sciences in 1939 and in 1958 an Academician. In
1941 he was awarded a Stalin Prize.

Pontryagin's main works are concerned with topology and
the theory of continuous groups. In 1932 he formulated the
general theory of duality, which fully solved the problem of determination of the Betty groups of an arbitrarily open set of
Euclidian space through the Betty groups of an additional closed
set. In connection with the proof of the theorem of duality,
Pontryagin set up a general theory of the character of commutative groups. This theory, and the theorems on the structure
of rather wide types of topological groups completely recon-
structed so-called topological algebra. The results obtained by
Pontryagin on the theory of topological groups are set forth in
the monograph "Continuous Groups" (1938), (Stalin Prize 1941).
Pontryagin also has worked in algebra, theory of the Lei
groups, and differential geometry.

Bibliography:
Continuous Groups, 2nd ed. Moscow: 1954.
Basis of Combinational Topology. Moscow-Leningrad: 1947.
Characteristic cycles of differentiating sets. Mat. Sbornik,
New Series, 1947, 21, #2, 233-284.

Vector topological theorem of duality for closed sets. Annals of Mathematics, II Series. Princeton-New York, 1934, 35, 904-14.
Vector fields on sets. Mat. Sbornik, 1949, 24, #2, 129-162.

Office: Mathematics Department
          Moscow University
          Moscow, USSR
Residence: Leninskii Prospekt, 13
          Moscow, USSR
Telephone: B2 53 76

POPKOV, VALERII IVANOVICH (Electrical Engineer)

V. I. Popkov was born February 3, 1908. He graduated in 1930 from the Moscow Institute of Energetics. In 1932-36, he worked at the All-Union Electro-Technical Institute. He began working in 1943 at the Institute of Energetics of the U.S.S.R. Academy of Sciences. Popkov has been a member of the Communist Party of the Soviet Union since 1951. In 1953 he was elected a Corresponding Member of the U.S.S.R. Academy of Sciences.

Popkov's main work is in high-voltage technology and electric discharge in gases at high voltage, physical processes in electric filters, and long-distance electric transmission.

Bibliography:

Theory of a bi-polar corona on conductors. Doklady Akad. Nauk S.S.S.R., 1947, 58, #5.

Theory of a bi-polar corona on conductors. Izvest. Akad. Nauk S.S.S.R., Otdel. Tekh. Nauk, 1948, #4.

The coefficient of recombination of ions in conditions of a corona discharge in the atmospheric air. Doklady Akad. Nauk S.S.S.R., 1948, 59, #1.

Theory of a unipolar corona of direct current. Electricity, 1949, #1.

and S. I. Ryabaya. Theory of a corona under constant voltage. Izvest. Akad. Nauk S.S.S.R., Otdel. Tekh. Nauk, 1950, #12.

and N. B. Bogdanova. Determining parameters in the scheme of replacing the corona lines. Izvest. Akad. Nauk S.S.S.R., Otdel Tekh. Nauk, 1951, #3.

and S. I. Ryabaya. Theory of a corona under constant voltage. Izvest. Akad. Nauk S.S.S.R., Otdel. Akad. Nauk, 1951, #1.

Electric field under a transitional unipolar corona. Izvest. Akad. Nauk S.S.S.R., Otdel. Akad. Nauk, 1954, #7.

and others. Experimental study of the movement of the volu-
metric charge in the field of a corona of alternating current. Izvest. Akad. Nauk S.S.S.R., Otdel. Tekh. Nauk, 1957,
#1.

and V. I. Levitov. Reactive effects of a corona of alternating current. Electricity, 1956, #7.

and N. B. Bogdanova. Methods of evaluating yearly losses
of energy on the corona. Electricity, 1957, #1.

Biography:
Corresponding Member of the U.S.S.R. Academy of Sciences,
V. I. Popkov. On the 50th Anniversary since the date of
birth and the 25th Anniversary of scientific activity. Electricity, 1958, #4, 94.

Office: Institute of Energetics of USSR Academy of
               Sciences
               Moscow, USSR
Residence: Novopeschanaya, 21
               Moscow, USSR
Telephone: D7 24 18

POPOV, YEVGENII PAVLOVICH (Automation Specialist)

Ye. P. Popov was born in 1914. In 1939, upon completion of
the Bauman Moscow Advanced Technical School, he served in
the Soviet Army until 1943 when he began to work at the A. F.
Mozhaiskii Air Force Engineering Academy in Leningrad
where, in 1949, he became chairman of the Department of Automation and Remote Control. At the same time he was working
as a senior scientific worker at the U.S.S.R. Academy of Sciences Institute of Electromechanics. He was awarded the degree of Doctor of Technical Sciences in 1947 and the rank of
professor in 1948. Since 1942 he has been a member of the
Communist Party of the Soviet Union. He was elected, in 1960,
a Corresponding Member of the U.S.S.R. Academy of Sciences.
In 1949 he was awarded a Stalin Prize.

Popov's works are primarily concerned with the theory of
automatic controls.

Bibliography:
On the approximate study of self and forced oscillations on
nonlinear systems. Doklady Akad. Nauk S.S.S.R. 95, 5, 943-
946 (1954). Applied Mechanics Reviews 9, 654 (1956).
Approximate calculation of self-excited and forced vibrations
in nonlinear systems of higher order on the basis of the
harmonic linearization of nonlinearity. Izvest. Akad. Nauk

S.S.S.R., Otdel. Tekh. Nauk, #5, 3-38 (1954). Applied Mechanics Reviews 9, 54 (1956).
Approximate determination of auto-oscillations and forced oscillations in systems of automatic control. Vol. 1 Moscow-Leningrad, Izd-vo Akad. Nauk S.S.S.R., 1955, 219-248. Referat. Zh. Mekh. #5, 1957. Rev. 5180. Applied Mechanics Reviews 12, 1959.
A generalization of the asymptotic method of N. N. Bogoliuboff in the theory of nonlinear oscillations. Doklady Akad. Nauk S.S.S.R. (N.S.) 111, 308-11 (1956).
Use of harmonic linearization method in automatic control theory. NACA-Tech. Memo, #1406, Jan. 1957, 6 p. (Eng. trans.) Doklady Akad. Nauk S.S.S.R. 106, #2, 211-14 (1956). Engineering Index, 1958, p. 87.
Isolation of regions of stability of nonlinear automatic systems based on harmonic lineation. Akad. Nauk S.S.S.R., Izvest. Otdel. Tekh. Nauk, Energetika i Automatika, #1, 53-64 (1959). Engineering Index, 1959, p. 104.
The effect of vibrational interference on the stability and dynamic quality of nonlinear automatic systems. Akad. Nauk S.S.S.R., Izvest. Otdel. Tekh. Nauk, Energetika i Automatika, #4, 97-105 (1959). Engineering Index, 1959, p. 107.
Approximate Methods of Study of Non-linear Automatic Systems. Fizmatgiz, Moscow: 1960 (includes bibliography of previous works and articles).
Automatic Regulation and Control. Fizmatgiz, Moscow: 1962 (Fizmatgiz, Moscow B-71, Leninskii Prospect, 15).
On the study of auto-oscillation systems with logic devices. Izvest. Akad. Nauk S.S.S.R., Otdel. Tekh. Nauk, Energetika i Automatika, #4, 1962.
On non-linear laws of control in automatics. Izvest. Akad. Nauk S.S.S.R., Otdel. Tekh. Nauk, Energetika i Automatika, #5, 1962.
Office: Institute of Electromechanics of USSR Academy of Sciences
Dvortsovaya Naberezhnaya, 18
Leningrad, USSR

PREDVODITELEV, A. S. (Physicist)
A. S. Predvoditelev was born August 30, 1891. He graduated from Moscow University in 1915 and has been a professor there since 1930. In 1938 he became Laboratory Chief at the U.S.S.R. Academy of Sciences Institute of Energetics. He was

elected to the U.S.S.R. Academy of Sciences as a Corresponding Member in 1939. In 1950 he was awarded a State Prize.

Predvoditelev's principal works have been in the field of molecular physics, hydrodynamics and thermal physics dealing with investigations in combustion processes, wave distribution in liquid and gas media, and with problems of gas dynamics of reactant media and physical properties of liquid. He developed a theory of heterogenous combustions which establishes a relationship between the chemical and physical processes facilitating carbon combustion.

Bibliography:

Carbon combustion, 1949 (monograph).

Molecular kinetics basis for hydrodynamic equilibria. Izvest. Akad. Nauk S.S.S.R., Otdel. Tekh. Nauk, 1948, #4.

The relationship between heat conductivity, heat capacity, and viscosity in viscous bodies. Zhur. Exptl. i Teoret. Fiz., 1934, 4.

Fluctuations in statistical systems. Journal of Moscow University, 1948, #4.

Physical Gas Dynamics. Editor in Chief. Akad. Nauk S.S.S.R. Energet. Inst. Translated by R. C. Murray and D. R. H. Phillips. New York: Pergamon Press, 1961. 183 p.

Physics of Heat Exchange and Gas Dynamics (Translation). New York: Consultants Bureau, 1962, 95 p.

and others. Charts for thermodynamic functions of air, for temperatures of 1000 to 12,000 K and pressures of 0.001 to 1000 atm. Glen Ridge, N. J. Translated and published by Associated Technical Services, 1962. 53 p.

Residence: Leninskiye gory, sekt. "K"

Moscow, USSR

Telephone: B9 19 54

PROKHOROV, ALEKSANDR MIKHAILOVICH (Radio Physicist)

A. M. Prokhorov was born in 1916. He graduated from Leningrad State University in 1939. In 1959, he became a professor. In 1941-1944, he served in the Soviet Army. From 1946 to 1954 he was the Senior Scientific Worker at the U.S.S.R. Academy of Sciences Lebedev Institute of Physics, and in 1954 he was made Chief of the Oscillation Laboratory of this institute. He received a Lenin Prize in 1959. Prokhorov has been a member of the Communist Party of the Soviet Union since 1960. He was elected, in 1960, a Corresponding Member of the U.S.S.R. Academy of Sciences.

In September 1959, Prokhorov visited the United States to attend the International Conference on Quantum Electronics Phenomena in Bloomingberg, New York, and in 1962, the annual meeting of the Optical Society of America in Washington. Prokhorov designed a molecular generator and amplifier.

Bibliography:

and A. M. Manenkov. A determination of the nuclear moments of Gd^{155} and Gd^{157} from the hyperfine structure of paramagnetic resonance. Zhur. Eksptl'. i Teoret. Fiz. 33, #5(11), 1116-18 (1957). SA(A) 61, 6214 (1958).

and L. S. Kornienko. A paramagnetic amplifier and generator using Fe^{3+} ions in corundum. Zhur. Eksptl'. i Teoret. Fiz. 36, #3, 919-20 (1959). SA(A) 62, 12476 (1959).

and T. M. Murina, E. A. Chayanova. The measurement of the absolute intensities of absorption lines. Radiotekhnika i Elektronika 3, #11, 1402-4 (1958). SA(A) 62, 7951 (1959).

and P. P. Pahinin. Measurements of the spin-lattice relaxation times of Cr^{3+} in corundum. Zhur. Eksptl'. i Teoret. Fiz. 34, #3, 777 (1958). Soviet Physics-JETP (New York), 34(7), #3, 535 (1958)(English trans.). SA(A) 62, 9811 (1959).

and G. M. Zverev. Electron paramagnetic resonance of Co^{++} in corundum. Zhur. Eksptl'. i Teoret. Fiz. 36, #2, 647-8 (1959). SA(A) 62, 12475 (1959).

and L. S. Kornienko, A. A. Manenkov, G. M. Zverev. A paramagnetic amplifier and generator using chromium corundum. Zhur. Eksptl'. i Teoret. Fiz. 34, #6, 1660-1 (1958). SA(A) 62, 2536 (1959).

and G. M. Zverev. The fine and hyperfine structure of the spectrum of paramagnetic resonance of Cr^{3+} in corundum. Zhur. Eksptl'. i Teoret. Fiz. 34, #2, 513-14 (1958). PB 141052T-1, Office of Tech. Services, U. S. Dept. Commerce, Washington, D. C. (English summary). SA(A) 62, 4828 (1959).

and S. D. Kaitmazov. Paramagnetic resonance of the free radicals obtained by freezing a plasma of H_2S. Zhur. Eksptl'. i Teoret. Fiz. 35, #2(8), 551 (1958). Soviet Physics-JETP (New York), 35(8), #2, (1959). SA(A) 63, 502 (1960).

and G. M. Zverev. Investigation of the electron paramagnetic resonance spectrum of V^{3+} in corundum. Zhur. Eksptl'. i Teoret. Fiz. 38, #2, 449-54 (1960). SA(A) 63, 8086 (1960).

and A. A. Manenkov. Spin-lattice relaxation in chromium corundum. Zhur. Eksptl'. i Teoret. Fiz. 38, #3, 729-3 (1960). SA(A) 63, 11940 (1960).

and V. V. Antonov-Romanovskii, V. G. Dubinin, Z. A. Trapezhikova, M. V. Fok. Detection of the ionization of Eu⁺⁺ in the phosphor SrS:Eu, Sm by the method of paramagnetic absorption. Zhur. Eksptl'. i Teoret. Fiz. 37, #5(11), 1466-7 (1959). SA(A) 63, 13713 (1960).

and S. D. Kaitmazov. Electronic paramagnetic resonance spectra of frozen OH radicals. Zhur. Eksptl'. i Teoret. Fiz. 36, #4, 1331-2 (1959). Soviet Physics-JETP (New York), 36 (9), #4, 944 (1959). SA(A) 63, 13868 (1960).

and L. S. Kornienko. Electron paramagnetic resonance of the Ti³⁺ ion in corundum. Zhur. Eksptl'. i Teoret. Fiz. 38, #5, 1651-2 (1960). SA(A) 63, 13873 (1960).

and G. M. Zverev. Electron paramagnetic resonances and spin-lattice relaxation of the Co²⁺ ion in corundum. Zhur. Eksptl'. i Teoret. Fiz. 39, #1(7), 57-63 (1960). SA(A) 63, 21074 (1960).

and G. M. Zverev. Electron paramagnetic resonance of vanadium in rutile. Zhur. Eksptl'. i Teoret. Fiz. 39, #1(7), 222-3 (1960). SA(A) 64, 1264 (1961).

and G. M. Zverev. Cross spin relaxation in the hyperfine structure of the electron spin resonance of Co²⁺ in corundum. Zhur. Eksptl'. i Teoret. Fiz. 39, (9), 545-7 (1960). SA(A) 64, 3940 (1961).

and P. P. Pashinin. Measurement of the spin-lattice relaxation time in compounds with strong covalent bonding. Zhur. Eksptl'. i Teoret. Fiz. 40, #1, 49-51 (1961). Soviet Physics-JETP (USA), 13, #1, 33-4 (1961). SA(A) 64, 14810 (1961).

Quantum counters. Zhur. Eksptl'. i Teoret. Fiz. 40, #5, 1384-6 (1961). Soviet Physics-JETP (USA) (English trans.). SA(A) 64, 19066 (1961).

and G. M. Zverev. Electronic paramagnetic resonance in the V³⁺ ion in corundum. Zhur. Eksptl'. i Teoret. Fiz. 40, #4, 1016-18 (1961). Soviet Physics-JETP (USA), 13, #4, 714-15 (1961). SA(A) 64, 2038 (1961).

and L. S. Kornienko, P. P. Pashinin. Spin-lattice relaxation time of ionic Ti³⁺ in corundum. Zhur. Eksptl'. i Teoret. Fiz. 42, #1, 65-6 (1962).

and A. A. Malenkov. Spin-lattice relaxation and cross-relaxation interactions in chromium corundum. Zhur. Eksptl'. i Teoret. Fiz. 42, #1, 75-83 (1962).

305   PTITSYN

and A. A. Malenko. Temperature relationship to spin-
lattice relaxation time. Zhur. Eksptl'. i Teoret. Fiz. 42,
#5, 1371-73 (1962).
Office: A. N. Lebedev Physics Institute of USSR Academy
             of Sciences
             Leninskii Prospekt, 53
             Moscow, USSR
Residence: Leninskii pr. 11
             Moscow, USSR
Telephone: B2 40 89

PTITSYN, BORIS VLADIMROVICH (Inorganic Chemist)
   B. V. Ptitsyn was born in 1903. In 1929 he graduated from
Leningrad State University. He worked as an assistant, docent,
and from 1940 to 1956 he was Chairman of the Chemistry Department at the Naval Medical Academy in Leningrad. He was
awarded a Doctor of Chemical Sciences degree in 1945. In
1956-1959, he was Chairman of the Department of General and
Analytical Chemistry at the Leningrad Technological Institute
of Food Industries. In 1959, he became Chairman of the Department of Complex Compounds at the U.S.S.R. Academy of
Sciences Siberian Branch Institute of Inorganic Chemistry, and
Chairman of the Department of General Chemistry at the Novosibirsk State University. He was elected to the U.S.S.R. Academy of Sciences as a Corresponding Member in 1960.
Bibliography:
   and V. F. Petrov. Oxidation potential of dichromate. J. Gen.
Chem. USSR 26, 3601-7 (1956) (Eng. trans.) C. A. 52, 15206c
(1958).
   and E. N. Tekster, L. I. Vinogradova, M. D. Morachevskaya.
Use of an oxalate-silver electrone to determine the instability constants of complex oxalates. Zhur. Neorg. Khim. 2,
2025-30 (1957). C. A. 52, 13382g (1958).
   and A. A. Grinberg, L. E. Nikolskaya, G. I. Petrzhak, F. M.
Filinov. Slightly soluble compounds of quadrivalent uranium
obtained with the aid of rongalite. J. Anal. Chem. USSR 12,
89-91 (1957) (Eng. trans.) C. A. 52, 7290i (1958).
   and M. D. Morachevskaya, V. S. Zlobin. Strontium adsorption by hydroxylapatite crystals. Biokhimiya 23, 564-7
(1958). C. A. 52, 20646i (1958).
   and A. A. Grinberg, G. I. Petrzhak, L. E. Nikolskaya, F. M.
Filinov. A new method of obtaining quadrivalent uranium.
Trudy Radievogo Inst. im. V. G. Khlopina 8, 166-9 (1958).
C. A. 53, 8907c (1959).

and L. N. Sheronov. The zirconium citrate complex. Zhur. Neorg. Khim. 4, 367-71 (1959). C. A. 53, 16790g (1959).
and E. N. Tekster. Determination of the instability constants for the uranyl oxalate complexes by the equilibrium displacement method. Zhur. Neorg. Khim. 4, 2248-54 (1959). C. A. 54, 14884g (1960).
and M. Morachevskaya. Determination of iodides in presence of bromides and chlorides with the aid of radioactive iodine. Zavodskaya Lab. 26, 269-71 (1960). C. A. 54, 13952d (1960).
and E. N. Tekster, L. I. Vinogradova. Determination of the instability constants of the complex oxalates of magnesium and uranyl with an oxalate silver electrode. Zhur. Neorg. Khim. 4, 764-8 (1959). C. A. 54, 8232f (1960).

Office: Department of General Chemistry
            Novosibirsk State University
            Novosibirsk, Siberia

PUSTOVALOV, LEONID VASIL'EVICH (Petrographer)
    L. V. Pustovalov was born August 8, 1902. He graduated from Moscow University in 1925. In 1934, he was professor at the Moscow Oil Institute and from 1943-1955 he was chairman of the Department of Petrography of Sedimentary Rock of the Institute of Geological Sciences at the U.S.S.R. Academy of Sciences. He was also chairman of the Council on the Study of Productive Forces of the U.S.S.R. Academy of Sciences in 1953. He was elected, in 1953, to the U.S.S.R. Academy of Sciences as a Corresponding Member. Since 1944, he has been a member of the Communist Party. He was awarded Stalin Prizes in 1940 and 1941, and in July 1962 the Order of the Red Banner of Labor.
    Pustovalov's main works deal with petrography and geochemistry of sedimentary rock. In 1933 he studied the problem of the geochemical species in sedimentary rock, having particular significance in understanding sedimentation processes. In particular, he demonstrated the differentiation in substances from a sedimentation zone, the periodicity in the formation of sedimentary rock and commercial minerals of sedimentary derivation. While studying conditions in the formation of oil producing rock masses of Azerbaijan, Pustovalov established a link between the mechanical, the mineralogical and the chemical composition of sedimentary rock (1946). In later years he has been occupied with the study of secondary changes of ancient sediments.

Bibliography:
  and others. Genesis of Lipetsk and Tula Iron Ore in View of
  the Geochemical History of the Southern Wing of Pre-
  Moscow Basin. Moscow-Leningrad: 1933.
  Geochemical facies and their meaning in general and applied
  geology. Problems of Soviet Geology, 1933, 1, #1.
  Ratofkite of Upper Volga Territories. Moscow-Leningrad:
  1937.
  Petrography of Sedimentary Rock, Part I-II. Moscow-
  Leningrad: 1940.
  Secondary changes of sedimentary rock and their geological
  meaning. Works of the Geological Institute of the U.S.S.R.
  Academy of Sciences, #5, Moscow, 1956.
Office: Institute of Geology of USSR Academy of Sciences
             Pyzhevskii Pereulok, 7
             Moscow, USSR
Residence: ul. Chaplygina 1-a
             Moscow, USSR
Telephone: B8 40 61

RABINOVICH, ISAAK MOISEEVICH (Structural Engineer)
  I. M. Rabinovich was born January 23, 1886. He graduated
from the Moscow Technical College in 1918. From 1918 to
1932, he worked at the Institute of Engineering Research for
the Scientific Technical Committee of the People's Commissariat in Roads and Communication. He also taught in a number of
universities and technical colleges of Moscow. In 1932 he became a professor at the Military Engineering Academy, and in
1933, at the Engineer Construction Institute. In 1944 he was
awarded the title Honored Scientist of the R.S.F.S.R. He has
held the rank of Major General in the Technical Engineering
Service, and was elected to the U.S.S.R. Academy of Sciences
as a Corresponding Member in 1946. He is a Corresponding
Member of the Academy of Construction and Architecture,
U.S.S.R.
  Rabinovich worked out a kinetic method in structural mechanics, originated effective methods for calculating complex,
and investigated statically indeterminate systems, theory of
guy trusses, and the dynamics of constructions. He led the
first systematic experimental investigations in the U.S.S.R. of
the dynamic action of different loads on the span of bridges and
on other engineering constructions. The results of multiple
investigations of Rabinovich are generalized in his Course in
Structural Mechanics of Rod Systems (two parts, 1938-40).

Bibliography:

Utilization of the Theory of Finite Differences in the Investigation of Continuous Beams. Moscow: 1921.

Investigation of Continuous Beams. Moscow: 1921.

Kinematic Method in Structural Mechanics in Connection with Graphic Kinematic and Static Plane Chains. Moscow: 1928.

On the Theory of Statically Indeterminate Trusses. Moscow: 1933.

Achievements of Structural Mechanics of Rod Systems in the U.S.S.R. Moscow: 1949.

On the theory of guy trusses. Techniques and Economics of Lines of Communication, 1924, 1, #1-4.

Method of Calculating Frames, Part I-III. Moscow-Leningrad: 1934-37.

The Basis of Dynamic Calculation of Structures on the Effects of Short-Term and Instantaneous Forces, Part I. Moscow: 1952.

Course in Structural Mechanics of Rod Systems, Part I-II, 2nd ed. Moscow-Leningrad: 1950-54.

Office: USSR Academy of Sciences
               Leninskii Prospekt, 14
               Moscow, USSR
Residence: Brusorskii pr. 7
               Moscow, USSR
Telephone: B9 44 55

RABOTNOV, YURII NIKOLAEVICH (Mechanics Physicist)

Yu. N. Rabotnov was born February 24, 1914. In 1935 he graduated from Moscow University. He taught at the Moscow Institute of Energetics from 1935 to 1946. In 1946 he was made Chief of the Laboratory of Strength of Materials of the Institute of Mechanics of the U.S.S.R. Academy of Sciences. Rabotnov became professor at Moscow University in 1947. Since 1951 he has been a member of the Communist Party of the Soviet Union. In 1953 he was elected Corresponding Member of the U.S.S.R. Academy of Sciences and in 1958, Academician.

Rabotnov's investigations are in the theory of envelopes, the theory of creep, and the theory of plasticity.

In April 1958, Rabotnov visited the United States to attend the Mechanics Organization.

Bibliography:

Main equations of the theory of envelopes. Doklady Akad. Nauk S.S.S.R., 1945, 47, #2.

Local stability of envelopes. Doklady Akad. Nauk S.S.S.R.,
1946, 52, #2.
Balance of elastic medium and its consequences. Priklad.
Mat. i Mekh., 1948, 12.
Approximate technical theory of elastic-plastic envelopes.
Priklad. Mat. i Mekh., 1951, 15, #2.
Some solutions to the zero-moment theory of envelopes.
Priklad. Mat. i Mekh., 1946, 10, #5-6.
Some questions on the theory of creep. Vestnik of the Mos-
cow State University, 1948, #10.
Resistance of Materials, 1950.
On some possibilities of describing unsettled creep with
application to study of the creep of rotors. Izvest. Akad.
Nauk S.S.S.R., Otdel. Tekh. Nauk, 1957, #5.
Office: Moscow University
           Moscow, USSR
Residence: Lomonosovskii prospekt, 14
           Moscow, USSR
Telephone: B9 11 48

RAKITIN, YURII VLADIMIROVICH (Plant Physiologist)

As of 1959 Yu. V. Rakitin has been working at the K. A.
Timiryazev Institute of Plant Physiology. In June 1962 he was
elected a Corresponding Member of the U.S.S.R. Academy of
Sciences.

Bibliography:
and A. D. Potapova. Effect of 2,4-d and chlorine -IPC on
transpiration and some colloidal properties of protoplasm.
Doklady Akad. Nauk S.S.S.R. 126, #3, 688-691 (1959).
and A. D. Potapova. Effect of herbicides on respiration and
photosynthesis of oats and sunflowers. Doklady Akad. Nauk
S.S.S.R. 126, #6, 1371-74 (1959).
Office: K. A. Timiryazev Institute of Plant Physiology
           Leninskii Prospekt, 33
           Moscow, USSR

RASPLETIN, ALEKSANDR ANDREEVICH (Radio Engineer)

A. A. Raspletin was born in 1908. He graduated from the
Leningrad Electrotechnical Institute in 1936, and has worked in
a number of scientific research organizations. He received a
Stalin Prize in 1951, has been a member of the Communist
Party of the Soviet Union since 1954, and was elected to the
U.S.S.R. Academy of Sciences as a Corresponding Member in
1958.

RAZUVAEV 310

Office: USSR Academy of Sciences
Leninskii Prospekt, 14
Moscow, USSR

RAZUVAEV, GRIGORII ALEKSEEVICH (Organic Chemist)
G. A. Razuvaev was born August 24, 1895. In 1925 he graduated from Leningrad University. He worked at the Laboratory
of High Pressures of the U.S.S.R. Academy of Sciences in 1924-
29, and in 1929-34 was the Chief of the Laboratory. He also
taught, in 1925-27, at the Military Technical Academy of the
Workers' and Peasants' Red Army. Razuvaev began teaching
at Gorkii University in 1946; in 1956 he became the Director of
the Scientific Research Institute of Chemistry at this University.
In 1958 he was elected a Corresponding Member of the U.S.S.R.
Academy of Sciences. For his works in the chemistry of free
radicals in solutions, in 1958 he was awarded a Lenin Prize.

Razuvaev studied free radicals of the phenarsazine series,
the displacement of mercury, tin, lead, arsenic, antimony from
metallo-organic compounds by hydrogen under high pressure.
He also studied chain reactions of free radicals in a liquid medium. He investigated photoreactions of series of mercury-
organic compounds and discovered the chain reactions in solutions of mercuric salts of organic acids which are initiated
by free radicals. He worked out a method of identifying radicals according to products of their interaction with a solvent.
Razuvaev also investigated the mechanism of decomposition of
organic peroxides in solutions. Candidate dissertation (1946):
"Meriquinoid phenarsazine derivatives." Doctor dissertation
(1946): "Free radicals in reactions of metallo-organic compounds."

In February 1960, Razuvaev visited the United States to attend Amexco Group meetings in Washington, D. C.
Bibliography:
Radicals in reactions of organic chemistry. Scientific
Papers of the Gorkii State University, 1947, 90, 13.
Free radicals in organic reactions. Scientific Papers of the
Gorkii State University, 1949, 81, 15.
and A. V. Savitskii. Reaction of symmetric organomercury
compounds with iodine. Doklady Akad. Nauk S.S.S.R. 85,
575 (1952). C. A. 47, 9911h (1953).
and Yu. A. Ol'dekop, L. N. Grobov. New method of synthesis
of organomercury compounds. Doklady Akad. Nauk S.S.S.R.
88, 77 (1953). C. A. 48, 142f (1954).

Reactions of free radicals in a liquid phase. Reaction ability
of acyloxy-radicals and polychloromethyl and ethyl radicals.
Questions of Chemical Kinetics, Catalysis and Reaction
Ability. Moscow: 1955, 790-797.

and E. V. Mitrofanova, N. S. Vyazankin. Reactions of acyl
peroxides with diethylmercury. Doklady Akad. Nauk S.S.S.R.
144, 132 (1962).

and Yu. I. Dergunov, N. S. Vyazankin. Homolytic reactions
of tinorganic compounds with alkyl halides induced by peroxides. Doklady Akad. Nauk S.S.S.R. 145, 347 (1962).

and V. S. Etlis. Interaction of 3-aminopropene-1,2-thio-
carbonate with ammonia and amines. Doklady Akad. Nauk
S.S.S.R. 143, 633 (1962).

and V. S. Etlis, V. R. Likhterov. The synthetic method of
asymmetrical acyl sulfoorganic peroxides. U.S.S.R. Patent
145230, 15.01.1962.

and G. G. Petukhov, S. F. Zhil'tsov, L. F. Kudryavtsev.
Thermal decomposition and oxidation of dicyclohexylmercury
in benzene. Doklady Akad. Nauk S.S.S.R. 144, 810 (1962).

and K. S. Minsker, R. P. Chernovskaya. The effect of organic compounds with a closed π-conjugated system of bonds
on stereospecific polymerization of propylene. Doklady
Akad. Nauk S.S.S.R. 147, #3, 636-38 (1962).

Office: Scientific Research Institute of Chemistry
              Gorkii University
              Gorkii, USSR
Residence: Arzamasskoye Shosse 15a, Apt. 7
              Gorkii 22, USSR

REBINDER, PYOTR ALIKSANDROVICH (Physical Chemist)

P. A. Rebinder was born October 2, 1898. In 1924 he graduated from Moscow University. He became, in 1923, a scientific
worker at the Institute of Physics and Biophysics of the U.S.S.R.
Academy of Sciences. In 1929 he was made professor at the
K. Liebknecht Pedagogical Institute in Moscow. He was appointed, in 1934, Chief of the Department of Dispersed Systems
at the Institute of Physical Chemistry of the U.S.S.R. Academy
of Sciences. In 1942 he became professor at Moscow University. Rebinder was elected Corresponding Member in 1933 and
in 1946 Academician of the U.S.S.R. Academy of Sciences. In
1942 he won a Stalin Prize.

Rebinder's investigations deal with surface adsorption layers
on solid-liquid boundaries and their influence on the properties
of dispersed systems. This work has had considerable

significance for the development of the theory of flotation of minerals. He has also studied the processes of dispersion and formation of a new crystalline phase and applied these to thixotropy, and to setting and hardening of cements, to the stabilization of foams, emulsions and suspensions, and to phase changes in emulsions. He investigated the mechanical properties of rheological systems and established the effect of small additions of adsorbing substances. Rebinder has indicated deformations can be eased and the mechanical stability of solids (in particular metals) can be lowered by adsorbing substances. This phenomenon is of particular significance for creep and fatigue breakdown of solids. This work of Rebinder has found application in a number of technological processes such as boring in solid rocks, grinding of the hard materials, and pressure processing and cutting of metals.

Bibliography:

with others. Physical Chemistry of Flotation Processes. Moscow-Leningrad: 1933.

with others. Physical Chemistry of Washing. Leningrad-Moscow: 1935.

and L. A. Shreiner and K. F. Zhigach. Depressors of Hardness in Drilling. Moscow-Leningrad: 1944.

as editor. Molecular surface phenomena in oil paints and varnishes. Physico-Chemical Basis of the Processes of Printing and Investigating Printing Inks. In works of the Publishing House of the Scientific Research Institute, #5, part 1, Moscow 1937.

as editor. On the physico-chemistry of flotation processes. New Studies in the Area of the Theory of Flotation. Moscow-Leningrad: 1937.

and others, editors. Investigations in the Area of Applied Physico-Chemistry of Surface Phenomena. Moscow-Leningrad: 1936 (contains a series of articles by Rebinder with co/authors).

Physico-chemical investigations of the processes of deformation of solid bodies. Anniversary Collection, devoted to the 30th Anniversary of the Great October Revolution, part 1, Moscow-Leningrad: 1947.

Some results of the development of the physico-chemical mechanics. Proc. Acad. Sci. U.S.S.R., Sect. Chem., 1957, #11.

Biography:
   A. B. Taubman. Laureate of the Stalin Prize Corresponding
   Member of the U.S.S.R. Academy of Sciences P. A. Rebinder.
   Uspekhi Khim., 1943, 12, #1.
   M. P. Volarovich and B. Ya. Yampol'skii. On the 50th Anni-
   versary since date of birth and 25th Anniversary of scientific
   activity of Academician P. A. Rebinder. Kolloid. Zhur.,
   1949, 11, #2.
Office: Institute of Physical Chemistry of USSR Academy
                 of Sciences
                 Leninskii Prospekt, 31
                 Moscow, USSR
Residence: Leninskii Prospekt, 13
                 Moscow, USSR
Telephone: B2 52 36

RENGARTEN, VLADIMIR PAVLOVICH (Geologist)

V. P. Rengarten was born July 24, 1882. Upon graduation
from the Mining Institute of Petersburg in 1908, he began to
work for the Geological Committee (later known as the All-
Union Scientific Research Geologic Institute). He has been
working in the U.S.S.R. Academy of Sciences since 1941. He
received a Stalin Prize in 1948 for his work on the geology of
the Caucasus. In 1946, he was elected to the U.S.S.R. Academy
of Sciences as a Corresponding Member.

   The works of Rengarten deal with the regional geology of the
Caucasus, the Eastern slope of the Urals, the Pamir and Amur
territory. Of particular significance is his work on the tectonics of the Caucasus and on the stratigraphy of chalk deposits. Rengarten has made paleontological investigations of
cretaceous cephalopodic pelecypods (particularly rudistids),
brachiopods, sea urchins. Under the editorship of Rengarten
the ninth and tenth volumes of Geology of the U.S.S.R. (1941-47)
were published, devoted to the North Caucasus and to the territory beyond the Caucasus.

Bibliography:
   Geological structure of the Murga-Istyk region of the Eastern Pamires. Geology and Paleontology of South Eastern
   Pamires. Leningrad: 1935.
   Rudistidic Facies of cretaceous deposits in territories
   beyond the Caucasus. Works of the Geological Institute of
   the U.S.S.R. Academy of Sciences, Moscow, 1950, #130, Geological series, #51.

Stratigraphy of cretaceous and tertiary deposits of Eastern territories near the Urals. Works of the Geological Institute of the U.S.S.R. Academy of Sciences, Moscow, 1951, #133, Geologic series, #54.

Paleontological substantiation of the stratigraphy of lower cretaceous era in the Greater Caucasus. In Memory of A. D. Arkhangel'skii. Questions of Lithology and Stratigraphy of the U.S.S.R. Moscow: 1951.

Office: USSR Academy of Sciences
              Leninskii Prospekt, 14
              Moscow, USSR

REUTOV, OLEG ALEKSANDROVICH (Organic Chemist)

O. A. Reutov was born September 5, 1920. He graduated from Moscow University in 1941 and from then until 1945 served in the military service. In 1945 he began teaching at Moscow University where in 1954 he was made professor. Reutov was elected a Corresponding Member of the U.S.S.R. Academy of Sciences in 1958. In 1942 he became a member of the Communist Party of the Soviet Union. Moscow University awarded him the first Lomonosov Prize in 1956 for his work in synthesis of metallo-organic compounds through diazo compounds.

Reutov worked out a large number of new methods for synthesizing metallo-organic compounds of mercury, arsenic, antimony, bismuth, lead and tin. He proposed new mechanisms of synthesis of metallo-organic compounds through diazo compounds. Reutov also studied the mechanism of carbon substitution reactions, particularly homolytic and electrophilic substitution reactions by the isotope exchange method. He organized a study of bactericidal properties of various metallo-organic compounds and developed an industrial method for obtaining a highly effective disinfectant called "Diotsid."

Bibliography:

Mechanism of reactions of diazo compounds with metals which lead to formation of metallo-organic compounds. Izvest. Akad. Nauk S.S.S.R., Otdel. Khim. Nauk, 1956, #8.

Investigation of electrophilic and homolytic substitution reactions of the isotope exchange method. Izvest. Akad. Nauk S.S.S.R., Otdel. Khim. Nauk, 1958, #6.

Theoretical Problems of Organic Chemistry. Moscow: 1956.

Office: Chemistry Department
              Moscow University
              Moscow, USSR

RIZNICHENKO, YURII VLADIMIROVICH (Geophysicist)

Yu. V. Riznichenko was born September 28, 1911. He graduated in 1935 from the Kiev Mining-Geological Institute. He became professor in 1947 at the U.S.S.R. Academy of Sciences Geophysical Institute where he had worked since 1938. In 1956 he began working at the Institute of Terrestrial Physics of the U.S.S.R. Academy of Sciences. Since 1950 he has been a member of the Communist Party of the Soviet Union. He was elected, in 1958, a Corresponding Member of the U.S.S.R. Academy of Sciences.

Riznichenko has studied the distribution of seismic waves and developed seismic methods for surveying. He has worked out a general kinematic method of interpreting seismic data-- method of the fields of time, the principles of which are set forth in his work "Geometric Seismics of Layered Media" (1946). Under his direction a new method of modeling seismic wave processes has been established.

Riznichenko has attended the Pugwash Conferences.

Bibliography:

Theory of a seismic hodograph. Izvest. Akad. Nauk S.S.S.R., Ser. Georgr. i Geofiz., 1939, #3.

Seismic properties of a layer of permafrost. Izvest. Akad. Nauk S.S.S.R., Ser. Geogr. i Geofiz., 1942, #6.

Seismologic speeds in layered media. Izvest. Akad. Nauk S.S.S.R., Ser. Geogr. i Geofiz., 1947, #2.

and others. Modeling of seismic waves. Izvest. Akad. Nauk S.S.S.R., Ser. Geofiz., 1951, #5.

and others. Correlative Method of Wave Refraction. Moscow: 1952.

Impulse seismic method for studying mountain pressure. Doklady Akad. Nauk S.S.S.R., 1955, 102, #3.

Development of supersonic methods in seismology. Izvest. Akad. Nauk S.S.S.R., Ser. Geofiz., 1957, #11.

Method of mass determination of the coordinates of centers of close earthquakes and speed of seismic waves in the area of the centers. Izvest. Akad. Nauk S.S.S.R., Ser. Geofiz., 1958, #4.

Study of the seismic regime. Izvest. Akad. Nauk S.S.S.R., Ser. Geofiz., 1958, #9.

Office: O. Yu. Shmidt Institute of Terrestrial Physics of USSR Academy of Sciences
Bolshaya Gruzinskaya Ulitsa, 10
Moscow, USSR

ROGINSKII, SIMON ZALMANOVICH (Physical Chemist)

S. Z. Roginskii was born March 25, 1900. He graduated in 1922 from Dnepropetrovsk University. From 1923 to 1928 he taught at the Dnepropetrovsk Mining Institute and, beginning in 1925, was also a scientific worker for the Ukrainian Institute of Physical Chemistry. He worked at the Institute of Chemical Physics of the U.S.S.R. Academy of Sciences in 1928-41 and at the Leningrad Polytechnic Institute. In 1941 he began work at the Institute of Physical Chemistry of the U.S.S.R. Academy of Sciences. Roginskii was elected in 1939 a Corresponding Member of the U.S.S.R. Academy of Sciences.

The works of Roginskii are devoted to study of catalysis, kinetics of heterogeneous reactions, and chemistry and use of isotopes. He showed that the surface of solids is not homogeneous in its adsorption and catalytic properties, and formulated a general theory of adsorption and catalysis for heterogeneous surfaces. He has used the electron microscope in studying the structure of catalysts. Roginskii proposed a microchemical theory for active surfaces. He is the author of the first Soviet article on isotope exchange and the use of artificial radioactive isotopes for studying chemical reactions. He worked out a series of isotope methods for studying surfaces of solid bodies. Roginskii is the author of a theory on the preparation of catalysts ("theory of supersaturation"), in accordance with which the catalytic activity of a solid body grows with the withdrawal of the system from the equilibrium in the process of preparing the catalyst. He studied the kinetics of reactions in the solid phase. Roginskii formulated a crystallization theory of topochemical reactions. He studied chemical reactions of free atoms hydrogen, oxygen, nitrogen and the kinetics of the decomposition of explosives.

Bibliography:

Adsorption and Catalysis on Heterogeneous Surfaces. Moscow-Leningrad: 1948.

and N. E. Brezhneva. Utilization of artificial radioactive elements as indicators. Uspekhi Khim., 1938, 7, #10.

Kinetics of topochemical reactions. Zhur. Fiz. Khim., 1938, 12, #4.

Theoretical basis in preparing catalysts. I. Zhur. Priklad. Khim., 1944, 17, #1-2.

Basis of the theory of a catalyst in problems of kinetics and catalysis. VI. Heterogeneous Catalysis. Works of the All-Union Conference on Catalysis. Moscow-Leningrad: 1949.

Theoretical Basis of Heterogeneous (Contact) Catalysis.
Part 1. Moscow: 1935.
Theoretical Basis in Use of Isotope Methods in the Study of
Chemical Reactions. Moscow: 1956.
Semi-Conducting Catalysis. Chemical Science and Industry,
1957, #2.
Electromicroscopic Investigations of Catalysts. Report of
the Meeting of the U.S.S.R. Academy of Sciences, January 15-
19, 1946. Moscow-Leningrad: 1946.

Office: Institute of Physical Chemistry of USSR Academy
            of Sciences
            Leninskii Prospekt, 31
            Moscow, USSR
Residence: Leninskii Prospekt, 13
            Moscow, USSR
Telephone: B2 45 55

ROZHKOV, IVAN SERGEEVICH (Geologist)

I. S. Rozhkov was born in 1908. In 1933 he graduated from
the Leningrad Mining Institute. From 1933 to 1957, he worked
in the gold-platinum industry. In 1957 he became Chairman of
the Yakutsk branch of the U.S.S.R. Academy of Sciences Siberian Branch, and in 1958, was made Director of the Geology Institute of the U.S.S.R. Academy of Sciences Yakutsk Branch.
Rozhkov was awarded Stalin Prizes in 1950 and 1951, and
served as a delegate and member of the Presidium at the fifth
convention of the Yakutsk A.S.S.R. Supreme Soviet. In 1952 he
was granted the degree of Doctor of Geologo-Mineral Sciences,
and the rank of professor in 1959. Since 1940 he has been a
member of the Communist Party of the Soviet Union. He was
elected, in 1960, a Corresponding Member of the U.S.S.R.
Academy of Sciences.
    Rozhkov's principal work is concerned with the geology and
geomorphology of ore deposits, metallurgy of gold and platinum, and also methods for surveying and prospecting for ore
deposits.
    As of 1961, Rozhkov was a Member of the Presidium of the
Siberian Branch U.S.S.R. Academy of Sciences.
Bibliography:
    and V. S. Koptev-Dvornikov and others. Geological cross-
    section of the Urals from Zlatovita to Chelyabinsk. Akad.
    Nauk S.S.S.R. Inst. Geol. Nauk, Moscow-Leningrad 1940.
    Bibliog. & Index of Geol. Exclusive of North America,
    Vol. 22, 1957. p. 461.

Office: Institute of Geology, Siberian Branch of USSR
Academy of Sciences
Yakutsk, Siberia

RYAZANSKII, MIKHAIL SERGEEVICH (Radio Engineer)

M. S. Ryazanskii was born in 1909. He graduated from the
Moscow Power Institute in 1935. A recipient of the Stalin Prize
in 1943, he became a member of the Communist Party in 1940.
In 1958, he was elected to the U.S.S.R. Academy of Sciences as
a Corresponding Member.

Office: USSR Academy of Sciences
Leninskii Prospekt, 14
Moscow, USSR

RYKALIN, NIKOLAI NIKOLAEVICH (Metallurgist)

N. N. Rykalin was born September 27, 1903. He graduated
from the Far East University in Vladivostok in 1929. From
1930 to 1937, he taught at the Far East Polytechnical Institute
and from 1936 to 1953, at the Moscow Technological College
where he became a professor in 1946. In 1943-1948, he taught
at the Moscow Institute of Construction Engineers. He was
elected, in 1953, to the U.S.S.R. Academy of Sciences as a
Corresponding Member.

In 1936-39, Rykalin worked at the Central Scientific Research Institute of Industrial Construction in Moscow, and in
1939-53, at the Institute of Machines and in the Section on the
Scientific Development of Problems of Electric Welding and
Electrothermics of the U.S.S.R. Academy of Sciences. From
1953 he has been working at the Institute of Metallurgy at the
U.S.S.R. Academy of Sciences.

The scientific works of Rykalin are devoted to developing of
theory and methods of calculating thermal processes in welding.

In 1961, Rykalin was Chairman of the National Committee of
U.S.S.R. for Welding.

Bibliography:
Thermal Basis of Welding. Moscow-Leningrad: 1947.
Calculation of Thermic Processes During Welding. Moscow:
1951.
Development of the theory of heat distribution during welding
in conformity with the distributed sources. Heat Processes
During Welding, Moscow, 1953, 10-58, 89-111, 140-63.

319   RZHANOV

Office: A. A. Baykov Institute of Metallurgy of USSR
              Academy of Sciences
              Leninskii Prospekt, 49
              Moscow, USSR

RYZHKOV, VITALY LEONIDOVICH (Biologist)
     V. L. Ryzhkov was born June 30, 1896. He worked in the
Artem Communist University in Kharkov from 1922 until 1930
when he went to Simferopol (now Krimsky) Teachers Institute.
In 1934 he was at the University of Kharkov. He began to work
in 1936 in the Institute of Microbiology at the U.S.S.R. Academy
of Sciences. Since 1946 he has been a Corresponding Member
of the U.S.S.R. Academy of Sciences.
     Ryzhkov has studied viruses and virus diseases. In 1938 he
developed a new process of obtaining the virus of tobacco mo-
zaic in a refined form, conducted a series of investigations into
the physiology of viruses and established the character in the
change of metabolism in superior plants produced by viruses.
     Ryzhkov is a Corresponding Member of the Academy of
Medical Sciences and a member of D. I. Ivanovskiy Institute of
Virology, Moscow, Academy of Medical Sciences U.S.S.R.
Bibliography:
     Basic Studies of Virus Diseases in Plants. 1944.
     Mutation and Disease of the Chlorophylic Grain. Moscow:
     1933.
     Virus Disease in Plants. Moscow-Leningrad: 1935.
     Genetics of Sex. Kharkov: 1936.
     Phytopathological Viruses. Moscow-Leningrad: 1946.
     Method of metabolism and anti-metabolism in the study of
     propagation of the virus in the mozaic disease of tobacco
     plants. Izvest. Akad. Nauk S.S.S.R., Ser. Biol., 1957, #1.
     On the basic principles of genetics. Botan. Zhur., 1956, 41,
     #2.
Office: Institute of Microbiology of USSR Academy of
              Sciences
              Leninskii Prospekt, 33
              Moscow, USSR
Residence: ul. Chkalova 21/2
              Moscow, USSR
Telephone: K7 62 34

RZHANOV, ANATOLII VASIL'EVICH (Radio Electronics
     Specialist)
     A. V. Rzhanov has been working at the P. N. Lebedev

Institute of Physics, U.S.S.R. Academy of Sciences. He visited
the United States in 1960 to attend the 20th Annual Conference
on Physical Electronics in Cambridge, Massachusetts. In June
1962 he was elected a Corresponding Member of the U.S.S.R.
Academy of Sciences.

As of November 1962, he was appointed Director of the new
Siberian Branch Institute of Solid State Physics and Semiconductor Electronics.

Bibliography:

Barium titanate--a new ferro-electric. Uspekhi Fiz. Nauk
38, 461-64 (1949).

and Yu. F. Novototskii-Vlasov, I. B. Neizvestnyi. The nature
of recombination surface centers on Germanium. Fiz.
tverdogotela 1, #9, 1471-74 (1959).

Using the stationary photoconductivity method for investigating the relationship of surface recombination rate to surface
potential. Fiz. tverdogotela 2, #10, 2431-38 (1960).

Surface charge changes in heated Germanium in a vacuum.
Fiz. tverdogotela 3, #6, 1718-22 (1961).

and A. F. Plotnikov. Germanium surface levels according to
infrared region photoconductivity. Fiz. tverdogotela 3, #5,
1557-1560 (1961).

and N. M. Pavlov, M. A. Selezneva. Temperature relationship to parameters of recombined surface centers in Germanium. Fiz. tverdogotela 3, #3, 832-840 (1961).

Office: P. N. Lebedev Institute of Physics of USSR Academy
of Sciences
Leninskii Prospekt, 53
Moscow, USSR

SADOVSKII, MIKHAIL ALEKSANDROVICH (Physicist)

M. A. Sadovskii was born November 6, 1904. He graduated
from Leningrad Polytechnic Institute in 1928. From 1930-1931,
he worked at the U.S.S.R. Academy of Sciences Seismological
Institute, and from 1941-1946, he was employed on the staff of
the U.S.S.R. Academy of Sciences Presidium. In 1946 he began
working at the Institute of Chemical Physics. Since 1941, he
has been a member of the Communist Party of the Soviet Union.
He was awarded the title Hero of Socialist Labor in 1949. He
has also been the recipient of a Stalin Prize. In 1953, he was
elected to the U.S.S.R. Academy of Sciences as a Corresponding
Member.

The scientific work of Sadovskii is devoted to the physics
and mechanics of explosions. He studied the destructive action

of a blast, experimentally studied shock waves of explosions in heterogeneous media and determined their basic parameters. Sadovskii substantiated the law of similarity during an explosion. He worked out a number of devices for investigating blast effects.

As of 1961, Sadovskii was Director of the Shmidt Institute of Terrestrial Physics of the U.S.S.R. Academy of Sciences.

Bibliography:
Experimental Investigations of the Mechanical Effect of Shock Waves from an Explosion. Moscow-Leningrad: 1945 (Works of the Seismologic Institute of the U.S.S.R. Academy of Sciences, #116.)
Seismic effect of explosions. Works of the All-Union Conference on Drill Explosive Works, Moscow-Leningrad, 1940.

Office: Institute of Chemical Physics of USSR Academy of Sciences
Vorob'evskoye Shosse 2
Moscow, USSR
Telephone: V2 22 22

SAKHAROV, ANDREI DMITRIEVICH (Physicist)
A. D. Sakharov was born May 21, 1921. He graduated in 1942 from Moscow University. In 1945 he began working at the Institute of Physics of the U.S.S.R. Academy of Sciences. He has been an Academician since 1953.

Sakharov's research is in theoretical physics. In 1950, together with I. E. Tamm, he proposed application of an electrical discharge in a plasma, which is placed in a magnetic field, for obtaining a controlled thermomolecular reaction.

Bibliography:
Generation of a hard component of cosmic rays. Zhur. Eksptl. i Teoret. Fiz., 1947, 17, #8.
Interaction of an electron and positron under origination of pairs. Zhur. Eksptl. i Teoret. Fiz., 1948, 18, #7.
Temperature of excitation in plasma of a gaseous discharge. Izvest. Akad. Nauk S.S.S.R., Ser. Fiz., 1948, 12, #4.

Office: A. N. Lebedev Institute of Physics of USSR Academy of Sciences
Leninskii Prospekt, 53
Moscow, USSR
Residence: Luzhnikovskaya 1/7
Moscow, USSR
Telephone: V1 09 00

SAKS, VLADIMIR NIKOLAEVICH (Geologist)

V. N. Saks was born April 22, 1911. He graduated from the Leningrad Mining Institute in 1933. From 1935 to 1940, and from 1944 to 1948, he worked at the All-Union Arctic Institute. He was employed, 1940-1944, in the mining geological department of the Main Directorate of the Northern Seaway. In 1948, he worked at the Scientific Research Institute of Arctic Geology. Since 1935 he has been a member of the Communist Party of the Soviet Union. He was elected, in 1955, a Corresponding Member of the U.S.S.R. Academy of Sciences. He has been awarded the Order of the Red Banner of Labor.

Saks' investigations are in quaternary geology, paleography, stratigraphy, and tectonics of Mesozoic deposits of the Soviet Arctic, and in the geology of its formation. He presented a general scheme on the separation of quaternary deposits of the Arctic, outlined the paleography of the Quaternary Period in the Arctic, and worked out the stratigraphy of Mesozoic deposits of oil-bearing territories of Northern Siberia.

Bibliography:

> Conditions in the Formation of Bottomset Beds in Arctic Seas of the U.S.S.R. Moscow-Leningrad: 1952 (Works of the Scientific Research Institute of Arctic Geology, 35.)
> Quaternary Period of the Soviet Arctic. 2nd ed. Moscow-Leningrad: 1953 (Works of the Scientific Research Institute of Arctic Geology, 77.)
> and Z. Z. Ronkin. Jurassic and Cretaceous Deposits of the Ust-Enisei Depression. Moscow: 1957.

Office: USSR Academy of Sciences
            Leninskii Prospekt, 14
            Moscow, USSR

SAMARIN, ALEKSANDR MIKHAILOVICH (Metallurgist)

A. M. Samarin was born August 14, 1902. In 1930 he graduated from the Moscow Institute of Steel where he remained as a teacher, and professor as of 1938. In 1955, he became deputy Director of the U.S.S.R. Academy of Sciences Institute of Metallurgy. Since 1925 he has been a member of the Communist Party of the Soviet Union. In 1946 he was elected a Corresponding Member of the U.S.S.R. Academy of Sciences.

Samarin's scientific work is in electrometallurgy of steel and ferroalloys; he has also been interested in the history of science and technology.

Samarin is Deputy Chairman of the State Committee for the Coordination of Scientific Research. In June 1962, he visited

323 SAPOZHNIKOV

the United States to attend the Chipman Conference on Physical Chemistry of Steelmaking at Cambridge, Massachusetts. Samarin, in July 1962, was awarded the Order of the Red Banner of Labor.

Bibliography:
The selection of slag with smelting of multi-carbonic ferrochrome. Works of the First All-Union Conference on Ferroalloys. Moscow-Leningrad: 1935.
Electrometallurgy. Steel Production. Moscow: 1943.
Influence of element-dioxidizers on the activity of oxygen dissolved in liquid iron. Problems of Metallurgy. Moscow: 1953.
Structure and Properties of Liquid Metals. Moscow, Acad. Sci. USSR, Baikov's Inst. of Metallurgy, 1960. [i.e. Washington, U. S. Atomic Energy Commission, 1962] 206 p.

Office: A. A. Baykov Institute of Metallurgy of USSR
Academy of Sciences
Leninskii Prospekt, 49
Moscow, USSR
Residence: Leningradskii prospekt, 13
Moscow, USSR
Telephone: D3 04 94

SAPOZHNIKOV, LEONID MIKHAILOVICH (Fuel Technologist)

L. M. Sapozhnikov was born April 29, 1906. After his graduation from the Dnepropetrovsk Mining Institute in 1930, he began to work at the Dnepropetrovsk Coal-Chemical Institute. In 1930 he taught at the Dnepropetrovsk Chemical-Technological Institute where he became a professor in 1935. In 1937 he began work as laboratory chief at the Institute of Fuel Minerals of the U.S.S.R. Academy of Sciences. He was elected, in 1946, a Corresponding Member of the U.S.S.R. Academy of Sciences.
The works of Sapozhnikov deal with the study of the coal coking process.

Bibliography:
and others. Investigating the Process of Coking, Classifying Coal and Calculating the Charge on the Basis of a Layer-Metric Method. Collection of Articles. Kharkov-Dnepropetrovsk: 1935.
Coal and Metallurgical Coke. Moscow-Leningrad: 1941.
and G. V. Speranskaya. Investigating Contemporary Principles of Coking Coal. Moscow: 1953.
Developing new methods of coking and concentration of coal. Coal and Chemistry, 1955, #1.

and A. Z. Yurovskaii. New Technics of Coking and Concentrating Coal. Moscow-Leningrad: 1956.
Office: Dnepropetrovsk Chemical-Technological Institute
Dnepropetrovsk, USSR

SATPAEV, KANYSH IMANTAEVICH (Geologist)

K. I. Satpaev was born April 11, 1899. He began his education in a two-grade village school. He went on to the Tomsk Technological Institute, where he graduated in 1926. He holds the degree of Doctor of Geological and Mineralogical Sciences and the title of professor. Satpaev has been a member of the Communist Party of the Soviet Union since 1944. In 1946 he became Academician of the U.S.S.R. Academy of Sciences and Academician of the Kazakh S.S.R. Academy of Sciences. He was elected Chairman of the Presidium of the Kazakh S.S.R. Academy of Sciences in 1941 and was made Director of the Institute of Geological Sciences of the Kazakh Affiliate of the Academy of Sciences U.S.S.R. (reorganized in 1946 as the Kazakh S.S.R. Academy of Sciences). He has received a State Prize and the Order of Lenin three times. In 1951 Tadzhik S.S.R. Academy of Sciences made him an Honorary Member. In March 1962, Satpaev was elected delegate from Kazakh S.S.R. to the Supreme Soviet. As of 1961 he was a member of the Presidium of the U.S.S.R. Academy of Sciences.

Satpaev early developed an interest in the potential mineral wealth of his native Kazakhstan. After graduation he worked with the Dzhezkazgan Geological Prospecting Group, 1926-1941. During this period, Satpaev directed explorations of abandoned copper mining areas. Helped by young Kazakhs returning from mining courses in Leningrad, this group discovered one of the richest ore deposits in the world, that of Great Dzhezkazgan. Subsequently, he surveyed the Karsakpay iron ore deposits, twin of the Krivoy Rog deposits, and found lignite. From 1926-1941 he also supervised a geological study of Tadzhik S.S.R. and found important ore deposits. He investigated various deposits of iron, manganese, brown coal, and lignite. During the early period of the war, manganese for steel was in very short supply, due to the German occupation of Nikopol. Satpaev suggested finding manganese in Dzhezda and organized its discovery and mining in record time. During this period, the Kazakh Affiliate of the Academy of Sciences of the U.S.S.R. conducted 350 expeditions resulting in 160 practical proposals to the government.

His major work is devoted to the study of the geology and mineral species of Central Kazakhstan, particularly the study of mineral formations and their use in the national economy. Satpaev supervised the discovery of large scale copper formations and deposits of other minerals in the Ulutau-Dzhezkazgansk Region. He compiled large scale maps for the prognosis for minerals.

Bibliography:
Main features of geology and metallogenesis of the Dzhezkazgansk copper ore region, Greater Dzhezkazgansk. Moscow-Leningrad: 1935.
On the prognostic metallogenic maps of central Kazakhstan. Izvest. Akad. Nauk S.S.S.R., Ser. Geol., 1953, #6.
On metallogenic epochs, formations, and belts of central Kazakhstan. Izvest. Akad. Nauk Kazakh S.S.R., #124, Ser. Geol., 1953, #17.
On some specific peculiarities of geology of copper-bearing sandstone of the Atbasar Tersakkansk Region. Izvest. Akad. Nauk Kazakh S.S.R., Ser. Geol., 1953, #18.
On specificity and main stages of development of metallogenesis of central Kazakhstan. Izvest. Akad. Nauk S.S.S.R., Ser. Geol., 1957, #3.

Biography:
N. G. Kassin and I. I. Bok. Kanysh Imantaevich Satpaev. Izvest. Akad. Nauk Kazakh S.S.R., #70, Ser. Geol., 1949, #11.
Vestnik of the Kazakh S.S.R. Akad. Nauk, 1949, #4 (Number devoted to the 50th anniversary of Satpaev.)
Office: President, Academy of Sciences Kazakh SSR
                Shevchenko Ulitsa, 28
                Alm-Alta, Kazakh SSR

SAUKOV, ALEKSANDR ALEKSANDROVICH (Geochemist)
     A. A. Saukov was born August 15, 1902. After graduating from the Leningrad Polytechnic Institute, he has worked at the U.S.S.R. Academy of Sciences. In 1949 he became Chairman of the Department of Geochemistry of the Institute of Geological Sciences. He was made professor in 1952 at Moscow University. In 1953 Saukov was elected a Corresponding Member of the U.S.S.R. Academy of Sciences. He has been a member of the Communist Party of the Soviet Union since 1945. For the monograph Geochemistry of Mercury he was awarded a Stalin Prize in 1947, and in 1952 he received a Stalin Prize for the second edition of Geochemistry.

Saukov's investigations are in the geochemistry of rare elements and of mercury. On the basis of a method developed by him for the determination of small quantities of mercury, he studied the distribution of mercury in various rocks and minerals; he studied the genesis of mercury deposits and proposed a method of prospecting for them based on a study of the so-called "dispersion halo." A number of investigations of Saukov deal with general questions of geochemistry, including energetics of natural processes and natural association of elements, problems of their migration, the geochemical methods of prospecting for deposits of commercial minerals. He is the author of a textbook, Geochemistry, which was translated into Bulgarian, German, Chinese, Polish and Czech, Rumanian, Georgian.

Bibliography:

Geochemistry of Mercury. Moscow: 1946.

Geochemistry, 2nd ed. Moscow: 1951.

and A. I. Perel'man. Geochemical methods of prospecting for deposits of commercial minerals. Papers of the All-Union Minerallogic Society, 2nd series, 1957, Part 86, #2.

Office: Moscow University
            Moscow, USSR
Residence: B. Kommunisticheskaya, 24
            Moscow, USSR
Telephone: ZH2 52 33

SAZHIN, NIKOLAI PETROVICH (Metallurgist)

N. P. Sazhin was born March 13, 1897. He received Stalin Prizes in 1946 and 1952. In 1953 he was elected to the U.S.S.R. Academy of Sciences as a Corresponding Member.

Office: USSR Academy of Sciences
            Leninskii Prospekt, 14
            Moscow, USSR
Residence: Komsomol'skii prosp. 45
            Moscow, USSR
Telephone: G5 29 55

SCHISHKIN, BORIS KONSTANTINOVICH (Botanist)

B. K. Schishkin was born April 19, 1886. He graduated from Tomsk University in 1911, and worked there as an assistant from 1914 to 1918, and as a professor from 1925 to 1930. In 1931 he became an associate of the U.S.S.R. Academy of Sciences Botanical Institute, and served as its Director from 1938 to 1949. He was awarded a State Prize in 1952. In 1943 he was elected to the U.S.S.R. Academy of Sciences as a Corresponding Member.

Schishkin conducted botanical investigations in Siberia, Middle Asia, the Caucasus and the Carpathians; also he made trips into Turkey, Algeria, Brazil, and French Guiana. He published numerous works, particularly on the flora of the U.S.S.R. A series of collective works (the majority of volumes devoted to "Flora of the U.S.S.R.", "Flora of Western Siberia" by P. N. Krylov, "Flora of the Leningrad Territory") was published under his editorship.

Bibliography:
Outlines of the Uryankhaiskii Territory. Tomsk: 1914.
Materials on the flora of Turkish Armenia. Proceedings of the Tomsk State University, 1928, 81, 409-490.
Botanico-geographic outline of the seaside slope on the Pontiiskii Ridge. Past- Caucasus Regional Study Collection. Series A, Natural Sciences, I. Tbilisi: 1930.
Family CXIX umbelliferae moris. Flora of the U.S.S.R., chief editor V. L. Komarov, 16-17. Moscow-Leningrad: 1950-51.

Biography:
I. A. Linchevskii. Boris Konstantinovich Schishkin (On the 60th Anniversary since the date of birth). Soviet Botany, 1946, #5 (contains bibliography of the works of Shishkin).
E. G. Bobrov. Boris Konstantinovich Schishkin (On the 70th Anniversary since the date of birth). Bot. Zhur., 1956, #6.
Office: V. L. Komarov Institute of Botany of USSR Academy of Sciences
Ulitsa Popova 2
Leningrad, USSR

SCHMALHAUSEN (SHMAL'GAUZEN), IVAN IVANOVICH
(Zoologist)

I. I. Schmalhausen, son of I. F. Schmalhausen (1948-1895, Russian botanist and one of the founders of paleobotany in Russia), was born April 23, 1884. In 1907 he graduated from Kiev University. He was professor at the Voronezh (1918), Kiev (1921) and Moscow (1938-48) Universities. From 1930 to 1941 he was Director of the Institute of Zoology and Biology of the Ukrainian S.S.R. Academy of Sciences, and from 1938 to 1948 he was also Director of the Institute of Evolutionary Morphology (now the Institute of Animal Morphology) of the U.S.S.R. Academy of Sciences. In 1948 he began working at the Zoological Institute of the U.S.S.R. Academy of Sciences. Schmalhausen

SCHMALHAUSEN

has been an Academician of the Ukrainian S.S.R. Academy of Sciences since 1922 and since 1935 Academician of the U.S.S.R. Academy of Sciences. In 1935 he was an Honored Scientist of the Ukrainian S.S.R., and in 1960, a fellow of the Academy of Zoology in Agra (India), and a fellow of the German Academy "Leopoldina" in Helle.

Schmalhausen, specialist in comparative anatomy, has worked in evolutionary morphology, on the regularities in the growth of animals, on factors and characteristics of the evolutionary processes. He has also been concerned with the history of development, and the comparative anatomy of unpaired fins of fish, and the origin of extremities of land vertebrates. He proposed a theory on the growth of animal organisms, based on the conception of a reverse ratio between the speed of growth of an organism and the speed of its change. He has formulated a theory of stabilizing selection as an essential factor in evolution. Since 1948 he has been studying the origin of land vertebrates (Tetrapoda).

Bibliography:

Unpaired fins of fish and their phylogenetic development. Dissertation, Kiev, 1913. (In German: Z. wiss Zool. Bd 400, 104, 107, 1912, 1913.)

Development of the extremities of amphibians and their significance in the question on origin of extremities in land vertebrates. Dissertation, Moscow, 1915.

Basis of Comparative Anatomy of Vertebrate Animals, 4th ed. Moscow: 1947.

The Organism as a Whole in Individual and Historical Development, 2nd ed. Moscow-Leningrad: 1942.

Ways and Regularities of Evolutionary Process. Moscow-Leningrad: 1939.

Factors of Evolution (Theory of Stabilizing Selection). Moscow-Leningrad: 1946. (English trans. Philadelphia-Toronto, 1949).

Problems of Darwinism. Moscow: 1946.

Office: Embryological Laboratory
Institute of Zoology of USSR Academy of Sciences
Leninskii Prospekt, 33
Moscow V-71, USSR

Residence: Ulitsa Chkalova 14/16
Moscow, USSR

Telephone: K7 47 13

SEDOV, LEONID IVANOVICH (Mechanics Physicist)

L. I. Sedov was born November 14, 1907. In 1931 he graduated from Moscow University and in 1937 was appointed professor there. He began work in 1931 at the Central Aerohydrodynamic Institute. In 1947 he started working at the Central Institute of Aviation Motor Building. Sedov is Chairman of the Interdepartmental Commission on Coordination and Control of Scientific Theoretical Research in the Area of Organization and Realization of Interplanetary Communication. In 1946 he was elected a Corresponding Member of the U.S.S.R. Academy of Sciences and in 1953 an Academician. The U.S.S.R. Academy of Sciences awarded Sedov in 1946 the Prize of S. A. Chaplygin. In 1952 he received a Stalin Prize.

Sedov investigated various problems of mechanics. He determined the aerodynamic forces during a non-stabilized movement of the wings, in particular during vibrations. Sedov generalized the theorem of N. E. Zhukovskii for arbitrary motion of the wing; formulated a mathematical method for solving problems of stream flow around wing profiles. This method was applied by him to the theory of a finite wing, and subsequently widely applied in the theory of waves, in elasticity, and in filtration. In his treatise "Plane Problems of Hydrodynamics and Aerohydrodynamics," Sedov formulated a theory on gliding which was applied in hydroaviation and ship building. Sedov studied the impact of bodies against water, ricocheting and other problems of heavy liquid hydrodynamics. He developed a method for visualizing the stream line flow of gas past a grating and worked out a method for investigating possible gas flows, widening the approximate method of S. A. Chaplygin. In the theory of similarity and dimensionality, Sedov constructed a theory of unstabilized gas motion, in particular the theory of dispersion of strong shock waves, obtained results on the theory of surface waves; established the law of pulsation in an isotropic turbulence. His work "Propagation of Strong Explosive Waves" (1946) is a study of strong shock waves. Sedov has also been concerned with problems of astrophysics.

Bibliography:

Propagation of strong explosive waves. Priklad. Mat. i Mekh., 1946, 10, #2.

On some unsettled movements of compressible liquid. Priklad. Mat. i Mekh., 1945, 9, #4.

Plane Problems of Hydrodynamics and Aerodynamics. Moscow-Leningrad: 1950.

Methods of Similarity and Dimensionality in Mechanics, 2nd
ed. Moscow-Leningrad: 1951.
Theory of construction of mechanical models of a continuous
media. Vestnik Akad. Nauk, #7, 26-38 (1960).
and M. E. Eglit. Construction of non-holomorphic models of
continuous media with allowance for the finite nature of
deformations and certain physico-chemical effects. Doklady
Akad. Nauk S.S.S.R. 142, #1, 54-57 (1962).

Biography:

N. D. Moiseev. General Outline of the Development of Me-
chanics in Russia and in the U.S.S.R. Mechanics in the
U.S.S.R. for 30 Years. Moscow-Leningrad: 1950.
E. A. Krasil'shchikova, G. V. Rudnev. Scientist, mechanic.
Priroda, 1952, #9.

Office: Interdepartmental Commission on Interplanetary
              Communication of USSR Academy of Sciences
              Leninskii Prospekt, 14
              Moscow, USSR
Residence: Leninskii gory, sekt. "I"
              Moscow, USSR
Telephone: B9 18 74

SEMENOV, NIKOLAI NIKOLAEVICH (Physical Chemist)
    N. N. Semenov was born April 15, 1896. In 1917 he gradu-
ated from Petrograd University. During the years 1920-31, he
worked at the Leningrad Physico-Technical Institute. He became Chief of the Institute of Chemical Physics of the U.S.S.R.
Academy of Sciences in 1931 and subsequently the Director. In
1928 he was made professor at the Leningrad Polytechnic Institute and in 1944 professor at the Moscow University. He was
a Corresponding Member of the U.S.S.R. Academy of Sciences
from 1929 until 1932 when he was elected Academician. In 1947
he became a member of the Communist Party of the Soviet
Union. He was awarded a Stalin Prize in 1941, and in 1956 the
Nobel Prize.
    Semenov's first scientific work was in molecular physics
and electron phenomena such as: vapor condensation on solid
surfaces, the ionization of vapors of salts under the influence
of an electron bombardment, and electric breakdown of dielectrics. And he also developed a thermal theory of the dielectric breakdown. The initial assumptions of this theory
were utilized by Semenov in his theory of thermal explosions of
gas mixtures. According to this theory, the cause of the explosion is the unattainment of the heat equilibrium during

chemical reaction, because the heat liberated does not have
time to leave the reaction zone. Semenov and his students
studied energy distribution in a flame, detonation, and combustion of explosives and powders. The investigations of Semenov on the theory of chain reactions is particularly significant.
On the basis of the study of critical phenomena, such as limit
of ignition, observed during oxidation of vapors of phosphorus,
hydrogen, carbon monoxide and other compounds, he discovered
branching reactions. In his monograph, "Chain Reactions"
(1934), he developed the theory of non-branching reactions and
showed the wide distribution of chain reactions in chemistry.
He and his associates developed theoretically and checked experimentally many ideas of the chain theory: the breaking of
reaction chains on walls and in the volume of a container, degenerate chain branching, positive and negative interaction of
chains. Also, he established the detailed mechanism in a series
of complex chain processes, and studied the properties of free
atoms and radicals with the aid of which the elementary stages
of these processes were realized. Semenov took active part
in organizing a physico-mechanical department at the Leningrad Polytechnic Institute and in starting scientific journals.
He trained many specialists in physics, chemical kinetics, and
the combustion theory.

In March 1962, Semenov was elected a delegate from
R.S.F.S.R. to the Supreme Soviet. As of 1961, he was Secretary
of the Department of Chemical Sciences of the U.S.S.R. Academy of Sciences.

In 1961 he was elected Candidate Member of the Central
Committee of the Communist Party.

Bibliography:

Chain Reactions. Leningrad: 1934.

Thermal theory of burning and explosions. Uspekhi Fiz.
Nauk, 1940, 23, #3; 24, #4.

On Some Problems of Chemical Kinetics and Reaction Ability. Moscow: 1954.

Biography:

Nikolai Nikolaevich Semyenov, compiled by N. M. Emanuel.
Moscow-Leningrad: 1946.

Yu. B. Khariton. Creator of the theory of chain chemical
reactions. Soviet Science, 1941, #4, p. 1621.

N. M. Emanuel. Contribution to the world of science. On
the awarding of the Nobel Prize to Academician N. M.
Semyonov. Priroda, 1957, #2.

Nikolai Nikolaevich Semyenov. On the 60th Anniversary
since the date of birth. Zhur. Eksptl. i Teoret Fiz., 1956,
<u>30</u>, #4.

Office: Institute of Chemical Physics of USSR Academy of
                  Sciences
              Vorob'evskoye shosse, 2
              Moscow, USSR

Telephone: B2 24 00

SEVERIN, SERGEI EVGEN'EVICH (Biochemist)

S. E. Severin was born December 21, 1901. He graduated
from Moscow University in 1924 and worked at the Physiology
Laboratory of the Institute of Professional Diseases in Moscow.
In 1932-48 he was professor at the Third Moscow Medical Institute and in 1933 at Moscow University. He was the Director of
the Institute of Nutrition in 1945-47, and in 1948-49, of the
Institute of Biological and Medical Chemistry of the U.S.S.R.
Academy of Sciences. Severin was Academician-Secretary of
the Department of Medico-Biological Sciences of the U.S.S.R.
Academy of Medical Sciences in 1949-57. He has been a member of the U.S.S.R. Academy of Medical Sciences since 1948
and since 1953 a Corresponding Member of the U.S.S.R. Academy of Sciences.

Severin's major investigations deal with muscle tissue biochemistry. In his investigation of carnosine and anserine in
the metabolism of the skeletal muscles, together with others,
he determined the time and the sequence of appearance of these
compounds in the development of the organism; he synthesized
phosphorous derivatives of a series of amino acids and peptides
and studied their properties; he showed the influence of carno-
side and anserine on raising the effectiveness of phosphory-
lation in the skeletal muscles which lead to the formation of
energy rich phosphorous compounds necessary for muscle
function. The early investigations deal with the biochemistry
of blood, particularly blood preservation.

Bibliography:

Les transformations de la carnosine dans l'organisme ani-
mal. Acta medica URSS, Moscow, <u>2</u>, #4, 1939.
Biochemical basis in favorable effect of glucose on the
conservation of blood. Biokhimiya, 1946, #2, 139-48.
<u>and N. P. Meshkova.</u> Practicum on the Biochemistry of
Animals, 1950.
<u>and P. P. Mitrofanov.</u> Textbook of Physical and Colloidal
Chemistry, 1941.

Distribution, transformation in the organism and the biological significance of carnosine and anserine. Uspekhi Biokhim., 2, 1954, 355-377.
and N. P. Meshkova. Influence of carnosine and anserine on the carbohydrate-phosphorus and oxygen metabolism in skeletal muscles. Questions on the Biochemistry of Muscles. Kiev: 1954, 193-206.
Office: Academy of Medical Sciences USSR
             Solyanka, 14
             Moscow, USSR
Residence: Novoslobodskaya, 57/65
             Moscow, USSR
Telephone: D1 69 87

SEVERNYI, ANDREI BORISOVICH (Astronomer)
A. B. Severnyi was born May 11, 1913. He graduated from Moscow University in 1935. In 1946 he started to work at the U.S.S.R. Academy of Sciences Crimean Astrophysical Observatory where he became Director in 1952. He was awarded a Stalin Prize in 1952 for his studies in solar chromospheric flares, and in 1958 was elected to the U.S.S.R. Academy of Sciences as a Corresponding Member.
Severnyi has worked in theoretical astrophysics and the physics of the sun.
Bibliography:
Stability and oscillations of gaseous spheres and stars. Publications of the Crimean Astrophysical Observatory, 1948, 1, #2.
and V. L. Khokhlova. Investigations of the movements and brightness of solar prominence. Publications of the Crimean Astrophysical Observatory, 1953, 10, 9-54.
and E. F. Shaposhnikova. Investigation of the development of chromospheric flares on the sun. Publications of the Crimean Astrophysical Observatory, 1954, 12, 3-32.
Investigation of the fine structure of emission of active regions and non-stationary processes on the sun. Publications of the Crimean Astrophysical Observatory, 1957, 17, 129.
Physics of the Sun. Moscow: 1956.
Investigation of magnetic fields connected with solar flares. Publications of the Crimean Astrophysical Observatory, 1960, 22, 12.

The fine structure of magnetic field and depolarization of radiation in sunspots. Astron. Journ. USSR, 1959, 36, 208.

Office: The Crimean Astrophysical Observatory of USSR
Academy of Sciences
Moscow, USSR

SHAFAREVICH, IGOR' ROSTISLAVOVICH (Mathematician)

I. R. Shafarevich was born June 3, 1923. He graduated in 1940 from Moscow University. In 1943 he began working at the Mathematics Institute of the U.S.S.R. Academy of Sciences. He also taught at Moscow University, beginning in 1944, and in 1953 was made professor. Since 1958 he has been a Corresponding Member of the U.S.S.R. Academy of Sciences.

The main works of Shafarevich are concerned with algebra and theory of algebraic numbers.

Bibliography:

On the normalization of topological fields. Doklady Akad. Nauk S.S.S.R., 1943, 40, #4.

On Galois groups of y-additative fields. Doklady Akad. Nauk S.S.S.R., 1946, 53, #1.

On p-expansions. Mat. Sbornik, 1947, 20 (62), #2.

General law of duality. Doklady Akad. Nauk S.S.S.R., 1949, 64, #1.

General law of duality. Mat. Sbornik, 1950, 26 (68).

On the structure of fields with a given Galois group in the order of 1^{alpha}. Izvest. Akad. Nauk S.S.S.R., Ser. Mat., 1954, 18, #3.

On the structure of fields of algebraic numbers with a given Galois group. Izvest. Akad. Nauk S.S.S.R., Ser. Mat., 1954, 18, #6.

and A. I. Kostrikin. Group of homologies of nilpotent algebras. Doklady Akad. Nauk S.S.S.R., 1957, 115, #6.

Office: Mathematics Department
Moscow University
Moscow, USSR

SHAKHOV, FELIKS NIKOLAEVICH (Geologist)

F. N. Shakhov was born October 24, 1894. Upon graduation from the Tomsk Technological (now the Polytechnic) Institute in 1922, he continued to work there where he became a professor in 1935. In 1944, he began work in the West Siberian branch of the U.S.S.R. Academy of Sciences, and since 1957 he has been at the U.S.S.R. Academy of Sciences Siberian Branch

Institute of Geology and Geophysics (Novosibirsk). He was
elected a Corresponding Member of the U.S.S.R. Academy of
Sciences in 1958.

Shakov has worked in the geology of ore deposits, in particular the formation of metals in various regions, the genesis of
various deposits, and methods of prospecting-survey work.
Lately, he has been conducting investigations in the field of the
geology of rare and radioactive elements.

Bibliography:
   Magmatic rocks of the Kuznets Basin. Proceedings of the
   Siberian Technological Institute, 1927, 47, #3.
   Materials on the geology of the Tanalyk-Baimakskii copper
   ore region in the Southern Urals. Proceedings of the Si-
   berian Technological Institute, 1928, 49, #1.
   Theory of Contact Deposits. Novosibirsk: 1947 (S.S.S.R.
   Akad. Nauk, Sibir. Otdel. Trudy Inst. Gor.-Geol., #1).
   The origin of granitic magmas. Mineral Sbornik, L'vov.
   Geol. Obshchestvo L'vov, Gosudarst. Univ. im. I. Franke
   1956, #10, 39-49. C. A. 53, 21487a (1959).
   Morphological Traits of Oxidation Zones. Novosibirsk:
   1960 (S.S.S.R. Akad. Nauk, Sibir. Otdel. Trudy Inst. Geol.-
   Geoph., 155.4).
   Textures of Ores. Moscow: 1961 (S.S.S.R. Akad. Nauk,
   Sibir. Otdel.).

Office: Institute of Geology and Geophysics
               Siberian Branch USSR Academy of Sciences
               Academgorolsk, Novosibirsk 72
               Siberia
Residence: Academiya Ul. 55, Apt. 6
               Novosibirsk 72, Siberia

SHAL'NIKOV, ALEKSANDR IOSIFOVICH (Physicist)
   A. I. Shal'nikov was born May 10, 1905. He graduated in
1928 from Leningrad Polytechnic Institute. He began working
in 1935 at the U.S.S.R. Academy of Sciences Institute of Physics, which he helped to organize. In 1938 he became professor
at Moscow University. Since 1946 he has been a Corresponding
Member of the U.S.S.R. Academy of Sciences. He has been
awarded a Stalin Prize.
   The work of Shal'nikov deals with low temperature experimental physics: the study of the properties of thin metallic
film and colloids. He investigated the structure of the intermediate state of super-conductors.

SHAPOSHNIKOV 336

Bibliography:
The methods of obtaining organosols of alkaline metals.
Zhur. Fiz. Khim., 1933, 4, #3.
Structure of super-conductors in the intermediate state.
Zhur. Eksptl. i Teoret. Fiz., 1946, 16, #9.
and A. Meshkovskii. Surface effects of super-conductors in
the intermediate state. Zhur. Eksptl. i Teoret. Fiz., 1947,
17, #10.
Office: Vorob'evskoye Shosse 2
Moscow, USSR
Telephone: B2 16 92

SHAPOSHNIKOV, VLADIMIR NIKOLAEVICH (Microbiologist)
V. N. Shaposhnikov was born February 24, 1884. He worked
at Moscow University after graduating from there in 1910, and
in 1938 became a professor at this University. From 1921 to
1935 he worked at the State Scientific Research Chemico-
Pharmaceutical Institute. In 1938 he became Chairman of a
Department in the Institute of Microbiology of the U.S.S.R.
Academy of Sciences. Shaposhnikov has been an Academician
of the U.S.S.R. Academy of Sciences since 1953. In 1949 he was
awarded a Stalin Prize.
Shaposhnikov's main investigations are in technical microbiology. While studying metabolism in microorganisms, he
worked out a classification of energy processes which reflect
processes of evolution of fermenting microorganisms. The investigations of Shaposhnikov had considerable significance for
organization and improvement of a number of industrial processes, which were based on the action of microorganisms.
His studies of the physiology of lactic bacteria allowed him to
work out an industrial scheme for producing lactic acid (the so-
called protein method); investigations of butyric and acetic acid
bacteria also led to the improvement of corresponding processes. In 1929 Shaposhnikov undertook the study of acetone-butyl
fermentation, at first in the laboratory and subsequently under
semi-plant conditions. The process data obtained were used
in planning and construction of the first U.S.S.R. Acetone-butyl
plant. His work on the mobility of sap in plants found a practical application in a new method of tapping pines.
Bibliography:
and others. New Tapping of the Pine Tree. Moscow: 1937.
On the significance of physiological signs in the systematics
of microorganisms. Mikrobiologiya, 1942, #1-2, 1-14; 1944,
#1, 1-22.

Technical Microbiology. Moscow: 1948.
Biography:
  Academician Vladimir Nikolaevich Shaposhnikov (On the 70th
  Anniversary since the date of birth). Mikrobiologiya, 1954,
  <u>23</u>, #2.
  Celebration in Honor of Academician V. N. Shaposhnikov.
  Vestnik Akad. Nauk S.S.S.R., 1954, #6.
Office: Moscow University
              Moscow, USSR
Residence: Leninskiye gory, sekt. "K"
              Moscow, USSR
Telephone: V9 23 91

SHCHEGLYAEV, ANDREI VLADIMIROVICH (Heat Engineer)

A. V. Shcheglyaev was born October 20, 1902. After gradu-
ating from Moscow Technical College in 1926, he taught there.
In 1924 he began working at the All-Union Heat Engineering
Scientific Research Institute. He joined the teaching staff of
Moscow Institute of Energetics in 1930 and in 1948 became pro-
fessor. Since 1953 he has been a Corresponding Member of the
U.S.S.R. Academy of Sciences. In 1948 and in 1952 he received
Stalin Prizes.
    Shcheglyaev studied heat processes of steam turbines and
their regulation systems in the testing of turbines. He partici-
pated in developing new systems of regulating turbines.
    In October 1962 Shcheglyaev was awarded the Red Banner of
Labor.
Bibliography:
  Steam Turbines, 3rd ed. Moscow-Leningrad: 1955.
  and N. G. Morozov. Testing of Steam Turbines. Moscow-
  Leningrad: 1937.
  Some Problems of Exploiting Steam Turbines. Moscow-
  Leningrad: 1947.
  Regulating Steam Turbines. Moscow-Leningrad: 1938.
Office: Moscow Institute of Energetics
              Moscow, USSR

SHCHELKIN, KIRILL IVANOVICH (Physicist)

K. I. Shchelkin was born May 17, 1911. He graduated from
the Pedagogical Institute in Simferopol' in 1932 and began to
work at the Institute of Chemical Physics of the U.S.S.R. Academy of Sciences. He has been a member of the Communist Party
of the Soviet Union since 1940. In 1953 he was elected a Corresponding Member of the U.S.S.R. Academy of Sciences.

Shchelkin made a considerable contribution to the development of gas dynamics of burning. He experimentally proved the presence of a considerable influence of turbulent flow in an initial mixture on flame acceleration and developed conditions for the transfer of slow burning into detonation. Shchelkin investigated burning in a turbulent flow. He studied spin denotation and the proposed theory for this phenomenon.

Bibliography:
On the theory of the origin of detonation in gas mixtures in pipes. Doklady Akad. Nauk S.S.S.R., 1939, 23, #7.
On the theory of detonation spin. Doklady Akad. Nauk S.S.S.R., 1945, 47, #7.
and Ya. B. Zel'dovich. Application of the theory of spreading of an arbitrary explosion in some cases of ignition of gases. Zhur. Eksptl. i Teoret. Fiz., 1940, 10, #5.
Influence of roughness of a pipe on the origin and spreading of a detonation in gases. Zhur. Eksptl. i Teoret. Fiz., 1940, 10, #7.
On transfer of slow burning into a detonation. Zhur. Eksptl. i Teoret. Fiz., 1953, 24, #5.
Detonation process. Vestnik Akad. Nauk #2, 12-20 (1960).
Office: Institute of Chemical Physics of USSR Academy of
              Sciences
              Vorob'evskoye Shosse 2
              Moscow, USSR

SHCHERBAKOV, DMITRII IVANOVICH (Geologist)

D. I. Shcherbakov was born January 13, 1893. After graduating in 1922 from Simferopol' University, he worked in institutions of the U.S.S.R. Academy of Sciences. He was a student of V. I. Vernadskii and A. E. Fersman, Russian geochemists. He also taught at Leningrad University, beginning in 1922 and from 1928 to 1932 at the Leningrad Polytechnic Institute. From 1939 to 1954, Shcherbakov was at the Institute of Geological Sciences of the U.S.S.R. Academy of Sciences. In 1953 he became Academic Secretary of the Department of Geological and Geographic Sciences of the U.S.S.R. Academy of Sciences. He was elected a Corresponding Member of the U.S.S.R. Academy of Sciences in 1946 and in 1953 an Academician.

Shcherbakov's main works are devoted to geology and geochemistry of rare metals and radioactive elements. He participated as a student in radium expeditions of the Academy of Sciences (from 1914). Later he participated in the Pamir Expedition (1928), in the Tadzhik-Pamir Expedition (until

1936) and also in expeditions on territories beyond the Baikal,
Kazakhstan, Crimea, Karelia, Central Urals, Kol'skii Peninsula
and other regions.   In 1927 Shcherbakov became acquainted
with some deposits of Central Europe and Sicily. In 1956 he
was the head of a U.S.S.R. delegation at the 20th Session of the
International Geological Congress in Mexico. Shcherbakov used
a comprehensive geochemical approach to study the distribution
of rare element deposits. He also studied the geology of Central Asia. Shcherbakov has also been active in popularizing
geology.
    As of 1961 Shcherbakov was Chairman of the Antarctic Com-
mission of the U.S.S.R. Academy of Sciences.
    In January 1961, he visited the United States to participate
in National Academy of Sciences conferences and meetings at
Stanford University, California.
Bibliography:
    The meaning of determination of the age of intrustions for
    practical geology. Works of the 1st Session of the Com-
    mission on Determination of the Absolute Age of Rocks
    (April 12-15, 1952), Moscow, 1954, 203-211.
    On survey maps for magmatogenic ore deposits. Izvest.
    Akad. Nauk S.S.S.R., Ser. Geol., 1952, #4, 9-15.
    High temperature ore formations of central caucasus.
    Questions of Mineralogy, Geochemistry and Petrography.
    Moscow-Leningrad: 1946, 219-27.
    Principles and methodology in compiling metallogenic maps.
    Soviet Geology, 1955, #5, 53-64.
    Source of raw materials of U.S.S.R. rare metals. Rare
    Metals, 1938, #1, 14-24.
    Genetic types of tin ore manifestation in Central Asia.
    Scientific Summaries of Works of the Tadzhik-Pamire Expe-
    dition. Moscow-Leningrad: 1936, 477-507.
Office: Joint Antarctic Commission of USSR Academy of
              Sciences
              Leninskii Prospekt, 14
              Moscow, USSR
Residence: n. Yakimanka, 3
              Moscow, USSR
Telephone: V3 24 52

SHCHUKIN, ALEKSANDR NIKOLAEVICH (Radioengineer)
    A. N. Shchukin was born July 22, 1900. In 1927 he graduated
from the Leningrad Electrotechnical Institute. He taught there
from 1929 to 1941 and in 1939 was made a professor. At about

the same time, 1933 to 1945, he was also teaching at the Leningrad Military-Naval Academy. He worked in several research institutions including the Leningrad Electrophysical Institute and the Central Radio Laboratory of a Trust for Low Voltage Plants. Shchukin has been a Major General in the Engineering-Technical Service. He became a member of the Communist Party of the Soviet Union in 1944. In 1946 he was elected a Corresponding Member of the U.S.S.R. Academy of Sciences and in 1953 an Academician.

Shchukin's main work is in the propagation of short waves and in short wave communication at great distances in two-way radiotelegraph broadcasting without power losses and methods of controlling pulse distortions, the study of non-stationary processes in resonance and band amplifiers.

Bibliography:
Propagation of Radiowaves (textbook), 1940.
Non-stationary processes in resonance and bank amplifiers. Izvest. Akad. Nauk S.S.S.R., Ser. Fiz., 1946, 10, #1.
Method of controlling impulse distortion to radio reception. Izvest. Akad. Nauk S.S.S.R., Ser. Fiz., 1946, 10, #1.

Biography:
A. N. Shchukin. Radio, 1947, #4.
F. Chestnov. In the World of Radio. Moscow: 1954.

Office: USSR Academy of Sciences
Leninskii Prospekt, 14
Moscow, USSR

Residence: Alekseeskogo studgorodka 3ii pr. 31
Moscow, USSR

Telephone: I3 07 74

SHEMYAKIN, MIKHAIL MIKHAILOVICH (Organic Chemist)

M. M. Shemyakin was born July 26, 1908. After graduating from Moscow University in 1930, he worked at the Scientific Research Institute of Organic Intermediates and Dyes until 1935. From 1930 to 1937 he was also at the Moscow Institute of Fine Chemical Technology and from 1935 to 1945 at the All-Union Institute of Experimental Medium. Shemyakin was made professor, in 1942, at the Moscow Textile Institute where he had been working since 1937. In 1945 he began work at the Institute of Biological and Medical Chemistry of the U.S.S.R. Academy of Sciences and in 1958 at the Institute of Organic Chemistry of the U.S.S.R. Academy of Sciences. He became a member of the Communist Party of the Soviet Union in 1951.

In 1953 he was elected a Corresponding Member of the U.S.S.R.
Academy of Sciences and in 1958 an Academician.

As of 1961 Shemyakin was Director of the Institute of Chemistry of Natural Compounds.

In May 1960, Shemyakin visited the United States on an exchange program at the California Institute of Technology.

Bibliography:
and A. S. Khokhlov. Chemistry of Antibiotic Substances, 2nd
ed. Moscow-Leningrad: 1953.

and L. A. Shchukina. Oxidizing-hydrolytic transformations
of organic compounds. Uspekhi Khim., 1957, <u>26</u>, #5.

and others. Chemistry of Antibiotics. <u>1-2</u>. Moscow: 1961.

Office: Institute of Natural Compounds of USSR Academy
              of Sciences
              1-y Akademicheskii Proyezd, 18
              Moscow, USSR

Residence: ul. Semashko, 5
              Moscow, USSR

Telephone: B8 31 72

SHEVYAKOV, LEV DMITRIEVICH (Mining Specialist)

L. D. Shevyakov was born January 15, 1889 in Vetluga in the
former Kostroma province. He received his secondary education at the Nizhnii-Novgorod gymnasium, and his higher education at the Ekaterinoslav (now Dnepropetrovsk) Mining Institute, from which he graduated in 1912 as a mining engineer.
The mining graduation project on which he worked as a student
was awarded the Kublin Prize, and his project on metallurgical
mechanics was given an honorable mention. Following one year
of work at the Donbas mines, he was enrolled as an assistant
in the mining faculty of the Ekaterinoslav Institute, and in 1916,
he was appointed a docent at the same faculty. After defending
his dissertation in 1919 on the subject "Discovery of Hard Coal
Deposits," he was awarded the degree of Mining Assistant (adjunct) and, in 1920, he was appointed professor in the mining
faculty.

Shevyakov served during his graduate work and after, until
1928, as professor and director of the mining faculty of the
Ekaterinoslav Mining Institute. In 1920-1922, he served with
B. I. Bokii, A. M. Terpigorev, A. A. Skochinskii, and V. A.
Guskov as a member of a Special Commission charged with the
restoration of the Donbas hard coal and anthracite industry.
After being sent on a mission by the VSNKh SSR (Supreme Council of the National Economy of the USSR) to Germany, U. S. A.,

England, and Scotland in 1925, he published a number of articles describing the status and trends of the development of the foreign mining industries. From 1929 to 1932, he served as professor at the Tomsk Technological Institute; from 1932 to 1944, as professor on the mining faculty at the Sverdlovsk Mining Institute, and from 1944 to 1950, as professor and director of the faculty for the mining of blanket deposits at the Stalin Moscow Mining Institute.

During these years, he served as permanent consultant and mining expert for numerous design establishments, main administrations, and individual mining enterprises, such as Donugol, Yugostal (Southern Steel Industry Trust), Soletrest, Kuzbasugol (State Association of the Hard Coal Industry of the Kuznetsk and Minusink Basins), Uralugol, Giproshakht (State Institute for the Design of Mine Construction in the Hard Coal Industry) and its Siberian affiliate, Gipromedruda (State Institute for the Design and Planning of Copper Mining Establishments). During the restoration of the Donbas, he was in charge of a design group in Dnepropetrovsk, which conducted numerous designs of mines in the Donets Basin. He was directly concerned with the development of design projects for high-capacity mines in the Kuznetsk Basin, and he acted as consultant in working out design projects for coal mines in many regions of Siberia.

The Ural affiliate of the Academy, which served the varied economy and industry of the Urals, expanded its scientific activities under his direction. During World War II, Shevyakov conducted extensive work in the Commission for mobilizing the resources of the Ural region, Western Siberia, and Kazakhstan to serve defense requirements. In 1942, Shevyakov, with A. A. Skochinskii, worked to restore the Donets and Moscow Basins destroyed by the Germans. In January 1942, he worked in the town of Karpinsk, where he determined the possibility of expanding coal production from the Bogoslovsk deposits in the Urals. In May 1942, he worked at the Ural Aluminum Plant in connection with the expansion of Bauxite production in Kamensk Region; in June-July 1942, he was in Kazakhstan where he increased coal production, ore production, and the smelting of metals. In September 1942, he worked in Korkino and Kopeysk where he served as consultant on a number of technical problems concerning the development of coal extraction by the open pit method.

In February-March of 1943, he was a member of the commission entrusted with the determination of the status of the available ore reserves supplying the Kuznetsk metallurgical plants, the determination of the production capacities of mines in the Kuznetsk Basin, and the improvement of power facilities in industrial centers of Western Siberia. In August-September of 1943, he was engaged in similar work in Krarganda. He worked in the Commission of the Peoples' Commissariat for the Coal Industry, which was charged with the establishment of rational systems for the extraction of the rich coal beds located at the Prokopyevsk-Kisel region of the Kuznetsk Basin, as well as the increased production of coking coal in the Osinovsk region. Almost immediately after the Mining Institute moved back to Moscow, Shevyakov worked there in establishments subordinate to the U.S.S.R. Academy of Sciences.

During the past 20 years, he was a member of the Presidiums of Technical Councils in the Ministry of the Coal Industry, the Ministry for the Building of Coal Enterprises, the Ministry of Nonferrous Metallurgy, and frequently served as the chairman of expert commissions to study important coal and ore mining technical problems.

In 1943, he was appointed a member, and in 1946, director of the Council for Scientific and Technical Consultation under the Gosplan (State Planning Commission of the USSR), which discussed the most important problems concerning the regional distribution and development of industry. From 1947 to 1957, he was a member of the Gosplan of the U.S.S.R. He has actively participated in All-Union Conferences, and works for close contacts between Soviet mining scientists and personnel employed in industry and in design and training institutes located in outlying districts. He is an active member of the All-Union Society for the Dissemination of Political and Scientific Knowledge. From 1947 to 1950, he served as a delegate of the Second Moscow City Council of Workers' Deputies; for many years, he was elected a member of the Orgbyuro (Organization Bureau) of the All-Union Scientific-Technical Mining Society. From 1941 to 1944, he served as president of the Orgbyuro of this society, and from 1953 to 1955, he acted as director of the section for underground mining of coal deposits.

Shevyakov is a member of the editorial boards of the following scientific-technical journals: Izvestia An SSSR, Otdelenie tecknicheskikh nauk (Bulletin of the USSR Academy of Sciences, Division of Technical Sciences), Ugol (Coal), Gornii Zhurnal (Mining Journal), Byulleten ITEIN (Bulletin of the Institute of Technical and Economic Information); he is also a member of the editorial council of Ugletekhizdat (State Scientific and Technical Publishing House of Literature on the Coal Industry).

He has frequently served as president of juries for All-Union contests involving the best design project of mining systems adapted to various conditions of complex mechanized equipment used on mine surfaces. He also constantly takes part in the examination and evaluation of projects submitted in competition for Lenin prizes, acting in the capacity of president of the mining and metallurgical section, and as a member of the Committee.

In 1939, he was elected an Academician of the U.S.S.R. Academy of Sciences, appointed Deputy Director of the Ural affiliate of it, and Director of the Mining and Geological Institute of the affiliate. In 1941, he was elected a member of the Bureau of the Section of Geological and Geographic Sciences, and served in this capacity until 1945. In 1942, he was awarded a Stalin Prize for participation in a study entitled "On the Development of the National Economy of the Urals Under Wartime Conditions," and, in 1943, together with workers in the coal industry, he was awarded the Order of the Red Banner of Labor for fulfilling government assignments calling for increased coal production under wartime conditions. He received a badge honoring him as an "Outstanding Worker" in socialist competition sponsored by the Peoples' Commissariat of the Coal Industry. In 1945, Shevyakov was awarded a second order of the Red Banner of Labor; in 1948, he was awarded the Order of Lenin and medals "For the Restoration of the Donbas" and "In Commemoration of Moscow's 800th Anniversary." In June 1956, he was awarded the title of honorary member of the Mining Society and in 1957, he received the badge, "Coal Miner's Glory," first degree as a reward for his activities aimed at the development of mining science and technology.

Shevyakov was awarded several prizes by the Presidium of the U.S.S.R. Academy of Sciences for his studies entitled, "Search for New Highly Productive Methods for Underground Mining of Rich Deposits of Hard Ores" (1956), and "Scientific Foundations of New Technical Equipment Used to Promote the Further Development of the Production of Coal, Ores and Other Minerals by the Open Pit Method" (1957).

The work of Shevyakov is concerned with problems of mine production and design, coal and ore mining for high production and efficiency, various problems presented by local mining situations, such as the Kursk magnetic anomaly.

Bibliography:
   Collected Articles on Mining.
   Analytical and Computation Articles.
   Mining Mineral Deposits.
   Mining Water Drains.
   Fundamentals of the Theory Involving the Planning of Coal
   Mines.
   Mechanization of Mining Operations.
   Bracing of Open Pit Mines.
   Sinking of Open Pit Mines.
   Miner's Library.
Biography:
   Lev Dmitrievich Shevyakov, Professor and Doctor of Techni-
   cal Sciences. Ugol, 1939, #3.
   A. A. Zvorikin. Academy of Sciences of the U.S.S.R. and the
   Development of Russian Mining Sciences. Ugol, 1945, #7-8.
   Lev Dmitrievich Shevyakov, Academician (To the 60th Anni-
   versary since the date of birth). Ugol, 1949, #1.
Office: USSR Academy of Sciences
               Leninskii Prospekt
               Moscow, USSR

SHIRKOV, DMITRII VASIL'EVICH (Theoretical Physicist)

D. V. Shirkov was born in 1928. In 1949 he graduated from
Moscow State University. From 1956 to 1960 he worked in the
Joint Institute of Nuclear Research, and in 1960 took a po-
sition at the Mathematics Institute of the U.S.S.R. Academy of
Sciences Siberian Branch. Shirkov was awarded the Doctor of
Physico-Mathematical Sciences degree in 1957. Since 1953 he
has been a member of the Communist Party of the Soviet Union.
He was elected, in 1960, a Corresponding Member of the
U.S.S.R. Academy of Sciences.
   Shirkov's principal work is in the field of the theory of
elementary particles.
Bibliography:
   Calculation of coulomb effects in the theory of surface con-
   ductivity. Zhur. Exptl. i Teor. Fiz. $\underline{37}$, #1, 179-186 (1959).
   The compensation equation in superconductivity theory. Zh.
   Ekspr. Teor. Fiz. $\underline{36}$, #2, 607-12 (1959). Phys. Sci. Abstr.
   $\underline{62}$, 9661 (1959).
   and M. E. Maier. On the two dimensional Thirring model.
   Doklady Akad. Nauk S.S.S.R. $\underline{122}$, #1, 45-7 (1958). Phys.
   Sci. Abstr. $\underline{62}$, 7791 (1959).

and N. N. Bogolyubov, A. A. Logunov. The method of dispersion relations and perturbation theory. Zh. Eksper. Teor. Fiz. 37, #3 (9), 805-15 (1959). Phys. Sci. Abstr. 63, 9258 (1960). Soviet Physics-JETP (New York), 37 (10), #3, 574-81 (1960).

and A. V. Efremov, V. A. Meshcheryakov. Pion-nucleon scattering at low energies. I. Zh. Eksper. Teor. Fiz. 39, #2 (8), 438-49 (1960). Phys. Sci. Abstr. 63, 20202 (1960).

and N. N. Bogolyubov. Certain problems of the quantum field theory. Trudy Tret'ego Vsesouyznogo, Matematicheskogo S'ezda, III, 5, 14-21 1956. Nucl. Sci. Abstr. 14, 4871 (1960).

and N. N. Bogolyubov. Introduction to the Theory of Quantized Fields. Translation Interscience Publishers, Inc. New York: 1959, 734 p. Nucl. Sci. Abstr. 14, 5982 (1960).

and N. N. Bogolyubov, V. V. Talmachev. A New Method in the Theory of Superconductivity Translation. Consultants Bureau, Inc., New York: 1959, 124 p. Nucl. Sci. Abstr. 14, 4870 (1960).

and I. F. Ginzburg. Asymptotic behavior of higher Green functions. Nauch. Doklady Vysshei Shkoly Fiz. Mat. Nauki #2, 143-51 (1959). Nucl. Sci. Abstr. 14, 3881 (1960).

and A. V. Efremov, V. A. Meshcheryakov. Equations for the low-energy meson-nucleon scattering. 1960. 18 p. CD-503. Nucl. Sci. Abstr. 14, 16174 (1960).

Office: Mathematics Institute of Siberian Branch of USSR
              Academy of Sciences
              Novosibirsk, Siberia

SHOSTAKOVSKII, MIKHAIL FEDOROVICH (Organic Chemist)

M. F. Shostakovskii was born in 1905. In 1929 he graduated from Irkutsk State University. From 1935 to 1938 he was a senior scientific worker at the U.S.S.R. Academy of Sciences Institute of Organic Chemistry. In 1939 he was appointed Chief of the Laboratory on Vinyl Compounds, and in 1957 became Director of the Irkutsk Institute of Organic Chemistry of the U.S.S.R. Academy of Sciences Siberian Branch. Since 1946 he has been a member of the Communist Party of the Soviet Union. He was elected, in 1960, a Corresponding Member of the U.S.S.R. Academy of Sciences. He has been awarded a Stalin Prize.

Shostakovskii developed a therapeutic balsam of polyvinyl pyrrolidon which is used as a blood substitute.

347   SHOSTAKOVSKII

Bibliography:

and Ye. P. Gracheva, N. K. Kul'bovskaya. Methods for synthesizing, and properties of substituted simple vinyl esters and substituted vinyl sulfides. Uspekhi Khim., #4, 493-516 (1961).

and A. V. Bogdanov, A. N. Volkov. Vinyl compounds in diene synthesis. Diene synthesis of simple vinyl esters and thioesters with anthracene. Izvest. Akad. Nauk S.S.S.R. Otdel. Khim. Nauk 11, 2072-75 (1961).

and A. M. Khomutov, I. A. Chekulaeva, N. M. Khomutora. Synthesis and polymerization of dialkyl tartrates. Izvest. Akad. Nauk S.S.S.R. Otdel. Khim. Nauk 11, 2075 (1961).

and P. P. Shorygin, E. N. Prilezhaeva, T. N. Shkurina, L. G. Stolyarova, A. P. Genich. Structure and spectra of vinyl sulfides. Izvest. Akad. Nauk S.S.S.R. Otdel. Khim. Nauk, #9, 157-77 (1961).

and D. N. Shigorin, V. I. Smirnova, G. S. Zhuravleva, Ye. P. Gracheva. E.P.R. Spectra of γ-irradiated acetylene and its derivatives. Doklady Akad. Nauk S.S.S.R. 140, #2, 419-22 (1961).

and N. V. Komarov, Yu. V. Maroshin. Synthesis and certain conversions of silanes of the vinyl acetylene series. Doklady Akad. Nauk S.S.S.R. 139, #4, 913-915 (1961).

and E. N. Prilezhaeva, L. V. Tsymbal. The comparative dienophyl reactability in a vinyl sulfide-vinyl sulfoxide-vinyl sulfone series. Doklady Akad. Nauk S.S.S.R. 138, #5, 1122-25 (1961).

and A. V. Bogdanova, G. M. Plotnikova. Stereo-directed syntheses on a diacetylene lease, and isomeric conversions of 1,4-bis(arylthio) butadienes-1,3 and their disulfides. Doklady Akad. Nauk S.S.S.R. 136, #3, 595-98 (1961).

and N. V. Komarov, V. B. Pukhnarevich. Synthesis and some conversions of secondary γ-silicon-containing acetyl alcohols. Doklady Akad. Nauk 136, #4, 846-48 (1961).

and I. A. Chekulaeva, L. V. Kondrat'eva. Reactability of nitrogen containing ethyl-vinyl compounds. Doklady Akad. Nauk S.S.S.R. 146, #2, 376-79 (1962).

and E. N. Prilezhaeva, A. V. Sviridova. Polymerization of vinyl ethyl sulfane under the effect of free radical initiators. Doklady Akad. Nauk S.S.S.R. 146, #4, 837 (1962).

Office: Institute of Organic Chemistry of Siberian Branch of USSR Academy of Sciences
Irkutsk, Siberia

SHTERN, LINA SOLOMONOVNA (Physiologist)

L. S. Shtern was born August 26, 1878 in Libava (Latvian S.S.R.). After graduating in 1903 from the University of Geneva, she remained there to work and in 1917 became a professor. In 1925 she moved to the U.S.S.R. and from 1925 to 1949 was professor at the Second Moscow Medical Institute (until 1930 the Medical Department of the Second Moscow University). About the same time, 1929-1949, she was also Director of the Institute of Physiology. In 1954 Shtern started working at the Institute of Biological Physics of the U.S.S.R. Academy of Sciences. She has been a member of the Communist Party of the Soviet Union since 1938. She is an Academician of the Ukrainian S.S.R. Academy of Sciences and in 1939 was elected Academician of the U.S.S.R. Academy of Sciences and in 1944 a member of the U.S.S.R. Academy of Medical Sciences. She was an Honored Scientist of the R.S.F.S.R. in 1934, and in 1954 she was a recipient of a Stalin Prize.

Shtern studied the chemical basis of physiological processes. Jointly with the Swiss scientist, F. Batteli, she investigated the respiration of isolated tissues and elucidated the role of various catalysts (in particular the catalase system) in biological oxidation. Shtern and her associates studied the hemato-encephalitic (blood-marrow) barrier which regulates the formation and the composition of cerebrospinal liquid.

Bibliography:

and others. Hematoencephalitic barrier. Collection of Works. Moscow-Leningrad: 1935.

Histohematic barriers, Regulators of the Direct Medium of the Organs. Moscow-Leningrad: 1938 (Works of the Institute of Physiology, 3).

Role of metabolites in regulating the functions of an organism, Regulators of the Direct Medium of the Organs. Moscow-Leningrad: 1938 (Works of the Institute of Physiology, 3, 238-249).

Direct nutritive medium of the organs and tissues and its regulating factors, Direct Medium of Organs and Tissues. Moscow-Leningrad: 1947 (Works of the Institute of Physiology, 4).

Active interference in physiological processes, Direct Medium of Organs and Tissues. Moscow-Leningrad: 1947 (Works of the Institute of Physiology, 4, 403-415).

Role of metabolites in the regulation of the functions of an
organism, Direct Medium of Organs and Tissues. Moscow-
Leningrad: 1947 (Works of the Institute of Physiology, 4,
238-249).
Biography:
  L. S. Shtern. Problems of Biology and Medicine. Collection
  Devoted to the 30th Anniversary of the Scientific, Pedagogi-
  cal and Social Activity of Honored Scientist Lina Solomonovna
  Shtern. Moscow-Leningrad: 1935.
Office: Institute of Biological Physics of USSR Academy of
              Sciences
              Leninskii Prospekt, 33
              Moscow, USSR
Residence: Dorogomilovskaya nab. 3
              Moscow, USSR
Telephone: G3 44 04

SHUBNIKOV, ALEKSEI VASIL'EVICH (Crystallographer)

  A. B. Shubnikov was born March 29, 1887. After graduating
from Moscow University in 1912 he did research and taught at
the People's University of Shanyanvskii in Moscow as assistant
to G. V. Vul'f (1863-1925, specialist in crystallography). From
1920 to 1925 he was visiting professor at the Urals Mining
Institute in Ekaterinburg (now Sverdlovsk). He has been with
the U.S.S.R. Academy of Sciences since 1925. In 1937 he was
made Chief of the Laboratory of Crystallography and in 1944,
Director of the Institute of Crystallography which he helped
found. Also, in 1953 he became a professor at Moscow University. He was elected a Corresponding Member of the Academy of Sciences in 1933, and in 1953 Academician. Shubnikov
was a member of the All-Union Mineralogical Society (1919),
honorary member of the British Mineralogical Society (1945),
and honorary member of the French Mineralogical Society
(1947). In 1946 and 1950 he was awarded Stalin Prizes, and in
1962 the Red Banner of Labor.
  Shubnikov's areas of research are growth of crystals, electric and optical properties of crystals, study of symmetry
(piezo-electric properties of crystals, methodics of cutting,
processing and polishing crystals).
  In 1962 Shubnikov was relieved of his position as Director of
the Institute of Crystallography.
Bibliography:
  How Crystals Grow. Moscow-Leningrad: 1935.
  Quartz and Its Application. Moscow-Leningrad: 1940.

and E. E. Flint, G. B. Bokii. Fundamentals of Crystallography. Moscow-Leningrad: 1940.
Symmetry. Moscow-Leningrad: 1940.
Piezo-Electric Textures. Moscow-Leningrad: 1946.
Optical Crystallography. Moscow-Leningrad: 1950.
Symmetry and Anti-Symmetry of Finite Figures. Moscow-Leningrad: 1951.
and others. Investigating Piezo-Electric Textures. Moscow-Leningrad: 1955.
Crystals in Science and Technology. Moscow: 1956.
and N. N. Sheftal', eds. Soveschanie po rostu kristallov.
2d, Moscow, 1959. Growth of crystals, v. 3; reports of 2d
Conf. on Crystal Growth, Moscow, Mar. 23-Apr. 1, 1959.
Translation from Russian. New York, Consultants Bureau, 1962. 357 p.

Office: Institute of Crystallography of USSR Academy of Sciences
Pyzhevskii Pereulok, 3
Moscow, USSR
Residence: pl. Vosstaniya, 1
Moscow, USSR
Telephone: D5 42 20

SHUIKIN, NIKOLAI IVANOVICH (Organic Chemist)
N. I. Shuikin was born March 30, 1898. He was a student of
N. D. Zelinskii (1861-1953, Russian catalytic chemist). In 1927
he graduated from Moscow University where he worked from
1930 and became a professor in 1943. In 1937 he began working
at the Institute of Organic Chemistry of the U.S.S.R. Academy
of Sciences. Shuikin has been a member of the Communist
Party of the Soviet Union since 1942. In 1953 he was elected a
Corresponding Member of the U.S.S.R. Academy of Sciences.

Shuikin has studied the preparation of catalysts for dehydrogenation of six and five membered cyclanes and alkanes. A
number of these catalysts are used for the production of aromatic hydrocarbons. He studied the hydrogenation and hydrogenolysis of the furan nucleus.

Bibliography:
Obtaining aromatic hydrocarbons from oil by the contact-catalysis. Uspekhi Khim., 1946, 15, #3.
and A. A. Balandin. Mechanism and Kinetics of a Heterogeneous Catalysis in Organic Chemistry. Moscow: 1955.

Transformation of hydrocarbons on oxide metal catalysts at
raised temperatures and pressures of hydrogen, Moscow,
1955 (Report at the IV International Oil Congress in Rome).
and N. F. Belskii. L'hydrogenolyse catalytique dans la serie
des composes Furanniques. Bulletin de Societe chimique de
France, 1956, #11-12, 1556-1634.

Office: N. D. Zelinskii Institute of Organic Chemistry of
              USSR Academy of Sciences
              Leninskii Prospekt, 31
              Moscow, USSR
Residence: 1-aya Cheremushkinskaya, 3
              Moscow, USSR
Telephone: B7 43 32

SHULEIKIN, VASILII VLADIMIROVICH (Geophysicist)

V. V. Shuleikin was born January 13, 1895. He initiated the
organization of the Black Sea Hydrophysical Station in the
Crimea in 1929, a marine hydrophysical laboratory in 1935, a
Department of Marine Physics at Moscow University in 1945, and
a sea laboratory of the Moscow Hydrometeorological Institute
in 1930. Shuleikin became a member of the Communist Party
of the Soviet Union in 1942. In 1929 he was elected a Corresponding Member and in 1946 an Academician of the U.S.S.R.
Academy of Sciences. The All-Union Geographic Society awarded him a medal of P.P. Semyonov-Tyan-Shanskii. And in 1942
he received a Stalin Prize.

Shuleikin's investigations are devoted to the physics of the
sea. He presented a theory on the heat balance of the sea, thus
allowing prediction of the presence of a deep warm current in
the Karsk Sea. He proposed a theory on heat interaction between the ocean, atmosphere, and land, and investigated
the oscillating phenomena in this system and the increase in
wind speeds against sharp-edged capes. On the basis of new
experimental data, he advanced a theory on sea waves. He explained the origin of sea and lake coloring. He obtained an
equation of a spectral curve of the sea and worked on other aspects of sea optics. He invented a series of devices for investigating the sea. He participated in several oceanic and sea
expeditions and was the head of a number of them.

Bibliography:
    The Physics of the Sea, 3rd ed. Moscow: 1953.
    Outline of the Physics of the Sea. Moscow-Leningrad: 1949.
    Theory on Sea Waves. Moscow: 1956.

Biography:
Russian Seafarers. Moscow: 1953, 574.
Office: Moscow University
                Moscow, USSR
Residence: ul. Vorovskogo 33/35
                Moscow, USSR
Telephone: D2 04 05

SHVETSOV, PYOTR FILIMONOVICH (Geologist)
P. F. Shvetsov was born January 27, 1910. After graduating
from Moscow Geological Survey Institute in 1935, he worked in
the Main Directorate of the Northern Seaway. In 1939 he began
working at the Institute of Permafrost of the U.S.S.R. Academy
of Sciences (1941-1945 he served in the Soviet Army). In 1948
he was made deputy Director and in 1956 Director of this
Institute. Shvetsov has been a member of the Communist Party
of the Soviet Union since 1940. In 1953 he was elected a Corresponding Member of the U.S.S.R. Academy of Sciences. He received in 1952 a Stalin Prize.
     Shvetsov's main works are devoted to the study of the regu-
larities in formation of underground water in regions of per-
petually frozen ground.
Bibliography:
Permafrost and Geological Engineering Conditions of the
Anadyr' Region. Leningrad: 1938.
and V. P. Sedov. Gigantic Icing and Underground Waters of
the Ridge of Tas-Khayatakh. Moscow-Leningrad: 1941.
Introductory Chapters to the Basis of Geocryology. Moscow:
1955. (Materials for basis in study of frozen zones of the
earth's crust), #1.
Office: V. A. Obruchev Institute of Permafrost of USSR
                Academy of Sciences
                Bol'shoy Cherkasskiy Pereulok 2/10
                Moscow, USSR
Residence: ul. Chkalova 39/41
                Moscow, USSR
Telephone: B7 19 15

SIDORENKO, ALEKSANDR VASIL'EVICH (Geologist)
A. V. Sidorenko was born October 19, 1917. He graduated
in 1940 from Veronezh University. In 1943-1950 he worked in
the Turkman branch of the U.S.S.R. Academy of Sciences. He
began working at the Kol'skii branch of the U.S.S.R. Academy
of Sciences in 1950 and in 1952 was elected Chairman of the

Presidium. Sidorenko has been a member of the Communist Party of the Soviet Union from 1942. In 1953 he was elected a Corresponding Member of the U.S.S.R. Academy of Sciences.

Sidorenko has studied the geomorphology and geology of the structure of deserts, processes of mineral formation in conditions of desert climate, and phenomena of hypergenesis. He also investigated phosphorous minerals and mineralogy of veined deposits of the Turkman S.S.R.

Bibliography:

Main characteristics of mineral formation in deserts. Questions of Mineralogy of Sedimentary Formations. Book 3-4. L'vov: 1956.

Eolian differentiation of substance in deserts. Izvest. Akad. Nauk S.S.S.R., Ser. Geogr., 1956, #3.

Experiment in separating continental rock masses of Kara-Kumy on the composition of gravel pebbled particles. Questions of the Geology of Asia, 2, Moscow: 1955.

Office: Presidium of the S. M. Kirov Kol'skii Branch of
              USSR Academy of Sciences
              Kirovsk, Murmansk Oblast', USSR

SIFOROV, VLADIMIR IVANOVICH (Radio Engineer)

V. I. Siforov was born May 31, 1904. He graduated in 1929 from the Leningrad Electro-Technical Institute and taught there in 1930-1941 and in 1946-1953; in 1938 he was made professor. From 1928-1941 he worked in the Central Radio Laboratory in Leningrad. He taught in 1941-1952 at the Leningrad Military Air Engineering Academy. In 1953 Siforov began working at the Scientific Research Institute of Communication and in 1955 at the Institute of Radiotechnics and Electronics of the U.S.S.R. Academy of Sciences. He has been a member of the Communist Party of the Soviet Union since 1941. In 1953 he was elected a Corresponding Member of the U.S.S.R. Academy of Sciences.

Siforov has worked on the theory, calculation, and design of radio receiving devices and amplifiers. He is the author of a widely known text "Receiving Devices" (1939, 5th edition, 1954).

Bibliography:

Resonant Amplifiers. Theory and Calculation. Leningrad: 1932.

Bandpass Amplifiers. Theory and Calculation. Leningrad-Moscow: 1936.

High-Frequency Amplifiers (Theory and Calculation). Moscow-Leningrad: 1939.

Ultra Short-Wave Receivers for Impulse Signals. Moscow: 1947.

and others. Theory of Impulse Radio Communication. Leningrad: 1951.

Receiving Devices. 5th Ed., 1954.

Receivers of Ultra-High Frequencies. 2nd ed. Moscow: 1957.

Office: Institute of Radiotechnics and Electronics of USSR
Academy of Sciences
Mokhovaya Ulitsa 11, K-9
Moscow, USSR
Residence: Chistoprudniy bulv. 2
Moscow, USSR
Telephone: K5 71 37

SISAKYAN, NORAIR MARTIROSOVICH (Biochemist)

N. M. Sisakyan was born January 25, 1907. He graduated from the K. A. Timiryazev Agricultural Academy, Moscow, in 1932, and in 1939 began working at the Institute of Biochemistry of the U.S.S.R. Academy of Sciences. Since 1937 he has been a member of the Communist Party of the Soviet Union. He was elected Corresponding Member of the Armenian S.S.R. Academy of Sciences in 1945, Corresponding Member of the U.S.S.R. Academy of Sciences in 1953, and in 1960 Academician. He was acting Academician Secretary of the U.S.S.R. Academy of Sciences 1958-60 and has been Academy Secretary for the division of biological sciences since 1960. Also he has been Chairman of the Soviet delegation to UNESCO. In 1949, the U.S.S.R. Academy of Sciences awarded him the A. N. Bakh Prize and in 1950 the I. I. Mechnikov Prize. He won a Stalin Prize in 1952.

The main scientific investigations of Sisakyan are the study of the action of enzymes in metabolism. While studying the biochemical properties and enzyme functions of submicroscopic structures of protoplasm, he showed that the plastides are rich not only in nucleoproteins but also in enzymes. He studied the biochemical nature of drought-resistance of plants, the biochemistry of wine production and others.

As of 1961 Sisakyan was Chairman of the Commission on International Scientific Relations of the U.S.S.R. Academy of Sciences.

Bibliography:
Enzyme Activity of Protoplasm Structures, Bakh Studies #5. Moscow, 1951.

Biochemical Characteristics of Drought-Resistance of Vegetation. Moscow-Leningrad: 1940.
Biochemistry of plastides in Problems of Botany, 1, pp. 195-223. Moscow-Leningrad: 1954.
Chemical nature and biochemical functions of plastides. Izvest. Akad. Nauk S.S.S.R., Ser. Biol. 1956, #5, 6.
and M. K. Veynova. Inclusion of tagged amino-acids and 8 C^{14} into nucleotidepeptides of baker's yeast Sacch, cerevisal. Doklady Akad. Nauk S.S.S.R. 147, #3, 731-34 (1962).

Office: Academician Secretary of Biological Sciences of
              USSR Academy of Sciences
              Leninskii Prospekt, 14
              Moscow, USSR
Residence: Leninskii Prospekt, 13
              Moscow, USSR
Telephone: B2 16 87

SKOBEL'TSYN, DMITRII VLADIMIROVICH (Physicist)

D. V. Skobel'tsyn was born November 24, 1892. After graduating from Petersburg University in 1915, he worked in the Polytechnic and Physico-Technic Institute in Leningrad. Subsequently he was at Moscow University and the Physics Institute of the U.S.S.R. Academy of Sciences. In 1951 he became Director of this Institute. He was a Corresponding Member of the U.S.S.R. Academy of Sciences from 1939 to 1946 when he was elected Academician. Skobel'tsyn has been active in public affairs also. He was Deputy to the U.S.S.R. Supreme Soviet and a member of the Commission on Foreign Affairs of the Soviet Union. In March 1962, he was re-elected a delegate from Ural SSR to the Supreme Soviet. In 1950 he was made Chairman of the Committee on the International Lenin Prize "For Strengthening Peace Between Peoples." He was awarded a Stalin Prize in 1951 and in 1952 the gold medal of S. I. Vavilov by the U.S.S.R. Academy of Sciences.

Skobel'tsyn carried out research in nuclear physics and cosmic rays. In 1923 he began research on the phenomena of interaction of substance with gamma rays from radium. In order to clarify the mechanism of these phenomena, Skobel'tsyn used the Wilson cloud chamber, with the aid of which he was able to view directly and photograph the recoil electrons knocked out by collisions of high energy photons (gamma rays) with gas atoms which filled the chamber. These studies gave direct support to the quantum character of the Compton effect. Subsequently Skobel'tsyn utilized these phenomena for studies

in gamma rays spectroscopy. The method proposed by Skobel'-
tsyn of using the Wilson cloud chamber in a magnetic field has
been widely used for studying beta and gamma rays spectra and
for basic investigations of properties of elementary particles.
In 1927-29 Skobel'tsyn studied cosmic rays. In the post war
years, he carried out research on the study of cosmic ray
showers.

In November 1962 Skobel'tsyn received the Order of Lenin.

Bibliography:

Cosmic Rays. Moscow-Leningrad: 1936.

Nature of cosmic radiation. Vestnik Akad. Nauk S.S.S.R.,
1950, #4, 31-45.

On the trend of a 'correlative' curve of auger showers over
a great distance. Doklady Akad. Nauk, 1949, 67, #2.

Über eine neue Art sehr schneller Betta Strahlen, Zeitschrift
für Physik, 1929, 54, #9-10.

Die spektrale Verteilung und die mittiere Wellenlänge der ra
gamma Strahlen. Zeitschrift fur Physik, 1929, 58, #9-10,
595-612.

Die Intensitatsverteilung in dem Spektrum der gamma Strahlen von RaC. Zeitschrift für Physik, 1927, 43, #5-6, 354-78.

Office: A. N. Lebedev Physics Institute of USSR Academy
              of Sciences
              Leninskii Prospekt, 53
              Moscow, USSR

SKRYABIN, KONSTANTIN IVANOVICH (Helminthologist)

K. I. Skryabin was born December 7, 1878. In 1905 he graduated from Yur'ev Veterinary Institute and until 1911 worked as
a veterinarian in Central Asia. He was professor at the Don
Veterinary Institute in Novocherkassk from 1917 to 1920 when
he became professor at Moscow Veterinary Institute (now the
Moscow Veterinary Academy). Also in 1920, he was made
Chairman of the Helminthological Department of the State Institute of Experimental Veterinary Sciences which he originally
organized and then, in 1931, reorganized into the All-Union
Institute of Helminthology. Skryabin has been the Director
since its founding. He was Chairman in 1921 to 1949 of the
Helminthological Department of the Tropical Institute (now the
Institute of Malaria, Medical Parasitology and Helminthology)
founded by him. In 1942 he became Chief of the Laboratory of
Helminthology of the U.S.S.R. Academy of Sciences. Skryabin
was elected an Academician of the U.S.S.R. Academy of Sciences
in 1939 and in 1944 a member of the U.S.S.R. Academy of

Medical Sciences. In 1943 to 1952 he was Chairman of the Presidium of the Kirghiz Branch of the U.S.S.R. Academy of Sciences. A member since 1935 of the Lenin All-Union Agricultural Academy, he was elected President in 1956. Skryabin is well known for his public activities also. He has been Deputy of the U.S.S.R. Supreme Soviet, second and third convocations. In 1922 he found and chaired the Commission of the Study of Helmintho Fauna of the U.S.S.R. and in 1940 reorganized it into the All-Union Society of Helminthologists of the U.S.S.R. Academy of Sciences of which he is currently President. He participates in domestic and international zoological and veterinary congresses and is a member and honorary member of several foreign scientific research organizations and societies. In 1927 he was an Honored Scientist of the R.S.F.S.R. Twice, 1941 and 1950, he was awarded Stalin Prizes. The Academy of Sciences of the U.S.S.R. awarded Skryabin the Gold Medal of I. I. Mechnikov in 1949. In 1954 he was an Honored Member of the Kirghiz S.S.R. and in 1958 a Hero of Socialist Labor. In 1957 he won a Lenin Prize. The All-Union Institute of Helminthology in Moscow and the Kirghiz Agricultural Institute in Frunze are named for him.

The investigations of Skryabin are in morphology, biology, phylogeny and systematics of parasitic worms, epidemiology (epizootology) and organization of measures to control helminthosis of man and domestic animals. Under the leadership of Skryabin there were conducted about 300 helminthologic expeditions in various regions of the U.S.S.R. He introduced (with R. S. Shul'ts) the concept of additional reservoir and transit hosts and gave an analysis of the processes of migration of various bladder worms in the bodies of a host; he introduced the concept of geo- and biohelminthosis, the concept of dehelminthization, devestation. The many instruction and reference books on control of helminthosis published by Skryabin are widely utilized in medical and veterinary practice. He outlined about 200 new types of bladder worms.

As of 1961, Skryabin was a Vice-President of the Lenin All-Union Agricultural Academy.

Bibliography:
and R.-Ed. S. Shul'ts. Helminthosis of Horned Cattle and Its Young Stock. Moscow: 1937.

and R.-Ed. S. Shul'ts. Basis of Helminthology. Moscow: 1940.

and R.-Ed. S. Shul'ts, N. P. Shikhobalova. Trychostrongyloidea of Man and Animals. Moscow: 1954.

Trematodes of Man and Animals. Basis of Trematodology, 1-12. Moscow-Leningrad: 1947-1956.
Devastation in the Struggle with Helminthosis and other Ailments of Man and Animals. Frunze: 1947.
and others. Indicator of Parasitic Nematode, 1-4. Moscow-Leningrad: 1949-1954.
Biography:
D. N. Antipin and N. P. Shikhobalova. Academician Konstantin Ivanovich Skryabin. Moscow: 1949.
Works on Helminthology (On the 75th Anniversary of date of birth of K. I. Skryabin. Collection of articles). Moscow: 1953.
Office: Laboratory of Helminthology of USSR Academy of
               Sciences
               Leninskii Prospekt, 33
               Moscow, USSR

SMIRNOV, NIKOLAI VASIL'EVICH (Mathematician)
N. V. Smirnov was born October 17, 1900. In 1926, he graduated from Moscow University. From 1937 to 1941, he was professor at the Lenin Moscow Pedagogical Institute. In 1938, he began work at the U.S.S.R. Academy of Sciences Institute of Mathematics. He was awarded a Stalin Prize in 1951. He was elected a Corresponding Member of the U.S.S.R. Academy of Sciences in 1960.
Smirnov's work is in the theory of probability and especially mathematical statistics. The theory of non-parametric methods of mathematical statistics was the contribution of Smirnov.
Bibliography:
Limited Laws of Distribution for Terms of Variational Series. Moscow: 1949.
and Dunin-Barkovskii. Theory of Probability and Mathematical Statistics in Technics. Moscow: 1955.
Mathematical statistics. Vestnik Akad. Nauk, #8, 53-58 (1961).
Office: V. A. Steklov Institute of Mathematics of USSR
               Academy of Sciences
               1-y Akademicheski Proyezd, 28
               Moscow, USSR
Residence: 1-aya Cheremushkinskaya 24/1
               Moscow, USSR
Telephone: B5 31 93

SMIRNOV, VLADIMIR IVANOVICH (Geologist)

V. I. Smirnov was born January 1910. He graduated from the Moscow Geological Survey Institute in 1934 and was an instructor there. From 1946 to 1951 he was U.S.S.R. Deputy Minister of Geology. At the same time, he was professor at Moscow Geological Survey Institute and at Moscow Institute of Non-Ferrous Metals and Gold. In 1951 he became a professor at Moscow University. He has been a member of the Communist Party of the Soviet Union since 1940. In 1958 he was elected Corresponding Member of the U.S.S.R. Academy of Sciences, and in June 1962, Academician.

Smirnov has worked with problems in the geology of ore deposits, their survey, and evaluation.

In January 1961, Smirnov visited the United States to attend National Academy of Sciences Conferences and meetings at Stanford University, California.

Bibliography:
An Inventory of Natural Resource Mineral Reserves. Moscow: 1950.
The Geological Basis for Surveying and Mining Ore Deposits, 2nd ed. Moscow: 1957.

Office: Department of Geology
                 Moscow University
                 Moscow, USSR

SMIRNOV, VLADIMIR IVANOVICH (Mathematician)

V. I. Smirnov was born June 10, 1887 in Leningrad (Petrograd). In 1910 he graduated from Petersburg University, in 1915 he began teaching there, and in 1926 he was made professor. From 1912 to 1930 Smirnov was professor at Petersburg Institute of Engineers of Means of Communication. He received the degree of Doctor in Physical-Mathematical Sciences in 1936. He worked from 1929 to 1935 in the Seismological and Mathematical Institutes of the U.S.S.R. Academy of Sciences. In 1932 he was elected a Corresponding Member of the U.S.S.R. Academy of Sciences and in 1943 an Academician. He was awarded a Stalin Prize in 1948.

Smirnov has worked primarily in theory of a function of a complex variable such as the uniformization of the many-valued analytical functions, the investigation of Fuchsian groups and Fuchsian functions in the presence of an infinite number of substitutions of corresponding groups, the reversal of a differential equation of the Fuchsian type with four singular points. In a series of investigations conducted with S. L. Sobolev,

Smirnov worked out a new method of solving some problems on the theory of the propagation of waves in elastic media with plane boundaries. He investigated the singular solutions of a wave equation and the equations for elasticity, and in connection with this, put forth a new method for investigating the oscillations of an elastic circle and sphere for a given external influence. For linear equations of elliptical type, with any number of variables, Smirnov studied cases when these equations allow functionally invariant solutions. This investigation was based on a concept introduced by Smirnov of conjugated function for Euclidian space or Riemannian space with a positive metric. Smirnov is the author of Course in Advanced Mathematics (5 volumes), 1924-47. He trained a large number of students.

Bibliography:
Problems of transformation of a linear differential equation of the secondary order with four singular points. Petersburg, 1918 (mimeographed).
Sur les formules de Cauchy et de Green et quelques problems qui s'y rattachent. Izvest. Akad. Nauk S.S.S.R., Otdel. Mat. i Est. Nauk, 1932, #3.
Solution of finite problems for a wave equation in the case of a circle and a sphere. Doklady Akad. Nauk, 1937, 14, #1.
Solution of finite problems in the theory of elasticity in the case of a circle and a sphere. Doklady Akad. Nauk, 1937, 14, #2.
On association functions. 1-3. Vestnik of the Leningrad University, 1953, #8, 11.
On conjugated functions in a multi-dimensional Euclidian space. Vestnik of Leningrad University, 1954, #5.
Biography:
A. P. Epifanova. Vladimir Ivanovich Smirnov. Moscow-Leningrad: 1949.
G. A. Ladyzhenskaya and G. M. Fikhtengolts. Vladimir Ivanovich Smirnov (On the 70th Anniversary since the date of birth). Vestnik of Leningrad University, 1957, #7.
Office: USSR Academy of Sciences
Leninskii Prospekt, 14
Moscow, USSR

SMIRNOV, VASILII IVANOVICH (Metallurgist)
V. I. Smirnov was born February 11, 1899. After graduating from the Leningrad Mining Institute in 1922, he worked as an engineer in the Katalinskii Copper Works (Urals) and supervised

the reconstruction of the Karabashskii Copper Smelting Plant from 1925 to 1927. In 1927-30, he was chief metallurgist of the Urals Copper Trust (Uralmed) and Deputy Technical Director. In 1930, he was appointed lecturer at the Ural Institute of Non-Ferrous Metals. He became a professor, in 1933, at the Ural Polytechnic Institute. In 1938 he was awarded the degree of Doctor of Technical Sciences. He is the recipient of two Orders of the Red Banner of Labor and a medal for "Valiant Labor during WWII." He was elected to the U.S.S.R. Academy of Sciences as a Corresponding Member in 1946, and became an Academician of the Kazakh S.S.R. Academy of Sciences in 1954.

Smirnov was sent abroad in 1928 on a scientific mission where he became acquainted with the operation of non-ferrous metallurgical plants of the United States and Canada. Upon his return he published a number of studies devoted to the scientific research and practical work of several American and Canadian copper smelting plants.

Smirnov's investigation is in the smelting of copper and nickel ores and concentrates.

Smirnov was an active participant in the Altai Session on the Development of the Productive Forces of this region. He is scientific consultant of the Institute of Metallurgy and Ore-Dressing of the Altai Mining and Metallurgical Institute of the Academy of Sciences of the Kazakh S.S.R.

Bibliography:
Hydrometallurgy of Copper. Sverdlovsk-Moscow: 1947.
Metallurgy of Copper and Nickel. Sverdlovsk-Moscow: 1950.
Reflection Smelting (Theory and Practice), 3rd ed. Sverdlovsk-Moscow: 1952.
Shaft Smelting in the Metallurgy of Non-Ferrous Metals. Sverdlovsk: 1955.
Pyrometallurgy of Copper.
The Firing of Copper Ores and Concentrates.
Office: Ural Polytechnic Institute of Kazakh SSR Academy of Sciences
1-uchebny korpus, Room 225
Sverdlovsk, USSR
Telephone: D1 37 08

SMIRNOV, VASILII SERGEEVICH (Metallurgist)
V. S. Smirnov was born in 1915. He graduated from the Ural Polytechnical Institute in 1937, and in 1937-38 and again in 1941-42, he worked in industry. From 1938 to 1941 he was

an assistant, senior laboratory technician, postgraduate, and from 1942 to 1949 was engaged in scientific and pedagogical work at the Ural Polytechnical Institute. In 1949 he became chairman of the department of Plastic Treatment of Metals at the M. I. Kalinin Leningrad Polytechnical Institute, where he was from 1954-56 deputy Director, and then became Director of this Institute. In 1948, he was granted the degree Doctor of Technical Sciences, and the rank of professor in 1950. Since 1940, he has been a member of the Communist Party of the Soviet Union. He was elected, in 1960, a Corresponding Member of the U.S.S.R. Academy of Sciences.

Smirnov's primary scientific activity deals with pressure treatment of metals (transverse spiral metal rolling, longitudinal periodic rolling, metal punching and pressing).

In June 1958, Smirnov visited the United States to attend the Gordon Research Conferences on Polymer Research at New London, New Hampshire.

Bibliography:
   Transverse Metal Rolling. Moscow: 1948.
   Calibration of Rollers by Coordinative Zones. Moscow: 1953.
   Transverse Rolling and Machine Building. Moscow: 1957.
   Longitudinal Periodic Rolling. Moscow: 1962.
   Fundamentals in the theory of metal rolling. Chps. 1-3, Metal Rolling Industry, Moscow, 1962.
Office: M. I. Kalin Leningrad Polytechnical Institute
             Polytechnical ul. 3
             Leningrad, K-64, USSR
Telephone: G2 85 80

SOBOLEV, SERGEI LVOVICH (Mathematician and Specialist in
        Mechanics)

S. L. Sobolev was born October 6, 1908 in Leningrad. He graduated from Leningrad University in 1929 and also holds the degree of Doctor of Physical-Mathematical Sciences from there. He then worked in the Seismological Institute of the U.S.S.R. Academy of Sciences. In 1932 he began working at the Mathematics Institute of the U.S.S.R. Academy of Sciences and in 1935 he became professor at Moscow University. Sobolev has been a member of the Communist Party of the Soviet Union since 1940. He was elected a Corresponding Member of the U.S.S.R. Academy of Sciences in 1933 and in 1939 an Academician. In 1941 he was awarded a Stalin Prize.

Sobolev has studied the dynamics of an elastic body. He formulated the theory of plane waves in an elastic semi-space with a boundary free from tension, and elucidated the general concept of a surface wave. Together with V. I. Smirnov, he worked out a new method of investigating the propagation and reflection of elastic waves from rectilinear boundaries—a method which is associated with functionally invariant solutions of wave propagation on a plane. Sobolev also worked out a new method of integrating linear and non-linear equations with partial derivates of the hyperbolic type. He carried out research on the boundary problem in an n-dimensional space for poly-harmonic equation in the presence of a degenerate boundary; he established an almost-periodic solution of the boundary problems of linear hyperbolic equations, investigated the dependence of the solutions of hyperbolic equations on disturbing forces, initial and final conditions, and solved new boundary problems for these equations. In his investigation Sobolev formulated a series of new concepts; generalized derivative, generalized solution of equations with partial derivatives, generalized differential operator. With the aid of these concepts, he was able to formulate and solve some fundamental problems in mathematical physics. Future development of these ideas of Sobolev led to the establishment of the theory of the so-called generalized functions. Sobolev also studied the properties of functional space.

As of 1961, Sobolev was a Member of the Presidium, Siberian Branch U.S.S.R. Academy of Sciences, and Director of the Institute of Mathematics and Computation Center, Siberian Branch U.S.S.R. Academy of Sciences.

Bibliography:

Some Uses of Functional Analysis in Mathematical Physics. Leningrad: 1950.

Equations of Mathematical Physics, 3rd ed. Moscow: 1954.

Formulae for mechanical curvatures in n-dimensional space. Doklady Akad. Nauk S.S.S.R. 137, #3, 527-30 (1961).

The interpolation of functions of n-variables. Doklady Akad. Nauk S.S.S.R. 137, #4, 778-81 (1961).

Cube formulae on a sphere, invariants in reformed finite groups of isolation. Doklady Akad. Nauk S.S.S.R. 146, #2, 310-13 (1962).

Number of formula branches on a sphere. Doklady Akad. Nauk S.S.S.R. 146, #4, 770-73 (1962).

Office: Moscow University
              Moscow, USSR

<u>SOBOLEV, VLADIMIR STEPANOVICH (Petrographer and
     Mineralogist)</u>
   V. S. Sobolev was born May 30, 1908 in the city of Lugansk
and spent his childhood in Vinnitsa. In 1930, he graduated from
the Leningrad Mining Institute. In 1936, his monograph, "Petrology of the Traprocks of the Siberian Plateau" was accepted
as his doctoral dissertation, and he received the title of professor. In 1951, he was elected Corresponding Member of the
Ukrainian Academy of Sciences, and on March 28, 1958, he was
elected Academician of the U.S.S.R. Academy of Sciences. He
is currently a member of the Council and the Editorial Council
of the Lvov Geological Society. He received a Stalin Prize in
1949.
   Sobolev started his research as a student first in 1928 in the
Geological Committee and then in the Central Scientific Research Institute of Geological Survey and the All-Union Geological Scientific Research Institute. He began his investigations in the Ukraine in 1936 and continued them in 1945,
following his transfer to the University of Lvov. He has been
teaching since 1931. In 1931-41 and 1942-45, he was employed
by the Leningrad Mining Institute and in 1939 was made professor. He also taught in the University of Irkutsk from 1941-
45. From 1943 to 1945, he served as Director of the Mineralogy Department of the Leningrad Mining Institute and as Director of the Fedorov Institute. In 1945, he joined the University
of Lvov as chairman of the Petrography Department. In 1947,
he began working at the Institute of the Geology of Minerals in
the Ukrainian S.S.R. in Lvov.
   Sobolev is the author of over 100 scientific papers dealing
chiefly with three subjects: petrography and mineralogy of
Siberia, petrography and mineralogy of the Ukraine, and theoretical aspects of mineralogy and petrography. He has devoted
many years to the study of the traprock of the Siberian Plateau.
He demonstrated that the formation of various rock minerals is
associated with the crystallization differentiation whose sensi-
tive index is the FeO:MgO ratio. His study of the mineralogy
of Siberia gave the first description of a rare paragenesis of
the contact calcium silicates--spurrite, merwinite, cuspidine.
In addition, he has discovered and described the magnetite deposits in the Ilimpeya River.
   In his monograph on traprock, Sobolev furnished a survey of
the corresponding formations of the earth's crust, stressing the
similarity of the Siberian plateau geology to that of the Karoo
plateau (South Africa). This analogy became more conclusive

when in 1937, having analyzed some petrographic samples collected by N. N. Urvantsev from the Taimir Peninsula, he succeeded in finding a unique basic rock resembling the ultrabasic
type. He concluded that this rock may be an analog of the South
African basic formations (melitite basalts) which accompany
the kimberlites. He also advanced the hypothesis concerning
the diamond-bearing potential of the northern Siberian plateau.
This hypothesis was confirmed first through the study conducted jointly with A. P. Burov of the geology of diamond deposits
in foreign countries, and by the discovery of extensive areas of
basic vulcanic rocks in Khatangi District. Rock samples from
this district were collected by members of the Arctic Institute
Expedition and tested by G. G. Moor in consultation with Sobolev, whereupon Moor confirmed the hypothesis on the occurrence
of diamonds. In his report for 1940 to Gosplan S.S.S.R. (State
Planning Committee of the U.S.S.R. Council of Ministers) he
wrote: "The Siberian plateau has the greatest coincidence with
the kimberlite deposits of South Africa. This coincidence is
amplified even more by the discovery by the author, on the
Taymir Peninsula, and by G. G. Moor (in consultation with the
author) in the Khatangi River area, of basic rocks of the lim-
burgite, augite, and alnoite type, resembling the South African
melitite basalts which accompany kimberlites. Each expedition
operating in the northern Siberian plateau should give serious
attention to prospecting for diamonds. It is especially important to diamond prospecting in the active placers of precious
metals in the Norilsk area and in Vilyuy." Thus, V. S. Sobolev
predicted the location of diamond kimberlites not only in the
northern Siberian plateau generally, but also in the Vilyuy area
in particular.

After the discovery of kimberlites, Sobolev was invited to
take part in the expedition. He paid visits to diamond deposits
(1955), advised in petrographic and mineralogical analysis of
the materials, and jointly with A. P. Burov served as the scientific editor of the first book on diamonds in Siberia.

Of Vladimir Stepanovich's writings on the petrography of the
Ukrainian S.S.R., one must mention first of all the monograph
on the petrology of the complex Korosten pluton which he feels
to have a direct connection with the petrology of traprock formations. In this book the author once again stresses the importance of the study of femic minerals of magmatic rocks. He
distinguishes the most important differences between the plateau
type of granites and those of folded areas, which are the result
of varying ferruginosity in femic minerals. He was the first to

find basic syenites and new deposits of piezo-electric crystals in this region of the Ukraine.

In post-war years, Sobolev has devoted much of his time to the study of young volcanic rocks in the Carpathian Mountains. Explorations in this region are being conducted jointly with a group of his students. In his writings on the mineralogy and petrology of the Ukrainian S.S.R. he described the ultra-basic rocks of Transcarpathia and established, within the metamorphic complex of this region, the occurrence of diaphtoresis; he has described a new find of pumpellyite from the Carpathian Mountains, pointing out the identity of this mineral to lotrite and others.

Sobolev is not only a petrographer but a mineralogist as well. He has published since 1944 a series of articles on the theoretical mineralogy of silicates, and in 1949 a book entitled Introduction to the Mineralogy of Silicates which was awarded a Stalin Prize, Second Class. In this treatise he attempted to make an interrelationship between the properties and genesis of minerals, on the one hand, and silicates and their crystal structure on the other. He has established a connection between the difference in ionic radii in isomorphic series and the type of fusibility curves; substantiated A. E. Fersman's ideas respecting the regularity of isomorphism; determined the relationship between the change in the coordinate number of aluminum during mineral formation and the physico-chemical equilibrium factors; clarified the relationship between the optical properties of silicates, including their color, and their structure. Moreover, he has generalized the data of paragenesis of igneous rocks in the form of multi-fascicular diagrams.

Certain structural features of various silicates, which had been predicted by V. S. Sobolev on the basis of mechanisms which he had evolved, have been verified by X-ray analysis. Thus, for example, the investigations conducted by N. V. Belov and I. M. Rumanova have corroborated his hypothesis concerning both the six-fold coordination of aluminum in epidote and the presence of a diortho group in the latter. Studies by Chinese authors have supported his hypothesis concerning the two types of coordination of aluminum in prehnite and others. ite and others.

Maintaining in his studies that hydroxyl in many silicates cannot substitute oxygen in oxysilicic tetrahedrons, V. S. Sobolev proposed in this connection a new way of computing the crystallo-chemical formulas of water-containing silicates. In 1949, he was the first to advance the hypothesis concerning the substitution of the potassium ion in micas with the oxonium ion. Sobolev has written a number of articles on theoretical petrography: metamorphism, formation of igneous rocks, granitization, genesis of lamprophyres, mineral formation at oriented pressure. He stresses the importance of studying femic minerals of rocks and proposes certain simplified diagrams which facilitate the approximate determination of biotite and hornblende (by their optical properties) in granitoids. Of special value are the tables of optical orientation of minerals which have been published as a supplement to the text Fedorov Method.

Bibliography:
Petrology of the Siberian Platform. Leningrad: 1936 (Trudy Arktich. Inst., 43).
Introduction to the Mineralogy of Silicates. Lvov: 1949.
Geology of Diamond Fields of Africa, Australia, Borneo and North America. Moscow: 1951.
The Fedorov Method. Moscow-Leningrad: 1954.
and others. Petrography of Non-molten Laval Types of the Soviet Carpathian Mountains. Kiev: 1955.
Office: Institute of Geology of Minerals
Ulitsa Kopernika 15
L'vov, Ukrainian SSR

SOBOLEV, VICTOR VICTOROVICH (Astronomer)
V. V. Sobolev was born September 2, 1915. In 1938 he graduated from Leningrad University. From 1941 he worked there, becoming a professor in 1948. He was elected, in 1958, a Corresponding Member of the U.S.S.R. Academy of Sciences.

Sobolev has worked in theoretical astrophysics. He has been concerned with physics of non-stationary stars and the theory of radiative transfer. He presented a theory on the luminosity of moving media, with the help of which he established the physical relationship of giant stars of early and late spectrum classes. He laid the basis for the theory of a non-stationary radiation field. He put forth a theory of shape of spectrum lines with consideration of frequency redistribution.

Sobolev's works are also concerned with the physics of gaseous mistiness, and investigation of planetary atmospheres.

Bibliography:
Moving Envelopes of Stars. Leningrad: 1947. (Harvard University Press, 1960).
and others. Course on Astrophysics and Stellar Astronomy (A. A. Mikhailov, ed.) Moscow-Leningrad: 1951.

and others. Theoretical Astrophysics (A. A. Ambartsumian, ed.) Moscow-Leningrad: 1952. (Pergamon Press, 1958) Transfer of Radiant Energy in the Atmospheres of Stars and Planets. Moscow: 1956.

Office: Leningrad University
Leningrad, USSR

SOTCHAVA, VIKTOR BORISOVICH (Geobotanist and Geographer)

V. B. Sotchava was born June 20, 1905. In 1924, he graduated from the Leningrad Agricultural Institute where he worked until 1926. From 1926 to 1936, and since 1943, he has been working at the U.S.S.R. Academy of Sciences Botanical Institute. He worked, in 1931-1935, at the Institute of Reindeer Breeding at the Lenin All-Union Academy of Agricultural Sciences. From 1935 to 1938, he was Chairman of the Department of Reindeer Breeding of the Arctic Institute. He taught at the A. I. Gertsen Pedagogical Institute in Leningrad from 1939 to 1950. Since 1938, he has been teaching at Leningrad University where he became a professor in 1944. He has been the recipient of several medals and the Order of Lenin. In 1958, he was elected to the U.S.S.R. Academy of Sciences as a Corresponding Member.

Sotchava has studied vegetation, landscapes of various zones of the U.S.S.R. Beginning in 1926, he took part in expeditions to the Far North, the Far East, Siberia, Urals, Caucasus, Carpathians, Moldavia and China, Rumania and Czechoslovakia. In a series of botanical-geographical outlines, he presented data on the vegetation of previously unexplored territories such as basins of the Anadyr, the Penzhin, and North Sikhote-Alin. He studied pastures of the Tundra zone, proposed some measures for organizing a food base for Soviet reindeer breeding. He studied the relationship between the forest and Tundra vegetation. He proposed a scheme of classifying vegetation based on ecologo-geographical and genetic factors and developed principles of classification of geobotanical and landscape sections. He published a summary work on the forest vegetation of the U.S.S.R. A series of his works deal with questions of paleography and the history of contemporary vegetation of the Far East, of polar countries, the Caucasus, of North and Central Siberia. He directed the compilation of a series of maps, the main among which is the "Geobotanical Map of the U.S.S.R." (scale 1/4,000,000) and the explanatory text to it.

Since 1950 Sotchava has been working out theoretical and
methodical aspects of vegetation mapping and problems of
comprehensive mapping of geographical environment. These
problems were elucidated in several articles and reports read
in the U.S.S.R. and at international symposiums. In 1960 Sotchava was honored with a silver medal of Pierre Fermat by the
Academy of Sciences, Inscriptions and Literature in Toulouse
(Academie des sciences, inscriptions et belles-lettres de Toulouse).

As of 1960, Sotchava has been Director of the Institute of
Geography of Siberia and the Far East, Irkutsk, Siberian Department, U.S.S.R. Academy of Sciences. He is also the Head
of the Laboratory of the Geography and Cartography of the
vegetation of the V. L. Komarov Institute of Botany of the
U.S.S.R. Academy of Sciences, Leningrad.

Bibliography:

Das Anadyrgebiet. Botanisch-geographische Beobachtungen
in aussersten Nordosten Asiens. Zeitschrift der Gesell-
schaft fur Erdkunde zu Berlin, 1930, 7-8.

Limits of forest in the mountains of the Lyapinskii Urals.
Works of the Botanical Museum of the U.S.S.R. Academy of
Sciences, 1930, 22.

Over the tundras in the basin of Penjin inlet. Proceedings
of the Geographical Society, 1932, 64, 4-5.

The vegetation of the Burein mountain range to the north of
Dulnikan pass. Transaction of the Council of the Study of
Productivity Factors, the Far East series, 1934, 2.

On the phylocoenogenetic systematics of vegetation association. Soviet Botany, 1944, I.

Elements of the vegetation cover of the North Sikhote-Alin
mountain range and their interrelations. Soviet Botany,
1945, I.

Floragenesis and phylocoenogenesis of the Manchurian mixed
forest. Materials on the History of the Flora and Vegetation
of the U.S.S.R. (chief editor: V. L. Komarov), 2.

Geographic connections of the vegetation on the territory of
the U.S.S.R. Scientific Papers of the Leningrad State Pedagogical Institute of A. I. Gertsen, 1948, 73.

Newest vertical movements of the earth's crust and vegetation. Geography, New Series, 1950, 3.

Principles of phytogeographical subdivision ("rayonization").
Principles of Geography. Collection of Articles. Moscow-
Leningrad: 1956.

and others. The Vegetational Cover of the U.S.S.R. Moscow-
Leningrad: 1956, I.
Vegetations classification, typology of physiographic facies
and biogeocoenoses. Problems of Vegetation Classification.
Sverdlovsk, 1961. (Transaction of the Institute of Biology of
the Ural Branch of the U.S.S.R. Academy of Sciences, 27.)
Mapping problems in geobotany. Principles and Methods of
Vegetation Mapping. Moscow-Leningrad: 1962.

Office: Botanical Institute of USSR Academy of Sciences
ul. Prof. Popova, 2
Leningrad 22, USSR

SOKOLOV, BORIS SERGEEVICH (Geologist and Paleontologist)
   B. S. Sokolov was born April 9, 1914. After graduating from
Leningrad University in 1937, he worked at the University. In
1943 he began working at the All-Union Scientific Research Oil
Institute. Since 1958 he has been a Corresponding Member of
the U.S.S.R. Academy of Sciences.
   Geological investigations were conducted by Sokolov in the
pre-Moscow basin and Tien Shan (until 1940), in middle and
central Asia (1941-45), in various regions of the European
section of the U.S.S.R. and on the Urals (1946-53), and in Siberia (from 1956). He has studied the stratigraphy of Paleozoic and late pre-Cambrian regional and oil geology. In the
area of paleontology he investigated Paleozoic corals, established the separation of tabulate corals as a particular sub-
class of higher polyps, formulated their new phylogenetic system, and established their stratigraphic significance.
Bibliography:
   Systematics and history of the development of paleozoic
   corals anthozoa tabulata. Questions of Paleontology, 1.
   (A. P. Bystrov, ed.) Leningrad: 1950.
   Chaetetida of the carboniferous of North Eastern Ukraine
   and adjacent territories. Leningrad-Moscow: 1950 (Works
   of the All-Union Scientific Research Oil and Geologic Prospecting Institute, #27.)
   Tabulate coral of the paleozoic era in the European part of
   the U.S.S.R. Preface and Part I-IV. Leningrad-Moscow:
   1951-1955 (Works of the All-Union Scientific Research
   Geological Prospecting Institute, #48, 52, 58, 62, 85.)
   Age of the ancient sedimentary sheet of the Russian platform. Doklady Akad. Nauk S.S.S.R., 1952, #5.

and Yu. K. Dzevanovskii. On the stratigraphic position and
age of sedimentary rock masses of late Pre-Cambrian.
Soviet Geology, 1957, #55.
Office: All-Union Scientific Research Oil Institute
             Moscow, USSR
Residence: Millionnaya, 13
             Moscow, USSR
Telephone: E3 52 88

SOKOLOVSKII, VADIM VASIL'EVICH (Mechanical Engineer)
    V. V. Sokolovskii was born October 17, 1912. In 1933 he
graduated from the Moscow Institute of Construction Engineers.
From 1936 to 1939 he worked at the Mathematics Institute, and
since 1939, at the U.S.S.R. Academy of Sciences Institute of
Mechanics. He became a professor in 1940. He was awarded,
in 1943 and in 1952, Stalin Prizes. Since 1956 he has been a
member of the Communist Party of the Soviet Union. In 1946
he was elected a Corresponding Member of the U.S.S.R. Academy of Sciences.
    The main works of Sokolovskii are devoted to the theory of
shells, statics of a loose medium and to theory of plasticity.
He obtained solutions to many problems of plane deformed conditions such as compression of plastic masses, pressing in of
punches, drawing of plastic strips. He developed the theory of
a plane plastic tense condition, and proposed new methods for
solving problems of plasticity in an analytical form. He developed a general method which allows solution of the main
problems of plane terminal equilibrium of loose and cohesive
media (the supporting power of bases, the form of stable slopes,
pressure on bulkheads).
Bibliography:
    Statics of a Loose Medium. Moscow-Leningrad: 1942; 2nd
    ed., Moscow-Leningrad: 1954.
    Theory of Plasticity, 2nd ed. Moscow-Leningrad: 1950.
Office: Institute of Mechanics of USSR Academy of Sciences
             Leningradskii Prospekt, 7
             Moscow, USSR
Residence: B. Cheremushkinskaya 6/1
             Moscow, USSR
Telephone: B3 10 76

SOTSKOV, BORIS STEPANOVICH (Automation Specialist)
    B. S. Sotskov was born in 1908. In 1931 he graduated from
the Military Technical Academy. From 1931 to 1938, he was

laboratory Chief, senior instructor, and departmental Chairman
of the Military Electro-technical Academy in Leningrad. He
was docent, 1938-42, at the Leningrad Polytechnical Institute.
From 1942 to 1960, he held positions as senior scientific
worker, laboratory supervisor and deputy Director respective-
ly of the U.S.S.R. Academy of Sciences Institute of Automation
and Remote Control where he became Chief of the Laboratory
in 1960. In the same year he was elected to the U.S.S.R. Academy of Sciences as a Corresponding Member.

Sotskov's principal work has been in the field of elemental
and technical media of automation and remote control.

Sotskov visited the United States in November 1961 to study
automatic controls.

Bibliography:

On the dimensions of electromagnetic elements. Automatika
i Telemekhanika 19, #9, 849-54 (1958). Automation Express
1, 1958-1959, #6, p. 25.

On the problem of reserve vacuum tubes of filament lamps.
Automatika i Telemekhanika 19, #12, 1126-28 (1958). Automation Express 1, 1958-1959, #6, p. 32.

The problem of dimension of electromagnetic elements in
automatics and remote control. Automatika i Telemekhanika
19, #9, 849-54 (1958). Engineering Index, 1959, p. 752.
Automation and Remote Control 19, 830-4 (1958) (Eng.
trans.)

Reliability characteristics of resistance and condensors in
automatics and remote control. Automation and Remote Control 21, #5, 439-42 (1960) (Eng. trans.) Engineering Index,
1960, p. 375.

Temperature stability and probable significance of strength
and tension on a collector for crystal triodes. Automatika i
Telemekhanika 20, #11, 1525-27 (1959).

Office: Institute of Automation and Telemechanics
            Kalanchevskaya Ulitsa 15-a
            Moscow, USSR
Residence: Novopeschanaya, 3
            Moscow, USSR
Telephone: D7 20 48

SPERANSKII, GEORGI NESTOROVICH (Pediatrician)

G. N. Speranskii was born February 20, 1873. He graduated
from the University of Moscow in 1898 and worked there until
1909. In 1934 he was awarded the title Honored Scientist of the
R.S.F.S.R., and Hero of Socialist Labor in 1957. He was elected

to the U.S.S.R. Academy of Sciences as a Corresponding Member in 1943, and became an active member of the U.S.S.R. Academy of Medical Sciences in 1944.

Speranskii founded in 1910 the first hospital in Moscow (with a clinic, consultation and milk kitchen) for infants. From 1922, he carried out his scientific work at the Central Scientific Research Institute for the care of mothers and infants; directed that institute (which later was reorganized into the Institute of Pediatrics) from 1925-30. At the same time he was president of the Central Institute for the Advancement of Doctors and in 1934 became professor there.

Speranskii's work is devoted to acute and chronic disturbances, digestion and acute gastric ailments in young children. He applied rational diethotherapy for dysentery. He devoted much time to the problem of pneumonia, grippe and septics in the newborn. He has also worked on pathology in older children, particularly rheumatism. He has organized and participated in many conferences on pediatricians, and has published numerous articles on this subject.

Bibliography:
and A. S. Rosenthal. The study of septics in children of an early age. Problems of Pediatrics. Moscow: 1947 (News of Medicine, #6).

Dysentery in children of pre-school age (clinical, pathogenesis and treatment). Problems of Prophylactics and the Treatment of Dysentery. Moscow: 1952.

and A. S. Rosenthal. Chronic Nutritive Disturbances in Young Children (hypothrophy I, II, III). Moscow: 1953.

Biography:
G. N. Speranskii. Problems of Pediatrics, 1951. Collection of works devoted to 50 years of scientific pedagogy and social activity.

Office: Academy of Medical Sciences of the USSR
             Solyanka 14
             Moscow, USSR
Residence: ul. Chaplygina, 22
             Moscow, USSR
Telephone: K7 03 64

SPITSYN, VIKTOR IVANOVICH (Chemist)

V. I. Spitsyn was born April 25, 1902. He graduated from Moscow University and taught there until 1931. In 1932 he was made professor at the K. Liebknecht Moscow Pedagogical Institute and in 1942 he became professor at Moscow University.

He was appointed, in 1949, Chief of the Laboratory of Biochemistry of the Institute of Physical Chemistry of the U.S.S.R.
Academy of Sciences, and in 1953, Director of this Institute. In
1941 he became a member of the Communist Party of the Soviet
Union. He was a Corresponding Member of the U.S.S.R. Academy of Sciences from 1946 until 1958 when he was elected an
Academician.

Spitsyn's main investigations are in the chemistry of rare
elements and in radiochemistry. He showed the reversibility
of reactions of chlorination of oxides at high temperature and
determined the cause of "sublimation" of some oxides in the
atmosphere of chlorine or hydrogen chloride. He investigated
thermal stability of alkaline salts of some oxyacids such as
tungstates and sulfate, and their volatility in various gaslike
media. He investigated the chemistry of heteropoly compounds,
and utilized "tagged atoms" in this investigation.

In March 1958, Spitsyn visited the United States to attend the
International Atomic Exposition in Chicago, Illinois.

Bibliography:

On the reduction of tungstates. Zhur. Fiz. Khim., 1926, 58,
#3-4, 474-490.

Das Chlorieren von Oxyden und ihren Gemischen mit Kohlen-
stoff. Leipzig: 1930.

Establishment of the Soviet Beryllium Industry. Rare
Metals, 1933, #5.

Soviet Chemistry Today. Washington, D. C. Academy of
Sciences. 1961.

and others. Techniques in the use of Radioactive Indicators.
Moscow: 1955.

Use of tagged atoms for study of the structure of some
aquopoly- and heteropolycompounds. Zhur. Neorg. Khim.,
1956, 1, #3.

Office: Institute of Physical Chemistry of USSR Academy of
Sciences
Leninskii Prospekt, 31
Moscow, USSR

Residence: Leninskii Prospekt, 13
Moscow, USSR

Telephone: B2 43 75

SPIVAKOVSKII, ALEKSANDR ONISIMOVICH (Transport
Engineer)

A. O. Spivakovskii was born January 29, 1888. In 1917 he
graduated from Petrograd Polytechnical Institute. In 1919 he

taught at the Dnepropetrovsk Polytechnical Institute and from 1921 to 1923 at the Dnepropetrovsk Mining Institute. In 1933 he became a professor at the Moscow Mining Institute. Since 1949, he has been working at the Moscow Mining Institute of the U.S.S.R. Academy of Sciences. He became a member of the Communist Party of the Soviet Union in 1941. He was elected, in 1946, a Corresponding Member of the U.S.S.R. Academy of Sciences. He was awarded a Stalin Prize in 1947.

Spivakovskii has worked in mining transportation. Together with others he participated in improving scraper conveyers and methods of transporting coal in long drifts in the mines of the Donbas (Stalin Prize 1947).

Bibliography:
Conveyer Units (4 parts, 1933-35).
Conveyers (Transport Machines of Continuous Action).
Moscow-Leningrad: 1941.
Mining Transport, 1949. (Translated into Chinese, Czech, Bulgarian, Hungarian and Rumanian.)
and N. F. Rudenko. Lifting and Transport Machines. General Course. Moscow: 1949.
Cable Conveyers. Moscow: 1951.
Office: Moscow Mining Institute of USSR Academy of Sciences
Moscow, USSR
Residence: Kutuzovskii Prospekt, 27
Moscow, USSR
Telephone: G9 36 72

SRETENSKII, LEONID NIKOLAEVICH (Mathematician)

L. N. Sretenskii was born February 27, 1902. In 1923 he graduated from Moscow University where he became a professor in 1934. In 1936, he was granted the degree of Doctor of Physico-Mathematical Sciences. From 1931 to 1941, he worked at the Central Aero-Hydrodynamics Institute. In 1951, he started to work at the U.S.S.R. Academy of Sciences Marine Hydrophysical Institute. He was elected, in 1939, a Corresponding Member of the U.S.S.R. Academy of Sciences.

The main works of Sretenskii deal with the theory of liquid wave movements, the tidal waves, waves of terminal amplitude, ship waves, and oscillation of liquid in containers. He has investigated the theory of figures of equilibrium of a rotating liquid, streamlining by gas flow, the movement of a heavy solid body around a fixed point, specific equations of mathematical physics, integral equations and differential geometry. Sretenskii's work has been applied in shipbuilding, geophysics and applied marine science.

Bibliography:
> Theory of Wave Movements of a Liquid. Moscow-Leningrad: 1936.
> Theory of Newton's Potential. Moscow-Leningrad: 1946.
> Theory of tides of long periods. Izvest. Akad. Nauk, Georg. i Geofiz. Ser., 1947, 11, #3.
> Movement of a gyroscope of Goryachev-Chapligin. Izvest. Akad. Nauk S.S.S.R., Otdel Tekh. Nauk, 1953, #1, 109-119.
> Space problem of settled waves of terminal amplitude. Moscow University Vestnik, 1954, #5. (Series of Physico-Mathematical and Natural Sciences, #3.)

Office: Marine Hydrophysics Institute of USSR Academy of
> Sciences
> Sadovaya Ulitsa 1
> Lyublino, Moscow Oblast', USSR

STARIK, IOSIF EVSEEVICH (Chemist)

I. E. Starik was born March 23, 1902. He was a student of V. I. Vernadskii (1863-1945, biogeochemist) and V. G. Khlopin (1890-1950, chemist in radioactivity). After graduating from Moscow University in 1924, Starik worked at the Institute of Radium. In 1946 he became professor at Leningrad University and deputy Director of the Radium Institute of the U.S.S.R. Academy of Sciences. Since 1946 he has been a Corresponding Member of the U.S.S.R. Academy of Sciences.

The studies of Starik deal with the investigation of colloidal conditions of radioelements in connection with their absorption properties, determination of geological age by radioactive methods, the study of conditions for the migration of radioelements and development of radiochemical analysis.

As of 1961, Starik was Chairman of the Commission on Absolute Age of Geological Formations, U.S.S.R. Academy of Sciences.

Bibliography:
> Question of colloidal properties of polonium. Works of the State Institute of Radium, 1-2. Leningrad: 1930-33.
> Radioactive Method of Determining Geologic Time. Leningrad-Moscow: 1938.
> Radiochemical analysis. Analysis of Mineral Raw Materials. Leningrad: 1936.

Form of occurrence and conditions of initial migration of
radioelements in nature. Uspekhi Khim., 1943, 12, #4.
Colloidal properties of polonium. Report. Izvest. Akad.
Nauk S.S.S.R., Otdel. Khim, Nauk, 1956, #7.
Role of secondary processes in determination of the age of
rocks by radioactive methods. Geokhimiya, 1956, #5, 18-29.
Condition of microquantities of radioelements in liquid and
solid phases. Uspekhi Khim., 1957, 26, #4, 389-398.
and Yu. A. Barbanel'. Investigation of several functions
characterizing the state of substances in solution. Doklady
Akad. Nauk S.S.S.R. 146, #6, 1352-55 (1962).

Office: Commission on Absolute Age of Geological For-
                mations, USSR Academy of Sciences
                Leninskii Prospekt, 14
                Moscow, USSR

STECHKIN, BORIS SERGEEVICH (Heat and Aeronautical
Engineer)

B. S. Stechkin was born July 24, 1891. In 1918 he graduated
from Moscow Higher Technical School. He was a student of
N. E. Zhukovskii, the founder of Russian aviation, and with him
helped found the Central Aerodynamic Institute. Stechkin is
one of the organizers of the Aeronautical Engineers' Academy
in Moscow where he became a professor in 1921. From 1918
to 1929 he also taught at the Moscow Higher Technical School
and from 1933 to 1937 at the Moscow Aviation Institute. In 1954
he was made Director of the Engine Laboratory of the U.S.S.R.
Academy of Sciences. He was elected a Corresponding Member
of the U.S.S.R. Academy of Sciences in 1946, and in 1953 an
Academician.

Stechkin calculated the heat balance for aviation engines and
developed methods for constructing aviation engines with rapid
and cool characteristics. He derived formulae for the calculation of air intake in aircraft engines, and for defining the
coefficient of air filling and indicator of useful work of aircraft
engines. In 1929, he published "A Theory of Jet Engines" which
presented a theory of jet propulsion. In technology, he further
improved the theory of jet engines and facilitated the development of their characteristics.

Bibliography:
Aviation Engines, I. Moscow: 1922.
On the heat calculus of engines. Air Force Technology,
1927, #2.

A Conspectus of Lectures on the Theory of Turbo-
Compressors. Moscow: 1944.

Biography:
    Akademik B. S. Stechkin. Air Force Journal, 1954, #2.
Office: Laboratory of Motors of USSR Academy of Sciences
              Krasnoproletarskaya Ulitsa, 32
              Moscow, USSR
Residence: Leninskii Prospekt, 13
              Moscow, USSR
Telephone: B2 54 96

STRAKHOV, NIKOLAI MIKHAILOVICH (Geologist)

N. M. Strakhov was born April 15, 1900. In 1928 he graduated from Moscow University. He began working in 1934 at the
Geological Institute of the U.S.S.R. Academy of Sciences. In 1953
he was made a member of the main editorial staff of the Bol'-
shaya Sovetskaye Entsykl. (Great Soviet Encyclopedia). He was
elected a Corresponding Member of the U.S.S.R. Academy of
Sciences in 1946, and in 1953 an Academician. In 1948 he was
awarded a Stalin Prize.

Strakhov's scientific activity is in the field of modern deposits, ancient sedimentary rock—iron ore, lime-dolomitic
rocks, oil shale, halogen deposition, and of the geochemistry of
iron, manganese, phosphorus, vanadium, chromium, nickel, and
a series of other elements. Continuing the work of his teacher,
A. D. Arkhangel'skii (1879-1940, geologist, professor at Moscow University, and Academician), Strakhov developed and established a comparative method of analysis in lithology. A
study of contemporary reservoirs (Black and Caspian Seas,
Lake Aral, Balkash and others) was made and an exact analysis
of contemporary sedimentation was presented. He studied the
role of diagenesis in the formation of sedimentary rock. He
published monographs on iron ore and lime-dolomitic species
of modern and ancient reservoirs and discovered new regularities in the formation of iron and carbonate rocks. He defined
the characteristics of sedimentation by the main structural
units of the earth's crust—platforms, geosynclines and the fore-
most depressions. He suggested a scheme of irreversible evolution in sedimentary rock formation during the history of the
earth, and indicated three important stages: Pre-Cambrian,
the Proterozoic-lower Paleozoic, and the modern (from the
Devonian to the present). In addition, he associated the periodic recurrence of similar rocks with the recurrence of major
transgressions and regressions of the sea. Recently he

has advanced the idea that four types, ice, humid, arid and sedimentary, are involved in sedimentary rock formation.

In 1960 Strakhov was awarded the Red Banner of Labor.

Bibliography:
Domanik Facies of Southern Urals. Moscow: 1939.
Iron Ore Facies and Their Analogies in the Earth's History. Moscow: 1947.
Basis of Historical Geology, 3rd ed., 2 parts, 1948.
Lime-Dolomitic Facies of Contemporary and Ancient Basins. Moscow: 1951.
Historico-geological types of sediment deposition. Izvest. Akad. Nauk S.S.S.R., Ser. Geol., 1946, #2.
On the periodic and irreversible evolution of sedimentation in the history of the earth. Izvest. Akad. Nauk S.S.S.R., Ser. Geol., 1949, #6.
and others. Sediment Deposition in Contemporary Basins. Moscow: 1954.
Types of sedimentation, and formation of sedimentary rocks. Izvest. Akad. Nauk S.S.S.R., Ser. Geol., 1956, #5 and #8.
On theoretical lithology and its problems. Izvest. Akad. Nauk S.S.S.R., Ser. Geol., 1957, #11.

Office: Geological Institute of USSR Academy of Sciences
Pyzhevskii Pereulok, 7
Moscow, USSR
Residence: Novopeschanaya, 3
Moscow, USSR
Telephone: D7 51 78

STRELETSKII, NIKOLAI STANISLAVOVICH (Structural Engineer)

N. S. Streletskii was born September 14, 1885. In 1911 he graduated from the Petersburg Institute of Engineers of Communication Lines. In 1915 he taught at the Moscow Technological College where he became a professor in 1918. In 1933 he was made a professor at the Moscow Institute of Construction Engineers. He has been a member of the U.S.S.R. Academy of Construction and Architecture since 1956, and was elected to the U.S.S.R. Academy of Sciences as a Corresponding Member in 1931. In 1944 he was awarded the title of Honored Scientist of the R.S.F.S.R.

In 1918-30 Streletskii organized and directed experimental investigations of bridge structures. He is the author of a static theory of the construction safety factor, the study of processes of destruction of steel structures and other questions

of supporting power of structures as a whole. He has developed
theories of calculating structures and established a scientific
basis for standardization of transportation and industrial structures.

Bibliography:

Methods of Calculating Non-Prop Beams with Parallel Belts
and a Junction Load. St. Petersburg: 1913.

Laws on Changing of Weight on Metal Bridges. Moscow:
1926.

New Ideas and Opportunities in Industrial Metal Construction. Moscow-Leningrad: 1934.

Course on Bridges. Metal Bridges, Part 1-2. Moscow:
1931.

and others. Course on Metal Construction, Part 1-3.
Moscow-Leningrad: 1940-44.

Basic premises in standardizing bridge constructions on the
U.S.S.R. ways of communication. Questions of Standardizing
Bridge Constructions, 1. Moscow: 1953.

Biography:

Nikolai Stanislavovich Streletskii. Moscow: 1946 (contains
list of works of Streletskii).

Nikolai Stanislavovich Streletskii (Anniversary of the scientist). Prikl. Mekhanika, 1956, 2, #2.

Office: Academy of Construction and Architecture USSR
            Pushkinshaya Ulitsa, 24
            Moscow, USSR

Residence: M. Levshinskii p. 14
            Moscow, USSR

Telephone: G6 60 42

STRELKOV, PETR GEORGIEVICH (Physicist)

P. G. Strelkov was born in 1899. In 1924 he graduated from
Leningrad Industrial Institute. He was engaged in scientific research, 1923-26, in Leningrad, and in 1936-56 he was a senior
scientific worker and then laboratory supervisor at the U.S.S.R.
Academy of Sciences Institute of Physical Problems. From
1956 to 1959 he was deputy Director and subsequently laboratory supervisor of the All-Union Institute of Physico-Technical
and Radiotechnical Measurements of the Commission on Measurements and Measuring Instruments. In 1959 he became a
departmental Chairman of the U.S.S.R. Academy of Sciences
Siberian Branch Institute of Thermal Physics. He was elected,
in 1960, a Corresponding Member of the U.S.S.R. Academy of
Sciences. In 1943 he was the recipient of a Stalin Prize.

Strelkov's works are primarily concerned with research in thermal and molecular processes.

Bibliography:

and S. I. Novikova. Thermal expansion of silicon at low temp. Fiz. tverdogo Tela, 1, #12, 1841-3 (1959). Phys. Sci. Abstr. 63, 13494 (1960).

and A. S. Borovik-Romanov, M. P. Orlova. Magnetic and thermal properties of three modifications of solid oxygen. Doklady Akad. Nauk S.S.S.R. 99, 699-702 (1954). Nucl. Sci. Abstr. 14, 24715 (1960).

and K. A. Karasharli. Thermodynamic investigations of 1,1-dicyclohexyldodecane, 1,1-diphenyldodecane, 1-phenyl-1-cyclohexyldodecane at low temperatures. Doklady Akad. Nauk S.S.S.R. 131, #3, 568-69 (1961).

and A. S. Borovik-Romanov, M. P. Orlova. Construction of a practical temperature scale in the range of 10-90° K. Technology of Measurements, #1, 34-35 (1960).

and D. N. Astrov, M. P. Orlov, D. I. Shaversaya. Collation of low temperature scales of platinum thermometer resistance. Technology of Measurements, #8, 29 (1959).

Office: USSR Academy of Sciences
Leninskii Prospekt, 14
Moscow, USSR

Residence: Vorob'evskoye Shosse, 2
Moscow, USSR

Telephone: B2 16 93

STRUMINSKII, VLADIMIR VASIL'EVICH (Mechanical Engineer)

V. V. Struminskii was born April 29, 1914. He graduated from Moscow University in 1938. In 1941 he began working at the Central Aero-Hydrodynamics Institute. He was elected, in 1958, to the U.S.S.R. Academy of Sciences as a Corresponding Member. In 1947 and 1948 he received Stalin Prizes.

Struminskii's main works deal with aerodynamics. He formulated a theory of a boundary layer on a sliding wing (1946), the general theory of a non-stationary boundary layer (1948) and the general theory on three-dimensional boundary layer for an arbitrary surface (1952).

Bibliography:

Sideslip of the wing in a viscous and compressed gas. Doklady Akad. Nauk S.S.S.R., 1946, 54, #9.

Sideslip of a wing in a viscous liquid. Doklady Akad. Nauk S.S.S.R., 54, #7.

Theory of non steady-state boundary layer. Collection of
Theoretical Works on Aerodynamics. Moscow: 1957.
and N. K. Lebed. Method of calculating the distribution of
circulation along the span of an arrow wing. Collection of
Theoretical Works on Aerodynamics. Moscow: 1957.
Theory of a space boundary layer on a sliding wing. Collection of Theoretical Works on Aerodynamics. Moscow:
1957.

Office: Central Aero-Hydrodynamics Institute of USSR
                 Academy of Sciences
                 Moscow, USSR

STYRIKOVICH, MIKHAIL ADOL'FOVICH (Heat Engineer)

M. A. Styrikovich was born November 16, 1902. He graduated in 1927 from the Leningrad Technological Institute. From
1928 to 1945 he worked at the Leningrad Province Scientific
Research Power Engineering Institute (now the Central Boiler-
Turbine Institute). He has also worked at the Institute of Energetics of the U.S.S.R. Academy of Sciences from 1938 and from
1939 at the Moscow Institute of Energetics. Since 1946 he has
been a Corresponding Member of the U.S.S.R. Academy of
Sciences.

Styrikovich worked on diesel generator units and steam
boiler processes and studied the movement of a steam mixture
through pipes and the heat transfer to a boiling liquid under
high pressure. He investigated the separation of steam and the
solubility of salts in high pressure steam. Styrikovich assisted
in establishing standards for heat and aerodynamic calculations
of boiler units.

In November 1962, Styrikovich was awarded the Order of the
Red Banner of Labor.

Bibliography:
and others. Course on Steam Boilers. Part 1-2. Leningrad-
Moscow: 1934-39.
Hydrodynamics and heat exchange in steam boilers and their
influence on the internal boiler physico-chemical processes.
Internal Boiler Physico-Chemical Processes. Moscow-
Leningrad: 1951.
Internal Boiler Processes. Moscow-Leningrad: 1954.
and others. Generation of Steam of Super High Parameter.
Moscow: 1950.
Working Processes of Continuously Operating Coil Boilers
of Super High Pressure (Report). Moscow: 1956.

Biography:
 On the 50th Anniversary of the Corresponding Member of the
 U.S.S.R. Academy of Sciences, M. A. Styrikovich. Boiler-
 Turbine Construction, 1953, #1.
 Office: USSR Academy of Sciences
               Leninskii Prospekt, 14
               Moscow, USSR
 Residence: Leninskii Prospekt, 13
               Moscow, USSR
 Telephone: B2 43 99

SUBBOTIN, MIKHAIL FEDOROVICH (Astronomer)
 M. F. Subbotin was born June 28, 1893. In 1914, he graduated from the University of Warsaw. In 1930, he became a
professor at Leningrad University. From 1922 to 1930, he was
Director of the Taskhent Observatory. He became, in 1942, the
Director of the U.S.S.R. Academy of Sciences Institute of Theoretical Astronomy. He was elected a Corresponding Member
of the U.S.S.R. Academy of Sciences in 1946.
 Subbotin has determined the orbits of planets and comets, investigated the general properties of motion of n-bodies, and
improved convergence of basic series used in celestial mechanics. He is the author of a three volume Course on Celestial
Mechanics (1933-49) in which all basic sections of celestial mechanics were presented for the first time in the Russian lan-
guage.
Bibliography:
 Determination of singular points of the analytical function.
 Mathematical Collection, 1916, 30, #3, 402-433.
 New form of the equation of Euler-Lambert and its appli-
 cation in calculating orbits. Russian Astronomical Journal,
 1924, 1, #1.
 Sur le problème des deux corps de masses variables. As-
 tron. Zhur., 1936, 13, #6.
 A new anomaly which contains as special cases the true and
 tangential anomalies. Doklady Akad. Nauk S.S.S.R., 1936,
 4, #4.
 The improvement of convergence of basic expansion of the
 theory of disturbed movement. Bulletin of the Institute of
 Theoretical Astronomy, 1947, 4, #1.
 Course on Celestial Mechanics, 1, 2nd ed. Leningrad-
 Moscow: 1941; 2-3, Leningrad-Moscow: 1937-49.

Astronomic and geodesic works of Gauss. Karl Friedrich
Gauss. Collection of articles under the general editorship
of Academician I. M. Vinogradov, Moscow, 1956 (241-310).

Office: Institute of Theoretical Astronomy
            Universitetskaya Naberezhnaya, 5
            Leningrad, USSR

SUKACHYEV, VLADIMIR NIKOLAEVICH (Botanist)

V. N. Sukachyev was born June 7, 1880. He graduated from
the Forestry Institute in Petersburg in 1902 and worked as an
assistant at the University. From 1912 to 1918 he was a junior
botanist at the Botanical Museum of the Petersburg Academy of
Sciences. He was a professor at the Institute of Forestry (later
Forest-Technical Academy) 1919-1941, at the Graphic Institute
1918-1925, and at Leningrad University 1925-1941. In 1924 to
1926, Sukachyev was Chairman of the Acclimatization Department of the Department of Geobotany, and in 1931 to 1933 of
the Main Botanical Garden of the U.S.S.R. Academy of Sciences.
He moved to Moscow in 1944 and became Director of the Institute of Forestry of the U.S.S.R. Academy of Sciences. He was
professor at the Moscow Forest-Technical Institute 1944-1948
and at Moscow University 1948-1951. Sukachyev was elected a
Corresponding Member of the U.S.S.R. Academy of Sciences in
1920, and in 1943 an Academician. Since 1937 he has been a
member of the Communist Party of the Soviet Union. In 1916
he was a member-founder and then became President in 1946
of the All Union Botanical Society. He has been President
(1955) of the Moscow Society of Naturalists, and Honored Member of the All Union Botanical Society and the Geographic Society of the U.S.S.R. The Geographical Society awarded him
prizes four times, 1912, 1914, 1929, 1947. In 1951 he was
awarded a Gold Medal of V. V. Dokuchaev by the U.S.S.R.
Academy of Sciences.

Sukachyev conducted many expeditions for studying the vegetation of various regions of the country. He spent much time
in studying swamps and worked out the theory of the formation
of swamps which he presented in a book (Swamps: their Formation, Development and Character, 1914). He also studied the
vegetative cover, working in phytocoenology. In geography, Sukachyev advocated a wide complex approach to the study of natural
phenomena and in particular to vegetation. In paleo-botany,
Sukachyev developed spore-pollen analysis for studying post-
glacial and mid-glacial deposits of the U.S.S.R. In the study of
forests, he proposed methods of characterization of types of

385 SVETOVIDOV

forests. He also has worked in systematics of wood (larch, birch, willow) and obtained a series of valuable sorts of willows. Scientific research on protective forest growing has been conducted under his leadership since 1949. He is the author of a series of textbooks and handbooks on dendrology, geobotany, the study of vegetation and especially on the study of the types of forests, and also work on some questions of Darwinism.

In 1960 Sukachyev was named an Honored Scientist of the R.S.F.S.R.

As of 1961, Sukachyev has been Chairman for the Study of the Quaternary Era, Moscow, Academy of Sciences U.S.S.R.

Biography:
 V. B. Sochava. Creative path of V. N. Sukachyev and his role in the development of geobotany and study of the landscale (on the 75th Anniversary since date of birth, and the 55th Anniversary of scientific activity). Proceedings of the All-Union Geographic Society, 1955, <u>87</u>, #5.
 To Academician V. N. Sukachyev on the 75th Anniversary since the date of birth. Collection of Works on Geobotany, Forestry, Paleogeography and Flora. Moscow-Leningrad: 1956.

Office: Laboratory of Forest Studies of USSR Academy of Sciences
 Moscow, USSR
Residence: Leninskii Prospekt, 13
 Moscow, USSR
Telephone: V2 23 52

SVETOVIDOV, ANATOLI NIKOLAEVICH (Ichthyologist)

A. N. Svetovidov was born November 3, 1903. He graduated in 1925 from the Faculty of Fisheries of the Moscow Agricultural Academy of K. A. Timiryazev. In 1932 he began work at the Institute of Zoology of the Academy of Sciences U.S.S.R., Leningrad. He has been a doctor and professor since 1928 and a Corresponding Member of the U.S.S.R. Academy of Sciences since 1953.

Svetovidov's work is concerned with the classification, morphology, geographical distribution, and historical origin of fish.

Bibliography:
 Materials on classification and biology of umber of the Lake Baikal. Trudy of the Baikal Limnological Station, 1931, 1.

Gadoid Fishes. Moscow-Leningrad: 1948. Fauna of the
U.S.S.R., Fishes, Vol. IX, #4.
Clupeoid Fishes. Moscow-Leningrad: 1952. Fauna of the
U.S.S.R., Fishes, Vol. II, #1.
Materials on the structure of the brain of fishes. Pt. I.
Codfish brain. Trudy Zoo. Inst. Akad. Nauk, 13, 1950.
Pt. II. Structure of herring brain. Trudy Zoo. Inst. Akad.
Nauk, 21, 1955.

SYRKIN, YAKOV KOVOVICH (Physical Chemist)
Ya. K. Syrkin was born December 5, 1894. In 1919 he graduated from the Ivanovo-Voznesensk Polytechnical Institute,
where he taught as a professor beginning in 1925. Since 1931,
Syrkin has been professor at the Institute of Fine Chemical
Technology. While at Karpov Physico-Chemical Institute, he
organized a department on molecular structure. From 1931 to
1952, he was scientific chairman of this department. In 1943,
he was elected to the U.S.S.R. Academy of Sciences as a Corresponding Member. He was awarded a Stalin Prize in 1943.

The works of Syrkin are concerned with chemical thermodynamics, kinetics of reactions in solutions, the mechanism of
Menshutkin reactions in solutions and in a gas phase, and in
particular, the study of molecular structure and chemical
bonds. He applied dipole moments in investigating molecular
structure and measured dipole moments for 500 substances.
He investigated mechanisms of chemical reactions with the aid
of labeled atoms, and intermolecular interaction by dielectric
polarization.

Bibliography:
and M. E. Dyatkina. Chemical Bonds and Structure of Molecules. Moscow-Leningrad: 1946.
and I. I. Moiseev. Mechanisms of some reactions with participation of peroxides. Uspekhi Khim. 29, 425-69 (1960).
C. A. 54, 17233c (1960).
and G. N. Kartsev. Dipole moments of some organosilicon
compounds. Izvest. Akad. Nauk S.S.S.R., Otdel. Khim. Nauk,
374-5 (1960). C. A. 54, 18000g (1960).
and M. E. Dyatkina. Stereochemistry of bimolecular substitution in complex compounds. Zhur. Neorg. Khim. 4, 1285-
90 (1959). C. A. 54, 8183b (1960).
and M. E. Djatkina. Contemporary state of quantum chemistry. Chem. listy 54, 332-43 (1960) - A review. C. A. 54,
12694 (1960).

and M. S. Kintenovo. Kinetics of alkylating 2-acetyl-
methylene-3-ethyl benzthioazoline (as related to the problem
of seven-membered active complexes). Doklady Akad. Nauk
S.S.S.R. 146, #1, 100-01 (1962).

Office: Karpov Physico-Chemical Institute of USSR Acade-
                my of Sciences
                Obukha Street, 10
                Moscow, USSR

TALMUD, DAVID L'VOVICH (Physical Chemist)
D. L. Talmud was born October 24, 1900. He graduated in
1923 from the Odessa Chemical Institute, and until 1925 taught
at the Odessa University. In 1930 he went to work at the Leningrad Institute of Chemical Physics. Beginning in 1934, he was
at the Institute of Biochemistry, U.S.S.R. Academy of Sciences.
Talmud was elected in 1934 a Corresponding Member of the
U.S.S.R. Academy of Sciences. He has been a member of the
Communist Party of the Soviet Union since 1940. In 1943 he
received a Stalin Prize.
    Talmud worked in physical chemistry of surface layers and
colloidal chemistry. He has also investigated the structure of
protein. Along with his scientific theoretical investigations,
Talmud has worked on problems connected with industry.
    Talmud is a member of the I. P. Pavlov Institute of Physi-
ology, Leningrad, U.S.S.R. Academy of Sciences, as well as a
member of the Institute of Biochemistry.
Bibliography:
    "Morphological" transformations of globular albumins. Suc-
    cesses of Biological Chemistry (annual), 1, Moscow, 1950.
    Structure of Albumin. Moscow-Leningrad: 1940.
    and S. E. Bresler. Surface Phenomena. Moscow-Leningrad:
    1934.
    and S. E. Bresler. On nature of globular albumins. Doklady
    Akad. Nauk S.S.S.R., 1944, 43, #7-8.
Office: A. N. Bakh Institute of Biochemistry of USSR
                Academy of Sciences
                Leninskii Prospekt, 33
                Moscow, USSR
Residence: Leninskii Prospekt, 13
                Moscow, USSR
Telephone: B2 54 35

TAMM, IGOR' EVGEN'EVICH (Physicist)

I. E. Tamm was born July 8, 1895. He graduated from Mcscow University in 1918 and then taught at several universities. From 1924 to 1941 and again in 1954, he was at Moscow University. Beginning in 1934, he has worked at the Physics Institute of the U.S.S.R. Academy of Sciences. Tamm was a Corresponding Member of the U.S.S.R. Academy of Sciences from 1933 until 1953 when he was elected an Academician. He was a Hero of Socialist Labor. In 1958 he received a Stalin Prize and also the Nobel Prize. All of Tamm's students are well known physicists and theoreticians.

Tamm's theoretical investigations are in quantum mechanics and its applications, in radiation, in cosmic rays, and interaction of nuclear particles. In 1932 he formulated a quantum theory on the scattering of light in solid bodies and developed the relativistic quantum mechanics theory of light scattering by electrons. In the quantum theory of metals, Tamm and S. P. Shubin gave a theory of the photoeffect in metals in 1931. In 1932 he predicted the existence of special surface states of electrons on crystals known as the Tamm levels. In 1934 he developed mathematically a quantitative theory of nuclear forces based on exchange interaction of electrons and neutrinos. In 1937 he and I. M. Frank worked out the theory of Cherenkov effect, the radiation emitted by a rapidly moving electron. For this work he received the Nobel Prize. In 1945 he gave an approximate method for calculating the interaction of nuclear elementary particles. Tamm, with A. D. Sakharov, proposed in 1950 the utilization of an electric discharge in plasma, which is placed in a magnetic field, for obtaining a controlled thermonuclear reaction. Tamm is the author of a textbook, Basis of the Theory of Electricity (1929, 6th ed., 1956).

Tamm has attended the Pugwash Conferences.

Bibliography:

Über die Wechselwirkung der freien Elektronen mit der Strahlung nach der Diraschen Theorie des Elektrons und nach Quantenenlektrodynamik. Zeitschrift fur physik, 1930, Bd 62, #7-8.

Über eine mögliche Art der Elektronenbindung an Kristalloberflächen. Physikalische Zeitschrift der Sowjetunion, 1932, 1, #6.

and S. Al'tshuler. Magnetic moment of the neutron. Doklady Akad. Nauk S.S.S.R., 1934, 1, #8.

Exchange forces between neutrons and protons and Fermi's theory. Priroda, 1934, 133, #3374.

Radiation emitted by uniformly moving electrons. Journal
of Physics, Moscow, 1939, 1, #5-6.
Relativistic interaction of elementary particles. Journal of
Physics, Moscow, 1945, 9, #6.
Biography:
    V. L. Ginzburg and E. L. Feinberg. Igor Evgen'evich Tamm
(On the 60th Anniversary since the date of birth). Uspekhi
Fiz. Nauk, 1955, 56, #4 (contains list of works of Tamm).
Academician Igor' Evgen'evich Tamm (On the 60th Anniver-
sary since the date of birth). Zhur. Eksptl. i Teoret. Fiz.,
1955, 29, #1 (7).
Office: P. N. Lebedev Physics Institute of USSR Academy
          of Sciences
          Leninskii Prospekt, 53
          Moscow, USSR
Residence: Nab. Gor'kogo 4/22
          Moscow, USSR
Telephone: B3 20 29

TANANAEV, IVAN VLADIMIRIVICH (Chemist)

I. V. Tananaev was born June 4, 1904. In 1925 he graduated
from Kiev Polytechnical Institute where he continued to work
until 1934. He was appointed, in 1939, Chief of the Laboratory
and, in 1949, Chief of the Department in the Institute of General
and Inorganic Chemistry of the U.S.S.R. Academy of Sciences.
From 1948 to 1954 he was Deputy Director of this Institute. In
1942 he became a member of the Communist Party of the Soviet
Union. He was a Corresponding Member of the U.S.S.R. from
1946 to 1958 when he became an Academician.

Tananev worked primarily in the fields of analytical and inorganic chemistry, especially in the study of fluorides, ferro-
cyanides of various metals, and also compounds or rare elements. He applies the physico-chemical methods for solving
problems of analytical chemistry.

In May 1960, Tananaev visited the United States and was at
the National Bureau of Standards on an exchange program.
Bibliography:
    On the solubility in an ice region in a triple system KF - HF
- H_2O. Proc. Acad. Sci. U.S.S.R., Sect. Phys. & Chem.
Anal., 1941, 14.
Physico-Chemical Analysis in Analytical Chemistry. Proc.
Acad. Sci. U.S.S.R., Sect. Phys. & Chem. Anal., 1950, 20.

Kurnakov Physico-Chemical Analysis in Analytical Practice.
Trudy Vsesoyuzn Knof. po Anal. Khim., <u>1</u>. Moscow-
Leningrad: 1939.
Investigation of the system K_2PdCl_4-KIH_2O according to the
method of light absorption. Zhur. Anal. Khim., 1948, <u>3</u>, #5.
<u>with N. V. Bausova.</u> Study of chemistry of fluorides of galli-
um and their utilization for separating gallium from other
metals. Khim. Redkikh El., #2. Moscow: 1950.
Biography:
  Ivan Vladimirovich Tananaev (to the 50th Anniversary since
  date of birth). Zhur. Anal. Khim., 1954, 9, #4.
Office: N. S. Kurnakov Institute of General Chemistry,
             USSR Academy of Sciences
             Leninskii Prospekt, 31
             Moscow, USSR
Residence: 1-aya Cheremushkinskaya 3
             Moscow, USSR
Telephone: B7 56 81

<u>TATARINOV, PAVEL MIKHAILOVICH (Geologist)</u>
  P. M. Tatarinov was born November 6, 1895. He graduated
in 1925 from the Leningrad Mining Institute. In 1924-49, he
worked in the Geological Committee (The All-Union Scientific
Research Geological Institute) and in 1954 he began working
there again. He went to teach at the Leningrad Mining Institute
in 1930 and in 1940 was made professor. Since 1953 he has
been a Corresponding Member of the U.S.S.R. Academy of
Sciences.
  Tatarinov has studied ore deposits and non-metallic industrial minerals of the U.S.S.R., particularly of the Urals.
Bibliography:
  Materials for Knowledge of the Deposits of Chrysotile-
  Asbestos of the Bazhenovsk Region of the Urals. Leningrad:
  1928 (Works of the Geological Committee. New series, #185).
  and others. Alapaevsk Intrusion of Ultrabasic Rock of the
  Urals and Chromite Deposits in It. Moscow-Leningrad:
  1940 (Works of the Central Scientific Research Institute of
  Geologic Prospecting, #120).
  <u>and others.</u> Course on Deposits of Commercial Minerals,
  2nd ed. Moscow-Leningrad: 1946.
  Conditions in the Formation of Deposits of Ore and Non-
  Metallic Commercial Minerals. Moscow: 1955.
  <u>and others.</u> Course on Non-Metalliferous Deposits, Part
  1-2. Moscow-Leningrad-Novosibirsk: 1934, 1935.

Biography:
  A. A. Ivanov. Pavel Mikhailovich Tatarinov. Collection of
  Information of the All-Union Scientific Research Geological
  Institute, 1956, #4.
Office: Leningrad Mining Institute
                 Leningrad, USSR

TERENIN, ALEKSANDR NIKOLAEVICH (Physical Chemist)
  A. N. Terenin was born May 6, 1896. In 1921 he graduated
from Petrograd (Leningrad) University, and in 1932 he became
a professor there. He was a student of D. S. Rozhdestvenskii,
the leading Russian optics specialist. In 1932 he was elected a
Corresponding Member of the U.S.S.R. Academy of Sciences
and in 1939 an Academician. He received a Stalin Prize in 1946
and in 1953 the S. I. Vavilov Prize, awarded by the U.S.S.R.
Academy of Sciences.
  Terenin's main works are devoted to study of the nature of
physical and chemical processes which take place in substances
under the influence of light. For discovering and analyzing
these processes Terenin worked out optical methods which are
based on observation of spectra and the intensity of luminescence of primary products of photoreactions. He showed the
possibility of selectively exciting emission of atomic spectral
lines of metal vapors and analyzing the energy level distribution. Terenin studied the dissociation of salt molecules in a
vapor state under the influence of light which is accompanied
by formation of luminescent atoms (1924). In this way he investigated many polyatomic molecules of inorganic and organic
compounds by irradiating them with a short-wave ultraviolet
radiation (1936). Terenin used fluorescence of aromatic molecules in a vapor state for establishing the mechanism in the
intramolecular and intermolecular transformations of energy
of excitation (1934). In 1943 he explained the phosphorescence
of molecules of complex organic compounds, and of their photochemical reactions based on excitation of molecules into a state
with two unpaired electrons (biradical). He was the first to obtain infra-red spectra of gases at several thousand atmospheres (1940). Terenin studied the optical properties of molecules, adsorbed on the surface of solid bodies and the nature of
catalyst activity (1934). In 1945 he studied the photochemical
reactions of chlorophyl and its analogs. In the 1950's Terenin
was investigating reactions of organic molecules by using light
to ionize electrons. Terenin is the leader of the school of
Soviet photochemists.

In May 1960, Terenin visited the United States to attend the
Gordon Conference on Infrared Spectroscopy, Meriden, New
Hampshire.

Bibliography:

Optical excitation of atoms and molecules. Zhur. Fiz. 31,
26-49 (1925); 37, 98-125 (1926).

Optical dissociation of salt molecules. Zhur. Fiz. 44, 713-
36 (1927).

Introduction to Spectroscopy. Leningrad: 1933.

Spectral investigation of chemical processes in organic compounds at low temperatures. Acta Physicochim. U.R.S.S.
12, 617-36 (1940); 13, 1-30 (1940).

Photo-luminescence and vibrational energy exchange in
complex molecules. Discussions Faraday Soc. 35, 39-43
(1939).

Photochemical processes in aromatic compounds. Acta
Physicochim. U.R.S.S. 18, 210-41 (1943) (in English).

Photochemistry of Dyes and Related Organic Compounds.
Moscow-Leningrad: 1947.

Infrared absorption spectra of adsorbed molecules. Doklady
Akad. Nauk S.S.S.R. 66, 885-8 (1949).

Photochemistry of chlorophyl and photosynthesis. Reported
at the 6th Annual Bach Conference, March 17, 1950. Moscow, 1951.

and V. B. Evstigneyev. Photoelectrochemical effect in
phthalocyanin, chlorophyll and pheophytin. Doklady Akad.
Nauk S.S.S.R. 81, 223-6 (1951).

and Yu. A. Klyvev. Effect of pressure on the oscillating
spectrum of chloroform absorption. Doklady Akad. Nauk
S.S.S.R. 147, #3, 653-55 (1962).

Biography:

V. N. Kondrat'ev. New directions in the development of
photochemistry (On the 50th Anniversary of Academician
A. N. Terenin). Zhur. Fiz. Khim., 1946, 20, #6.

A. T. Vartanyan. Academician A. N. Terenin. Zhur. Fiz.
Khim., 1956, 30, #5.

G. G. Neuimin. Aleksandr Nikolaevich Terenin (On the 60th
Anniversary since the date of birth). Optika i Spektroskopiya, 1956, 1, #4.

Office: Institute of Physics
        The University
        Leningrad B-164, USSR

TERENT'EV, ALEKSANDR PETROVICH (Organic Chemist)

A. P. Terent'ev was born January 20, 1891. He graduated from Moscow University in 1913 and continued working there. In 1934 he became a professor. In 1953 he was elected a Corresponding Member of the U.S.S.R. Academy of Sciences. He was awarded in 1948 a Stalin Prize.
Terent'ev worked on methods in organic functional analysis. He worked on synthesis of sulfonic compounds. He also investigated the chemistry of pyrrole, furan, indole and other heterocyclic compounds, as well as stereochemistry and the nomenclature of organic compounds.

Bibliography:
Sulfonation of Acidophobic Compounds. 1947.
and M. M. Buzlanova, S. I. Obtemperanskaya. Determination of acrylonitrile with the aid of piperidine. Zhur. Anal. Khim. 14, 506 (1959). C. A. 54, 9611g (1960).
and K. I. Litvin, E. G. Rukhadze. Method of nascent reagents. II. Use of dioxane in the determination of calcium and strontium as sulfates. Zhur. Anal. Khim. 14, 288-93 (1959). C. A. 54, 8444a (1960).
and R. A. Gracheva, V. A. Dorokhov. Preparation of α-amino acids from furan derivatives. II. Synthesis of aspartic acid. Zhur. Obshchei Khim. 29, 3474-8 (1959). C. A. 54, 15262h (1960).
and M. N. Preobrazhenskaya, G. M. Sorokina. Introduction of substituents in the benzene ring of indole. V. Synthesis of ketones of the indole series. Zhur. Obshchei Khim. 29, 2875-81 (1959). C. A. 54, 12098d (1960).

Office: Chemistry Department
            Moscow University
            Moscow, USSR
Residence: Leninskii gory, sekt, "L"
            Moscow, USSR
Telephone: B9 14 65

TIKHOMIROV, VIKTOR VASIL'EVICH (Radio Engineer)

V. V. Tikhomirov was born December 23, 1912. In 1940 he graduated from the Moscow Institute of Energetics, after which he worked in a number of scientific research institutes. He has been a member of the Communist Party of the Soviet Union since 1948. In 1953 he was elected to the U.S.S.R. Academy of Sciences as a Corresponding Member. He has been awarded Stalin Prizes.

Office: USSR Academy of Sciences
              Leninskii Prospekt, 14
              Moscow, USSR
Residence: 1-aya Cheremushkinskaya, 3
              Moscow, USSR
Telephone: B7 34 56

TIKHONOV, ANDREI NIKOLAEVICH (Mathematician and Geophysicist)

A. N. Tikhonov was born October 30, 1906 in Gzhatsk, Smolensk Oblast. He graduated in 1927 from Moscow University. He holds the Doctor of Physical-Mathematical Sciences degree and in 1936 became a professor at Moscow University. He is also at the Institute of Terrestrial Physics. In 1939 he was elected a Corresponding Member of the U.S.S.R. Academy of Sciences.

The first investigations of Tikhonov were in theoretical topology. He introduced the concept of the product of topological spaces ("Tikhonov Product"). He then worked in mathematical physics and geophysics such as on theorems of uniqueness for equations of the parabolic type, distribution of electromagnetic fields, investigation of commercial minerals, and electromagnetic sounding of deep layers of the earth's crust with the aid of variation of the electromagnetic field of the earth.

Bibliography:

On determining the electric characteristics of deep layers of the earth's crust. Doklady Akad. Nauk S.S.S.R., 1950, <u>73</u>, #2.

On the singleness of solving the problems of electrosurveying. Doklady Akad. Nauk S.S.S.R., 1949, <u>69</u>, #6.

and A. A. Samarskii. Equations in Mathematical Physics. 2nd Ed. Moscow: 1953.

Office: Moscow University
              Moscow, USSR
Residence: Leninskii Prospekt, 13
              Moscow, USSR
Telephone: B2 46 95

TIMOFEEV, PYOTR VASIL'EVICH (Electrical Engineer)

P. V. Timofeev was born June 25, 1902. In 1925 he graduated from Moscow University. In 1928 he began working at the All-Union Electro-Technical Institute. He has taught at Moscow University, the Moscow Institute of Energetics and other

colleges and universities. He was awarded Stalin Prizes in
1946 and 1951, and was made an Honored Scientist of the
R.S.F.S.R. in 1947. In July 1962, he received the Order of the
Red Banner of Labor. In 1953 he was elected to the U.S.S.R.
Academy of Sciences as a Corresponding Member.
Timofeev studied photoeffect, the secondary emission of
electrons, discharge in gases, and electronic optics. He has
designed photocells, electronic multipliers, transmitting tubes.
Together with others he designed a series of new electronic
devices.

Bibliography:
   On the mechanism of secondary emission of electrons from
   complex surfaces. Zhur. Tekh. Fiz., 1940, 10, #1.
   Photocells with multistage amplification of the photocurrent
   with the aid of secondary emission of electrons. Zhur. Tekh.
   Fiz., 1940, 10, #1.
   and V. V. Sorokina. On the form of the field for electro-
   static lenses. Zhur. Tekh. Fiz., 1948, 18, #4.
   Emission of electrons from complex surfaces. Radiotekh-
   nika i Electronika, 1957, 2, #1.
Office: USSR Academy of Sciences
                 Leninskii Prospekt, 14
                 Moscow, USSR
Residence: Fil'skoe sh. 5.
                 Moscow, USSR
Telephone: G9 00 03, Ext. 180

TOROPOV, NIKITA ALEKSANDROVICH (Physical Chemist)

N. A. Toropov was born June 28, 1908. He graduated in 1930
from Leningrad Polytechnical Institute. From 1930 to 1941 and
1944 to 1953, he worked at Lensovet Leningrad Technological
Institute where, in 1940, he became professor. He had worked
from 1941 to 1944 at the "Giprocement" Institute. In 1953, he
became Director of the U.S.S.R. Academy of Sciences Institute
of Silicate Chemistry. Toropov has been an Active Member of
the U.S.S.R. Academy of Construction and Architecture since
1957. As of June 1962 he was elected Corresponding Member
of the U.S.S.R. Academy of Sciences. In 1952 he received a
State Prize.
   Toropov's work deals with mineralogy of silicates and physical chemical investigation of silicate systems. He also investigated problems in physical chemistry of semi-conductors and
ferrite materials.

Bibliography:
and V. F. Zhuravlev. Physical and Colloidal Chemistry of
Silicates. Moscow-Leningrad: 1941.
and K. S. Evstrop'ev. The Chemistry of Silicon and the
Physical Chemistry of Silicates. 2nd ed. Moscow: 1956.
and L. N. Bulak. A Course in Mineralogy and Petrography
with Fundamentals of Geology. Moscow: 1953.
and A. I. Borisenko. Physical chemical investigations of
magnetic ceramics. Trudy of the Lensovet Leningrad Technological Institute, 1952, #24, pp. 13-59.
Chemistry of Cements. Moscow: 1956.
Office: Institute of the Chemistry of Silicates of USSR
             Academy of Sciences
             Makarova, 2
             Leningrad V-164, USSR
Telephone: A2 71 43

TRAPEZNIKOV, VADIM ALEKSANDROVICH (Scientist in
       Automation and Electric-Machine Building)
V. A. Trapeznikov was born November 28, 1905. After
graduating from the Moscow Technological Institute in 1928, he
worked until 1933 at the All-Union Electro-Technical Institute.
From 1930 to 1941, he taught at the Moscow Institute of Energetics and in 1939 became a professor there. In 1941 Trapeznikov began working at the Institute of Automation and Telemechanics of the U.S.S.R. Academy of Sciences, and in 1951 was
made the Director. He has been a member of the Communist
Party of the Soviet Union since 1951. In 1953 he was elected a
Corresponding Member of the U.S.S.R. Academy of Sciences
and in 1960 an Academician. He was awarded a Stalin Prize in
1951.
    Trapeznikov proposed calculating transverse field electric
machines, methods and techniques of economic analysis, and
the construction of electrical machines and transformers. In
the area of automation, he investigated automatic control of
geometric sizes, construction of high-speed automatic devices
and the design of aggregate systems of automatic control and
regulation. Under his leadership methods were worked out for
modeling systems of automatic control and he designed electronic modeling units.
    As of 1961, Trapeznikov was Chairman of the National
Committee of the Soviet Union for Automatic Control.

Bibliography:
Basis of Planning Series of Asynchronous Machines.
Moscow-Leningrad: 1937.
Generalized conditions of proportionality and optimal geome-
try of a transformer. Electricity, 1948, #2.
and others. Automatic Control of Linear Dimensions of
Products. Moscow: 1947.
Biography:
Corresponding Member of the U.S.S.R. Academy of Sciences,
V. A. Trapeznikov (On the 50th Anniversary of date of
birth). Automat. i Telemekh., 1956, 17, #2.
Office: Institute of Automation and Telemechanics of USSR
Academy of Sciences
Kalanchevskaya Ulitsa 15-a
Moscow, USSR

TROFIMUK, ANDREI ALEKSEEVICH (Geologist in the Oil
        Field)
A. A. Trofimuk was born August 16, 1911. After graduating
from Kazan' University in 1933, he worked in the oil industry.
In 1953 he joined the staff of the All-Union Oil-Gas Scientific
Research Institute and in 1953 to 1955 was deputy Director,
then in 1955 to 1957 Director. In 1957 he became Director of
the Institute of Geology and Geophysics of the Siberian Branch
of the U.S.S.R. Academy of Sciences. Trofimuk has been a
member of the Communist Party since 1941. In 1944 he was a
Hero of Socialist Labor. He was elected a Corresponding Member of the U.S.S.R. Academy of Sciences in 1953 and in 1958 an
Academician. In 1946 and in 1950 he was awarded State Prizes
of the First Degree.
Trofimuk's main investigations are in the field of tectonics
and the Volga-Ural oil bearing territory. Under his leadership,
large-scale geologic surveys were carried out in this territory.
As a result of the studies of lithology of oil bearing Ishimbaevo
limestone, Trofimuk substantiated methods of prospecting for
new oil deposits of the Ishimbaevo type. In cooperation with
others, he divided the Volga-Ural territory into tectonic districts. He has worked on increasing the oil output from limestone collectors and also in particular in developing methods of
flooding the oil fields.
As of 1961, Trofimuk was Chairman of the Commission for
Conservation of Nature of the Siberian Branch U.S.S.R. Academy
of Sciences.

Bibliography:
and V. I. Nosal' and Yu. A. Pritula. Outline of Tectonics and
oil bearing of the Volga-Urals territory, 1939, #2.
Oil Bearing of Paleozoic Bashkir. Moscow-Leningrad:
1950.
Conditions in the Formation of Oil Deposits of the Ural-
Volga Oil Bearing Territory. Moscow: 1955.
and M. F. Mirchink, K. R. Chepikov. Specific Features of
the Geological Structure of Platform Regions in the Soviet
Union in Relation to Their Oil and Gas Saturation. Works of
the Fifth World Petroleum Congress, 1959, Sec. I.
Oil and gas saturation of Siberian platform. Geologia i Geo-
fizika, 1960, #7.

Office: Institute of Geology and Geophysics
              Siberian Branch of USSR Academy of Sciences
              Novosibirsk 72, Akademgorodok
              Siberia

TROSHIN, AFANASII SEMENOVICH (Cytologist)

A. S. Troshin was born in 1912. In 1936 he graduated from
Leningrad State University, and completed his postgraduate
work in 1940 at the Physiological Institute of the University.
In 1940-41 he worked at the All-Union Institute of Experimental
Medicine. He served in the Soviet Army from 1941-46, after
which he worked as a senior scientific worker at the Institute of
Experimental Medicine until 1950. From 1950 to 1951 he was
at the U.S.S.R. Academy of Medical Sciences Institute of Oncology, and from 1951-1957, at the U.S.S.R. Academy of Sciences
Institute of Zoology. In 1957 he became supervisor of the Laboratory on Cell Physiology of the U.S.S.R. Academy of Sciences
Institute of Cytology, where in 1958, he became Director. In
1959 he was named Chief Editor of the journal "Cytology." He
has been a member of the Communist Party of the Soviet Union
since 1944. He was elected, in 1960, to the U.S.S.R. Academy
of Sciences as a Corresponding Member.

Troshin's basic works deal with the study of cell permeability and the nature of bioelectric phenomena.

Bibliography:
and V. S. Kirpichnikov, A. N. Svetovidov. Labelling of Cy-
prinus carpio with radioactive phosphorous and calcium
isotopes. Doklady Akad. Nauk S.S.S.R. 111, #1, 221-24
(1956).
and V. S. Kirpichnikov, A. N. Svetovidov. Absorption and
output of radioactive calcium by Daphnia, cyclops and

Lebistes reticulates. Doklady Akad. Nauk S.S.S.R. 110, #6, 1122-25 (1956).
and N. B. Ilinskala. The marking of flies and insects by means of radioactive phosphorus. Zoologicheski Zhur. 33 (4): 841-847, 1954. Biol. Abstr. 30, 6302 (1956).
Concerning the regulation of water content of protoplasm. Akad. Nauk S.S.S.R., Trudy Zoologicheskovo Instituta 13, 420-433. 1953. Biol. Abstr. 31, 7210 (1957).
and A. A. Vareninov, S. A. Krolenko, N. N. Nikol'skii. History of the physiological science: Dimitrii Nikolaevich Nasonov. Fiziol. Zhur. S.S.S.R. (Trans.) 44 (11/12): 1124-1129. 1958. Biol. Abstr. 35, 25682 (1960).
Concerning an article by L. M. Chailakhian—Modern concepts of the nature of the resting potential. Biofizika (Trans.) 5 (1): 104-111, 1960. Biol. Abstr. 35, 69156 (1960).
On the question of research in the problem "the main questions of cytology." Tsitologia 2 (2): 131-137, 1960, Referat. Zhur. Biol., 1961, #1A131 (Trans.) Biol. Abstr. 36, 39488 (1961).
Symposium on the theme, "Membrane transport and metabolism." Vestnik Akad. Nauk S.S.S.R. 11: 111-112. 1960, Referat. Zhur. Biol. 1961. #9A127 (Trans.) Biol. Abstr. 36, 71235 (1961).
Das Problem der Zellpermeabilitat. Jena: 1958.
Office: Institute of Cytology of USSR Academy of Sciences
           Prospekt Maklina, 32
           Leningrad F-121, USSR

TSELIKOV, ALEKSANDR IVANOVICH (Mechanical Engineer)
    A. I. Tselikov was born April 20, 1904. He graduated from the Moscow Technical College in 1928. He worked as a constructor in "Hammer and Sickle" steel plant, the Izhevsk plant and others. Since 1935, he has been teaching at colleges and universities, and in 1945 began working at the Central Construction Bureau of Metallurgical and Mechanical Engineering. He was awarded Stalin Prizes in 1947, 1948 and 1951. In 1945, he became a member of the Communist Party, and in 1953 he was elected a Corresponding Member of the U.S.S.R. Academy of Sciences.
    Tselikov has constructed rollingmills and studied the theory of rolling. He has developed an original method of calculating rollingmills. Under his direction new, highly productive mechanized rollingmills (including blooming continuous sheet, pipe and wire mills, mills for rolling the thinnest ribbon, and section

of a variable and periodic cross-section—spheres, semi-axis)
were constructed.
Bibliography:
Calculation for Constructing Rolling Machines. Moscow-
Leningrad: 1938.
Rollingmills. Moscow: 1946.
Mechanisms of Rollingmills. Moscow: 1946.
Influence of external zones on the widening and distribution
of speeds and tension along the width of a rolled strip.
Problems of Metallurgy, 1953.
Progressive processes of processing by pressure on plants
of mass machine building. Up-to-Date Technology of Ma-
chine Building. Moscow: 1955.
Office: Central Construction Bureau of Metallurgical and
Mechanical Engineering
Moscow, USSR
Residence: B. Afanas'evskii, p. 3
Moscow, USSR
Telephone: G6 01 11

TSITSIN, NIKOLAI VASIL'EVICH (Botanist and Plant Breeder)
N. V. Tsitsin was born December 18, 1898. He graduated
from the Institute of Agriculture and Melioration in Saratov in
1927 and worked at the All-Union Southeastern Scientific Research Institute of Agriculture. In 1932 he began working at
Omsk Regional Experimental Station (later the Siberian Scientific Research Institute of Agriculture) and from 1936 to 1938
was the Director. In 1938-1949 and 1954-1957 Tsitsin was Director of the All-Union Agricultural Exhibit in Moscow; 1938-
1948 Chairman of the State Commission on Quality Testing of
Grain, Oil-bearing Plants and Grasses; in 1940-1949 Director
of the Scientific Research Institute of the Non-Black Soil Belt
Grain Economy. He was made Director, in 1945, of the Chief
Botanical Gardens of the U.S.S.R. Academy of Sciences which
he had organized. From 1938 to 1948, he was Vice President
of the Lenin All-Union Agricultural Academy. Tsitsin has been
a member of the Lenin All-Union Agricultural Academy since
1932 and an Academician of the U.S.S.R. Academy of Sciences
since 1939. In 1938 he became a member of the Communist
Party of the Soviet Union. He was elected an Honorary Member
of the Rumanian Academy of Sciences in 1946 and, in 1947, of
the Czech Academy of Agriculture. In 1958 he was made Chairman of the Society of Soviet-Indian Cultural Relations. He has

been a Deputy to the U.S.S.R. Supreme Soviet, first, third, and fourth convocations. In 1943 he was awarded a Stalin Prize.

Tsitsin's main investigations are in the field of hybridization, such as crossing grassy plants with woody plants, and cultured plants with wild growing ones. According to Soviet sources, he created a new form of perennial wheat. Tsitsin and his associates claim that wild rye (sandy and gigantic) can be crossed with wheat, barley, and rye; and also rye with quack grass. He has also obtained hybrids between ordinary and tree-like tomatoes, and produced new forms of stable hybrid variety of winter branching wheat.

Bibliography:
Distant Hybridization of Plants. Moscow: 1954.
Problem of Wheat and Perennial Wheat. Moscow: 1935.
What Will Crossing Wheat with Quack Grass Produce? Moscow: 1937.
Investigating vegetative-sexual hybridization of grassy plants with woody plants. Works of the Zonal Institute of Agriculture of the Non-Chernozem Belt of the U.S.S.R., 1946, #13.
Ways of Creating New Cultured Plants. Moscow: 1948.
Role of Science and Advanced Practices in Raising the Agricultural Economy. Moscow: 1954.
Office: Main Botannical Garden of USSR Academy of
              Sciences
              Ostankino, USSR

TSYTOVICH, NIKOLAI ALEKSANDROVICH (Geophysicist)

N. A. Tsytovich was born May 13, 1900. He graduated from Leningrad Institute of Civil Engineers in 1927. In 1930 he began to teach in a number of institutions of higher learning in Leningrad. He became, in 1951, professor of the Moscow Engineering Structural Institute. From 1947 to 1953, he was Chairman of the Presidium of the U.S.S.R. Academy of Sciences Yakut Branch. In 1943 he began work in the Institute of Permafrost of the U.S.S.R. Academy of Sciences where from 1948-1953, he was deputy Director. He has been a Corresponding Member of the U.S.S.R. Academy of Sciences since 1943 and an Active Member of the Academy of Construction and Architecture of the U.S.S.R. Academy of Sciences since 1956.

Tsytovich's main works deal with the study of frozen ground mechanics.

In 1950, Tsytovich was the recipient of a Stalin Prize.

Bibliography:
and M. I. Sumgin. Fundamentals in the Mechanics of Frozen
Grounds. Moscow-Leningrad: 1937.
Estimation of Foundation Depressions. Moscow-Leningrad:
1941.
Ground Mechanics. 3rd ed. Moscow-Leningrad: 1951.
and M. I. Sumgin. Principles of Mechanics of Frozen
Ground. U. S. Snow, Ice, and Permafrost Research Es-
tablishment. Trans. 19 Apr. 1959, 288 p. Engineering In-
dex, 1960, 1359.
Office: V. A. Obrachev Institute of Permafrost
Bol'shoy Cherkasskii Pereulok, 2/10
Moscow, USSR

TUDOROVSKII, ALEKSANDR ILARIONOVICH (Physicist)

I. I. Tudorovskii was born August 24, 1875. He graduated in
1897 from Petersberg University. In 1902-1919 he taught at
the Petersberg Polytechnic Institute, in 1919-1929 at the
Petersberg University (Leningrad). Tudorovskii was named,
in 1916, the head of the first Russian Calculating Bureau on the
calculation of optical systems. In 1918 he began work at the
State Optical Institute. He has been a Corresponding Member
of the U.S.S.R. Academy of Sciences since 1933. He was awarded the Stalin Prizes in 1942 and in 1946, and in 1956 he was an
Honored Scientist of the R.S.F.S.R.

The works of Tudorovskii deal with problems of geometrical
optics and optical techniques and also with electromagnetic
phenomena. Tudorovskii organized optics calculations in
U.S.S.R. He used vector methods in calculating mirror and
prism systems and aberrations of the third order. He completed, together with associates, large-scale works on the
calculation and development of new types of photographic
lenses.

Bibliography:
Electricity and Magnetism. Part 1-2. Leningrad, Moscow:
1933-35.
Theory of Optical Devices. 1-2, 2nd ed. Moscow-Leningrad:
1948-52.
Dependence of aberrations of the third order of the optical
system on the position of planes of the inlet pupil and the
object. Zhur. Tekh. Fiz., 1942, 12, #8, 496.
Calculation of the aberrations of the third order by the
formulas of Lange. Zhur. Tekh. Fiz., 1943, 13, #4-5,
230-258.

On the coefficient of chromatic aberrations of the first
order. Zhur. Tekh. Fiz., 1945, 15, #9, 585-597.
Influence of errors in the production of reflection prisms on
the passing of rays in them. Zhur. Tekh. Fiz., 1934, 4, #4,
719-747.
Reflection systems with three mutually perpendicular planes
in the case of minor deviations of angles from the right
angle. Works of the State Optical Institute, 1941, 15, #112-
120, 137-147.
Biography:
   A. I. Tudorovskii—Honored Scientist of the R.S.F.S.R. Zhur.
   Tekh. Fiz., 1956, 26, #9, 2125.
Office: USSR Academy of Sciences
             Leninskii Prospekt, 14
             Moscow, USSR

TUMANOV, IVAN IVANOVICH (Plant Physiologist)

   I. I. Tumanov was born June 30, 1894. He graduated from
the Kiev Agricultural Institute in 1923. From 1925 to 1942, he
worked at the All-Union Institute of Horticulture in Leningrad.
In 1940, he worked at the U.S.S.R. Academy of Sciences Institute of Plant Physiology where he became a professor in 1947.
In 1953, he was elected to the U.S.S.R. Academy of Sciences as
a Corresponding Member.
   Tumanov's work is in winter endurance, drought-resistance,
water treatment and fruit-yields of agricultural crops. He developed methods of laboratory determination of drought-
resistance and frost-resistance of plants; he studied in detail
the process of adaption of plants to winter conditions, and
worked out a laboratory method of determining frost-resistance
of field cultures. He carried out experimental studies on the
physiology of rotting, the destruction of plants through excess
moisture and under an ice crust. He has also worked on the
physiology of fertility in cultured plants.
Bibliography:
   Physiological Basis of Frost-Resistance of Cultured Plants.
   Moscow-Leningrad: 1940.
   Main Achievements of Soviet Science in the Study of Frost-
   Resistance of Plants. Moscow: 1951.
   and E. Z. Gareev. Influence of organs of fertility on the
   female plant. Works of the Institute of the Physiology of
   Plants of K. A. Timeryazev, 1951, 7, #2.

Office: K. A. Timiryazev Institute of Plant Physiology of
              USSR Academy of Sciences
              Leninskii Prospekt, 33
              Moscow, USSR
Residence: Sokol'nicheskaya slob. 14/18
              Moscow, USSR
Telephone: E1 40 13

TUPOLEV, ANDREI NIKOLAEVICH (Aeronautical Engineer)
A. N. Tupolev was born October 29, 1888. In 1909 he entered
Moscow Higher Technical School where he was a pupil of N. E.
Zhukovskii, founder of Russian Aviation. While still an under-
graduate, he designed the first wind tunnel. Tupolev also participated in the work of the aeronautical group of the Moscow
Higher Technical School and designed and built training gliders,
in one of which he became a pilot. After his graduation from
the Moscow Higher Technical School, he assisted in the organization of the Central Aerodynamic Institute and from 1918 to
1935 was the Director. Tupolev is a Lieutenant General in the
Engineer-Technical Service. In 1933 he was elected Corresponding Member of the U.S.S.R. Academy of Sciences and in
1953 Academician. He was made an Honored Scientist of the
R.S.F.S.R. in 1933 and a Hero of Socialist Labor in 1945. Tupolev was awarded a Stalin Prize and, in 1957, a Lenin Prize. He
has been a Deputy of the Supreme Soviet (third through fifth
convocations).

In 1922, a bureau of design, in the Central Aerodynamic
Institute, under the direction of Tupolev, designed and constructed the single-seat ANT-1, built wholly of wood. In 1923-
24, Tupolev designed a glider, a hydroplane, and the two-seat
airplane, ANT-2, made entirely from duraluminum. Under his
direction, more than 100 various types of airplanes were designed and constructed. Tupolev also designed and constructed
medium and heavy bombers: TB-1, ANT-9, TB-3, ANT-25
(RD), TB-7, SB, TU-2, TU-4, TU-104, and the TU-114. In
planes designed by Tupolev, a series of Russian flights were
carried out in Europe and to America (flights of V. P. Chkalov
and M. M. Gromov across the North Pole in an ANT-25 airplane), landings of polar expeditions on drifting ice floes, the
rescue of the crew of the steamship "Chelyuskin," and other important tasks were accomplished. Tupolev airplanes were used
for attacking enemy objectives at long distances.

The TU-104 (1955) is the Soviet jet airplane. Its cruising
flight speed: 800 kilometers/hr. The cabin of the airplane is

hermetically sealed, which permits use of flight altitudes at
10,000 meters. Through further improvement of this type of
aircraft, there appeared the more comfortable, multi-seat (170)
passenger airplane, the TU-114 (1956) with turboprop engines.
Continuing the work of N. E. Zhukovskii, Tupolev worked on
aerodynamic calculation for airplanes and on the strength of
material. Besides the designing of airplanes, Tupolev constructed various types of naval torpedo boats.
    In March 1962, Tupolev was re-elected Deputy from
R.S.F.S.R. to the Supreme Soviet. He has attended Pugwash
Conferences.
Office: USSR Academy of Sciences
               Leninskii Prospekt, 14
               Moscow, USSR

USHAKOV, SERGEI NIKOLAEVICH (Organic Chemist)

S. N. Ushakov was born September 16, 1893. In 1921 he
graduated from the Petrograd Polytechnic Institute. He was
made professor at the Leningrad Technological Institute in
1930; at the same time, 1931-41, he worked at the Scientific
Research Institute of Plastics of which he was Director in 1931-
38. In 1945-49, he was Director of the Scientific Research
Institute of Polymerized Plastics. He was also the Director,
in 1948-53, of the Institute of High Molecular Compounds of the
U.S.S.R. Academy of Sciences. Ushakov has been a member of
the Communist Party of the Soviet Union since 1943. He was
elected, in 1943, a Corresponding Member of the U.S.S.R.
Academy of Sciences. In 1942 and 1950 he received Stalin
Prizes, and in 1943 was an Honored Scientist of the R.S.F.S.R.
    The investigations of Ushakov are concerned with phenol
aldehyde condensation, the synthesis of vinyl polymers, cellulose esters, the polymerization and copolymerization of unsaturated compounds, the preparation of polyvinyl alcohol and its
acetals, and the reactions of high molecular compounds. He
developed the technology of producing synthetic camphor, ethyl
cellulose, benzyl cellulose, poison of phenolic resins, polyvinyl
acetate, and polyvinyl alcohol.
Bibliography:
    Artificial Resins and Their Utilization in the Varnish Indus-
    try. Leningrad: 1929.
    Plastics from Esters of Cellulose. Moscow-Leningrad:
    1932.
    Esters of Cellulose and Plastics on Their Basis. Leningrad-
    Moscow: 1941.

Biography:
I. A. Arbuzova and E. N. Rostovskii. Laureate of the Stalin
Prize S. N. Ushakov. Uspekhi Khim., 1943, 12, #1.

Office: Institute of High Molecular Compounds of USSR
Academy of Sciences
Birzhevoy Prospekt, 6
Leningrad, USSR

VAINSHTEIN, BORIS KONSTANTINOVICH (Physicist)
B. K. Vainshtein is a Doctor of Physico-Mathematical Sciences. In April 1962, he was made the Director of the U.S.S.R.
Academy of Sciences Institute of Crystallography. He was
elected a Corresponding Member of the U.S.S.R. Academy of
Sciences in June 1962. In 1958 he received a prize awarded by
the Academy of Sciences Presidium for his "Structural Electro-
nography."

Bibliography:
New equations relating structural factors. Doklady Akad.
Nauk S.S.S.R. 124, #1, 87-90 (1959).
Symmetry of chain molecules. Kristallografia 4, #6, 842-48
(1959).
A new type of bonds between structural factors. Kristallo-
grafia 4, #1, 3-12 (1959).
Antisymmetry in Fourier formations of figures with a
special point. Kristallografia 5, #3, 341-345 (1960).
Problem of the atomic structure of biological molecules.
Vestnik Akad. Nauk S.S.S.R., #12, 20-26 (1960).
and A. N. Lobachev. Electronographic investigation of urea.
Kristallografia 6, #3, 395-401 (1961).
Developmental tendencies in contemporary crystallography.
Vestnik Akad. Nauk S.S.S.R. 4, 99-104 (1961).
and L. I. Tatarinova. Electronographic investigation of
poly-γ-methyl L-glutamate. Doklady Akad. Nauk 139, #6,
1347-50 (1961).
and N. V. Nikolaeva, R. E. Kruglyakova, N. A. Kiselev,
N. M. Emanuel'. Reducing the destructive degree of DNA
molecules during irradiation in the presence of propylgal-
late. Doklady Akad. Nauk 142, #3, 713-15 (1962).
Office: Institute of Crystallography of USSR Academy of
Sciences
Pyzhevskii Pereulok, 3
Moscow, USSR

VANICHEV, ALEKSANDR PAVLOVICH (Power Specialist)
In June 1962, A. P. Vanichev was elected Corresponding
Member of the U.S.S.R. Academy of Sciences.

VARENTSOV, MIKHAIL IVANOVICH (Geologist)
M. I. Varentsov was born January 20, 1902. In 1929 he
graduated from Moscow Mining Academy. He was Director of
the Institute of Geological Sciences in 1949-55; and in 1956 he
became Chief of the Laboratory in the Institute of Oil of the
U.S.S.R. Academy of Sciences. In 1953 he was elected a Corresponding Member of the U.S.S.R. Academy of Sciences.
Varentsov has further developed the studies of his teacher,
I. M. Gubkin (1871-1939, geologist), on the main problems of
oil geology. In 1929-49 he studied regional geological investigations in tectonics, stratigraphy, and oil geology of Sakhalin
Island, North Caucasus, Tamanskii Peninsula, Turkmeniya,
Georgia, Azerbaijan, Armenia, Volga-Ural oil bearing territory, Venskii and Pannonskii Basins. In 1935-49 he was leader
of expeditions into the territory beyond the Caucasus, Turkmen, Volga-Bashkir and Georgia.
Bibliography:
    and I. M. Gubkin. Geology of Oil and Gas Deposits of the
    Tamanskii Peninsula. Baku-Moscow: 1934.
    Oil deposits in Turkmen. International Geological Con-
    gress. Works of the XVIIth Session of the U.S.S.R., 1937, 4.
    Moscow: 1940.
    Problem of the oil-bearing of Turkmen in view of new
    data. Geology and Commercial Minerals of Middle Asia.
    Moscow-Leningrad: 1940 (U.S.S.R. Academy of Sciences).
    Geology and oil-bearing of the Venskii Basin. Collection of
    Geological Works Devoted to the Memory of Academician
    I. M. Gubkin. Moscow-Leningrad: 1948.
    Geological Structure of the Western Part of the Kurinsk De-
    pression. Moscow-Leningrad: 1950.
    New oil-bearing province of the Pannonskii Basin of South-
    Eastern Europe and its possible analogs. Collection of Geo-
    logical Works Devoted to the Memory of Academician I. M.
    Gubkin. Moscow-Leningrad: 1950.
    and V. T. Mordovskii. Geological Structure of the Northern
    Edge of Gori-Mukhranskaya Depression. Moscow: 1954.
Office: Institute of Oil, USSR Academy of Sciences
                 Moscow, USSR

VDOVENKO, VIKTOR MIHAILOVICH (Chemist)

V. M. Vdovenko was born January 5, 1907. He graduated from the Kiev Chemico-Technological Institute of Food Industry in 1930 and worked from then until 1935 at the Institute of Chemical Physics of the U.S.S.R. Academy of Sciences. In 1935 he began teaching at Leningrad University and in 1953 was made professor. He joined the staff of the Radium Institute of the U.S.S.R. Academy of Sciences and in 1953 became the Director. Vdovenko has been a member of the Communist Party of the Soviet Union since 1929. In 1953 he was elected a Corresponding Member of the U.S.S.R. Academy of Sciences.

The work of Vdovenko is in radiochemistry, inorganic and physical chemistry. He studied the behavior of ions in complex systems such as solutions containing gelatin, or solid electrolytes, the action of atomic hydrogen on inorganic compounds, chemical protection against war gases, and the adsorption of radium on glass as a function of the pH and radium ion concentration. Vdovenko investigated the distribution of radioactive elements between two immiscible solvents, which could make possible the utilization of an extraction method for separating and purifying these elements. He also investigated the systems: radioactive element-water-organic solvent, determined the solubility and forms of state of some radioelements in nonaqueous solutions, established the connection between the structure of organic solvents and their extractability.

Bibliography:

and S. A. Shchukarev. Mechanism of the movement of chloride and hydrogen ions in the presence of gelatin. Zhur. Fiz. Khim., 1934, 5, #4.

Investigating the action of atomic hydrogen on inorganic compounds. Works of the Anniversary Scientific Session. Leningrad State University. Section on Chemical Sciences. Leningrad: 1946, 112-122.

Adsorption of ions and the potential discontinuity at the border of a solid electrolyte-solution. Scientific Papers of the Leningrad University, 1936, #11. Series on Chemical Sciences, #2, 48-102.

and B. A. Nikitin. Adsorption of radium on glass. Works of the State Radium Institute, 1937, 3, 256-65.

Extraction methods of separating elements. Zhur. Anal. Khim., 1957, 12, #5, 593-599.

Extraction as a method of separating and studying radioactive element. Zhur. Neorg. Khim., 1958, 3, #1, 145-54.

and D. N. Suglobov, G. A. Romanov. Structure of UO2-
(NO3)2-NO2. Doklady Akad. Nauk S.S.S.R. 146, #5, 1078-80
(1962).

Office: V. G. Khlopin Radium Institute of USSR Academy of
           Sciences
           Ulitsa Roentgena 1
           Leningrad, USSR

VEKSHINSKII, SERGEI ARKAD'EVICH (Electronics Physicist)

S. A. Vekshinskii was born October 15, 1896. He studied at
Leningrad and Don Polytechnic Institutes. From 1922 to 1928
he was chief engineer of the Electrovacuum plant in Leningrad.
He became Chief of the Vacuum Laboratory of "Svetlana" in
1928. He was chief engineer from 1936 to 1939 and a consultant
from 1939 to 1941 at this plant. Vekshinskii was made Director
of the Scientific Research Vacuum Institute in 1947. In 1940 he
became a member of the Communist Party of the Soviet Union.
In 1946 he was elected Corresponding Member of the U.S.S.R.
Academy of Sciences and in 1953 Academician. He received a
Stalin Prize in 1946, and in 1956 he was a Hero of Socialist
Labor. In 1962 he was awarded the A. S. Popov Gold Medal.

Vekshinskii has worked on a new method of obtaining and
investigating metallic alloys. The results of this work are set
forth by Vekshinskii in his monograph, "New Method of Metallographic Study of Alloys" (1944, Stalin Prize 1946). He designed
a whole series of new electronic devices which were utilized in
industry. At the Scientific Research Vacuum Institute, he
directs the development of vacuum apparatus for various
branches of industry.

Bibliography:
A new method of Metallographic Study of Alloys. 1944.
and M. I. Menshikov, I. S. Rabinovich. High-vacuum pumps
and units for accelerators. Vacuum (GB) 9, 201-6 (1959).
SA(A) 64, 9426 (1961).

Biography:
E. V. Gurvich. S. A. Vekshinskii. Radiotekh. i Elektron,
1956, 1, #12.

Office: USSR Academy of Sciences Scientific Research
           Institute
           Moscow, USSR

VEKSLER, VLADIMIR IOSIFOVICH (Physicist)

V. I. Veksler was born March 4, 1907. In 1931 he graduated
from Moscow Institute of Energetics. He was at the All-Union

Electrotechnical Institute from 1930 until 1936 when he began work at the Institute of Physics of the U.S.S.R. Academy of Sciences. In 1956 he started working at the Joint Institute of Nuclear Research. He became a Corresponding Member of the U.S.S.R. Academy of Sciences in 1946 and in 1958 an Academician.

Veksler has worked on development of experimental methods used in investigations of x-rays, atomic nucleus, and cosmic radiation such as the use and mode of action of Geiger-Muller and proportional counters. He also studied electron-nuclear showers in cosmic rays. Well known is Veksler's work on the theory of particle accelerators. In 1944, he proposed a principle of phase stability of particles and used it as a basis of new types of accelerators--synchrotrons and synchrocyclotrons.

In November 1959, Veksler visited the United States on a Nuclear Science Exchange program in New York City.

Bibliography:
New method of accelerating of relativistic particles. Doklady Akad. Nauk S.S.S.R., 1944, 43, #8.

and L. Groshev, B. Isaev. Ionization Methods in Irradiation Research. Moscow-Leningrad: 1949.

Office: Joint Institute of Nuclear Problems
          Dubno, Moscow, USSR
Residence: ul. Chkalova 21/2
          Moscow, USSR
Telephone: K7 39 56

VEKUA, ILYA NESTOROVICH (Mathematician)

I. N. Vekua was born May 6, 1907 in Sheshelety, Georgian S.S.R. In 1930 he graduated from Tbilisi University and holds the degree of Doctor of Physical-Mathematical Science. He began working at Moscow University in 1952 and in 1953 at the Mathematics Institute of the U.S.S.R. Academy of Sciences. In 1946 he was elected Academician of the Georgian S.S.R. Academy of Sciences, also a Corresponding Member of the U.S.S.R. Academy of Sciences, and in 1958 Academician. He was awarded in 1950 a Stalin Prize.

Vekua has utilized methods of the theory of analytical functions of a complex variable for the solution of differential and integral equations, which are met in problems of physics and mechanics, particularly the theory of elasticity. He obtained solutions to equations of steady-state oscillations of an elastic cylinder, thin plates and sloping shells, and torsion and bending of rods of heterogeneous material. The main results of Vekua in singular integral equations are included in the monograph of N. I. Muskhelishvili, "Singular Integral Equations" (1946). The work of Vekua in differential and integral equations has been utilized in the solution of problems in the theory of elasticity. Vekua also studied the general properties of the solutions of a wide range of elliptical partial differential equations and investigated the general boundary problems, which are important in the bending of the surfaces and in the theory of elastic shells.

As of 1961, Vekua was a Member of the Presidium of the Siberian Branch U.S.S.R. Academy of Sciences.

Bibliography:
New Methods of Solving Elliptical Equations. Moscow-Leningrad: 1948.
Systems of differential equations of the first order of the elliptical type, and boundary problems with their use in the theory of shells. Mat. Sbornik, New Series, 1952, 31, #2.
Stationary singular points of generalized analytical functions. Doklady Akad. Nauk S.S.S.R. 145, #1, 24-27 (1962).

Biography:
A. G. Kurosh and others, eds. Thirty Years of Mathematics in the U.S.S.R., 1917-1947. Collection of articles. Moscow-Leningrad: 1948.

Office: V. A. Steklov Institute of Mathematics of USSR
               Academy of Sciences
               1-y Akademicheskii Proyezd, 28
               Moscow, USSR
Residence: Novopeschanaya, Korp. 25
               Moscow, USSR
Telephone: D7 19 60

VELIKANOV, MIKHAIL ANDREEVICH (Hydrologist and Hydrodynamicist)

M. A. Velikanov was born January 22, 1879. After graduating from the Institute of Engineers of Lines of Communication, he worked as an engineer on the Siberian rivers Ob' and Yenisei, and in 1912-1921 on field studies of the rivers: Sukhona, North Dvina, Bug, Berezina, Volga, and Tom'. He taught in 1922-1929 at the Moscow Technical College, in 1930-1941 at the Moscow Hydrometeorological Institute, in 1942-1943 at the Central Asiatic University in Tashkent, in 1945-1954 at the Moscow University. Since 1939 he has been a Corresponding

Member of the U.S.S.R. Academy of Sciences. In 1948 he was made an Honored Scientist of the R.S.F.S.R.

Velikanov initially engaged in the study of flow stations (organized by him) and water balance. In 1932 he transferred to an experimental study of problems of river-bed hydrology in laboratories established under his direction for the Hydrometeorological Service and the U.S.S.R. Academy of Sciences. Velikanov studied water balance, large scale turbulence of river streams, mechanism of water pumps and the behavior of river beds. He took part in many large scale hydraulic projects.

Bibliography:

Hydrology of Continents; 1925.

Dynamics of a River-Bed Stream, 1-2., 3rd ed. Moscow: 1954-55.

Kinematic structure of a turbulent river bed stream. Izvest. Akad. Nauk S.S.S.R., Ser. Georgr. i Geofiz., 1946, 10, #4.

Structural forms of river-bed turbulence. Izvest. Akad. Nauk S.S.S.R., Ser. Geofiz., 1951, #3.

Basis of the gravitational theory of the movement of pumps. Izvest. Akad. Nauk S.S.S.R., Ser. Geofiz., 1954, #4.

Energo-balance of a deposit-bearing stream. Izvest. Akad. Nauk S.S.S.R., Ser. Geofiz., 1956, #6.

Biography:

G. V. Lopatin. On the 70th Anniversary of Mikhail Andreevich Velikhanov. Proceedings of the All-Union Geographical Society, 1949, 81, #5.

Celebration in honor of Mikhail Andreevich Velikanov. Bulletin of Moscow University, Series on Physico-Mathematical and Natural Sciences, 1954, 4, #6.

Office: USSR Academy of Sciences
              Leninskii Prospekt, 14
              Moscow, USSR
Residence: Leninskii Prospekt, 13
              Moscow, USSR
Telephone: V2 50 96

VERESHCHAGIN, LEONID FEDOROVICH (Physicist)

L. F. Vereshchagin was born in 1909. In 1930-32, he was a postgraduate student, and 1932-34 he worked as a senior engineer at a turbogenerator plant. He was an engineer, 1934-39, and subsequently chief engineer at the Physico-Technical Institute in Khar'kov. From 1939-1954, he was laboratory supervisor at the U.S.S.R. Academy of Sciences Institute of Organic

Chemistry, and from 1954-58, he was Chief of the U.S.S.R.
Academy of Sciences Laboratory in Ultra-High Pressures in
Moscow. In 1958 he became Director of the U.S.S.R. Academy
of Sciences Institute of High Pressure Physics. He attained the
rank of professor at Moscow University in 1953, and in 1960
was elected to the U.S.S.R. Academy of Sciences as a Corresponding Member. In 1952 he was awarded a Stalin Prize.
Vereshchagin's basic works are in the field of the physics
and technology of ultra-high pressures.
In July 1958, Vereshchagin visited the United States to attend
the Gordon Research Conference in Meriden, New Hampshire.
Bibliography:

and A. I. Likhter. Compressibility of the elements as a
function of atomic number. Translated into French from
Doklady Akad. Nauk S.S.S.R. 86, 745-8 (1952). Nucl. Sci.
Abstr. 14, 9847 (1960).

X-ray study of linear compression of graphite at pressures
up to 16000 kg/cm^2. Doklady Akad. Nauk S.S.S.R. 131, 300-2
(1960). Nucl. Sci. Abstr. 14, 17015 (1960).

and Demyashkevich. Indicator for high-pressure gas compressor. Pribory i Tekh. Ekspt. #1, 118-22 (1960). Nucl.
Sci. Abstr. 14, 19074 (1960).

and Yu. N. Ryabinin. Peculiarities of rheological behavior
of metals extruded by a hydraulic press. Translated into
French from Izvest. Akad. Nauk S.S.S.R. Otdel. Tekh. Nauk,
#5, 48-55 (1957). Nucl. Sci. Abstr. 14, 5567 (1960).

and A. A. Semerchan, S. V. Popova. Variation of the electrical resistance of praseodymium, dysprosium, erbium and
ytterbium at high pressures up to 250,000 kg/cm^2. Doklady
Akad. Nauk S.S.S.R. 139, #3, 585-86 (1961).

and A. A. Semerchan, N. N. Kuzin, S. V. Popova. Variation
of the electrical resistance of certain metals up to pressures
of 250,000 kg/cm^2. Doklady Akad. Nauk S.S.S.R. 138, #1,
84-85 (1961).

and A. A. Semerchan, N. N. Kuzin, S. V. Popova. Variation
of the electrical resistance of certain metals up to pressures
of 200,000 kg/cm^2. Doklady Akad. Nauk S.S.S.R. 136, #2,
320-21 (1961).

and Yu. N. Ryabinin, A. Ya. Preobrazhenskii, V. A. Stepha-
nov. Growth of metallic monocrystals at high hydrostatic
pressures. Doklady Akad. Nauk S.S.S.R. 135, #1, 45-47
(1961).

and F. F. Voronov, V. A. Goncharov. Effect of hydrostatic
pressure on the elastic properties of cerium. Doklady Akad.
Nauk S.S.S.R. 135, #5, 1104-07 (1960).
and A. A. Semerchan, N. N. Kuzin. Temperature dependence
of electrical resistance of polycrystalline graphite at pressures of up to 250,000/Kg.cm^2. Doklady Akad. Nauk S.S.S.R.
146, #2, 803-04 (1962).

Office: Institute of Physics of High Pressures of USSR
            Academy of Sciences
            Leninskii Prospekt, 31
            Moscow, USSR
Residence: Dorogomilovsk. nab. 9
            Moscow, USSR
Telephone: G3 59 68

VERNOV, SERGEI NIKOLAEVICH (Physicist)

S. N. Vernov was born July 11, 1910. He graduated from
Leningrad Polytechnic Institute in 1931. From 1930 to 1935 he
worked in the Institute of Radium of the U.S.S.R. Academy of
Sciences. In 1935 he went to work in the Physics Institute of
the U.S.S.R. Academy of Sciences, and in 1943 he became a
professor at Moscow University. He became Director, in 1946,
of the Scientific Research Institute on Nuclear Physics at Moscow University. Since 1953 he has been a Corresponding Member of the U.S.S.R. Academy of Sciences. In 1949 he was awarded a Stalin Prize. He was awarded a Lenin Prize in 1960 for
his participation in the discovery of and investigation of the
earth's external radiation belt and studies of the magnetic earth
and moon.

Vernov studied the nature and properties of cosmic rays in
the upper atmosphere. He investigated cosmic rays with the
aid of automatic devices, elevated to high altitudes by pilot-
balloons and transmitting their findings by radio. Vernov and
his associates discovered considerable effects due to cosmic
rays in the stratosphere. They showed that the primary particles are composed of protons, studied transition effects in the
stratosphere and ascertained the origin of a soft component.

Bibliography:

Latitude effect of cosmic rays in the stratosphere and test-
ing of the cascade theory. Works of the Physics Institute of
P. N. Lebedev, 1945, 3, #1.
Research on cosmic rays. (Collection of articles). Doklady
Akad. Nauk S.S.S.R. New Series, 1948, 61, #5-6, 62, #2-4.

Study of the interaction of a primary component of cosmic
rays with a substance in the stratosphere. Zhur. Eksptl. i
Teoret. Fiz., 1949, 19, #7.

Biography:
    Grigorov, N. L. Investigation of Cosmic Rays in the Strato-
    sphere. On the Work of the Laureate of the Stalin Prize,
    Professor S. N. Vernov. Successes of Contemporary Sci-
    ences. Moscow-Leningrad: 1950.
Office: Physics Department
             Moscow University
             Moscow, USSR
Residence: Leninskiye gory, sekt. "L"
             Moscow, USSR
Telephone: B9 34 17

VINOGRADOV, ALEKSANDR PAVLOVICH (Geochemist and
    Analytical Chemist)
    A. P. Vinogradov was born August 21, 1895. In 1943 he be-
came a Corresponding Member of the Academy of Sciences of
the U.S.S.R., and since 1953 he has been an Academician. He
was made, in 1949, a hero of Socialist Labor.
    Vinogradov graduated from the Medical Military Academy
and Leningrad University in 1924. He was a pupil and close
collaborator of B. I. Vernadskii, the founder of the Russian
School of Geochemistry. In 1948 he became Director of the
Institute of Geochemistry and Analytical Chemistry, U.S.S.R.
Academy of Sciences. Both in 1949 and 1951, he was winner of
Stalin Prizes.
    His fields of interest are the distribution of chemical ele-
ments in the upper part of the earth's crust, the investigation of
primary rock from which the sedimental part of the earth's
surface was formed, and the role played by vulcanic materials
in the formation of this upper part. While studying the salts in
the ocean, he came to the conclusion that cations of the sea
water are products of the erosion of magmatic rocks and that
anions are of vulcanic origin.
    Vinogradov has worked predominantly with rare and widely
dispersed chemical elements. In geochemistry of the individual
elements (halogen, boron, strontium, etc.), he emphasized the
importance of knowing, not only absolute amounts of the elements but also the ratios of the closely related elements, as
that of chlorine to bromine or strontium to calcium. He described geochemically more than forty rare and widely dispersed elements for different soil zones and showed their roles

in various soil-forming processes. He has investigated the
association of heavy metals such as vanadium and nickel with
bitumen. He has been active in the use of isotopes (sulfur,
hydrogen, oxygen, carbon, etc.) in geochemistry and has used
oxygen isotope O^{18} as an indicator of geochemical processes.
In photosynthesis, he found that plants liberate oxygen from
water and not from carbon dioxide. Also he showed that natural
hydroxides of iron, manganese, etc. obtain oxygen from water
rather than from the air. In the biogeochemical field, he investigated the changes produced by surroundings in the chemical composition of marine organisms. He found that the majority of chemical elements exist in all the organisms and that
elemental chemical composition of a species is its characteristic feature. Vinogradov also developed a theory of biogeochemical regions and by his study of areas with deficient and
excessive content of chemical elements, he evolved a theoretical basis for ordinary fertilizers and those containing microelements. His investigations in biogeochemical regions also
explained the effect of the chemical environment on the evolution of flora and fauna during different geological ages. In
analytical chemistry, Vinogradov developed many methods of
separation of numerous stable and unstable chemical elements
and introduced instrumental methods of analysis such as polarography, spectrometry, radiometry, mass spectrometry,
x-ray, and luminescence.

As of 1961, Vinogradov was Director of the Siberian Branch
U.S.S.R. Academy of Sciences Institute of Geochemistry and of
the U.S.S.R. Academy of Sciences Institute of Geochemistry and
Analytical Chemistry.

Bibliography:

Elementary chemical composition of marine organisms.
Works of the Biogeochemical Laboratory at the U.S.S.R.
Academy of Sciences, 3, 4, 6, parts 1 to 3. Moscow-
Leningrad: 1935-44.
Biogeochemical regions. Works of the Jubilee Session Dedi-
cated to the Centennial Birthday of V. V. Dokuchaev.
Moscow-Leningrad: 1949.
Geochemistry of dispersed elements in the sea water. Us-
pekhi Khim. 1944, 13, #1.
Geochemistry of Dispersed Elements in Soils. Moscow:
1957, 2nd edition.

Biography:

Academician Aleksandr Pavlovich Vinogradov (for 60th birthday). Vestnik Akademii Nauk S.S.S.R., 1956, #2, 97-98.

Vinogradov Aleksandr Pavlovich. Vestnik Akademii 1954,
   #4, 70.
Office: V. I. Vernadskii Institute of Geochemistry and
            Analytical Chemistry, USSR Academy of Sciences
            Vorob'evskoye Shosse 47-a
            Moscow, USSR
Residence: 2-aya Filevskaya, 10
            Moscow, USSR
Telephone: G9 00 07, Ext. 529

VINOGRADOV, IVAN MATVEEVICH (Mathematician)

I. V. Vinogradov was born September 14, 1891. He graduated from the Petersburg University in 1914 and remained
there to prepare for a doctor's degree. From 1918-1920 he
was a reader and professor at the Perm University, 1920-1934
a professor at Leningrad Polytechnical Institute, and in 1925
professor at the Leningrad University. In 1932 Vinogradov became Director of the Mathematics Institute of the U.S.S.R.
Academy of Sciences. He has been an Academician of the
U.S.S.R. Academy of Sciences since 1929. In 1945 he was recipient of a Stalin Prize and also a Hero of Socialist Labor.

Vinogradov's scientific activity pertains to the area of analytical theory of numbers. His first work is devoted to questions of determining errors of approximate formulas, which
express the sums of values of various arithmetical functions.
In 1937 Vinogradov derived the formula for a number of representations of the odd number in the form of a sum of three
simple numbers, and used them to obtain a solution of the
Goldbach problem.

In 1961 Vinogradov was awarded the Order of Lenin.
Bibliography:
   Selected Works. Moscow: 1952 (contains bibliography of the
   works of Vinogradov).
   New Method in Analytical Theory of Numbers. Leningrad-
   Moscow: 1937 (Works of the Mathematics Institute of V. A.
   Steklov, 10).
   Basis of Theory of Numbers, 6th ed. Moscow-Leningrad:
   1952.
Biography:
   editorship of A. G. Kurosh and others. Thirty years of
   Mathematics in the U.S.S.R., 1917-1947. Collection of
   articles. Moscow-Leningrad: 1948 (contains bibliography
   of works of Vinogradov).

K. K. Mardzhanishvili. Ivan Matveevich Vinogradov (On the
60th Anniversary since the date of birth). Uspekhi Mat.
Nauk, 1951, 6, #5.
Office: V. A. Steklov Mathematics Institute of USSR
Academy of Sciences
1-y Akademicheskii Proyezd, 28
Moscow, USSR
Residence: ul. Gor'kogo 22-a
Moscow, USSR
Telephone: B1 45 24

VLADIMIRSKII, VASILLII VASIL'EVICH (Physicist)

V. V. Vladimirskii has been working at the U.S.S.R. Academy
of Sciences Institute of Theoretical and Experimental Physics.
In June 1962 he was elected a Corresponding Member of the
U.S.S.R. Academy of Sciences.
Bibliography:
Magnetic mirrors, canals and flasks for cold neutrons.
Zhur. Ekspt'l. i Teoret. Fiz. 39, #4, 1062-1070 (1960).
and V. N. Andreev. Non-preservation of stability in strong
interactions, and nuclear fission. Zhur. Ekspt'l. i Teoret.
Fiz. 41, #2, 663-65 (1961).
Office: Institute of Theoretical and Experimental Physics
of USSR Academy of Sciences
Moscow, USSR

VLASOV, KUZMA ALEKSEEVICH (Geochemist and Mineralogist)

K. A. Vlasov was born November 14, 1905. He graduated in
1931 from Timiryazev Moscow Agricultural Academy. From
1932 to 1952 he worked at the Institute of Geological Sciences
at the U.S.S.R. Academy of Sciences. In 1953 he became Chief
of the Laboratory of Mineralogy and Geochemistry of Rare
Elements, and in 1956 Director of the Institute of Mineralogy,
Geochemistry, and Crystallography of Rare Elements of the
U.S.S.R. Academy of Aciences. Vlasov has been a member of
the Communist Party of the Soviet Union since 1939. In 1953 he
was elected a Corresponding Member of the U.S.S.R. Academy
of Sciences. He has been awarded two orders and also medals.
Vlasov has studied the genesis and classification of granite
pegmatites and other deposits of rare elements.
In November 1958, Vlasov visited the United States to attend
the American Geological Society meetings in St. Louis,
Missouri.

Bibliography:
Texture-paragenetic classification of granite pegmatites.
Izvest. Akad. Nauk S.S.S.R., Ser. Geol., 1952, #2.
Genesis of Rare Metallic Granitic Pegmatites. Moscow:
1955.
Factors in the formation of various types of rare metal
granite pegmatites. Izvest. Akad. Nauk S.S.S.R., Ser. Geol.,
1956, #1.
Office: Institute of Mineralogy, Geochemistry and Crystal-
             lography of Rare Elements of USSR Academy of
             Sciences
             Ulitsa Kuybysheva, 8
             Moscow, USSR
Residence: Lavrushinskii p. 17
             Moscow, USSR
Telephone: V1 85 90

VOEVODSKII, VLADISLAV VLADISLAVOVICH (Physical Chemist)

V. V. Voevodskii was born July 25, 1917. He graduated from
the Leningrad Polytechnic Institute in 1940 and remained to do
graduate work. In 1944 he became a senior scientific research
worker of the Institute of Chemical Physics at the U.S.S.R.
Academy of Sciences. He taught from 1946 to 1952 at Moscow
University. In 1953 he began work at the Moscow Physico-
Technical Institute and in 1955 was made professor there.
Voevodskii was elected a Corresponding Member of the U.S.S.R.
Academy of Sciences in 1958. In 1952 he was awarded the D. I.
Mendeleev Prize.

Voevodskii's work is in chemical kinetics and the chemistry
of free radicals. He has worked in combustion theory, and
oxidation of hydrocarbons, heterogeneous and homogeneous
catalysis, and structure and properties of free radicals. He
established a number of important details in the mechanism of
a chain reaction of hydrogen oxidation. Together with N. N.
Semyonov and F. F. Vol'kenshtein, he demonstrated the possibility of radical chain mechanisms in heterogeneous-catalytic
processes.

Bibliography:
and Ya. B. Zel'dovich. Thermal Explosion and Velocity of
Flames in Gases. Moscow: 1947.
and A. B. Nalbandyan. Mechanism of Oxidation and Combustion of Hydrogen. Moscow-Leningrad: 1949.

Office: Institute of Chemical Physics of USSR Academy of
            Sciences
            Vorob'evskoye Shosse, 2
            Moscow, USSR

VOL'FKOVICH, SEMEN ISAAKOVICH (Inorganic Chemist)
S. I. Vol'fkovich was born October 11, 1896. He graduated
from Moscow University of National Economy in 1920. In 1921
he began working at the Scientific Research Institute for Fertilizers and Insectifungicides and is the scientific director. In
1929, he was appointed professor at Moscow Military Technical
School, and in 1932 he was made professor at the Military Academy of Chemical Defense. In 1947 he was made professor at
Moscow University. He has been an Academician since 1946.
        With E. I. Zhukovskii he made a study of electrothermal
distillation of phosphorus from native phosphates in 1922. On
the basis of this study, electric furnace plants were built for
the first time in the U.S.S.R. From 1923 to 1929, he supervised
the production of superphosphates from native phosphates and
apatites. He worked also on the acid conversion of phosphates
to concentrated fertilizers. Then he developed a process for
obtaining potassium salts from sylvinite. In 1926, Vol'fkovich
and his co-workers worked out a coordinated treatment of phosphates with nitric acid to obtain phosphorus, nitrogen, and complex fertilizers, fluorine salts, and rare earths. For this work
he received a Stalin Prize in 1941. In 1930 and 1931 with A. P.
Belopol'skii, he studied a physico-chemical treatment of mira-
bilite to obtain soda and ammonium sulfate. Vol'fkovich initiated a number of studies on crystal chemistry of ammonium nitrate. And he also proposed a method of obtaining boric acid
from native datolites. With co-workers he developed a hydrothermal method of phosphate treatment. From 1945 to 1950, he
worked out new methods for obtaining fluorine compounds, ammonium nitrates and sulfates, phosphides, chlorides, and phosphorus compounds. He also developed procedures for obtaining
a number of metallo organic compounds.
        In June 1958, Vol'fkovich visited the United States to attend
the 50th Annual American Institute of Chemical Engineers in
Philadelphia, Penna.
Bibliography:
        Production of Potassium Chloride. Leningrad: 1930.
        Treatment of Khibin Apatites for Fertilizers. Leningrad:
        1932.
        Technology of Nitrogen Fertilizers. Moscow: 1935.

with others. General Chemical Technology, Vol. 1-2.
Moscow-Leningrad: 1940-1946.
with others, editors. Technology of phosphoric acid, double
phosphate and ammonium phosphates (collection of research
works). Moscow-Leningrad: 1940.
Physico-chemical and technological analysis of phosphate
decomposition with nitric acid and obtaining of fertilizers.
Izvest. Akad. Nauk S.S.S.R., Ser. Khim. 1940, #5.
Biography:
O. E. Zvyagintsev. Semen Isaakovich Vol'fkovich (for 60th
birthday). Zhur. Priklad. Khim., 1946, 19, #12.
A. M. Dubovitskii and M. E. Pozin. Semen Isaakovich Vol'f-
kovich (for 60th birthday). Zhur. Priklad. Khim., 1956, 29,
#11.
Office: Chemistry Department
                Moscow University
                Moscow, USSR
Residence: M. Bronnaya 19/6
                Moscow, USSR
Telephone: B3 11 37

VOLOGDIN, ALEKSANDR GRIGOREVICH (Geologist)
    A. G. Vologdin was born March 11, 1896. In 1925 he gradu-
ated from the Leningrad Mining Institute. He worked, in 1920,
for the Geological Committee and subsequently in organizations
developing from it. In 1943 he worked at the Paleontological
Institute of the U.S.S.R. Academy of Sciences. He was elected
to the U.S.S.R. Academy of Sciences in 1939 as a Corresponding
Member.
    Vologdin worked in the geology and minerals of Yuzhno-
Krasnoyarskii Kray, in paleontology (particularly the archaeocyathus and the most ancient algae), in stratigraphy, in hydrogeology, in geologic engineering, and in search for minerals of
commercial importance.
Bibliography:
Archaeocyatals of Siberia, 1-2. Surveys. Moscow-Leningrad:
1931-32.
Tubinsko-Sisimskii Region of the Minusinko-Khahaskii Ter-
ritory. Moscow-Leningrad: 1932.
Kizir-Kazyrskii Region (with one map). Moscow-Leningrad:
1931.
Archaeocyathus and Algae of Cambrian Limestone of
Mongolia and Tuva. I. Moscow-Leningrad: 1940.

and others. Geology and Commercial Minerals of Northern
Bukovina and Bessarabiya. Moscow-Leningrad: 1946.
Office: Institute of Paleontology of USSR Academy of
           Sciences
           Leninskii Prospekt, 33
           Moscow, USSR
Residence: Berezhkovsk. nab. 40
           Moscow, USSR
Telephone: G3 37 33

VOL'SKII, ANTON NIKOLAEVICH (Metallurgist)

A. N. Vol'skii was born June 24, 1897. In 1924 he graduated
from the Moscow Institute of National Economy. From 1928 to
1948 he worked in the State Scientific Research Institute of Non-
Ferrous Metals. He began teaching in the Moscow Institute of
Non-Ferrous Metals and Gold in 1929, and in 1934 he was made
a professor there. From 1953 he was a Corresponding Member of the U.S.S.R. Academy of Sciences, and since 1960 an
Academician.

Vol'skii has studied chemical equilibriums in melts during
metallurgical smelting in non-ferrous metallurgy. He completed a series of investigations of great practical significance.
Bibliography:
     Extraction of Zinc and Lead from Waste Products of Metal-
     lurgical Plants. Moscow: 1934.
     Theory of Metallurgical Processes, I. Moscow-Leningrad:
     1935.
     The Basis of Theory of Metallurgical Smelting. Moscow:
     1943.
     Interaction between sulfides and oxides during the smelting
     of ores and Bessemerizing of mattes. Anniversary Col-
     lection of Scientific Works 1939-1940, #9. Moscow-
     Leningrad: 1940.
Office: Moscow Institute of Non-Ferrous Metals and Gold
           Moscow, USSR

VONSOVSKII, SERGEI VASIL'EVICH (Physicist)

S. V. Vonsovskii was born September 2, 1910. After graduating from Leningrad University in 1932, he worked in the Urals
Physico-Technical Institute in Sverdlovsk. In 1939 he began
working in the Institute of Physics of Metals in the Urals branch
of the U.S.S.R. Academy of Sciences, now U.S.S.R. Academy of

Sciences, and in 1944 he was also a professor at Urals University. Since 1953 he has been a Corresponding Member of the U.S.S.R. Academy of Sciences.
In order to explain the electrical and magnetic properties of metals and semiconductors, Vonsovskii (with S. Shubin) developed the so-called "polar" and (s-d) exchange theories, treating the system of electrons in a crystal lattice as a single interacting system. Besides the processes of exchange, he also took into account transfer processes, which lead to the establishment of polar states. On the basis of these models, Vonsovskii and associates constructed a general theory on ferromagnetics close to the Curie point, and explained fractional atomic moments, the optic, magnetooptic, electric and other phenomena in ferromagnetics, an indirect exchange in ferrites, and the general theories of transition metals with magnetic atomic orders.
Bibliography:

and Ya. S. Shur. Ferromagnetism. Moscow-Leningrad: 1948.
Contemporary Theory on Magnetism. Moscow: 1953.
and S. Schubin. Zur elektronentheorie der Metalle. I-II. Physikalische Zeitschrift der Sowjetunion, 1935, $\underline{7}$, #3, 292-328; 1936, $\underline{10}$, #3, 348-77.
On the exchange interaction of valent and internal electrons in ferromagnetic (transition) metals. Zhur. Ekspt'l. i Teoret. Fiz. $\underline{16}$, #11 (1946).
and E. A. Turov. On the exchange interaction of valent and internal electrons in crystals (s-d)—exchange model of transition metals. Zhur. Ekspt'l. i Teoret. Fiz. $\underline{24}$, #4 (1953).
Theory of interaction of electrons in a crystal lattice. Izvest. Akad. Nauk S.S.S.R., Ser. Fiz. $\underline{12}$, #4 (1948), and Uspekhi Phys. Nauk $\underline{48}$, 289 (1952).
Some questions on multiple-electron theory of semiconductors. Zhur. Tekh. Fiz. $\underline{25}$, #12 (1955).
and Yu. M. Seidov. On indirect exchange interaction. Doklady Akad. Nauk S.S.S.R. $\underline{107}$, #1 (1956).
and E. A. Turov. On the phenomenological treatment of ferro- and antiferromagnetism. J. Appl. Phys. $\underline{29}$, #9 (1959).
and Yu. A. Izumov. On the statistical properties of electrons in transition metals. Fiz. Metal, Metalloved $\underline{10}$, 321 (1960).
and Yu. A. Izumov. Electron theory of transition metals. Uspekhi Fiz. Nauk 77, 377 (I) (1962); $\underline{78}$, 1 (II).

Office: Institute of Physics of Metals USSR Academy of
             Sciences
             S. Kovalevskaya Ul. 13
             Sverdlovsk, USSR

VOROZHTSOV, NIKOLAI NIKOLAEVICH (Organic Chemist)

N. N. Vorozhtsov, son of N. N. Vorozhtsov (1881-1941, organic chemist), was born June 5, 1907. He graduated from the Moscow Technological College in 1928, and from then until 1930 he worked in the Laboratory of the Commission on the Study of the Natural Productive Forces of the U.S.S.R. Academy of Sciences in Moscow. In 1930-38, he was at the State Institute of High Pressures in Leningrad; in 1938-43 he taught at the Kazakh State University where, in 1939, he was made professor. He was Director of the Scientific Research Institute of Organic Semiproducts and Dyes from 1943 to 1947, and in 1945 was Chairman of the Department of the Moscow Mendeleev Chemico-Technological Institute. In 1958 he was elected a Corresponding Member of the U.S.S.R. Academy of Sciences. He became a member of the Communist Party of the Soviet Union in 1942. He received a Stalin Prize in 1952.

The investigations of Vorozhtsov are in organic chemistry, technology of organic dyes and intermediates. He investigated exchange reactions of aryl halides, catalytic isomerization, halogen-naphthalenes, halogenation of aromatic and aliphatic compounds, sulfonation and the transformation of sulfo acids. A part of the work of Vorozhtsov deals with the structure of natural products. He supplemented and prepared for publication the 3rd and 4th editions of a well-known monograph of N. N. Vorozhtsov, Sr., "Basis of Synthesis of Intermediate Products and Dyes," (3rd ed., 1952).

As of 1961, Vorozhtsov was the Director of the Institute of Organic Chemistry of the Siberian Branch U.S.S.R. Academy of Sciences.

Bibliography:

Chemistry of Natural Tanning Substances. Moscow-Leningrad: 1932.

and V. A. Kobelev. Kinetics and mechanism of a catalytic exchange of chlorine for an amine group. Doklady Akad. Nauk S.S.S.R., 1934, 3, #2.

and V. A. Koptyug. Study of the mechanism of catalytic isomerization of monochlornaphthalene by the method of tagged atoms. Zhur. Obshchei Khim., 1958, #2.

425   VUL

Office: Moscow Mendeleev Chemico-Technological Institute
             Moscow, USSR

VUL, BENTSION MOISEEVICH (Physicist)

B. M. Vul was born May 22, 1903. He graduated in 1928
from the Kiev Polytechnic Institute. In 1932 he went to work at
the Physics Institute of the U.S.S.R. Academy of Sciences. He
has been a member of the Communist Party of the Soviet Union
since 1922. In 1939 he was elected a Corresponding Member
of the U.S.S.R. Academy of Sciences. He was the recipient in
1946 of a Stalin Prize.

Vul's works deal with the physics of dielectrics. While
studying electric strength of dielectrics, he established the
nature of the end-effect in the breakdown of dielectrics and the
particularitites of the breakdown of compressed gases in sharp-
ly heterogeneous fields. He discovered (1944) a new ferro-
electric-barium titanate ($BaTiO_3$) which has a very high dielectric constant.

In March 1960, Vul visited the United States to attend the
20th Annual Conference on Physical Electronics in Cambridge,
Massachusetts.

Bibliography:

Consecutive breakdown of solid dielectrics. Zhur. Tekh.
Fiz., 1932, 2, #3-4.

and I. M. Gol'dman. Substances with a high and super-high
dielectric constant. Electricity, 1946, #3.

and I. M. Gol'dman. Breakdown of compressed gas in a
heterogeneous electric field. Doklady Akad. Nauk S.S.S.R.,
1934, 2, #9.

The dielectric constant of rutile compositions. Doklady
Akad. Nauk S.S.S.R., 1944, 43, #7.

and I. M. Gol'dman. The dielectric constant of titanates of
metals of the second group. Doklady Akad. Nauk S.S.S.R.,
1945, 46, #4.

On the nature of piezoelectric properties of the titanate of
barium. In memory of Sergei Ivanovich Vavilov. Moscow:
1952, 319-323.

On the dielectric properties of transition layers in semi-
conductors. Zhur. Tekh. Fiz., 1955, 25, #1, 3-10.

On the Breakdown of Transition Layers in Semiconductors.
Zhur. Tekh. Fiz., 1956, 26, #11, 2403-2416.

and E. I. Zavaritskaya, L. V. Keldysh. Impurity conductivity
of germanium at low temperatures. Doklady Akad. Nauk
S.S.S.R. 135, #6, 1361-63 (1960).

Electric current in gamma-rayed dielectrics. Doklady Akad.
Nauk S.S.S.R. 139, #6, 1339-41 (1961).
Office: A. N. Lebedev Physics Institute of USSR Academy
        of Sciences
        Leninskii Prospekt, 53
        Moscow, USSR

WWEDENSKY (VVEDENSKII), BORIS ALEKSEEVICH
(Electronics Physicist)

B. A. Wwedensky was born April 19, 1893. After graduating
from Moscow University in 1915, he worked in several scientific research organizations. From 1927 to 1935, he was at the
All-Union Electrotechnical Institute where he was made professor in 1929. He worked at the Physics Institute of the
U.S.S.R. Academy of Sciences from 1941 until 1944. Wwedensky, in 1941-1944, served as a member of the Presidium of the
U.S.S.R. Academy of Sciences. In 1944-1951 he was Chairman
of the Section on Development of Problems in Radioengineering
of the U.S.S.R. Academy of Sciences and, in 1946-1951, he was
Academician Secretary of the Department of Technical Sciences
of the U.S.S.R. Academy of Sciences. He became a member, in
1949, of the main editorial board and the chief editor, in 1951,
of the Great Soviet Encyclopedia. Since 1959, he has been
Chairman of the Scientific Council of the Soviet Encyclopedia.
In 1953 he began working at the Institute of Radioengineering
and Electronics of the U.S.S.R. Academy of Sciences. Wwedensky was elected Corresponding Member of the U.S.S.R. Academy
of Sciences in 1934, and in 1943 Academician. In 1954 he be-
camė a Corresponding Member of the German Academy of Sciences, Berlin. He has received the following awards: in 1949
the Gold Medal of A. S. Popov; in 1952 the State Prize; in 1945
and 1953, the Order of Lenin; in 1953 and 1962, the Red Banner
of Labor.

    Wwedenskii's main work is concerned with the study of the
propagation of ultra-short waves, and also with investigations
in magnetism. Under his leadership an ultra-short wave broadcasting station (RV-61) was built in 1929. In 1932-1933 he
organized expeditions for the study of the propagation of meter
and decimeter waves over the sea surface. The expedition
proved the possibility of the propagation of ultra short waves
beyond the horizon (diffraction propagation) and allowed a determination of the relationship between the propagation of ultra
short waves and meteorological conditions (phenomenon of refraction). Wwedensky introduced the "diffraction formula,"

according to which the field of ultra short waves beyond the horizon could be calculated (1935-1936). Wwedensky's publications on the propagation of ultra short waves are: Basis of the Theory of Propagation of Radiowaves (1934); Propagation of Ultra Short Waves (1934); Propagation of Ultra Short Waves (1938; together with A. G. Arenberg). His investigations in magnetism are presented in the monograph, Contemporary Study of Magnetism (1929; together with Academician G. S. Landsberg).

Bibliography:

Über die Magnetische Viskositat in sehr dünnen Eisendrähten und ihre Abhängigkeit von der Magnetisierung und der Temperatur. Annalen der Physik, 1921, 66, 110-129.

Über die Wirbelströme bei der spontanen Änderung der Magnetisierung. Annalen der Physik, 1921, 64, #67, 609-620.

and S. M. Rzhevkin. Die Messung von Kapazitäten und grossen Widerständen mittels intermittierenden Rohrengenerators. Physikalische Zeitschrift, 1922, 23, 150-153.

Physical Phenomena in Electron Tubes, 4th ed. Moscow-Leningrad: 1932.

and A. G. Arenberg. Questions on Propagation of Ultra Short Waves, Part I. Moscow: 1948.

On diffraction propagation of radiowaves. Zhur. Tekh. Fiz., 1936, 6, #1, 163-176; #11, 1837-1847; 1937, 7, #16, 1647-1657. Technical Physics in the U.S.S.R., 1935, 2, #2, 624; 1936, 3, #11, 915-925; 1937, 4, #8, 579-591. (English trans.)

and M. I. Ponomarev. Utilizing method of geometrical optics for determining trajectory of ultra short radiowaves in heterogeneous atmosphere. Izvest. Akad. Nauk, Otdel. Tech. Nauk, 1946, #9, 1201-1210.

and A. G. Arenberg. Long distance tropospheric propagation of ultra short waves. Radiotechnics, 1957, #1-2.

Physical Phenomena in Cathode Tubes, 4th ed. 1932.

Biography:

Academician B. A. Wwedenskii (On the 60th Anniversary since date of birth). Radiotekh., 1953, 8, #3.

Office: Chairman of the Scientific Council "Soviet
              Encyclopedia"
              State Scientific Publishing House
              Pokrovskii Blvd. 8
              Moscow ZH-28, USSR

Telephone: K7 26 19

Residence: Leninskii Prospekt, 13
Moscow, USSR
Telephone: B2 11 13

YAKOVLEV, ALEKSANDR SERGEEVICH (Aircraft Designer)
A. S. Yakovlev was born April 1, 1906. He was a Colonel-
General in the Engineering Technical Service. In 1931, he
graduated from the Military Air Engineering Academy in Moscow. In 1934 he was Chief, and in 1957, he became General
Designer of the Experimental-Designing Bureau. From 1940-
1948 he was deputy of the People's Commissariat and subsequently deputy Minister of the Aviation Industry. He was a
delegate to the Supreme Soviet at the second and fifth convocations. Yakovlev has been a member of the Communist Party
since 1938. He has been awarded the title Hero of Socialist
Labor, and was the recipient of a Stalin Prize in 1941, 1942,
1943, 1946, 1947, and 1948. In 1943 he was elected to the
U.S.S.R. Academy of Sciences as a Corresponding Member.
Yakovlev designed a number of planes for different purpos-
es--sports, training, passenger, fighters, bombers and helicopters. Among the training and passenger airplanes, these
are outstanding: training planes UT-1 and UT-2, planes for
communication YAK-12, which is utilized in agriculture and as
a light passenger airplane, the YAK-18 for beginners' study and
training. Yakovlev has also designed combat, piston and jet
airplanes, primarily fighters and fighter-interceptors. In
the beginning of World War II he designed a fighter, the YAK-1,
which was widely employed. Also well known is the fighter
YAK-9 and particularly the YAK-3 which was one of the main
fighters among those participating in World War II (1941-45)
and which had high speed and maneuverability. Under the
leadership of Yakovlev, the first jet fighter, the YAK-15 was
designed in 1945, and subsequently the jet fighters YAK-17,
YAK-23 and later a series of jet supersonic fighters. Yakovlev
also designed helicopters, including the twin-engine helicopter,
the "Flying Car"--the YAK-24. He is the author of memoirs
"Stories of an Aircraft Designer" (1957).
In March 1962, Yakovlev was elected to the Council of
Nationalities.
Office: USSR Academy of Sciences
Leninskii Prospekt, 14
Moscow, USSR

Residence: Metrostroevskaya 1
            Moscow, USSR
Telephone: G5 36 21

YAKOVLEV, N. N. (Geologist-Paleontologist)
      N. N. Yakovlev was born April 27, 1870. He worked on the
Geological Committee (now the All-Union Scientific Research
Geological Institute in Leningrad) in 1895. From 1900-1930, he
was professor at the Petersburg (Leningrad) Mining Institute.
In 1923-26, he was Director of the Geological Committee. He
was awarded the title Honored Scientist of R.S.F.S.R. in 1930.
In 1948 the U.S.S.R. Academy of Sciences awarded Yakovlev the
A. P. Karpinskii Prize for his scientific investigations. He was
elected, in 1921, to the U.S.S.R. Academy of Sciences as a
Corresponding Member.
      Yakovlev conducted geological investigations in various
regions of the country. In the Donbas, from 1892, he participated in a geological survey conducted by the Geological Committee and studied the structure of the Bakhmut salt-bearing
basin. He worked out and paleontologically substantiated the
stratigraphy of lower Permain sediments. In the Urals, Yakovlev conducted geological investigations on deposits of coal, iron
and other ores; the Caucasus and territories beyond the Caucasus, he studied various mineral sources. He was the first to
make paleoecological investigations of invertebrates in Russia,
particularly of the three Paleozoic groups of animals—brachiopods, tetracorals and pelma echinoderms. He investigated the
origin of structural festures of organisms and the change of
these features under the influence of external factors.
Bibliography:
      Studies on the Coral Rugosa. Works of the Geological Com-
      mittee, New Series, 1914, #96.
      Fauna of the upper part of the Paleozoic deposits in the
      Donetz Basin, I-III. Works of the Geological Committee,
      New Series, 1903-1912, 79, #4-12.
      Attachment of brachiopods as a basis of their species and
      genus. Works of the Geological Committee, New Series,
      1908, #48.
      Extinction of animals and plants and reasons according to
      geologic data. Proceedings of the Geologic Committee, 41,
      #1, Petrograd, 1922.
      Crinoids and Blastoids of Carboniferous and Permian De-
      posits of the U.S.S.R. Moscow: 1956.

The organism and the environment. Articles on Paleoecology of Invertebrates, 1913-1956. Moscow-Leningrad: 1956.
Biography:
  A. Ryabinin. Nikolai Nikolaevich Yakovlev (On the 70th Anniversary since the date of birth). Annual of the All-Russia Paleontological Society, 12, 1936-1939, Moscow-Leningrad, 1945 (contains bibliography of the works of Yakovlev.)
  V. V. Menner. Nikolai Nikolaevich Yakovlev. Izvest. Akad. Nauk S.S.S.R., Ser. Geol., 1951, #3.
  I. I. Gorskii. N. N. Yakovlev (On the 70th Anniversary since the date of birth). Annual of the Paleontological Society, 14, 1948-53, Moscow-Leningrad, 1953.
  V. P. Nekhoroshev. On the work of N. N. Yakovlev in the field of geology. Annual of the Paleontologic Society, 14, 1948-53.
Office: USSR Academy of Sciences
             Leninskii Prospekt, 14
             Moscow, USSR
Residence: ul. Marksa i Engelsa 16
             Moscow, USSR
Telephone: K5 12 19

YANSHIN, ALEKSANDR LEONIDOVICH (Geologist)

A. L. Yanshin was born March 28, 1911. In 1923 he graduated from Moscow Geological Survey Institute and had been working since 1929 in the Mining-Geological Department at the Scientific Institute for Fertilizers. From 1936 he worked at the Geological Institute of the U.S.S.R. Academy of Sciences and in 1956 was made Chairman of the Department on Regional Tectonics at this Institute. Yanshin was elected an Academician of the U.S.S.R. Academy of Sciences in 1958. In 1953 he was awarded the A. P. Karpinskii Prize for his work on "Geology of the North." He was the recipient of three orders and also some medals.

Yanshin's investigations are in tectonics, stratigraphy, lithology, and hydrogeology primarily of the Western territory of the Kazakh S.S.R., and of the Southern Urals. In the Southern Urals, he located a wide development of continental Mesozoic sediments and distinguished in them a series of formations. He worked out the stratigraphy of Tertiary sedimentation of the Aralo-Turgaisk depression, in connection with which he critically examined some general questions in paleogenic stratigraphy. In biostratigraphic examinations, he adhered to the idea of

non-simultaneous appearance and disappearance of the same or
similar species in dissimilar zoophyto-geographic territories.
In tectonics he studied so-called "young" platforms with a
Paleozoic folded base. In particular, he suggested new ideas on
folded structures of the Urals, Tien Shan, and Mangishlak, and
of the deep geological structure of the plains surrounding the
Aral Sea. The presence of oil deposits in this territory was
predicted by Yanshin. He took part, in 1952 and 1956, in the
compilation of tectonic maps of the U.S.S.R. He studied lignites, iron ores, bauxite, phosphorite, potassium salt, and
cement raw materials, and he discovered industrial deposits of
these minerals. He also found a series of artesian basins.
Bibliography:
    Methods of studying buried folded structures as an example
    of elucidation of the correlation of the Urals, Tien Shan, and
    Mangishlak. Izvest. Akad. Nauk S.S.S.R., Ser. Geol., 1948,
    #5.
    Views of A. D. Arkhangelskii on the tectonic character of
    southeastern surroundings of the Russian platform, and con-
    temporary views on this question. In Memory of Academici-
    an A. D. Arkhangelskii. Questions on Lithography and
    Stratigraphy of the U.S.S.R. Moscow: 1951.
    Geology of Northern Territories Close to the Aral Sea.
    Moscow: 1953.
Office: Department of Regional Tectonics
              USSR Academy of Sciences Institute of Geology
              Pyzhevskii Pereulok, 7
              Moscow, USSR
Residence: Leninskii Prospekt, 25
              Moscow, USSR
Telephone: V4 00 27, Ext. 8

YUNUSOV, SABIR YUNUSHOVICH (Organic Chemist)
    Yunusov was born November 11, 1909, in Tashkent. In 1935
he graduated from the Chemical Faculty of the Central Asia
University. Since 1943 he has been Chief of the Laboratory of
Alkaloid Chemistry of the Uzbèk S.S.R. Academy of Sciences
Institute of Plant Chemistry, and he is Director of this insti-
tute. In 1948 Yunusov received his Doctor of Chemical Sciences
degree. He has been a member of the Communist Party of the
Soviet Union since 1950. In 1952 he was elected Academician
of the Uzbek Academy of Sciences, and in 1958 a Corresponding
Member of the U.S.S.R. Academy of Sciences. From 1952 to

1962 he was Vice-President of the Uzbek S.S.R. Academy of Sciences.
Yunusov's investigations are in alkaloid chemistry. He has studied the alkaloid content of over four thousand plant flora of Uzbekistan and Central Asia. From twenty-five hundred plant types he isolated one hundred and forty alkaloids of which ninety-five were new. Yunusov established the structure of twenty-eight alkaloids and found a number of them to have medicinal properties. He has also conducted research on alkaloid storage in various parts of plants with respect to their period of growth.

Bibliography:
Alkaloids of Ungernia severtzovii. Structure of ungerine. Zhur. Obshchei Khim. 29, 1724-8 (1959). C. A. 54, 8871c (1960).

and Kh. A. Abduazimov. Galanthamine hydrobromide. U.S.S.R. Patent 128, 111, Apr. 28, 1960. C. A. 54, 23206e (1960).

and S. T. Akramov. Alkaloids of Lolium cuneatum. II. Zhur. Obshchei Khim. 30, 677-82 (1960). C. A. 54, 24831c (1960).

and S. T. Akramov. Structure of norloline, loline, and lolinine. Doklady Akad. Nauk Usbek. S.S.R., #4, 28-31 (1959). C. A. 54, 11028i (1960).

Office: Uzbek SSR Academy of Sciences Institute of Plant Chemistry
Ulitsa Kuibysheva, 14
Tashkent, Uzbek SSR
Telephone: 34686 and 28465

ZABABAKHIN, EVGENII IVANOVICH (Physicist)

E. I. Zababakhin was born in 1917. After graduating from the Military Air Engineering Academy in 1944, he taught there. He has been a member of the Communist Party of the Soviet Union since 1949. In 1958 he was elected a Corresponding Member of the U.S.S.R. Academy of Sciences.
Zababakhin's work was in gas dynamics.
Bibliography:
and M. N. Nechaev. Shock waves of fields and their cumulation. Zhur. Eksptl. i Teoret. Fiz., 1957, 33, #2(8).
Office: USSR Academy of Sciences
Leninskii Prospekt, 14
Moscow, USSR

ZAVALISHIN, DMITRII ALEKSANDROVICH (Electrotechnolo-
  gist)
    D. A. Zavalishin was born in 1900. In 1925 he graduated
from Leningrad Polytechnical Institute, where he worked until
1939. From 1939 to 1941 he was Chairman of the Department
of Electric Machines of the S. M. Buden Military Electrotechnical Academy, and from 1941 to 1946 he was professor on the
faculty of special electrotechnology of the Armed Forces Advanced School of Engineering-Technology. He became, in 1946-
1959, Chairman of the Department of Electrical Machines of the
Leningrad Institute of Aeronautical Instrument Construction.
In 1959, he became Chief of the Laboratory on Scientific Fundamentals of Automatized Electrical Apparatus of the U.S.S.R.
Academy of Sciences Institute of Electromechanics. He was
elected, in 1960, a Corresponding Member of the U.S.S.R. Academy of Sciences. In 1957 he was awarded the title of Honored
Scientist and Technologist of the R.S.F.S.R.
    Zavalishin's principal work is in the field of electrical ma-
chines, electron-ionic and semiconductor equipment.
Bibliography:
    and S. V. Zakharevich, V. A. Tikan. A model study of in-
    verter and rectifier performance of an electric locomotive
    thermionic converter. Elektrichestvo, 1959, #6, 1-8. Elec.
    Eng. Sci. Abstr. 62, 5736 (1959).
    and A. I. Vazhnov, E. V. Tolvinskaya, I. A. Gordon, I. A.
    Glebov. Synchronous capacitors for long distance power
    transmission. Elektrichestvo, 1958, #10, 43-7. Elec. Eng.
    Sci. Abstr. 62, 1943 (1959).
Office: Institute of Electromechanics of USSR Academy of
            Sciences
            Dvortsovaya Naberezhnaya 18
            Leningrad, USSR

ZAVOISKII, EVGENII KONSTANTINOVICH (Physicist)
    E. K. Zavoiskii was born September 28, 1907. In 1930 he
graduated from the University of Kazan' and has taught there
since 1933, becoming a professor in 1945. He has been working
at U.S.S.R. Academy of Sciences departments since 1947. In
1957 he was awarded the Lenin Prize. He was elected, in 1953,
a Corresponding Member of the U.S.S.R. Academy of Sciences.
    Zavoiskii discovered in 1944 the phenomenon of electronic
paramagnetic resonance. On the basis of an analysis of experimental data, together with S. A. Al'tschuller and B. M. Kozyrev,
he established a series of relationships between the form of

resonant lines. From 1947 he has been developing the use of
image converters for a scintillation chamber, and for investigating processes of a comparatively short duration (10^{-9} -
10^{-14} seconds).
Bibliography:

and S. A. Al'tshuller, B. M. Kozyrev. New method of in-
vestigating paramagnetic absorption. Zhur. Eksptl. i Teoret.
Fiz., 1944, #10-11.
Paramagnetic Absorption in solutions with parallel fields.
Zhur. Eksptl. i Teoret. Fiz., 1945, #6.
and S. A. Al'tshuller, B. M. Kozyrev. Paramagnetic re-
laxation in liquid solutions with perpendicular fields. Zhur.
Eksptl. i Teoret. Fiz., 1945, #7.
Paramagnetic abscription in some salts in perpendicular
magnetic fields. Zhur. Fiz., Moscow, 1946, 10, #2.
Spin magnetic resonance in the decimeter-wave region.
Zhur. Fiz., Moscow, 1946, 10, #2.
and others. Scintillation chamber. Doklady Akad. Nauk
S.S.S.R., 1955, 100, #2.
Office: Physics Department
               University of Kazan'
               Kazan', Tatar ASSR

ZAYMOVSKII, ALEKSANDR SEMYONOVICH (Metallographer)
    A. S. Zaymovskii was born October 9, 1905. Upon gradu-
ation from the Moscow Mining Academy in 1928, he taught
there, and subsequently at the Moscow Institute of Steel, and at
Moscow University from 1932-1941. From 1928-43, he worked
at the All-Union Electro-Technical Institute. Since 1945 he has
been a member of the Communist Party of the Soviet Union. In
1958, he was elected to the U.S.S.R. Academy of Sciences as a
Corresponding Member. He received a Stalin Prize.
    Zaymovskii's main works are in metallography, the pro-
duction of new alloys with special physical properties. Zaymovskii aided the production in the U.S.S.R. of new magnetic and
conducting alloys. He investigated conducting and transforming
steel, electro-technical iron, Permalloys and powdered magnetic dielectrics.
Bibliography:

and others. Metals and Alloys in Electrical Engineering,
3rd ed., 1-2. Moscow-Leningrad: 1957.
Office: USSR Academy of Sciences
               Leninskii Prospekt, 14
               Moscow, USSR

ZEL'DOVICH, YAKOV BORISOVICH (Physicist)

Y. B. Zel'dovich was born March 18, 1914. He studied at Leningrad University. In 1931 he began working at the Institute of Chemical Physics of the U.S.S.R. Academy of Sciences. He was elected Corresponding Member of the U.S.S.R. Academy of Sciences in 1946 and Academician in 1958. In 1943 he was awarded a Stalin Prize.

Zel'dovich examined the statistics of heterogeneous surfaces based on the measurement of the adsorption isotherm. In the period 1935-1939 he and associates ascertained the mechanism of nitrogen oxidation during an explosion. Together with Yu. B. Khariton, Zel'dovich proposed a calculation of the chain reaction in uranium fission in 1939-1940. In 1938-1943, he and D. A. Frank-Kamenetskii worked out a theory of the flame propagation and proposed a mechanism for chemical reaction in a shock wave.

Bibliography:

and Yu. B. Khariton. The question of chain decay of the main isotope of uranium. Zhur. Eksptl. i Teoret. Fiz., 1939, 9, #12.

and Yu. B. Khariton. The chain decay of uranium under the influence of slow neutrons. Zhur. Eksptl. i Teoret. Fiz., 1940, 10, #1.

Theory of Burning and Detonation of Gases. Moscow-Leningrad: 1944.

Theory of Shock Waves and Introduction to Gas Dynamics. Moscow-Leningrad: 1946.

and P. Ya. Sadovnikov, D. A. Frank-Kamenetskii. Oxidation of Nitrogen During Combustion. Moscow-Leningrad: 1947.

and A. S. Kompaneets. Theory of Detonation. Moscow: 1955.

Movement of gas under the influence of a shock wave. Akust. Zhur., 1956, 2, #1.

Development of the theory of anti-particles, charging of elementary particles and properties of heavy neutral mesons. Uspekhi Fiz. Nauk, 1956, 59, #3.

Experimental investigation of spherical gas detonation. Zhur. Tekh. Fiz., 1956, 26, #8.

Problems of contemporary physics and astronomy. Uspekhi Fiz. Nauk 78, #4, 549 (1962).

and G. I. Barenblatt, R. L. Salganik. Quasi periodic sediment fallout in interdependent diffusion of two materials (Lisegang ring). Doklady Akad. Nauk S.S.S.R. 140, #6, 1281-84 (1961).

Office: Institute of Chemical Physics of USSR Academy of
              Sciences
              Vorob'evskoye Shosse 2
              Moscow, USSR

ZENKEVICH, LEV ALEXANDROVICH (Oceanographer)

L. A. Zenkevich was born June 17, 1889. He was a graduate
of the Law Faculty in 1912, and in 1916 of the Moscow University Department of Physico-Mathematical Faculty. Upon his
graduation, he worked there as a professor since 1930. He
also worked at the Institute of Oceanography at the Academy of
Sciences in 1927. He became a Corresponding Member of the
U.S.S.R. Academy of Sciences in 1953.

Zenkevich took an active part in organizing the Floating
Scientific Marine Institute (later known as the State Oceanographic Institute) where he worked from 1921-30. He took part
in many expeditions for comprehensive study of the northern
seas, the Caspian, the Far East Seas and the Pacific Ocean
(1949-52); he directed the expedition on the "Vitiaz." His basic
work is devoted to the fauna of the Russian seas. He introduced
a quantitative system for the study of marine benthic fauna. He
has developed ration methods of feeding of fish. To improve
the food base of the Caspian, he acclimatized the clamworm.
He studied the evolution of motive power of invertebrates.
From 1955 he was a member of the Advisory Committee on
Marine Science at the UNESCO and vice president of the Special
Committee on Oceanographic Research at the International
Council of Scientific Unions.

In August 1959, Zenkevich visited the United States to attend
the International Oceanographic Conference in New York City.
As of 1961 he was Chairman of the Oceanographic Committee
of the U.S.S.R. Academy of Sciences.

Bibliography:
    Fauna and the Productivity of the Seas, 1947, 1-2.
    The Seas of U.S.S.R., their Fauna and Flora, 2nd ed., 1956.
    and others. Animal Geography, 1946.

Office: Chairman of Oceanographic Committee
              USSR Academy of Sciences
              Leninskii Prospekt, 14
              Moscow, USSR
Residence: Lomonosovskii Prospekt, 14
              Moscow, USSR
Telephone: B9 25 56

437 ZHAVORONKOV

ZERNOV, DMITRII VLADIMIROVICH (Electronics Expert)

D. V. Zernov was born March 20, 1907. Upon graduation in 1930 from Moscow University, he worked at the All-Union Electro-Technical Institute until 1934. From 1932 to 1938, he taught at the Moscow Institute of Transport Engineers. From 1936 to 1939, he worked at the Scientific Research Institute of Cinematography and Photography. In 1939, he worked at the Institute of Automation and Telemechanics of the U.S.S.R. Academy of Sciences, and in 1953 at the U.S.S.R. Academy of Sciences Institute of Radiotechnology and Electronics. He was elected, in 1953, a Corresponding Member of the U.S.S.R. Academy of Sciences.

In the early 1930's, Zernov was the first in the Soviet Union to construct sodium vapor fluorescent lamps. Under his leadership a television system with a large multi-grain screen was developed, for which he created a multi-contact, electron-beam commutator. In later years, Zernov continued work on the improvement and investigation of electron-beam devices of the commutator type. He studied electronic emission of thin dielectric layers under the influence of a field of a positive surface charge which is formed by electron bombardment.

Bibliography:
Electric discharge in sodium vapors as a source of light. Zhur. Tekh. Fiz., 1933, 3, #8.
Investigation of autoelectronic emission of thin dielectric films. Izvest. Akad. Nauk S.S.S.R., Otdel. Tekh. Nauk, 1944, #3.
Mechanics of an electric breakdown of solid dielectrics. Izvest. Akad. Nauk S.S.S.R., 1950, #6.
Utilization of electron-beam tubes for regulating and track homing. Elektrichestvo, 1945, #10.

Office: Institute of Radio Engineering and Electronics of
USSR Academy of Sciences
Mokhovaya Ulitsa 11, K-9
Moscow, USSR

ZHAVORONKOV, NIKOLAI MIKHAILOVICH (Chemical Technologist)

N. M. Zhavoronkov was born August 7, 1907. Upon graduation from the Moscow Chemical-Technological Institute in 1930, he joined the Institute's faculty, and in 1942 became a professor. In 1948 he became Director of the Institute. Beginning in 1944, he has been working at the L. A. Karpov Physico-Chemical Institute. Since 1939, he has been a member of the

Communist Party of the Soviet Union. He was elected, in 1953,
a Corresponding Member of the U.S.S.R. Academy of Sciences,
and in June 1962, an Academician. In June 1958, Zhavronkov
visited the United States to attend the 50th Anniversary of the
Institute of Chemical Engineers in Philadelphia, Penna.

In the beginning of his scientific career, Zhavoronkov studied
processes for obtaining hydrogen and a nitrogen-hydrogen mixture and their purification from carbon dioxide and carbon
monoxide for production of synthetic ammonia. In 1936-50 he
investigated hydro-aerodynamics of scrubbers and fractional
columns. For this work in 1950 the Academy of Sciences
awarded him the D. I. Mendeleev Prize.

The works of Zhavoronkov in later years dealt with the processes of separating liquid and gas mixtures by absorption,
rectification, molecular distillation and chemical ion exchange.
Together with others, he completed a series of works on the
theory of processes of concentration of stable isotopes and
worked out methods for isolating isotopes of hydrogen, carbon,
nitrogen, oxygen, boron and other light elements.

In September 1962, Zhavoronkov was appointed Director of
the U.S.S.R. Academy of Sciences Institute of General and Inorganic Chemistry.

Bibliography:

Hydraulic Basis of the Scrubber Process and Heat Transfer
in Scrubbers. Moscow: 1944.
and V. A. Malyusov. Molecular distillation. Chemical
Industry, 1950, #11-12.
Nitrogen in Nature and in Technology. Moscow: 1951.
Sources of Technical Combined Nitrogen. Moscow: 1951.
and V. A. Mamosov, N. A. Malafeev. Mass transfer in the
process of film absorption. Chemical Industry, 1951, #8,
1953, #4.
and A. I. Maier. Separation of mixtures by methods of molecular distillation. Methods and Processes of Chemical
Technology. Collection 1. Moscow-Leningrad: 1955.
and V. A. Mamosov, N. N. Umnik. Separation of mixtures by
method of high vacuum rectification. Methods and Processes
of Chemical Technology. 1. Moscow-Leningrad: 1955.
and O. V. Uvarov, N. N. Sevryugova. Physico-chemical
constants of heavy oxygen water. Utilization of Labelled
Atoms in Analytic Chemistry. Moscow: 1955.
and S. I. Babkov. Industrial method of obtaining concentrates
of the heavy isotope of nitrogen. Chemical Industry, 1955,
#7.

and V. A. Mamosov, N. N. Umnik. Mass of exchange in the processes of film rectification. Doklady Akad. Nauk S.S.S.R., 1955, 105, #4-5.

and V. A. Mamosov, N. N. Umnik. Investigation of the rectification in columns with a rotating rotor. Doklady Akad. Nauk S.S.S.R., 1956, 106, #1.

and N. N. Sevryugova, O. V. Uvarov. Determining the coefficient of the division of the isotopes of boron during equilibrium of evaporation of BCl_3. Atomic Energy, 1956, #4.

and O. V. Sokol'skii. Fractional column for obtaining heavy oxygen water. Chemical Industry, 1956, #7.

Chemical industry and research in the Soviet Union. Canadian Chemical Processing, 1956, 40, #5.

K. A. Timiryazev and the problem of nitrogen. Chemical Industry, 1956, #6.

Office: Institute of General and Inorganic Chemistry of
               USSR Academy of Sciences
               Leninskii Prospekt, 31
               Moscow, USSR
Residence: N. Basmannaya 16
               Moscow, USSR
Telephone: E1 79 73

ZHURKOV, SERAFIM NIKOLAEVICH (Physicist)

S. N. Zhurkov was born May 16, 1905. He graduated in 1929 from Voronezh Institute. In 1930 he began working at the Leningrad Physico-Technical Institute and in 1947 became professor. He has been a member of the Communist Party of the Soviet Union since 1944. In 1958 he was elected a Corresponding Member of the U.S.S.R. Academy of Sciences.

Zhurkov's main works are the physics of solids and polymers. He has carried out research on the strength of brittle materials and polymers, temperature-dependent breakdown, and the duration of action of mechanical stress. Zhurkov conducted investigations on the molecular mechanism of transition into a solid state (vitrification) of polymers and amorphous substances, relating the temperature dependence of mechanical properties of such substances to the nature of intermolecular interaction. On the basis of these studies he developed the theory of polymer plastification.

Bibliography:
Molecular mechanics of the solidification of polymers. Doklady Akad. Nauk S.S.S.R., 1945, 47, #7.

and B. N. Narzullaev. Temporary dependence of the strength
of solids. Zhur. Tekh. Fiz., 1953, 23, #10.
and T. P. Sanfirova. Temperature and temporary dependence
of the strength of pure metals. Doklady Akad. Nauk S.S.S.R.,
1955, 101, #2.

Office: Leningrad Physico-Technical Institute
             Leningrad, USSR

ZVEREV, MITROFAN STEPANOVICH (Astronomer)
    M. S. Zverev was born April 16, 1903. In 1929, he graduated
from the Moscow Conservatory, and in 1931 from Moscow University. From 1931-1951, he worked at the Shternberg State
Astronomical Institute in Moscow. He was a member of the
teaching staff at Moscow University from 1938-1952, and was
made professor in 1948. In 1951 he was appointed deputy Director of U.S.S.R. Academy of Sciences Main Astronomical
Observatory in Pulkovo. He was elected to the U.S.S.R. Academy of Sciences as a Corresponding Member in 1953. Since
1947 he has been a member of the Communist Party of the
Soviet Union.
    For many years Zverev made observations on the meridian
circle in Moscow and Pulkovo. He compiled a series of cata-
logs on stars, including a catalog on geodesic stars, a catalog
on fundamental, faint stars. Zverev developed an idea of a new
fundamental system of coordinates--a catalog on faint stars.
He also worked on time service, gravimetry and on variable
stars.
    In May 1959, Zverev visited the United States to attend the
Second World Astrometric Conference in Cincinnati, Ohio.
Bibliography:
    Untersuchungen des Lichtwechsels von helleren verader-
    lichen Sternen (1921-1934). Publications of the Sternberg
    Astronomical Institute; Vol. VIII. Moscow: 1936.
    Investigating results of astronomical observations of the
    time service of the Sternberg State Institute of Astronomy
    in 1941-44. Publications of the Sternberg State Astronomi-
    cal Institute, Vol. XVIII, p. 1, 1949 and p. 2, 1950.
    Catalog of faint stars. Astron. Zhur., 1940, 17, #5. Trans-
    actions I.A.U., Vol. VIII, 755, 1952.
    Fundamental astronomy. Uspekhi Astron. Nauk, 1950, 5,
    1954, 6.
Office: Main Astronomical Observatory of USSR Academy
             of Sciences
             Leningrad M-140, Pulkovo, USSR

Telephone: K8 22 42
              K8 84 14
              K8 84 11

ZVONKOV, VASILII VASIL'EVICH (Transport Engineer)

V. V. Zvonkov was born January 6, 1891. He graduated in
1917 from the Moscow Institute of Lines of Communication
Engineers. Until 1929 he worked in various transport organizations and in 1929-1933 at the Moscow Institute of Lines of
Communication Engineers. From 1935 to 1955 he was professor at the Military Transport Academy. He began working
in the section on the scientific solution of transportation problems at the U.S.S.R. Academy of Sciences in 1939, and in 1955
at the Institute of Complex Transportation Problems at the
U.S.S.R. Academy of Sciences. He has been a Corresponding
Member of the U.S.S.R. Academy of Sciences since 1939. In
1948 he was made an Honored Scientist of the R.S.F.S.R. Since
1956 he has been a member of the Communist Party of the
Soviet Union.

From 1922 Zvonkov has worked on the restoration, planning,
and development of water transport in the U.S.S.R.

As of 1961, Zvonkov was Chairman of the Council for Water
Economy. In 1962 he requested to be relieved of his duties as
Chairman.

Bibliography:
Organization of Navigation. Calculations. Moscow: 1929.
Commercial Calculation for Ships, with Examples of Practi-
cal Solutions, 2nd ed. Moscow-Leningrad: 1932.
Controller's System for Water Transport, 2nd ed. Moscow-
Leningrad: 1932.
Complex Typification of Technical Means of International
Water Transport. Moscow: 1948.

Biography:
Vasilii Vasil'evich Zvonkov. Moscow: 1957.

Office: Institute of Complex Transportation Problems
               USSR Academy of Sciences
               Moscow, USSR

Residence: Kotel'nicheskaya nab. 1/15
               Moscow, USSR

Telephone: B7 42 27